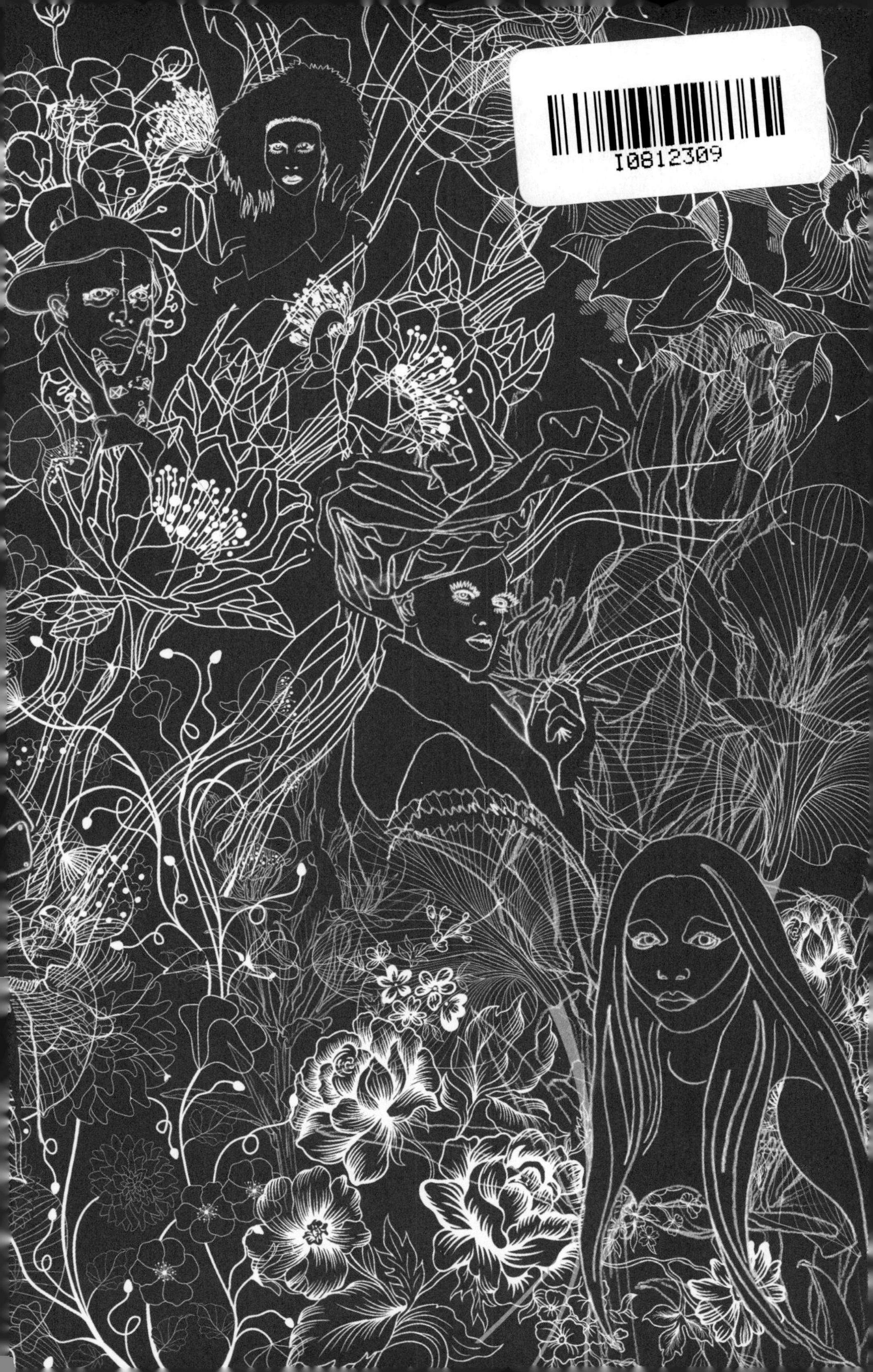

night flowers

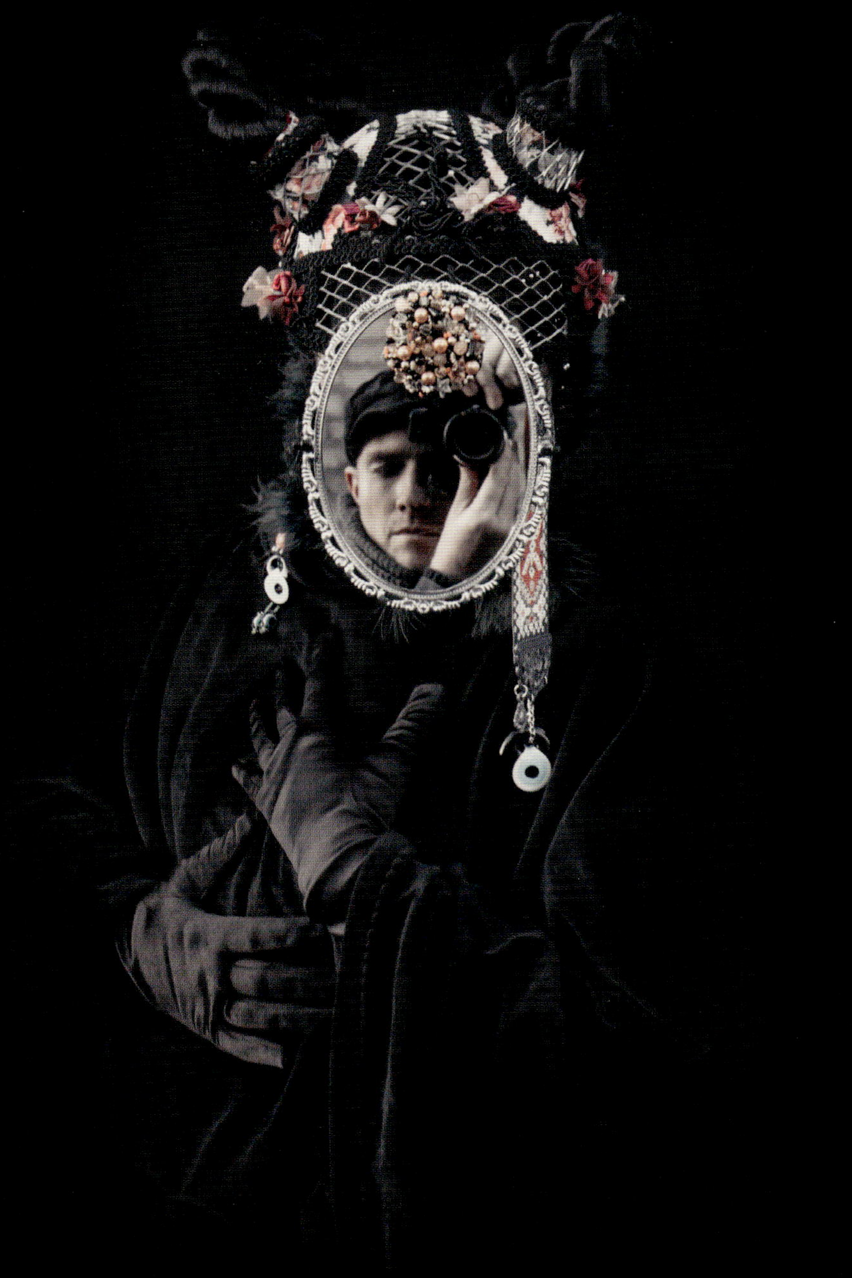

DAMIEN FROST

night flowers

from avant-drag to extreme haute couture

foreword by boy george

MERRELL
LONDON • NEW YORK

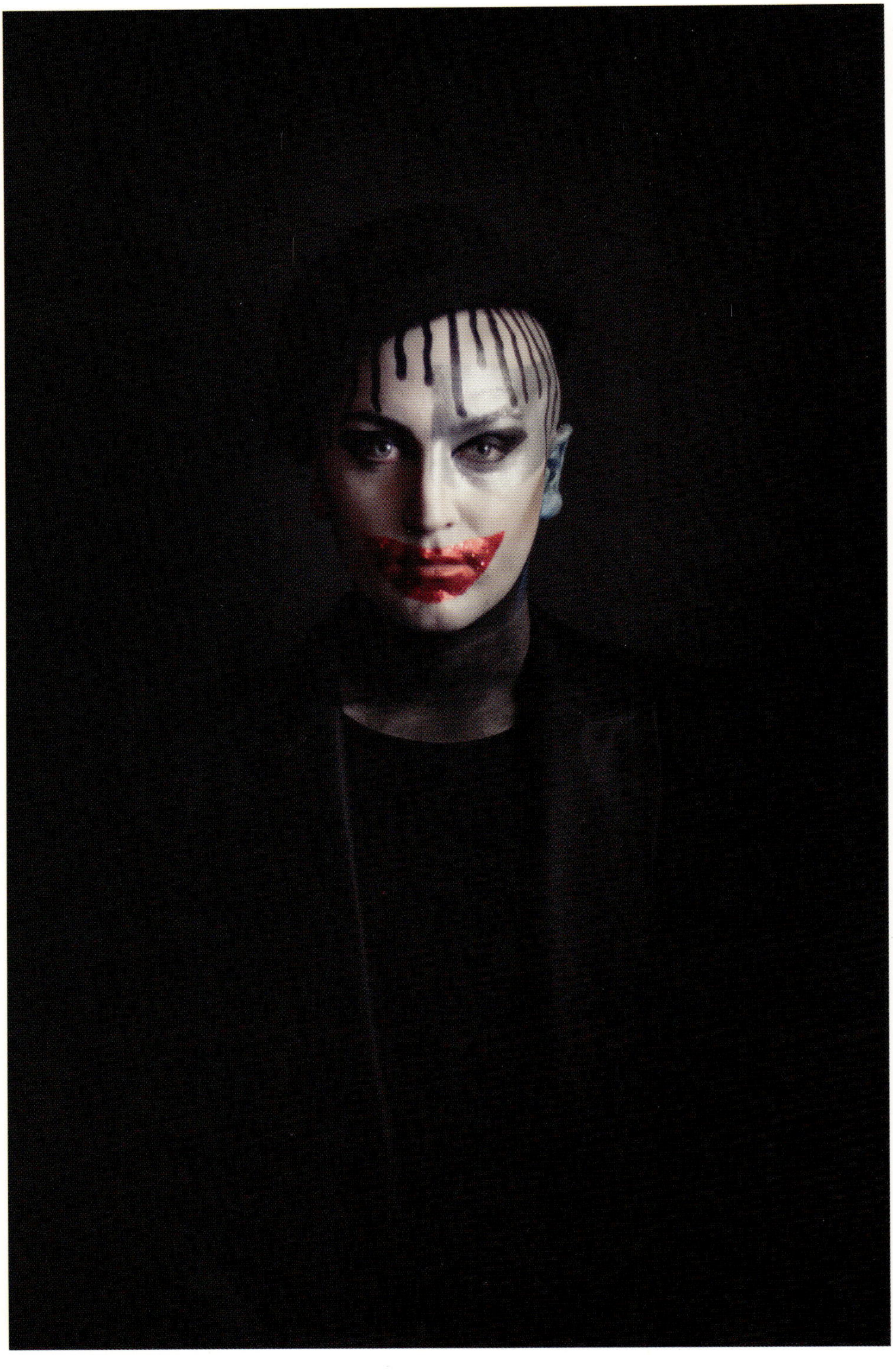

4 | luke harris (after boy george/leigh bowery) at cirque le soir

foreword

boy george

If Jack the Ripper had been armed with a camera, there would have been far less blood – and his photographs might have looked like these portraits by Damien Frost. There's something very gothic about Damien's images, with their stark black backgrounds, but you are undeniably forced to concentrate on the subjects and their beautiful costumes and painted cheeks. One can't help but think of David Bowie singing, 'We're painting our faces and dressing in thoughts from the skies'.

These exotic attention-seekers, glittering guttersnipes and bearded ladyboys have been hunted down on the London streets, where their souls have been robbed by the simple click of Damien's Leica. Making use of street lamps or the reflected light from bus stops and shop doorways, the pictures are seriously raw, stunning, even kamikaze. Damien has captured the spirit of the capital's new exhibitionism and slack drag. I can't wait for the next volume!

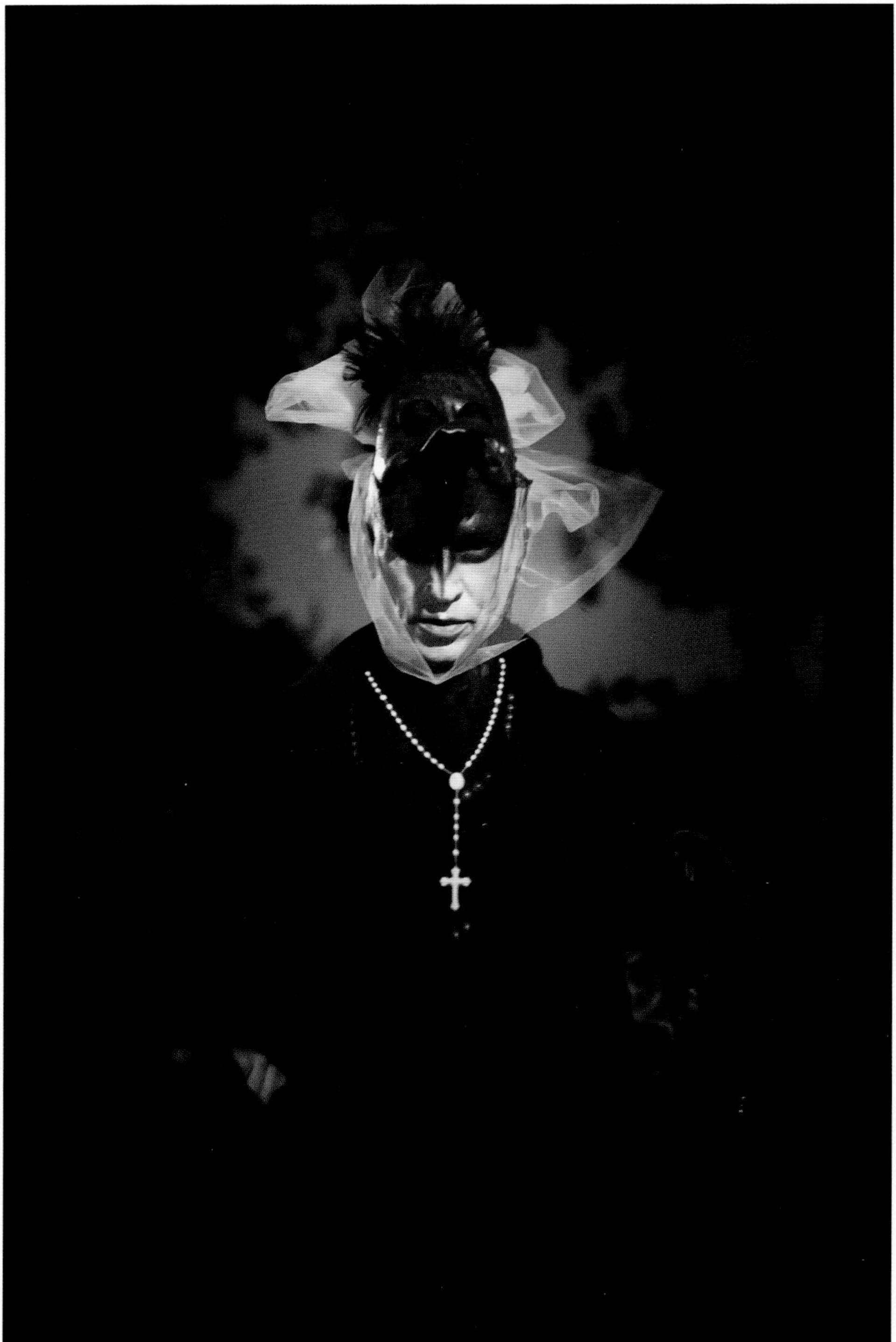

 dahc dermur viii on goldsmith's row

introduction

It's a familiar sight in late-night London: the rush of people sneaking drunken kisses and fumbling exchanges before they stumble down the steps around midnight to catch the last Tube home, lest their golden carriages should turn into pumpkins and their horses into mice. But travelling in the opposite direction, dashing to make the last Tube towards the centre of the capital, are a select few whose glass slippers come on only at midnight and who are just beginning their evening's revelries as most people are tucking themselves into bed. These 'Night Flowers' are a loose-knit community of drag queens and kings, club kids, alternative queer, transgender and gender-queer people, goths, artists, and cabaret, burlesque and fetish performers who bloom at night and burn bright among the neon lights of inner-city London.

The term 'Night Flowers' isn't in common use, but it's a poetic way to describe those people who constitute the more colourful elements of London's alternative club, queer, performance and arts scene. Like their namesakes in the natural world, they blossom after sundown, lending the night an element of mystery, grandeur and beauty. It was the performer Maxi More who first coined the term, and she describes her fellow 'Night

Flowers' as an 'amorphous mix of characters and creatures who paint the dark corners of the city with colour'.

The portraits in this book grew out of a project I began in early 2014, when every day for 365 days – no matter the weather or whatever was going on in my life – I wandered the streets of London after work in search of its most fascinating and vibrant inhabitants, seeking to photograph some of the people who help to give the city its character, charm and edge. It was in so doing that I started to document the world of the 'Night Flowers', capturing the personalities and their wild array of looks and creative expression at a time when, owing to the increasing pressures of gentrification, the very venues to which many of these people were going were under threat or being closed down.

At first, I chose to place the portraits within the context of the street, and used the location where I 'found' my subject as the backdrop. However, as the make-up and fashions I was photographing became more outlandish, I began to avoid the urban setting, because it seemed to distract from the idiosyncrasies and subtle detail. So I attempted to situate my subjects outside of a time and a place; this gave rise to the dark backgrounds and

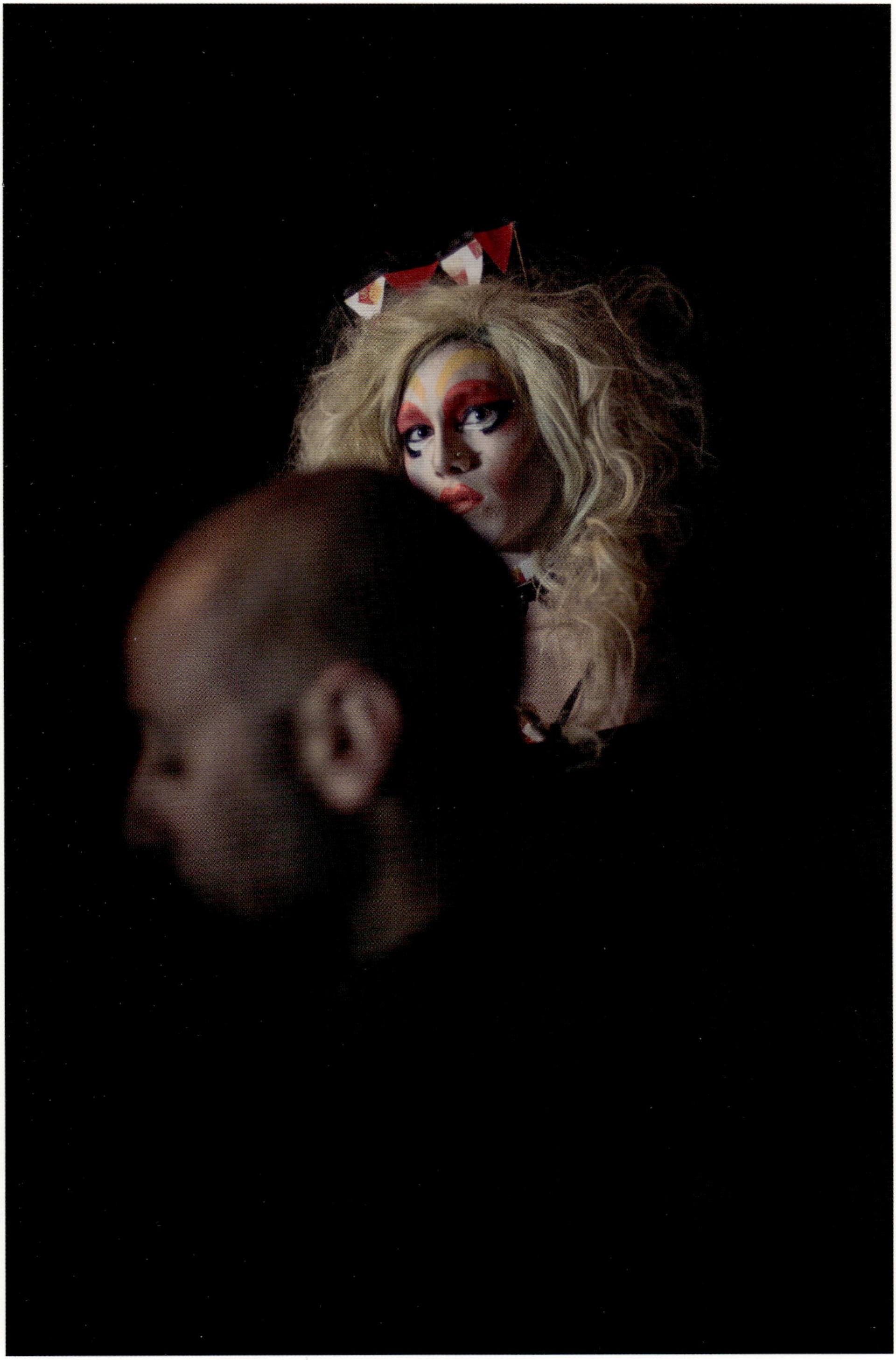

9 | charity kase (with passer-by) on tisbury ct

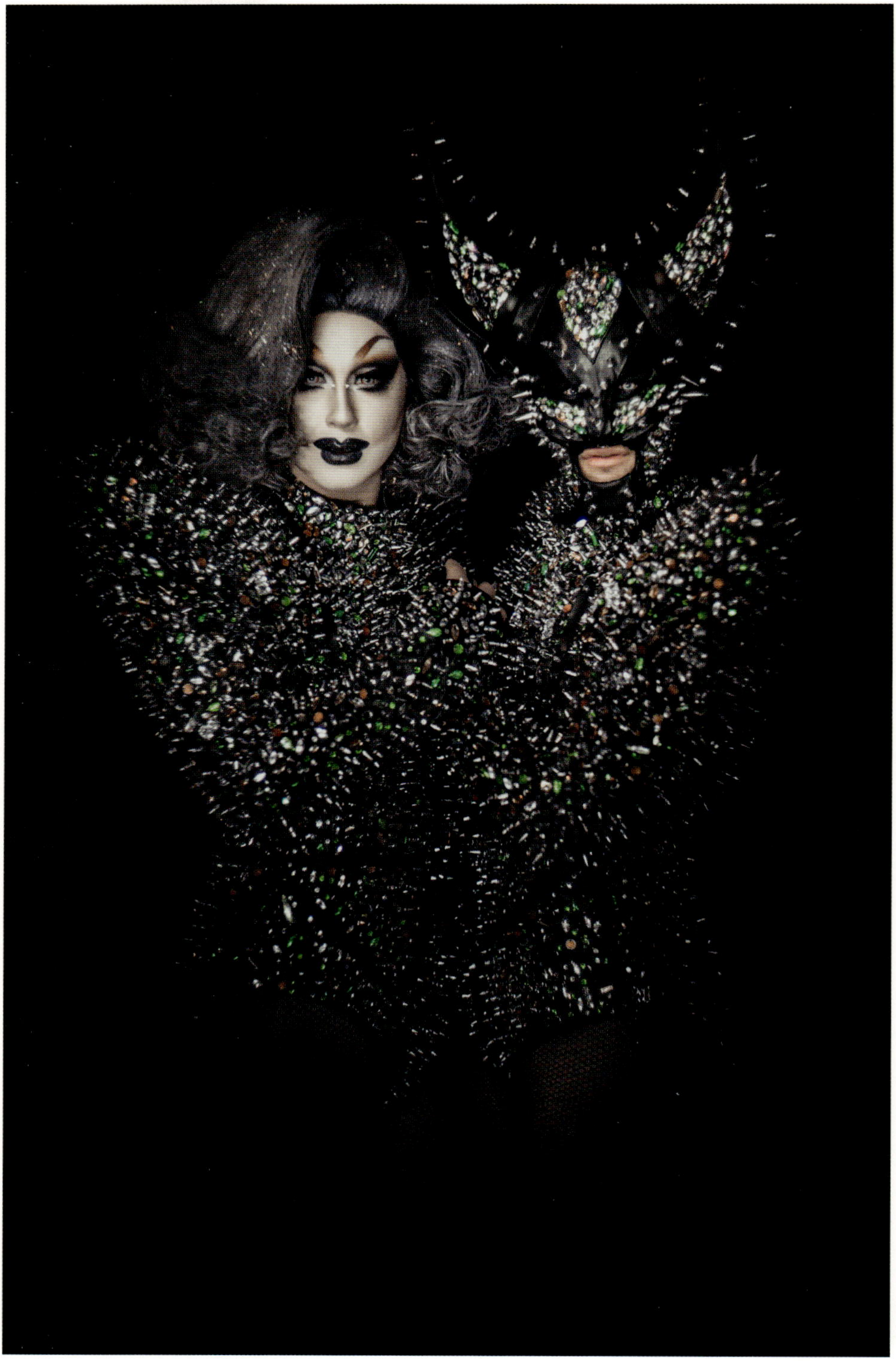

increasingly traditional poses of the photographs. But frequently it meant convincing the sitter – whom I had usually only just met – to agree to walk with me until we could find a suitable background against which to shoot. Sometimes this would take the form of a dark wall (often down a seedy alleyway), but just as easily it could be a brightly lit shopfront or bus stop that would illuminate the subject and force the background to fade away, and at the same time entertain people waiting for their evening bus ride.

As a graphic designer who works in the world of stage productions, I already had an appreciation of all things theatrical, and so became ever more intrigued by the brief glimpses of people who appear in the public domain as if in their own personal theatre, who use the streets as both catwalk and stage, and turn themselves into a walking piece of art. This ephemeral artwork may last a few hours at most – often much less than the amount of time spent creating and sourcing the look. Some members of the drag and club-kid community pride themselves on the vast range of looks they can conjure up, with some making a point never to be seen in the same look twice. Once they've worn it, they consider it 'burnt' and not to be repeated.

The portraits shown here represent only a small proportion of the people who comprise London's alternative night scene. They are incidental portraits, taken after chance encounters on the street or at parties, drag balls or performances, and backstage in clubs, more often than not shot in cramped, insalubrious conditions. The poise and grace of a subject may belie the fact that the photograph was taken at the side of a packed dance floor in a hot, sweaty club; down a dingy, unpleasant alley; or on a crowded street, where we were met with quizzical or amused looks, taunts and other comments from passers-by, even not-so-accidental 'bumps' as they walked past.

The extravagant looks of the sitters, all sequins and glitter on initial impression, hide the difficulties and sometimes outright danger that the people wearing them may face on a daily basis, where they are constantly questioned, catcalled, prodded and poked by strangers. Their very existence seems to stop people in their tracks; sometimes the onlookers stare in awe and with respect, but just as frequently in indignation. Even in an area considered as liberal as London's Soho, it's not unusual to hear of unprovoked attacks from strangers late at night on members of this

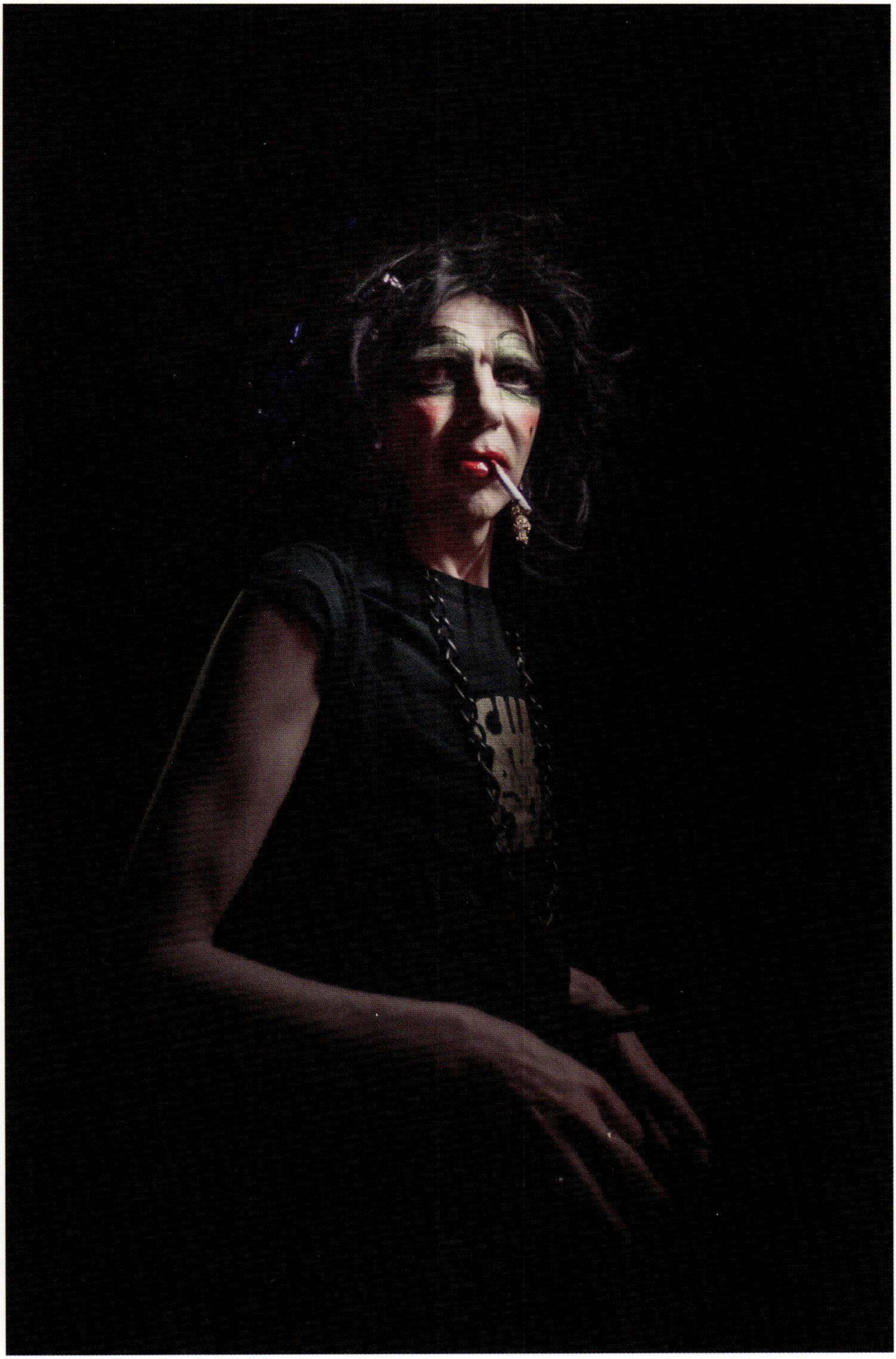

13 | david hoyle backstage at kaos

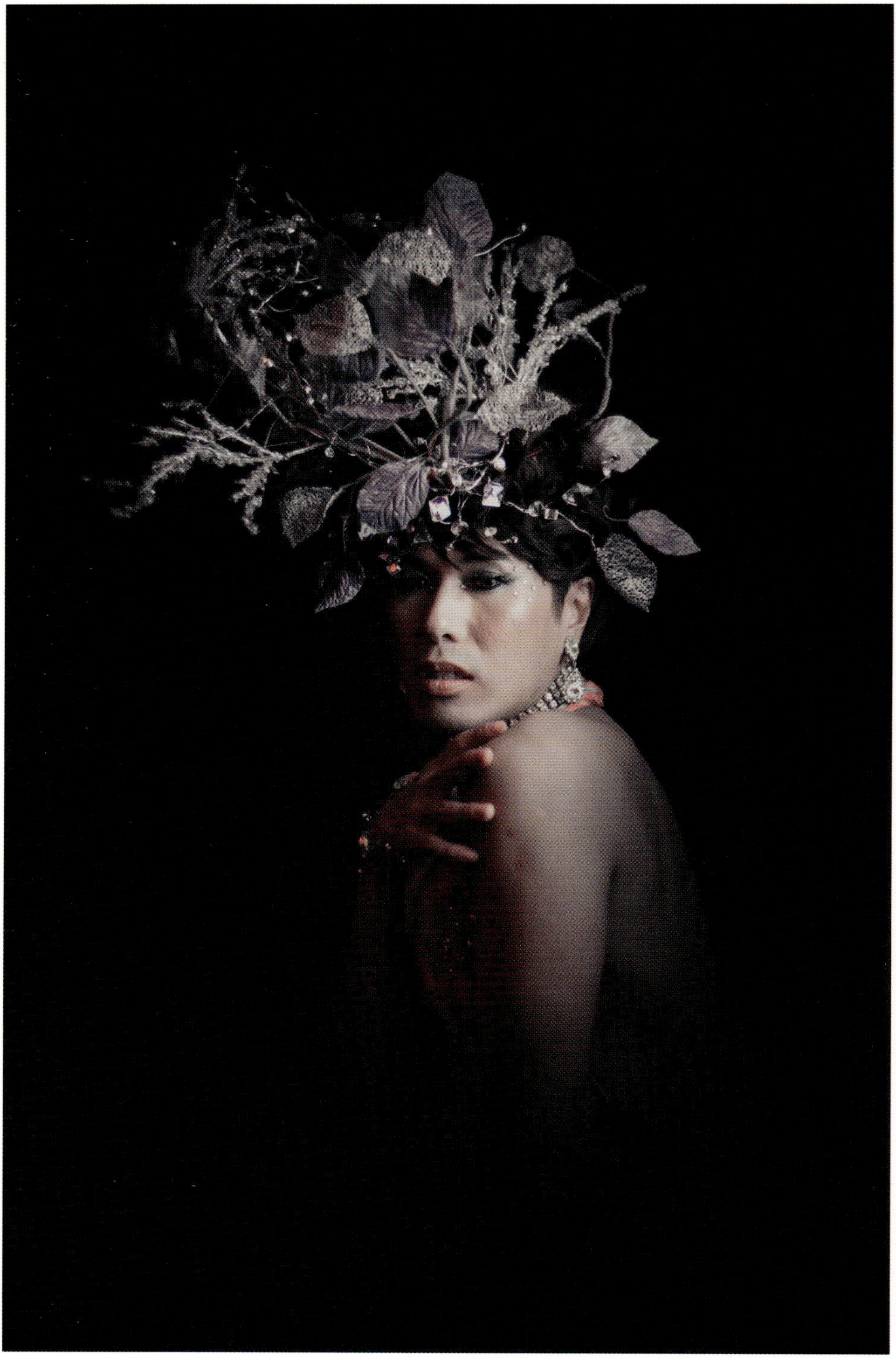

community. In a world where everything is packaged according to age-old market demographics, it's easy to regard these 'Night Flowers' as being the torch-bearers of an anti-establishment ethos of 'true' punk, as much as they are the precursors to many fashion and pop-culture trends. There's a transgressive spirit of rebellion that's inherent in many of the looks, whether it's rebelling against binary gender roles or simply what's viewed as 'normal' or in good taste.

In Plato's *Symposium*, in his speech in reference to the androgynes – humans who were both male and female, described appropriately as 'children of the moon' – Aristophanes claims, 'Terrible was their might and strength, and the thoughts of their hearts were great, and they made an attack upon the gods'. It could be argued that, even today, these 'children of the moon' still have the ability to attack the gods, to confound expectation and to provoke reaction, intentionally or not, just by exercising their freedom to be who they choose to be. It's my hope that these portraits document them in both their might and strength (and also their great hearts). If the images go even just a small way towards attacking the gods, then it will have been a worthwhile cause.

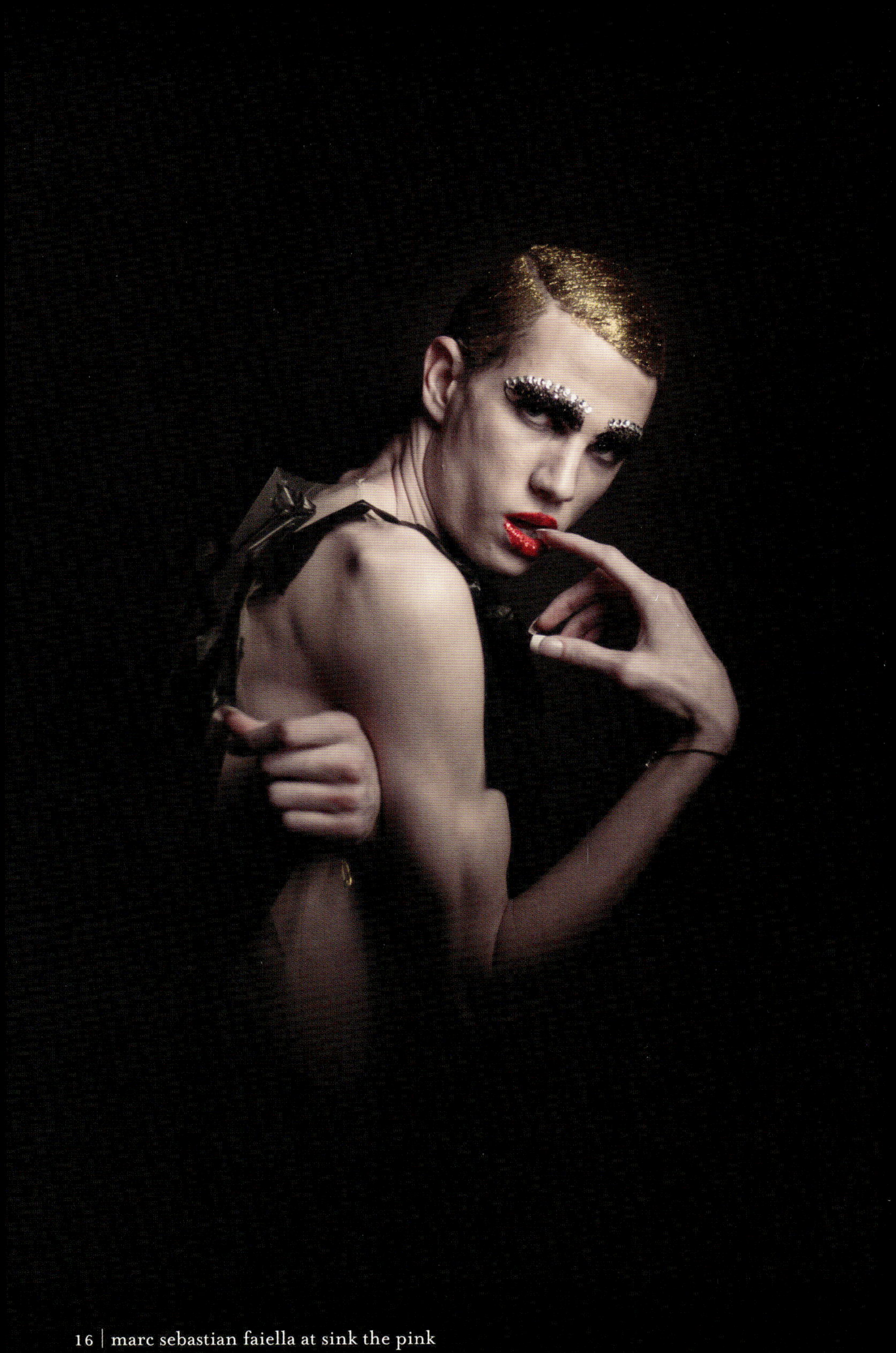

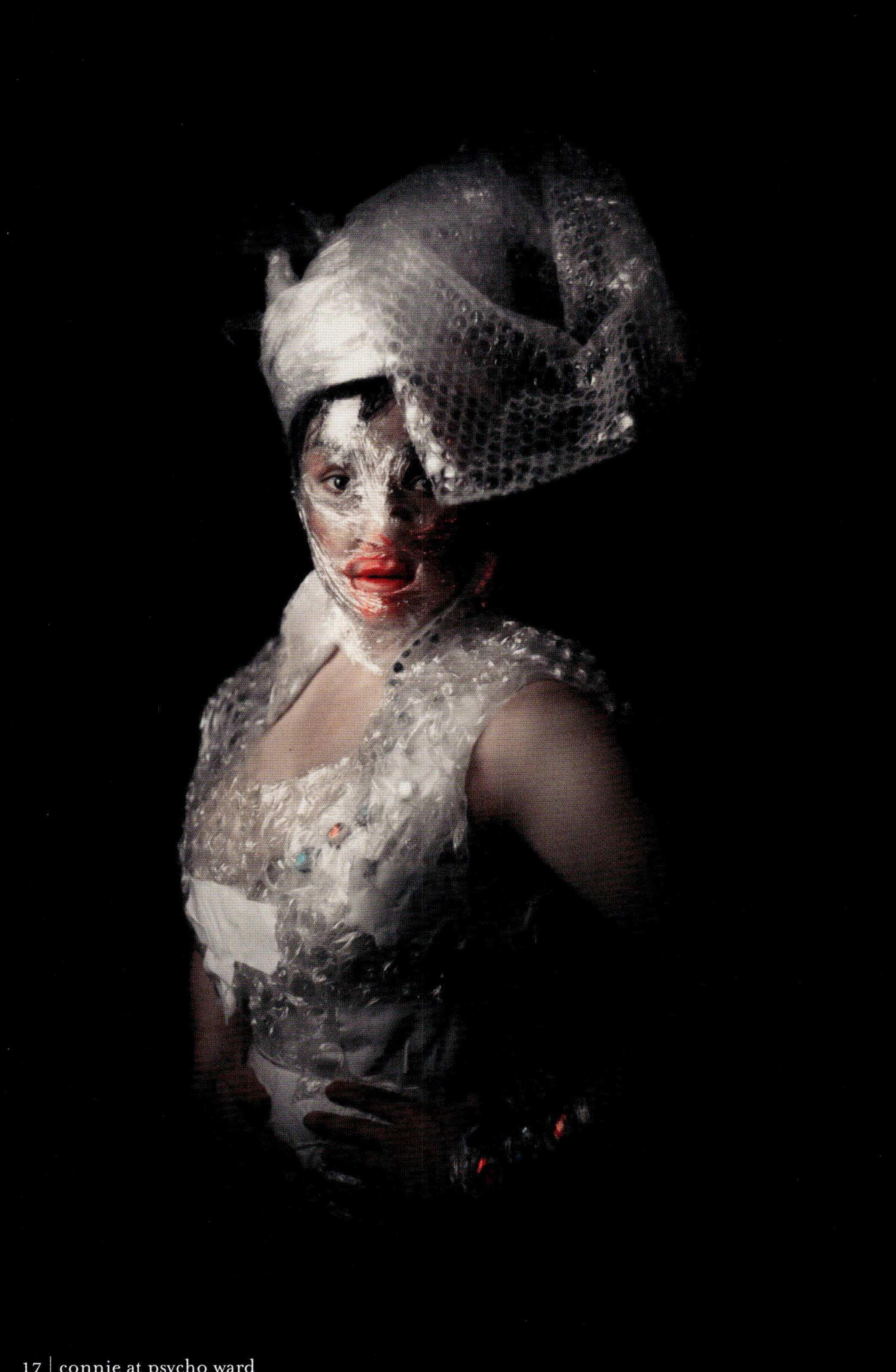

17 | connie at psycho ward

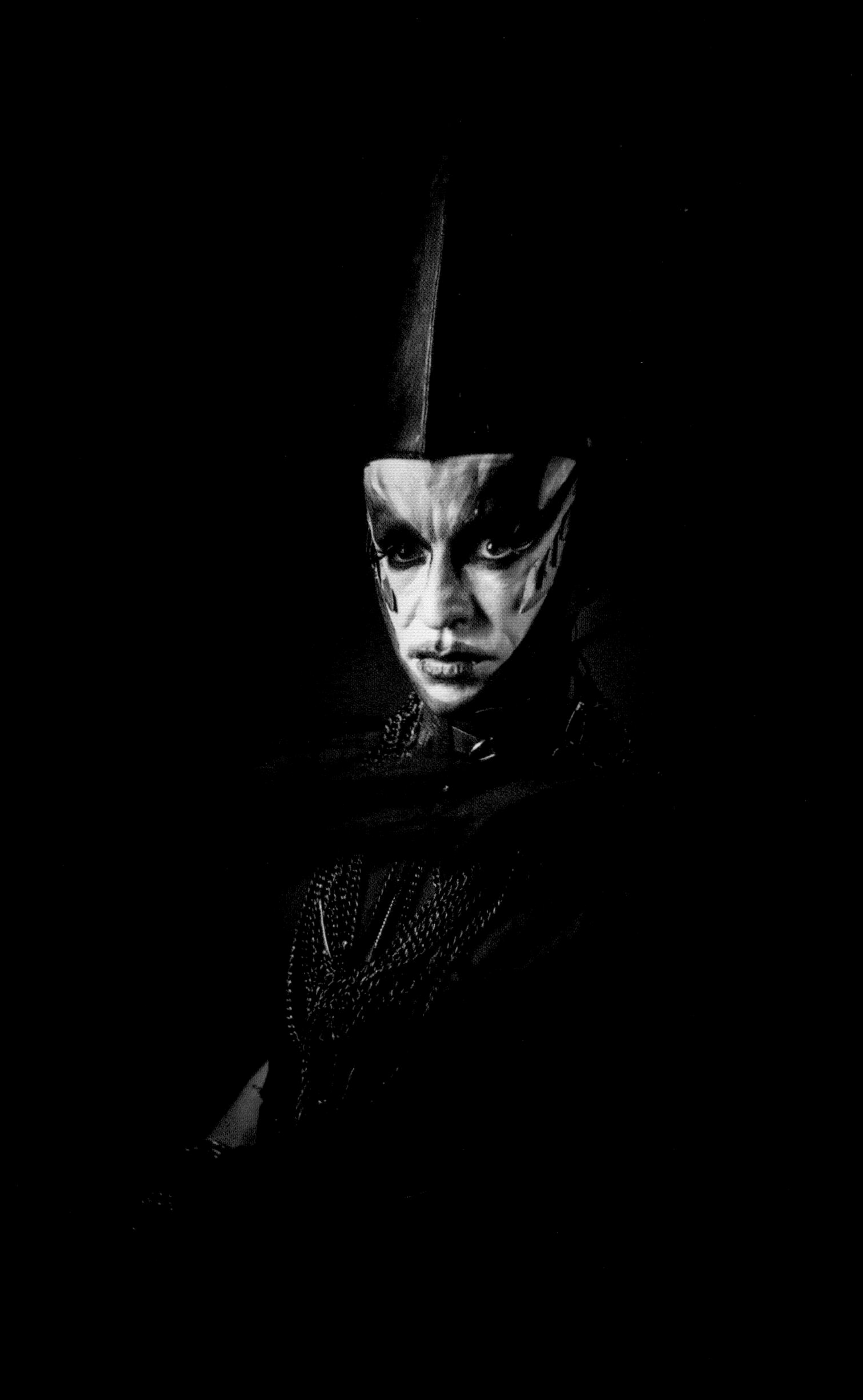

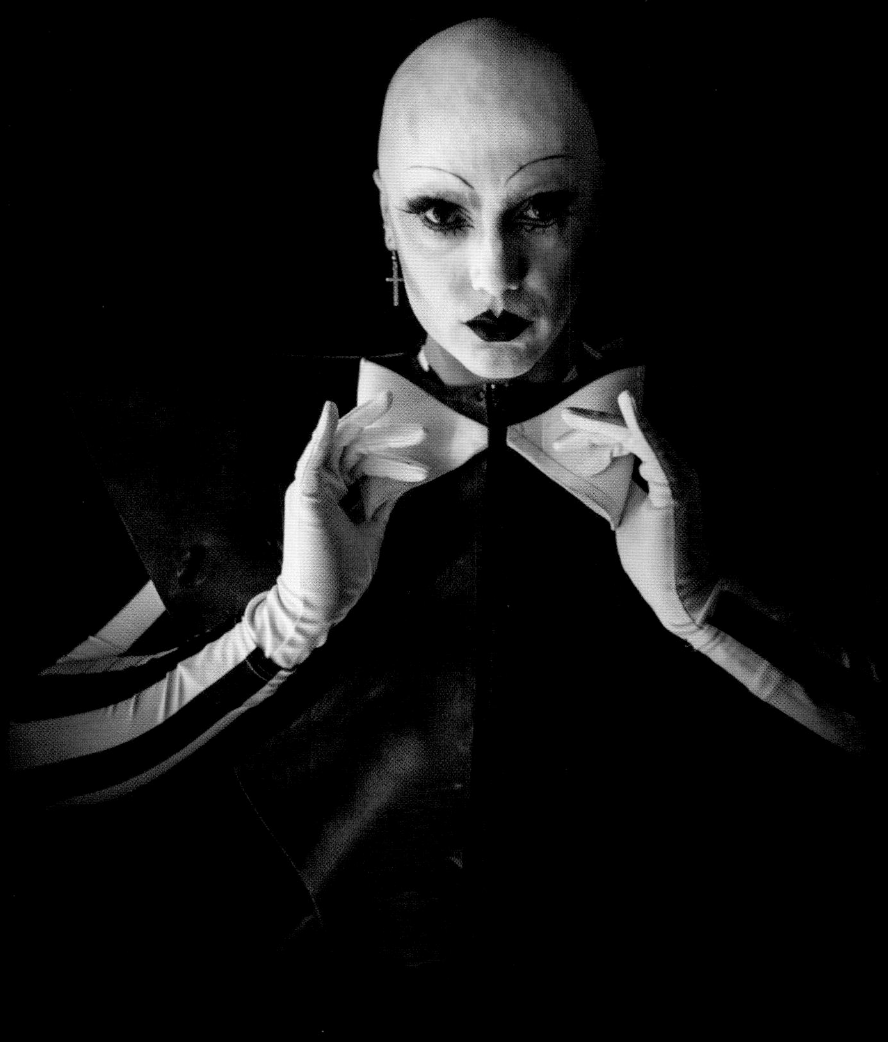

19 | le pustra on theobald's rd

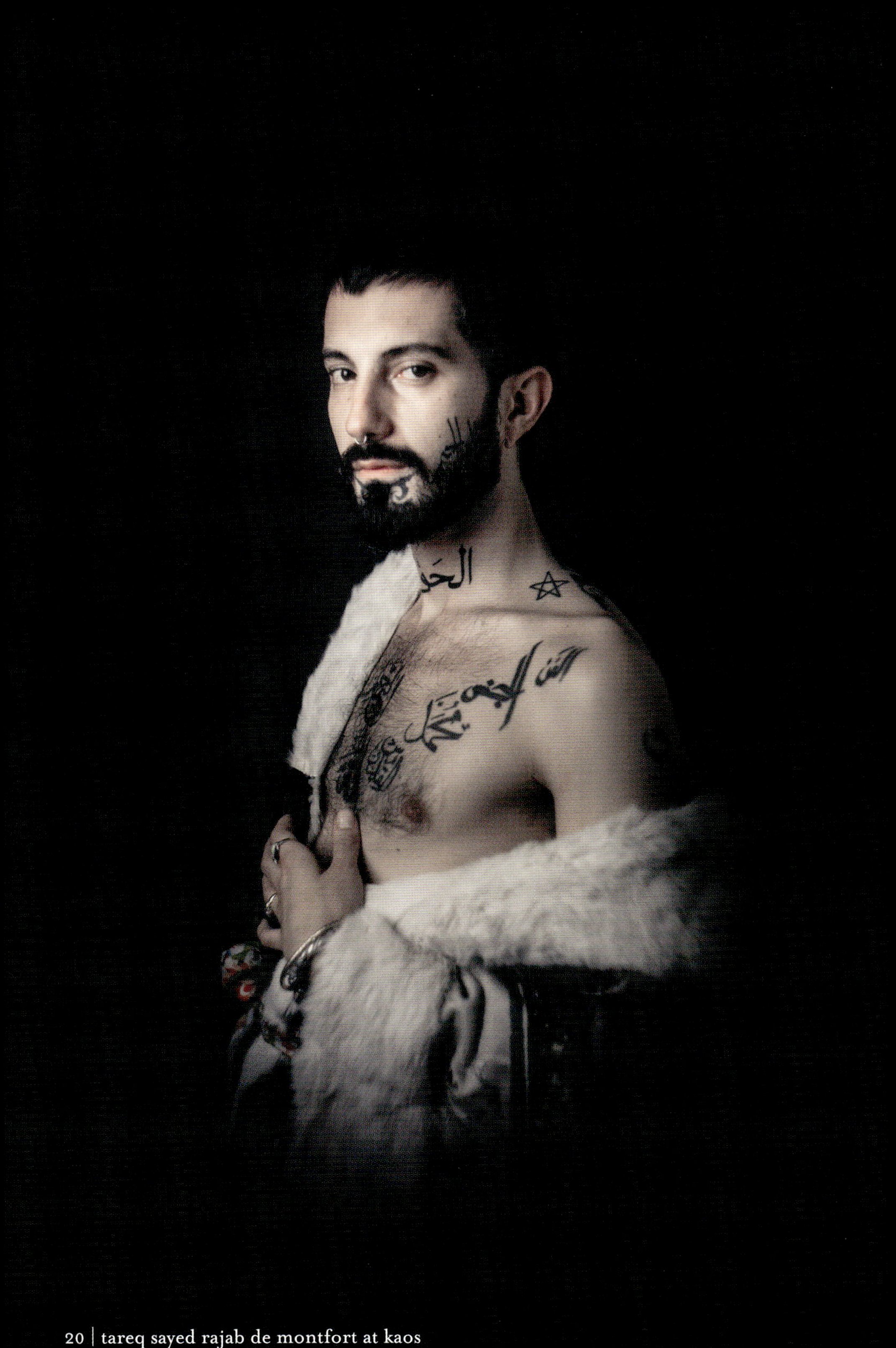

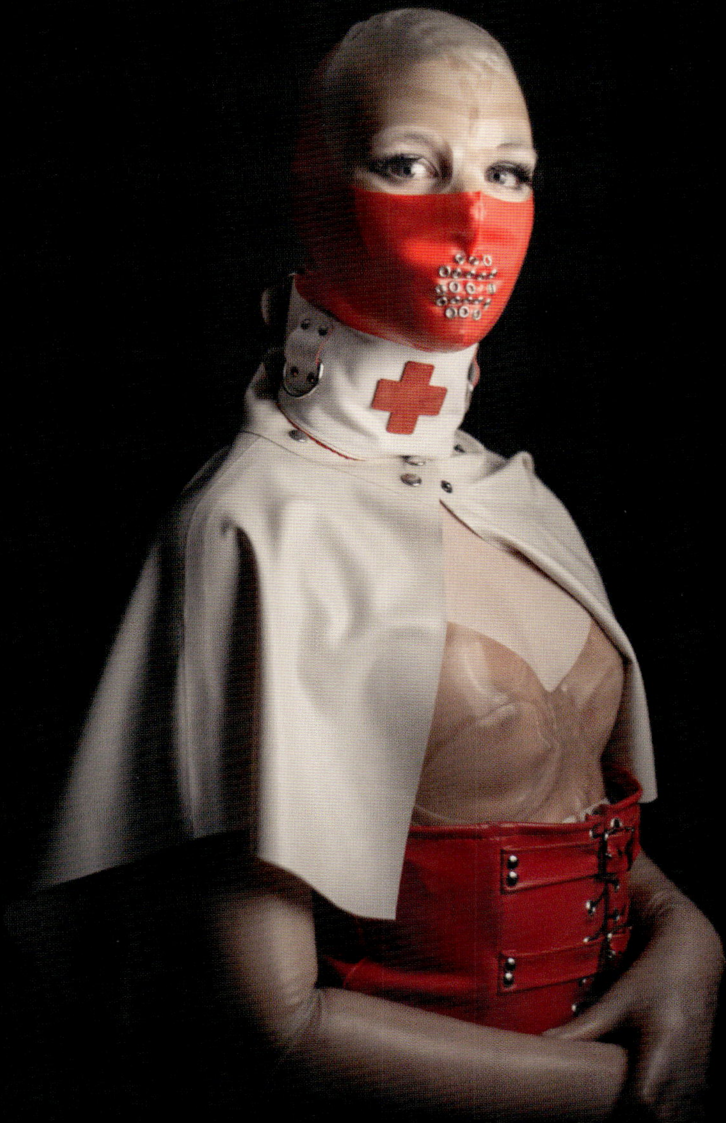

21 | cynth icorn at psycho ward

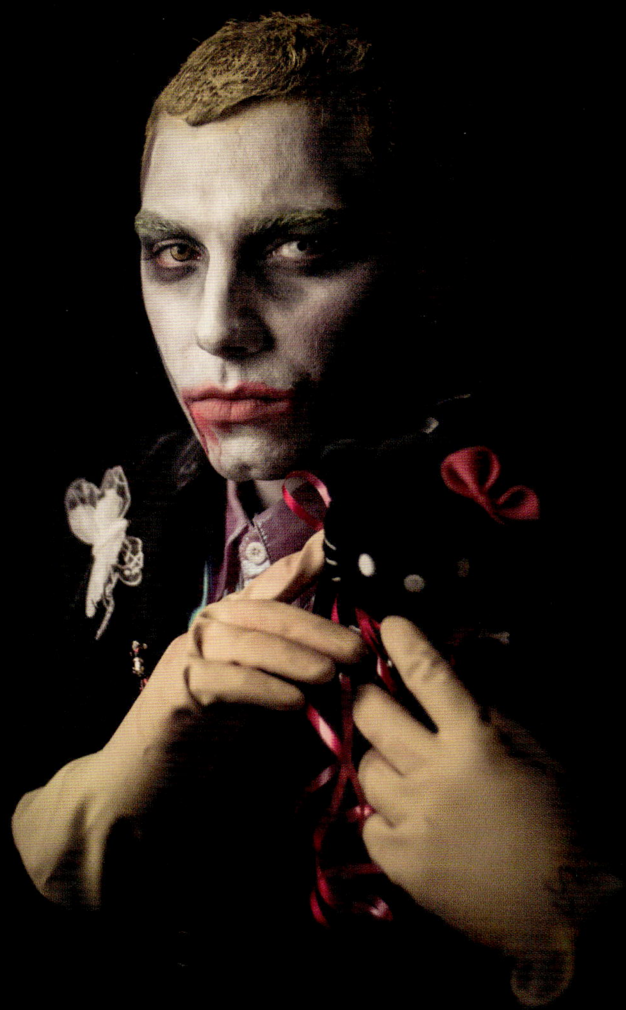

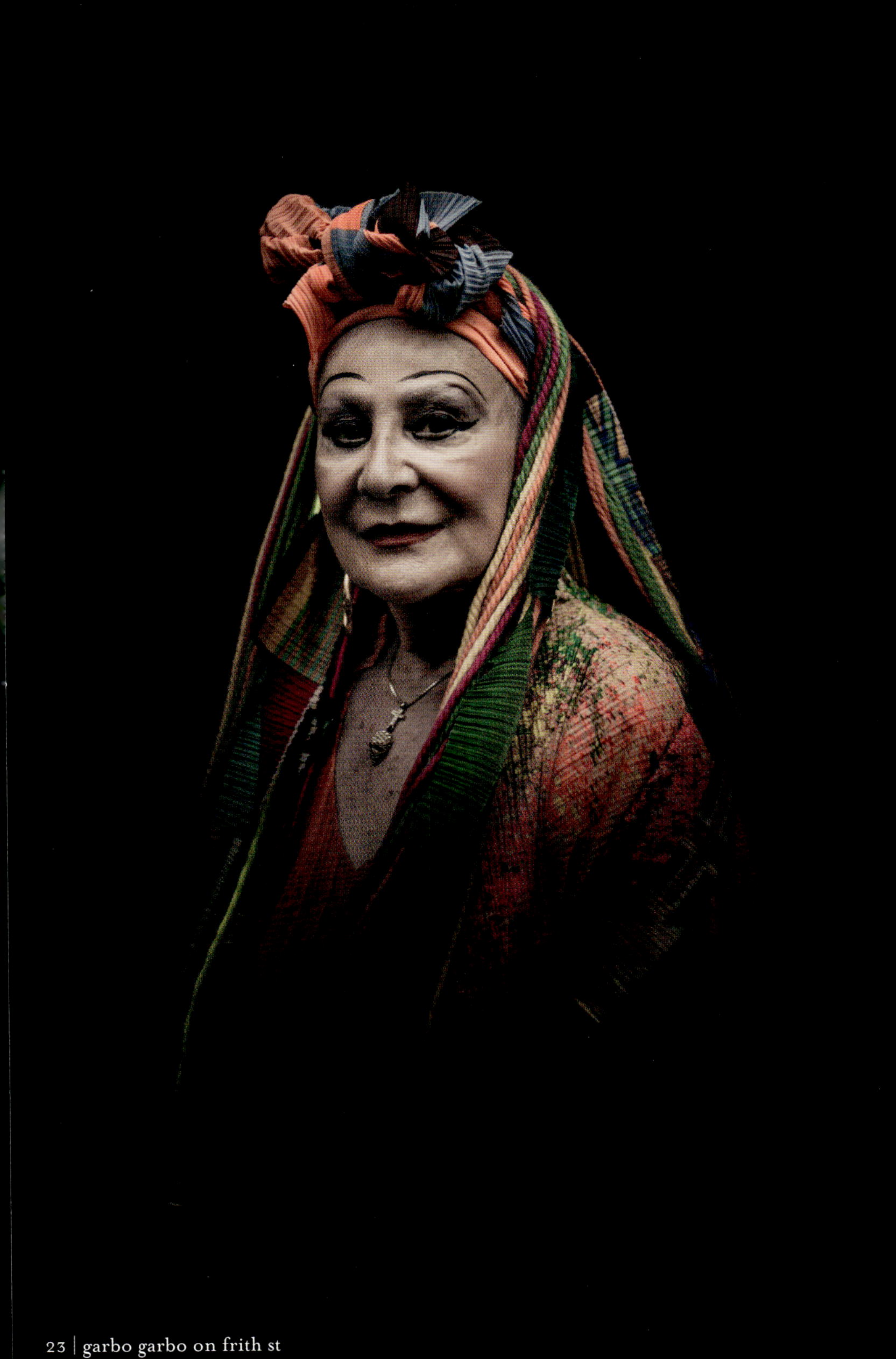

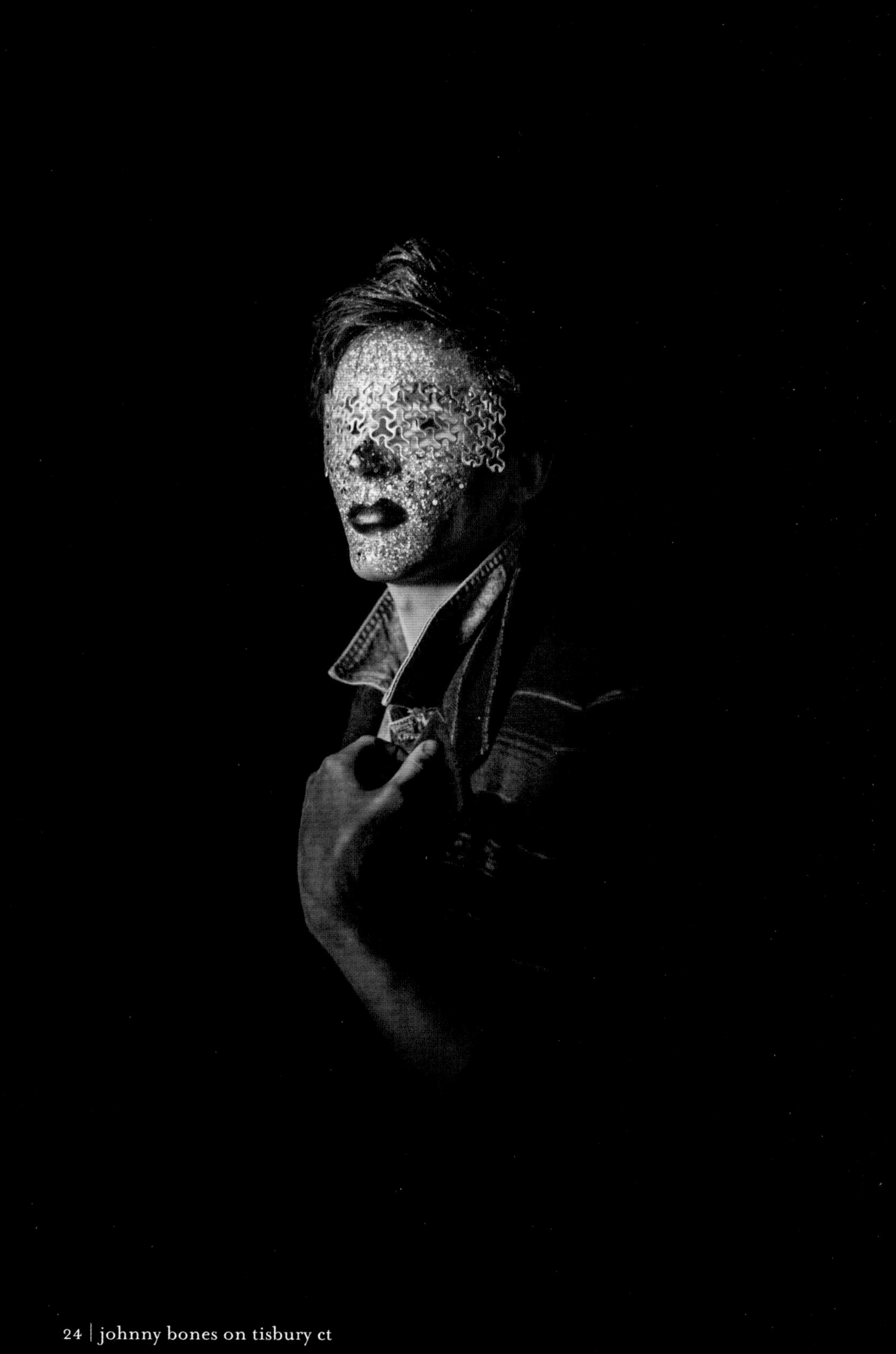

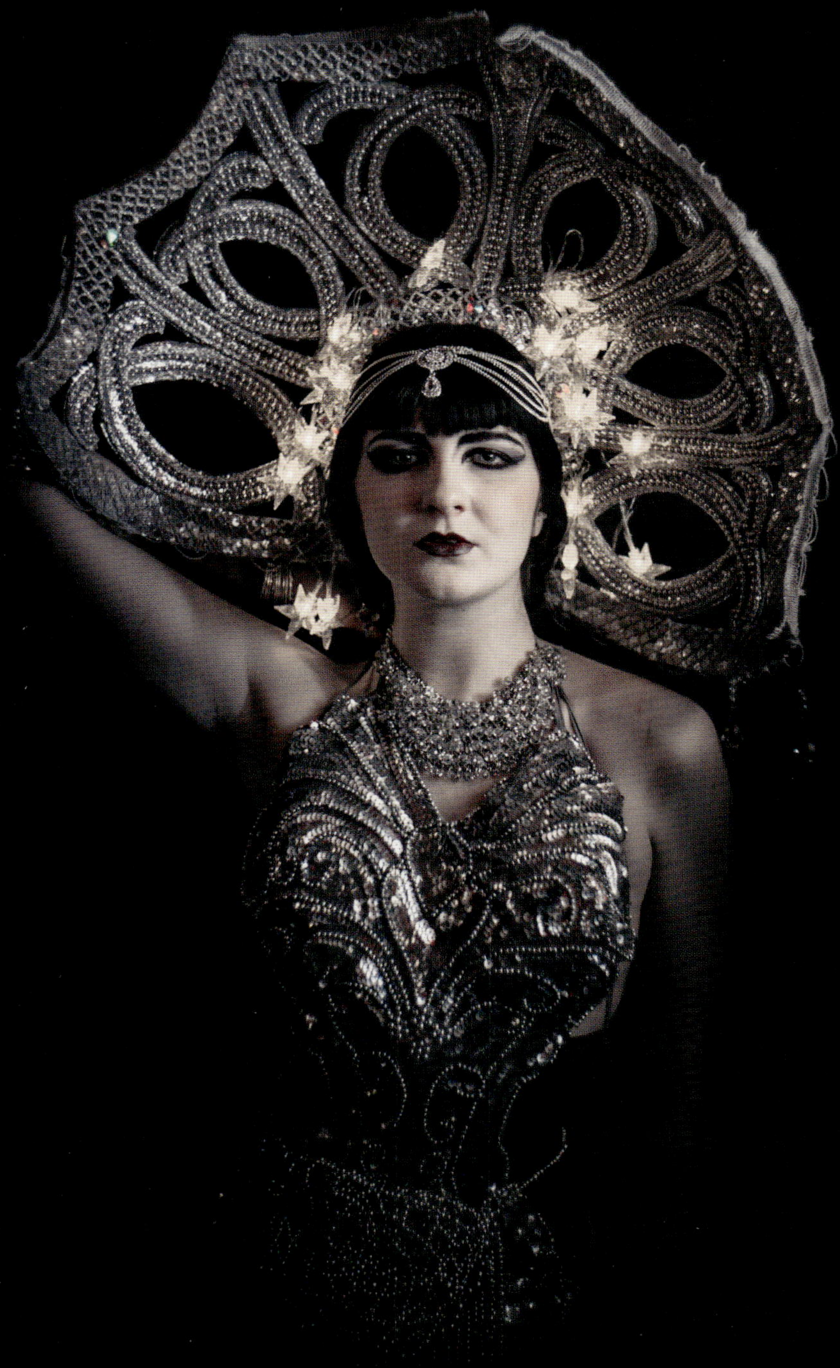

 charlotte vka at cirque le soir

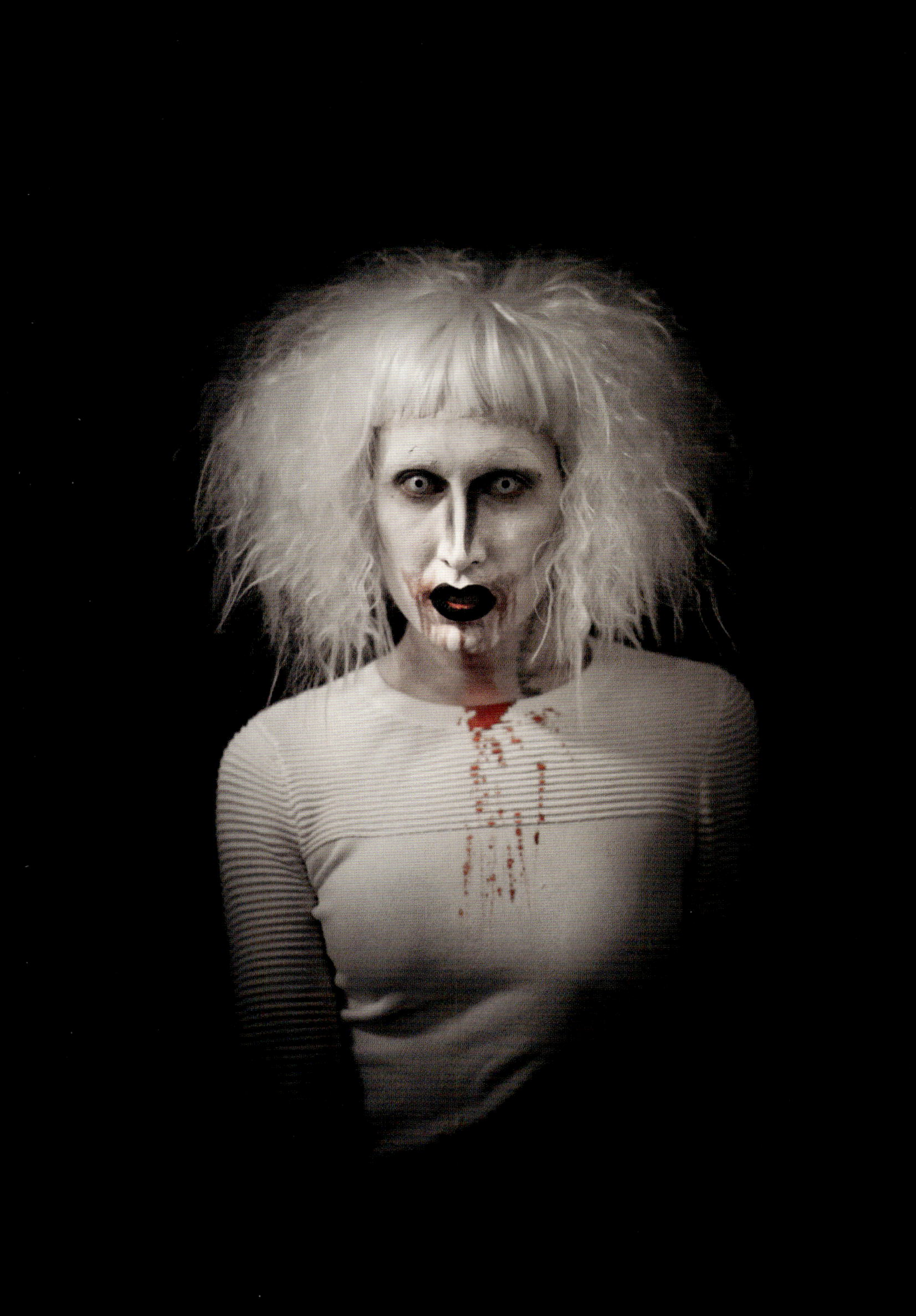

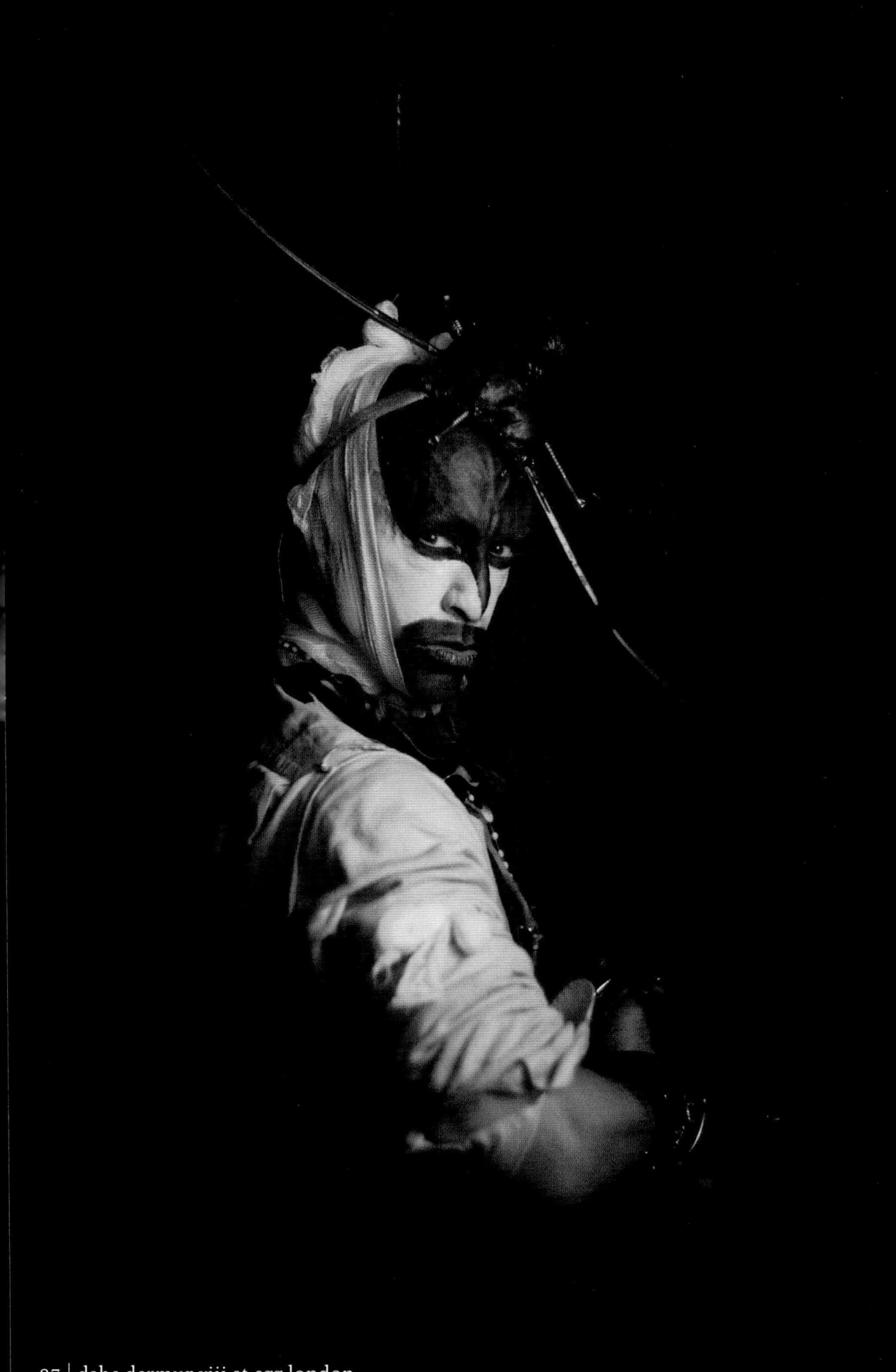

27 | dahc dermur viii at egg london

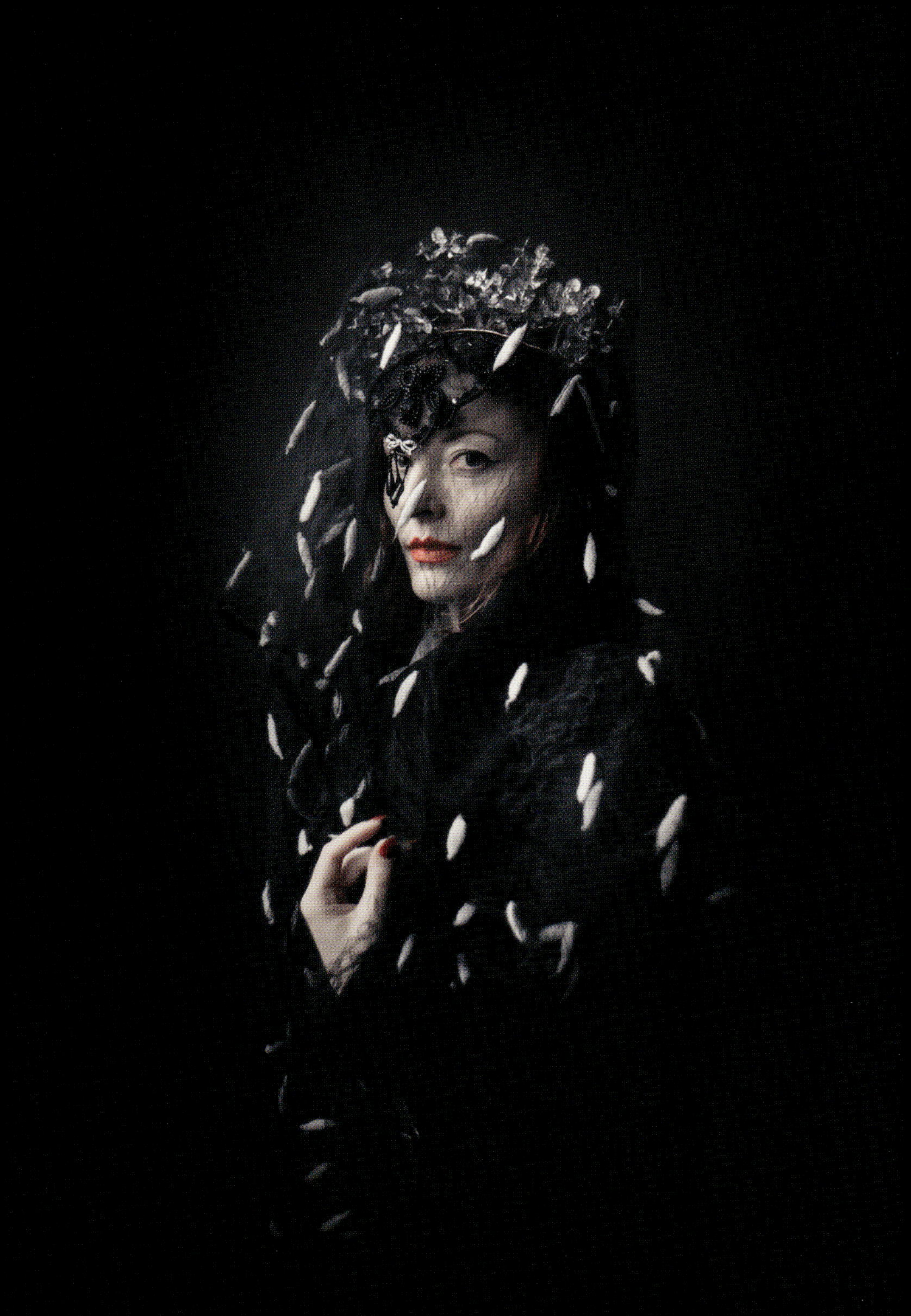

 | lucy february at shoreditch high st station

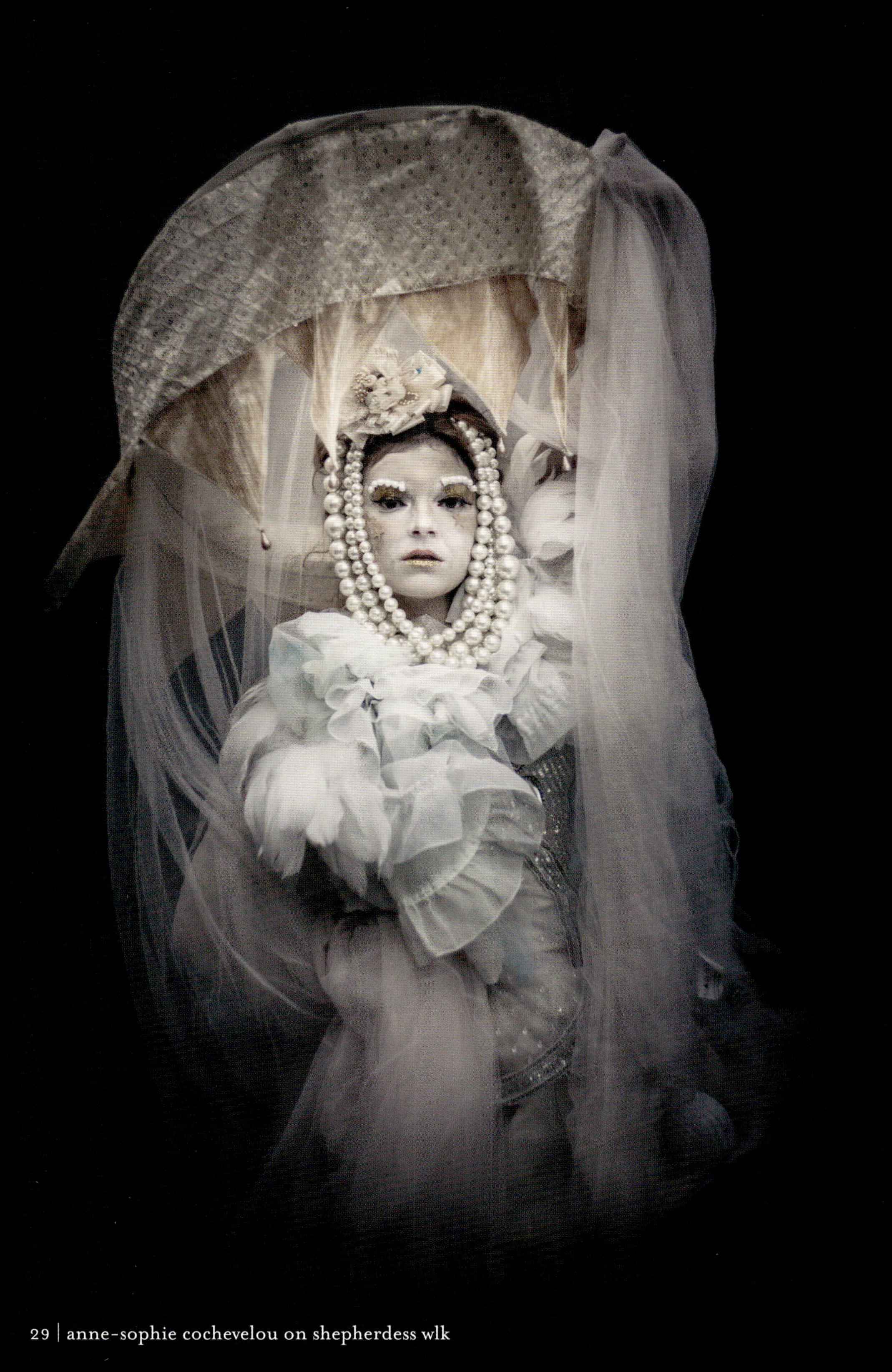

29 | anne-sophie cochevelou on shepherdess wlk

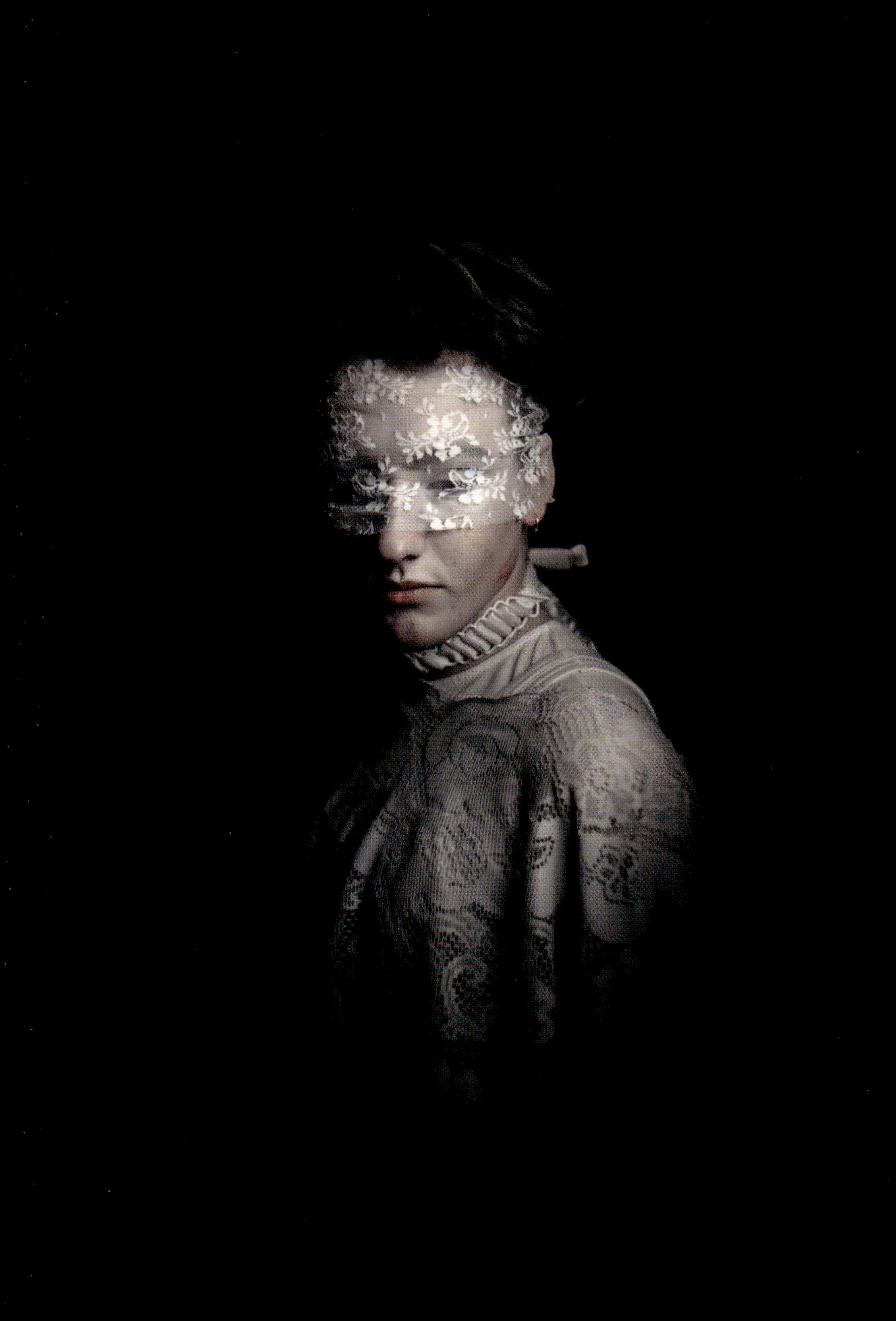

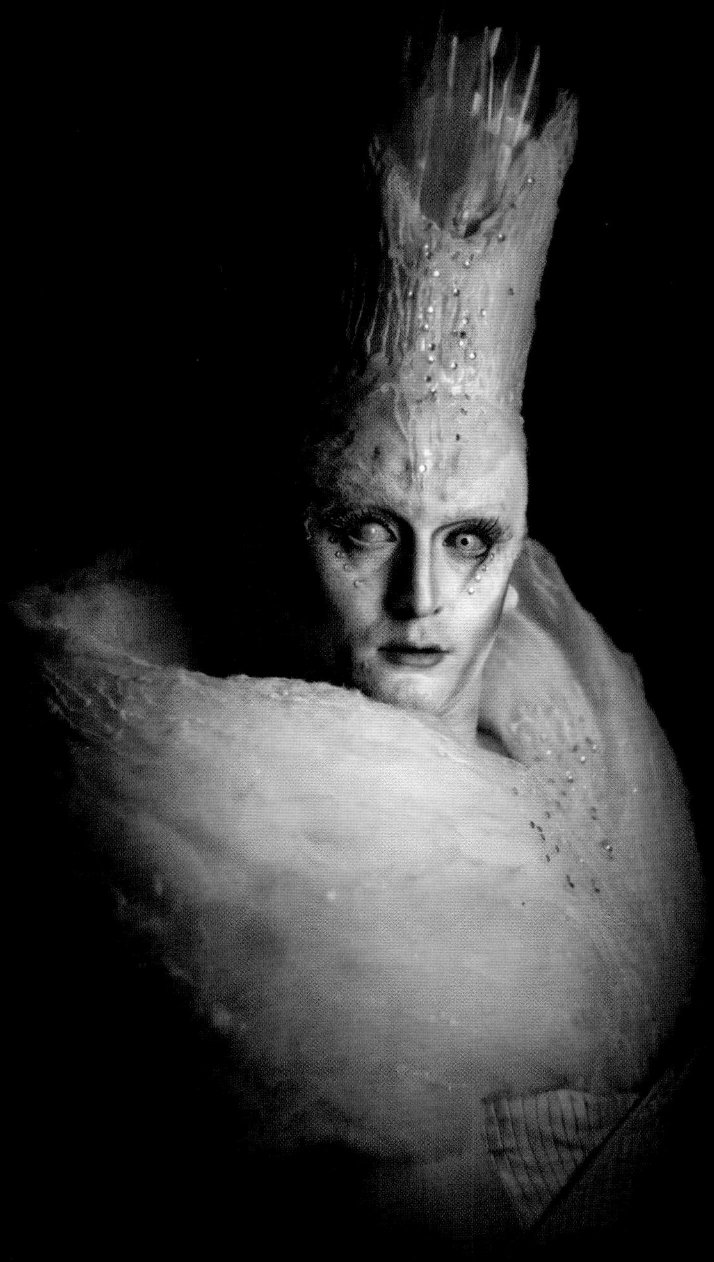

31 | luke harris at the sink the pink winter ball

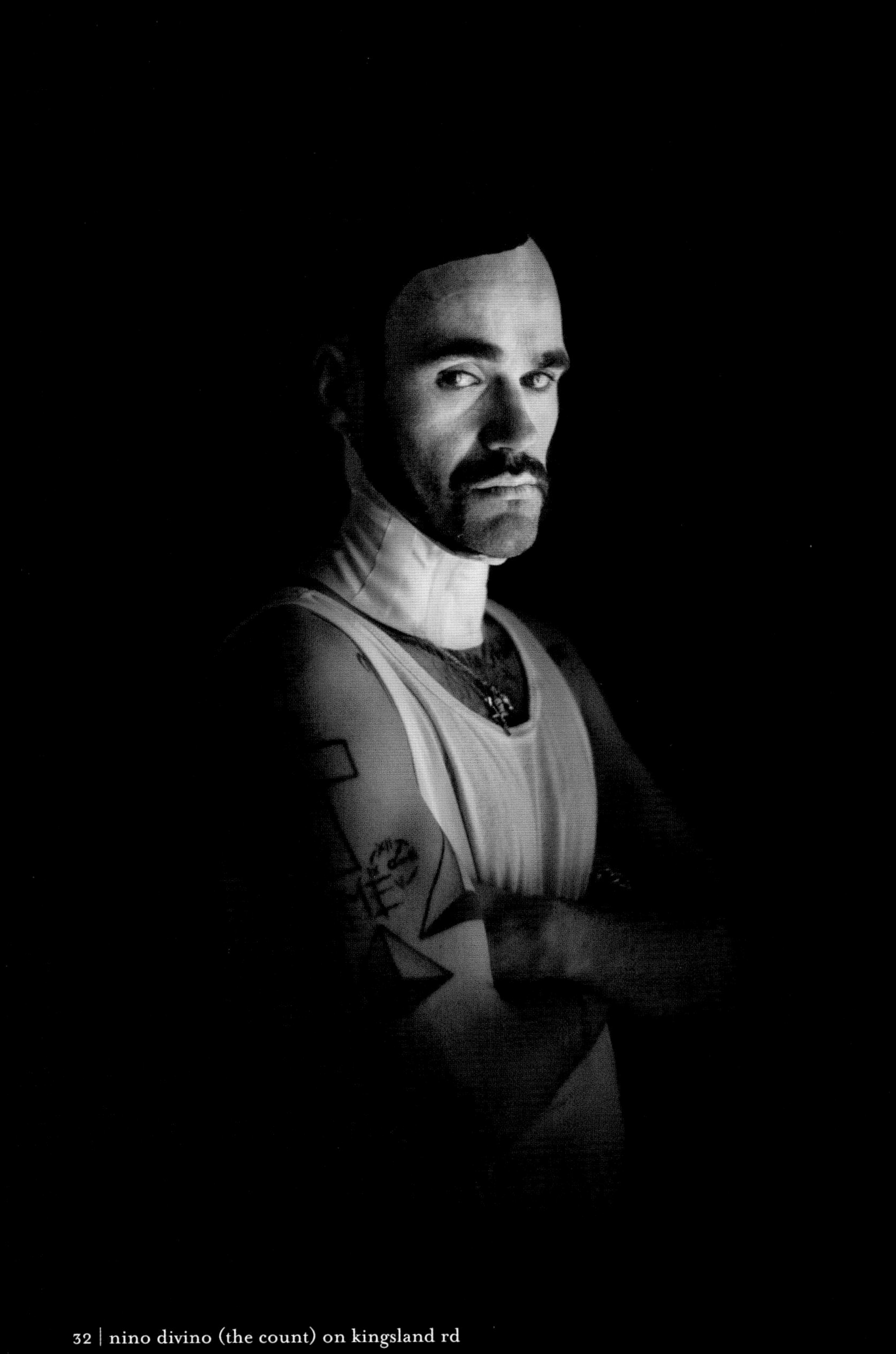

 nino divino (the count) on kingsland rd

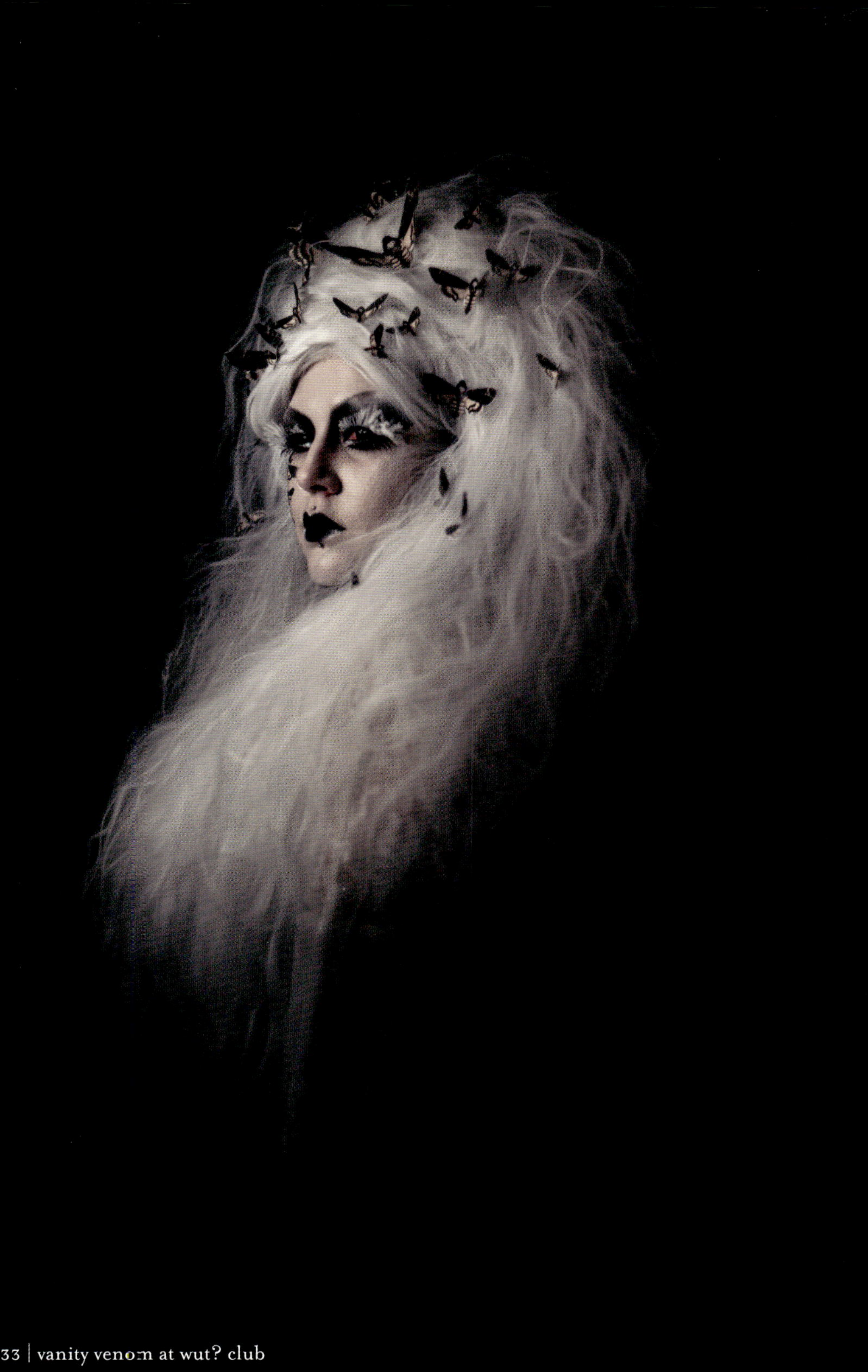

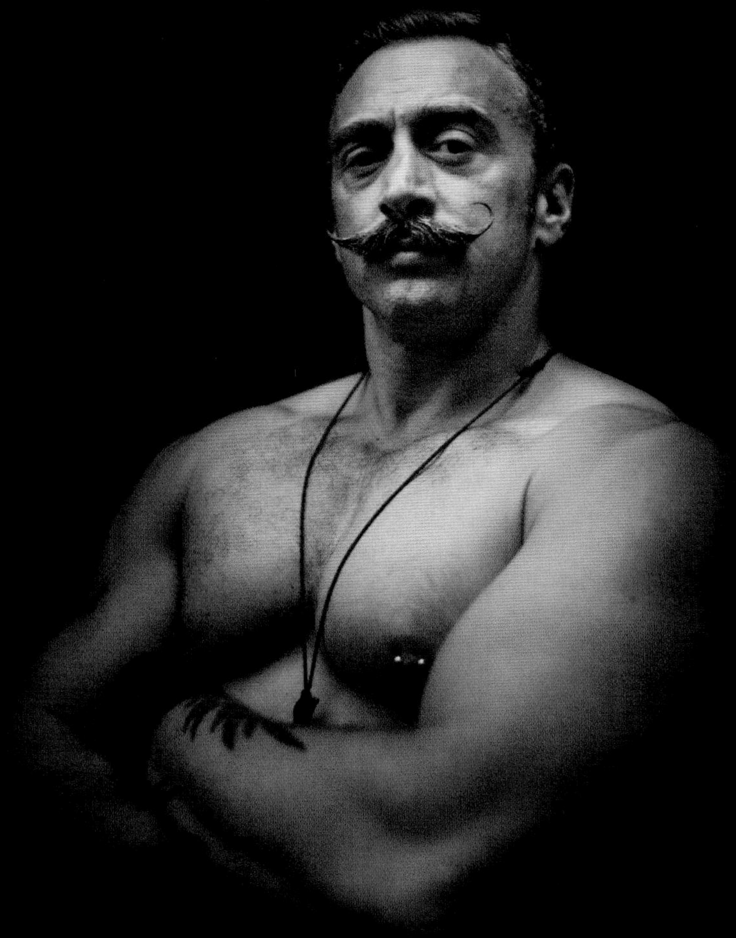

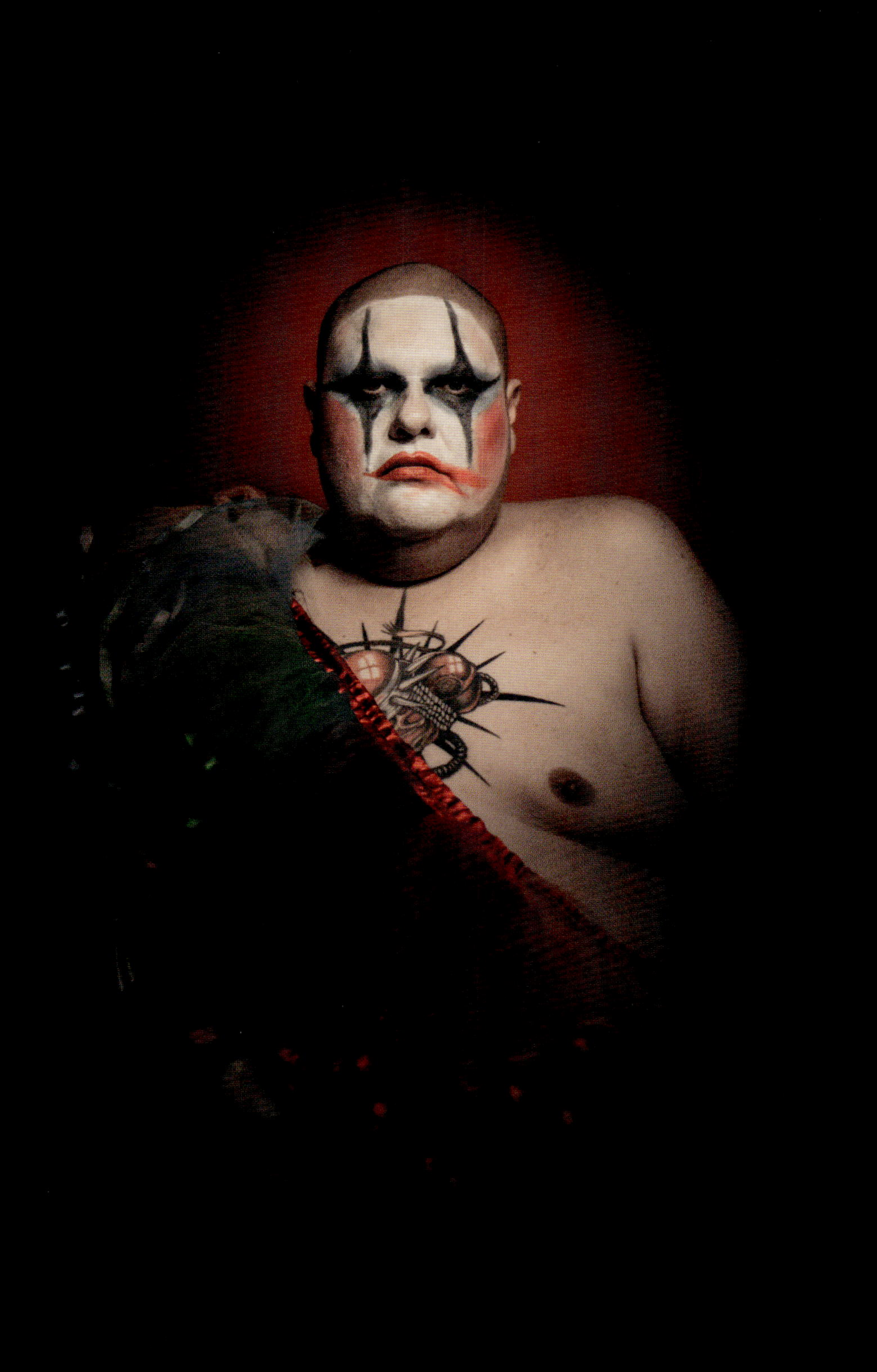

35 | the infamous boom boom at cirque le soir

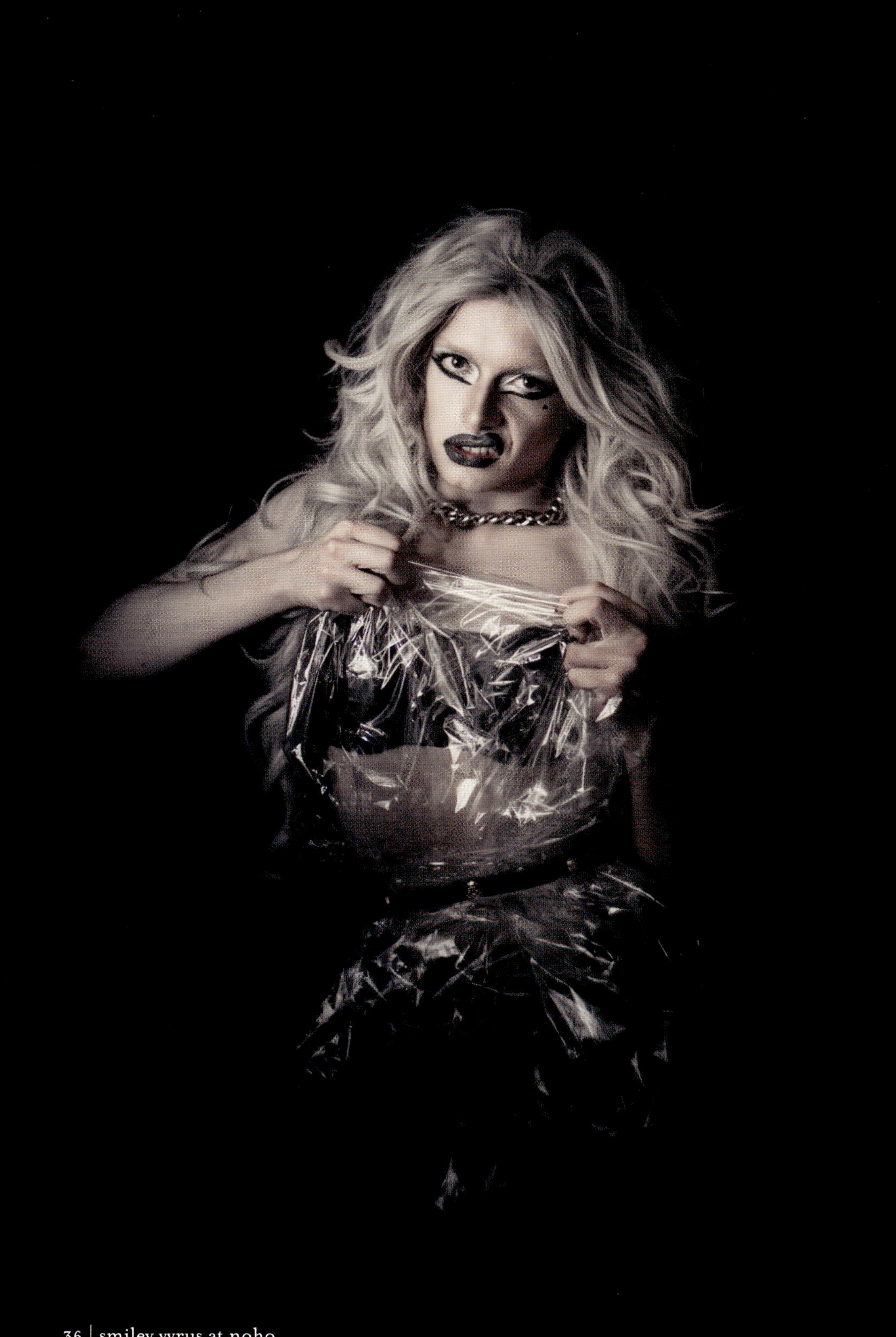

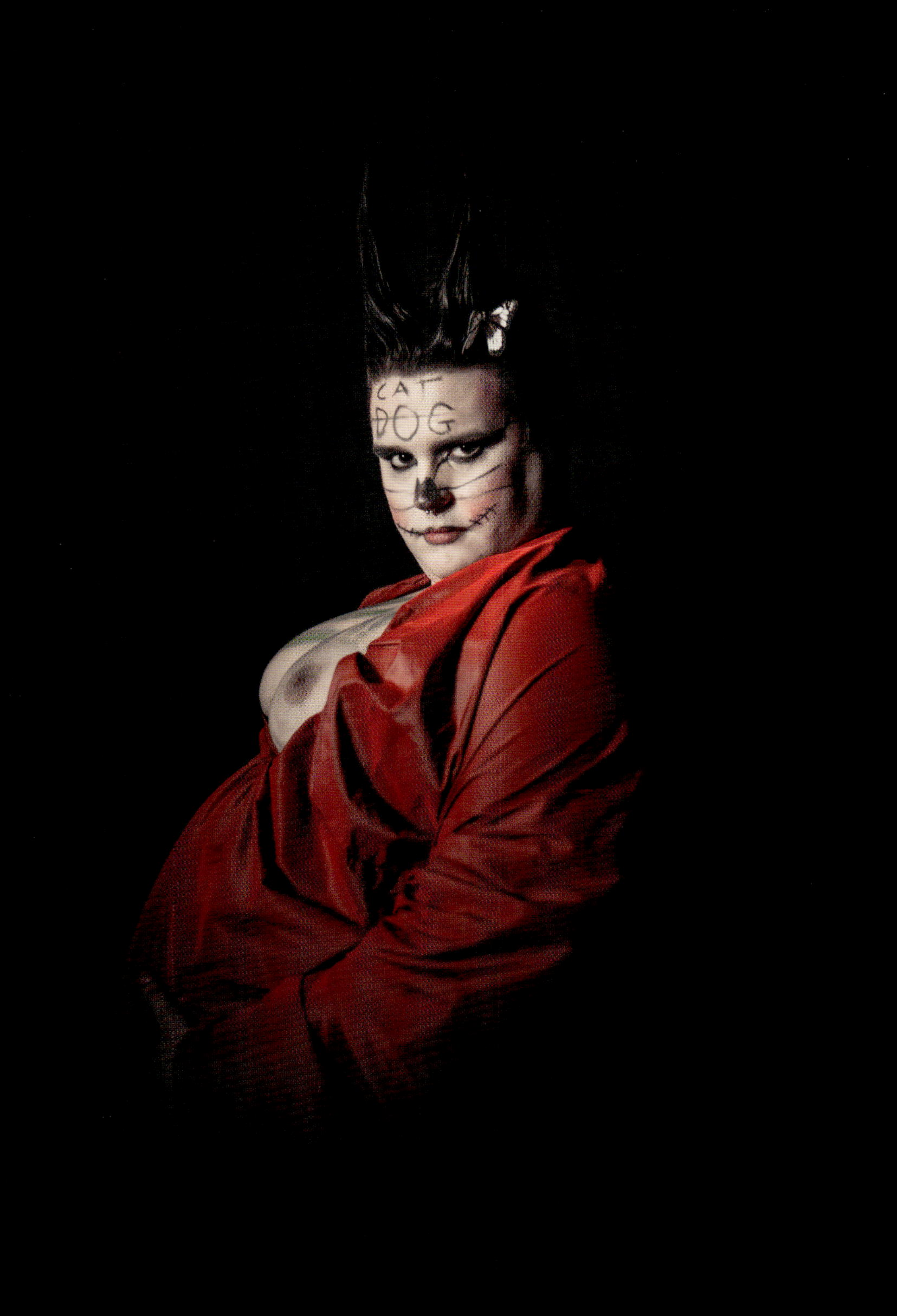

37 | sam buttery on sloane sq.

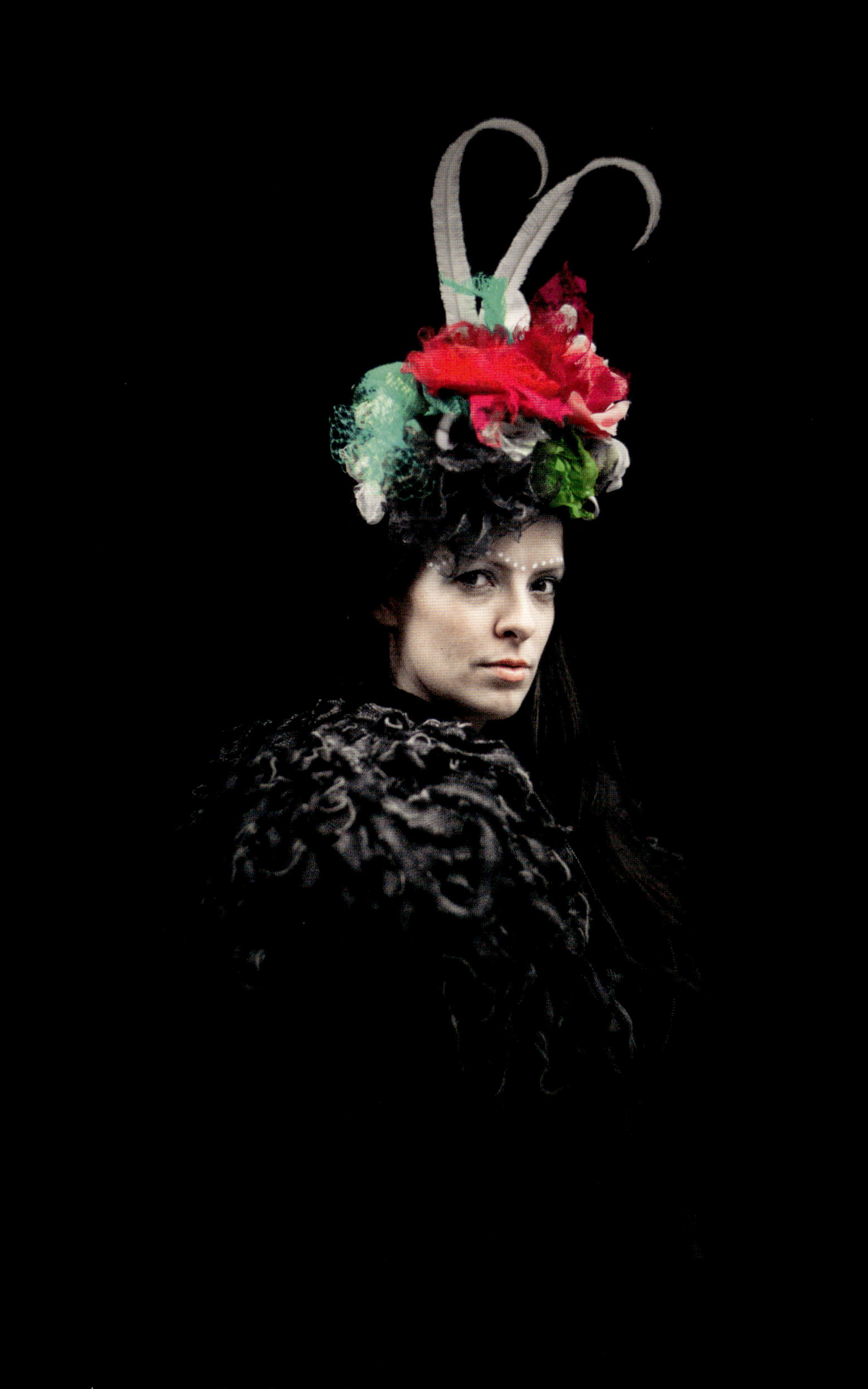

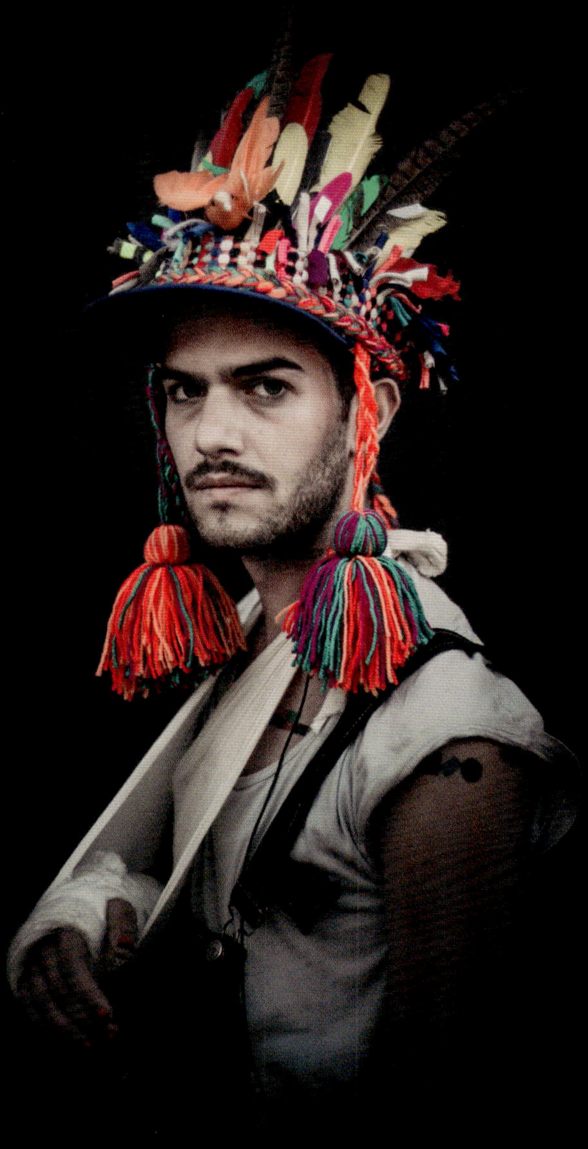

39 | mátyás vasicza on shoreditch high st

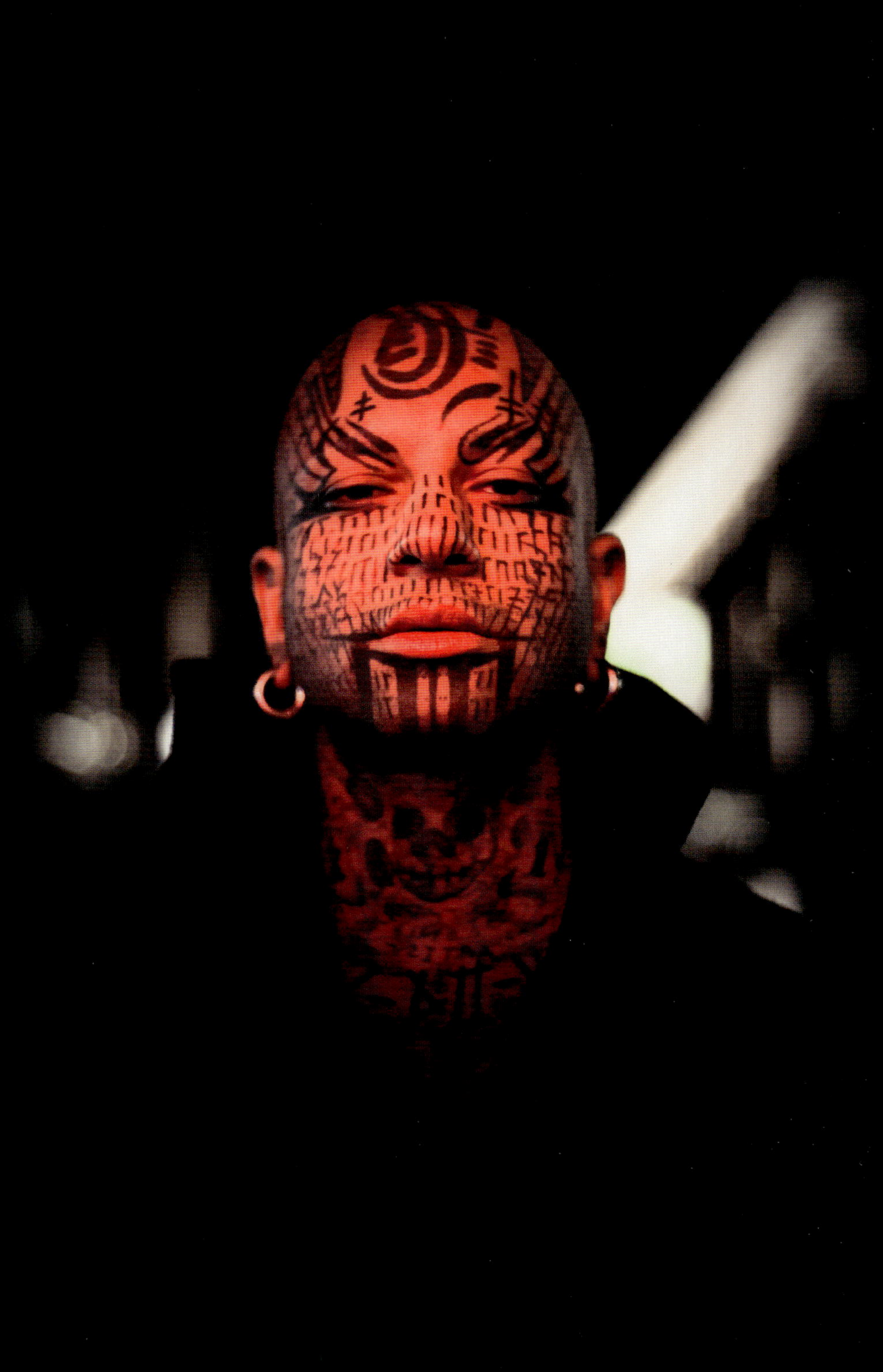

 | touka voodoo on old compton st

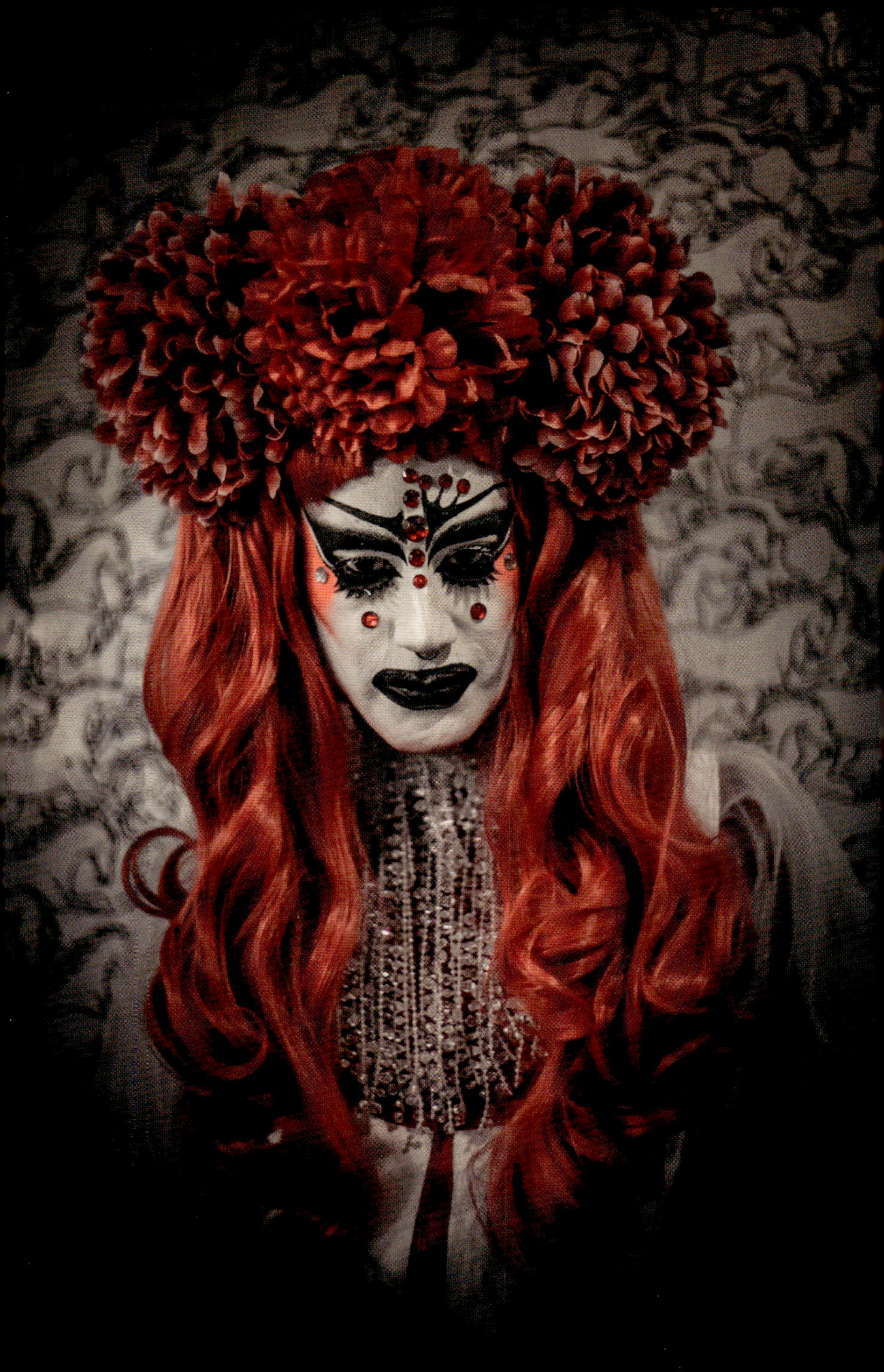

1 | twiggy birmingham on brewer st

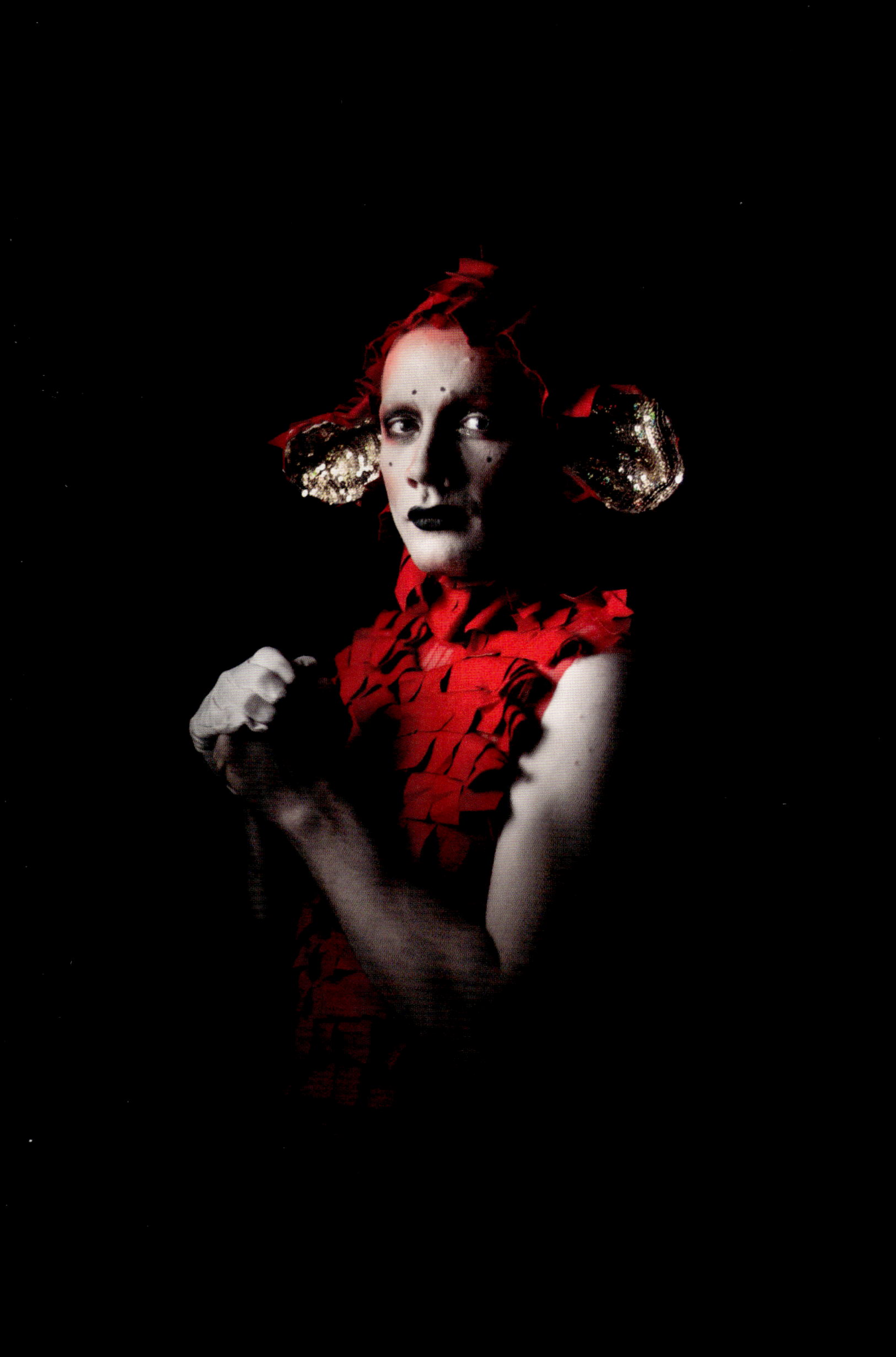

 | ginger johnson at sink the pink

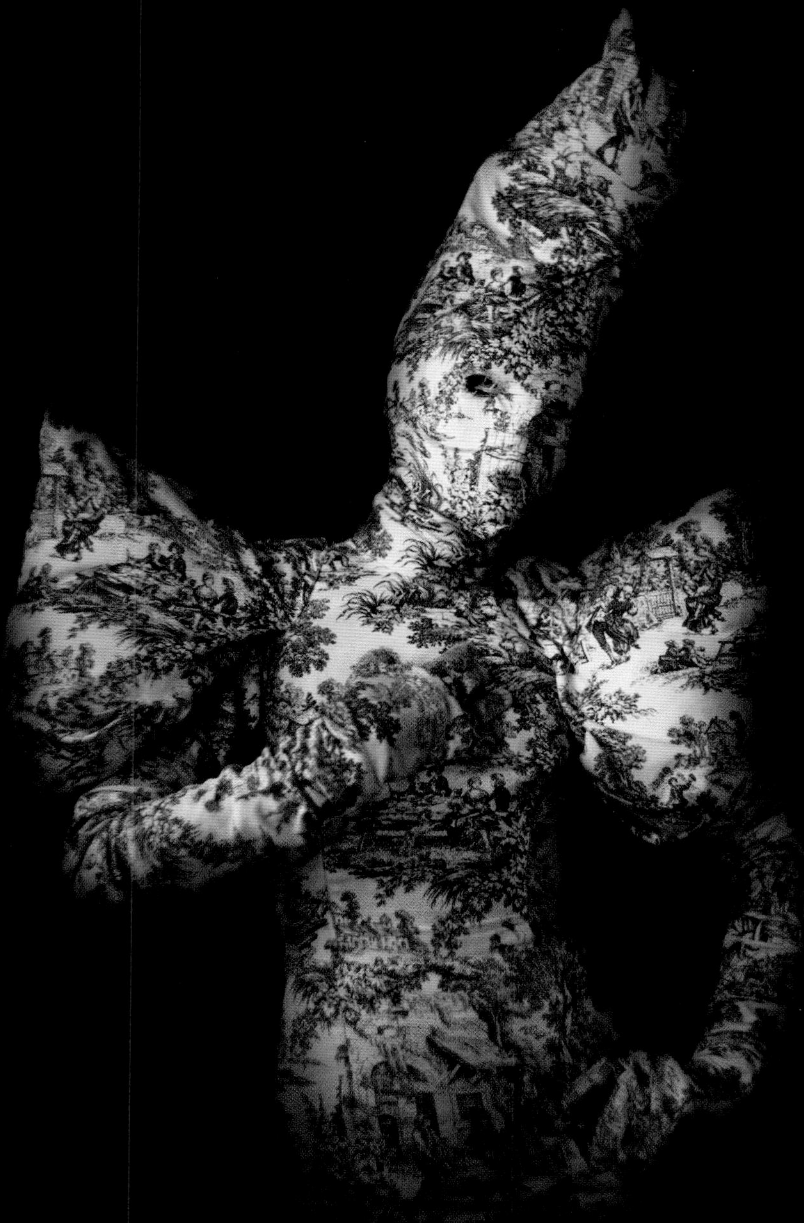

43 | yozmit walker on old compton st

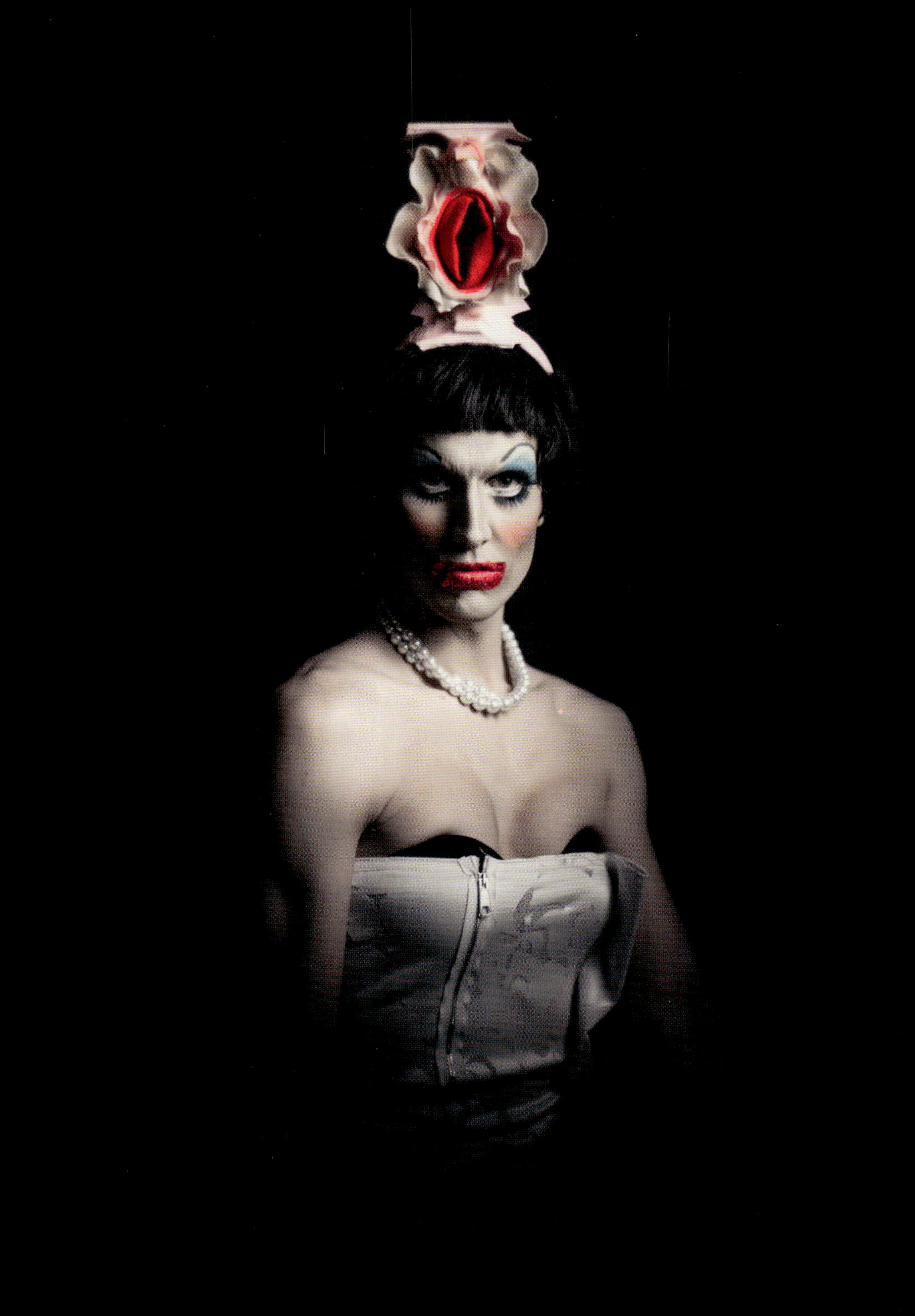

 | daniel mcilwraith (after isabella blow) at sink the pink

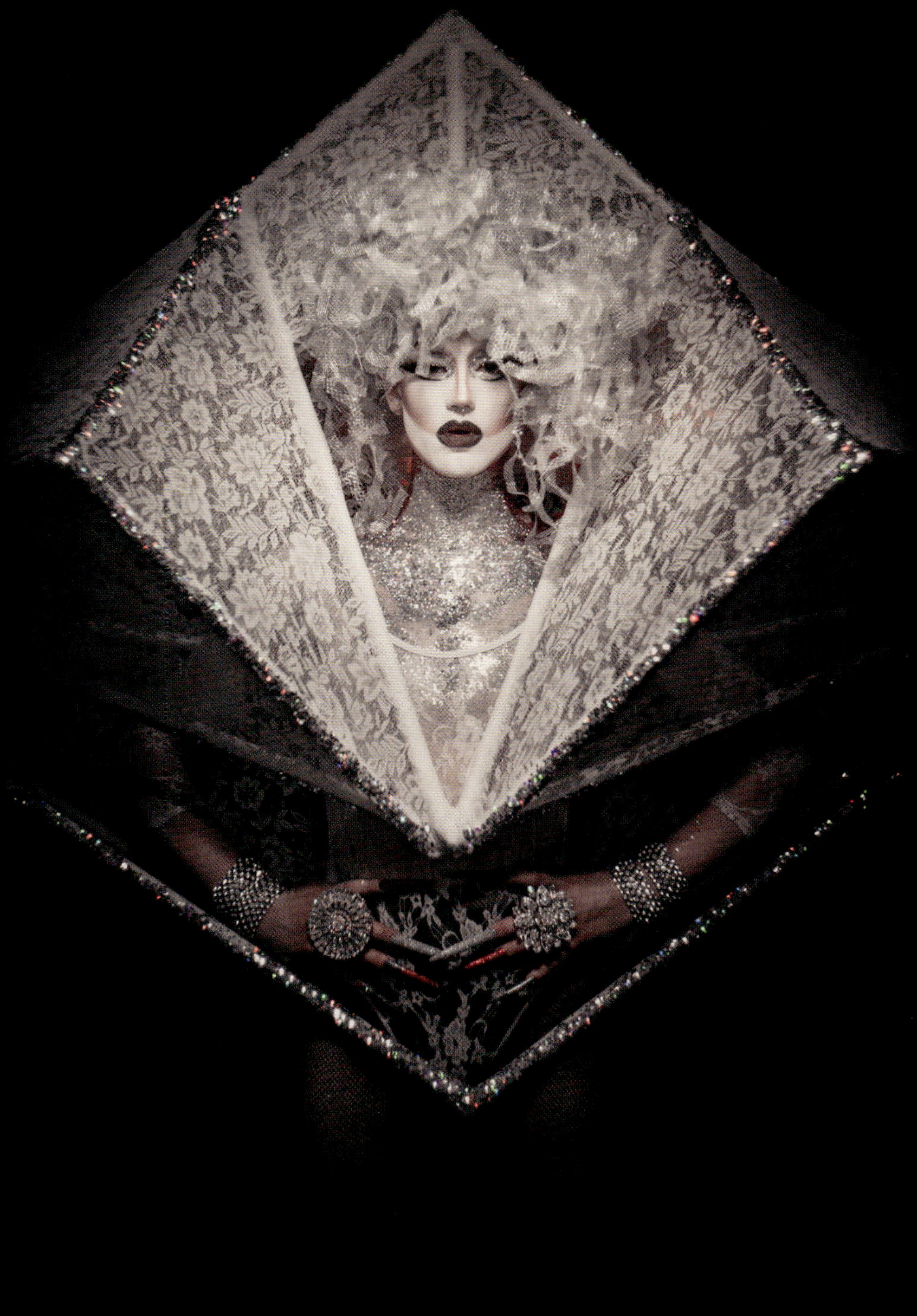

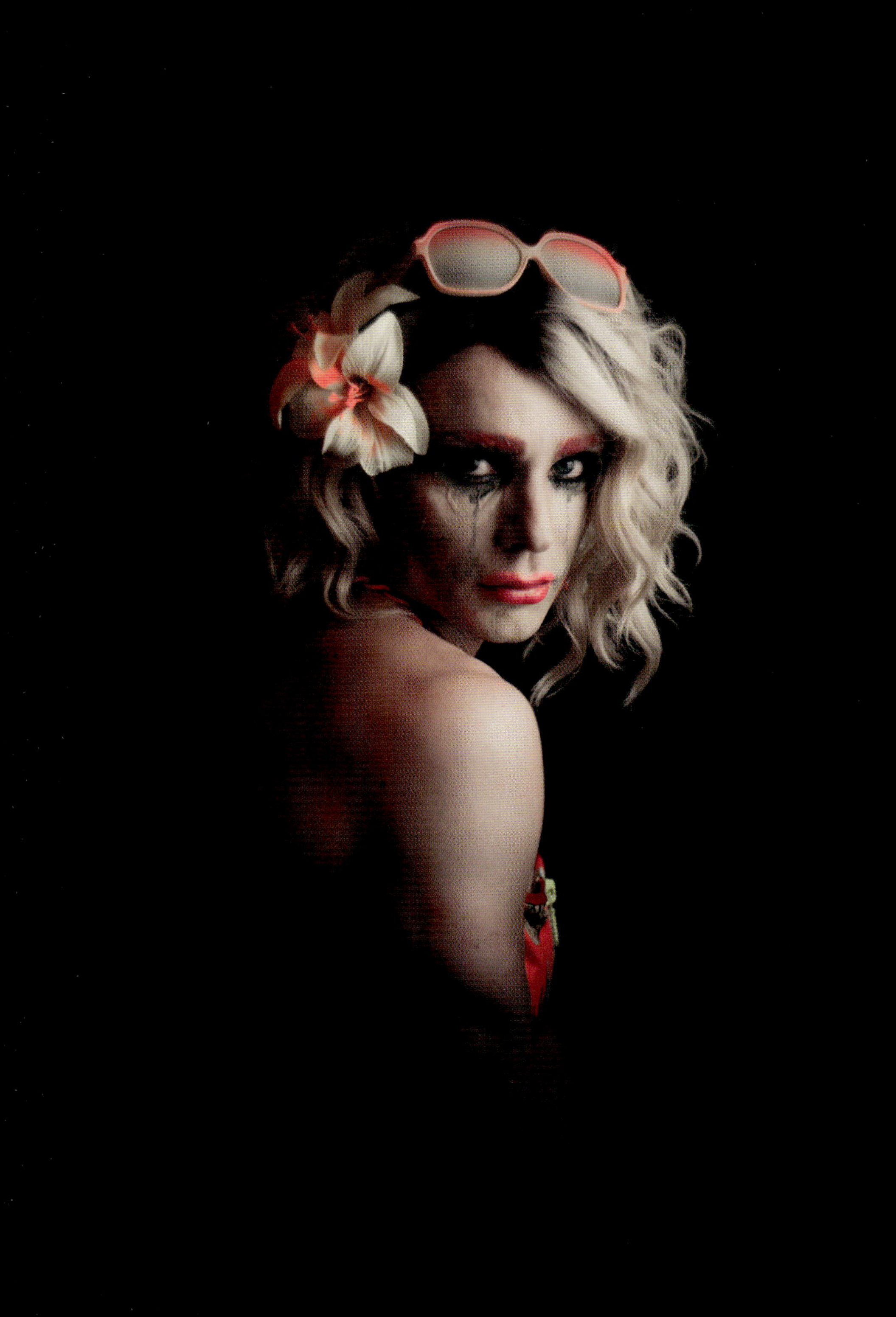

 | jordi hulshof at the sink the pink summer ball

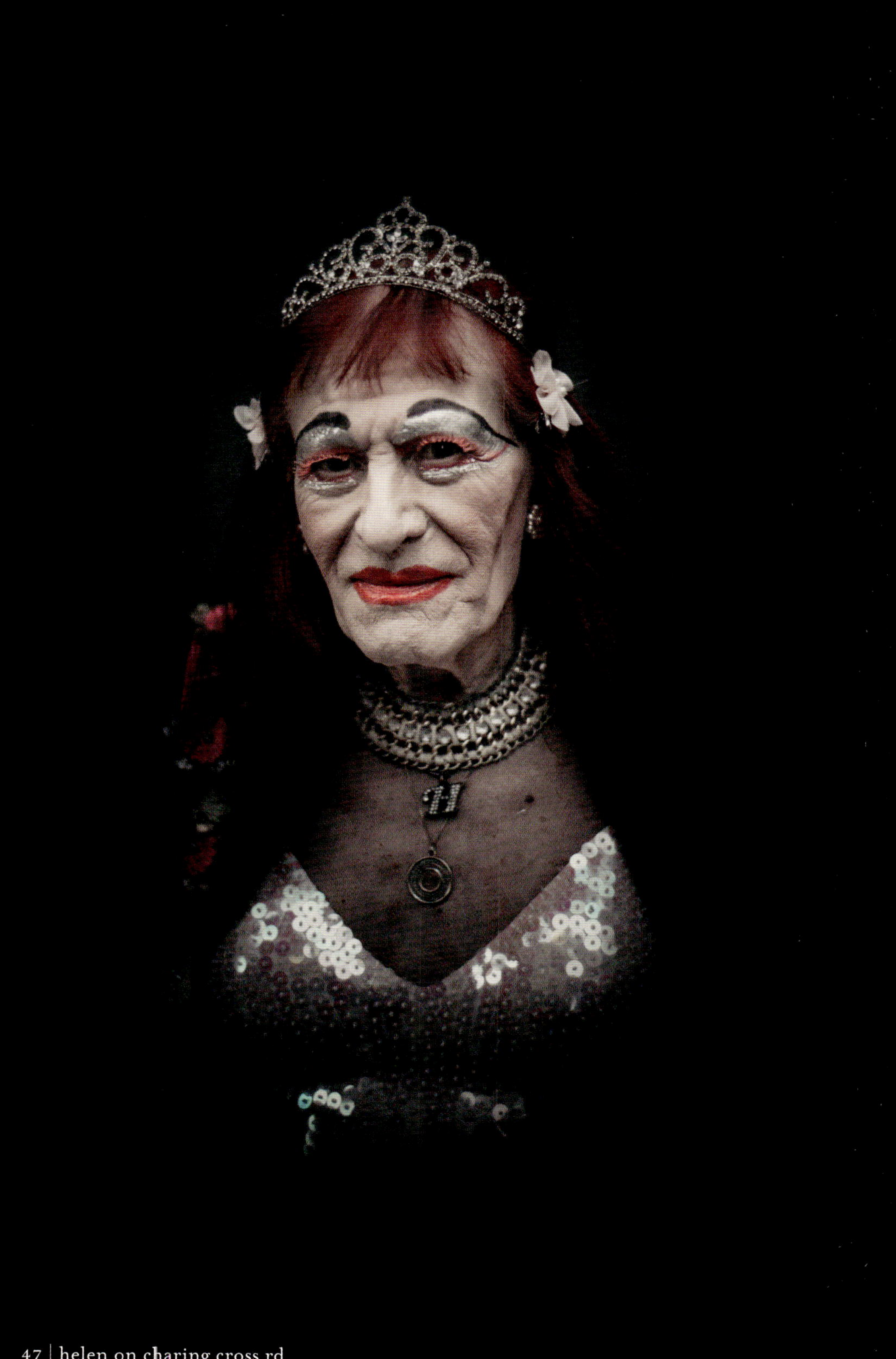

 | helen on charing cross rd

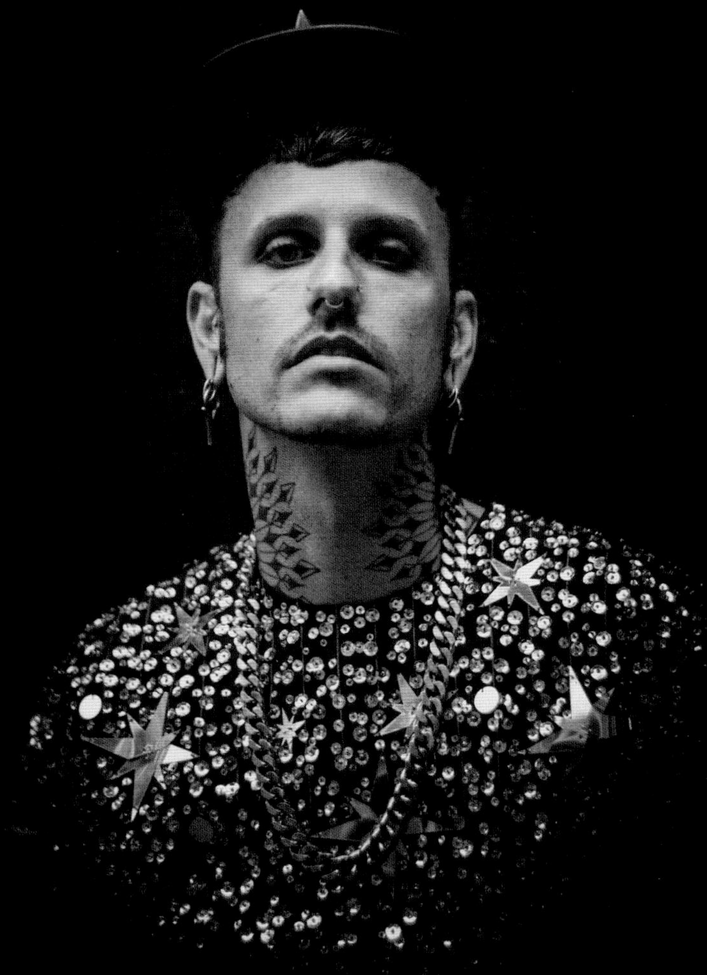

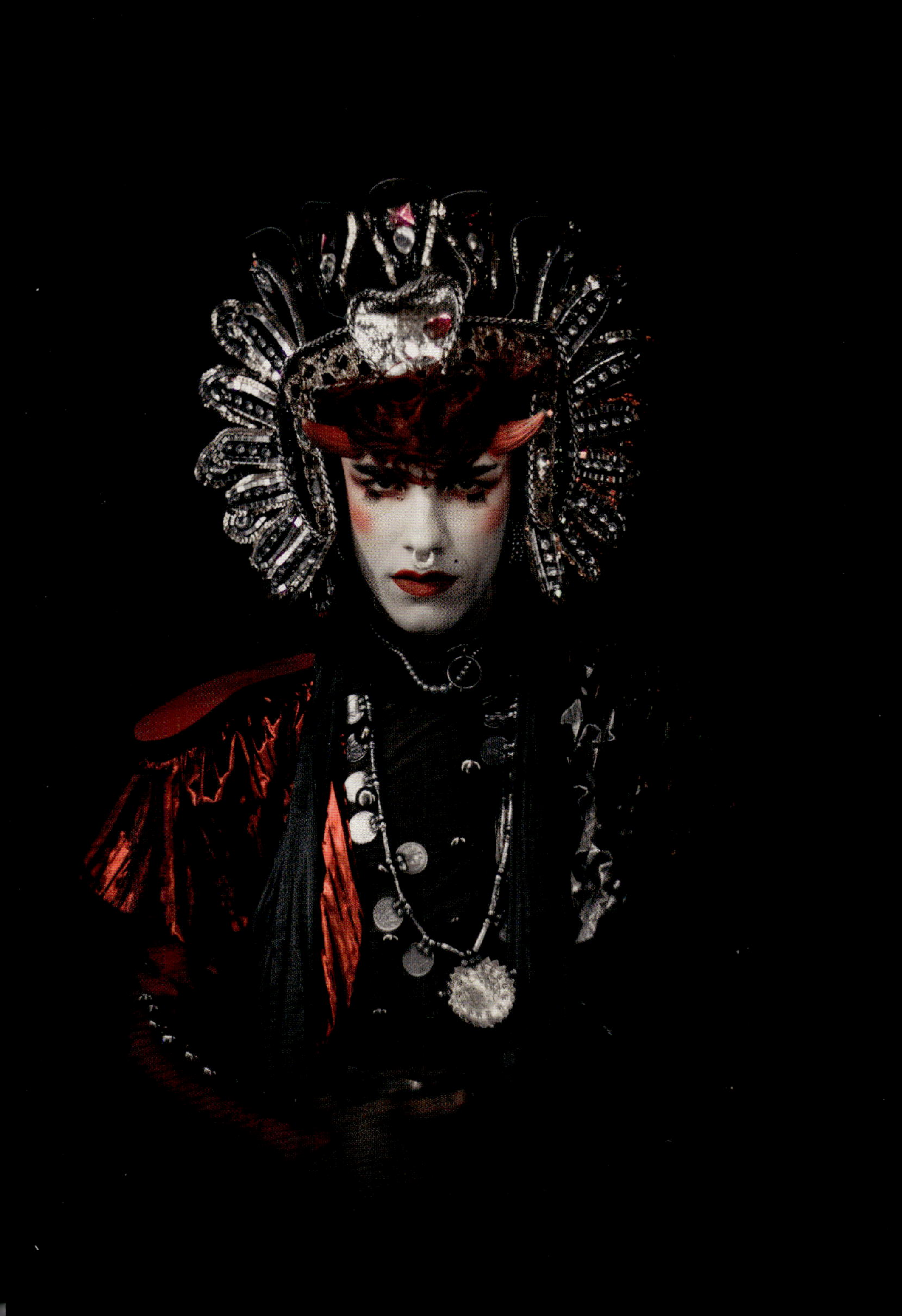

 | jenkin van zyl on old compton st

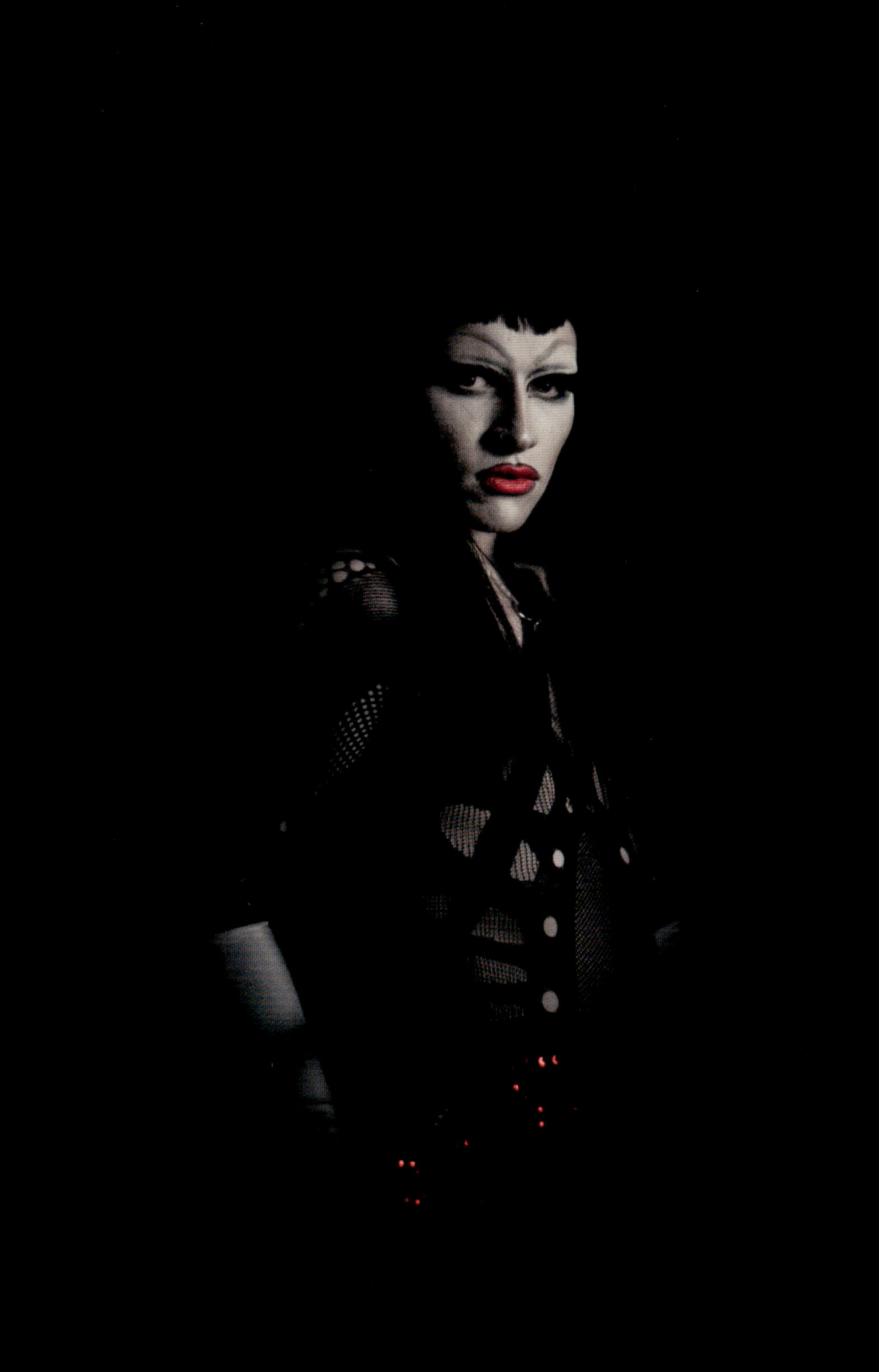

 | china dethcrash at sink the pink

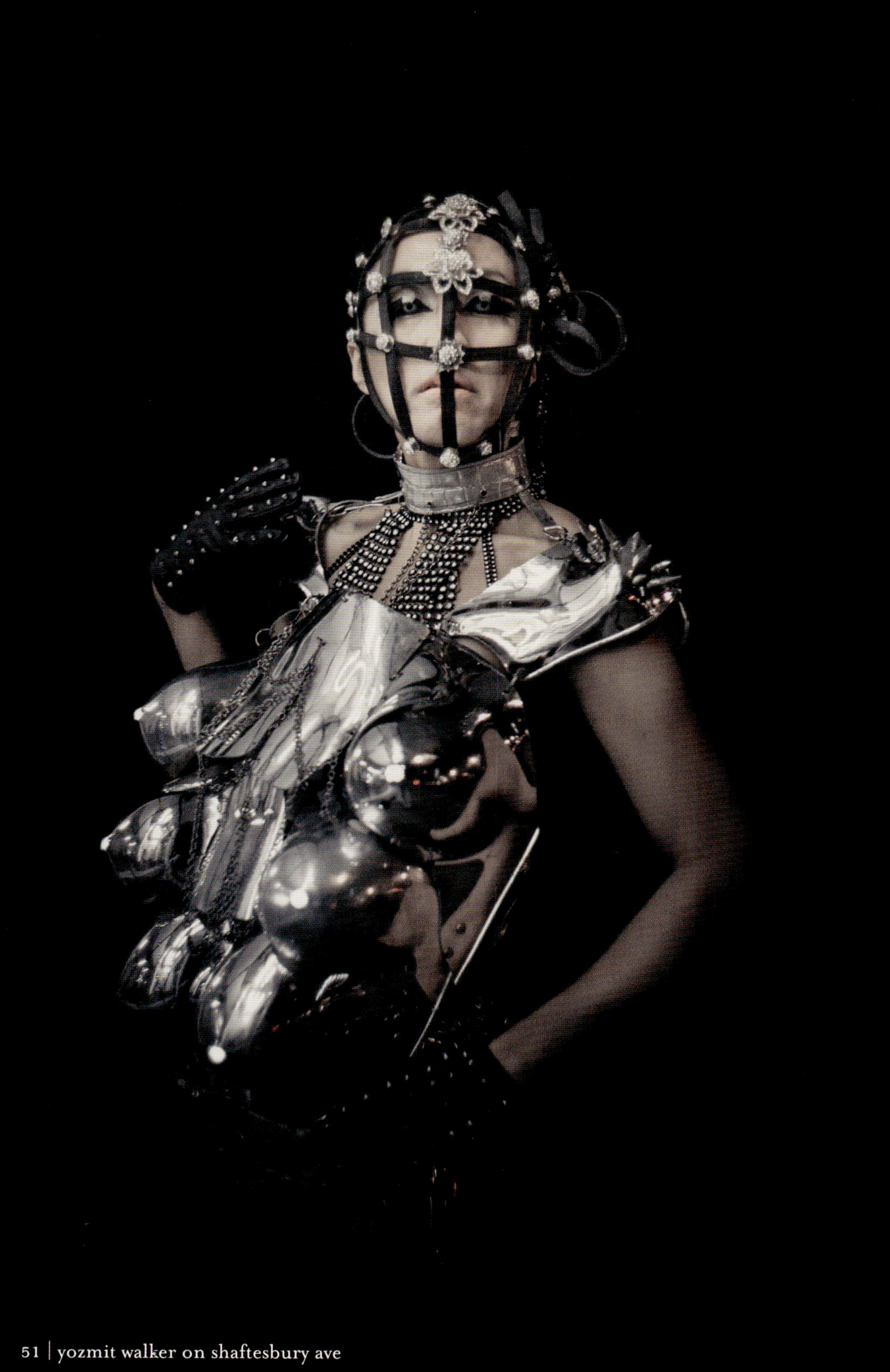

 | yozmit walker on shaftesbury ave

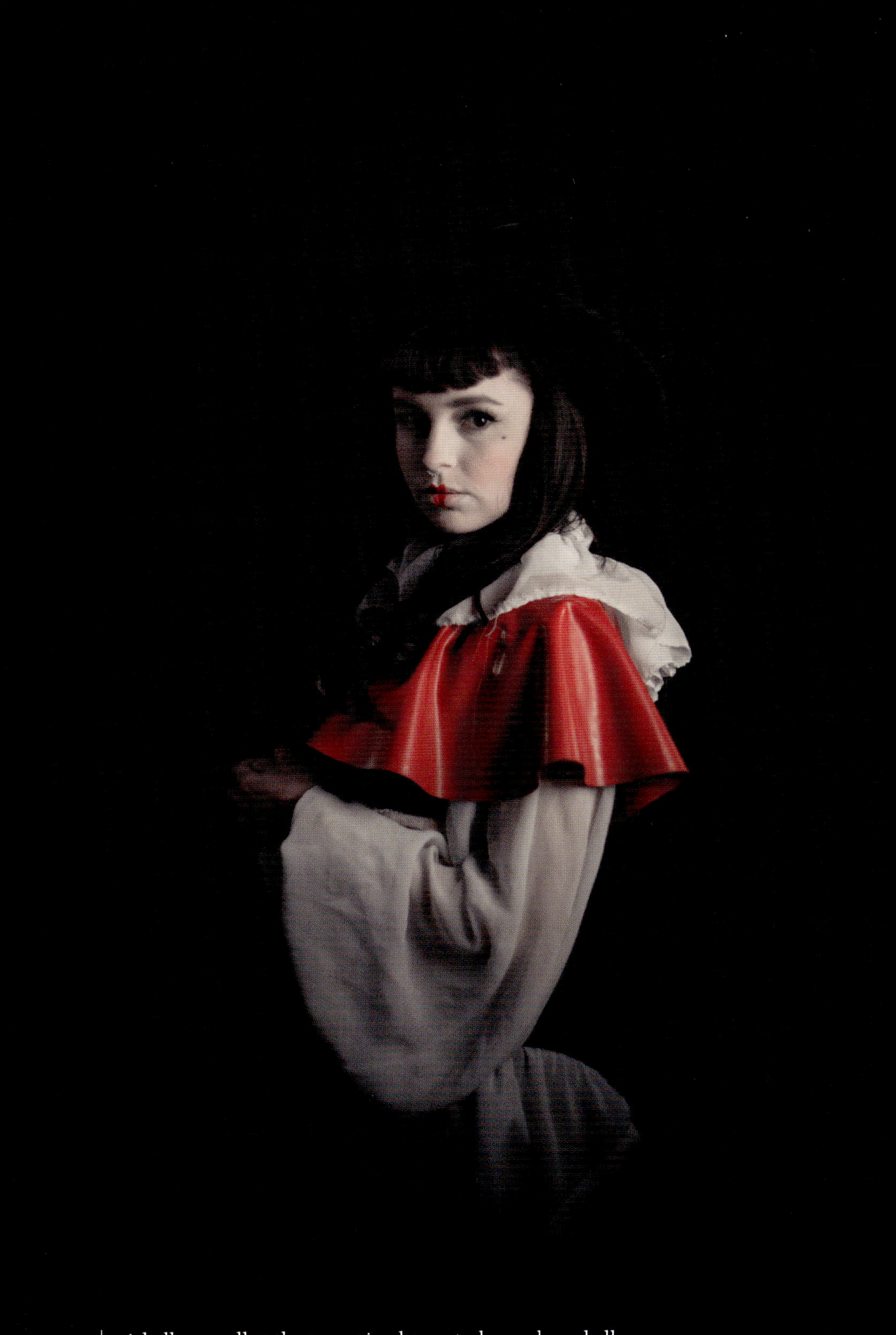

 michelle carroll at the amy grimehouse tudor realness ball

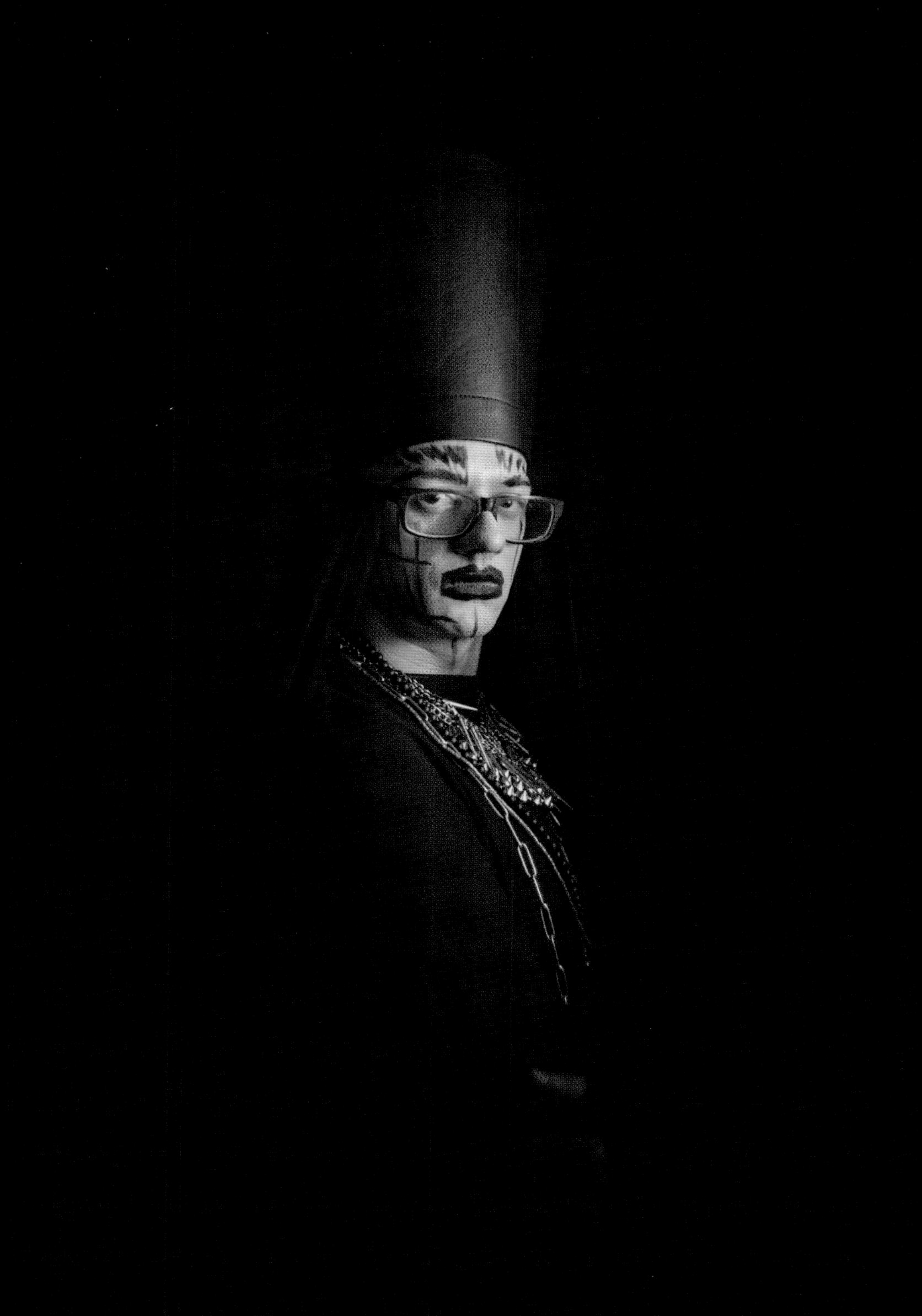

 | adrian rybak on tisbury ct

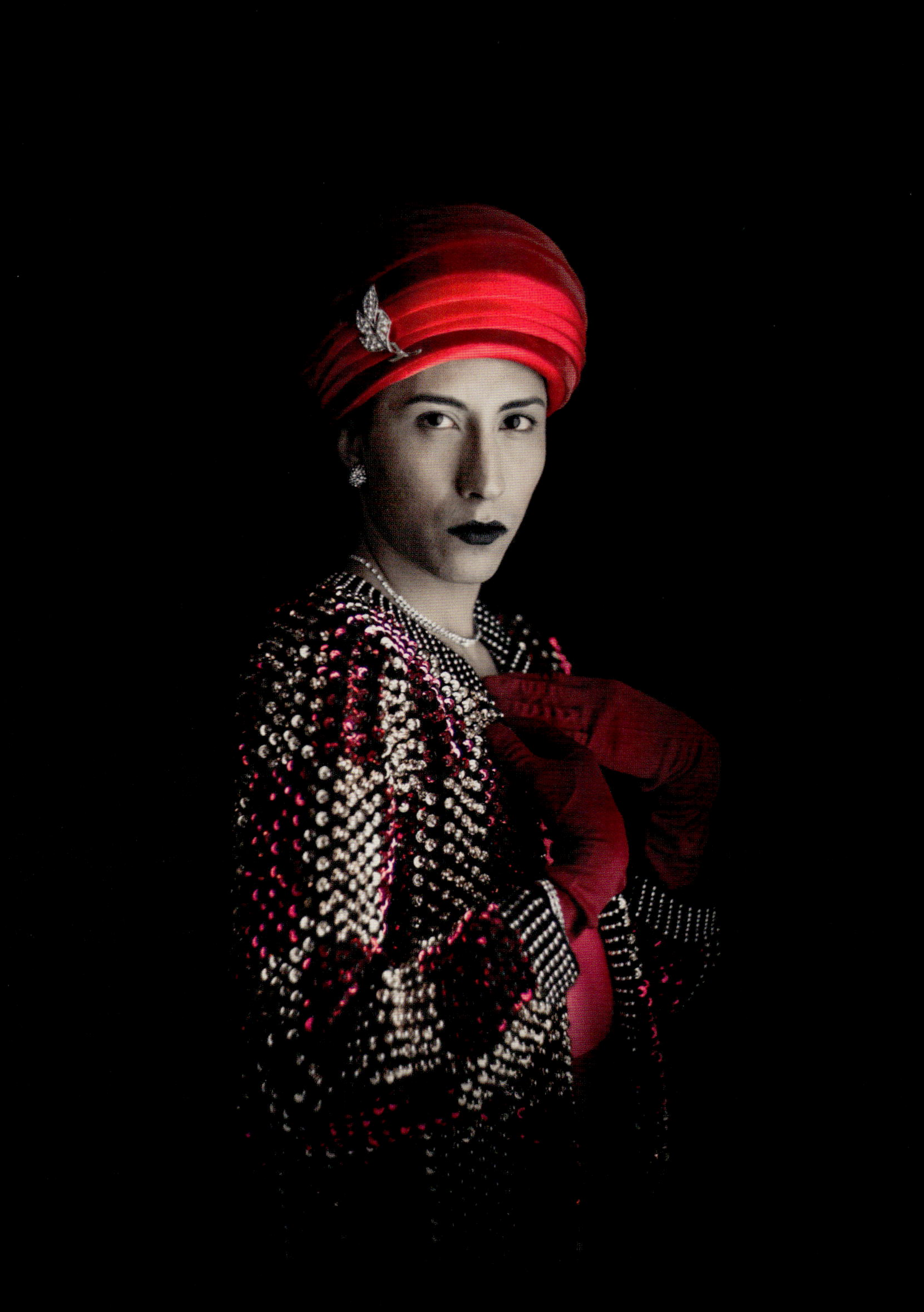

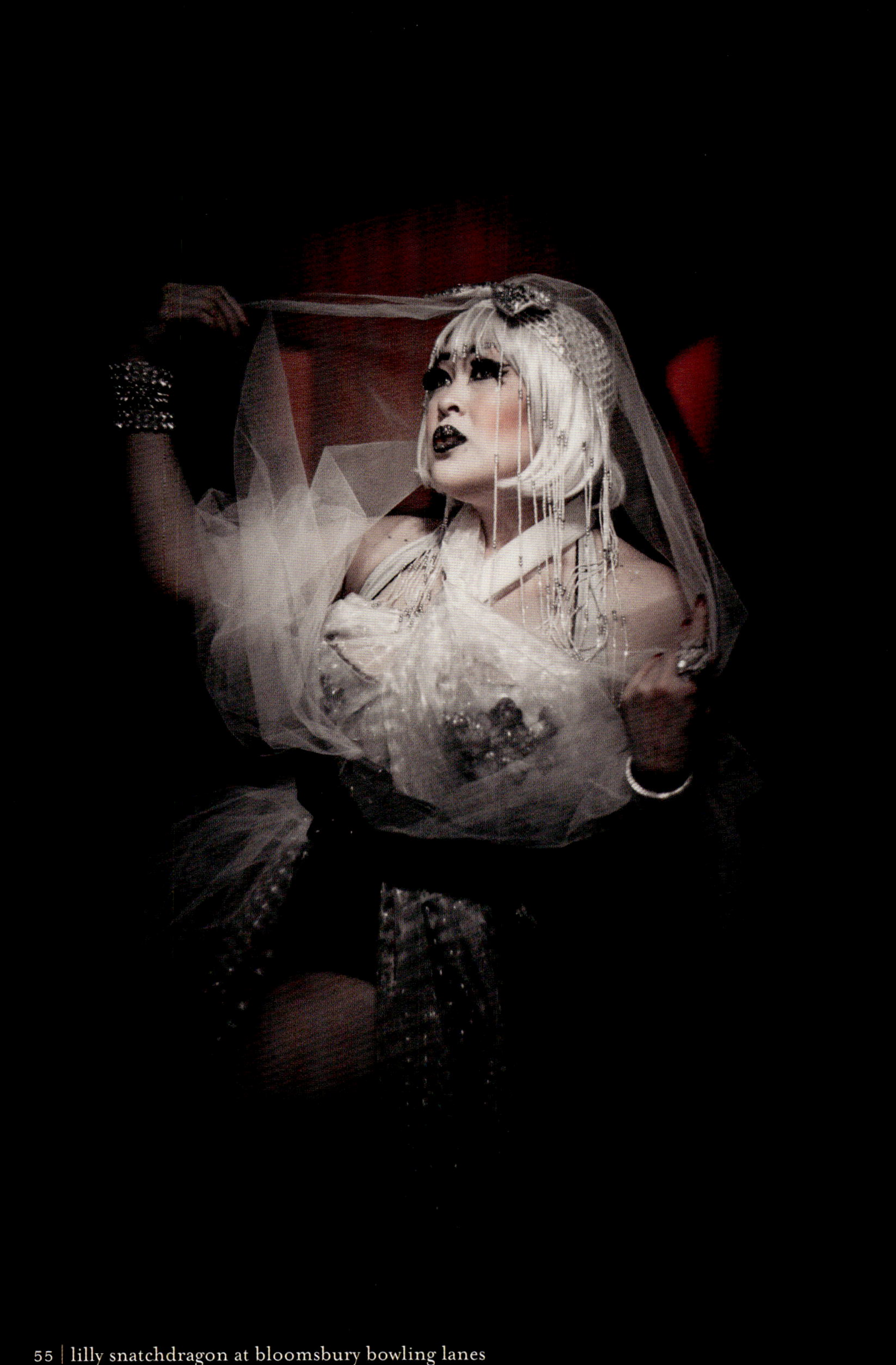

 | lilly snatchdragon at bloomsbury bowling lanes

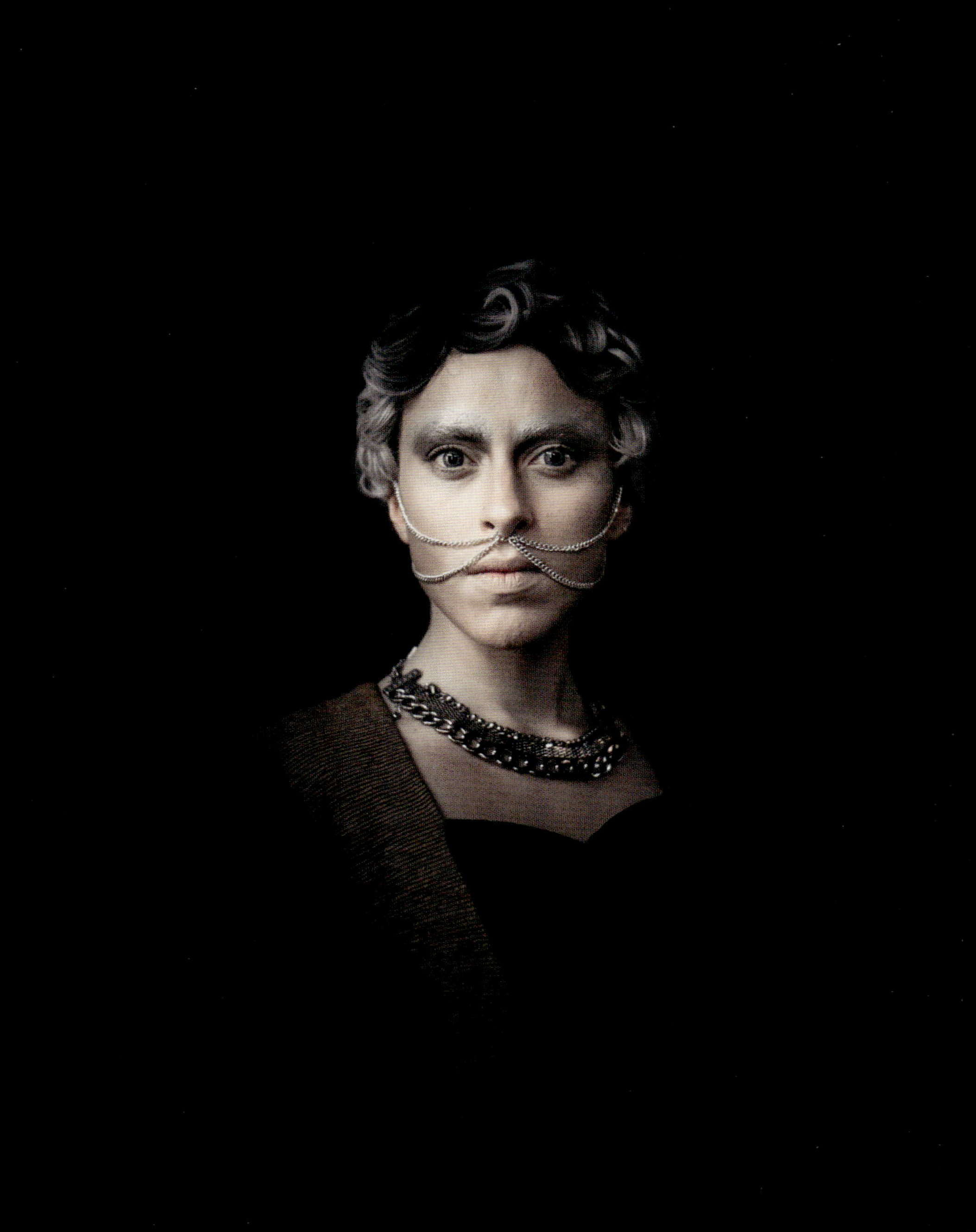

 | eleanor jean on old compton st

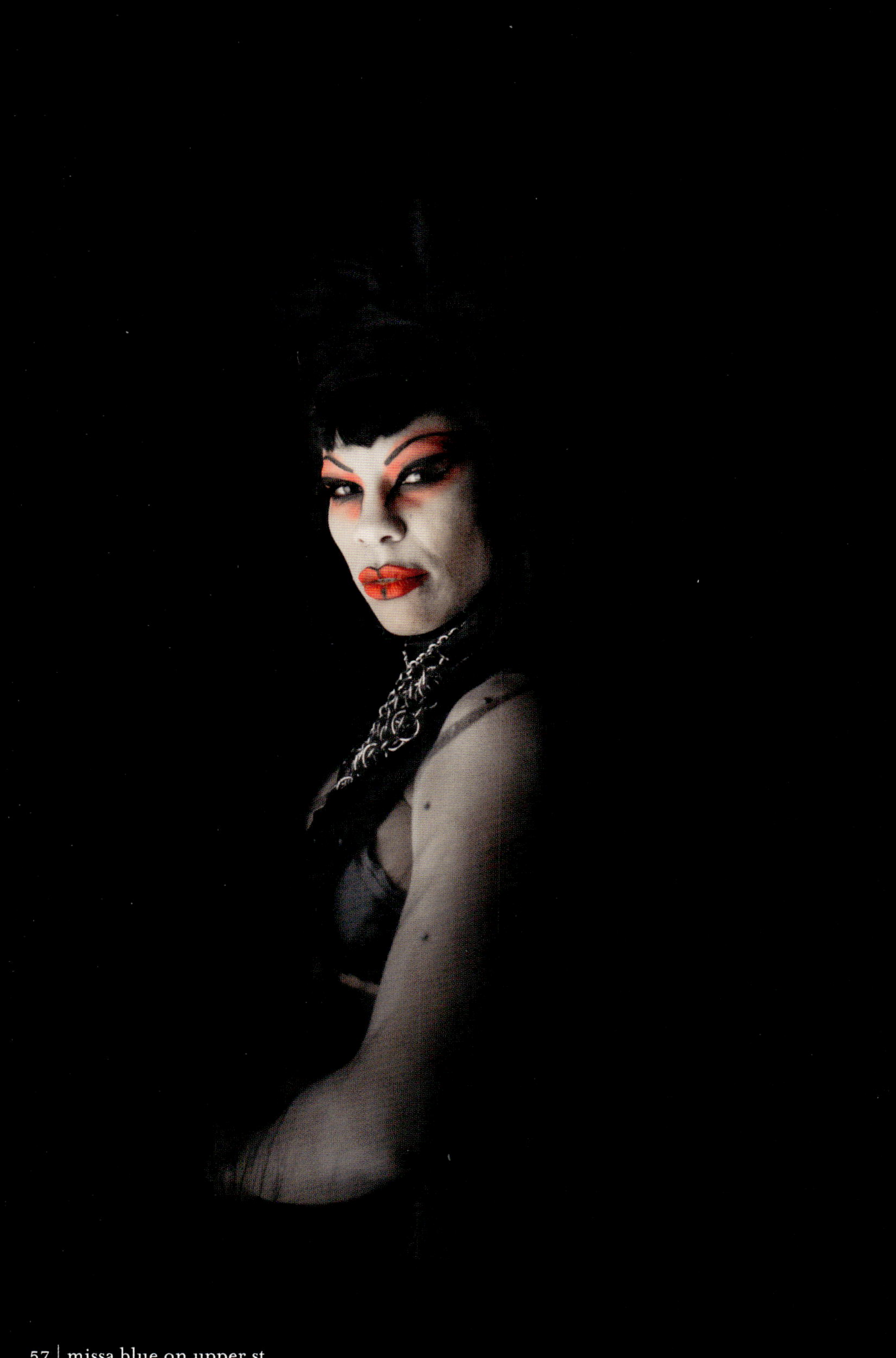

57 | missa blue on upper st

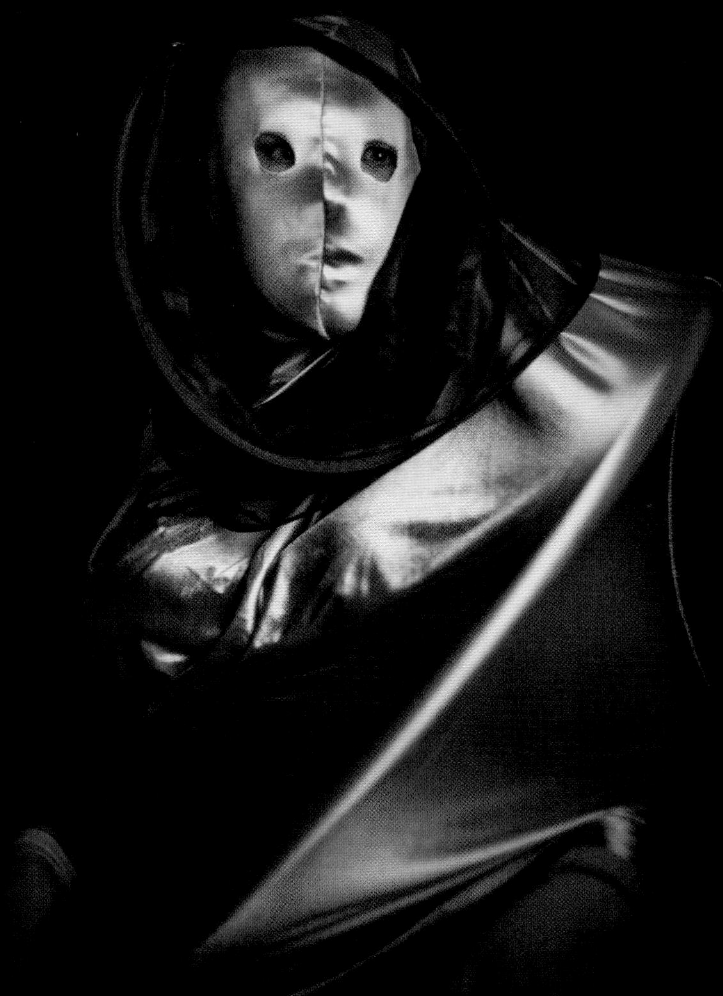

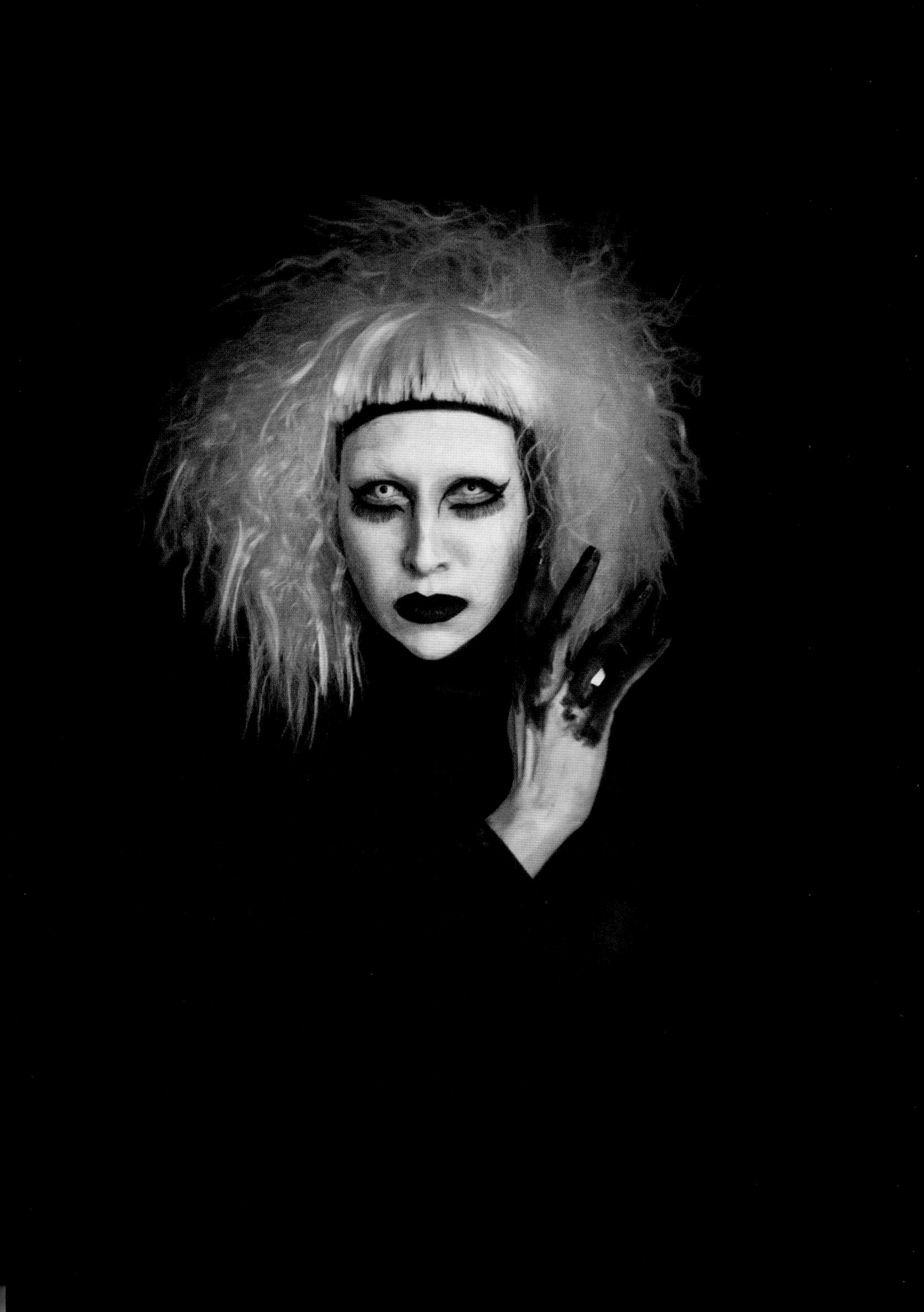

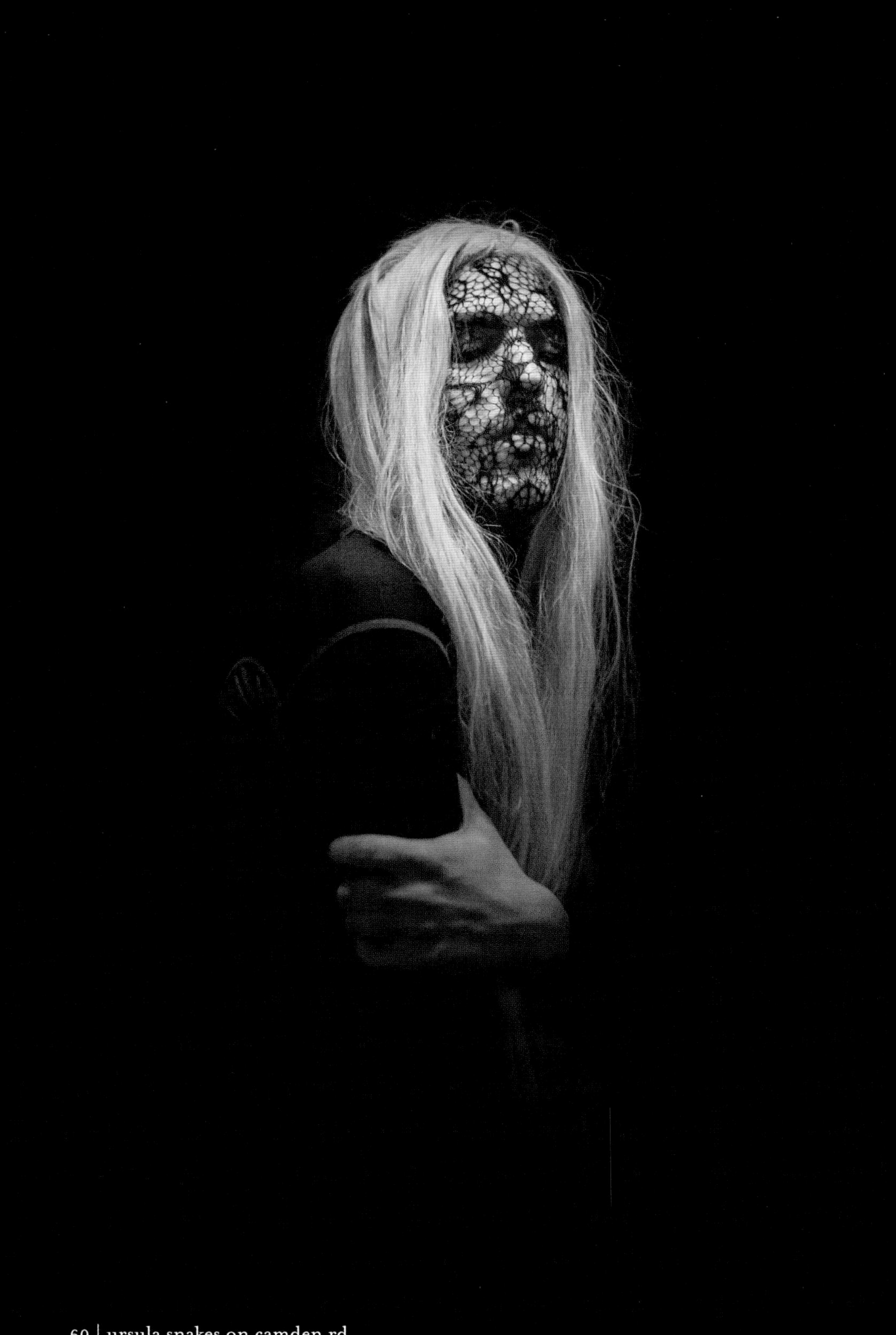

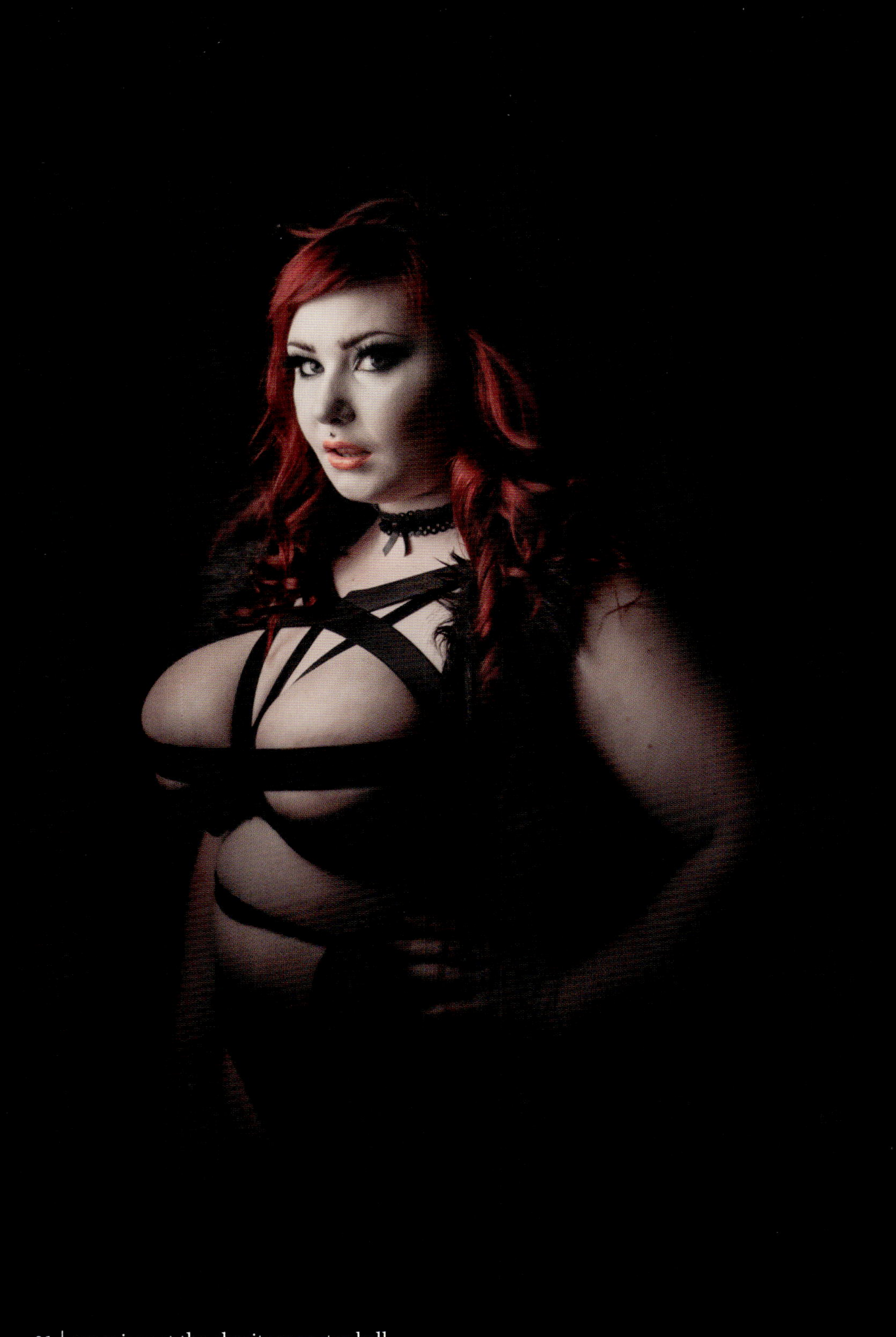

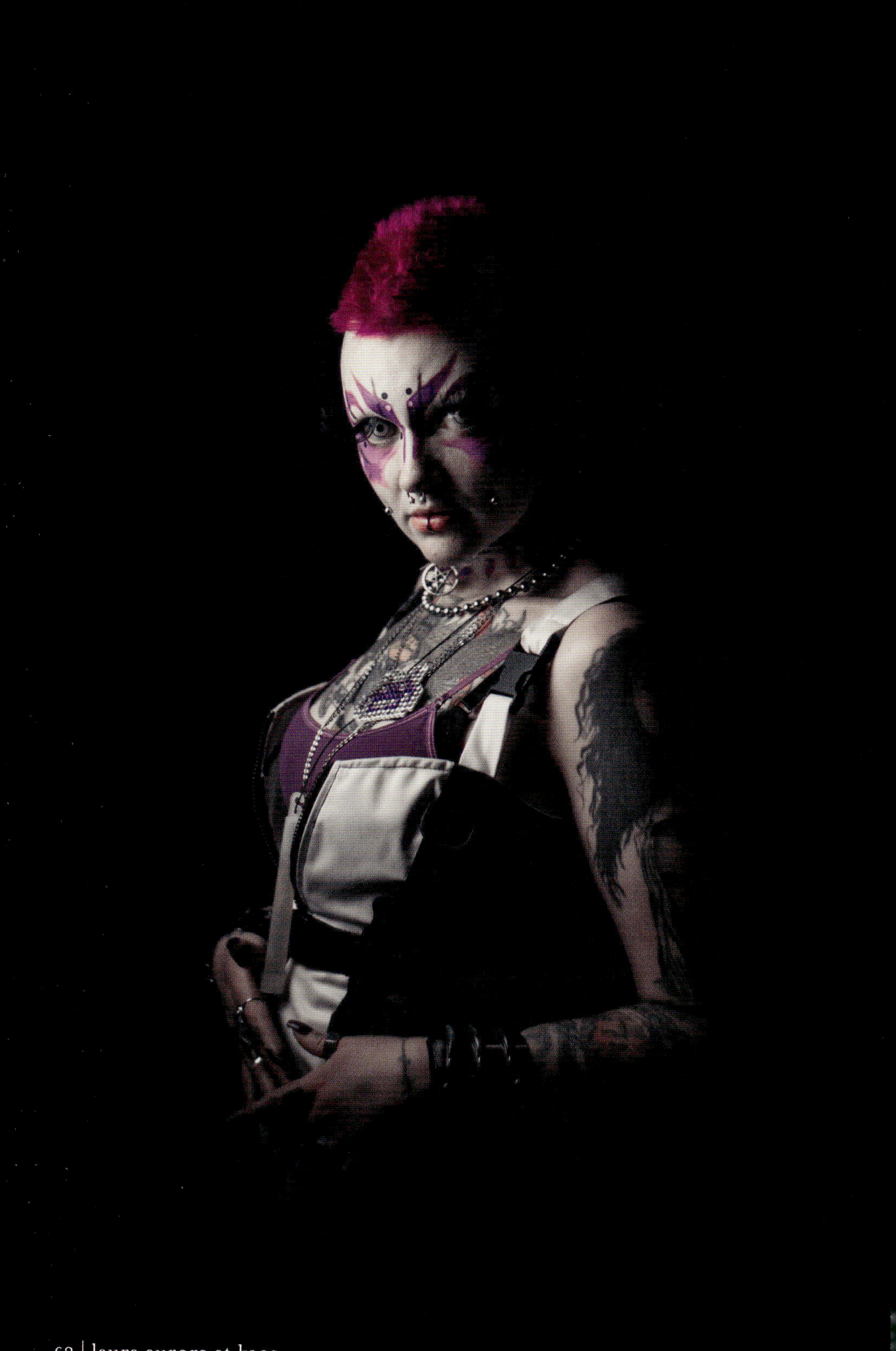

 | laura aurora at kaos

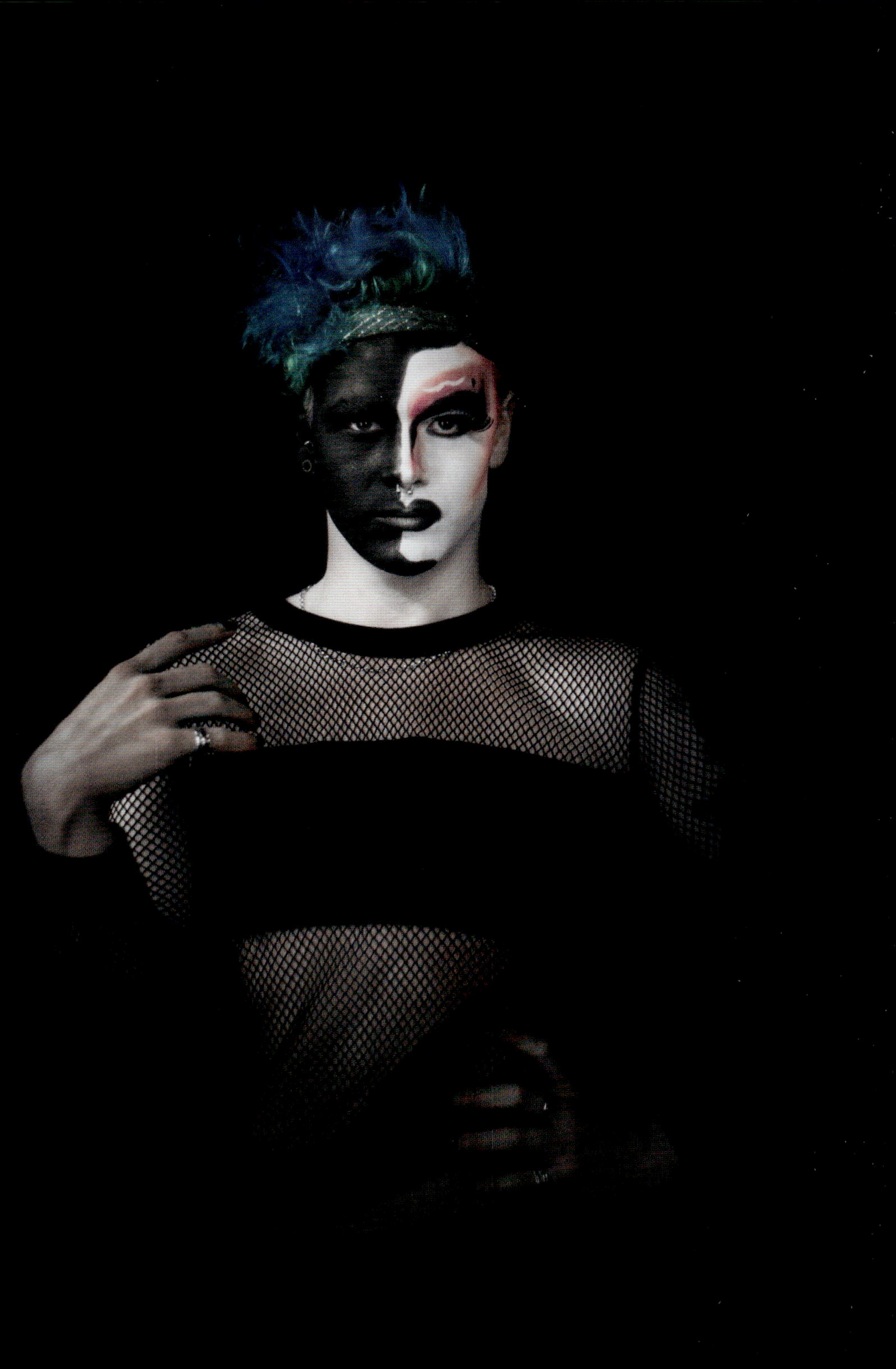

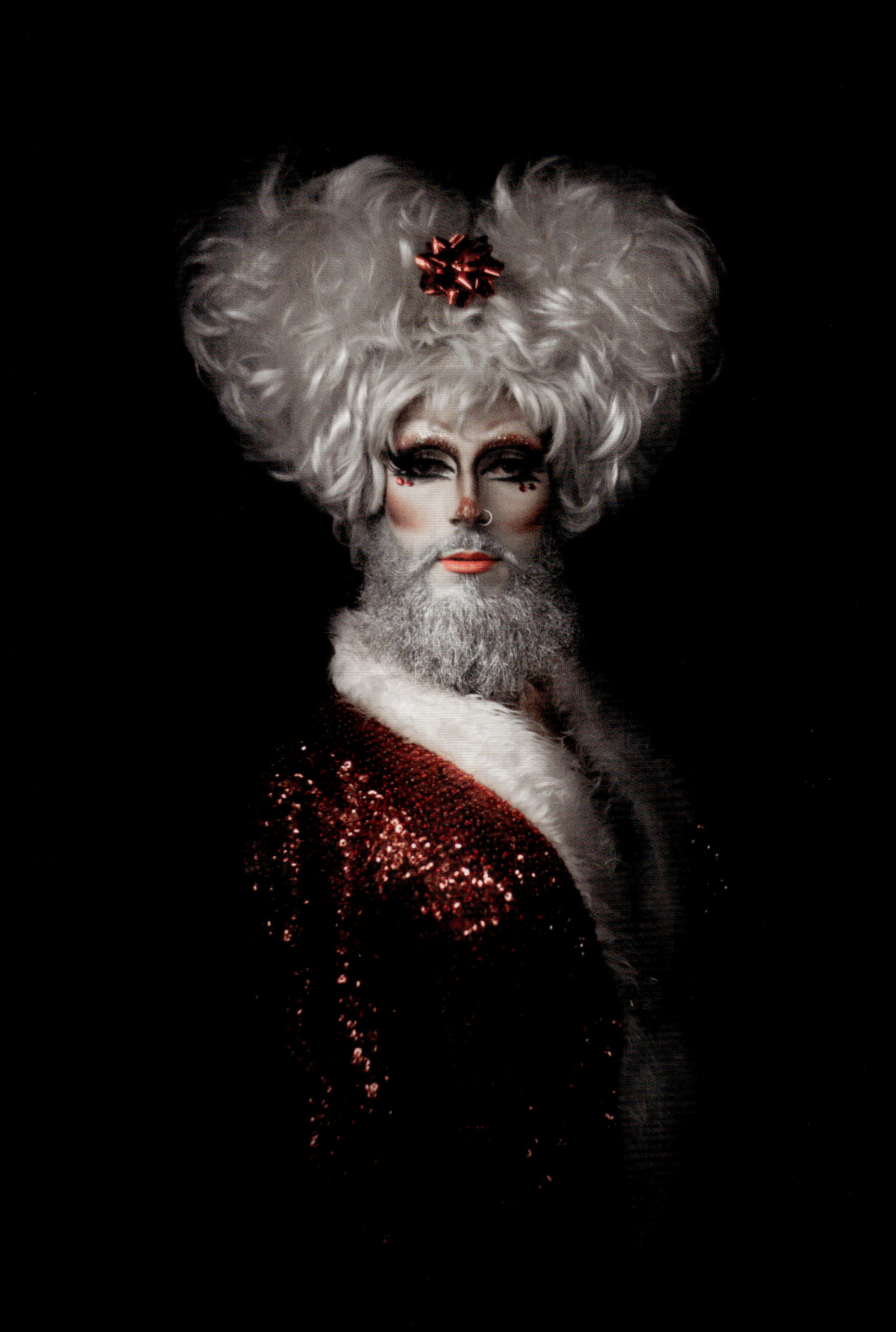

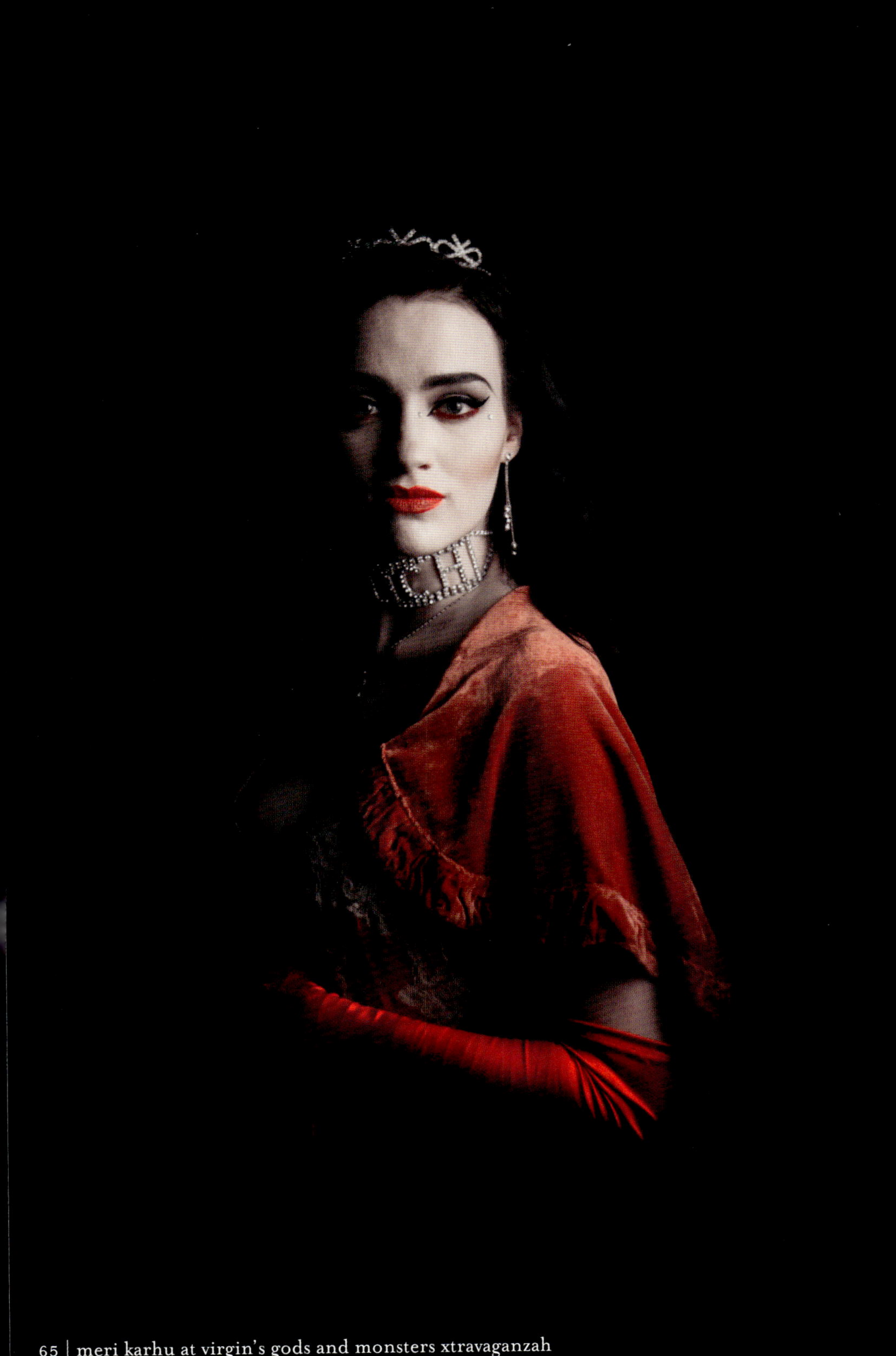

65 | meri karhu at virgin's gods and monsters xtravaganzah

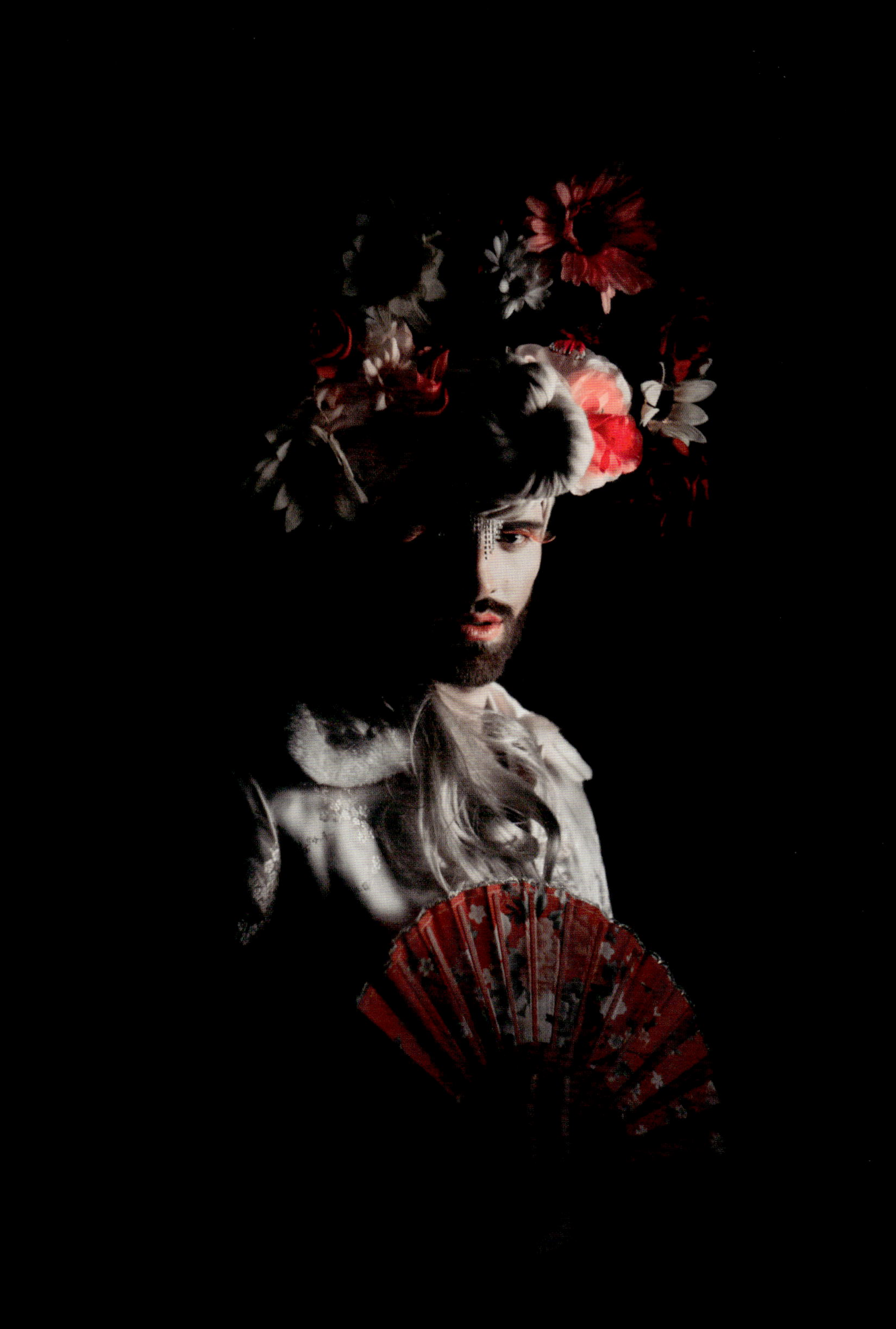

 | daniel joseph hibbs-woodings at sink the pink

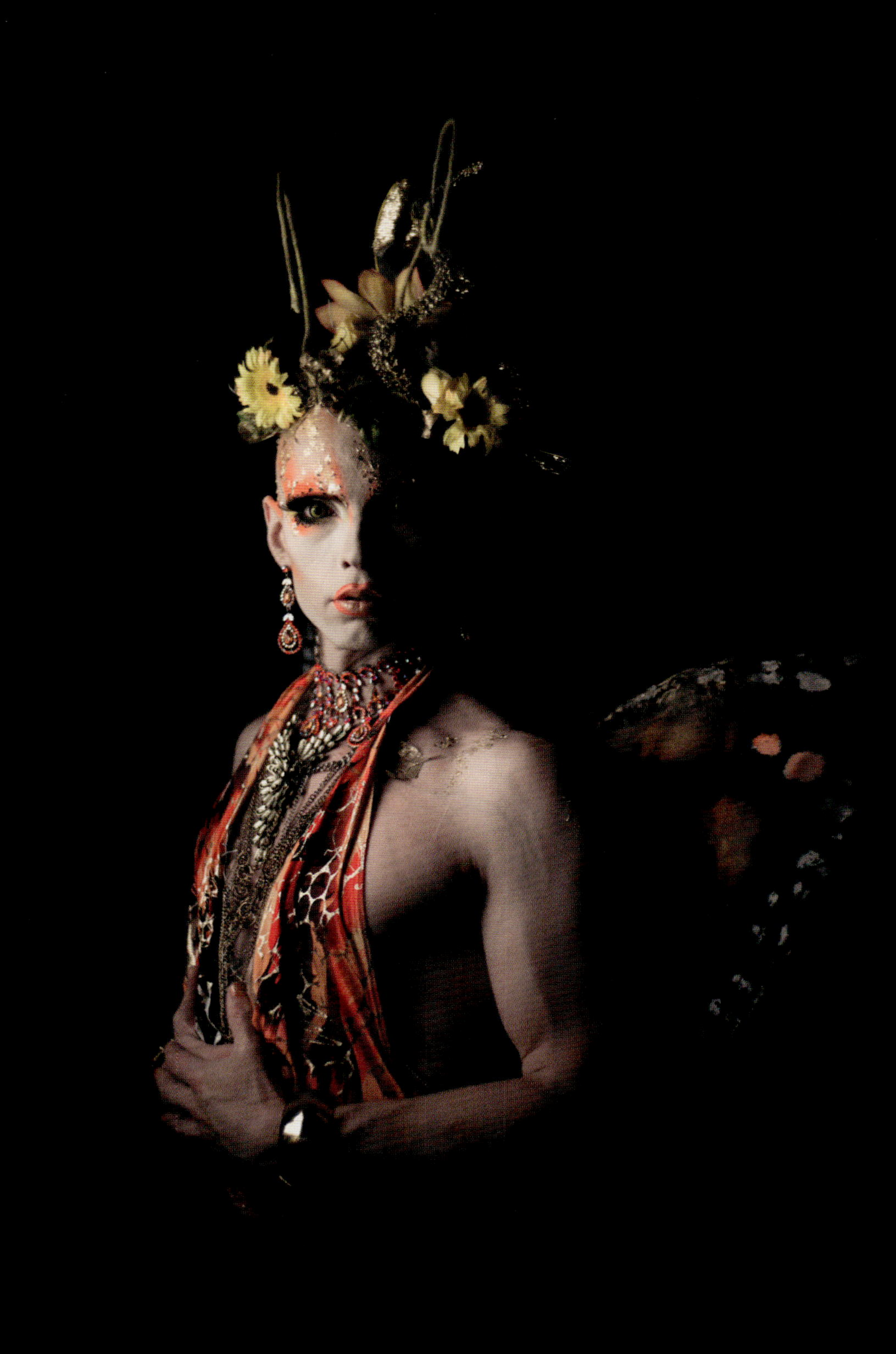

 cheddar gorgeous at the queerest of the queer festival

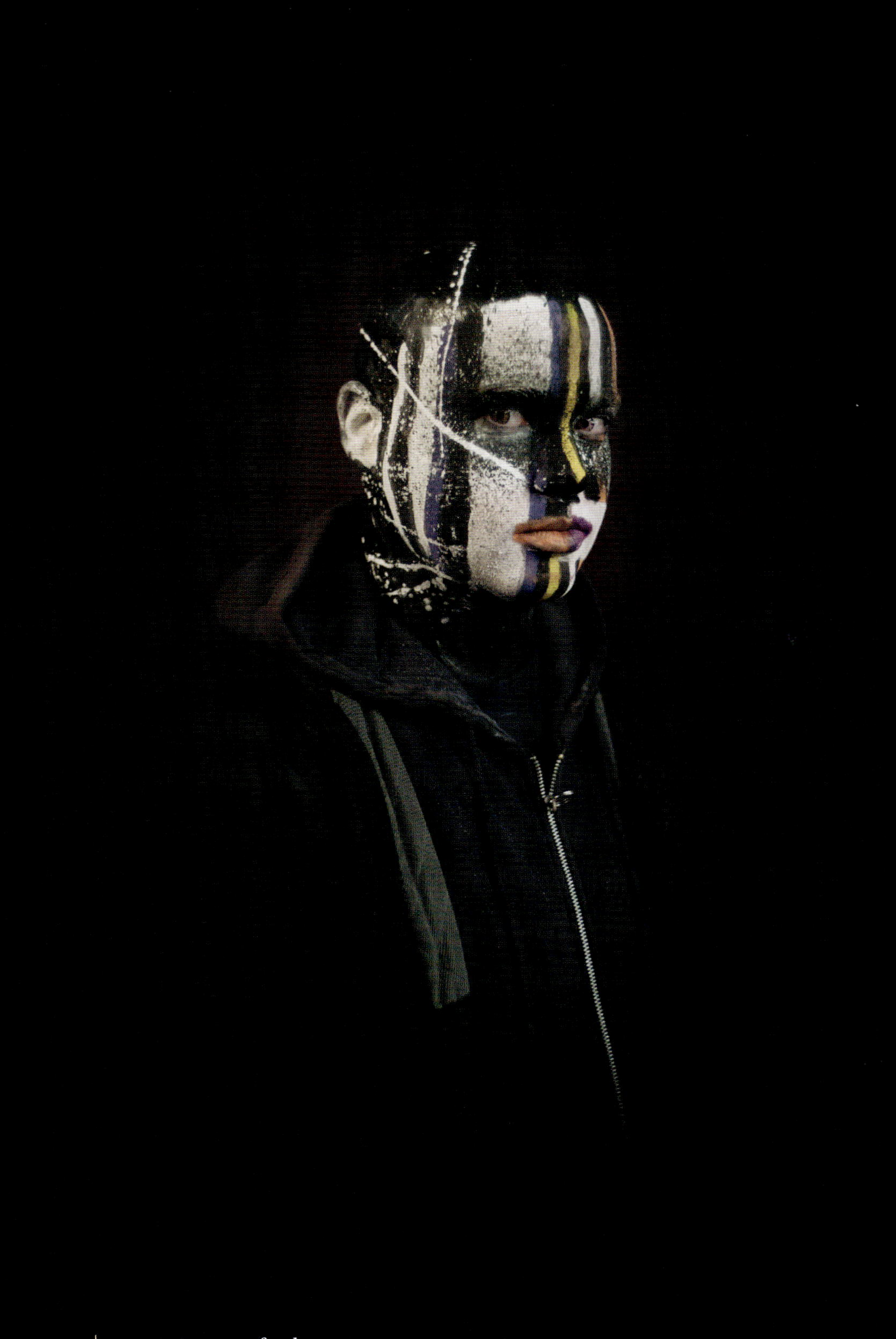

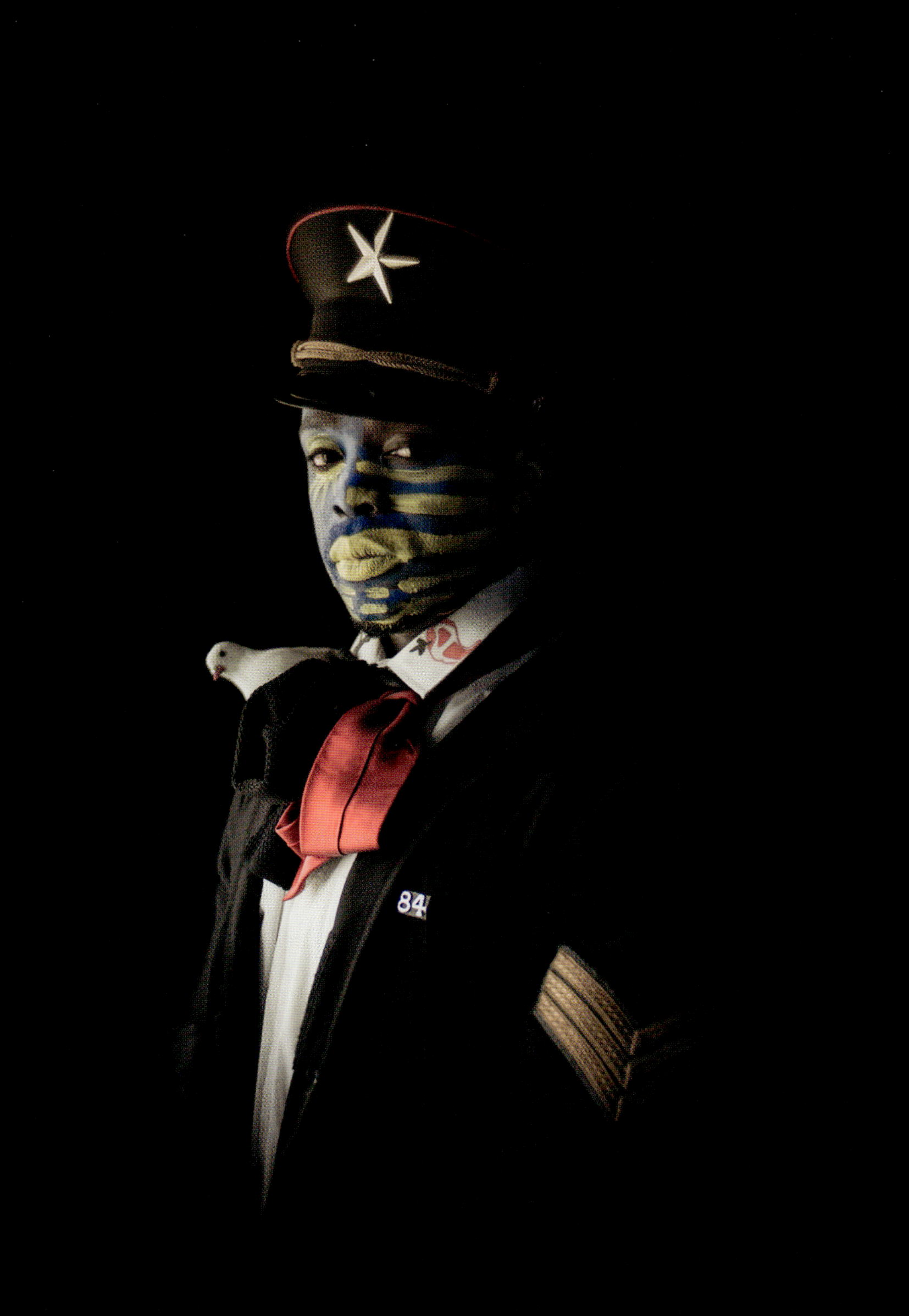

69 | eugene ankomah on dalston sq.

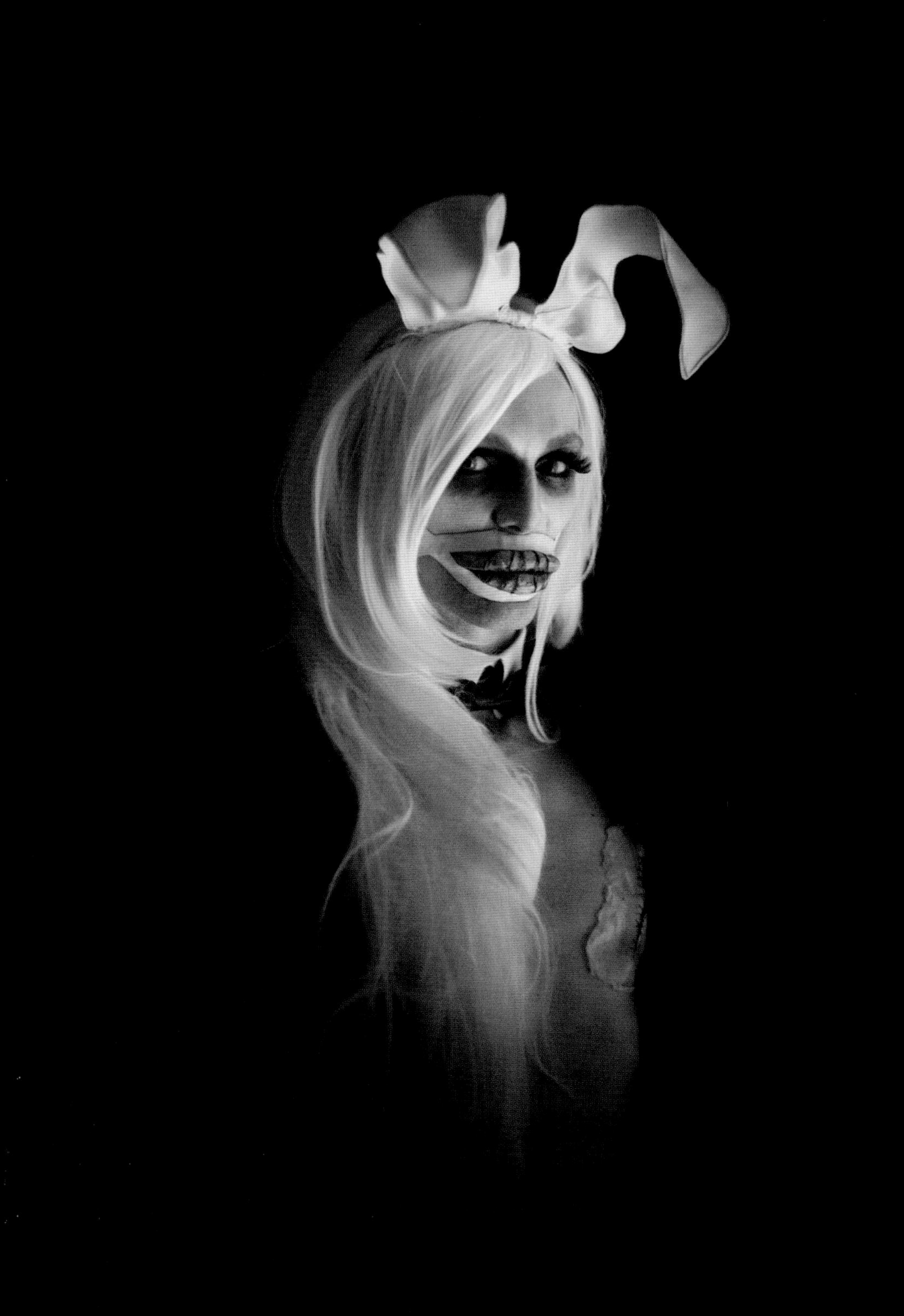

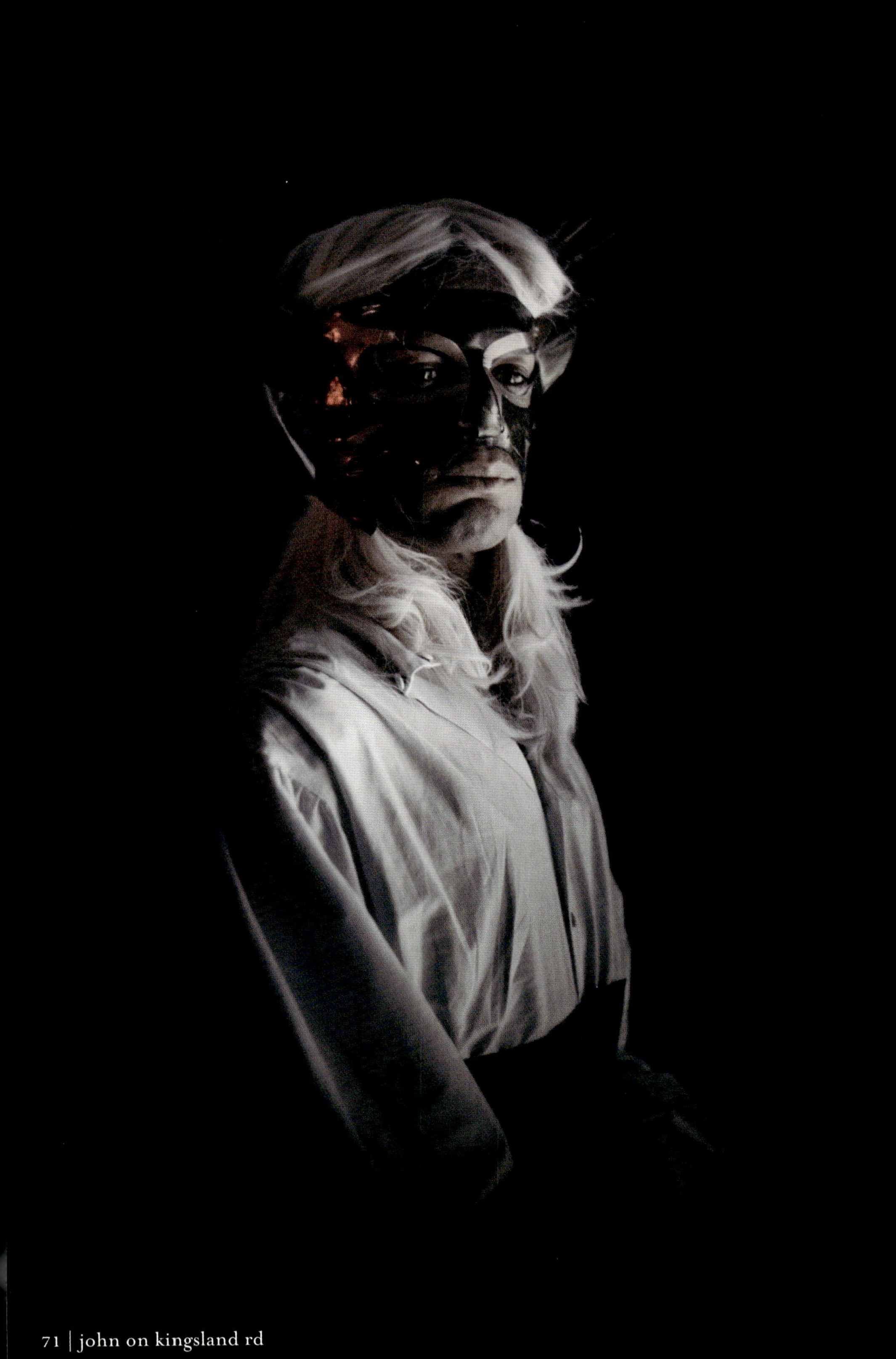

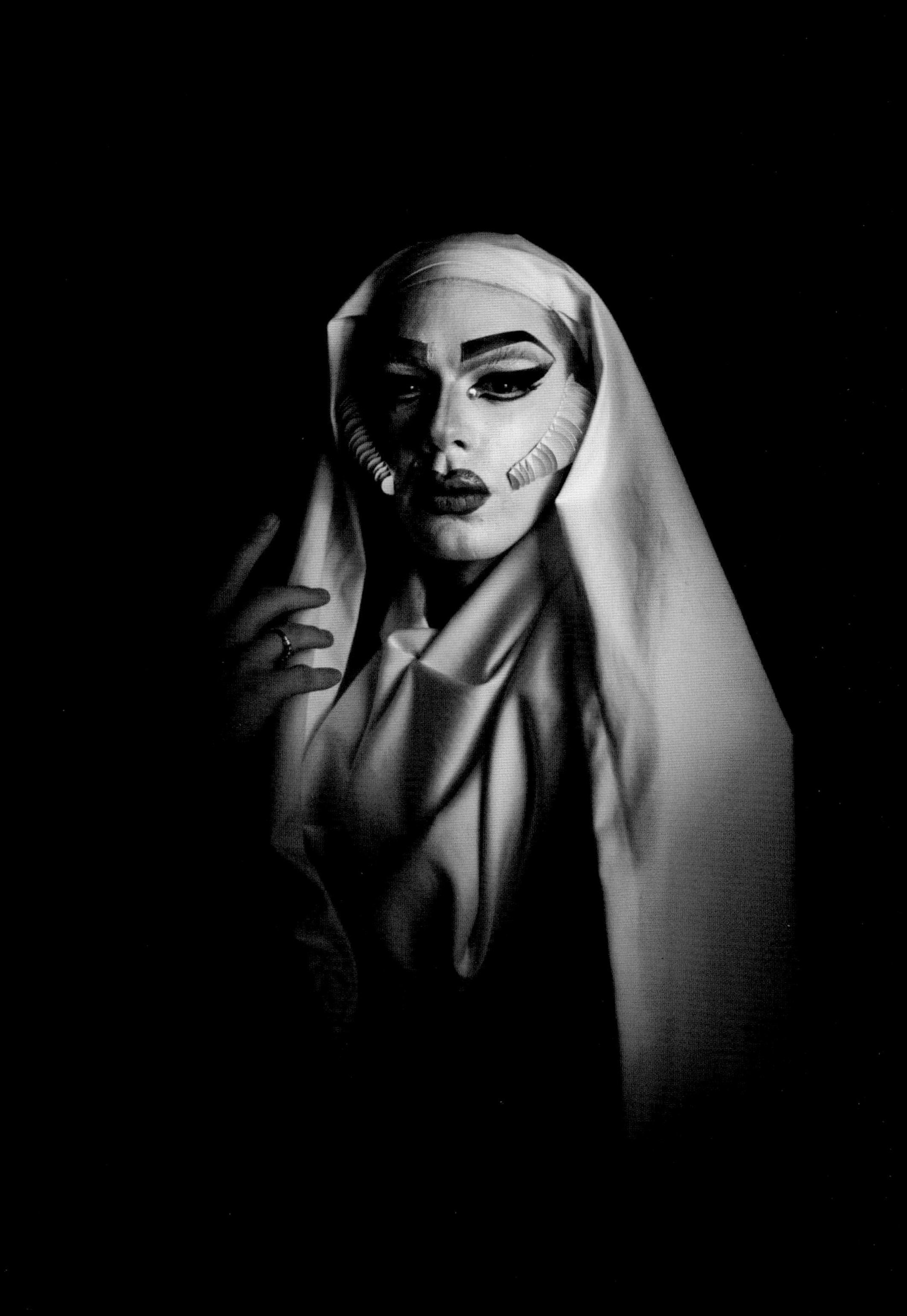

 simon peters at the sink the pink winter ball

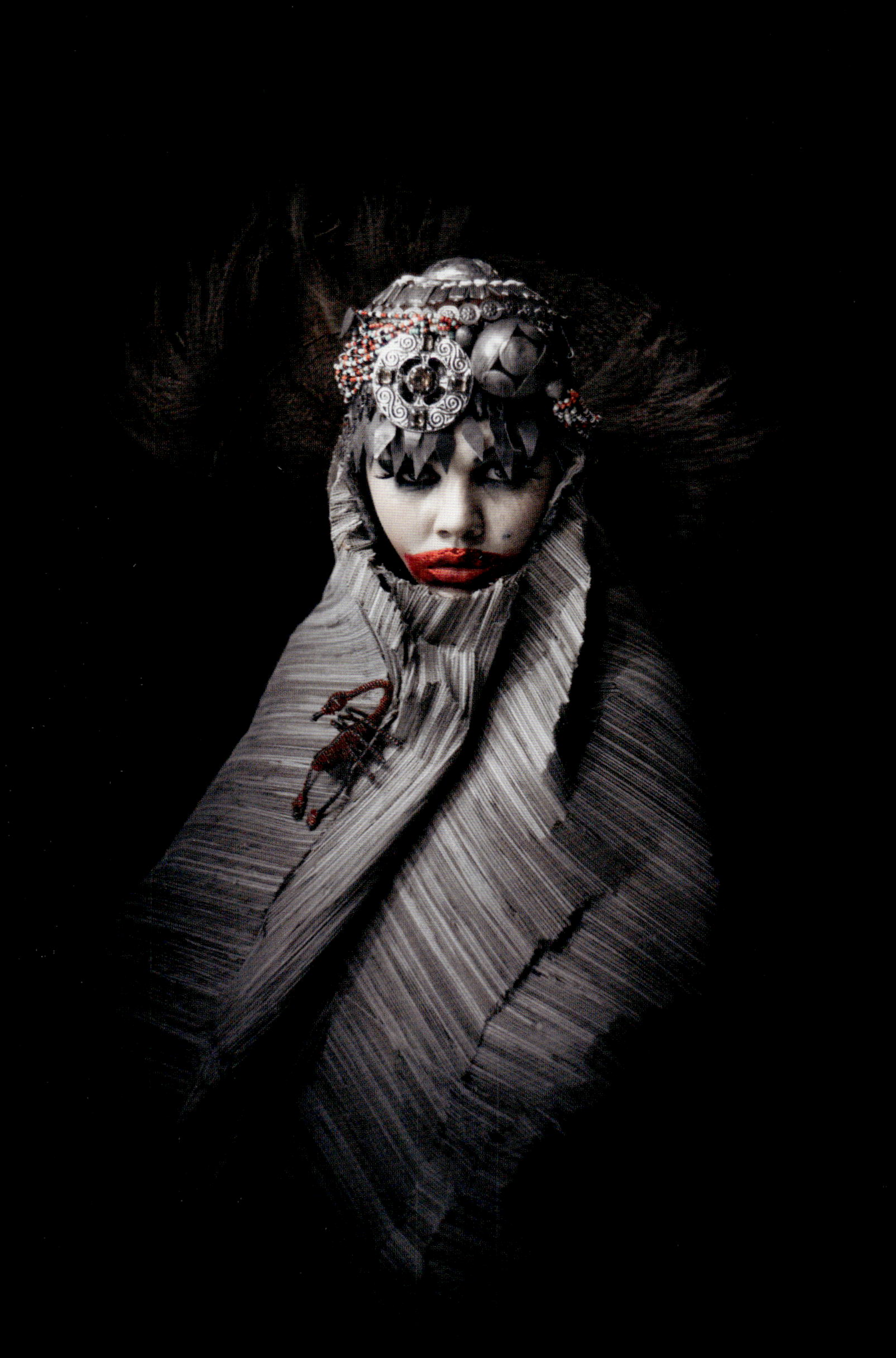

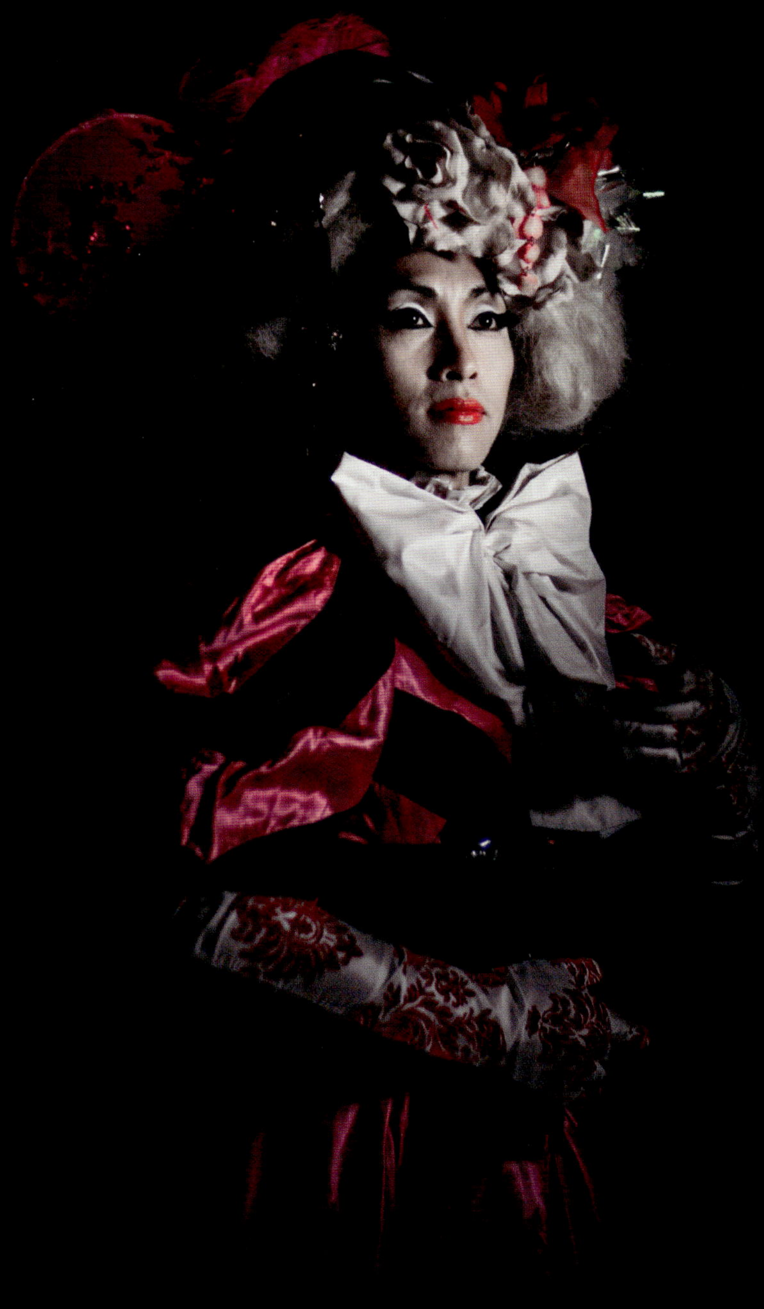

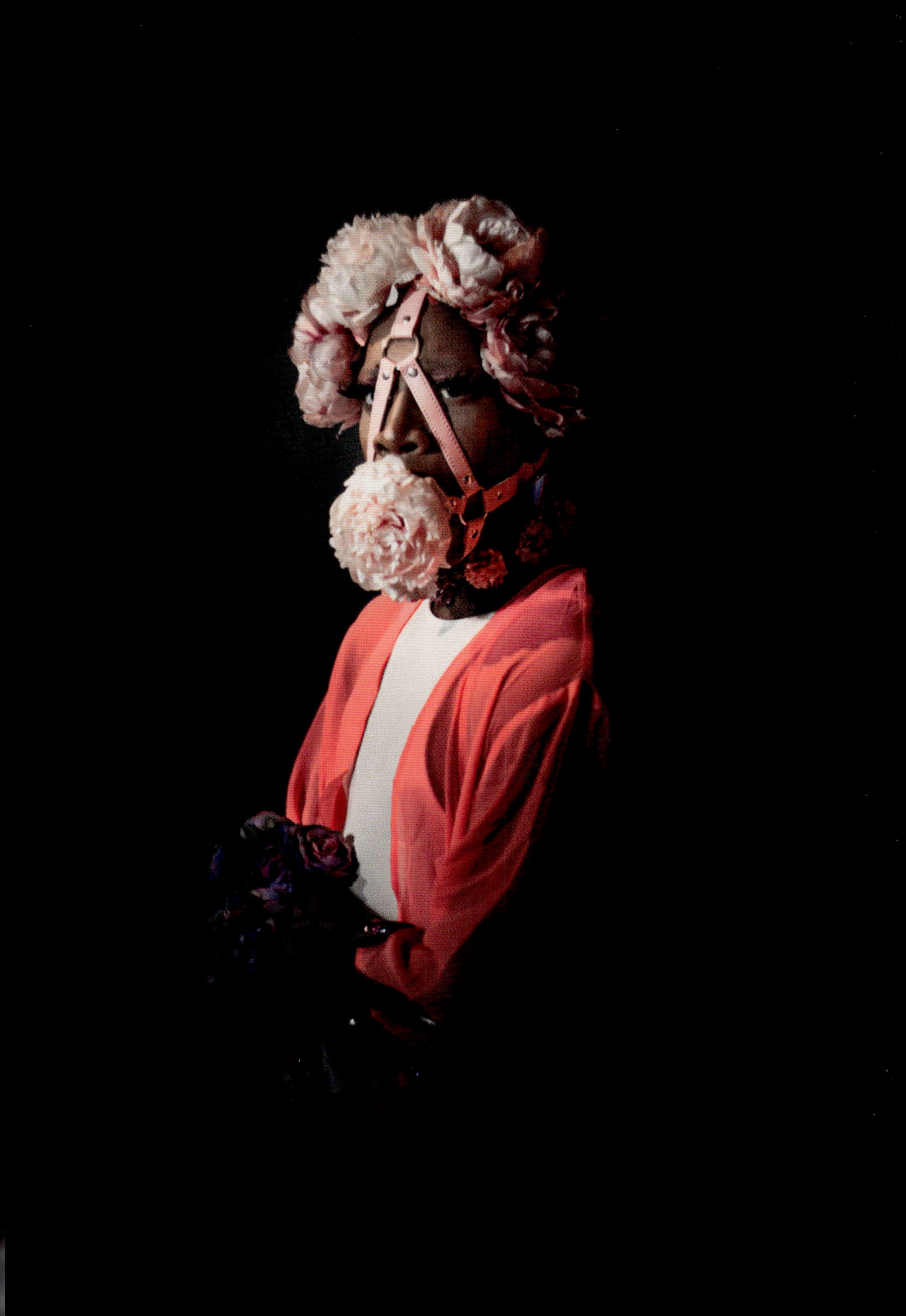

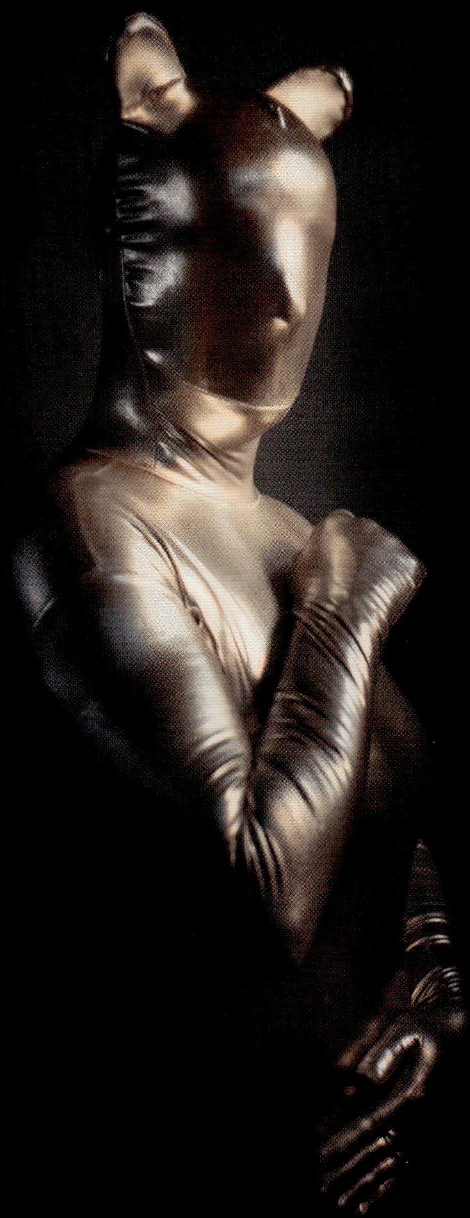

 miss pro flaps at cirque le soir

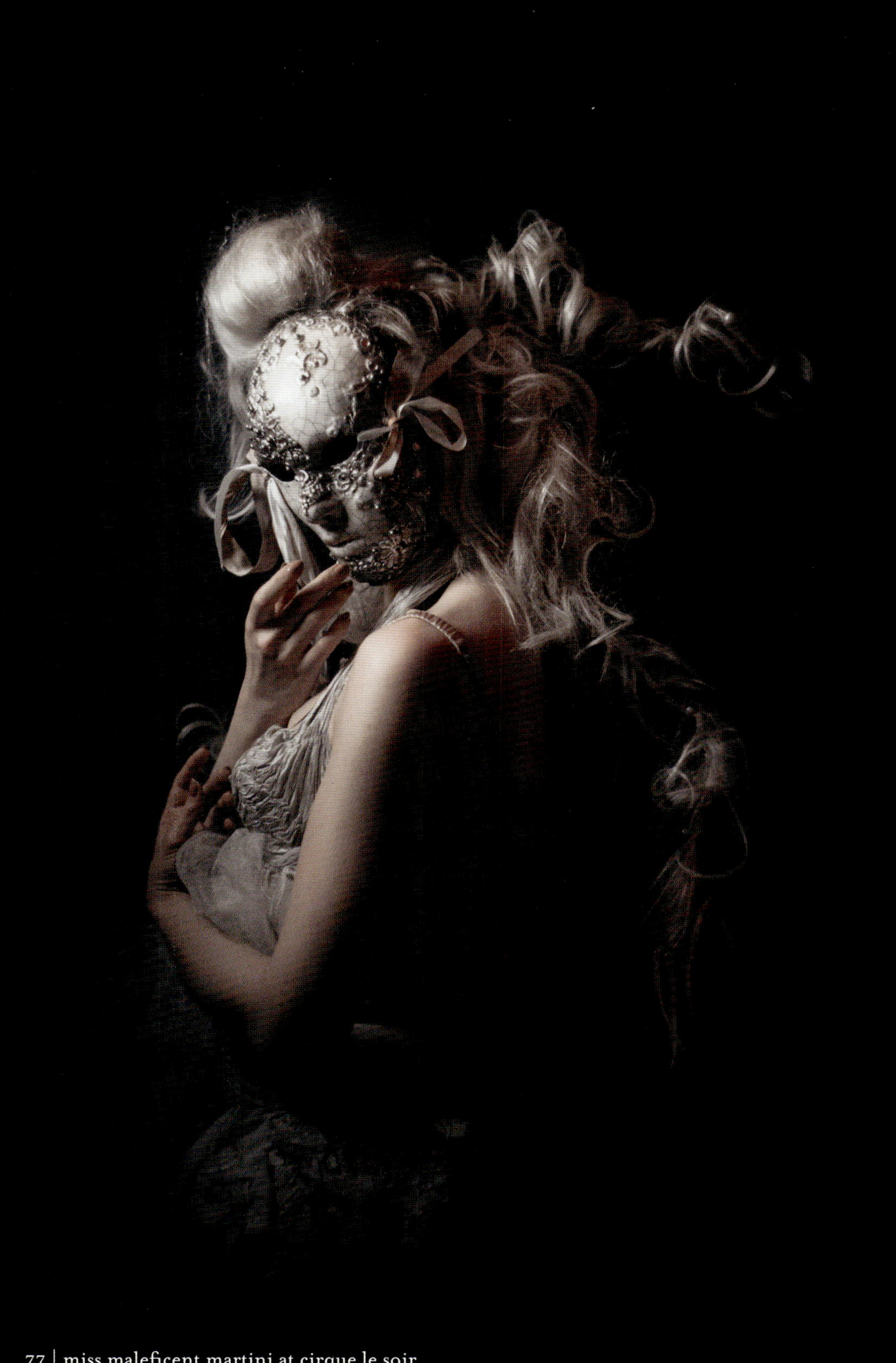

 miss maleficent martini at cirque le soir

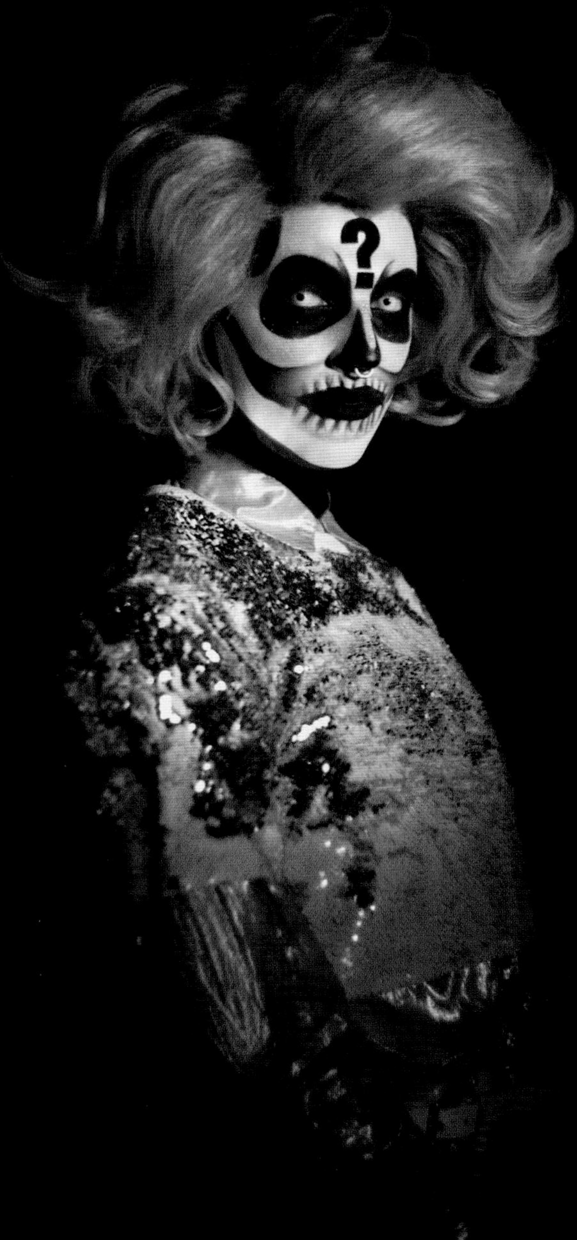

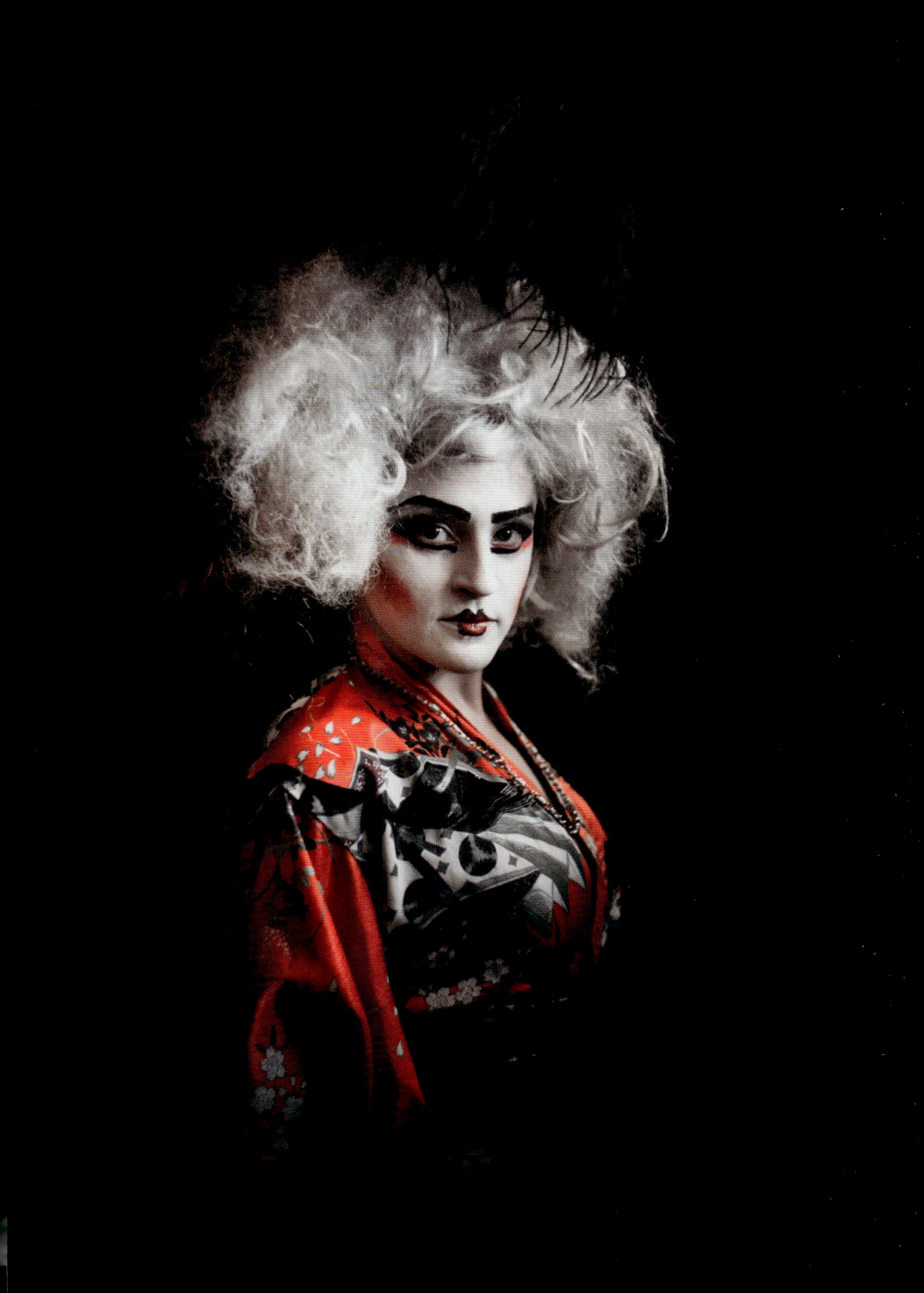

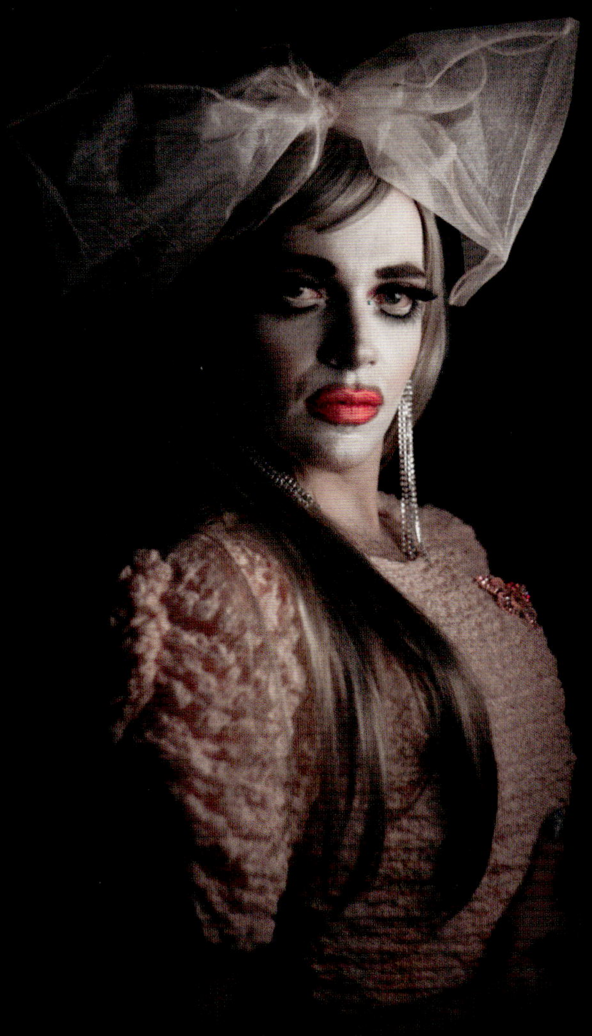

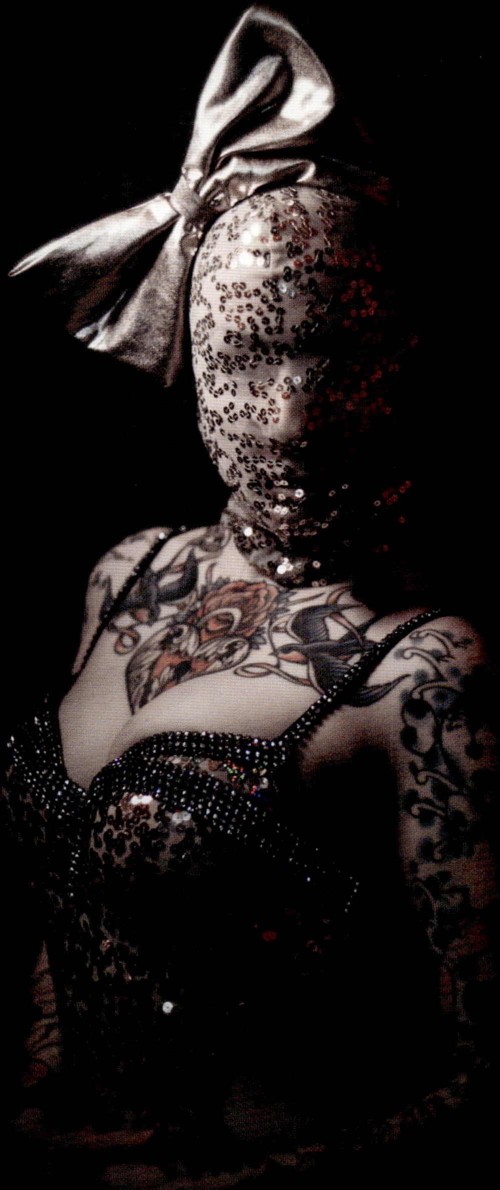

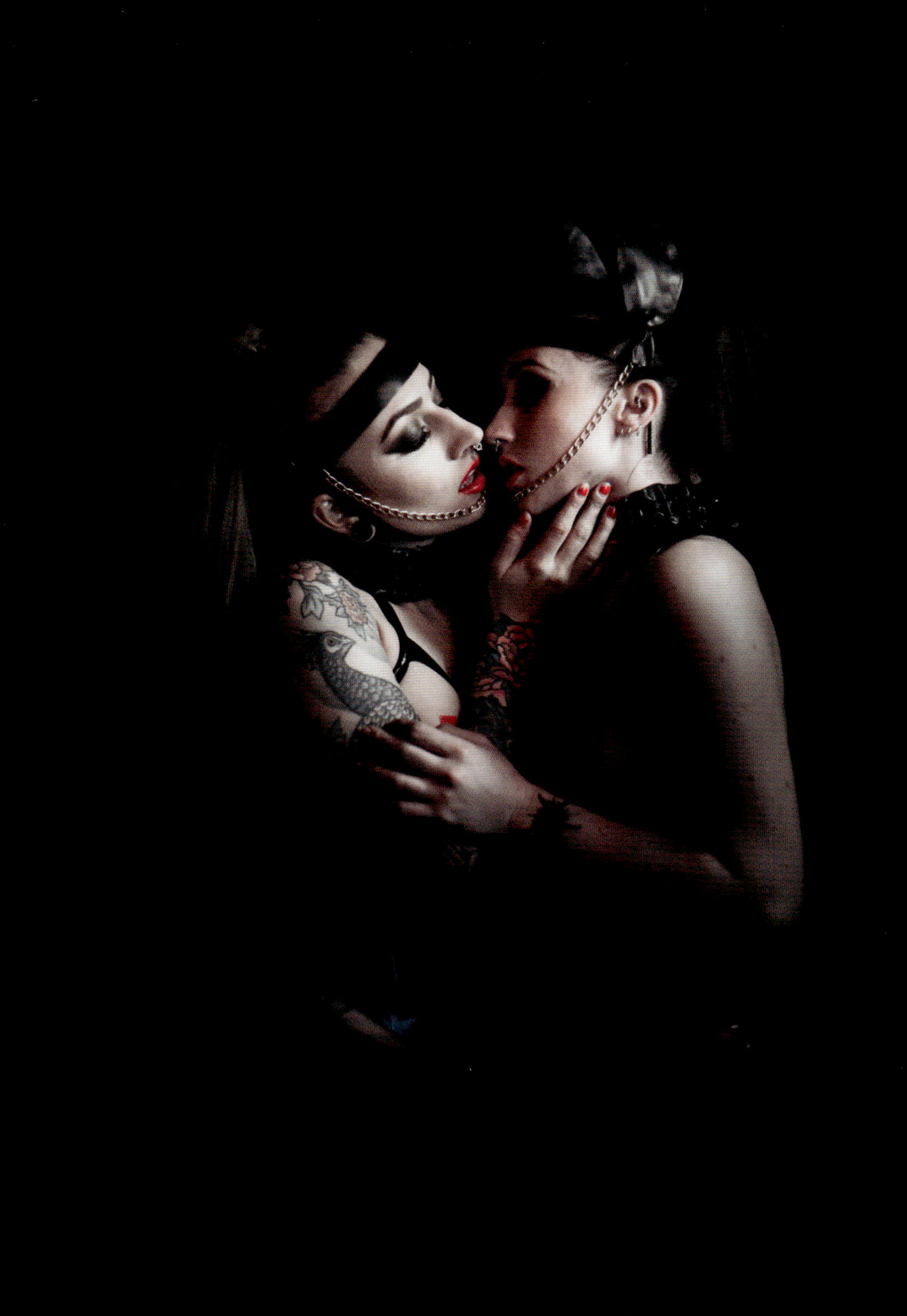

 | charlotte moran and shavonne wager at cirque le soir

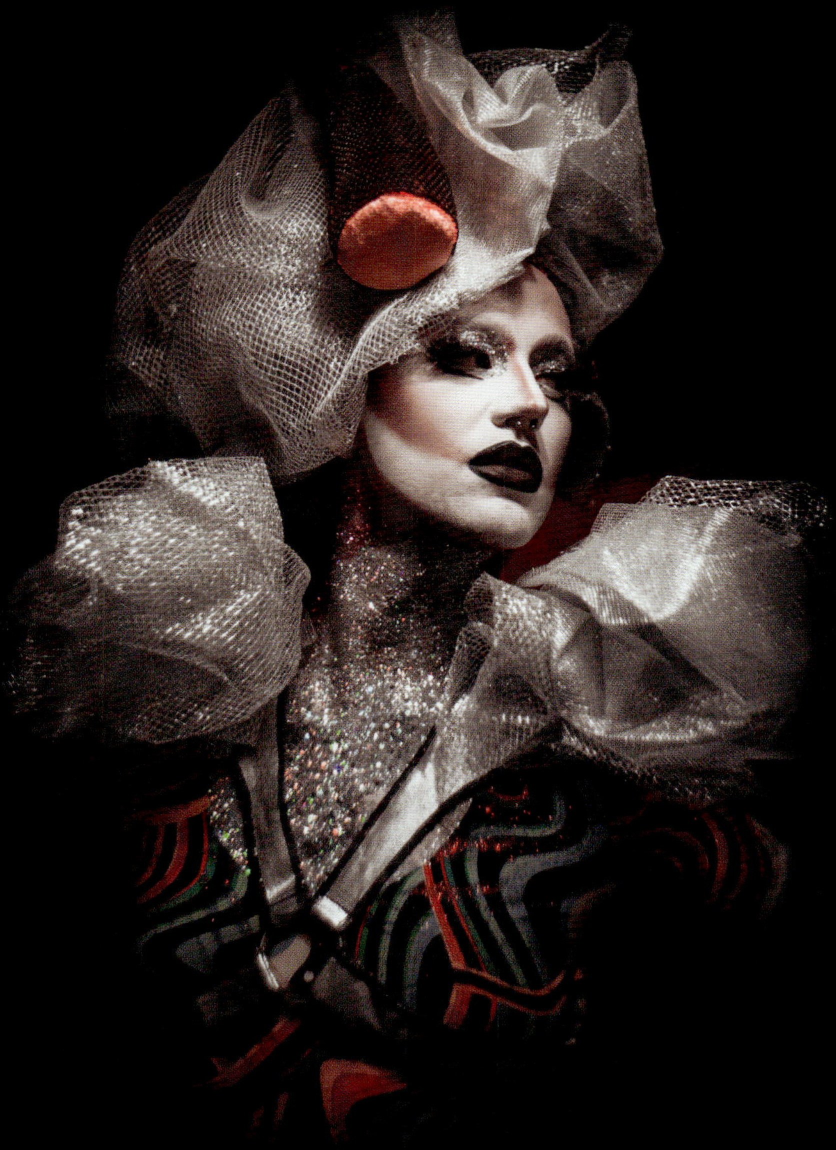

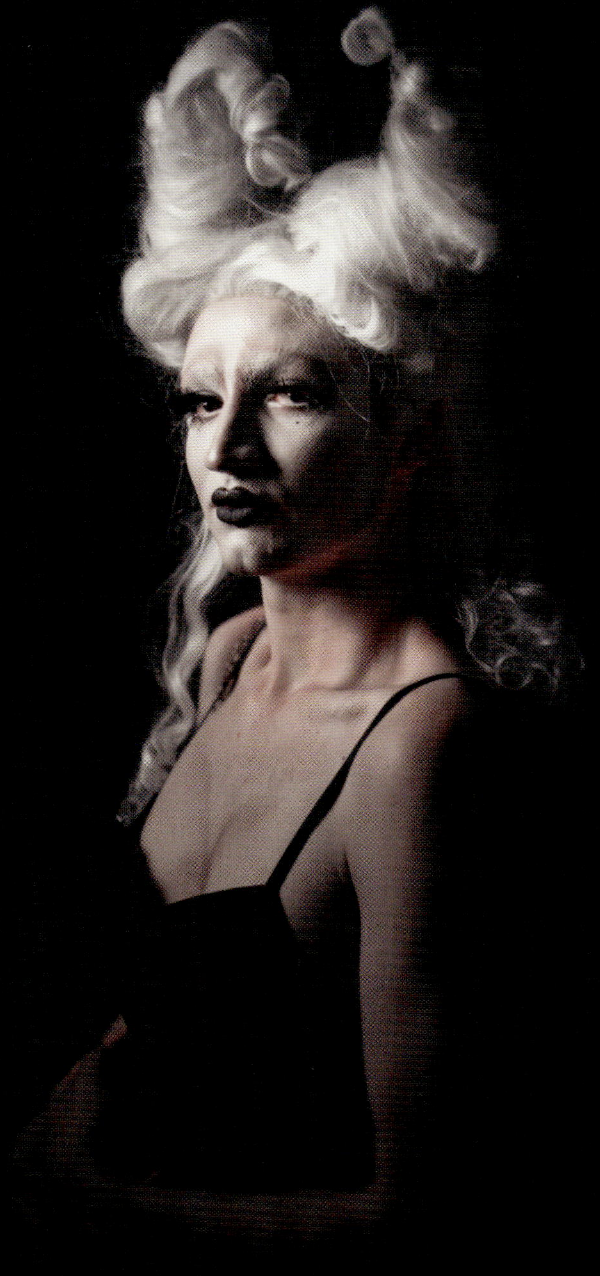

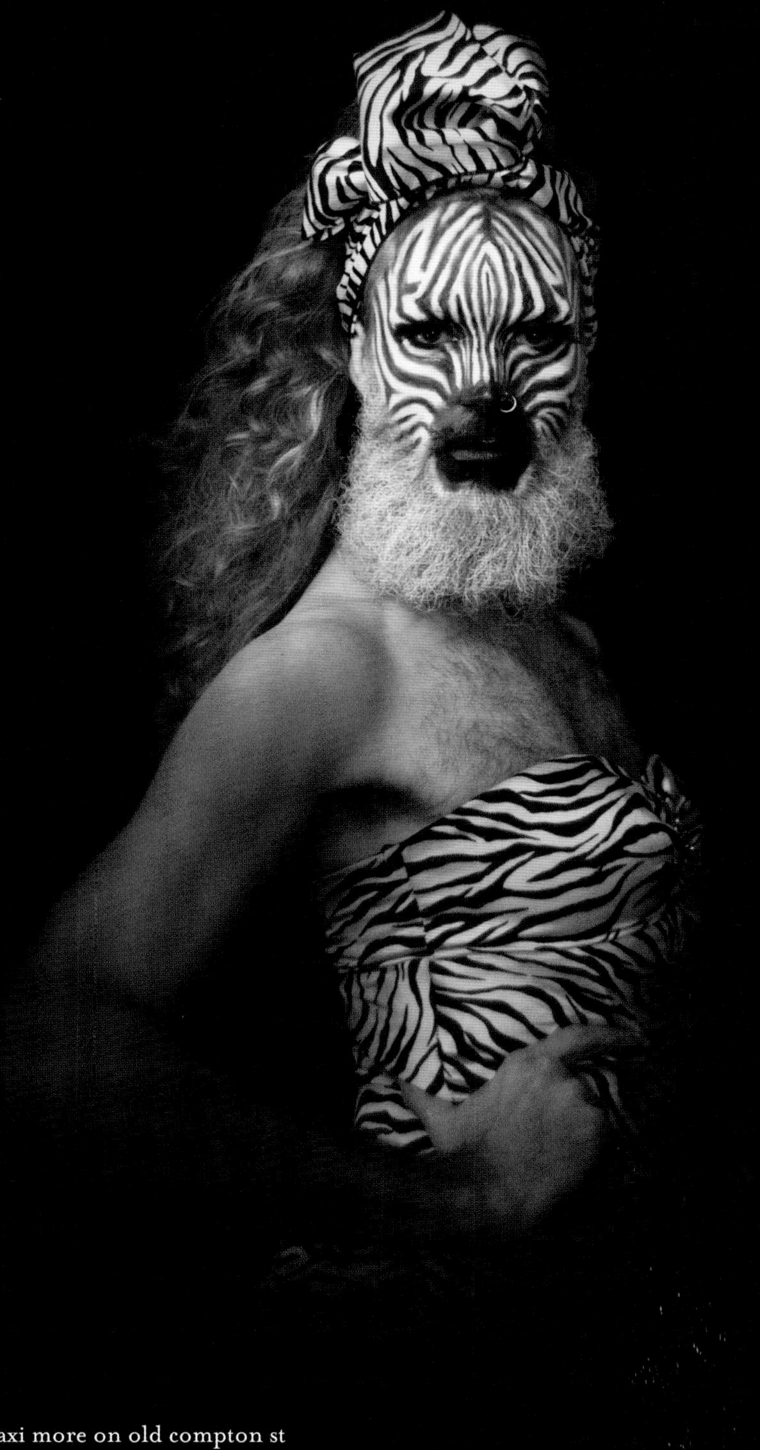

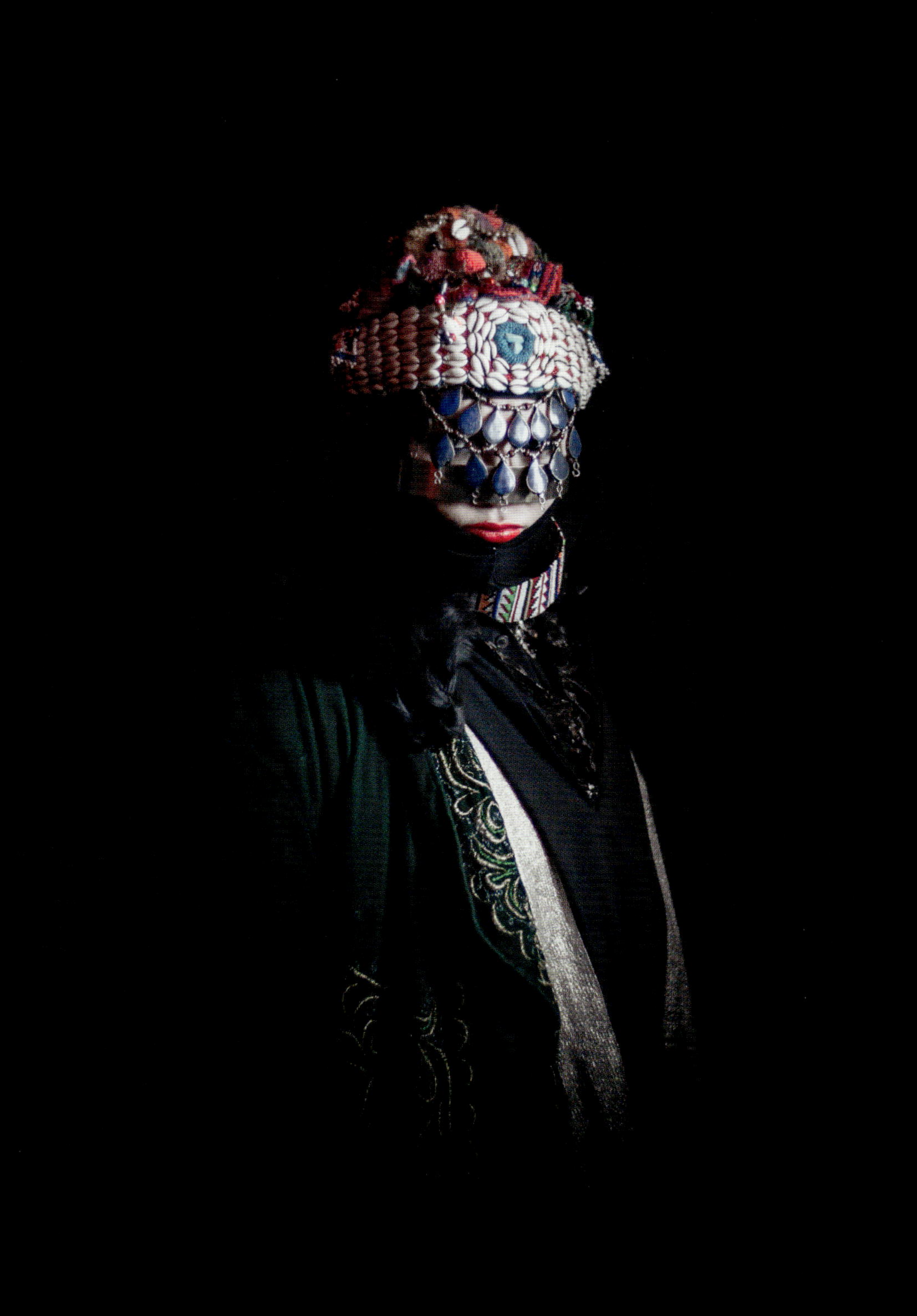

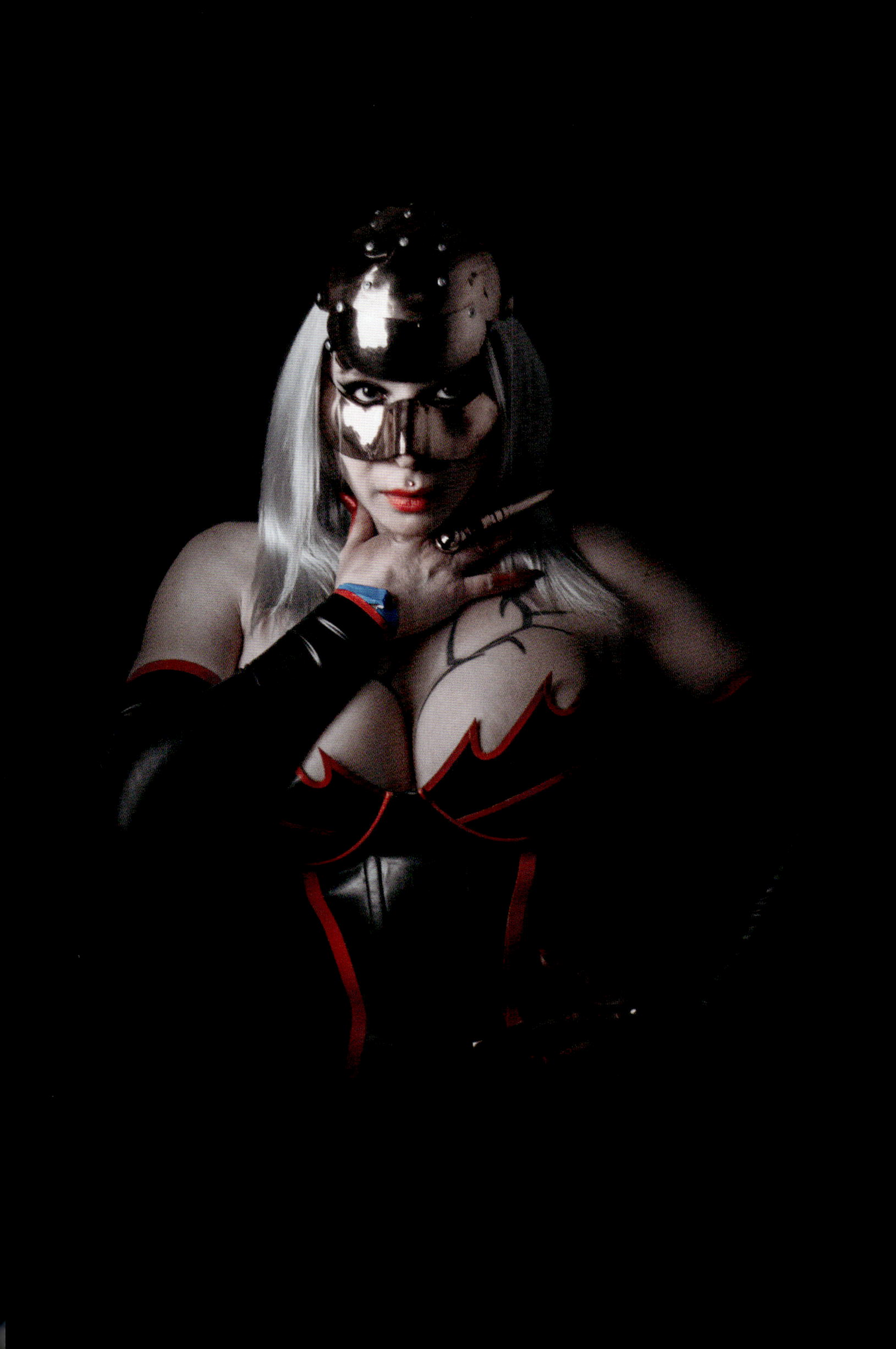

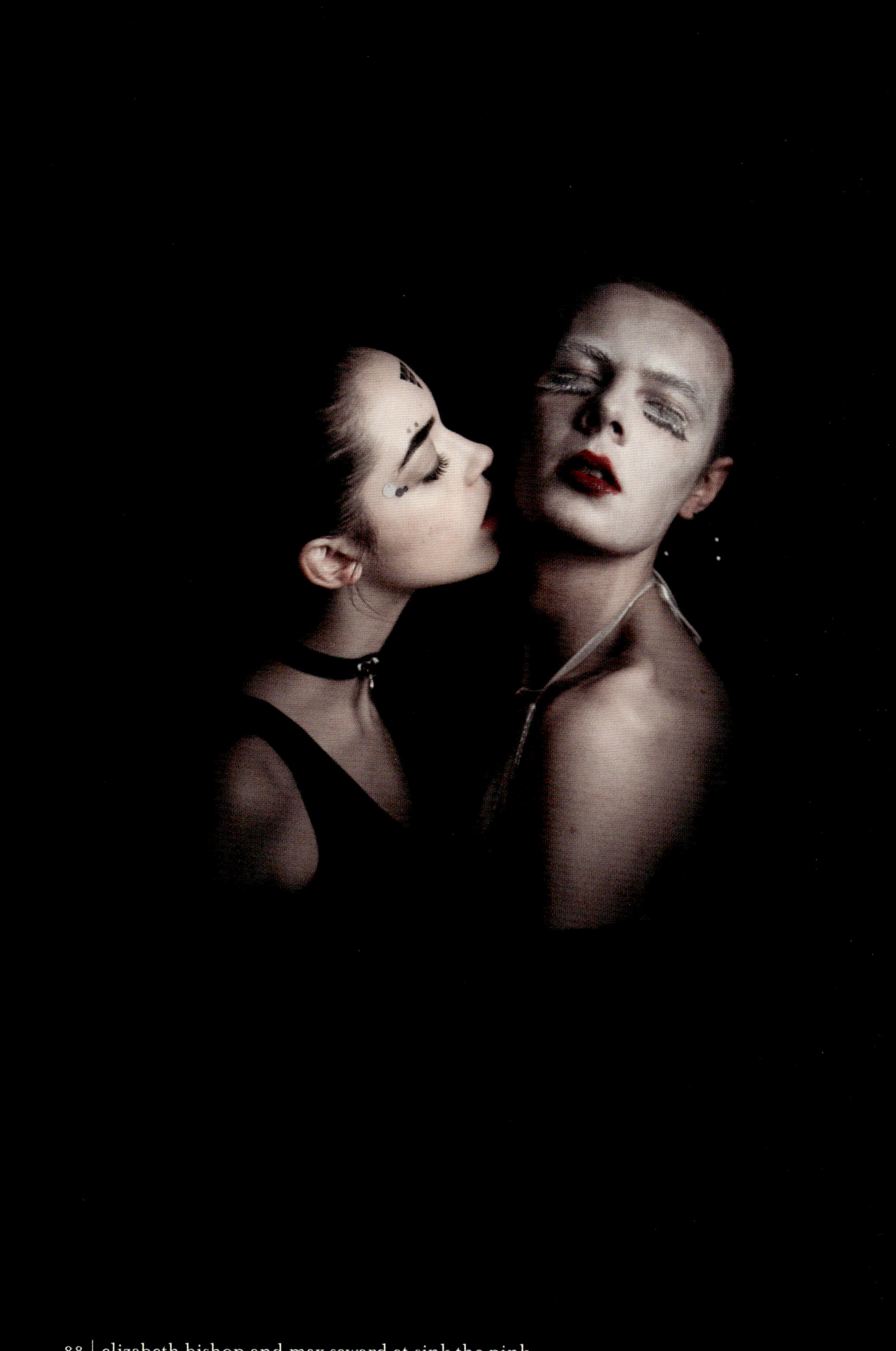

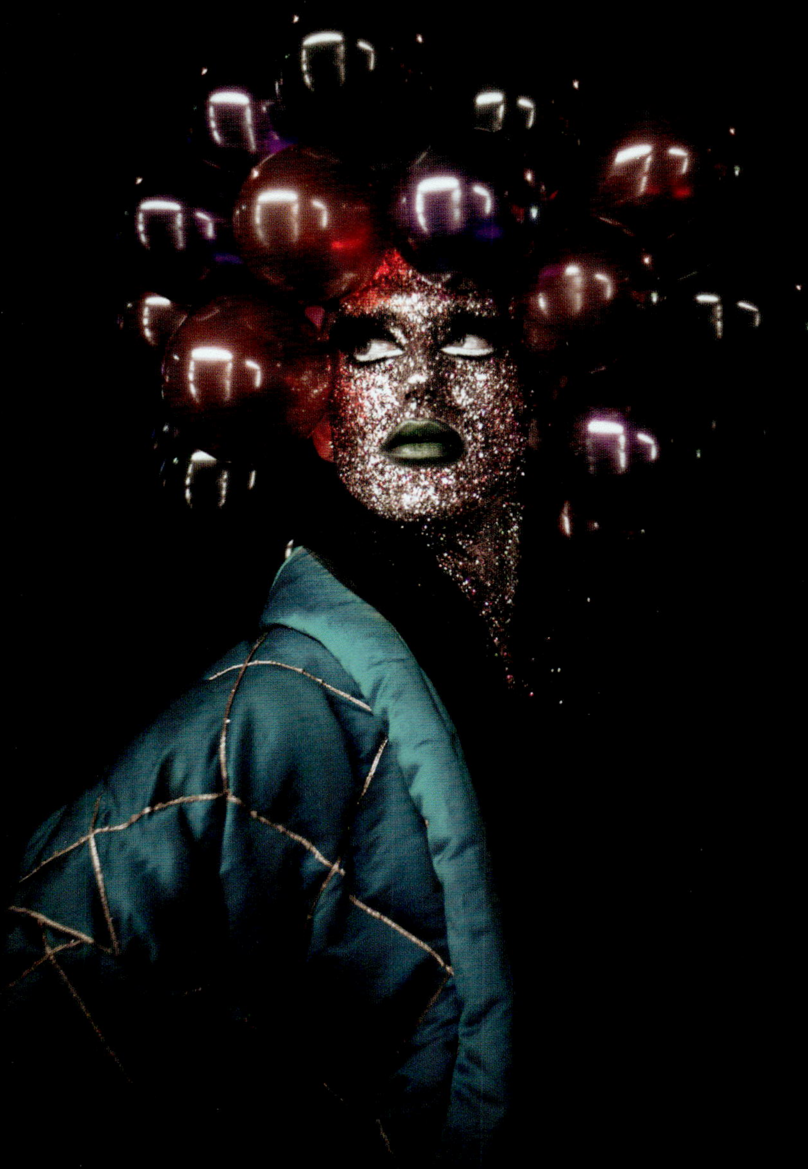

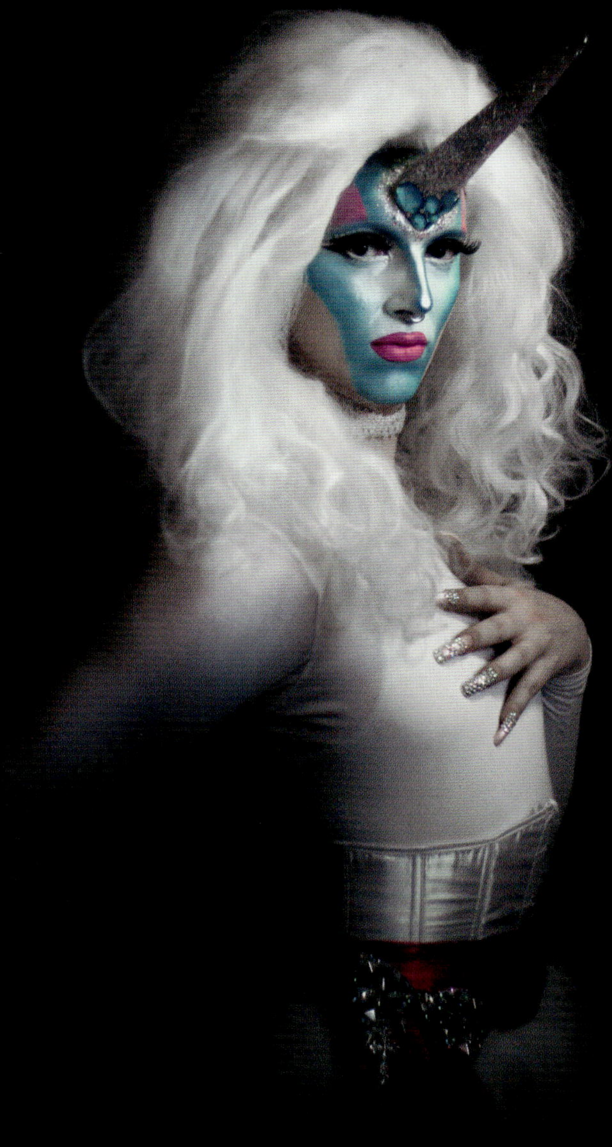

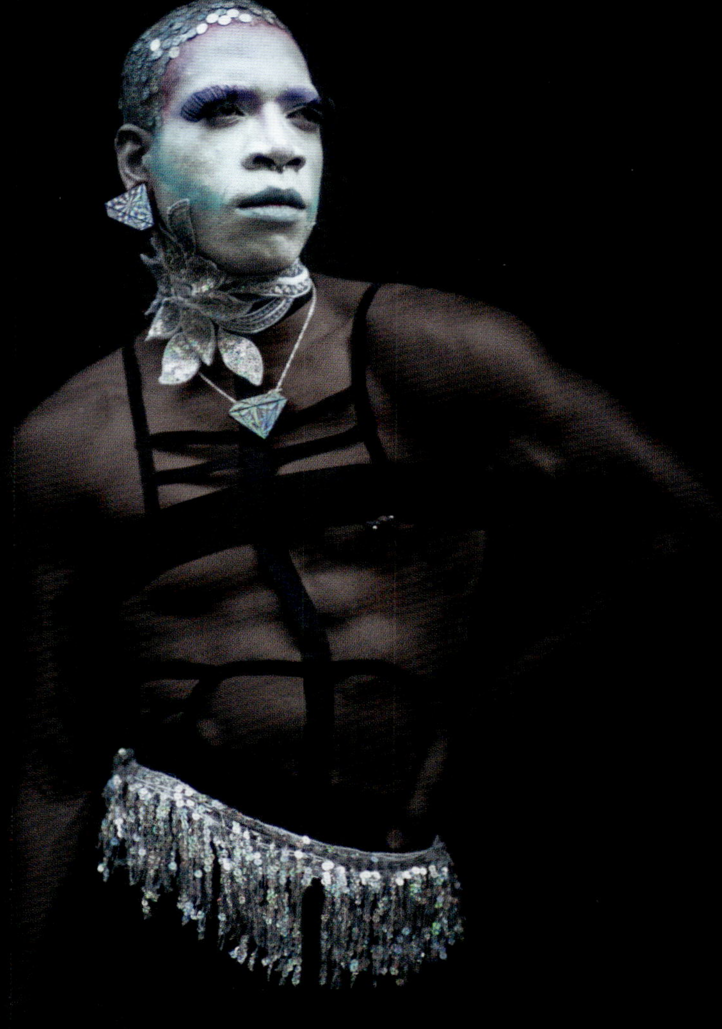

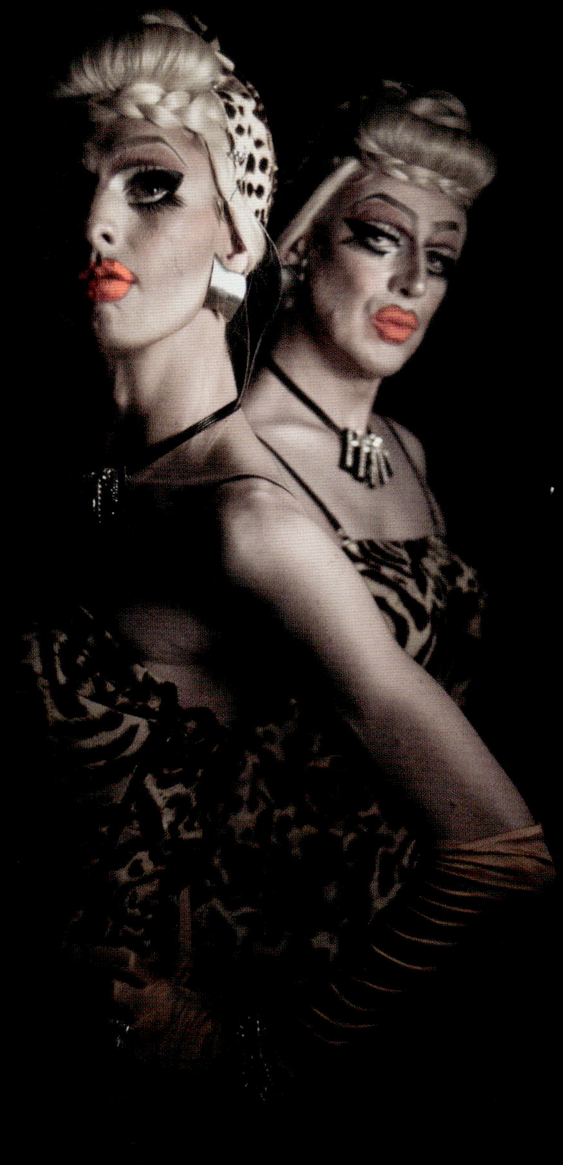

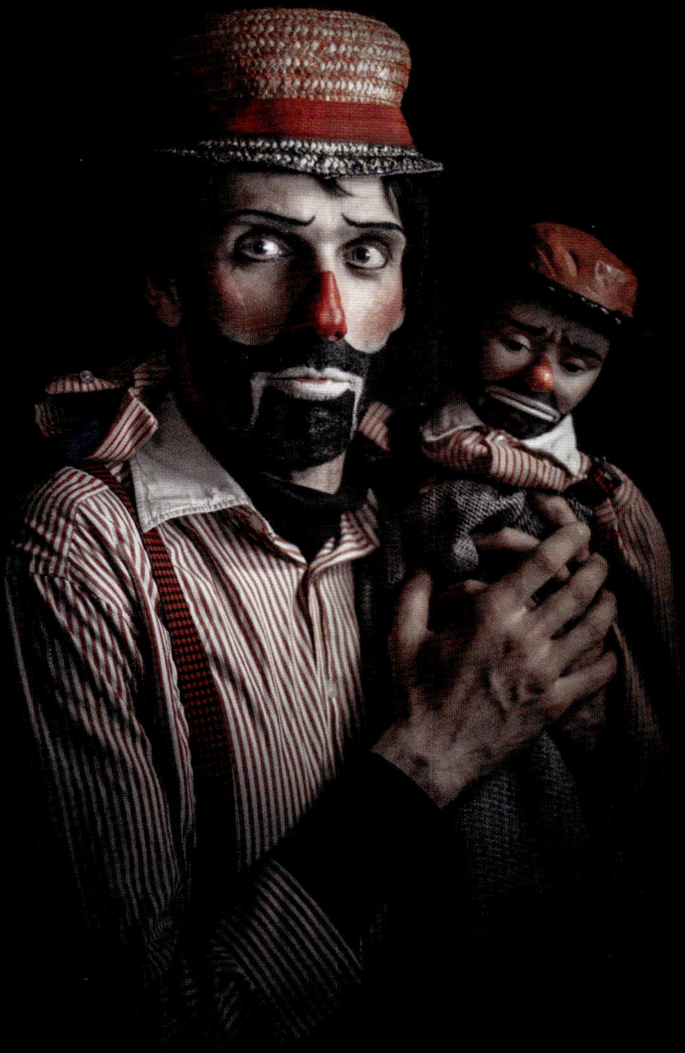

93 | anton (and friend) at cirque le soir

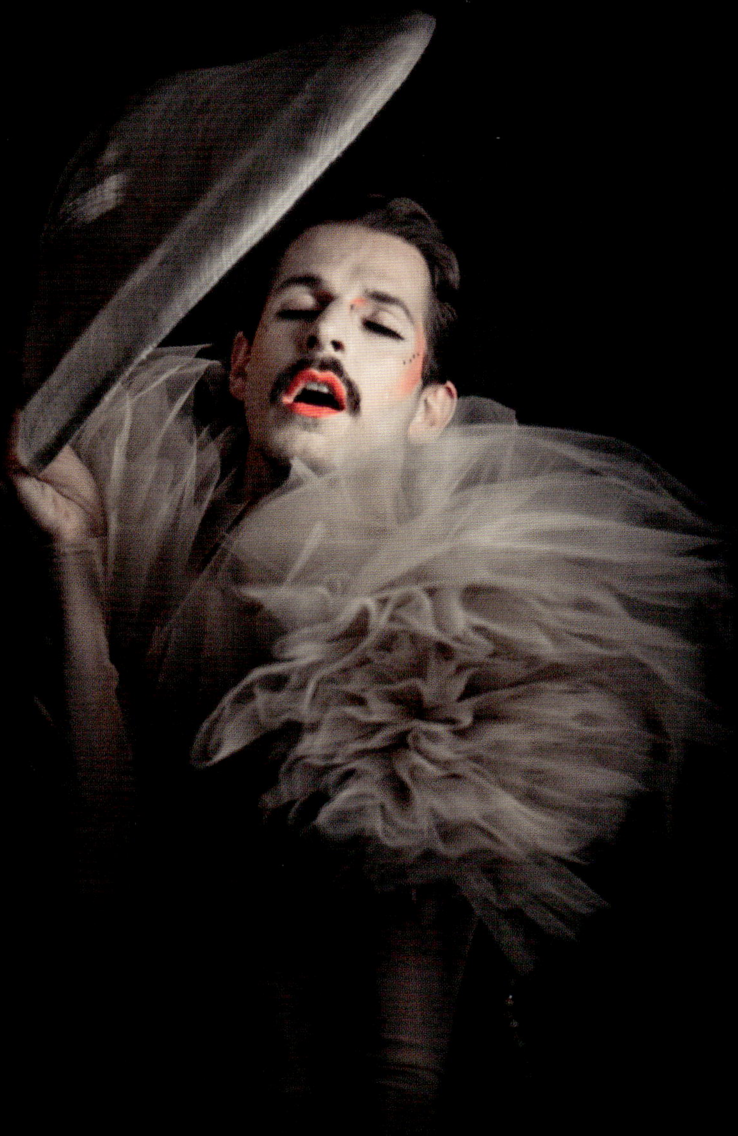

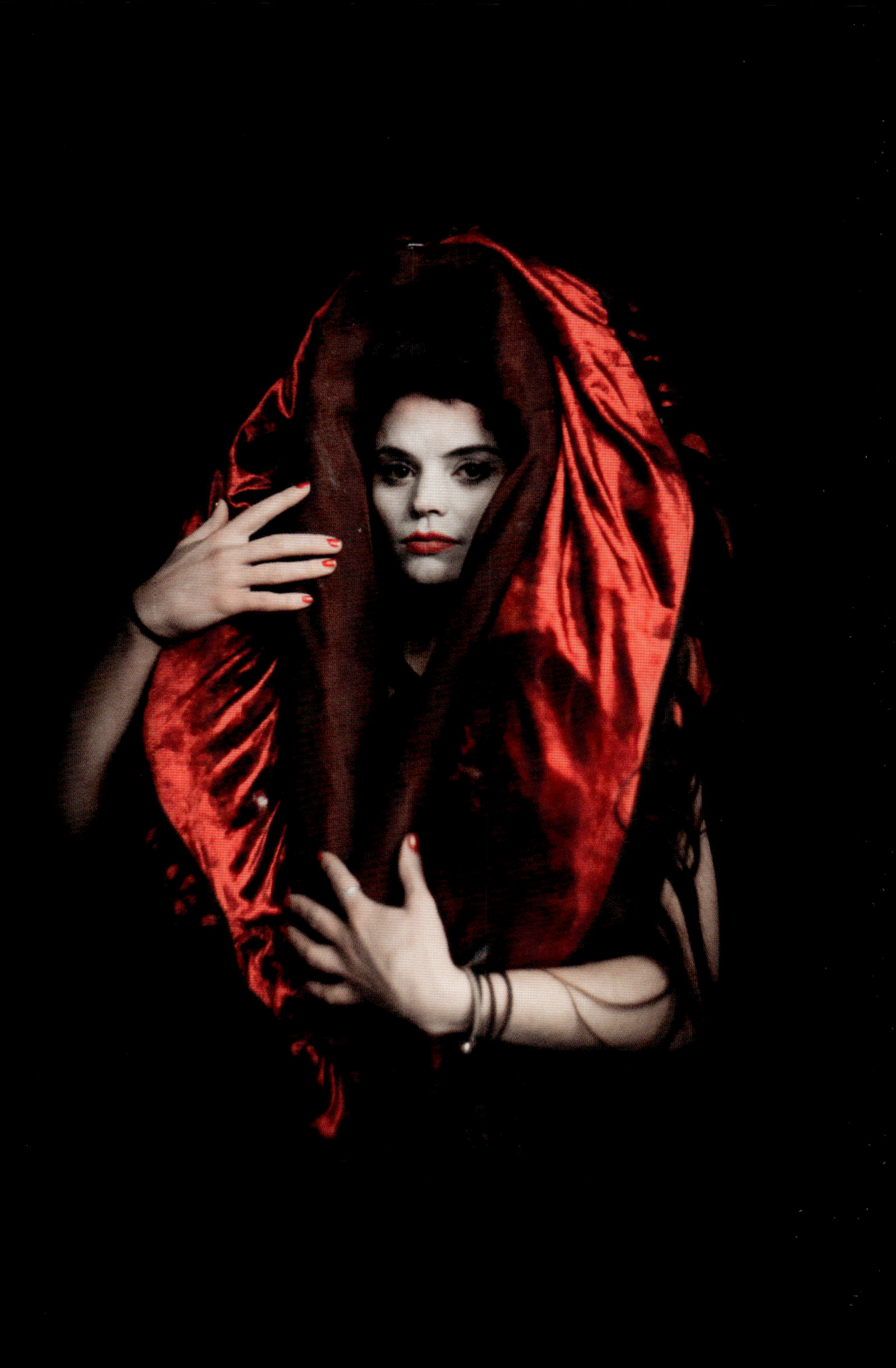

95 | edythe woolley (lady vagina) on hackney rd

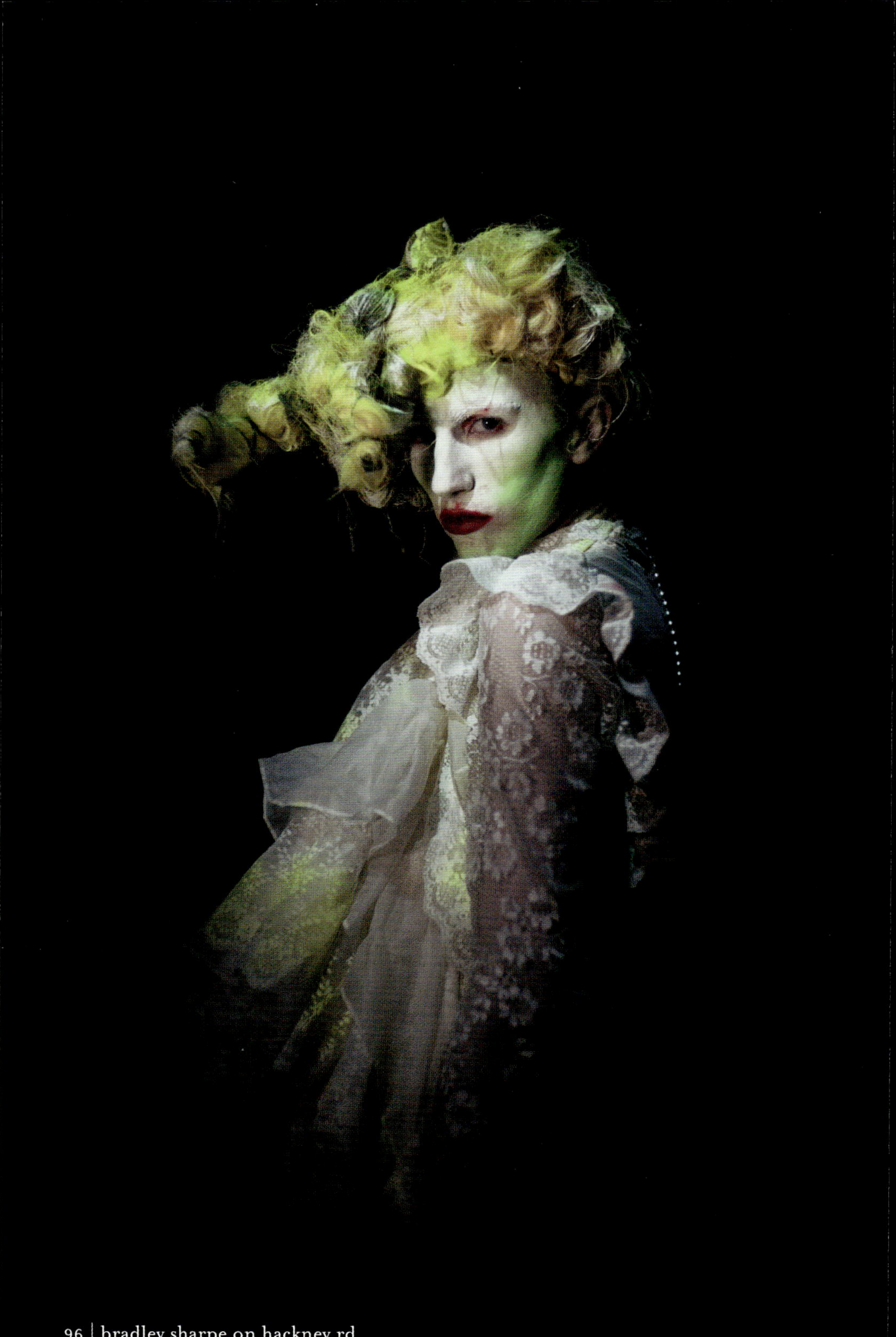

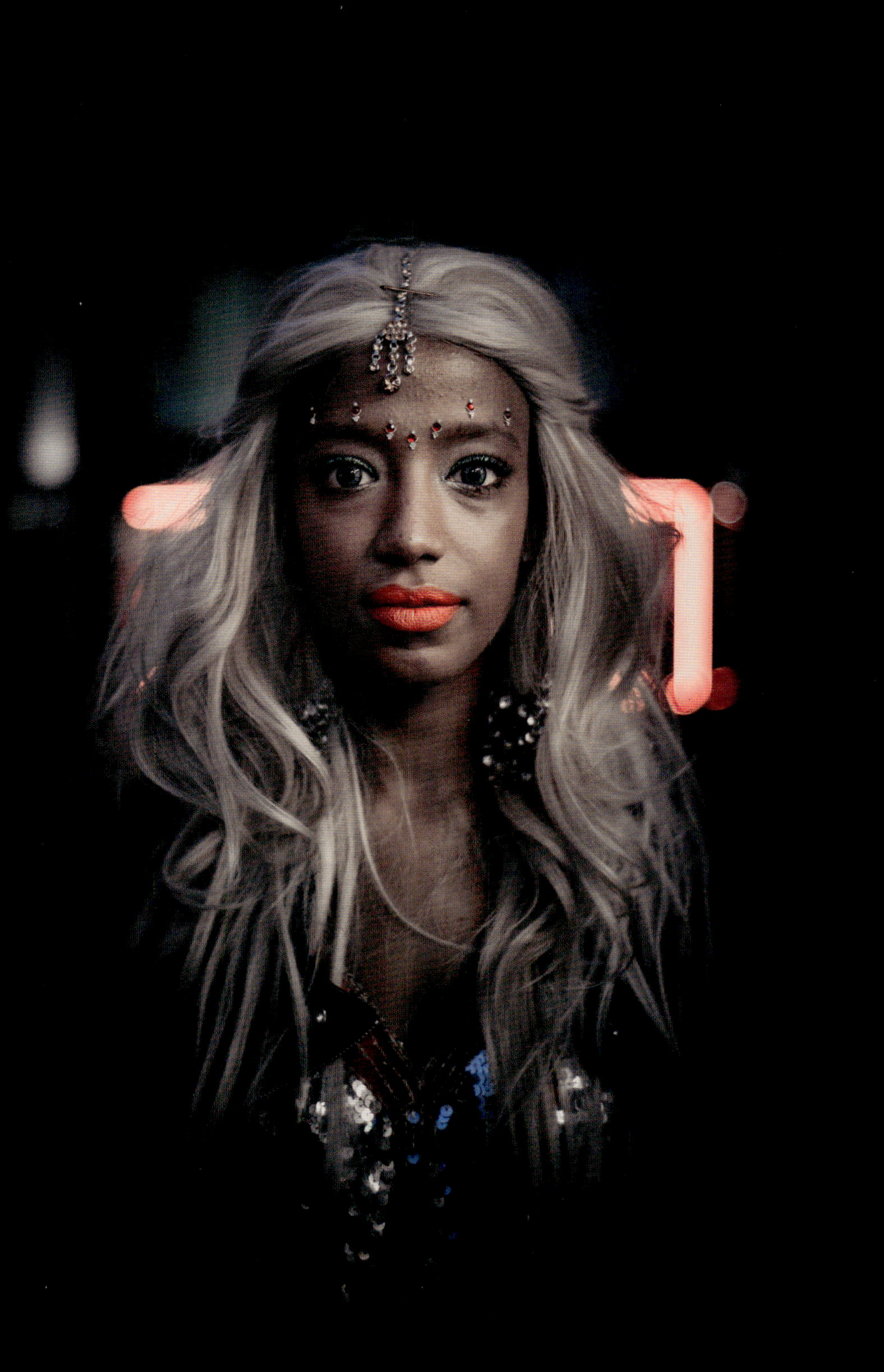

7 | emma darling on old compton st

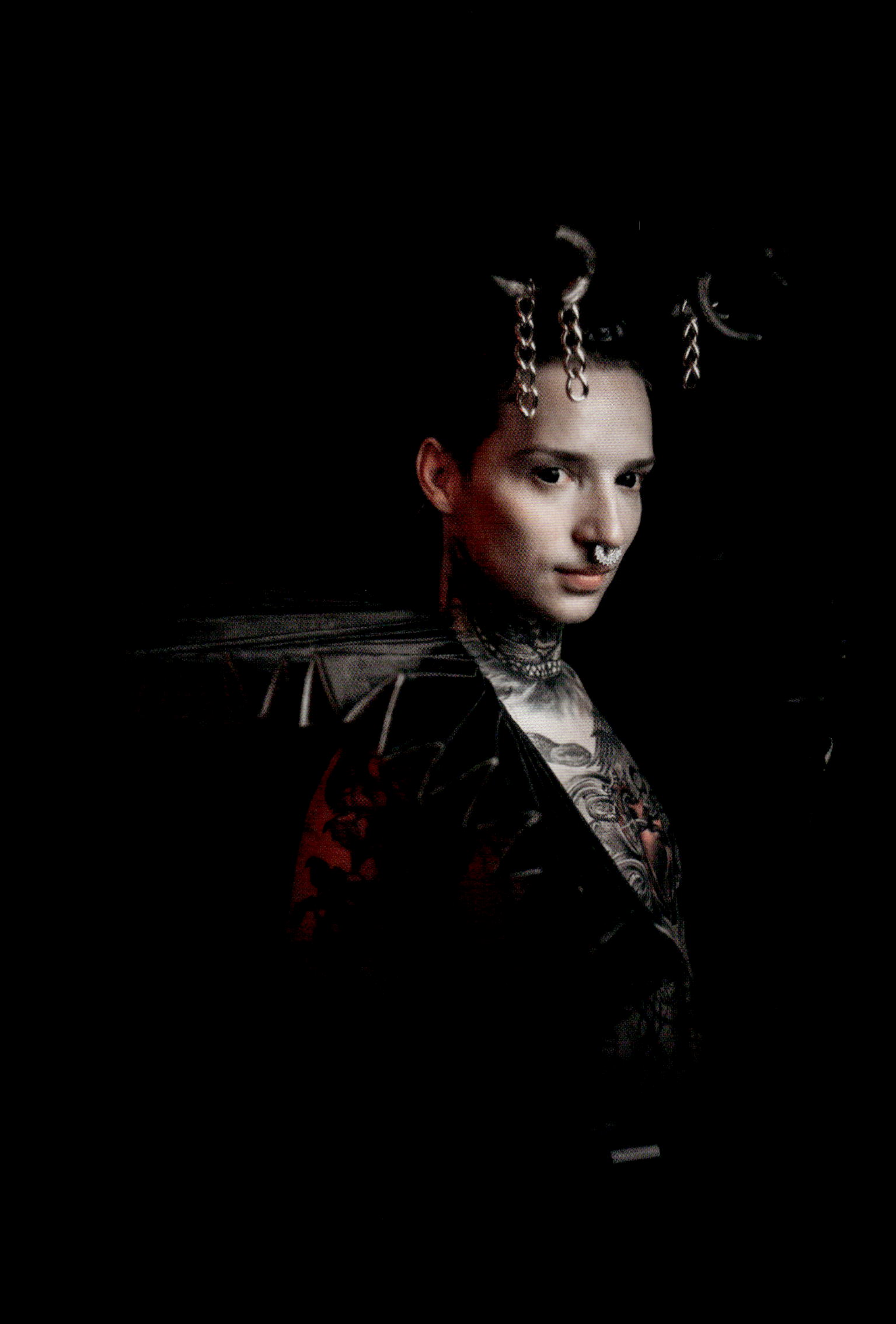

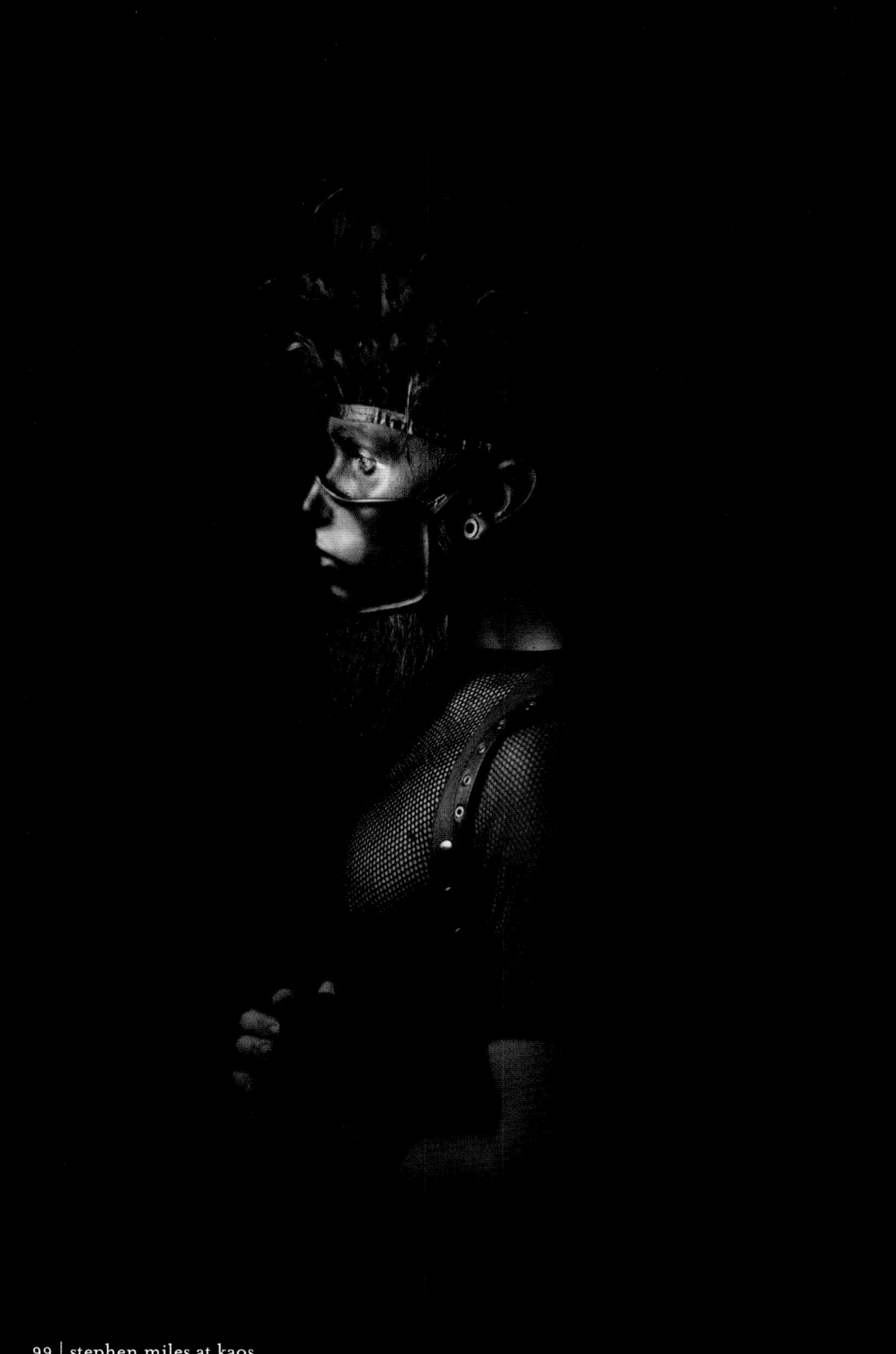

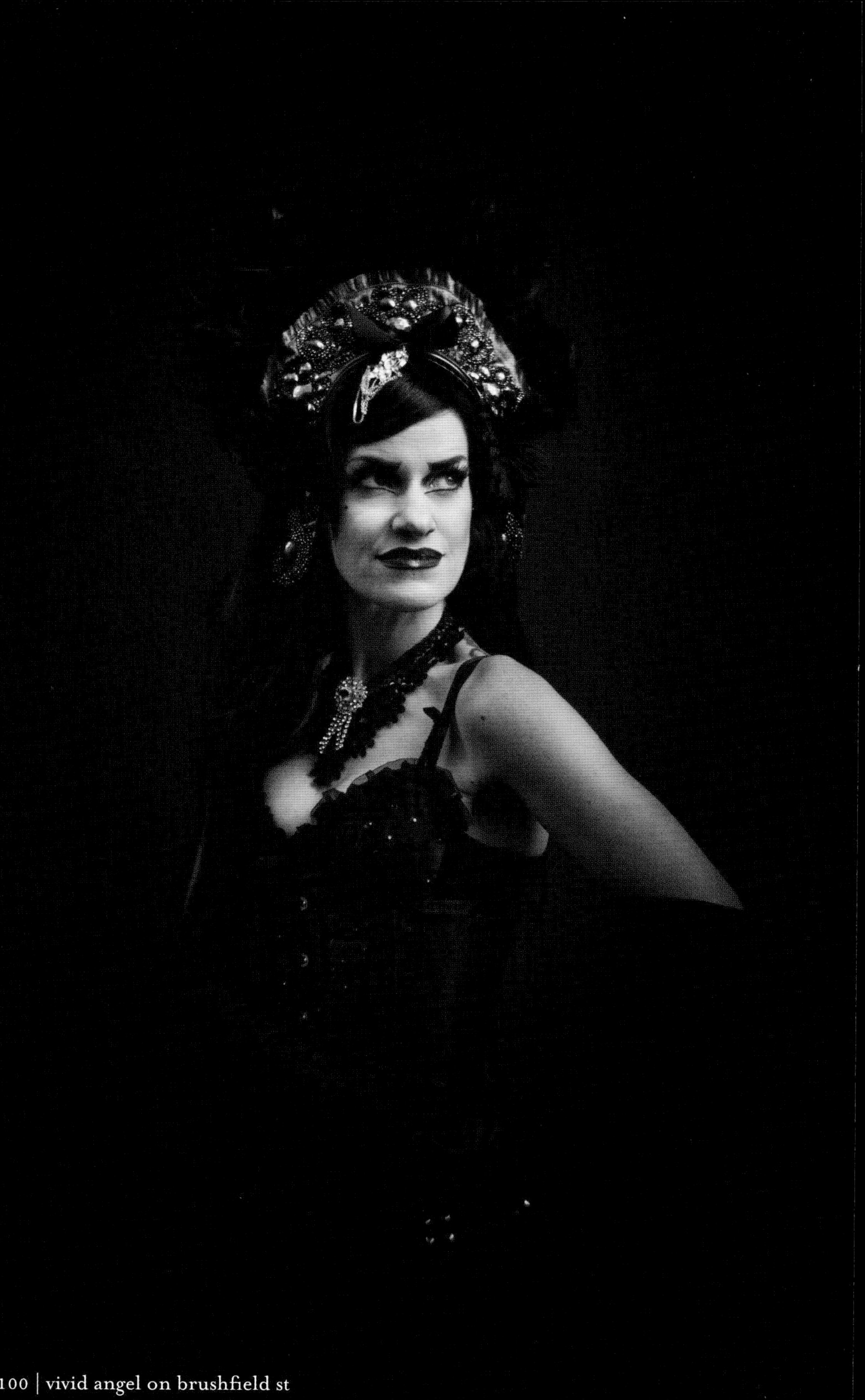

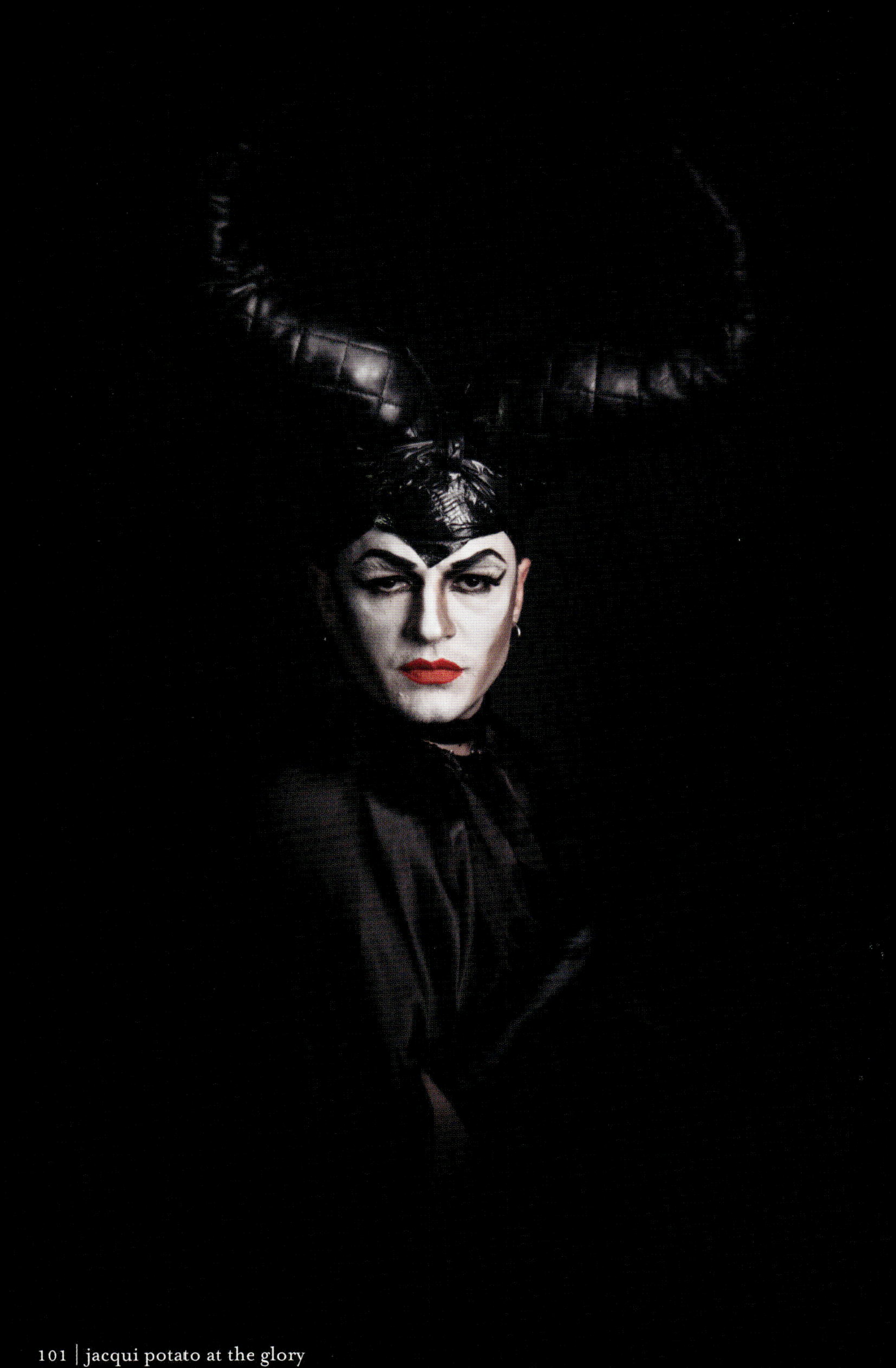

 | jacqui potato at the glory

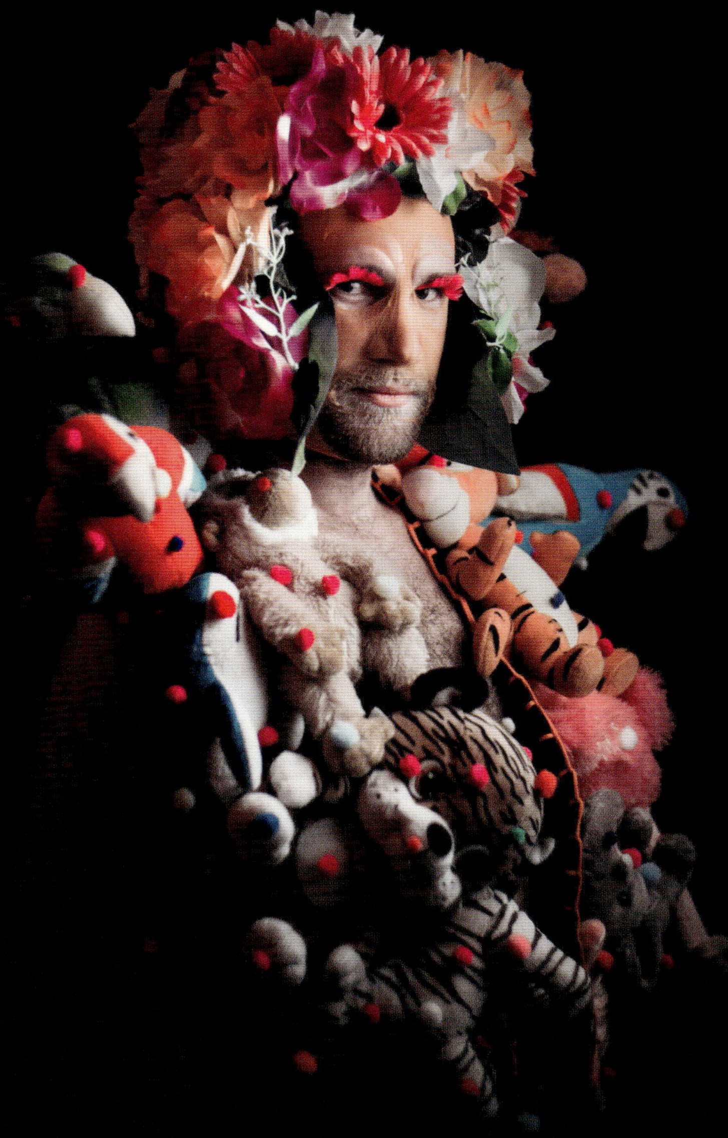

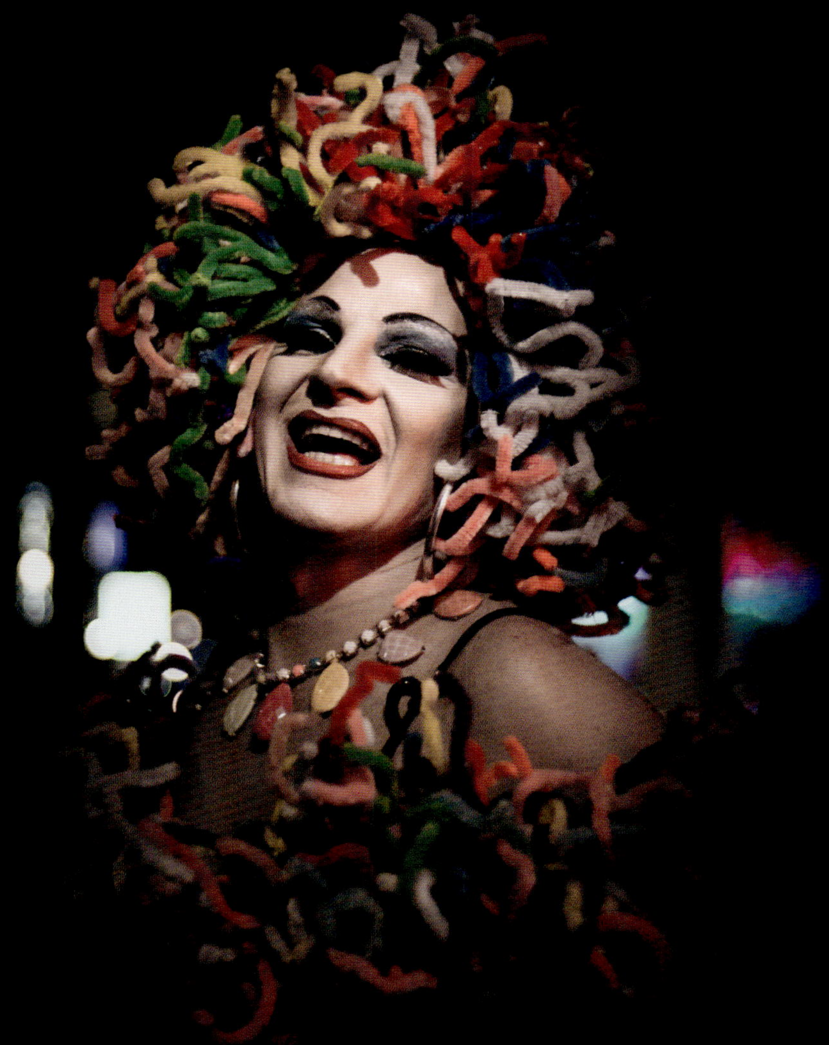

 sidney bueno on walker's ct

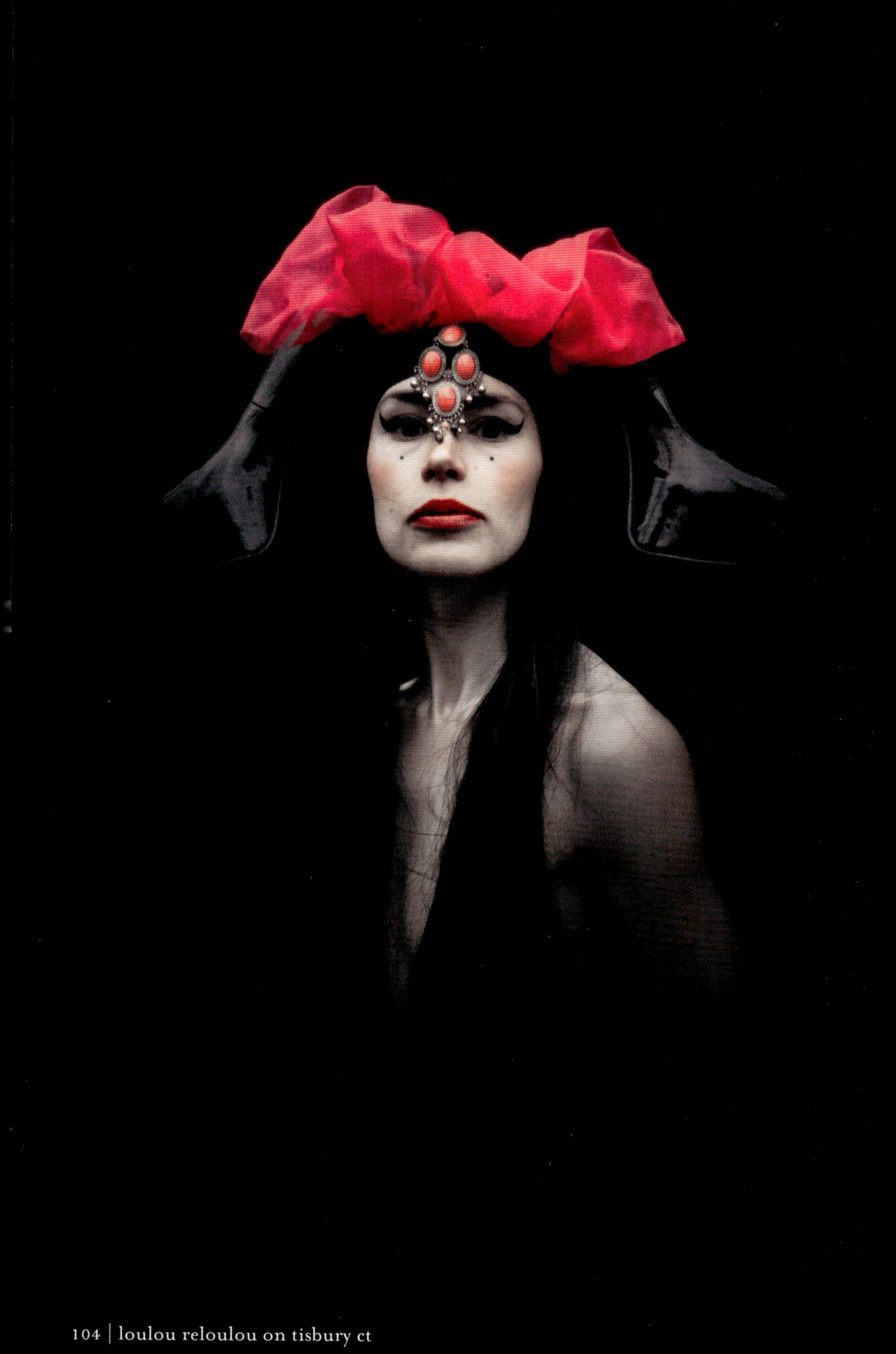

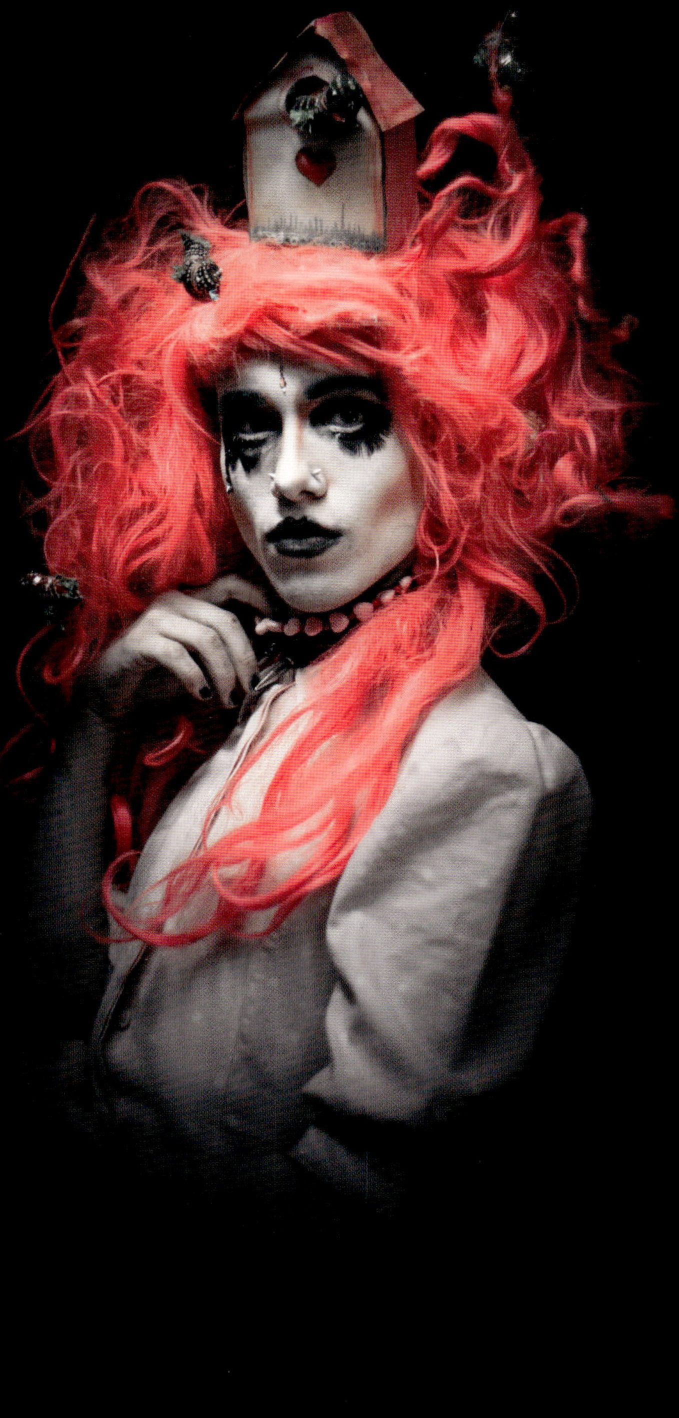

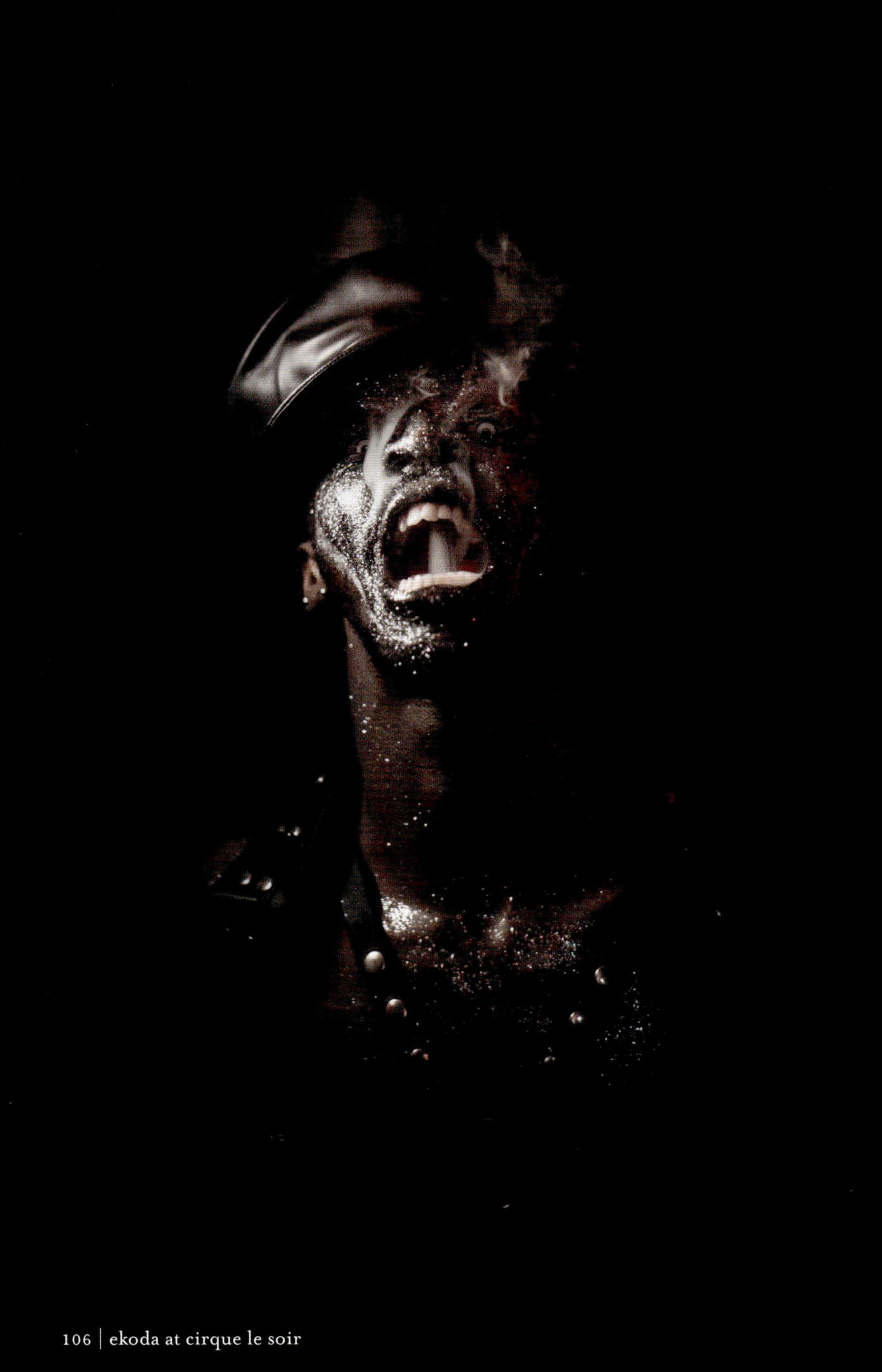

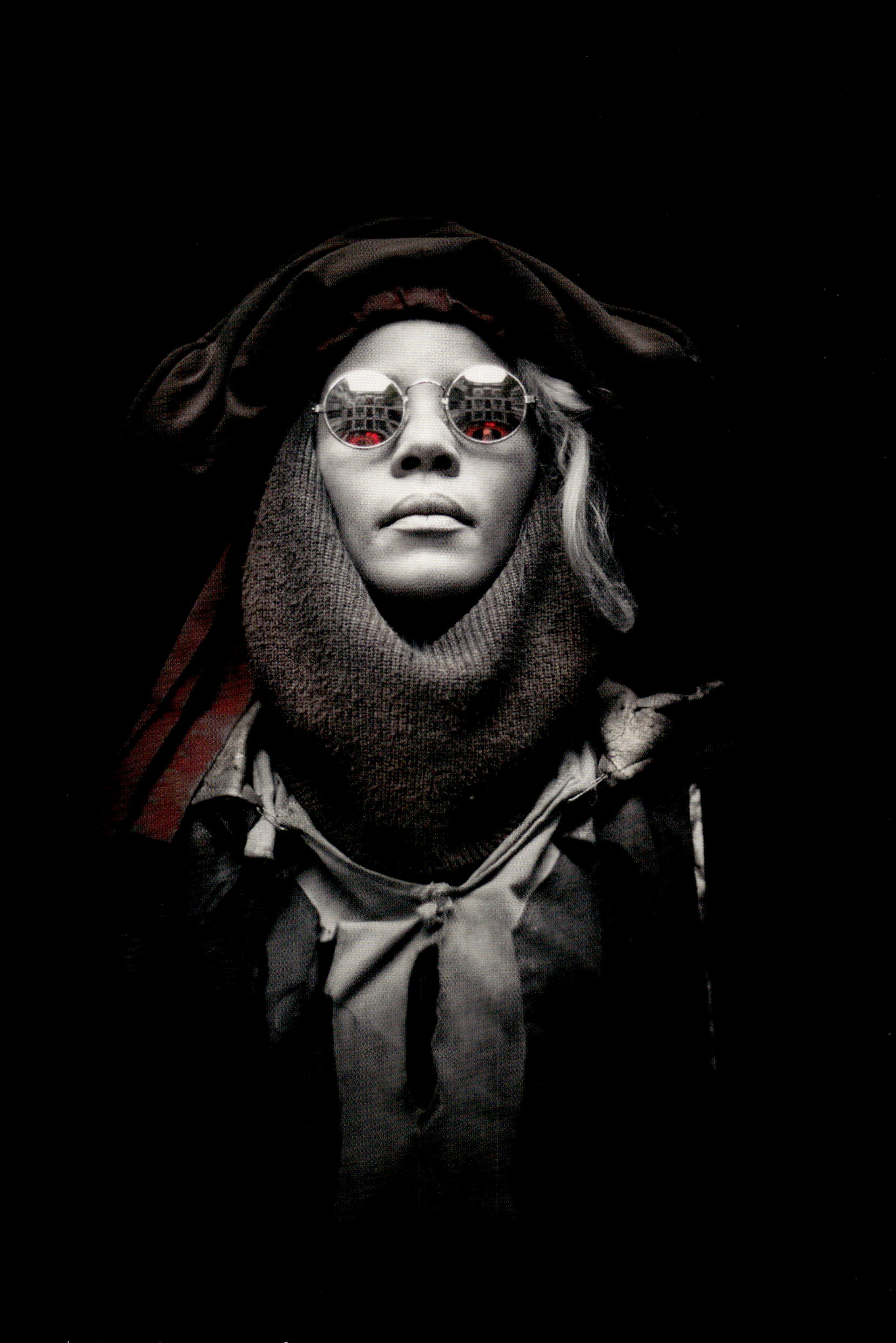

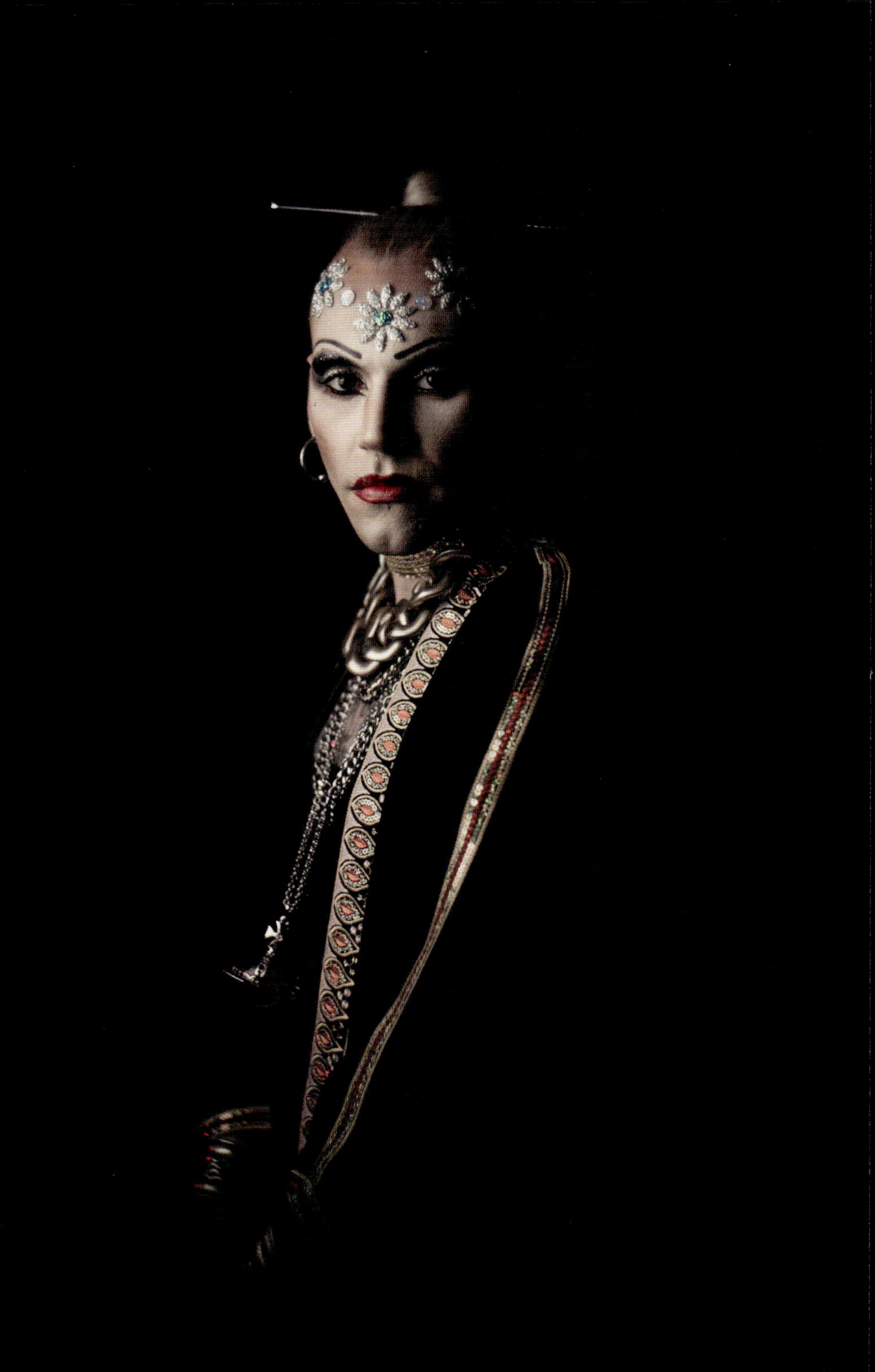

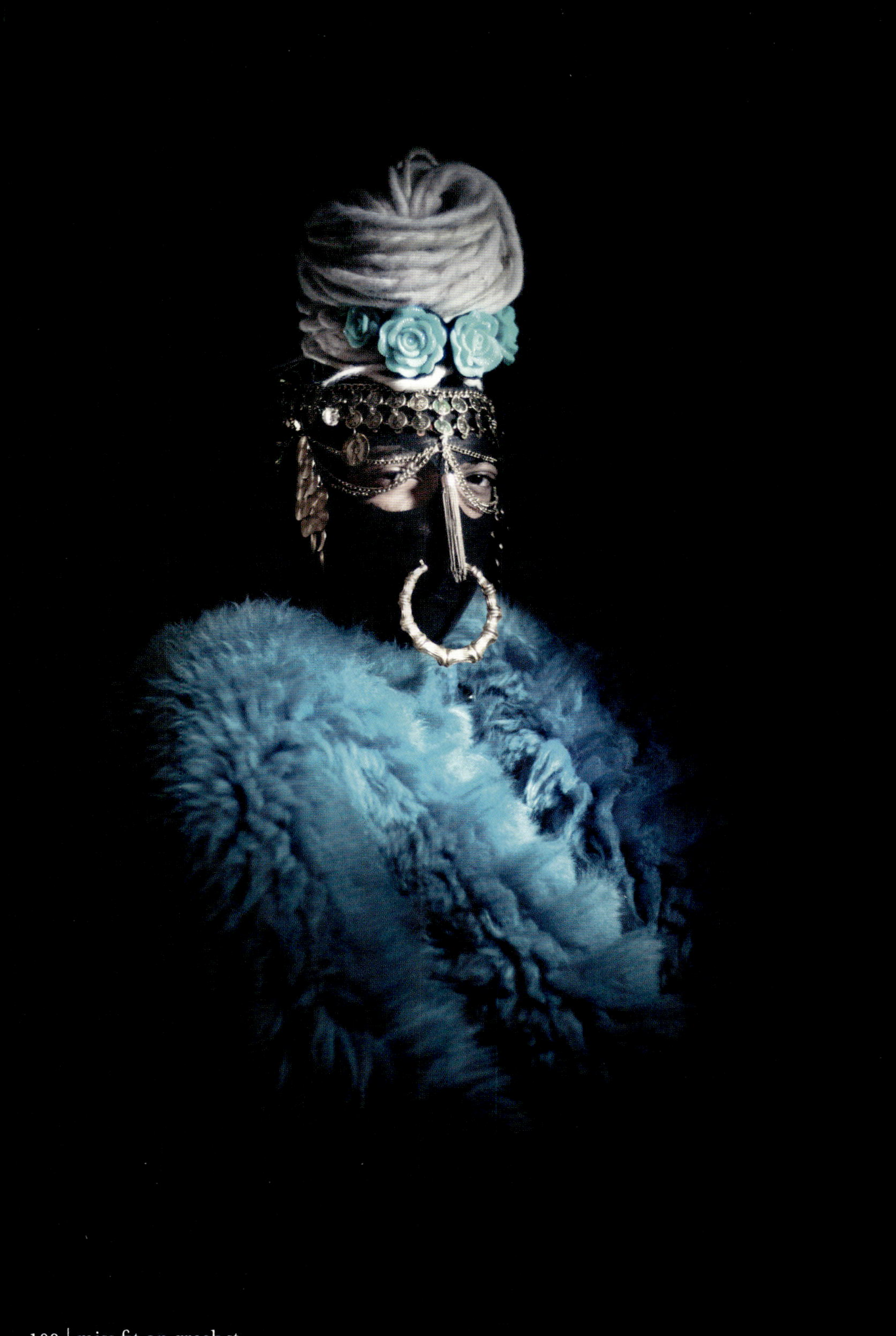

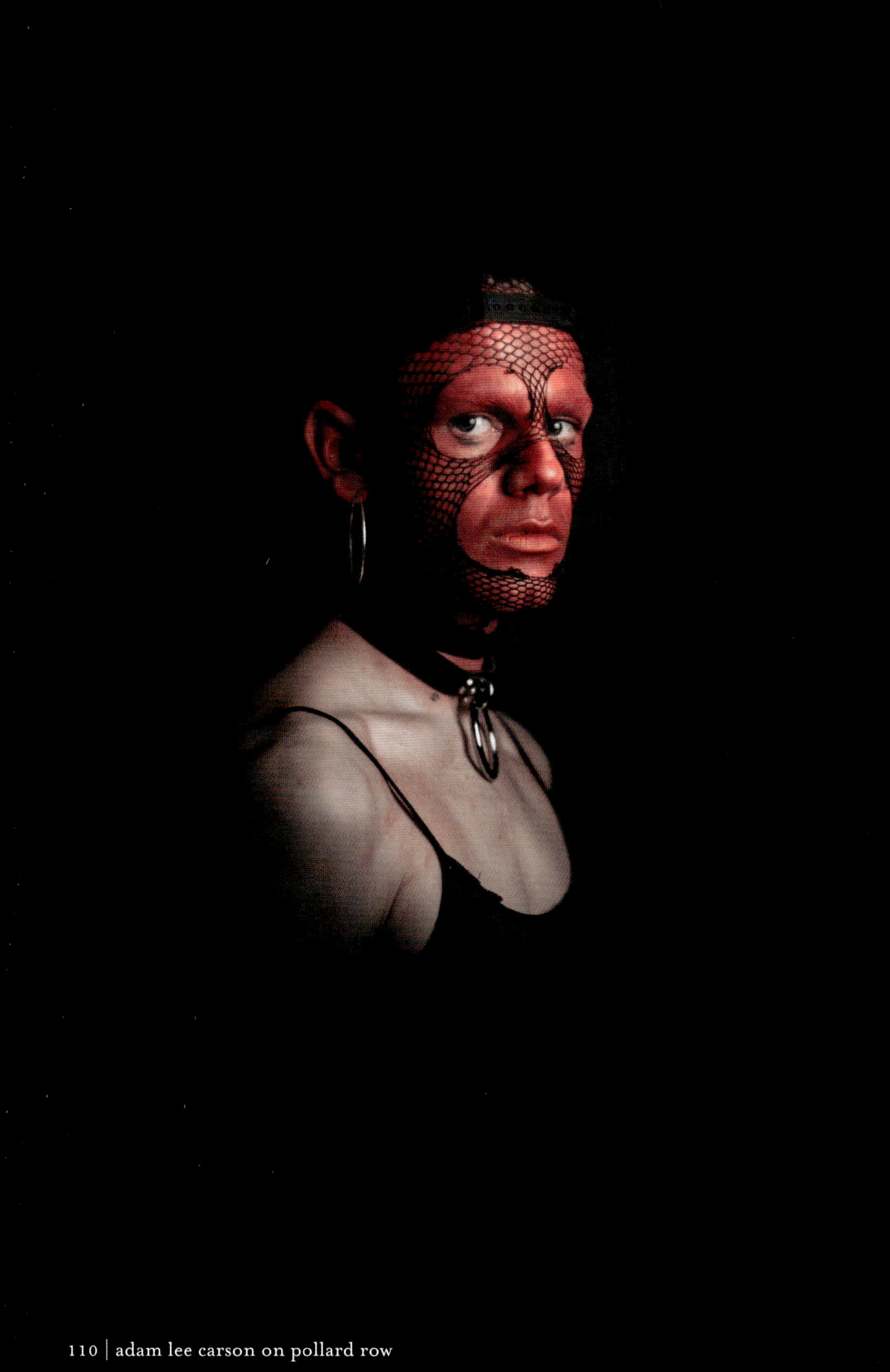

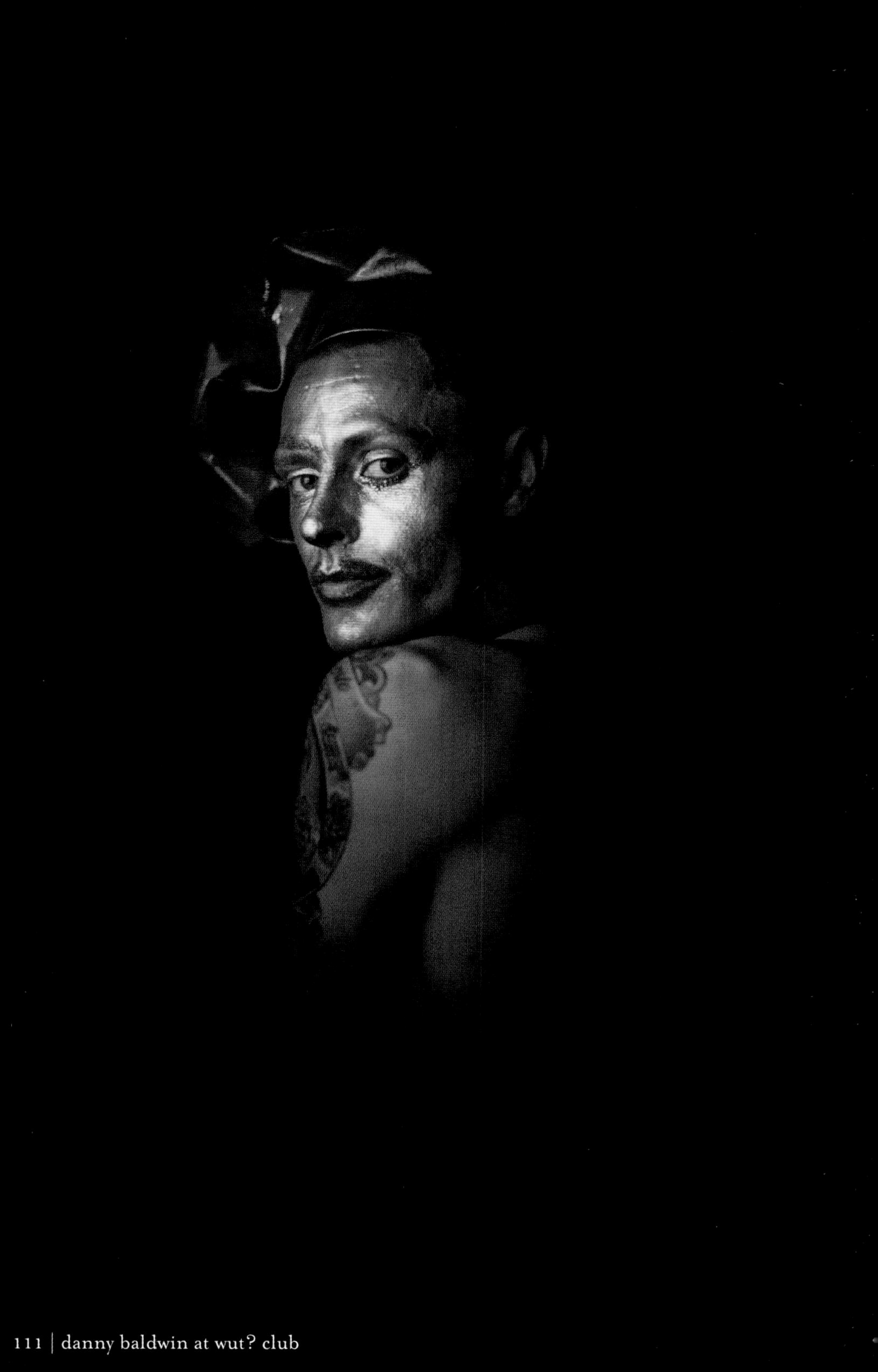

111 | danny baldwin at wut? club

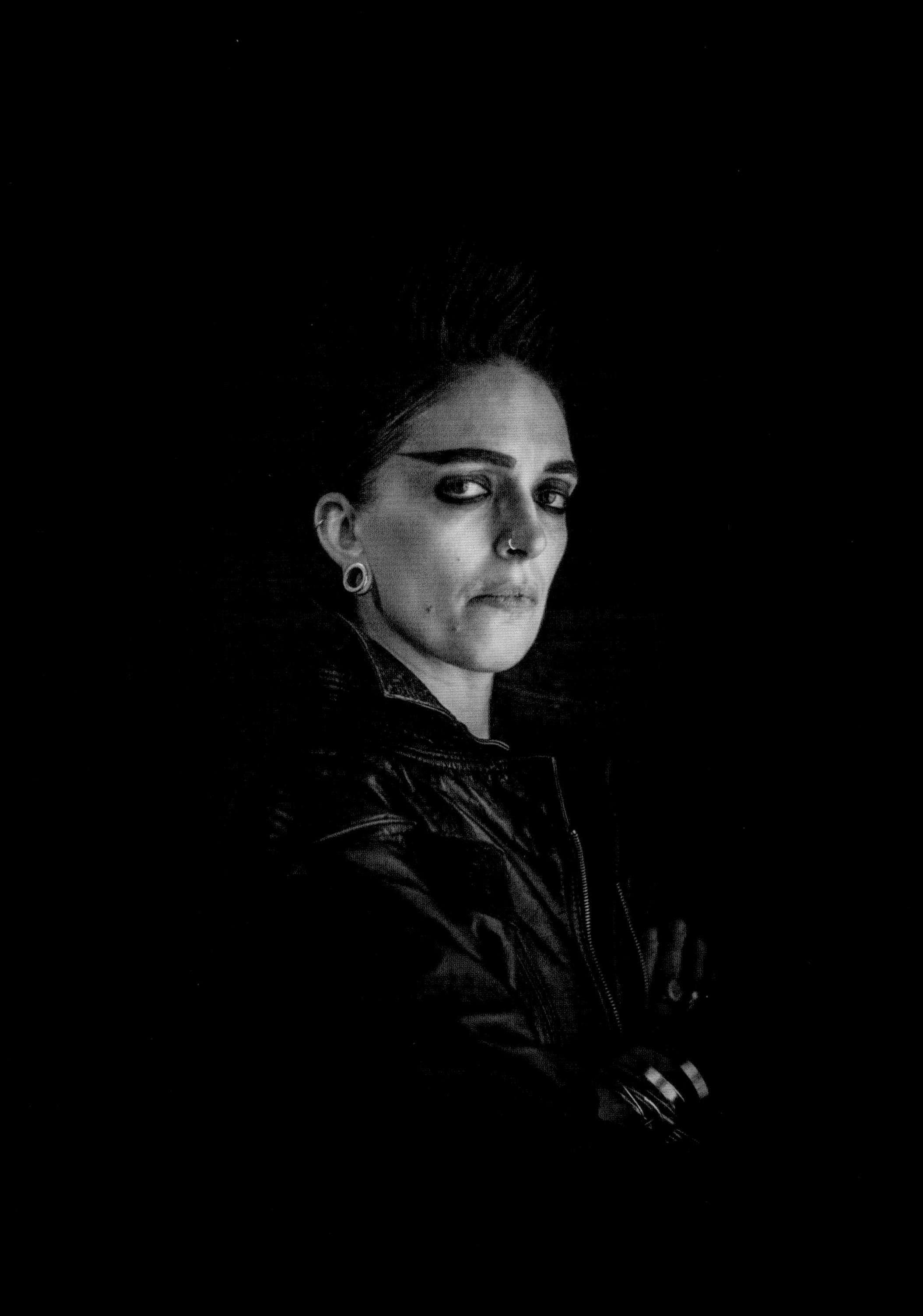

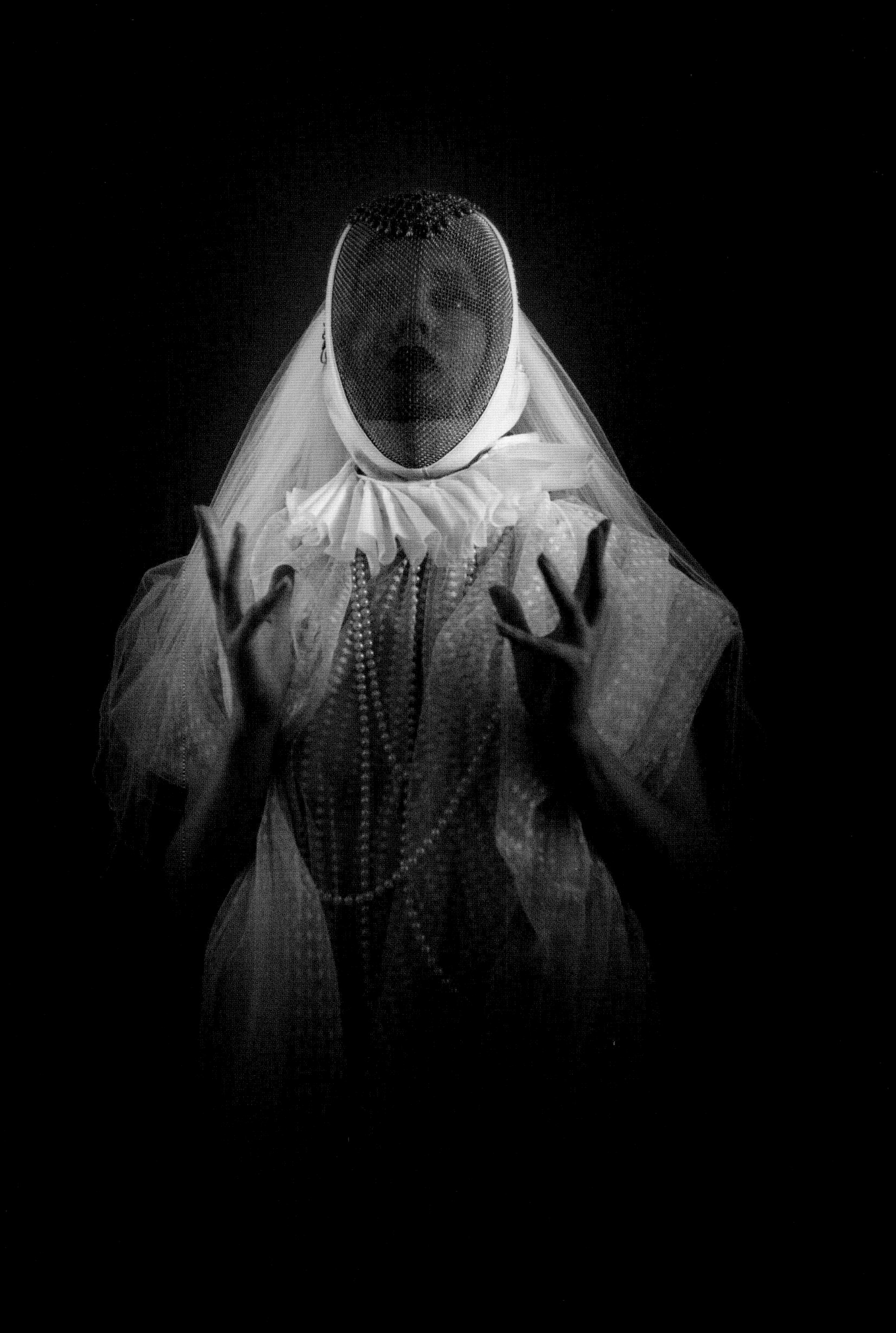

113 | amy kingsmill at nun

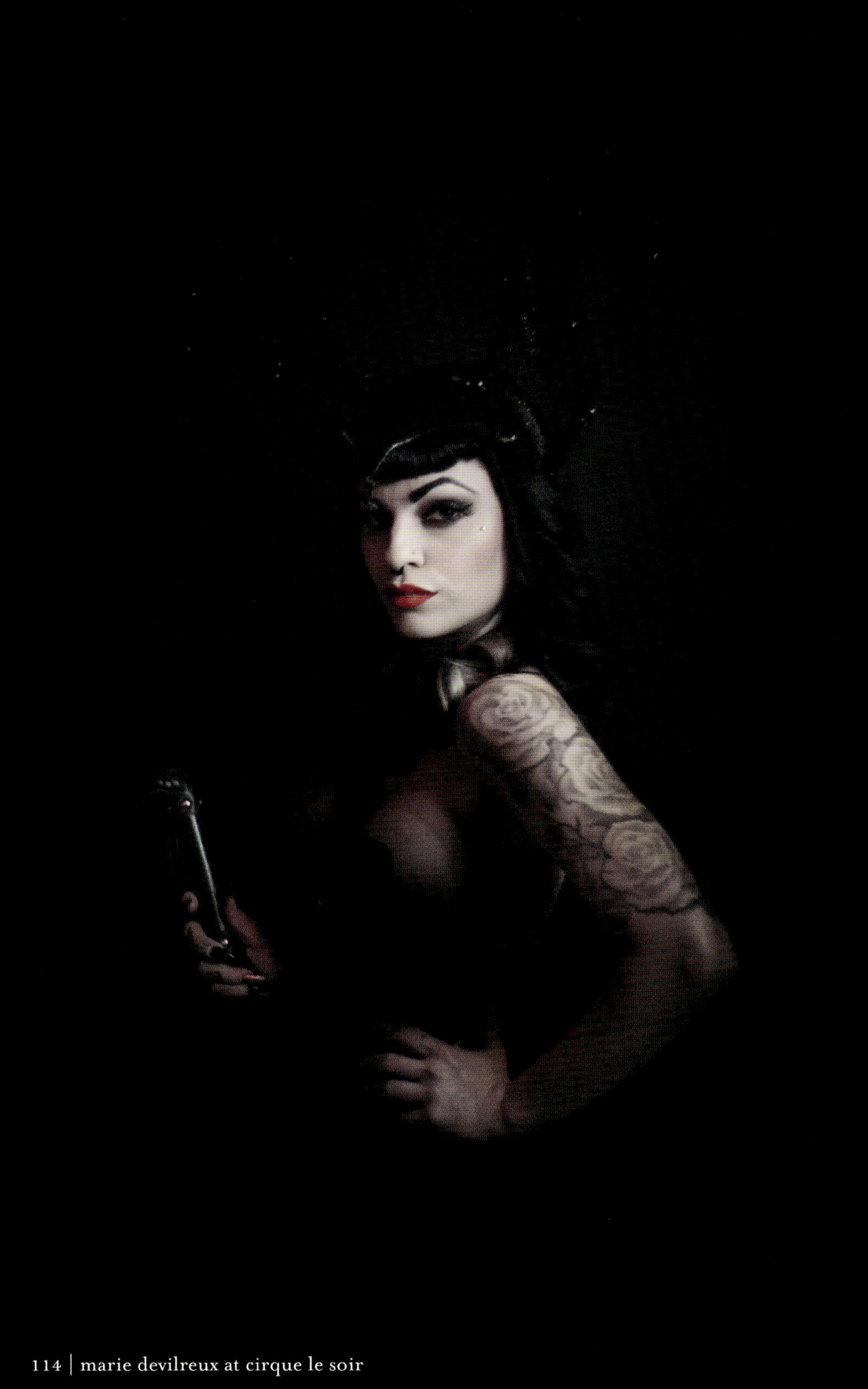

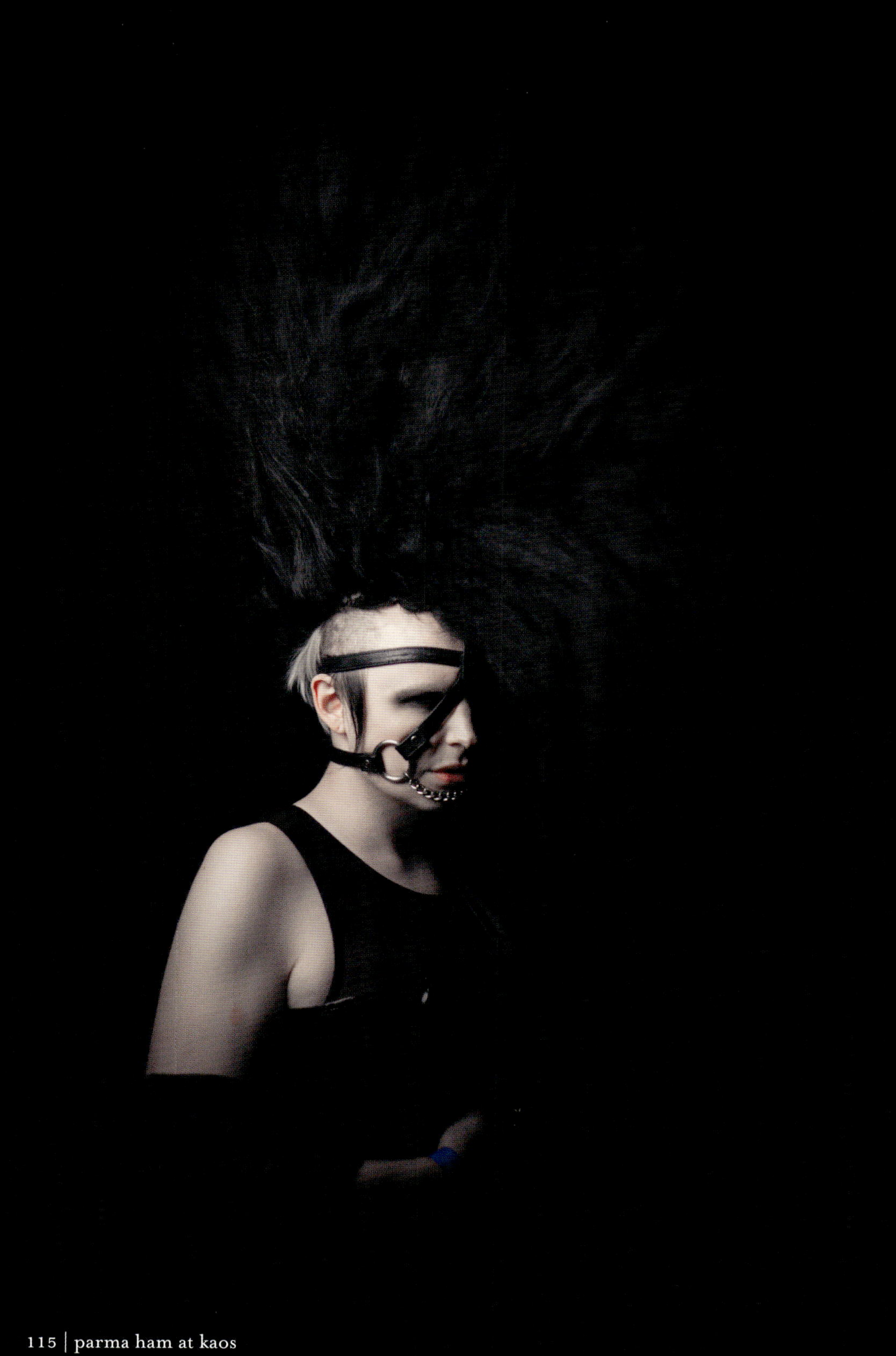

 parma ham at kaos

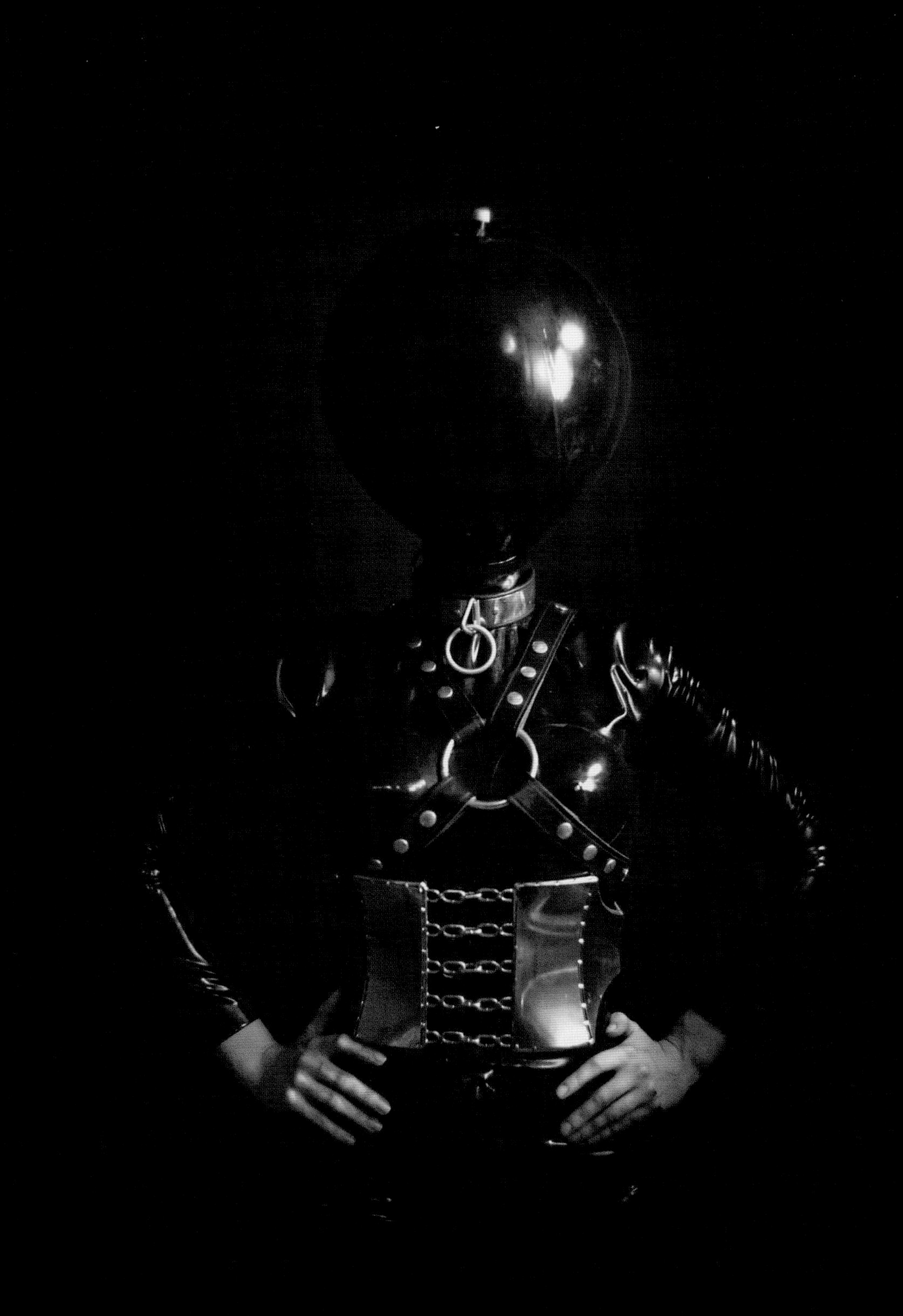

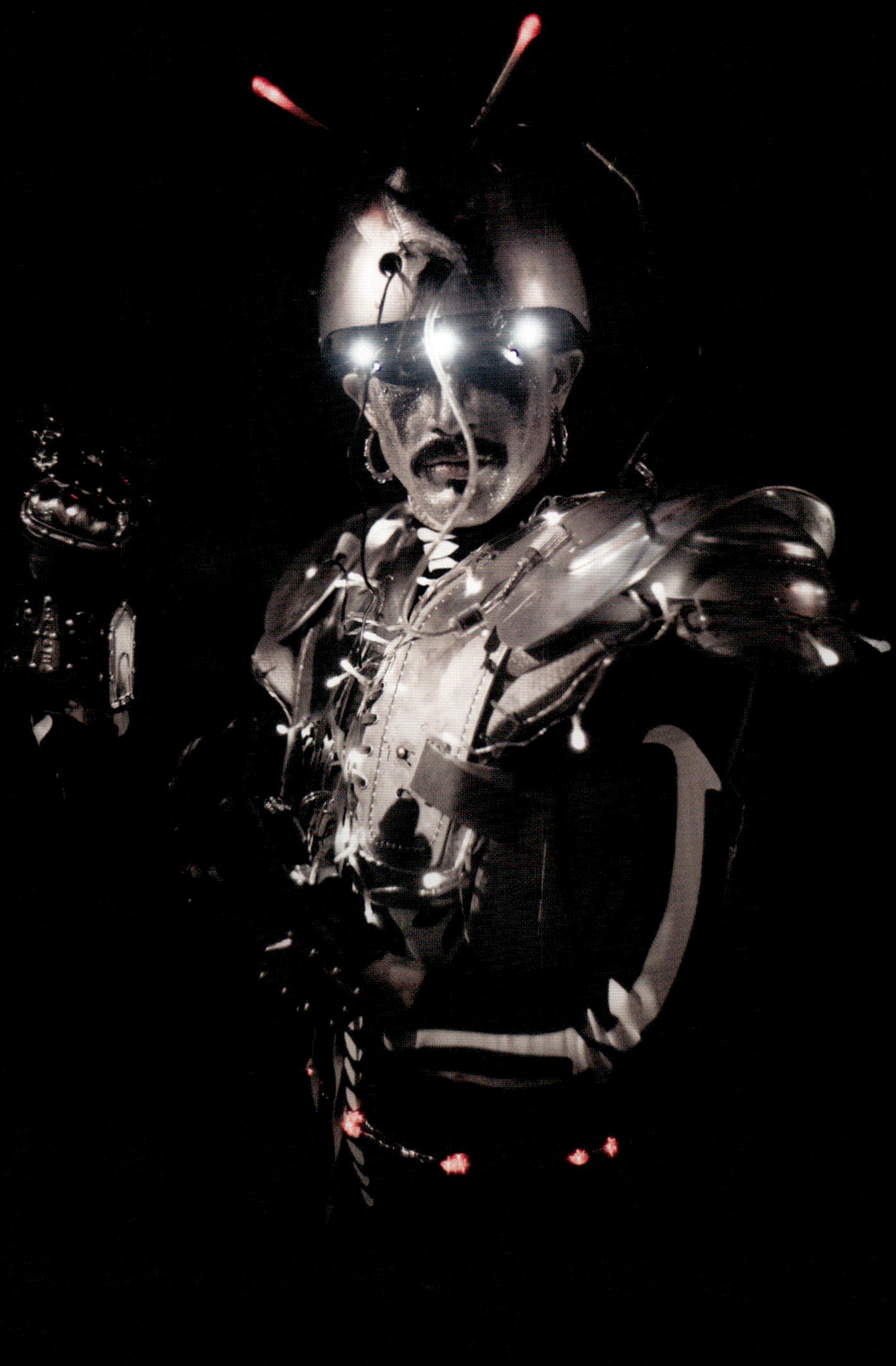

117 | olly innes on tisbury ct

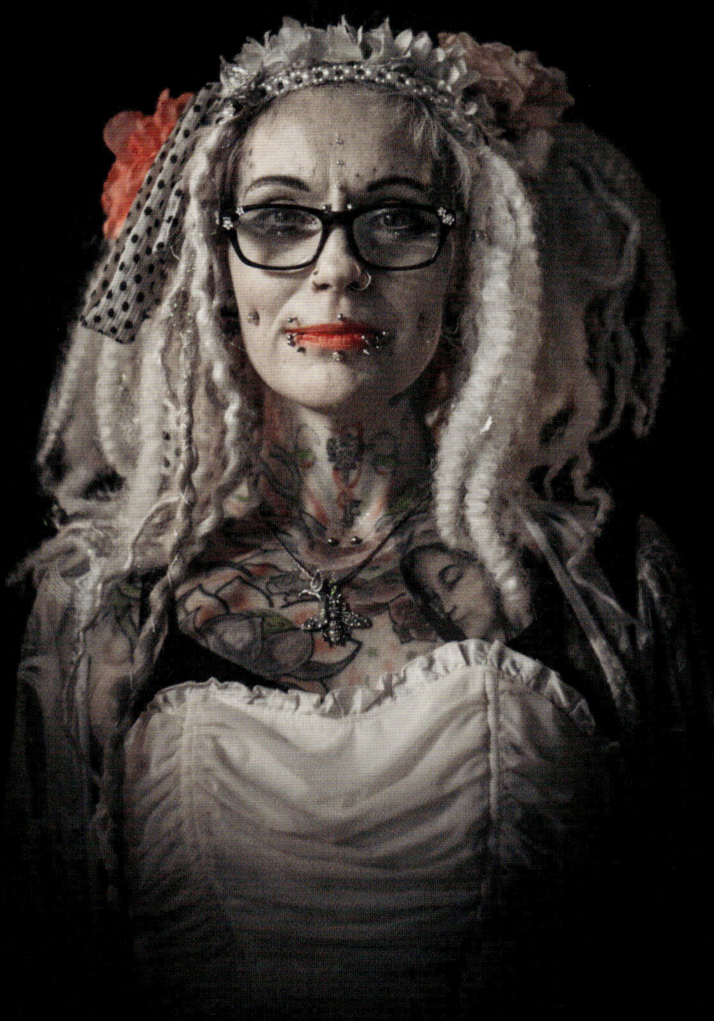

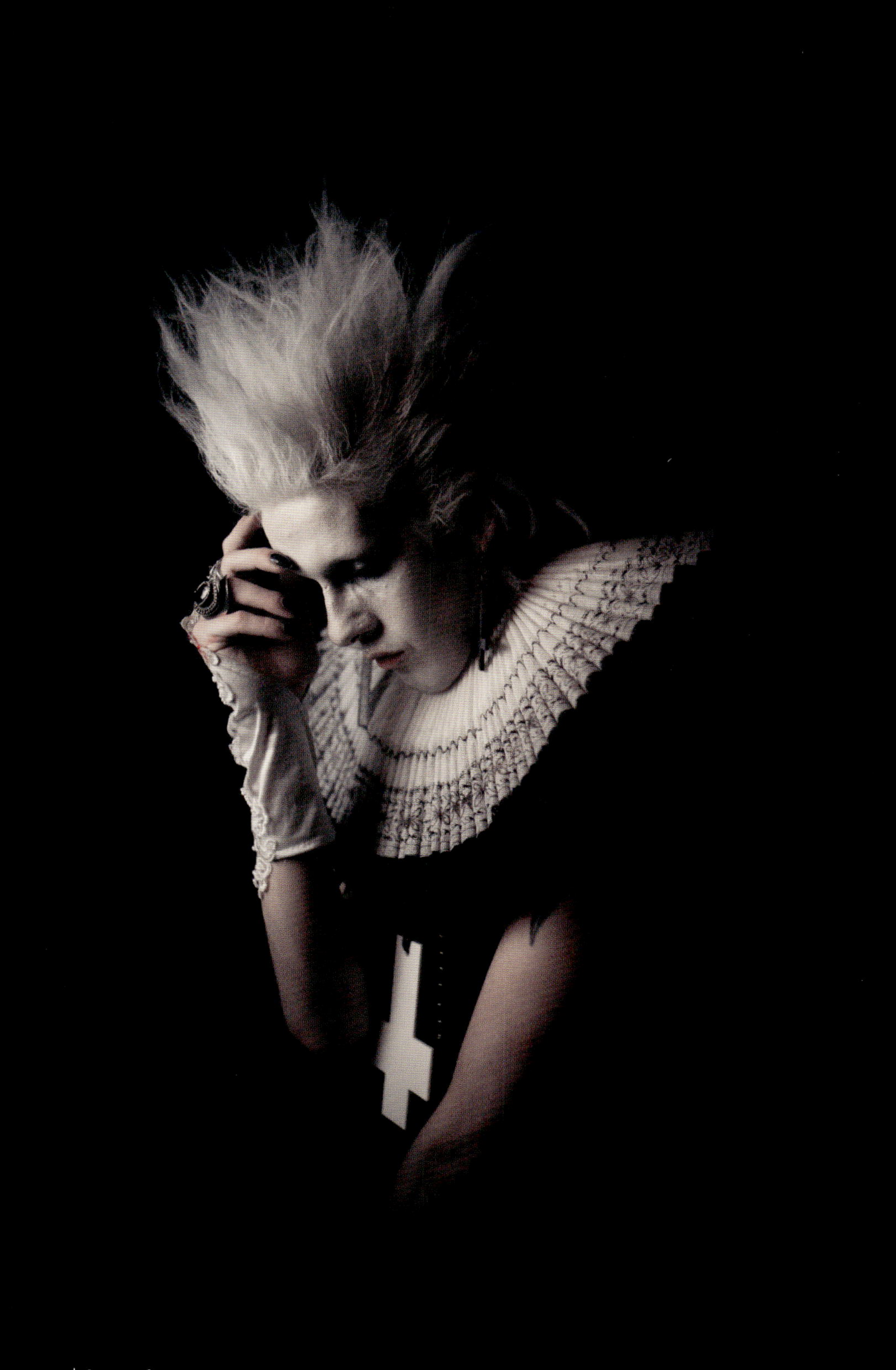

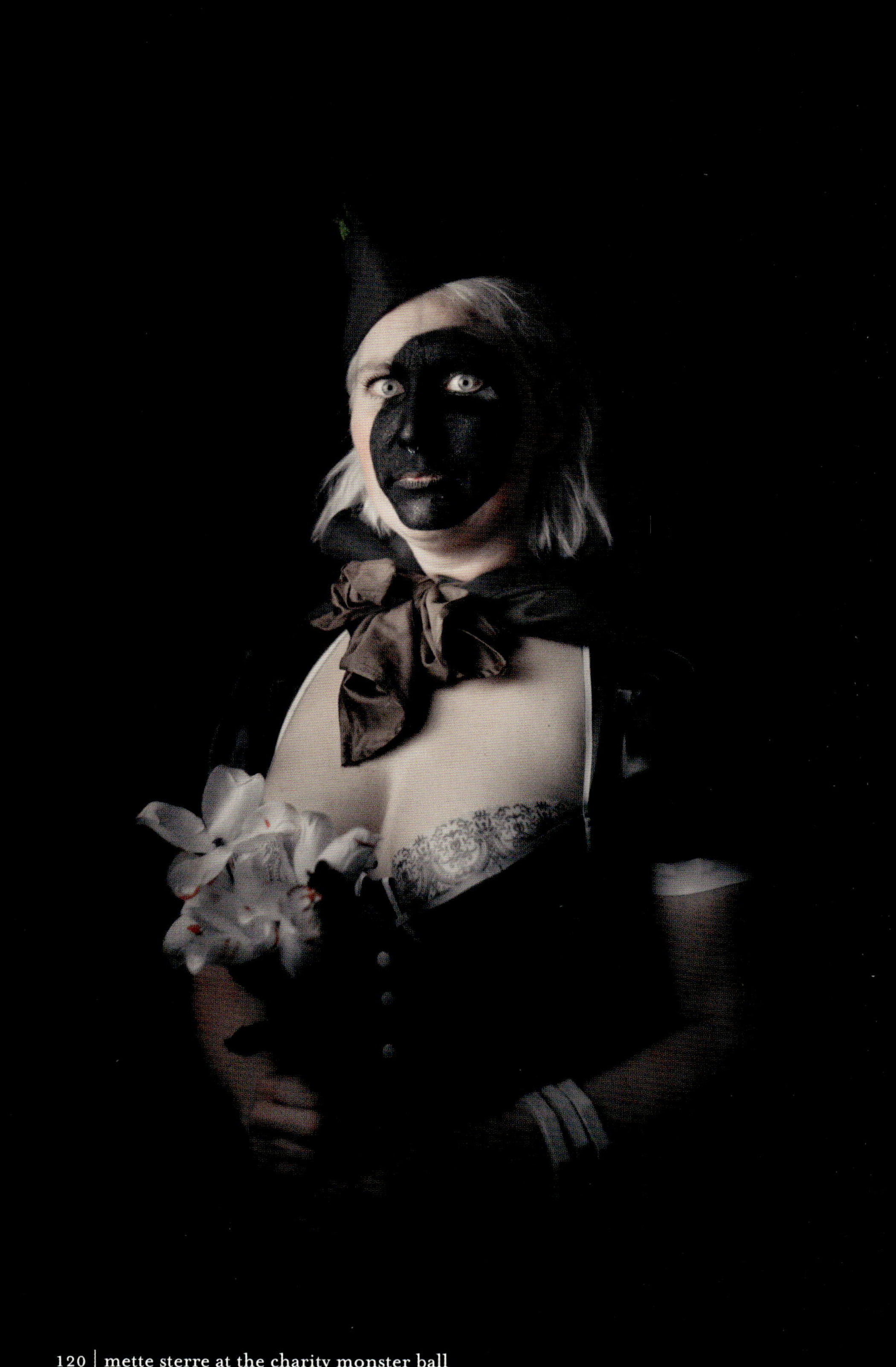

mette sterre at the charity monster ball

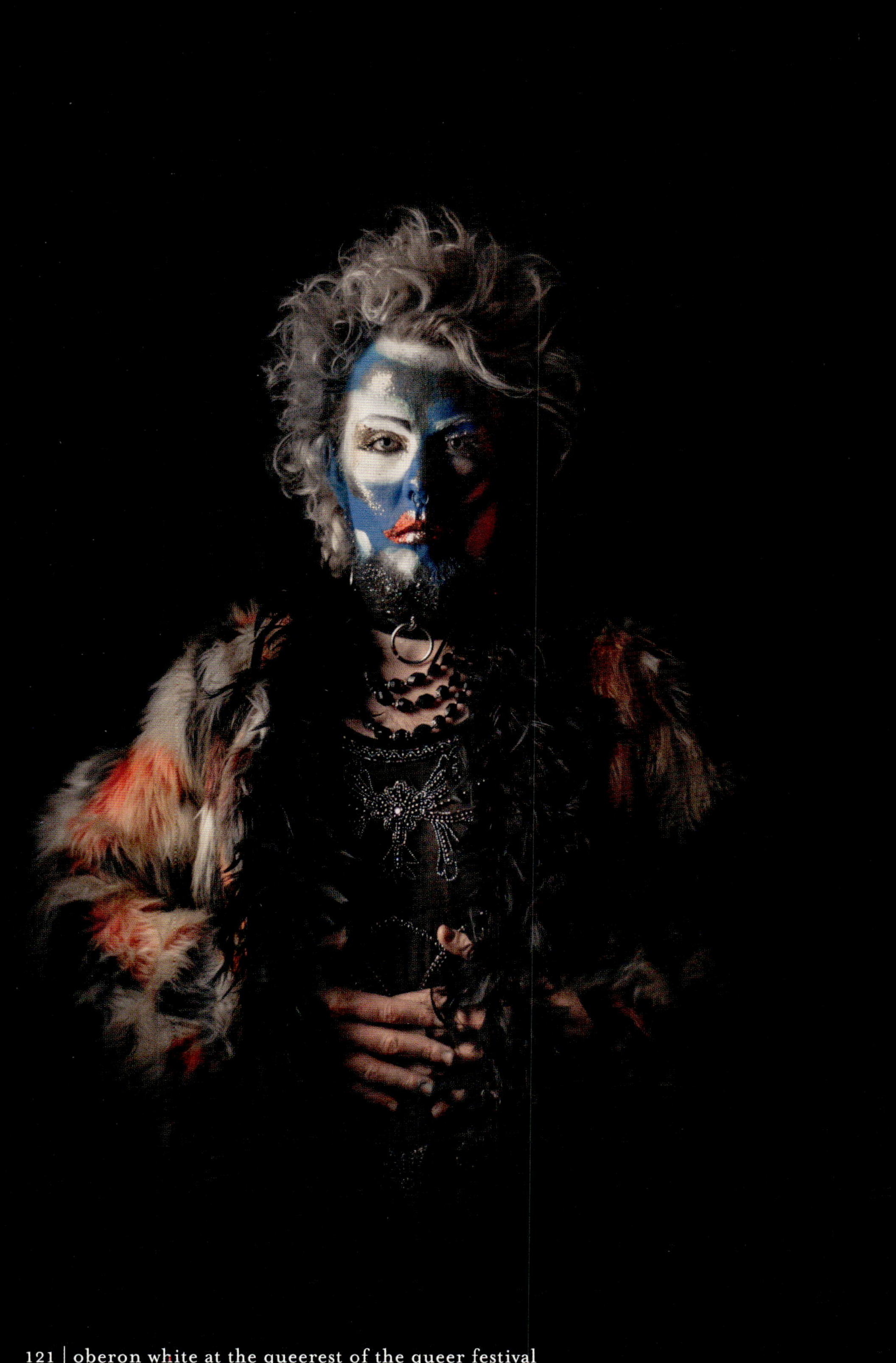

121 | oberon white at the queerest of the queer festival

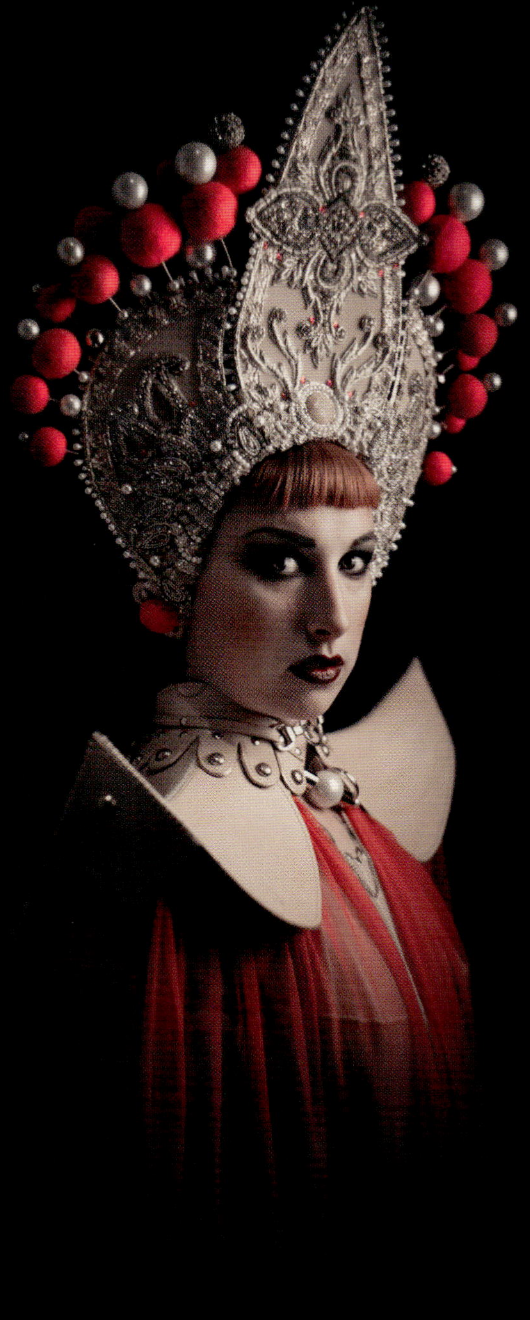

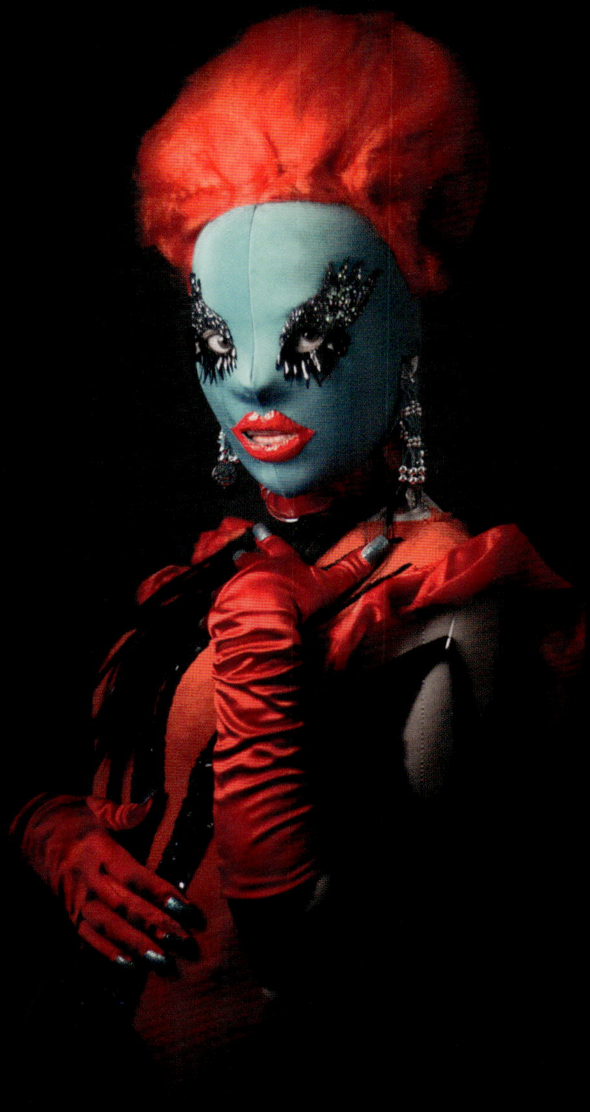

123 | monsterlune on claredale st

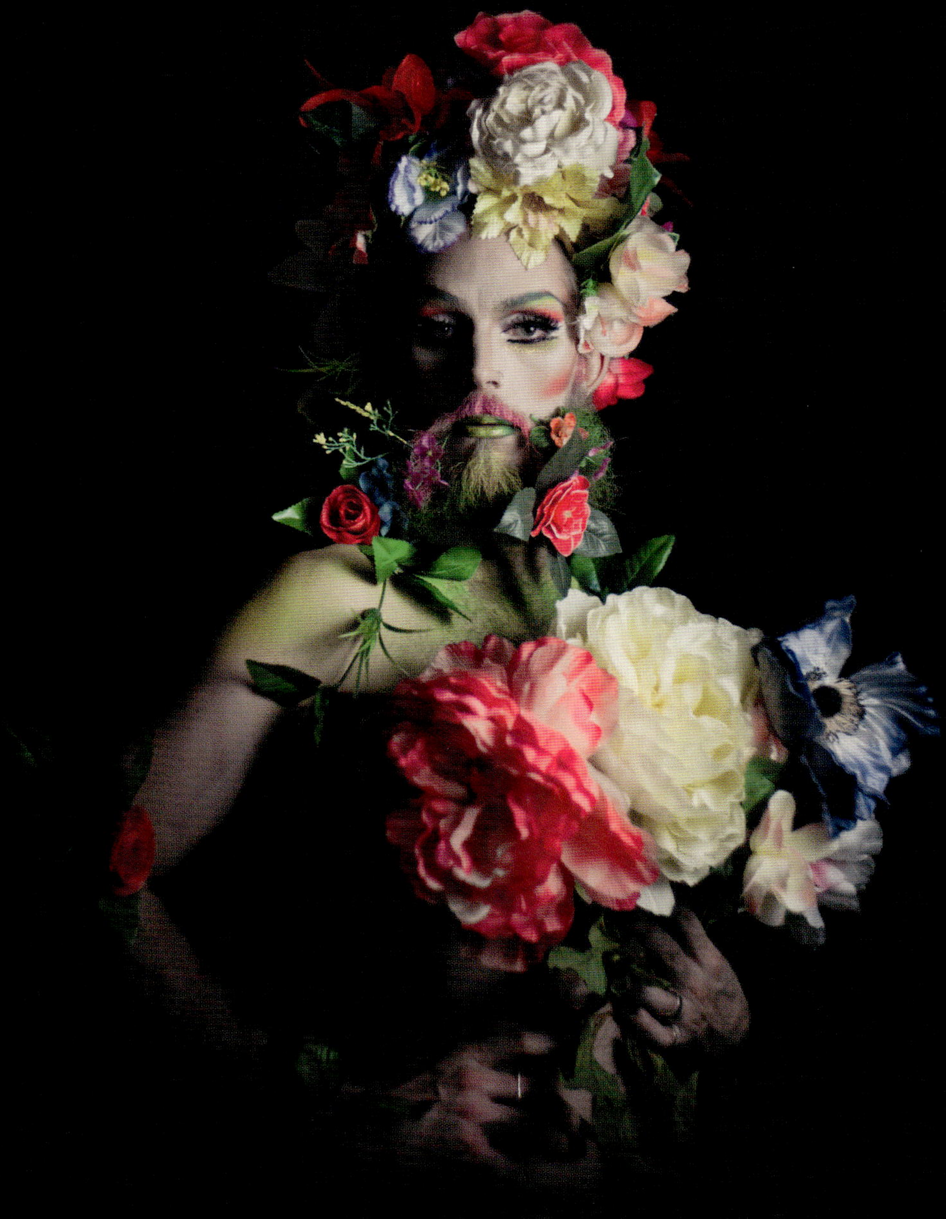

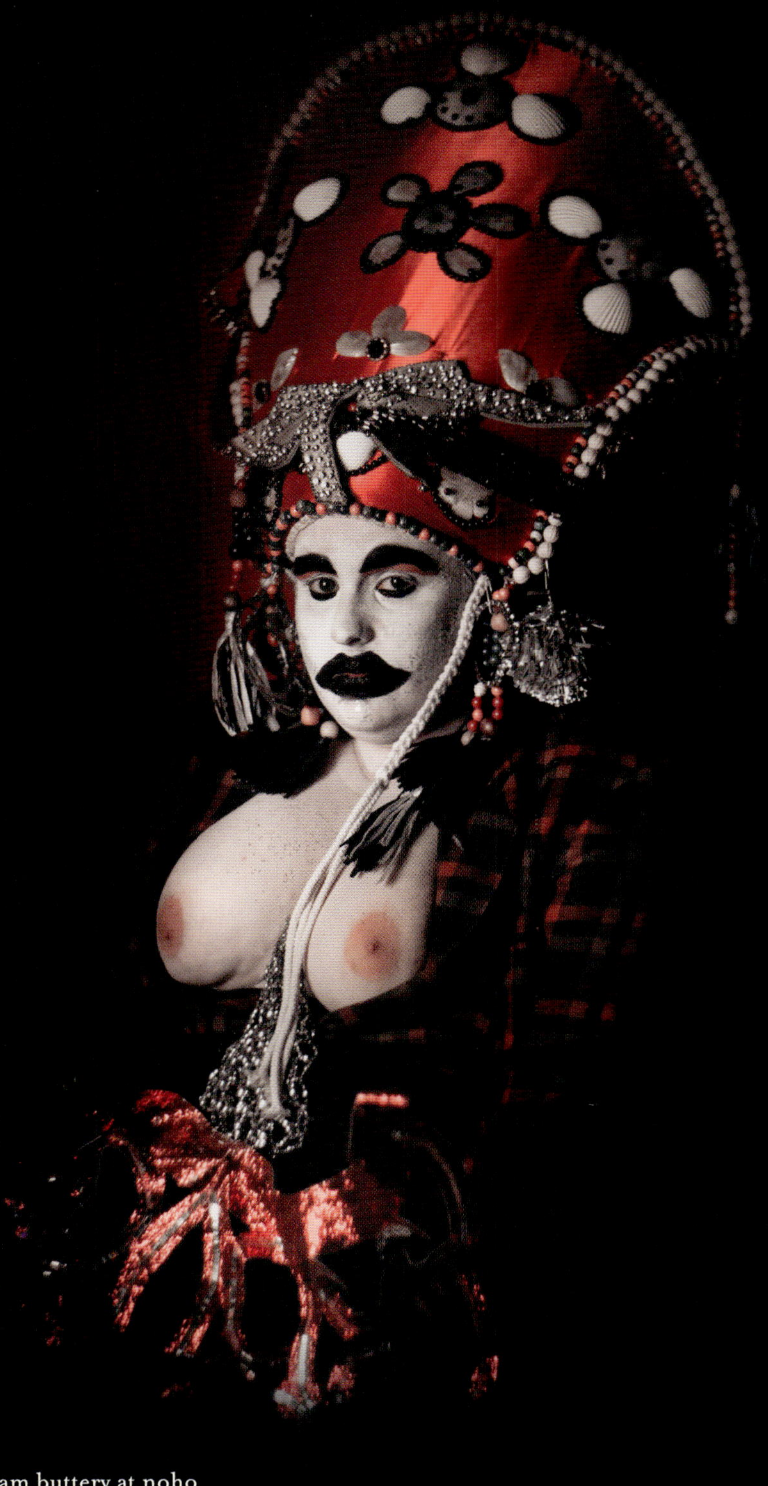

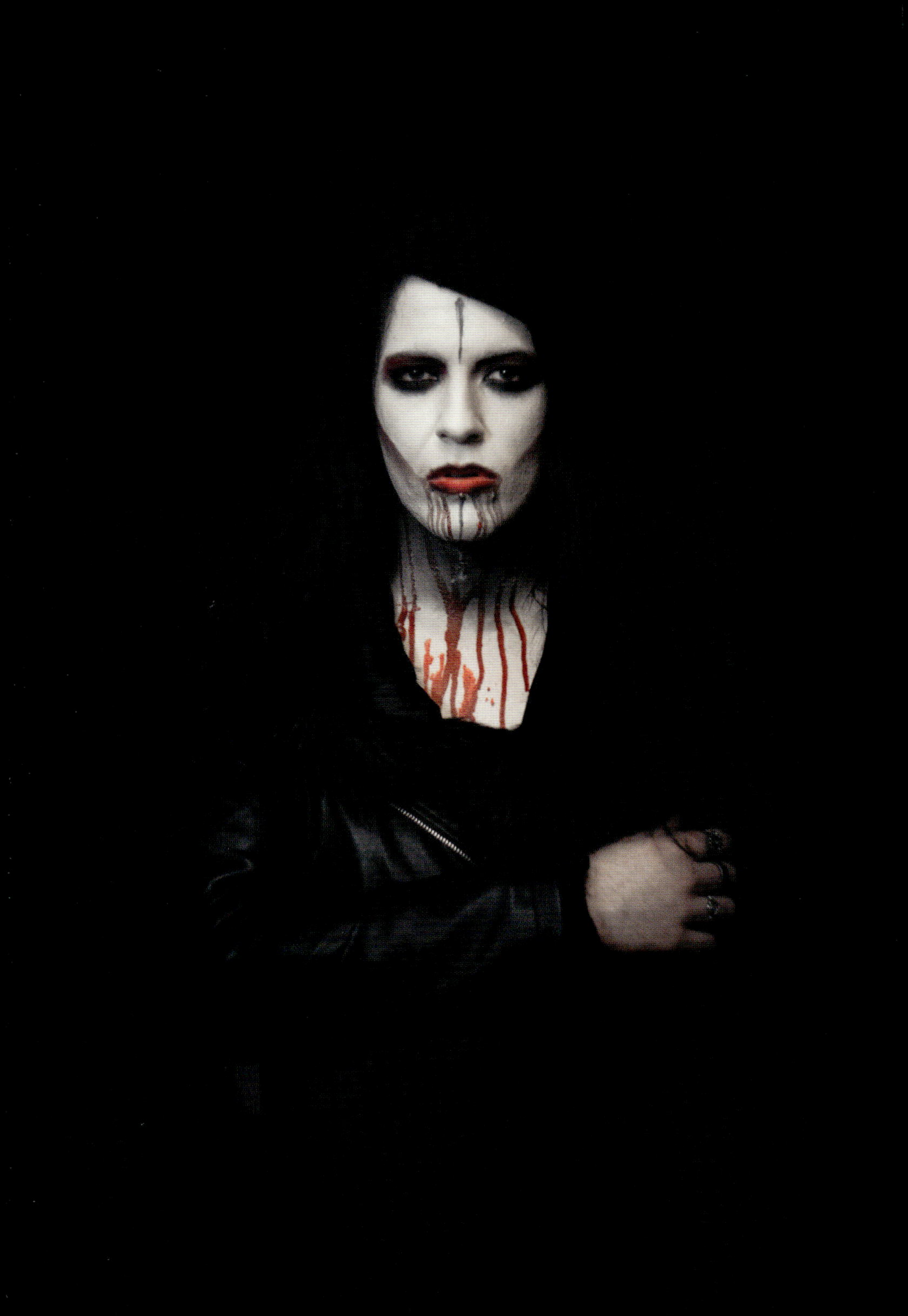

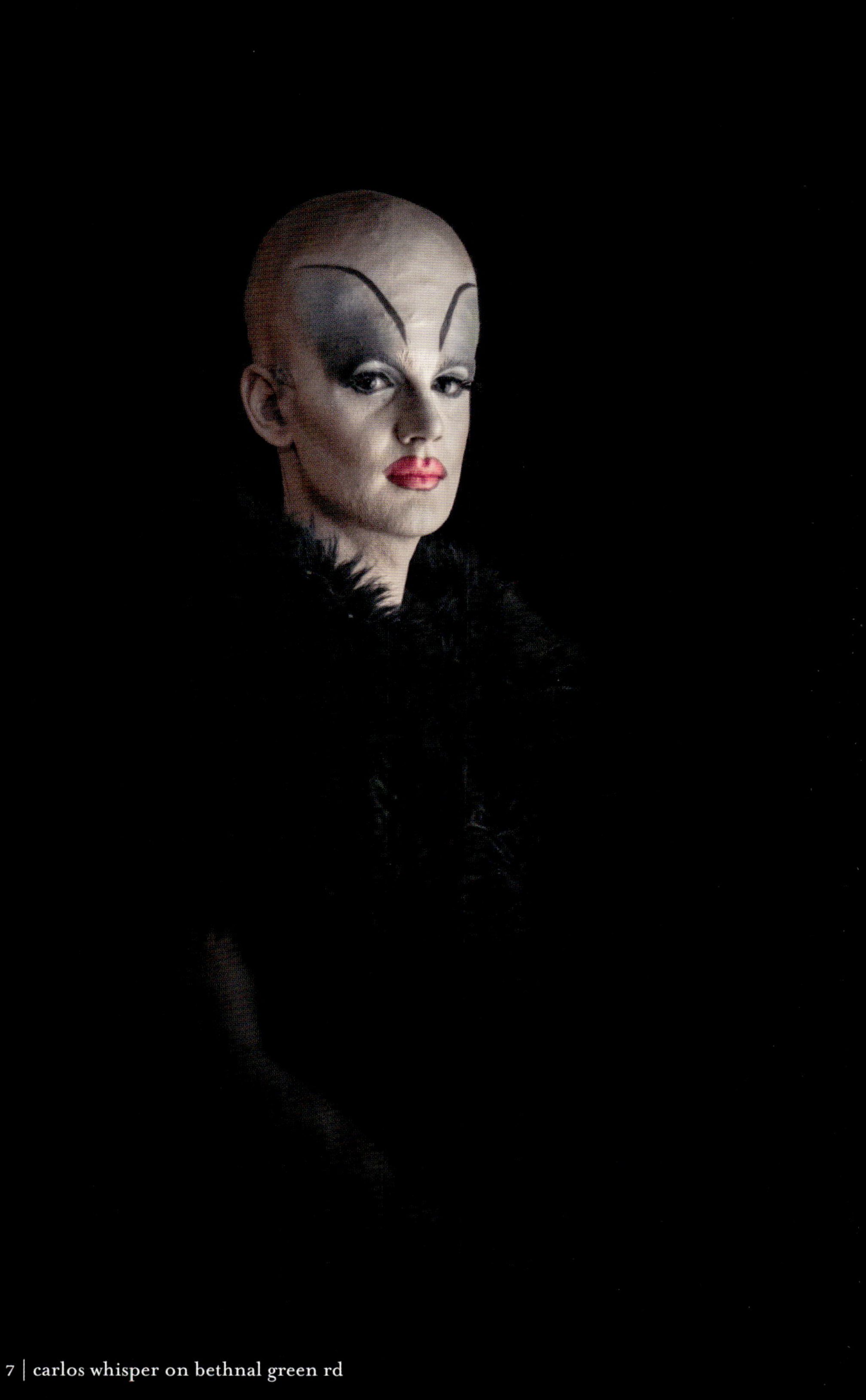

7 | carlos whisper on bethnal green rd

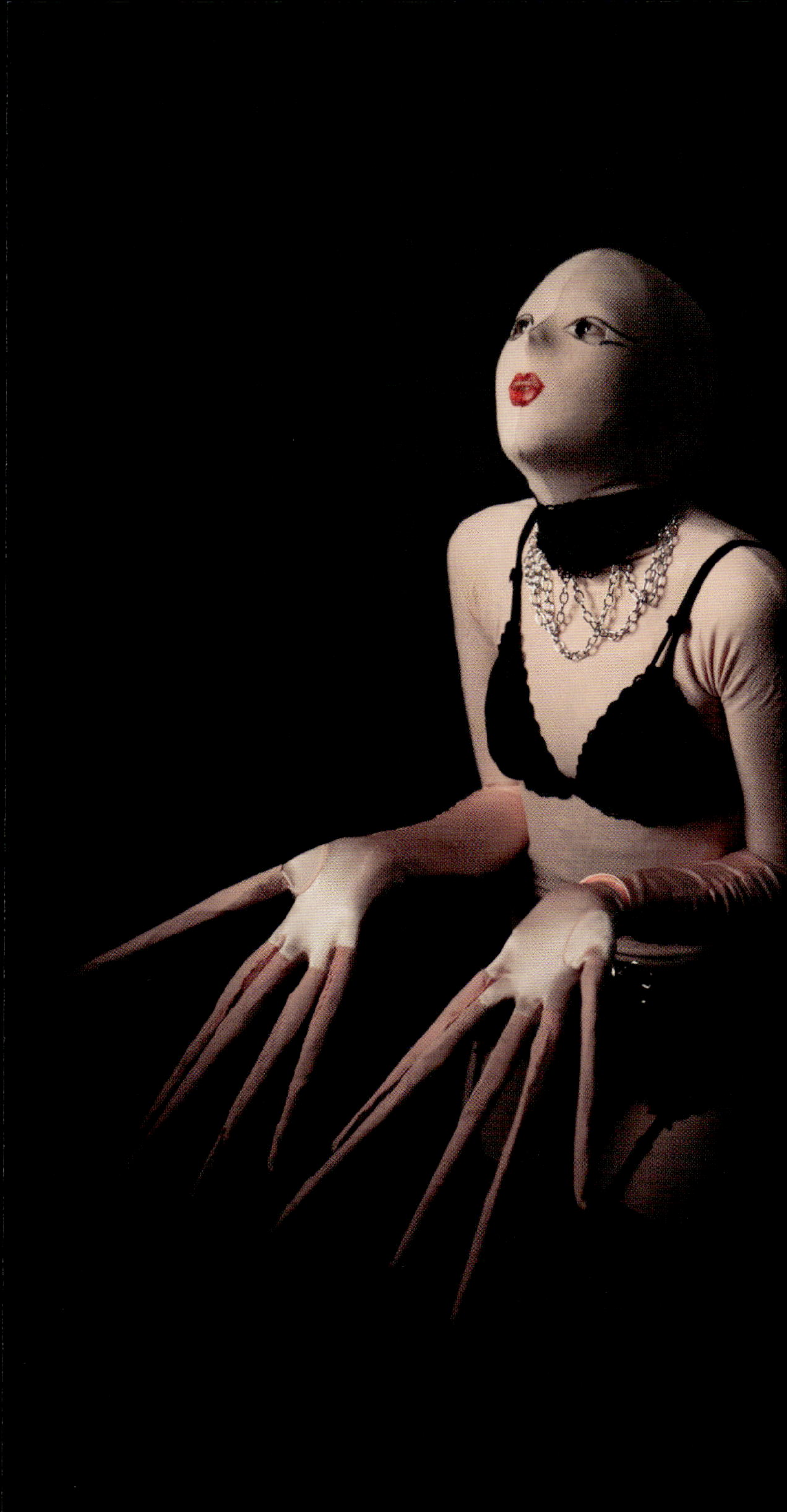

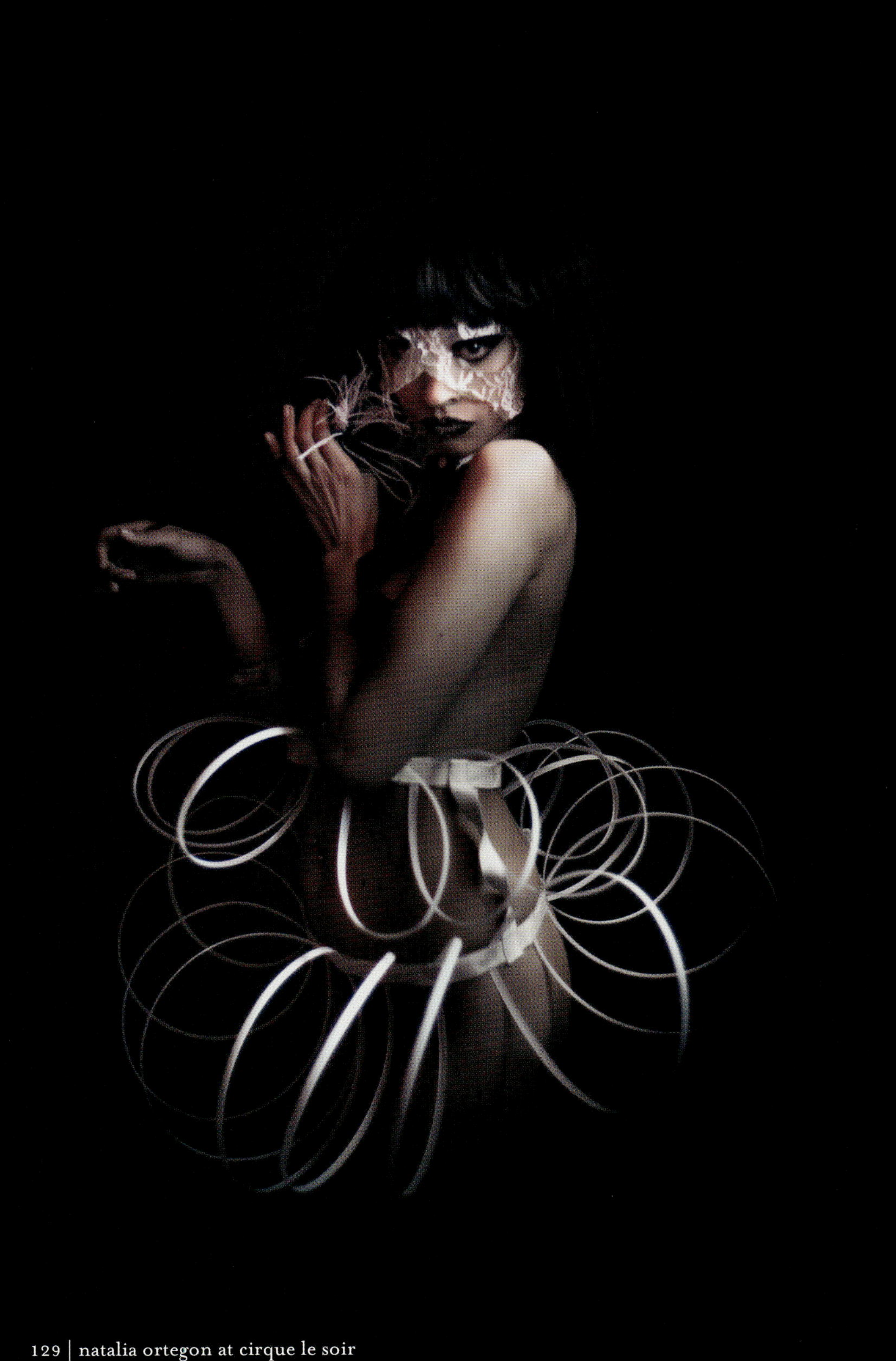

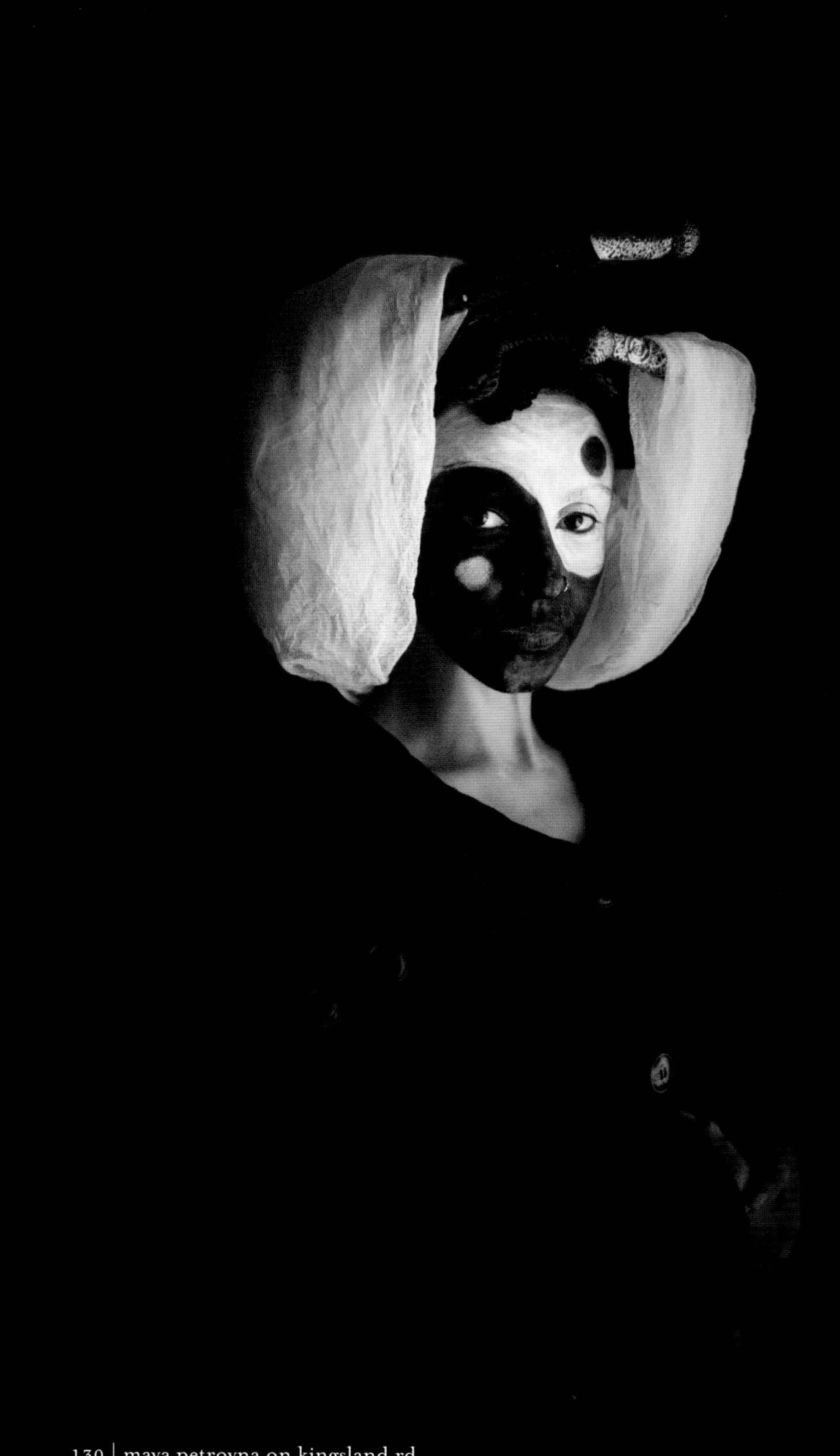

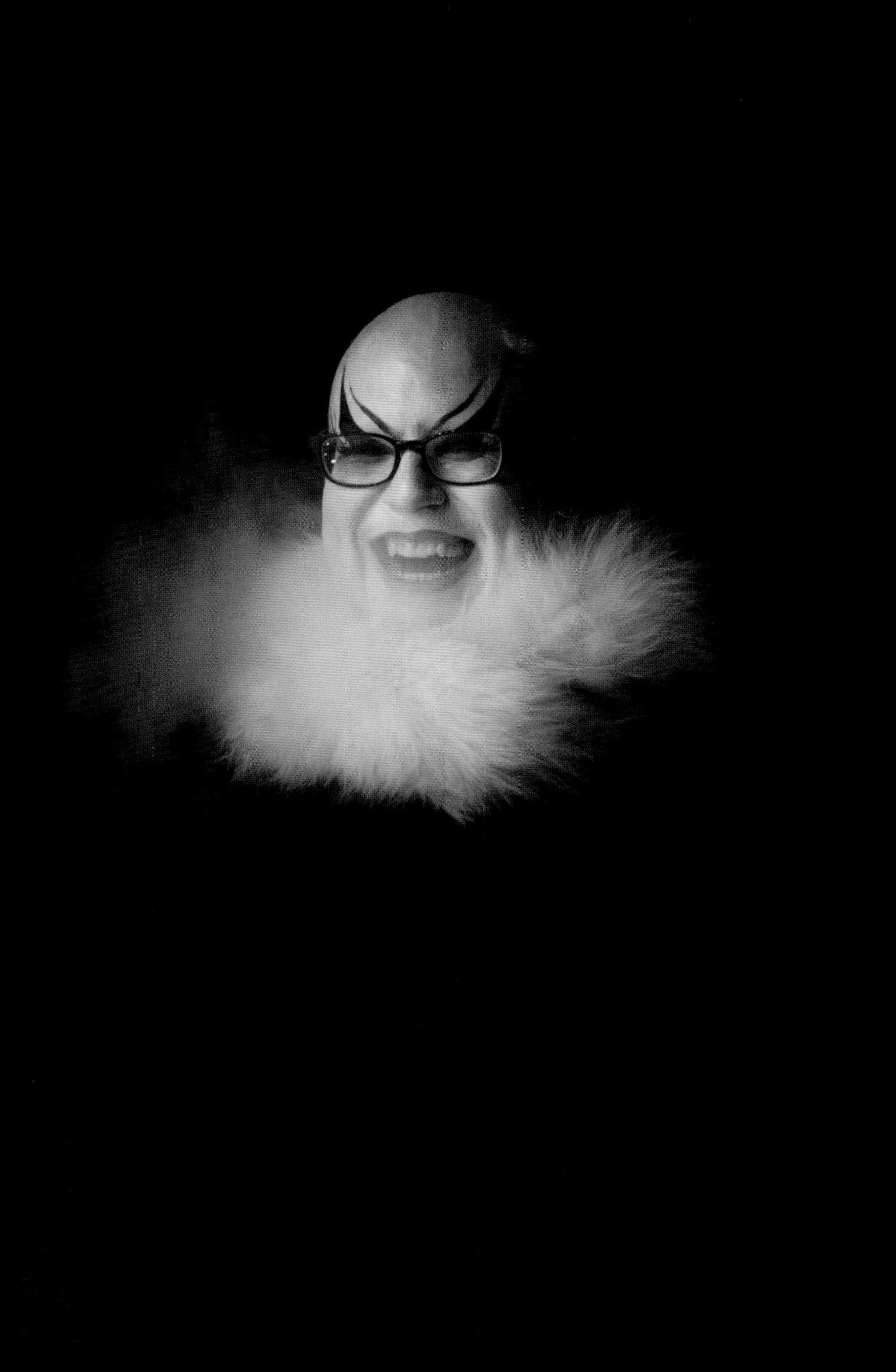

31 | lewis g burton on dover st

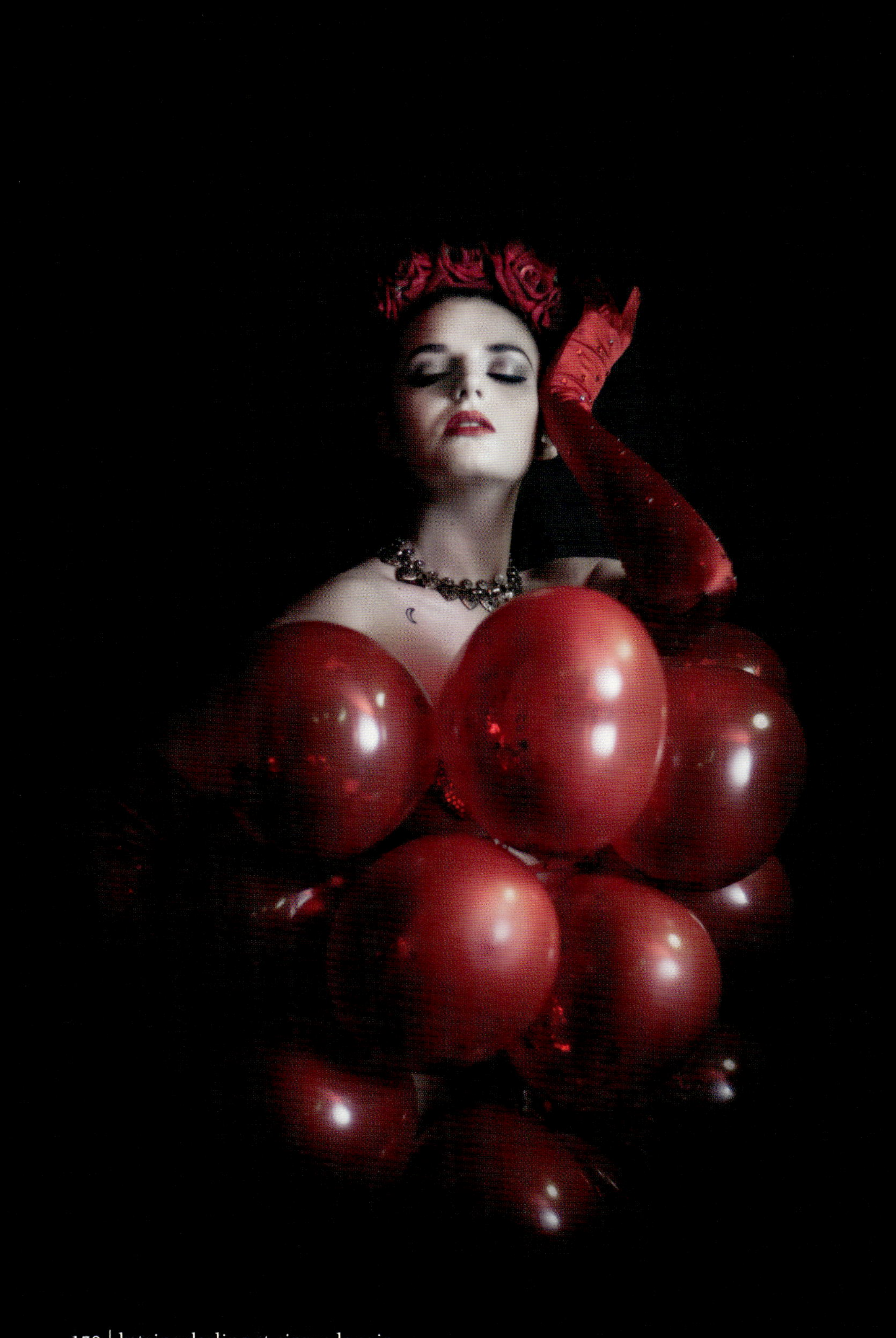

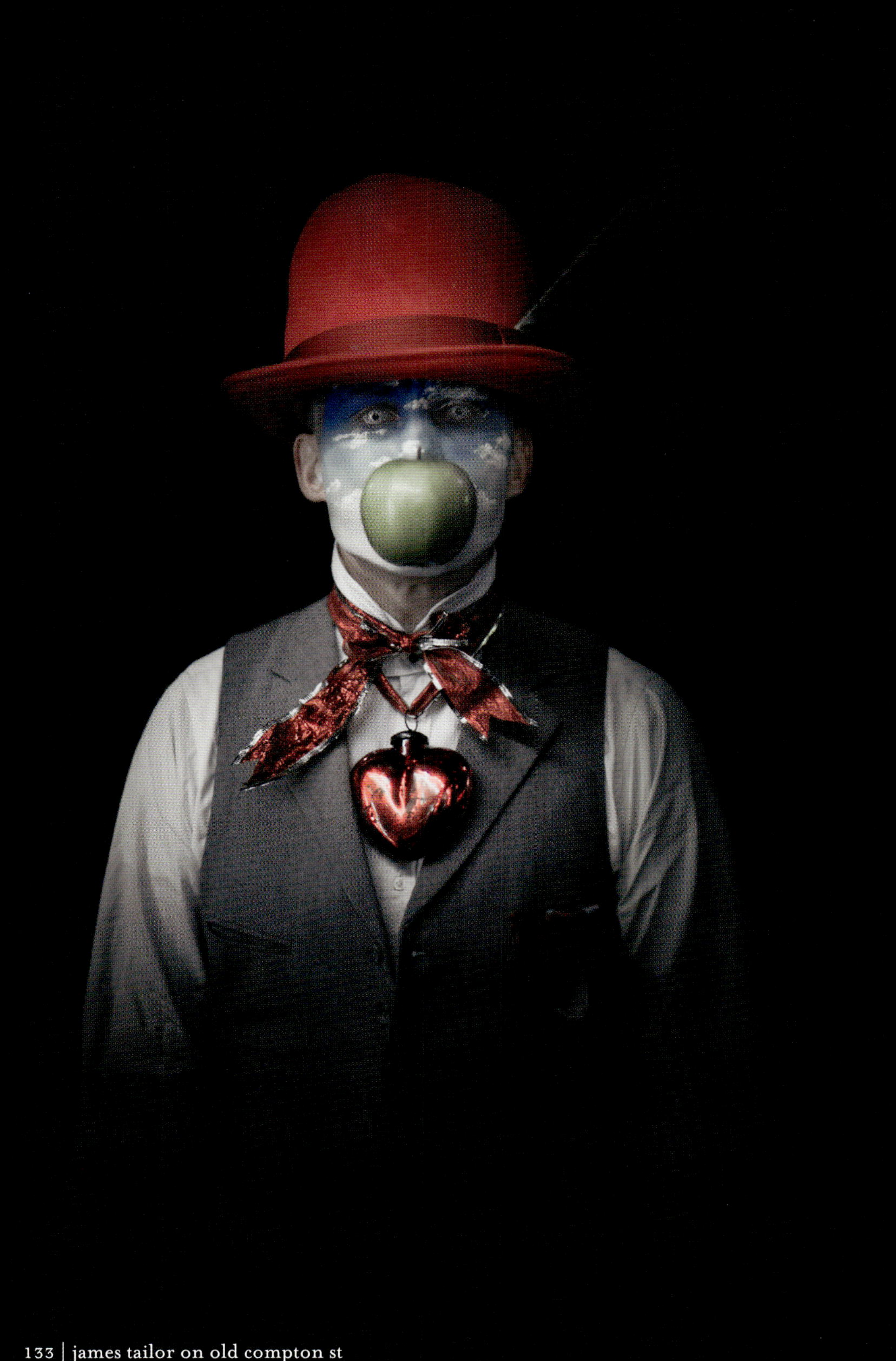

 | james tailor on old compton st

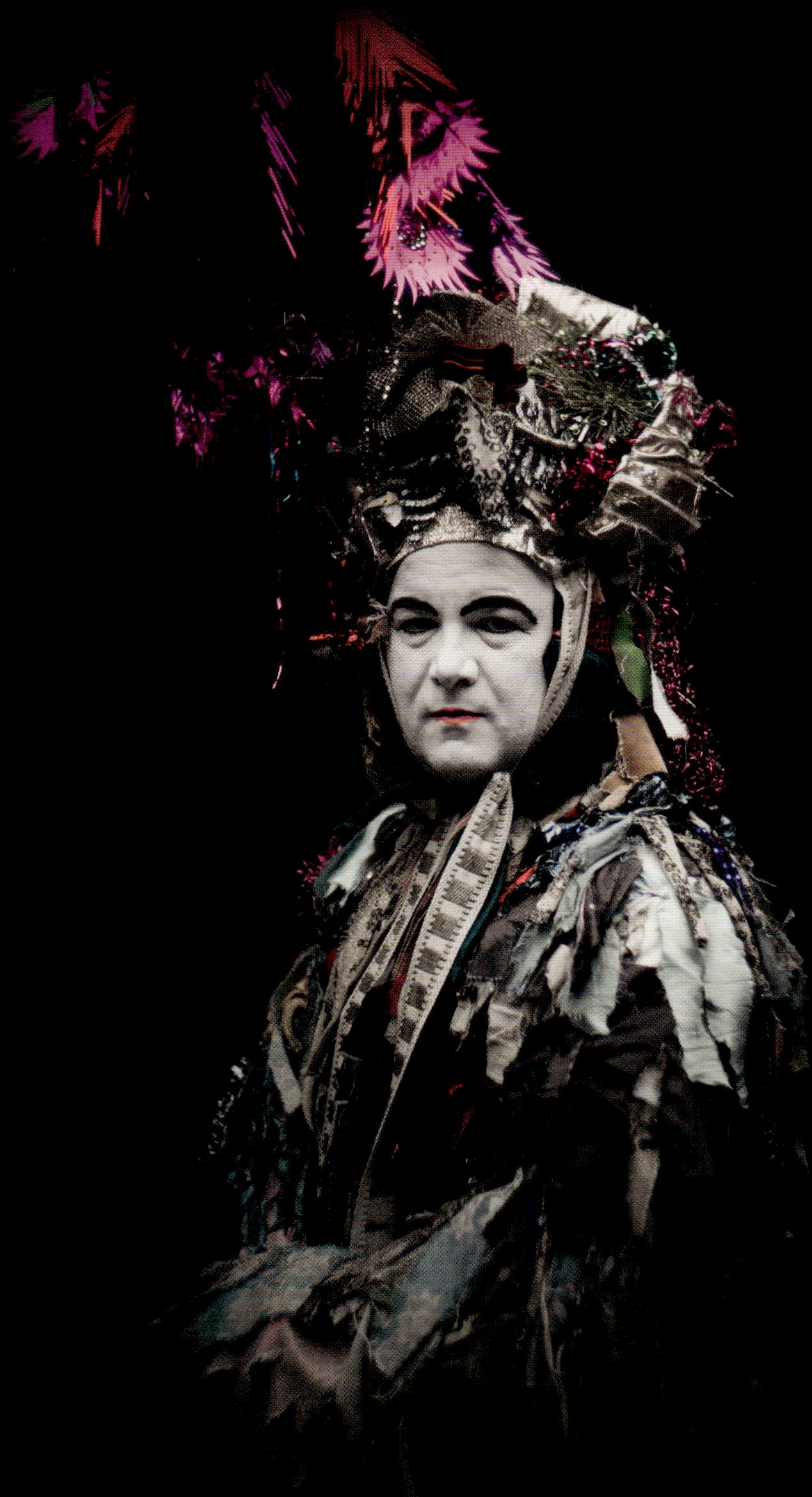

 | danny hopkins on borough high st

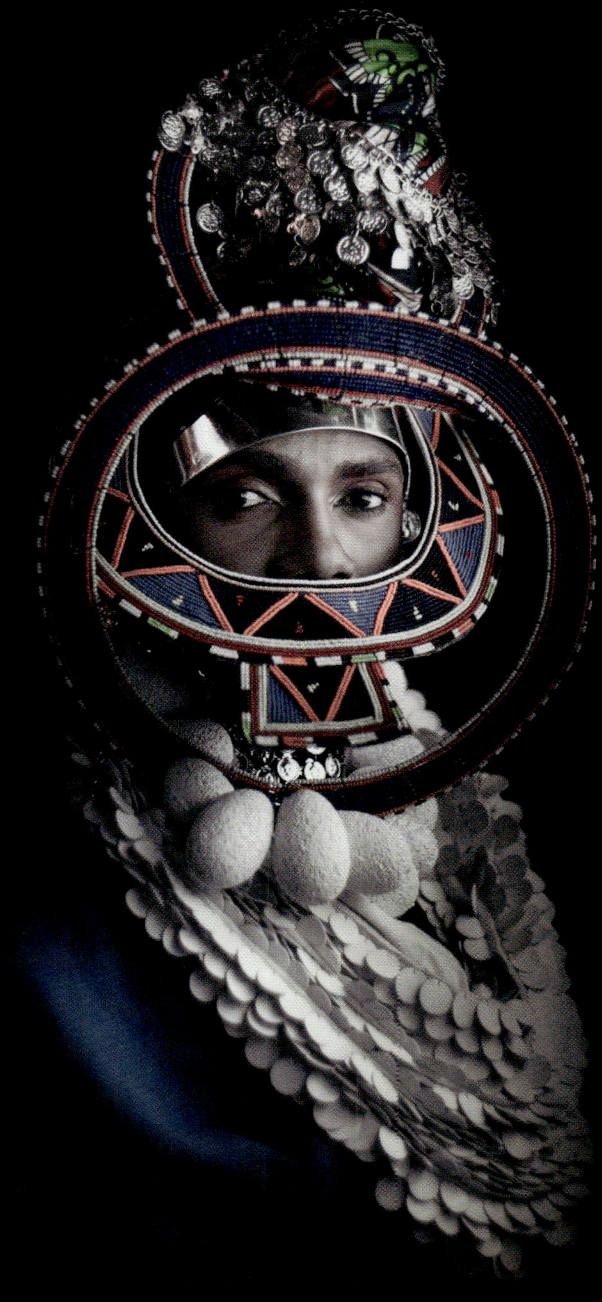

135 | julius reuben on chalk farm rd

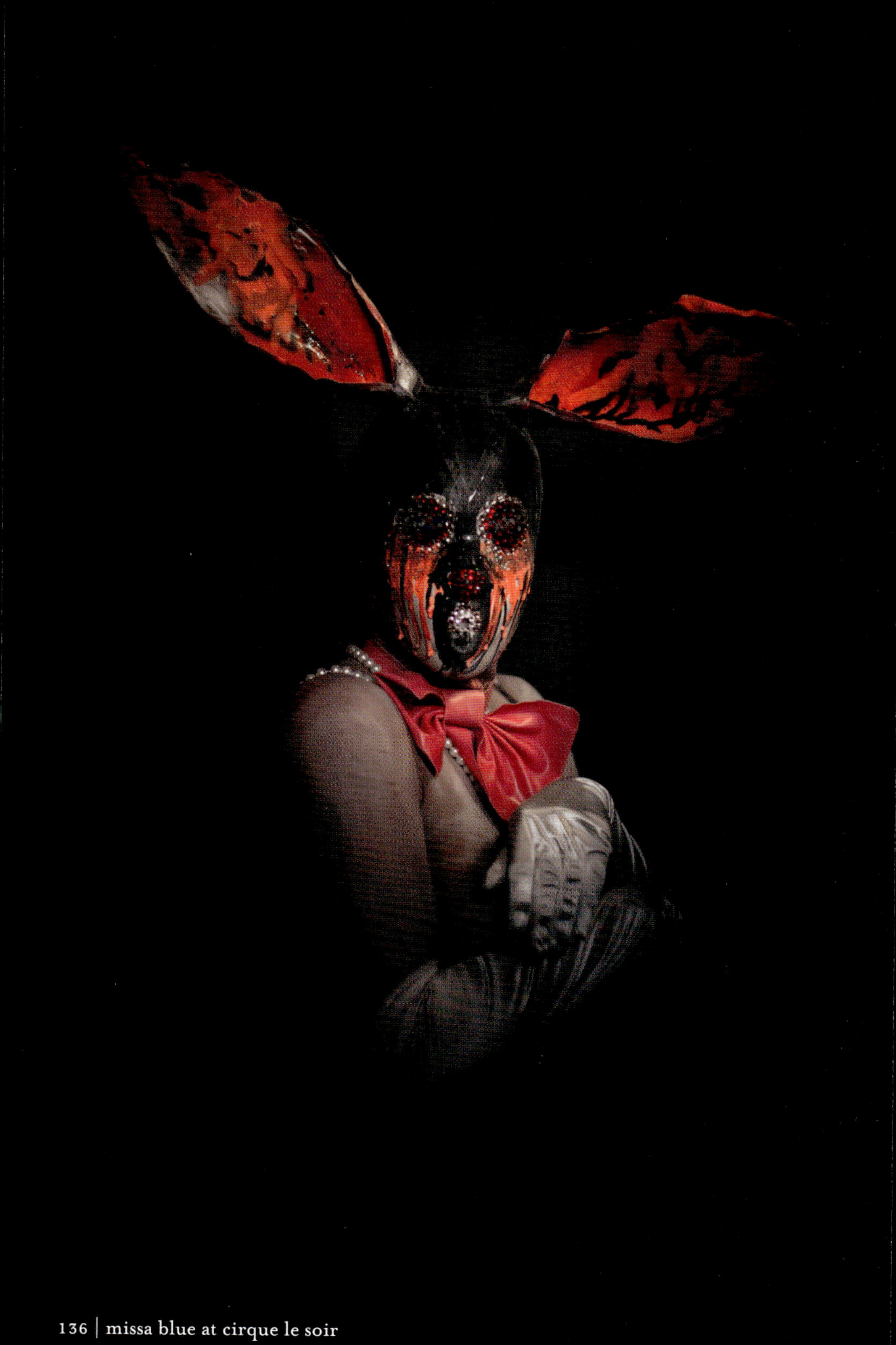

 missa blue at cirque le soir

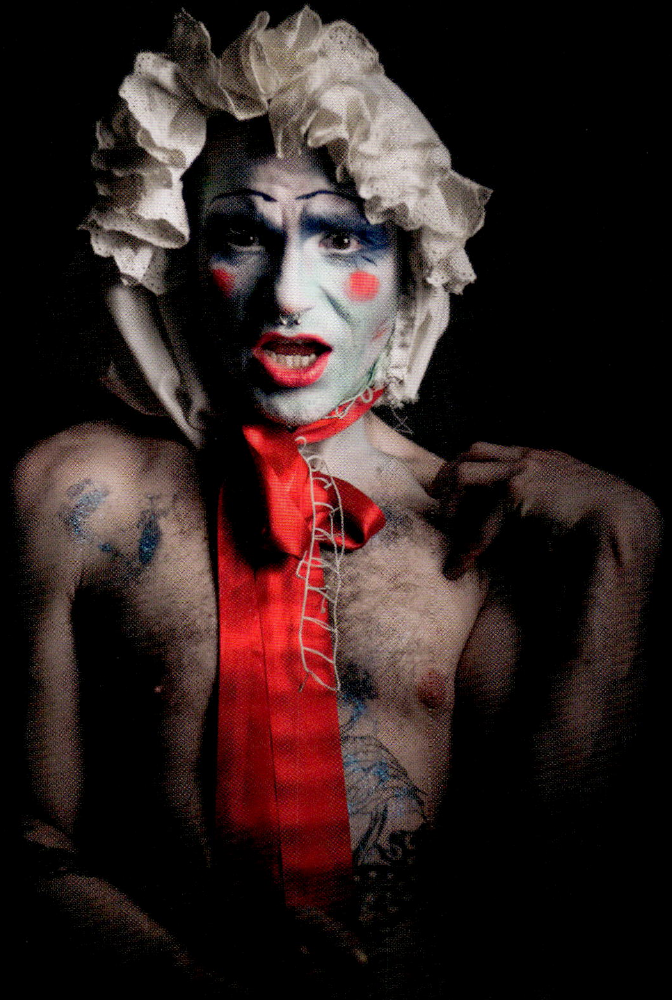

 | oozing gloop at sink the pink

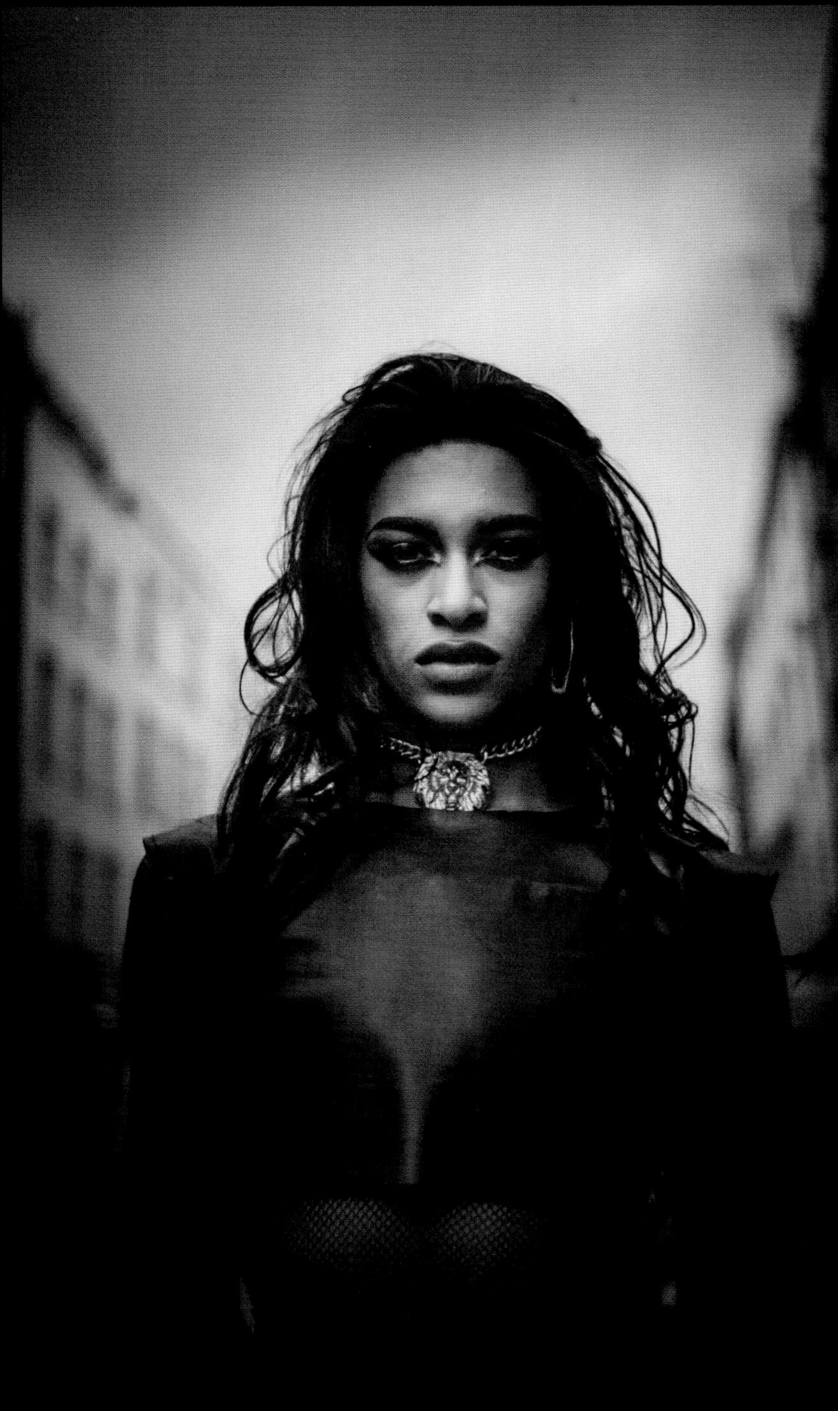

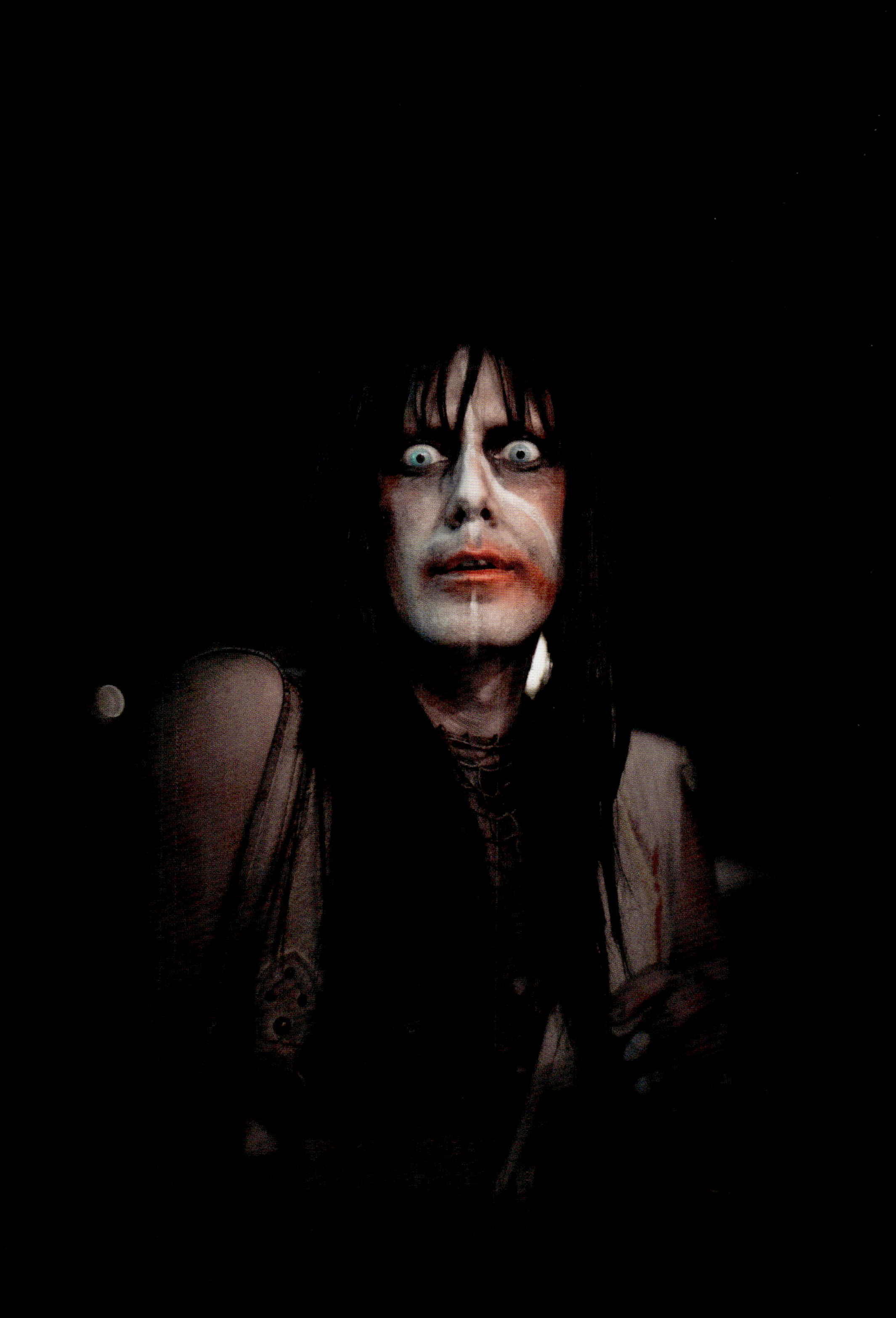

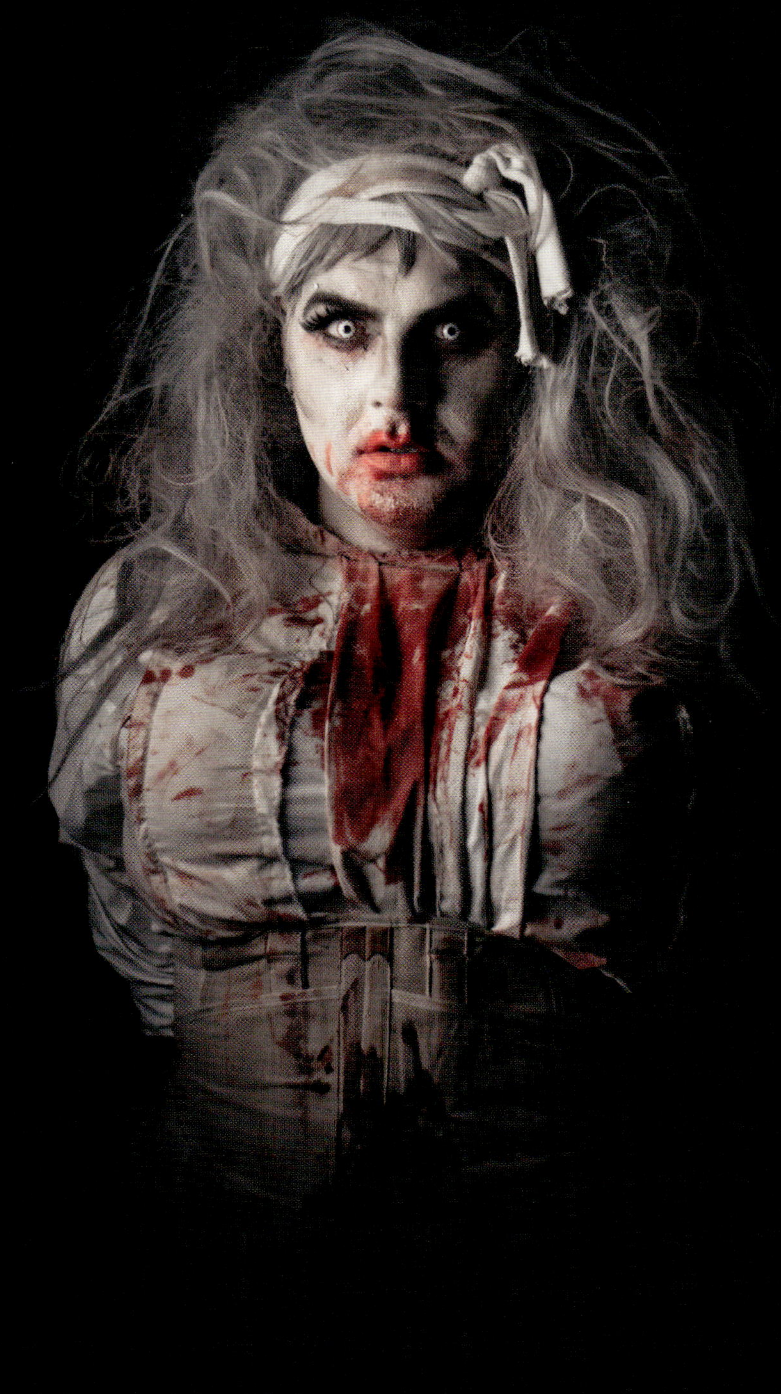

 death ditto at sink the pink

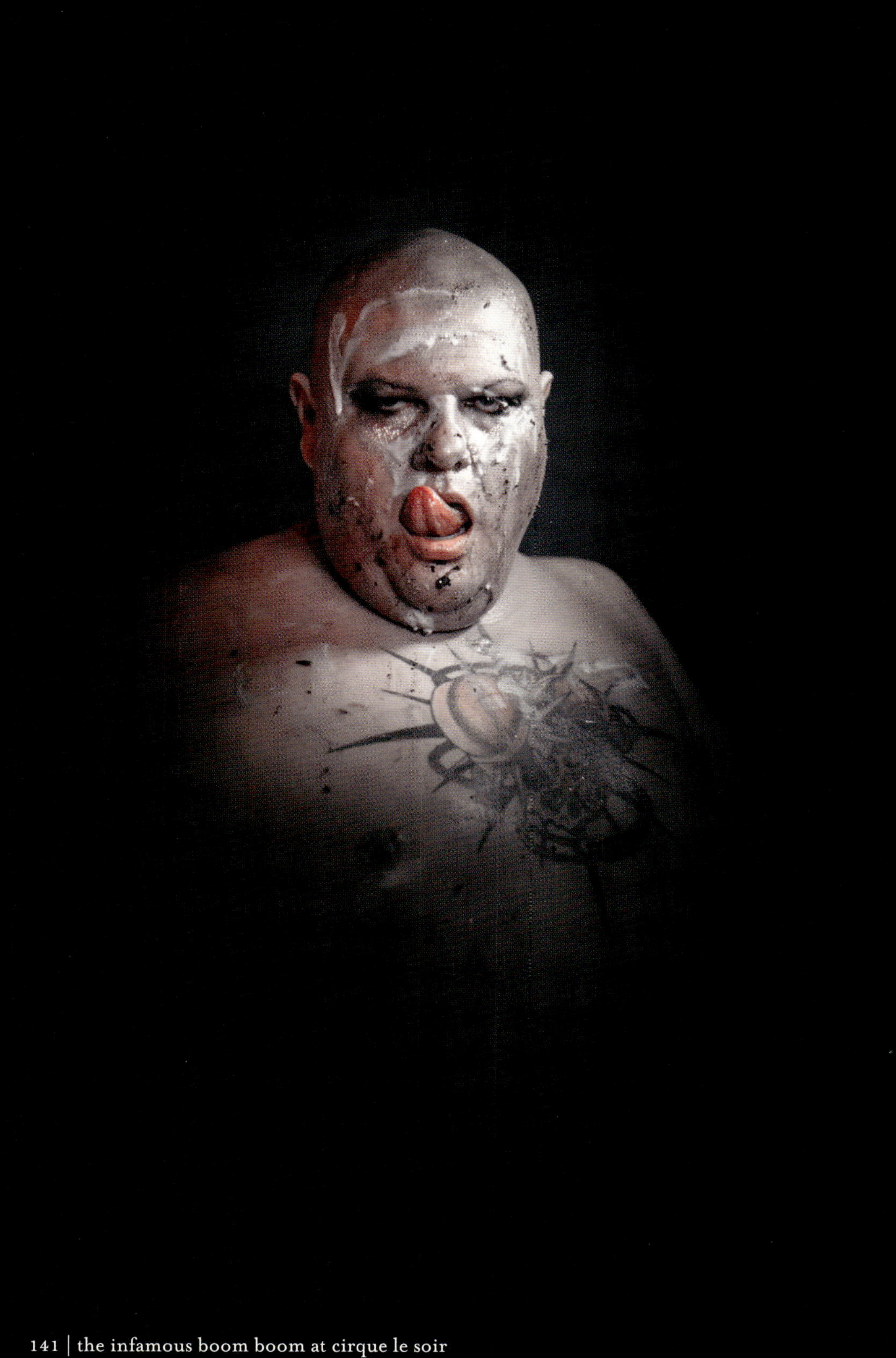

 | the infamous boom boom at cirque le soir

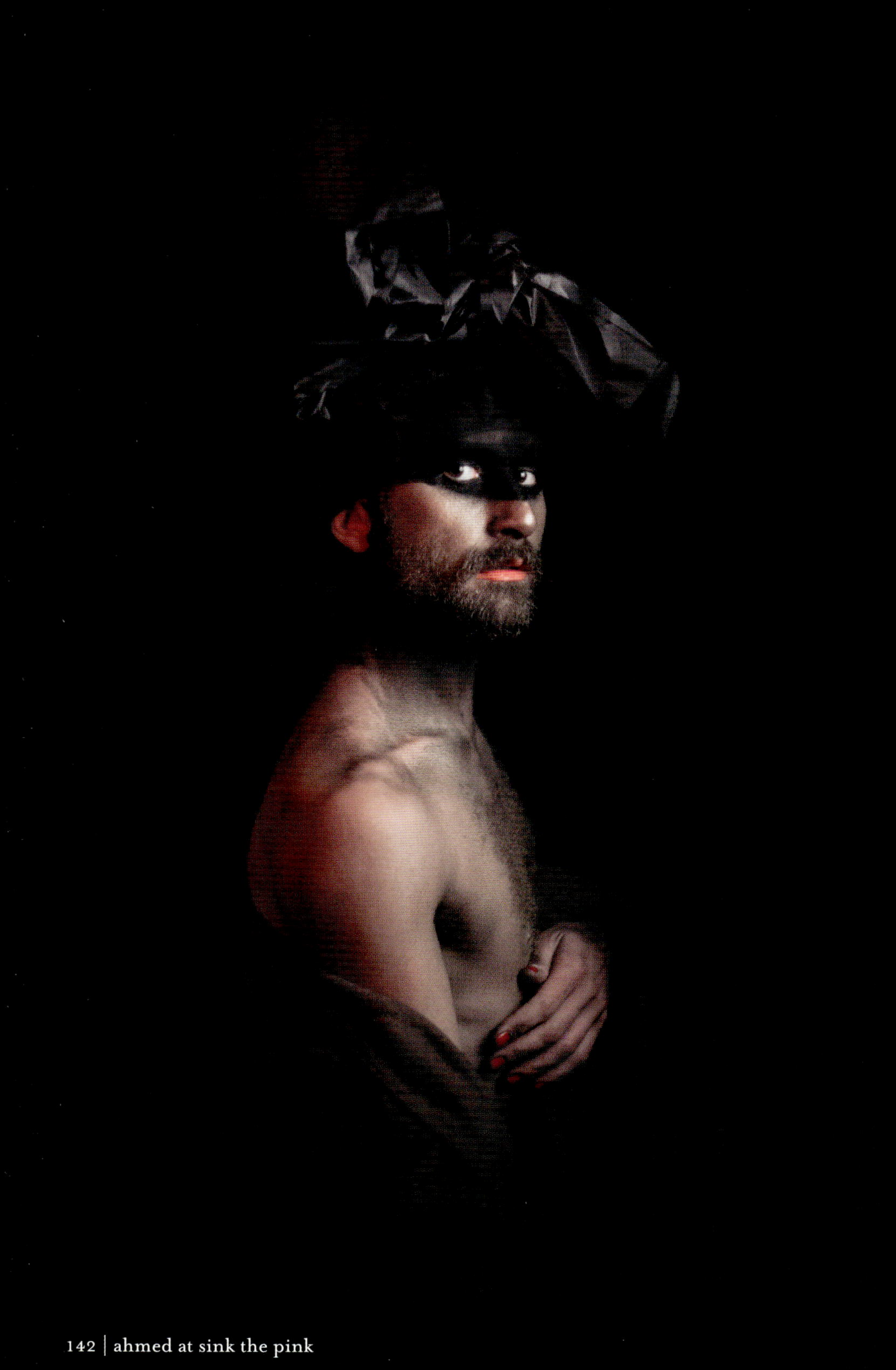

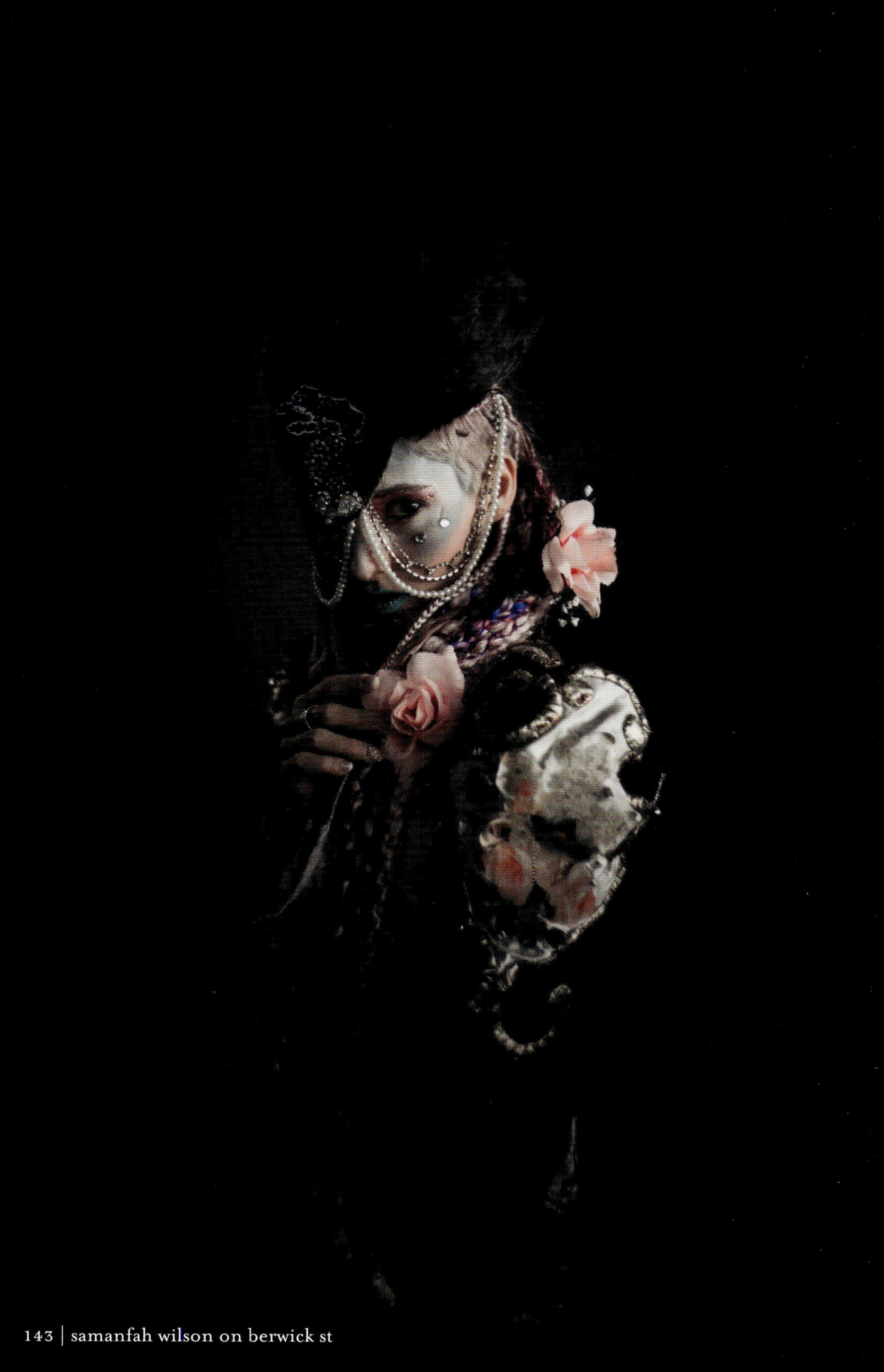

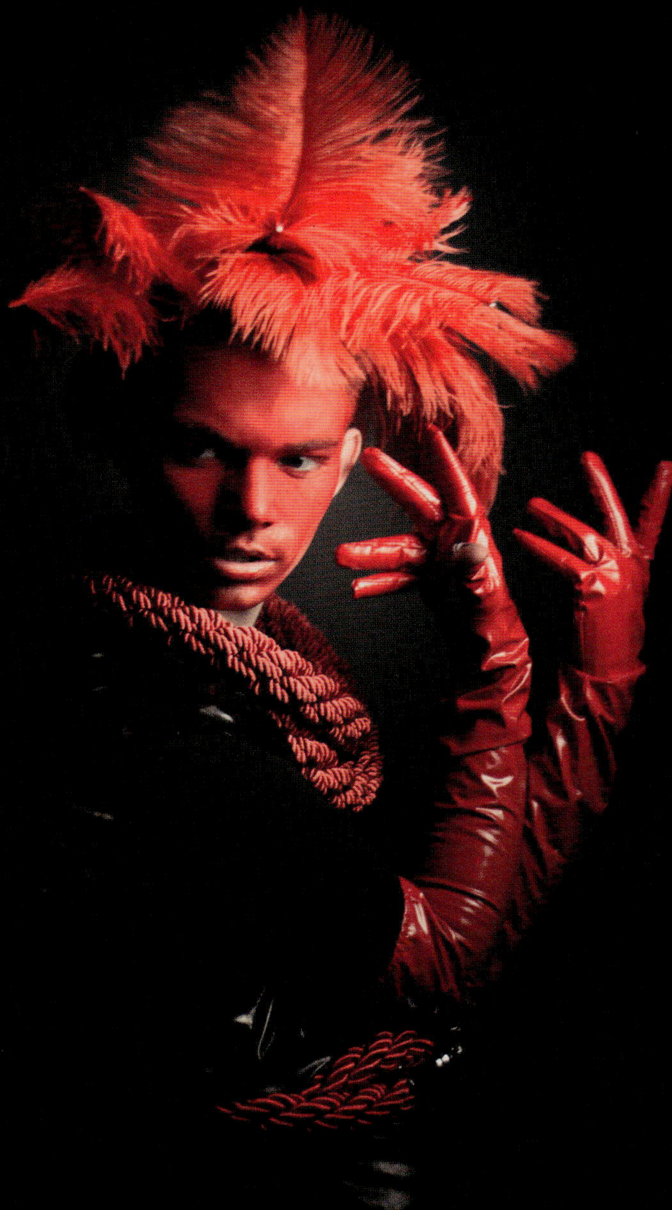

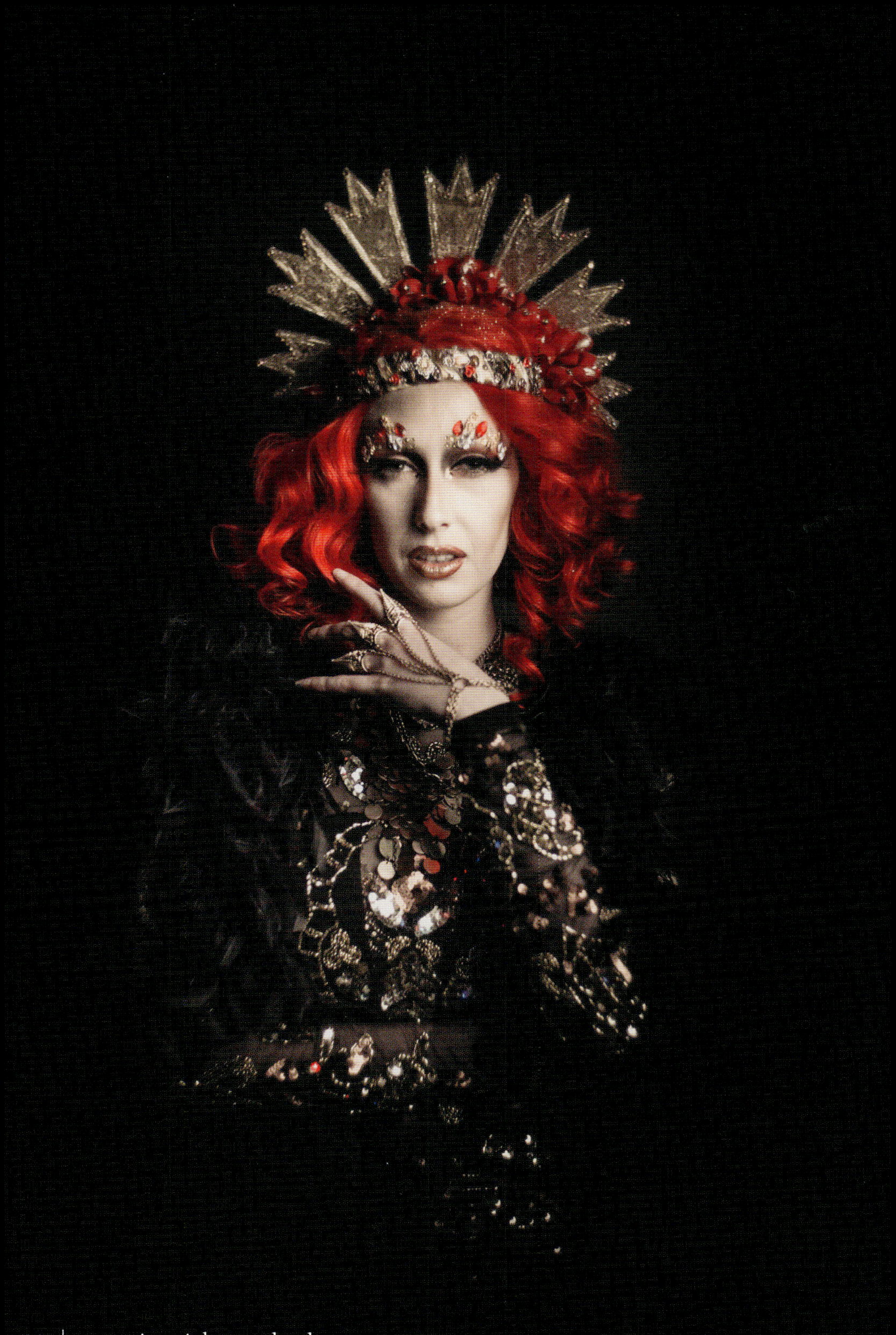

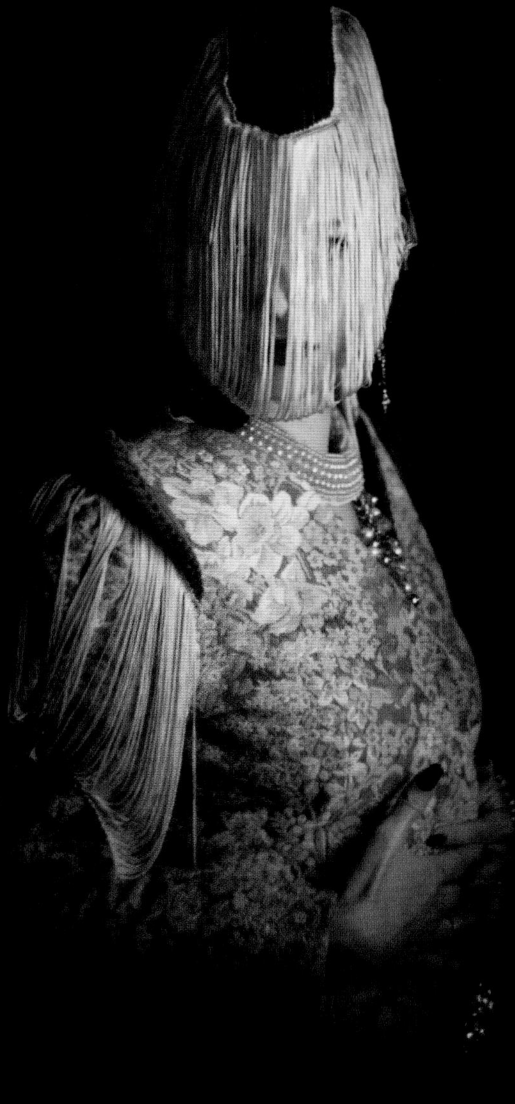

146 | rachel at the amy grimehouse tudor realness ball

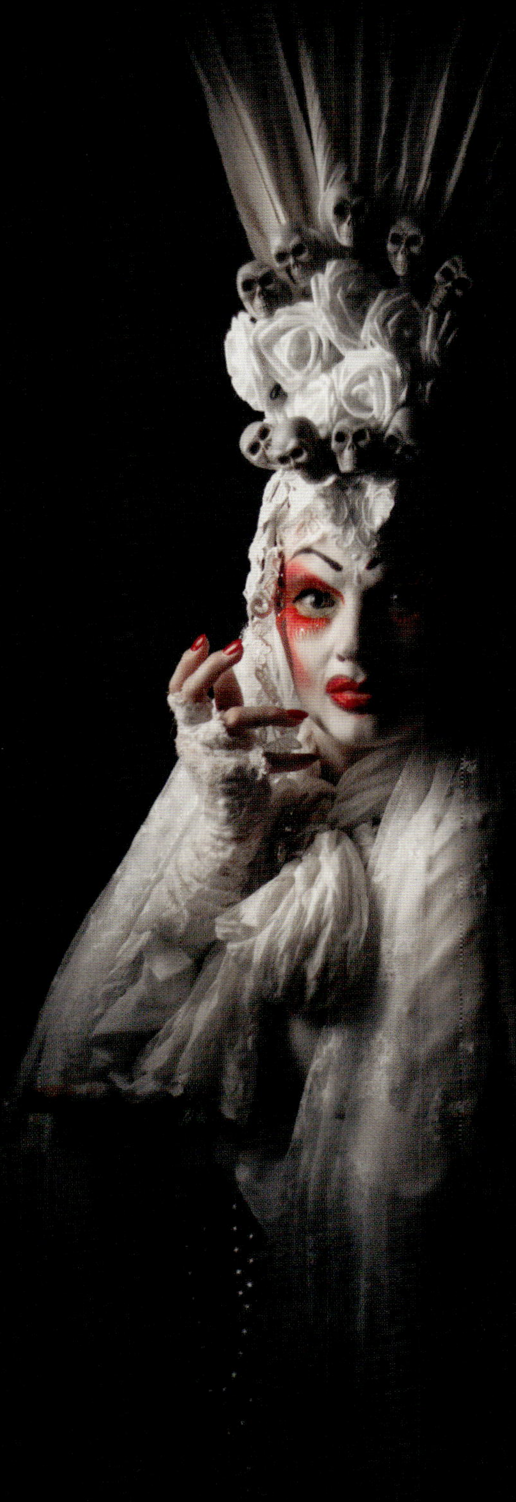

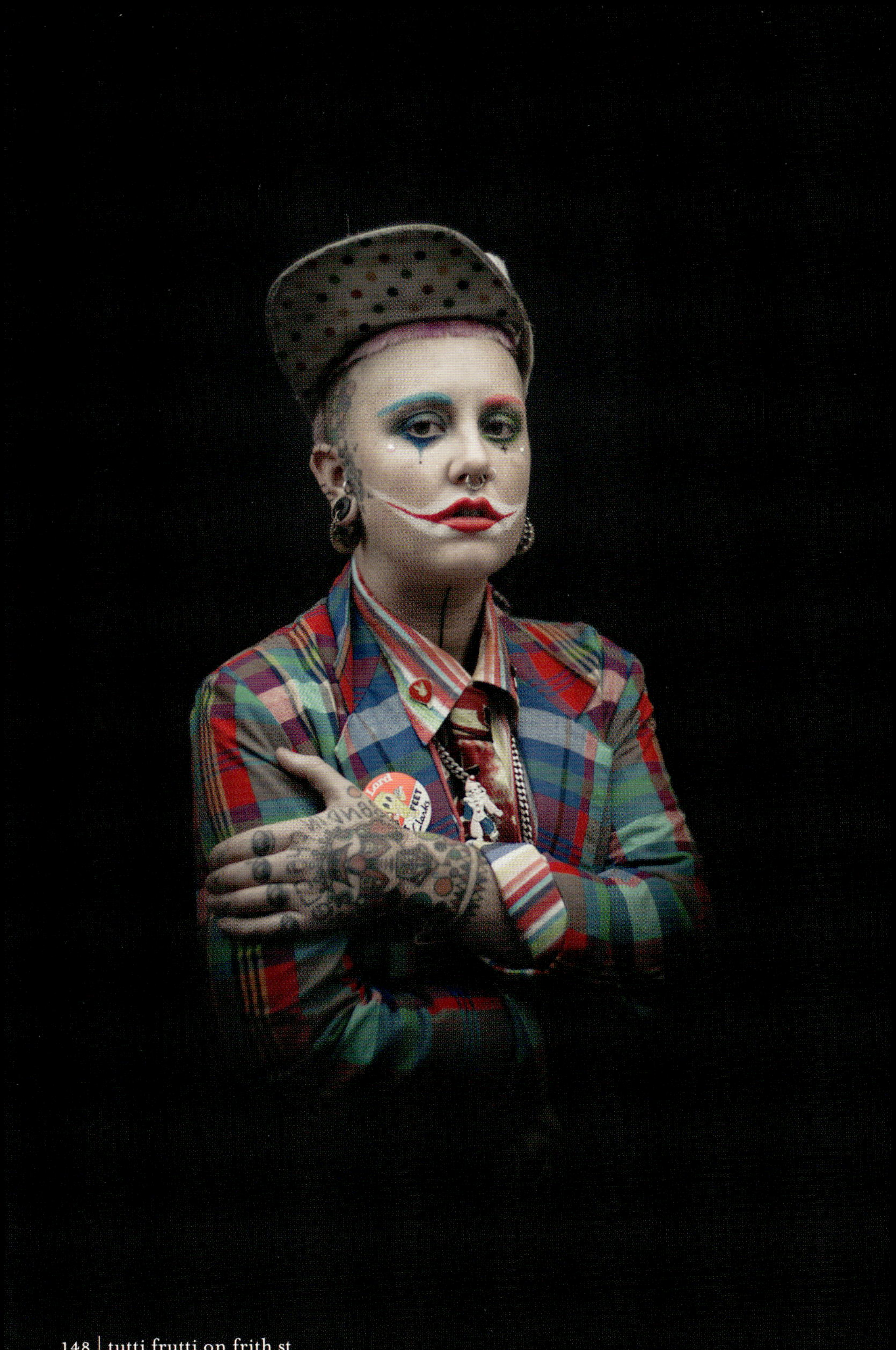

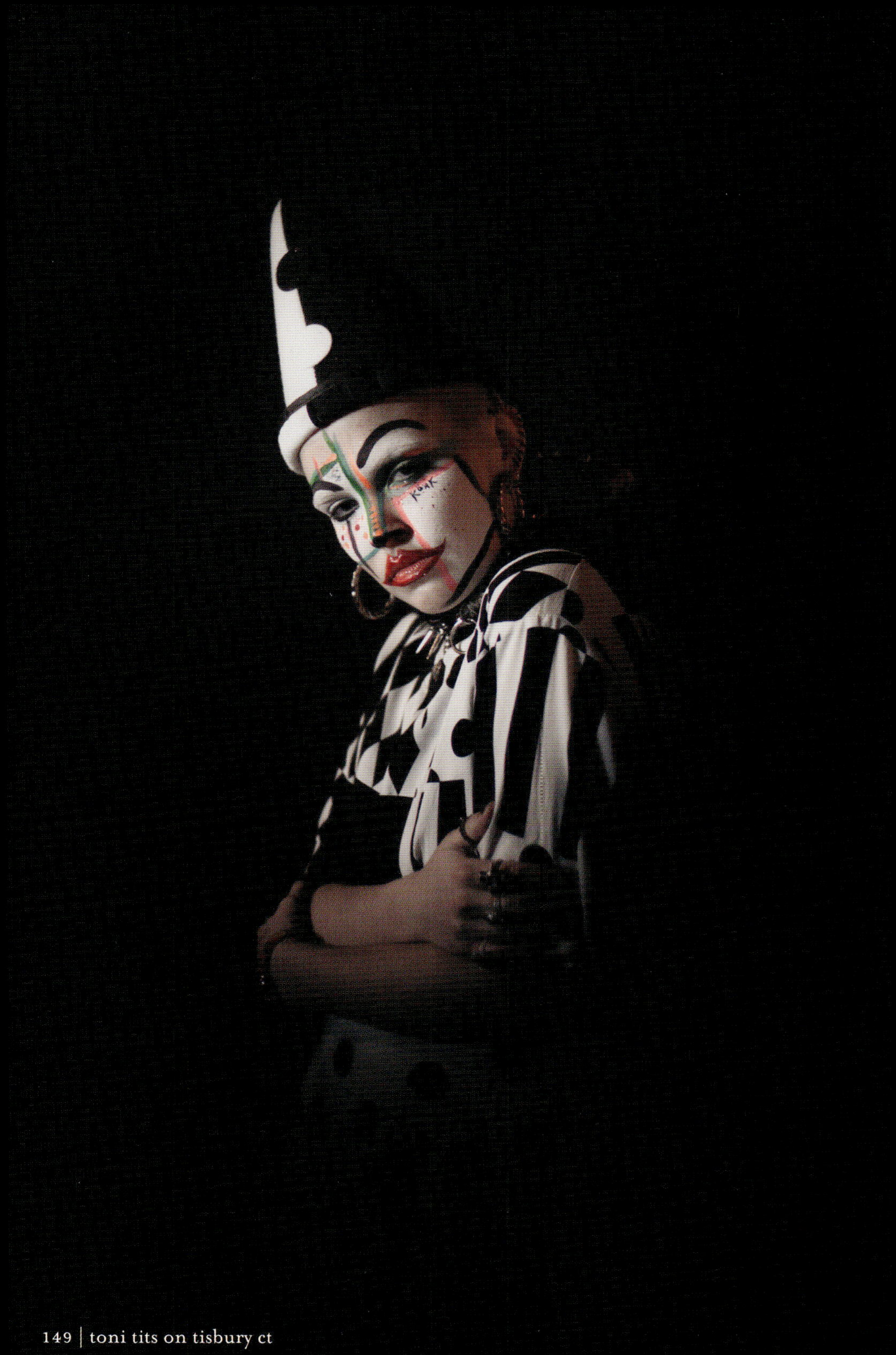
KOAK

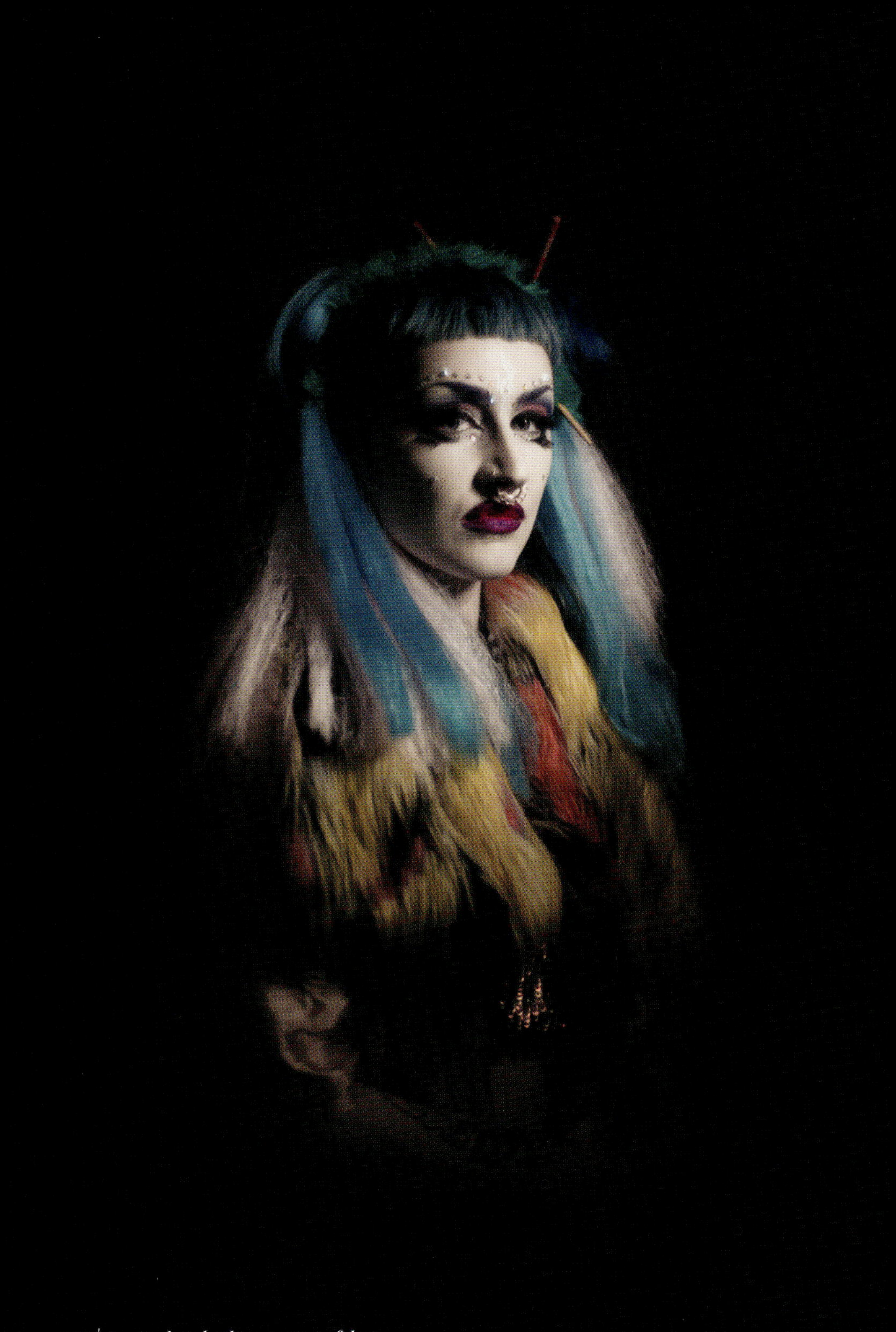

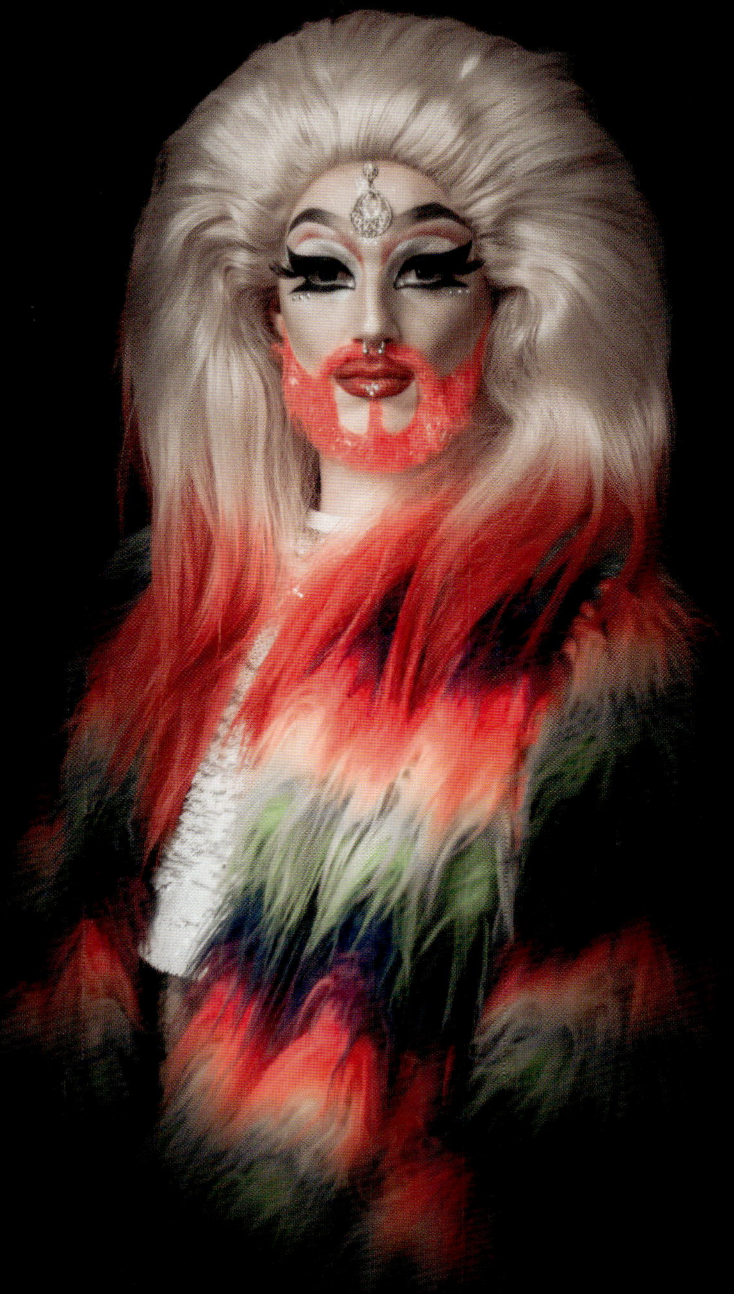

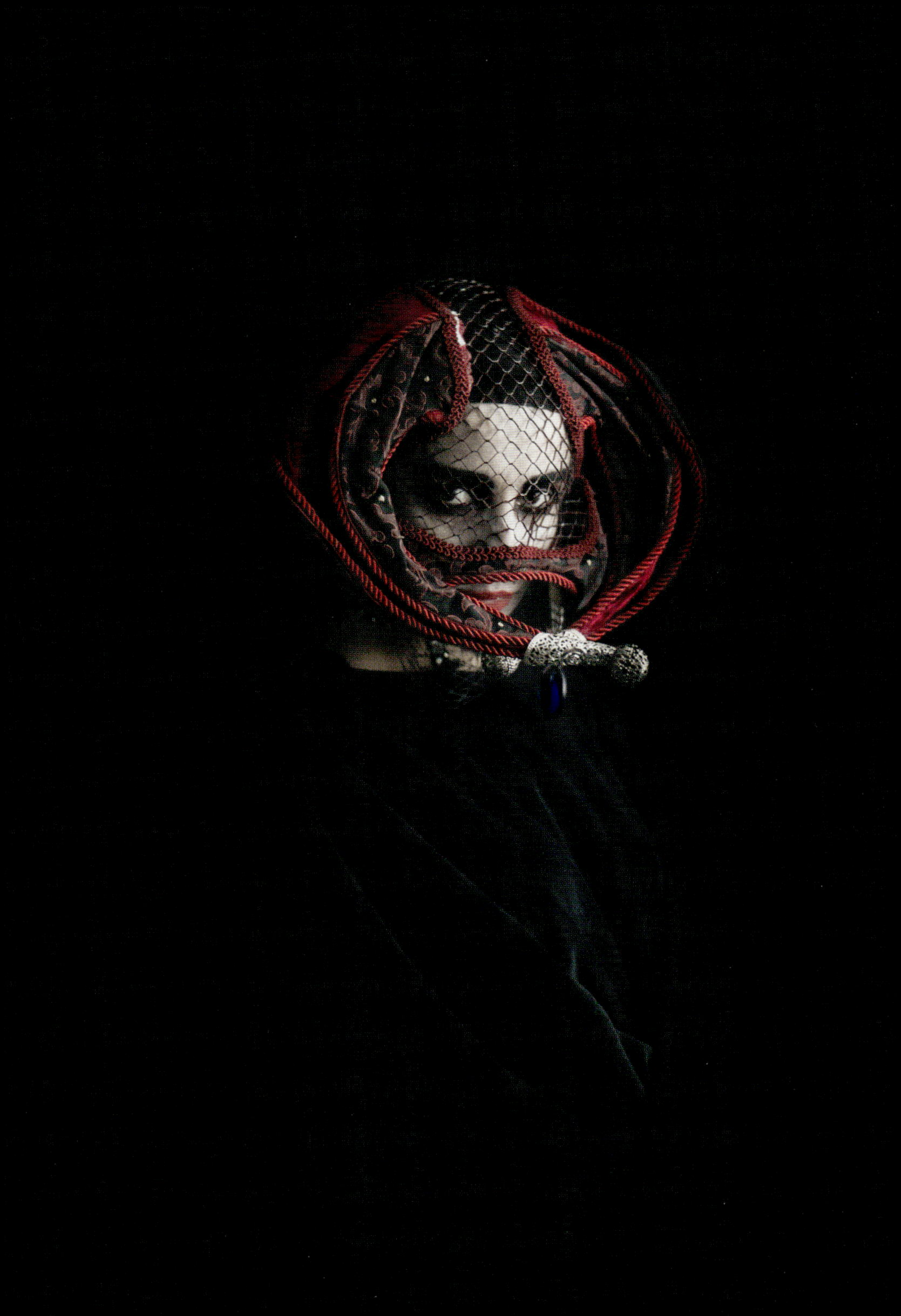

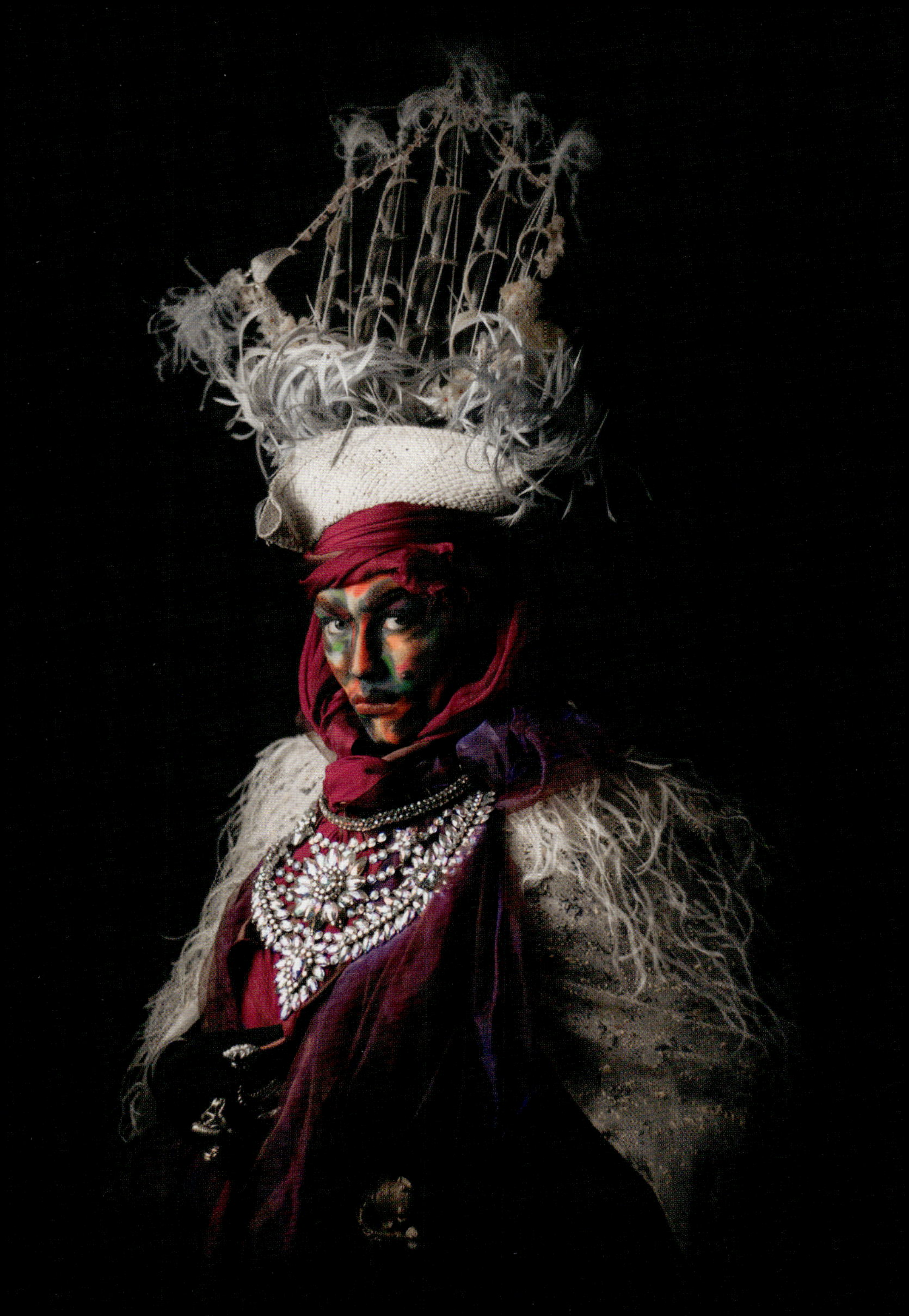

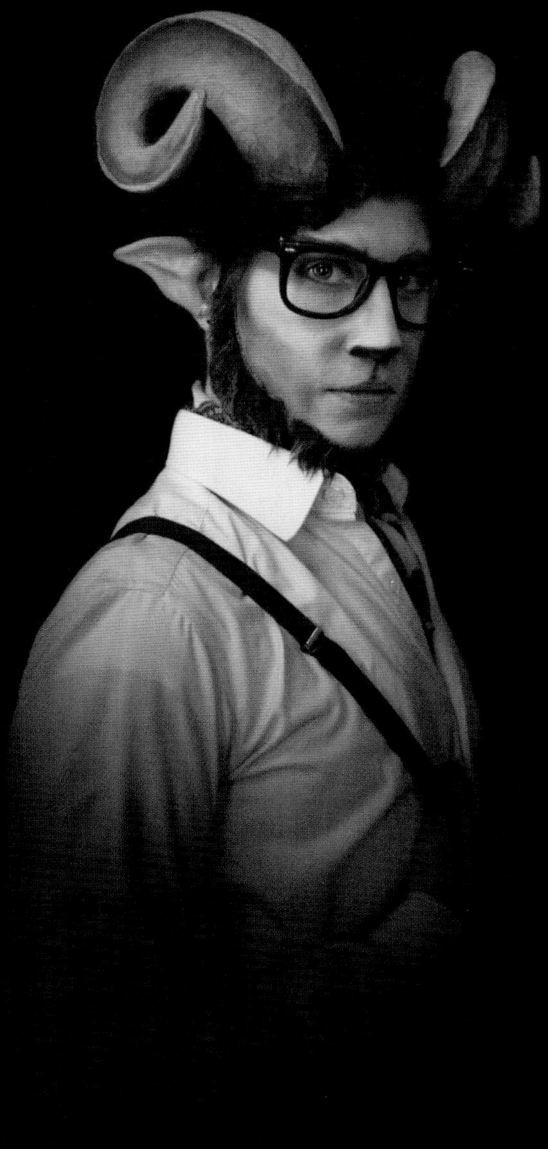

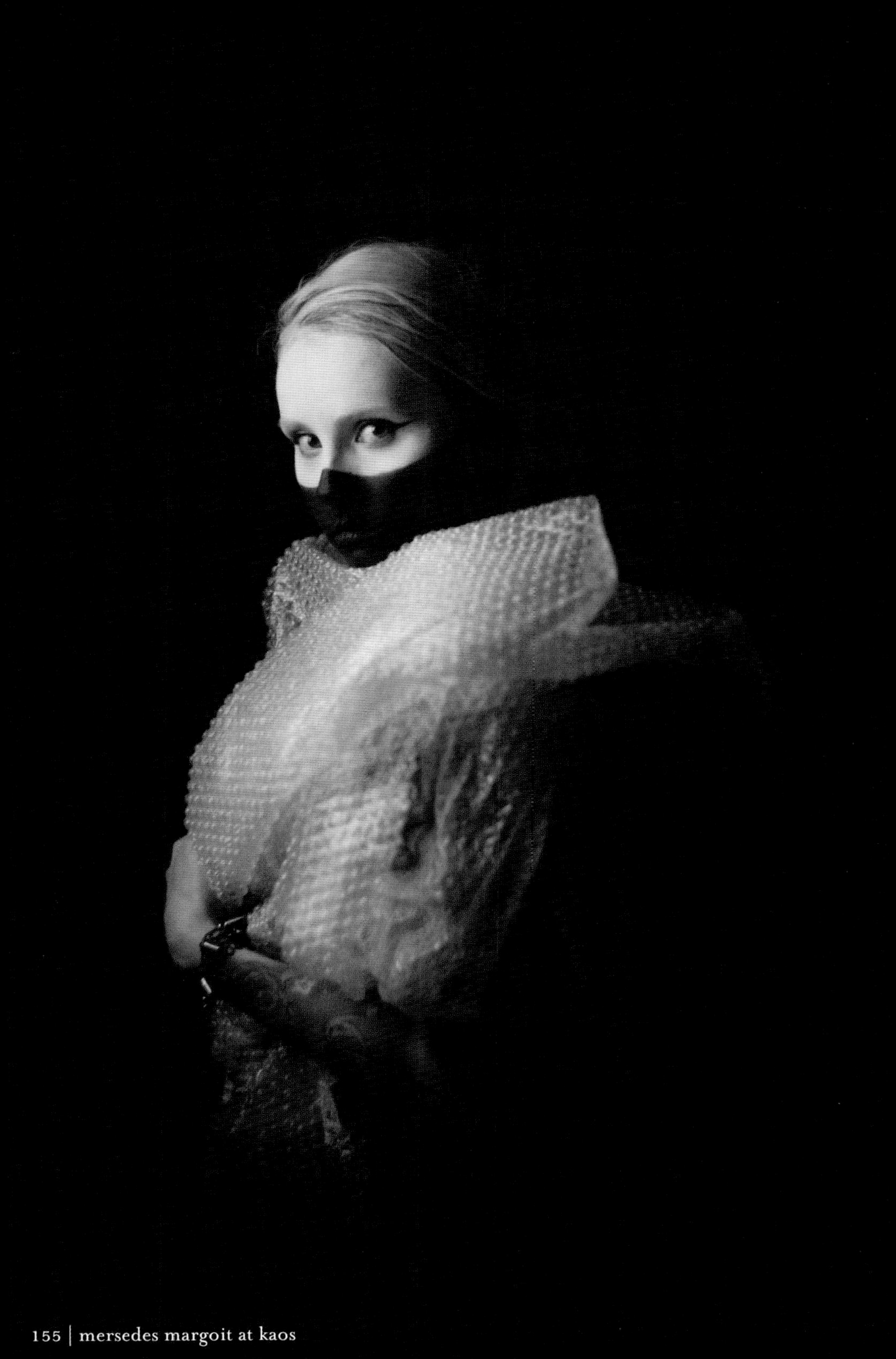

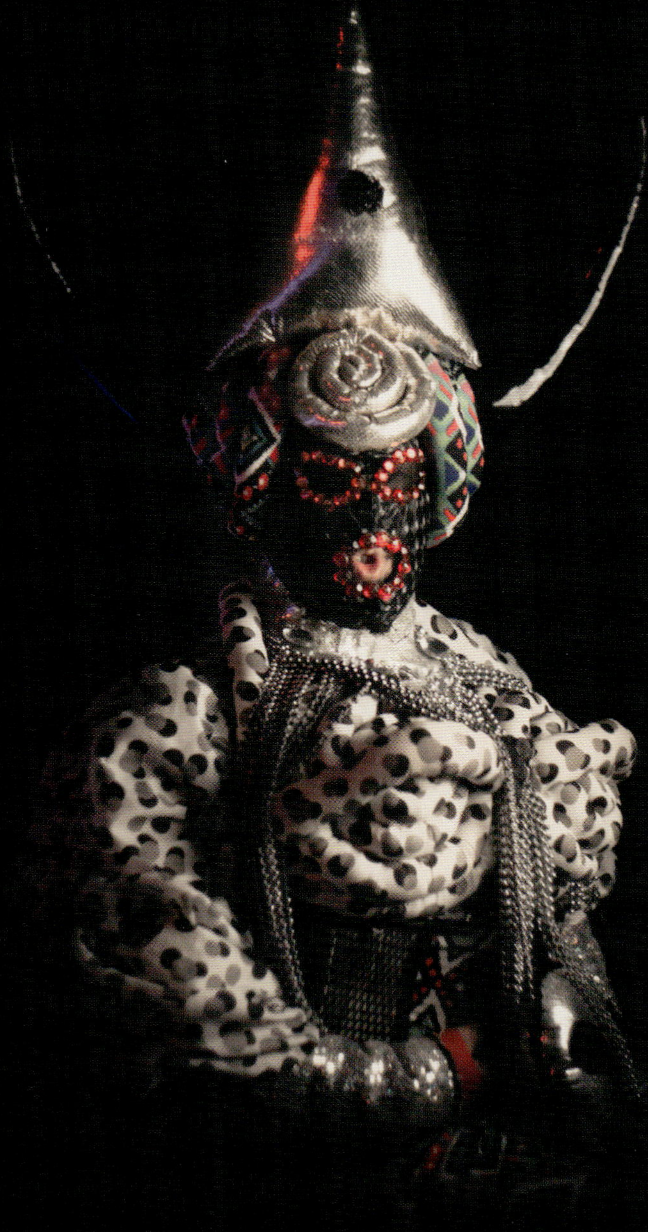

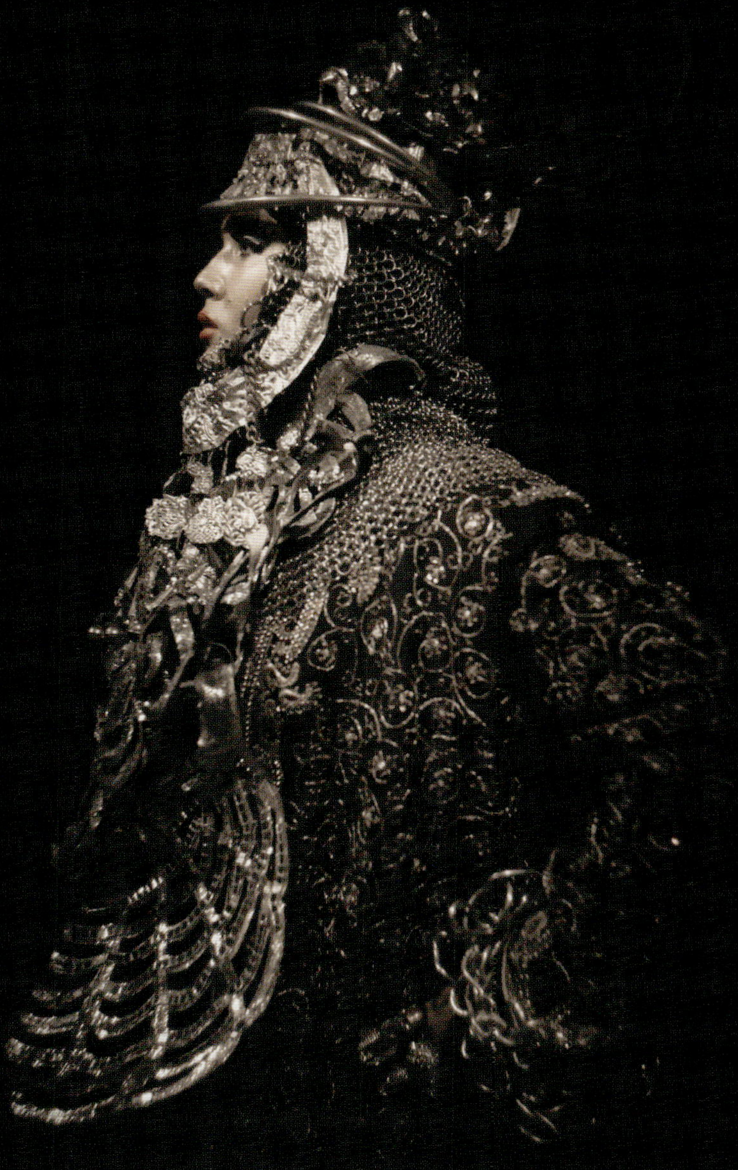

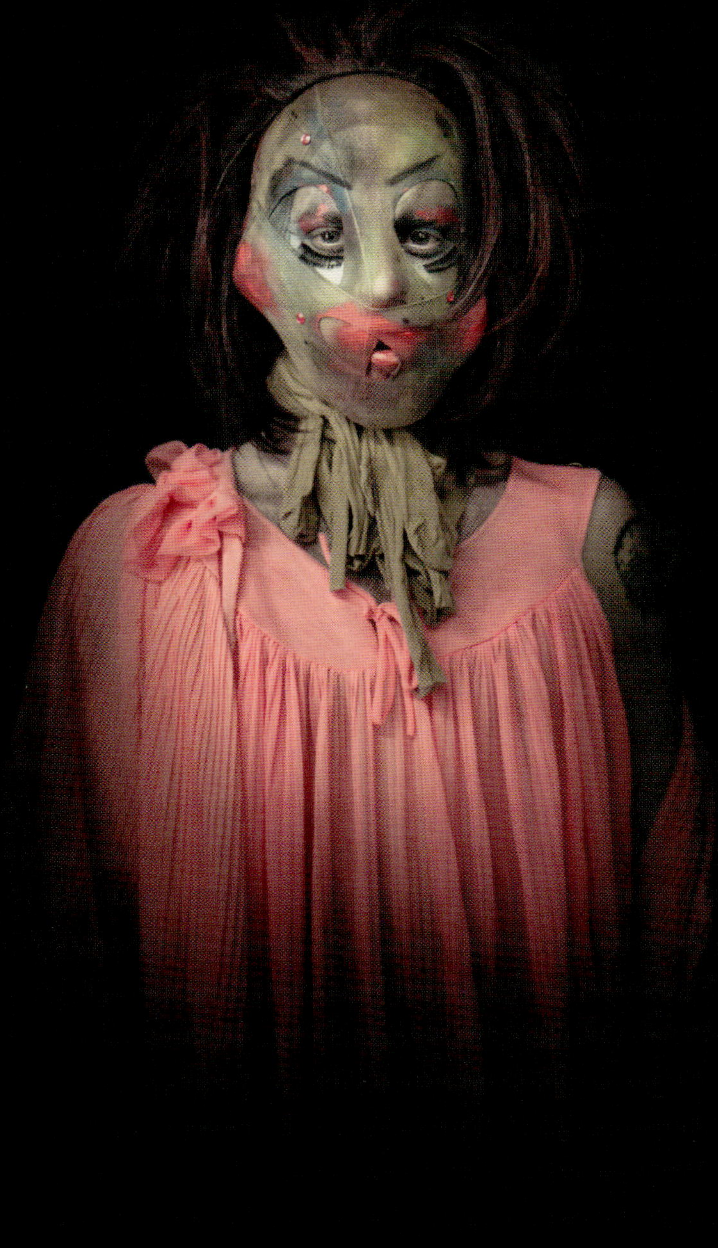

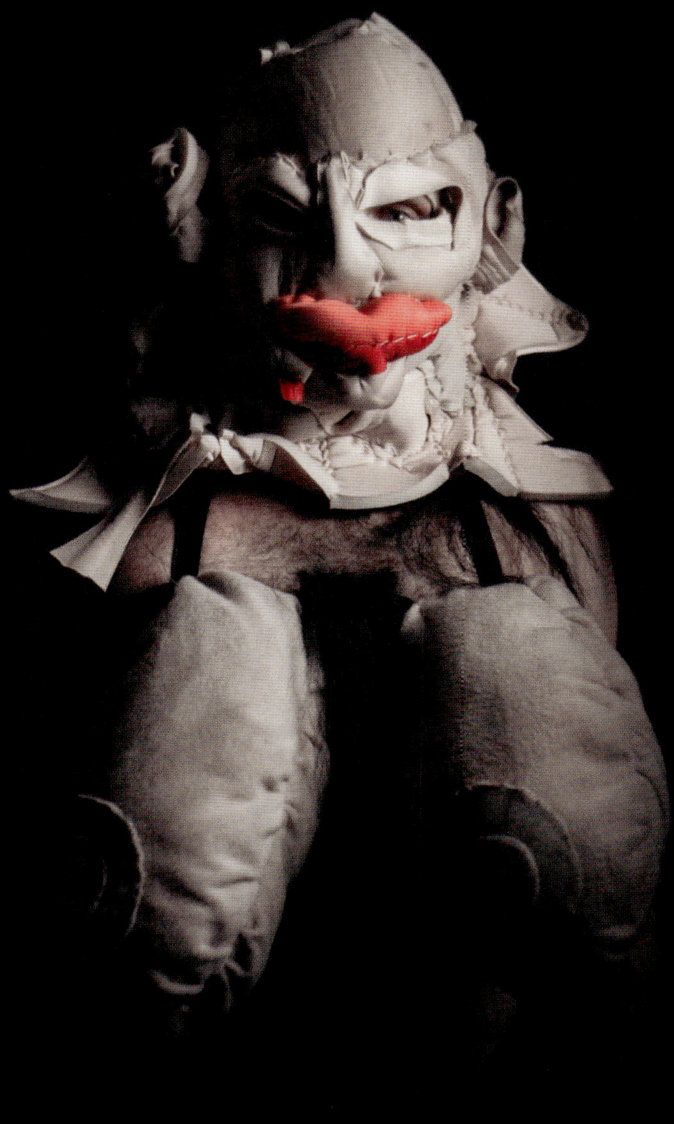

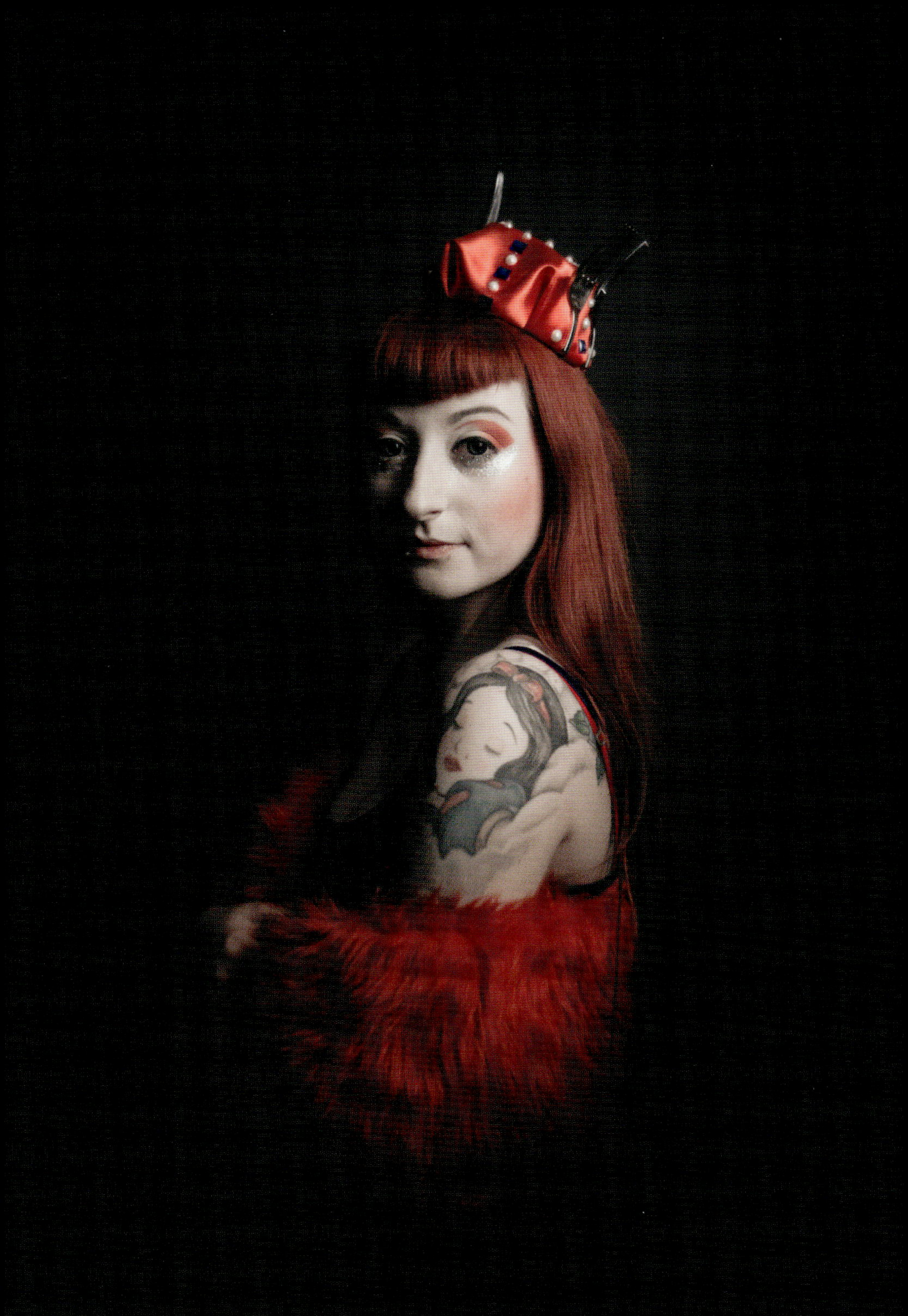

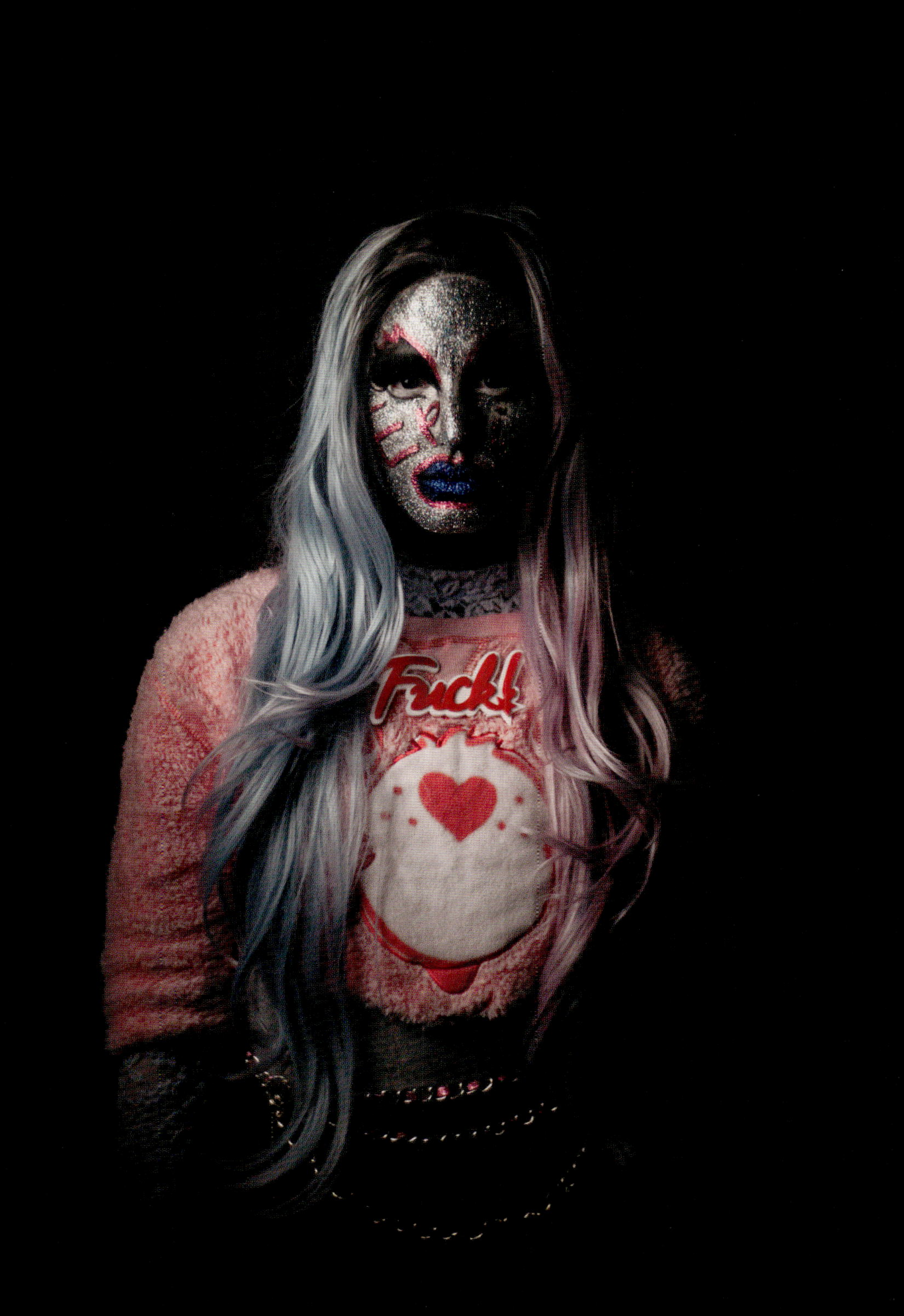

161 | eppie on old compton st

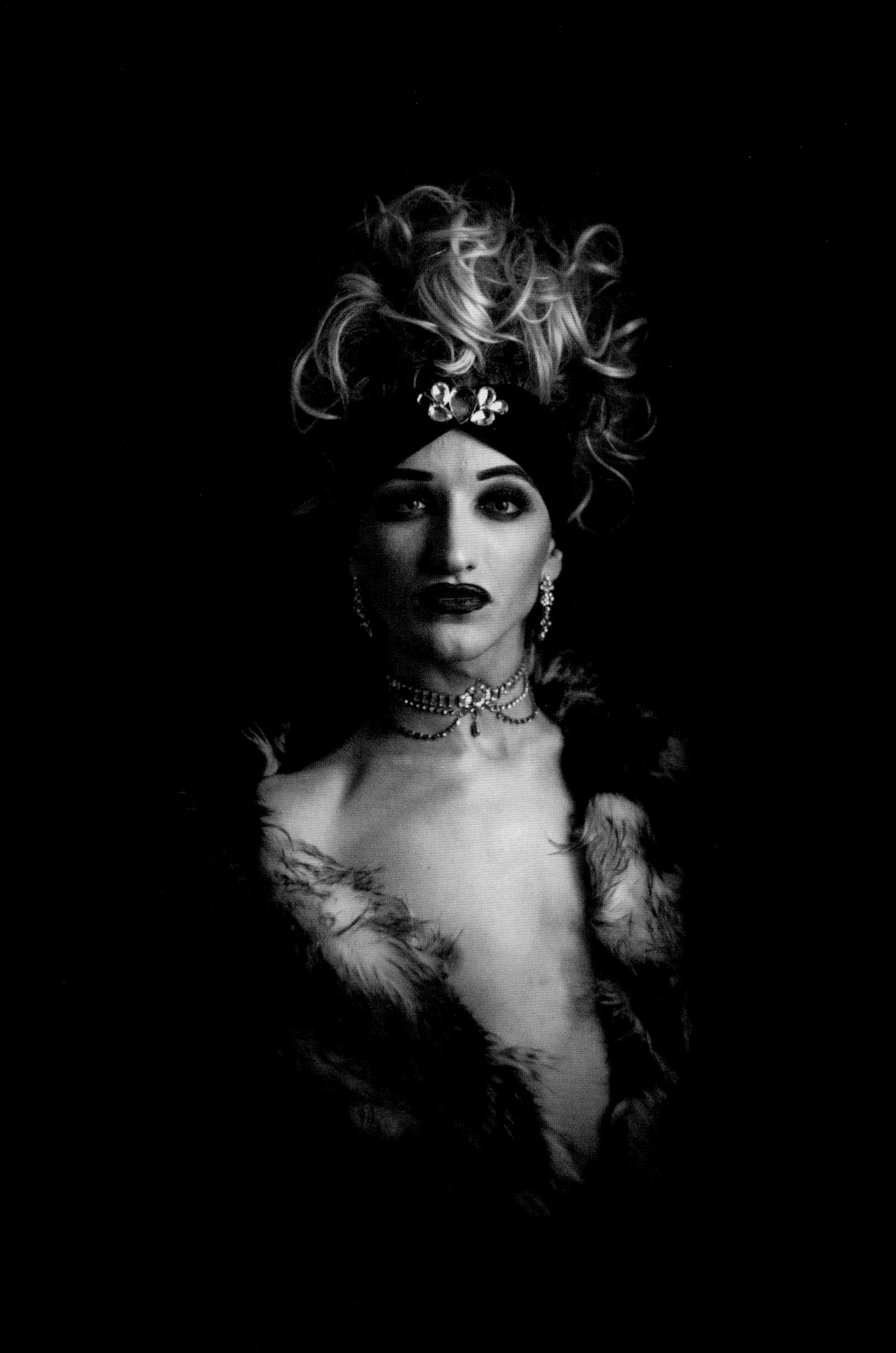

 anna wintoral at sink the pink

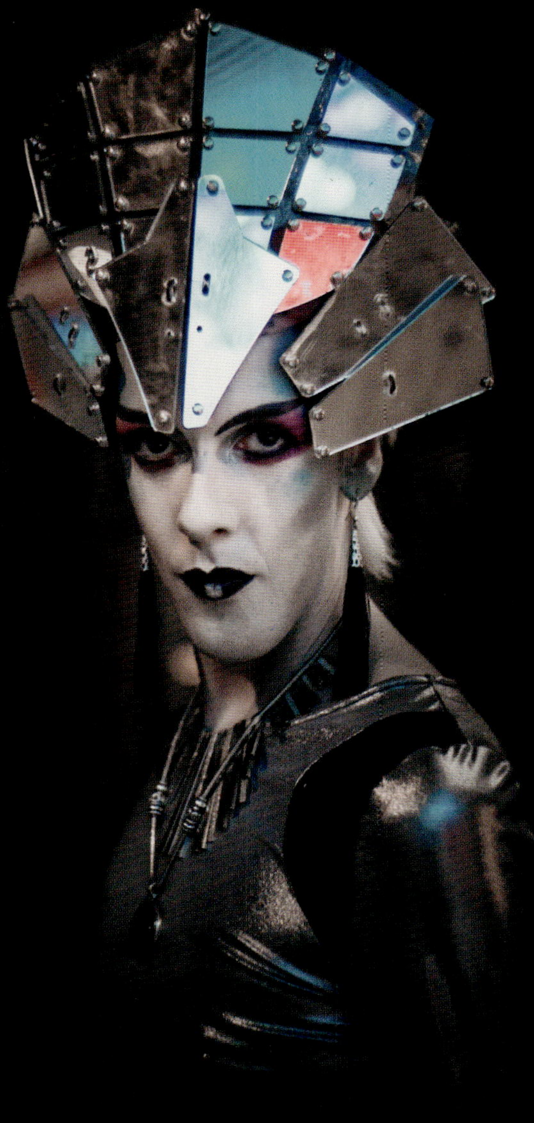

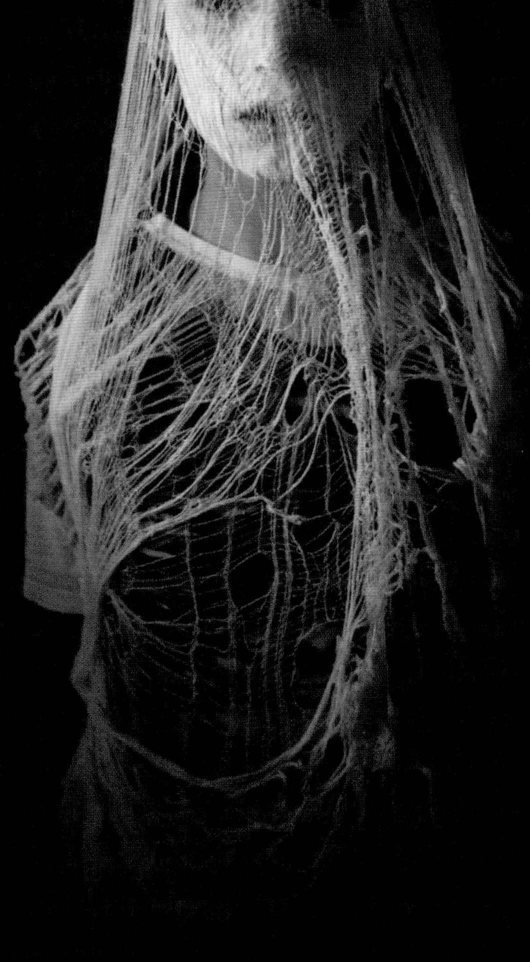

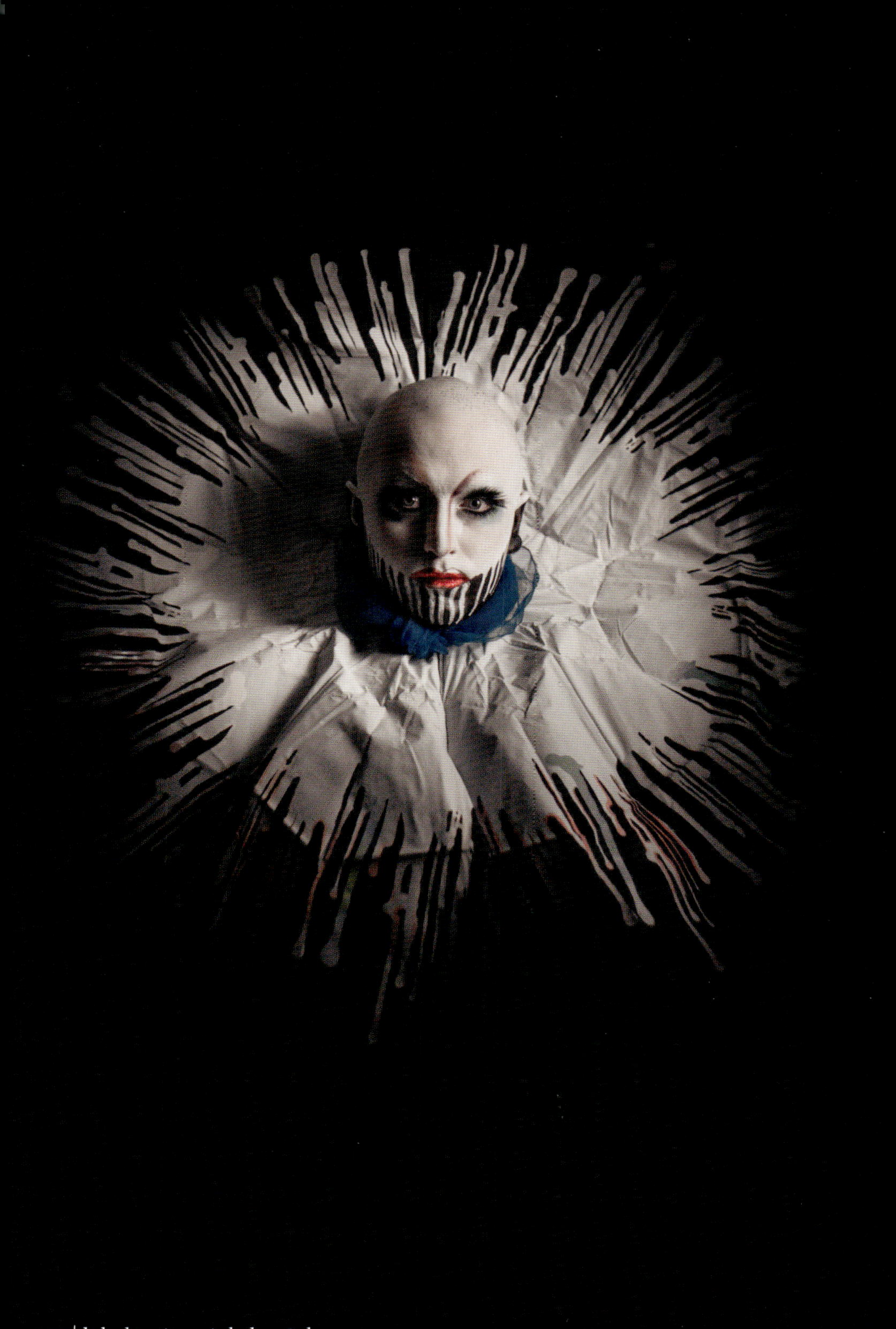

 luke harris at sink the pink

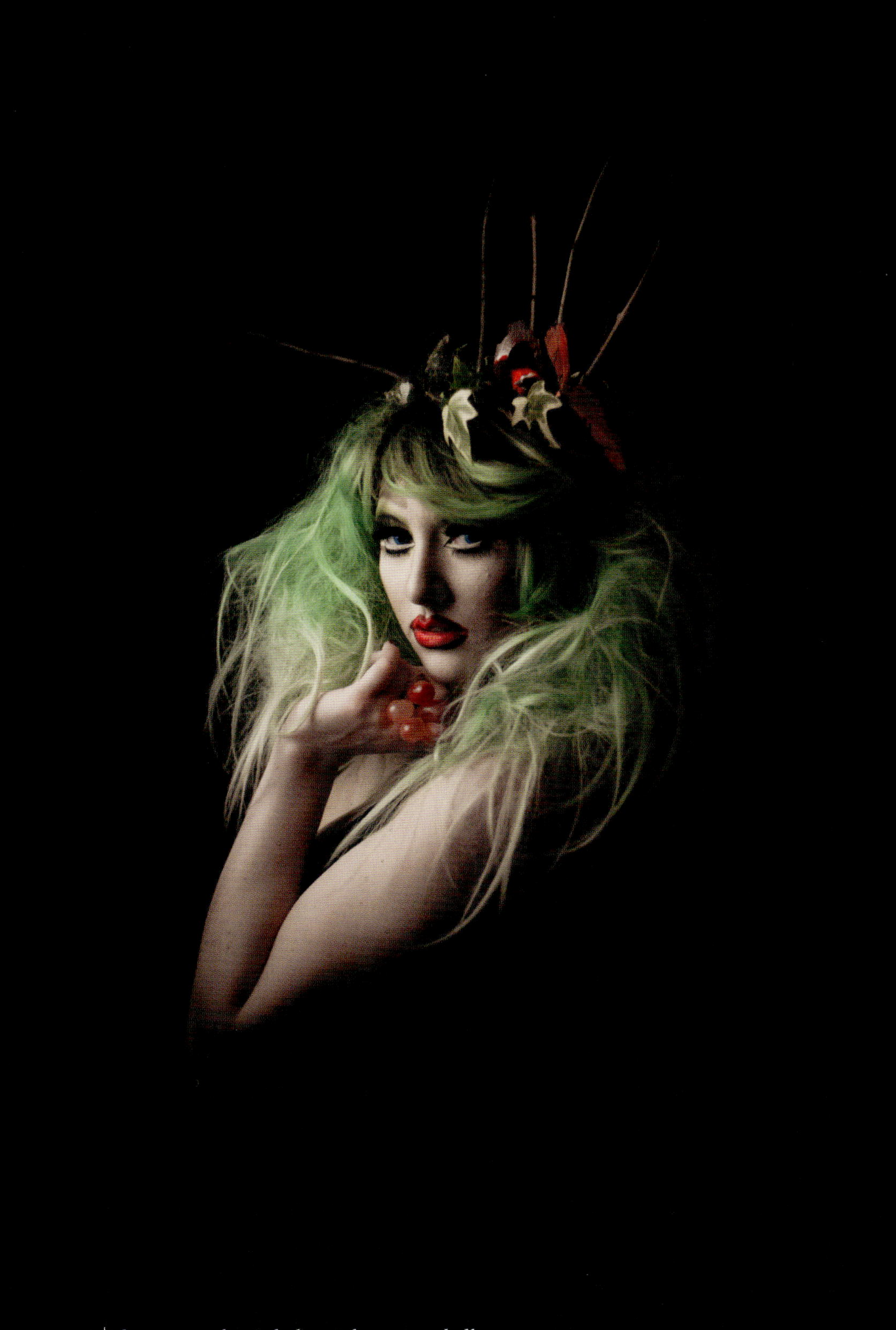

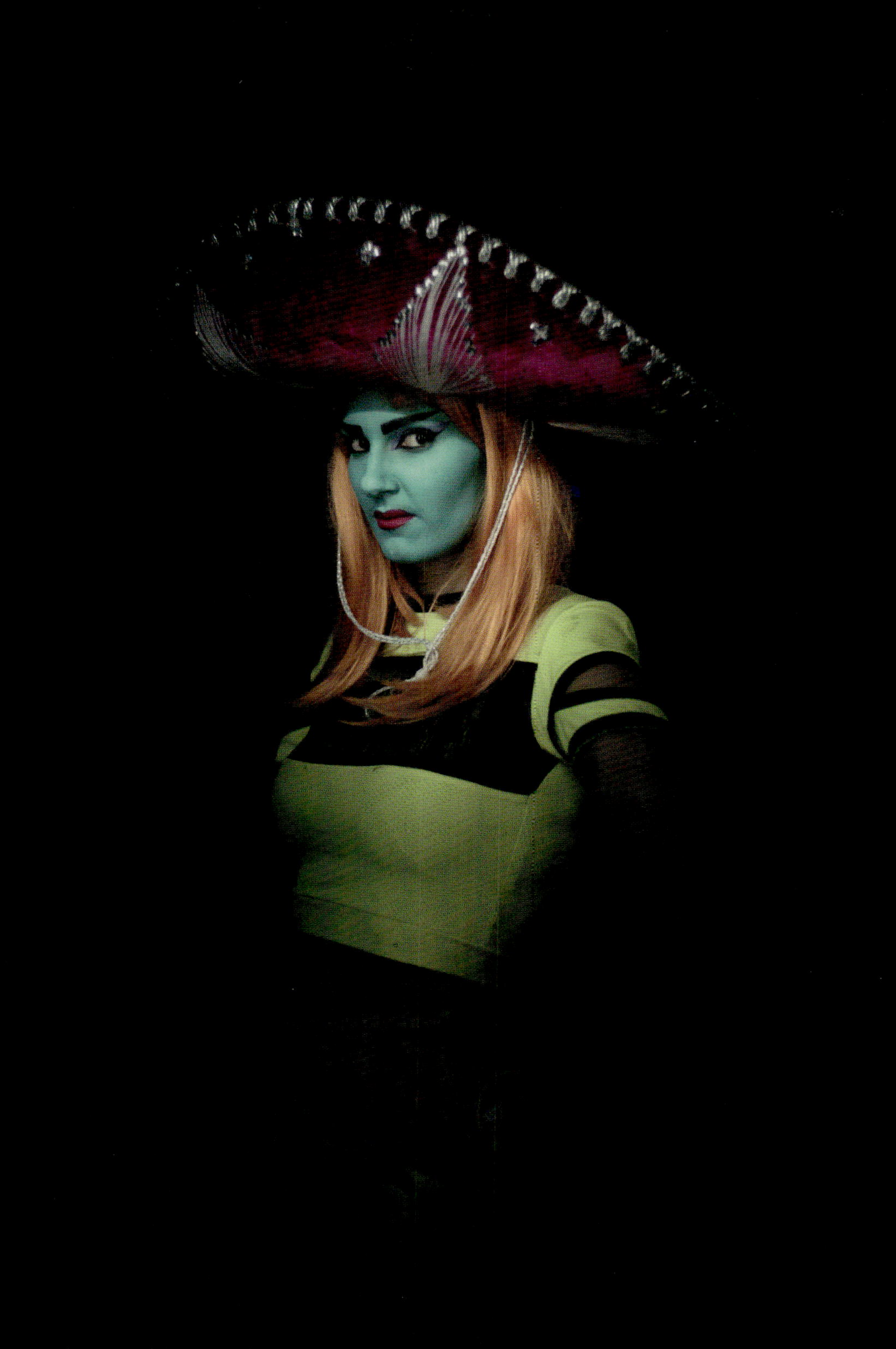

 gaffy gaffiero on old compton st

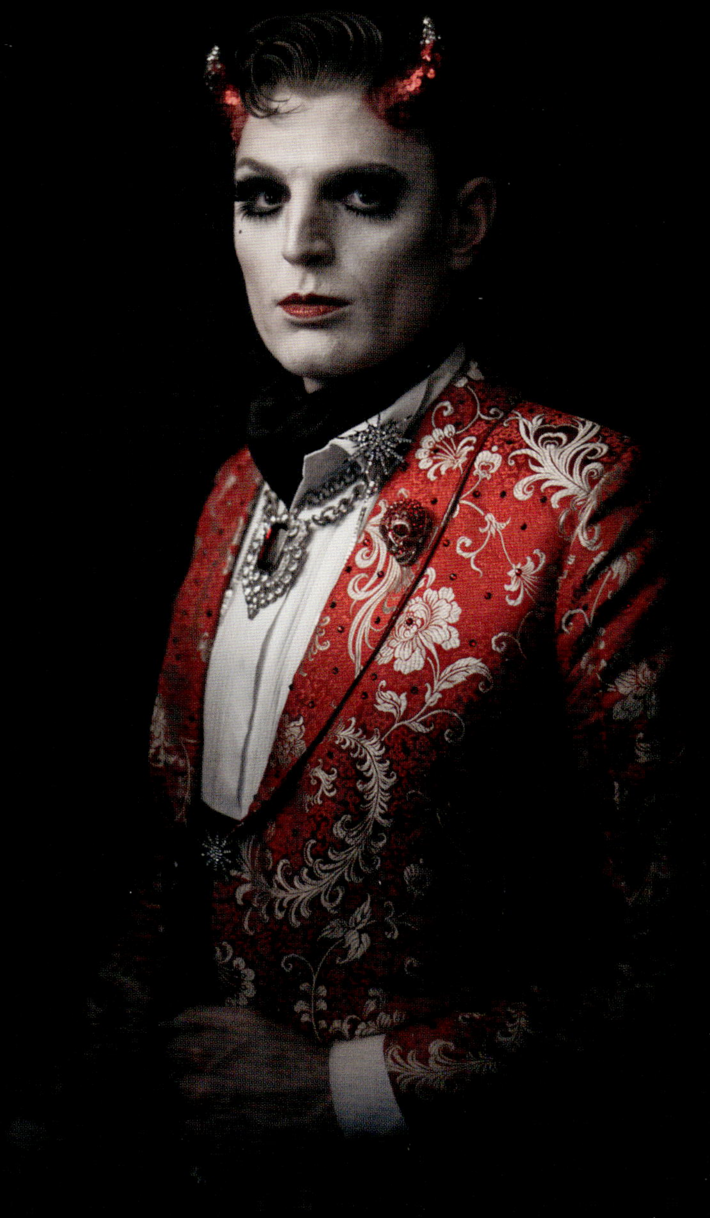

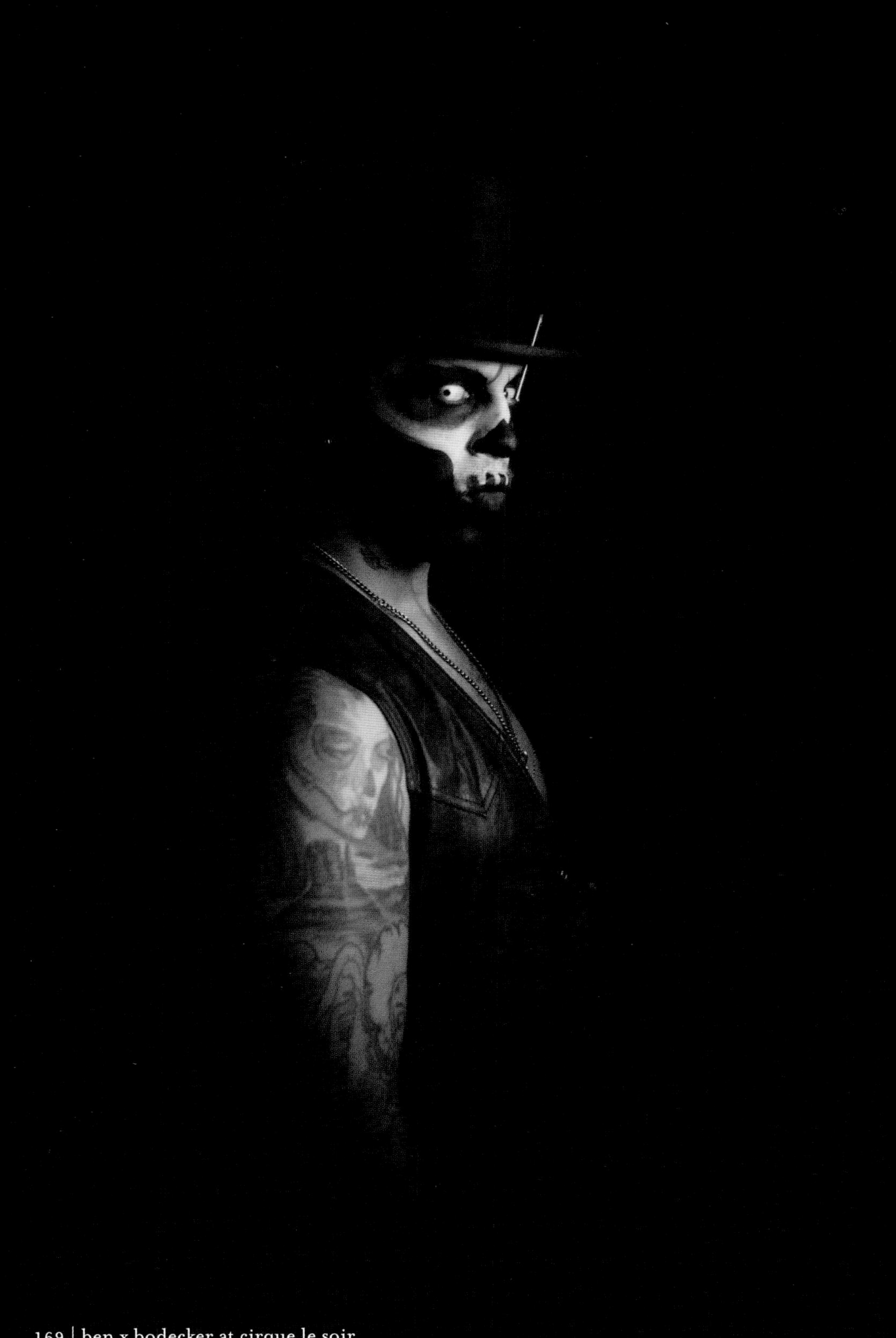

 | ben x bodecker at cirque le soir

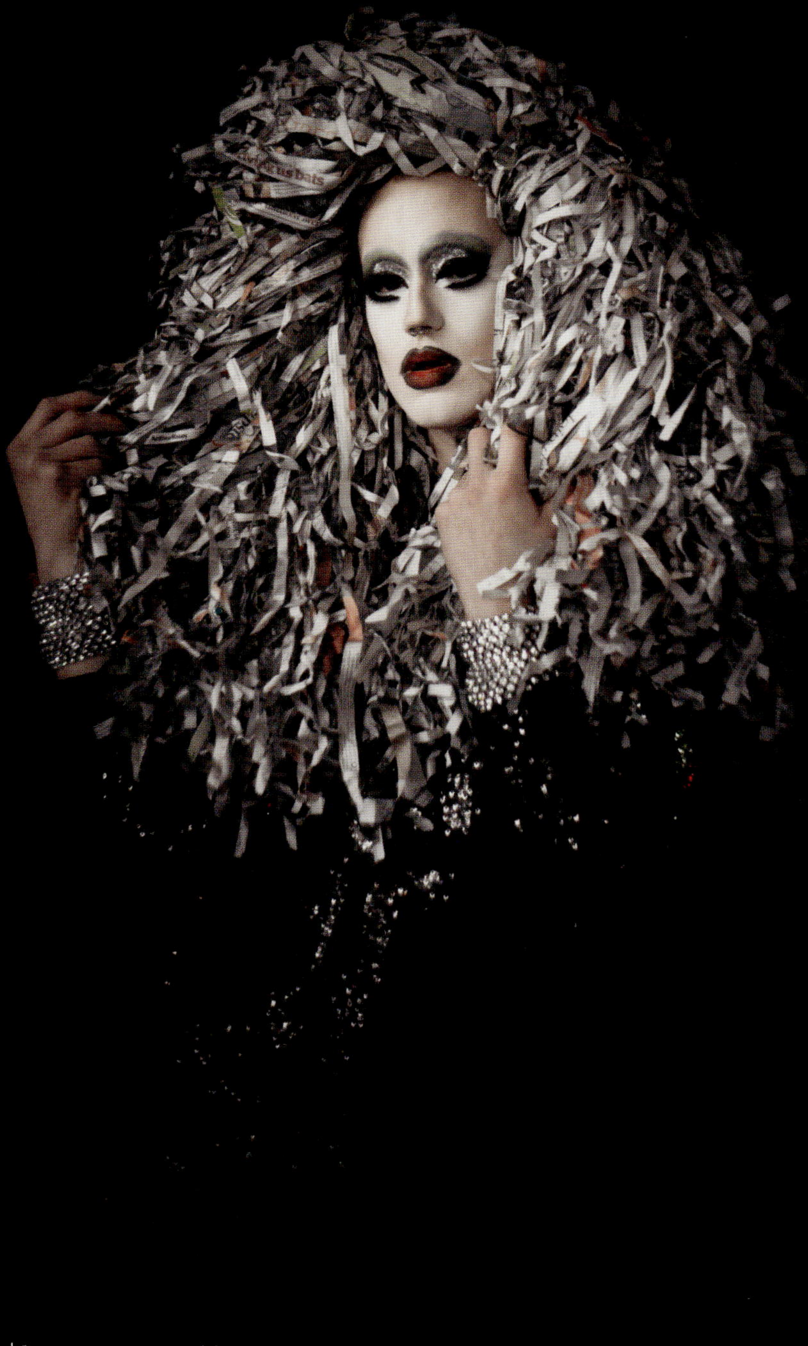

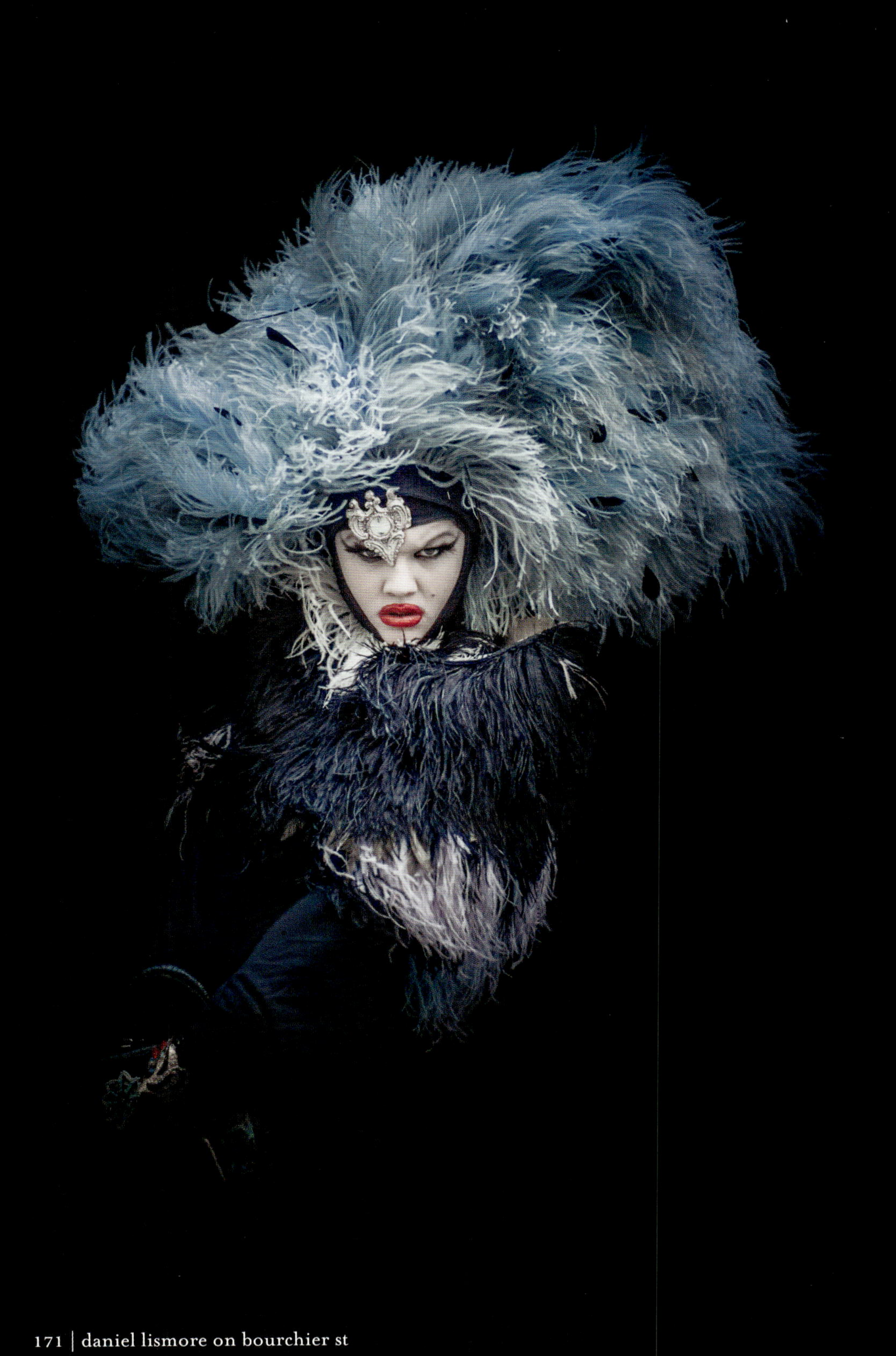

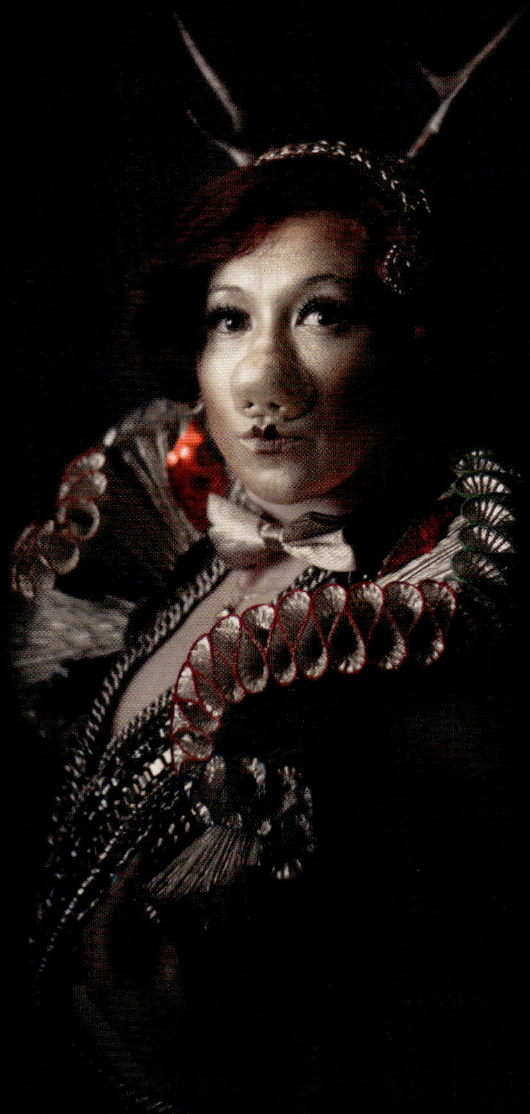

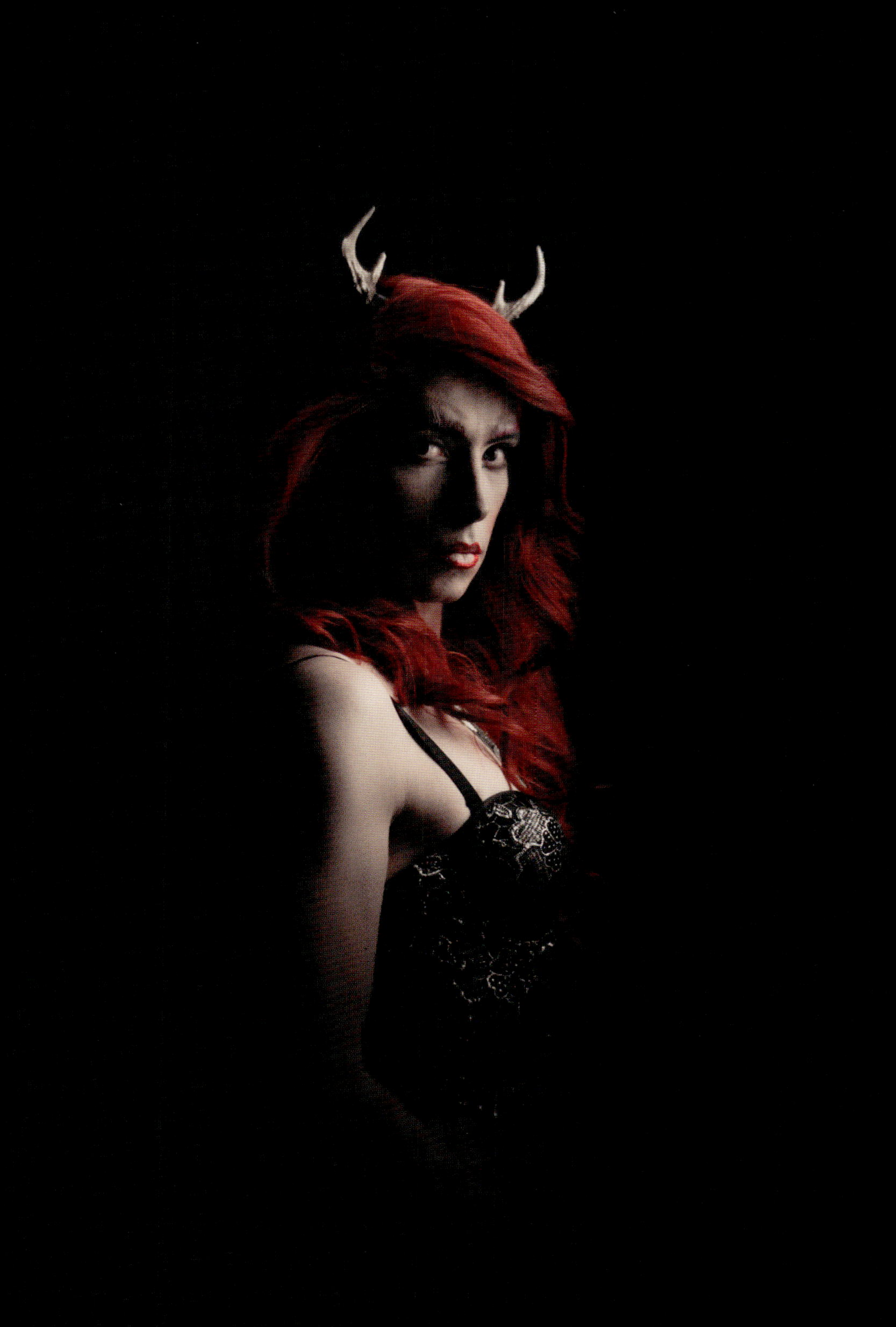

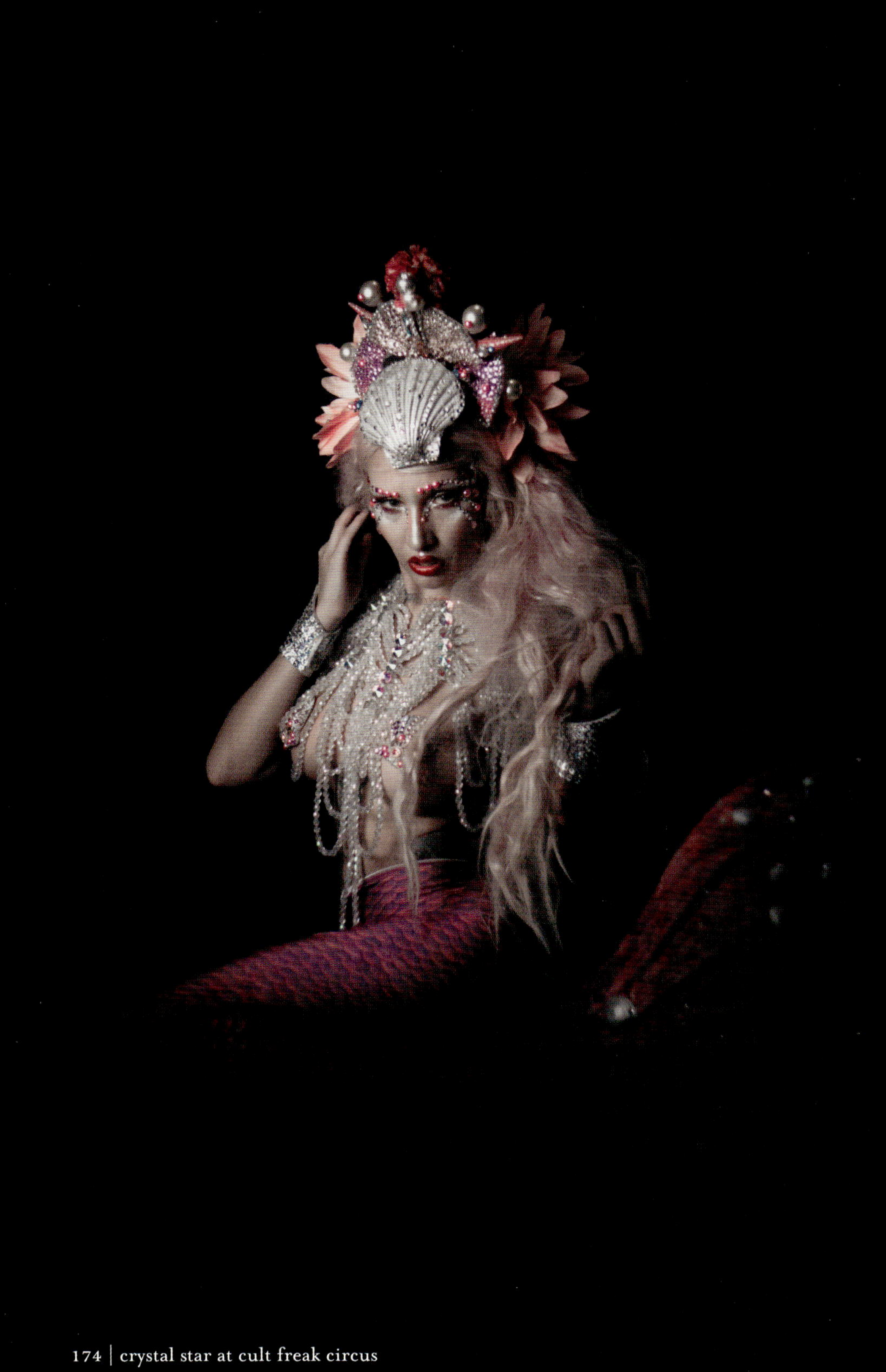

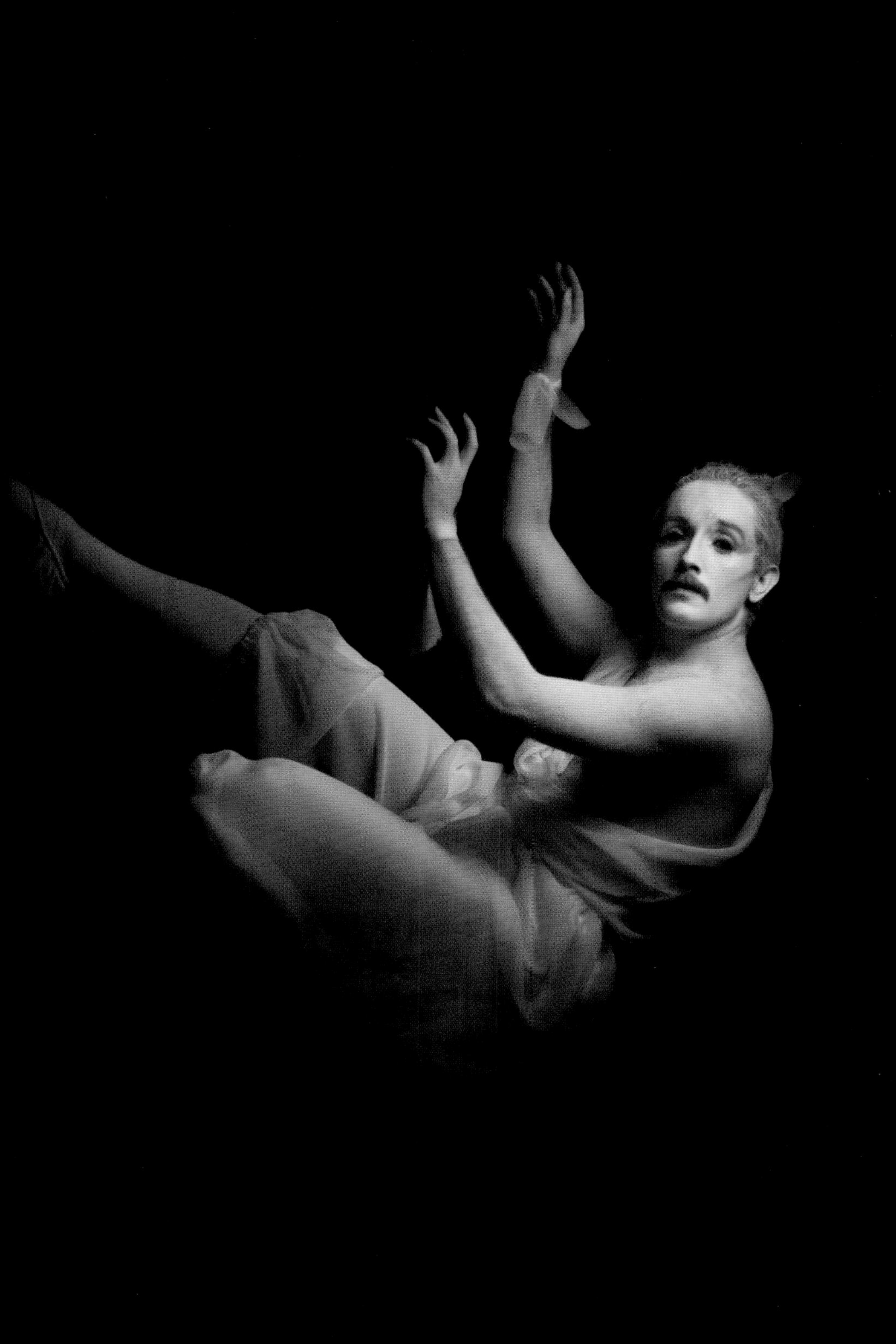

 | pi the mime at bethnal green working men's club

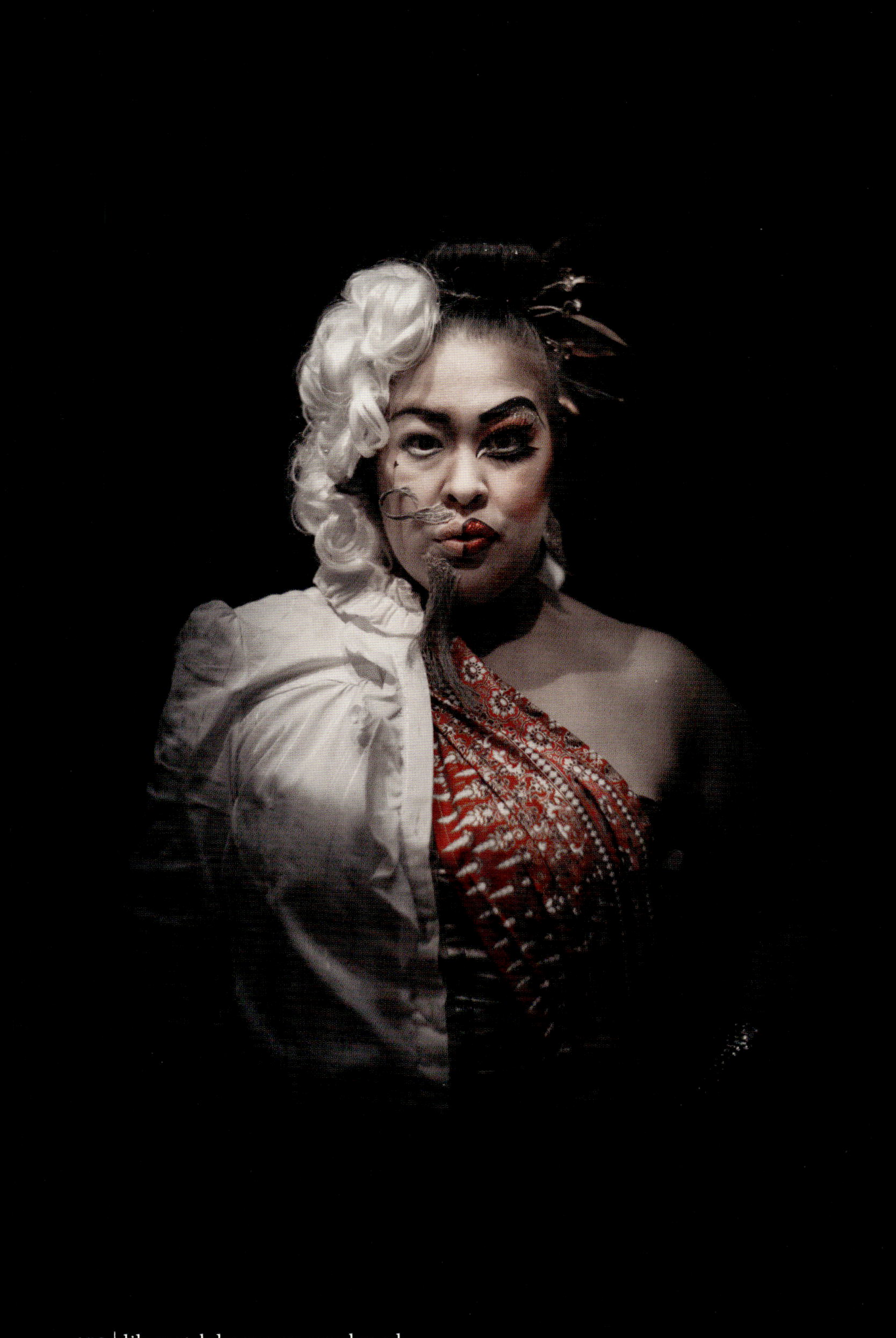

 | lily snatchdragon on camden rd

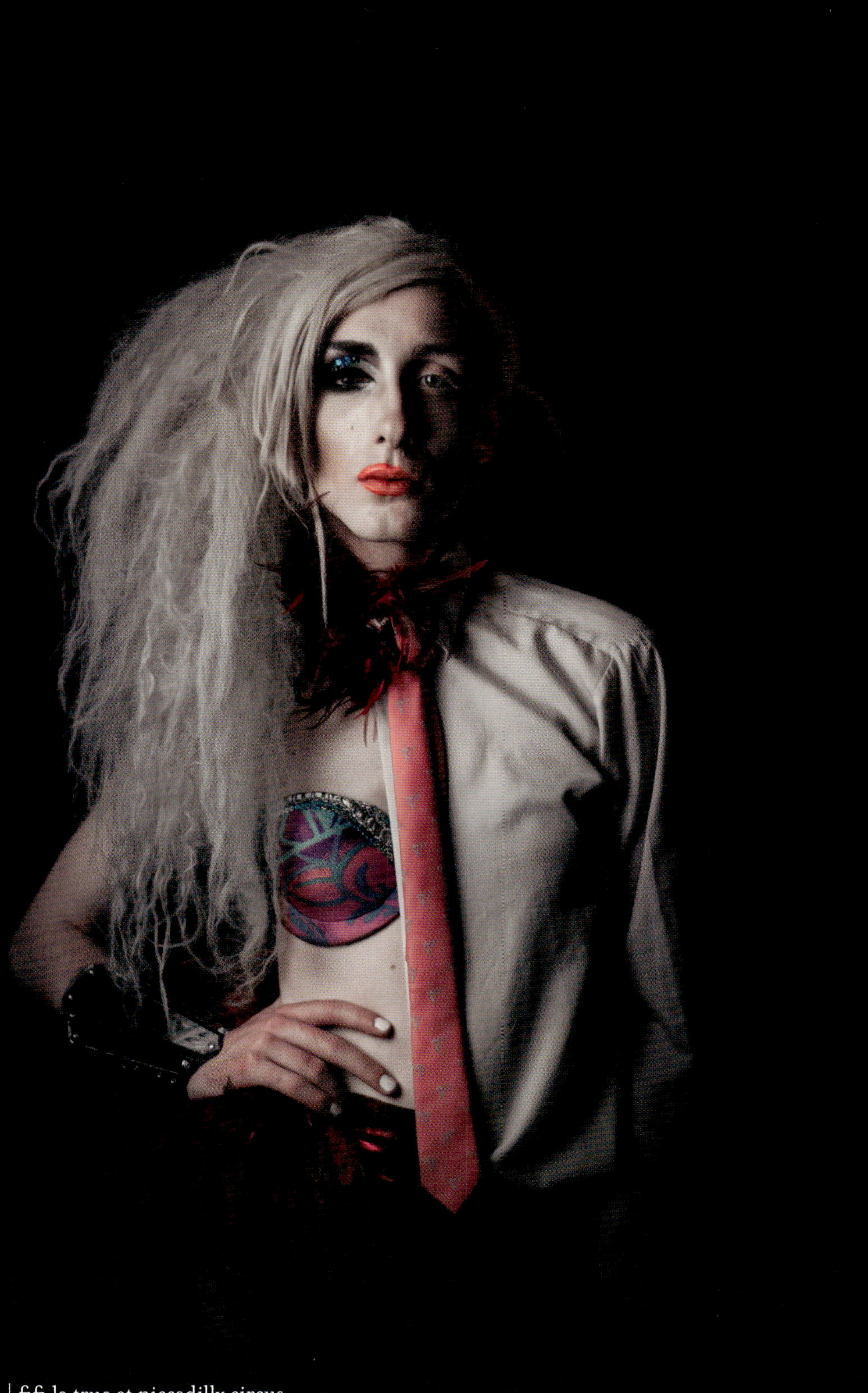

| fifi la true at piccadilly circus

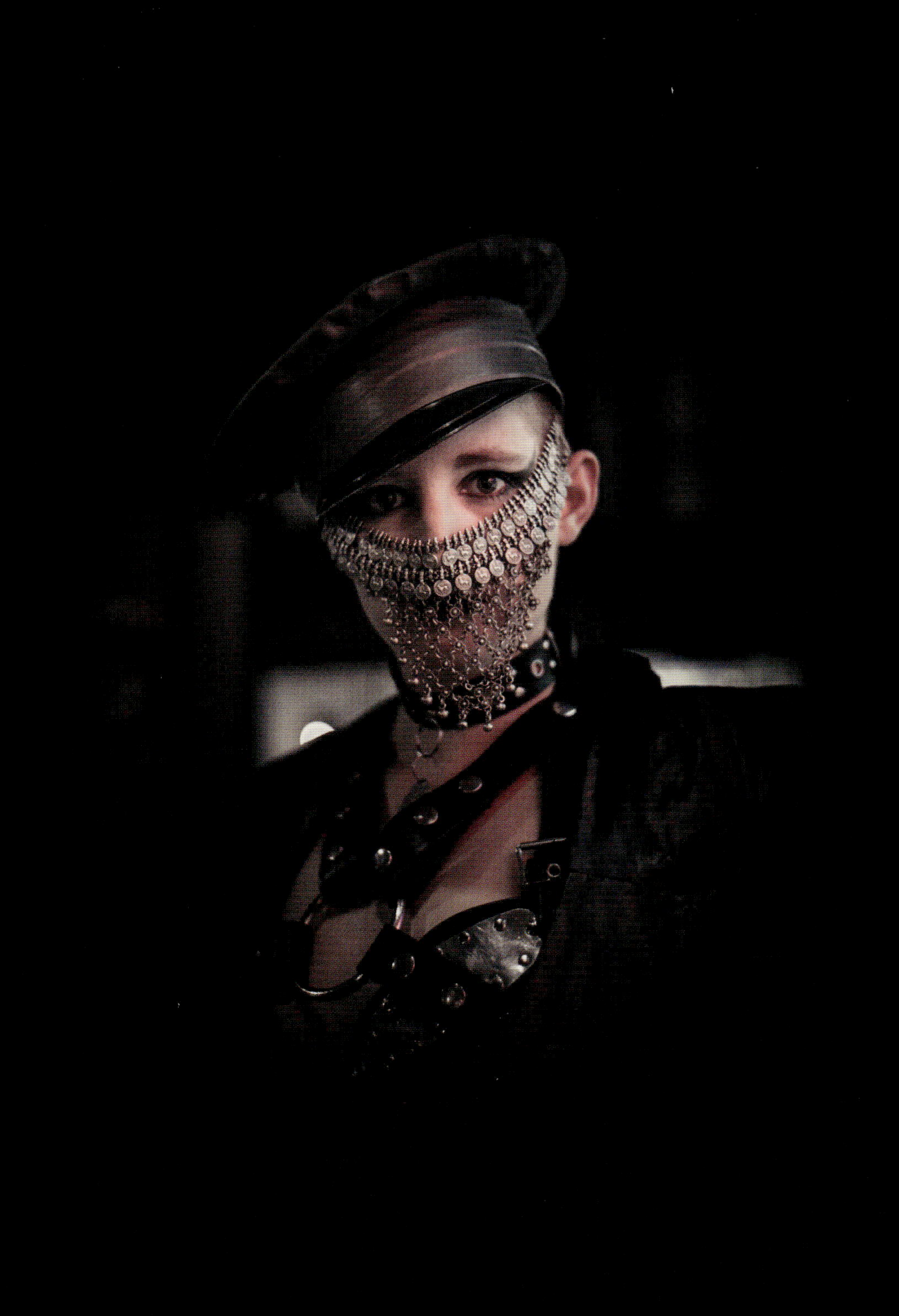

178 | amy kingsmill on brewer st

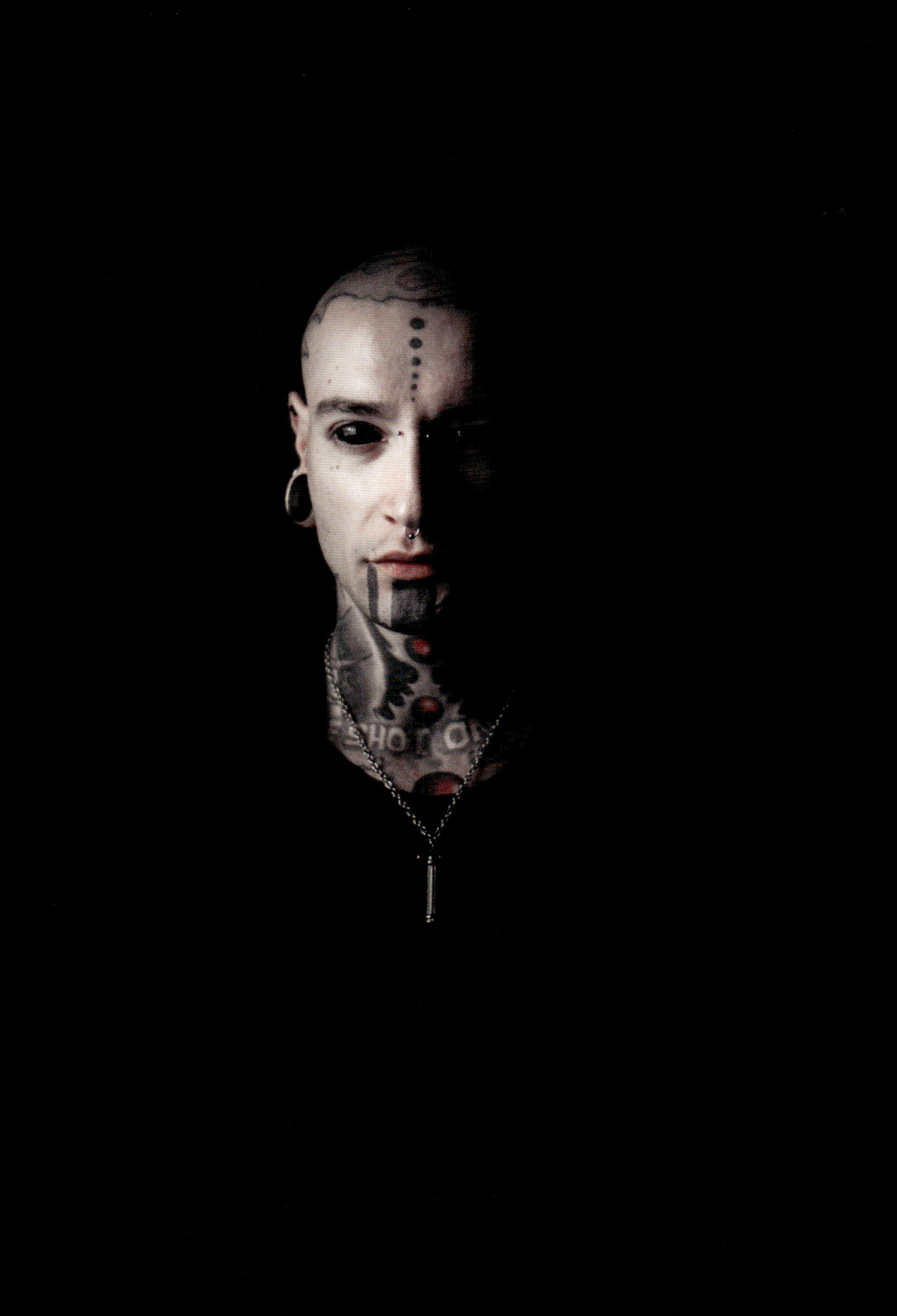

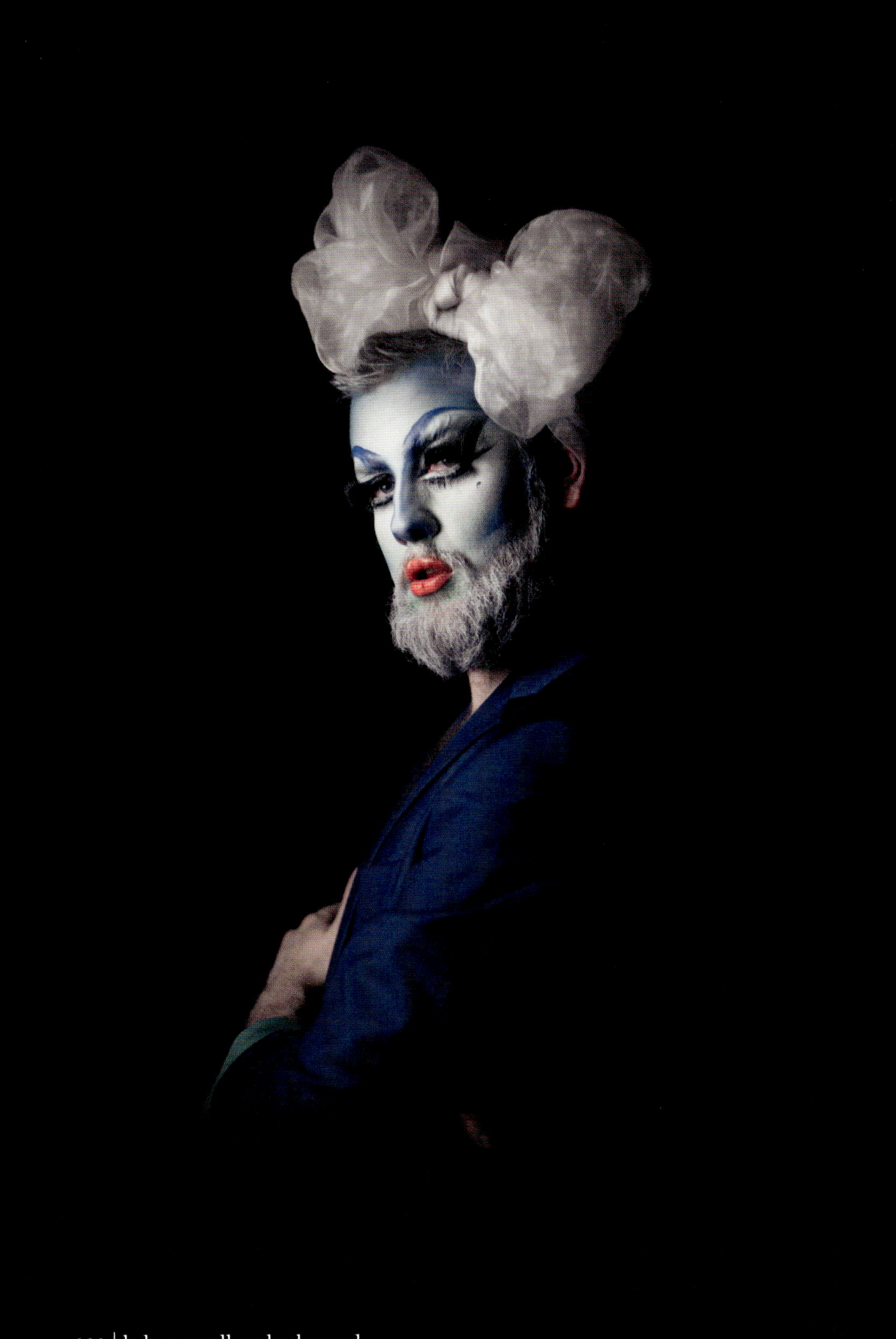

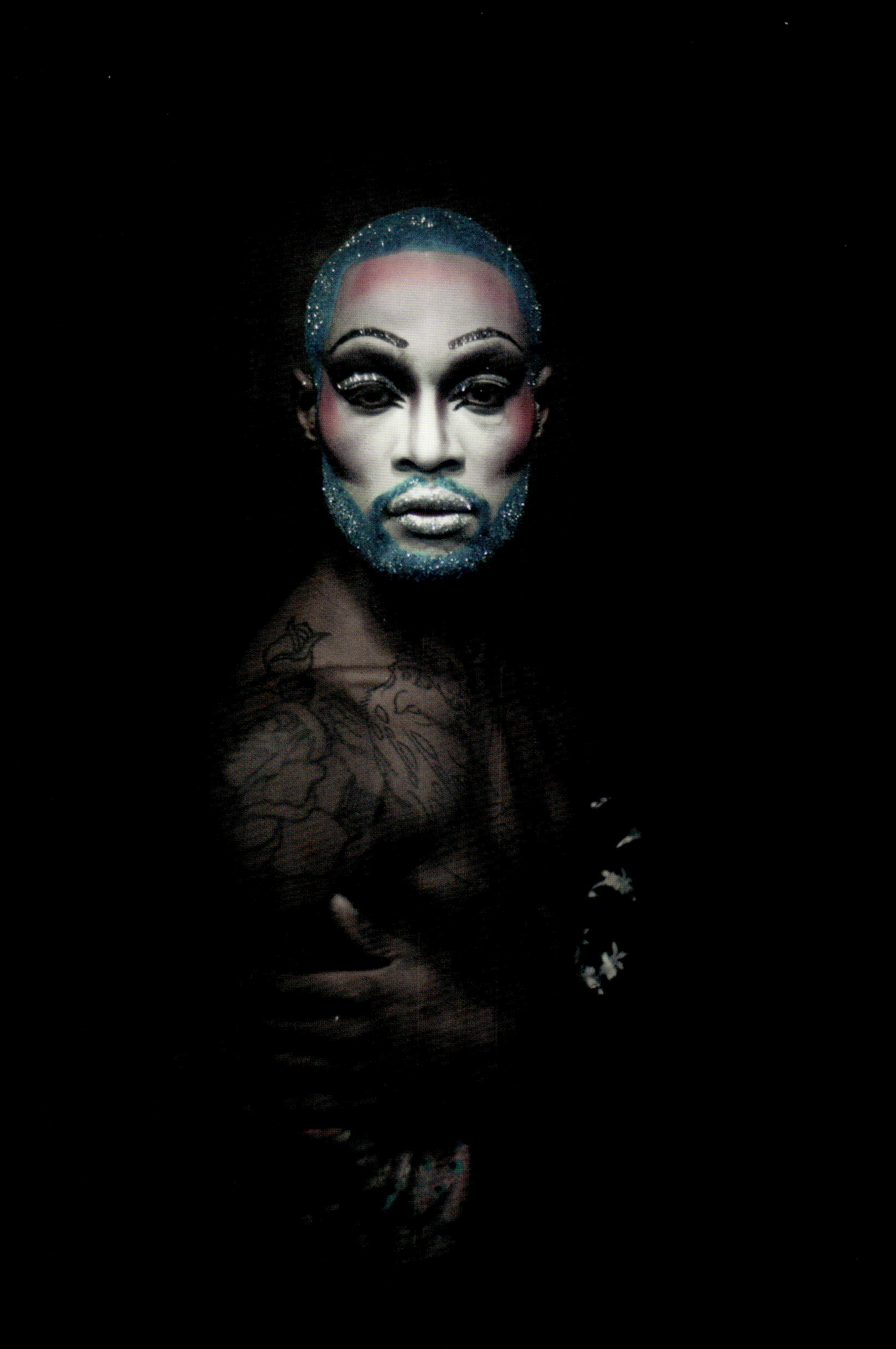

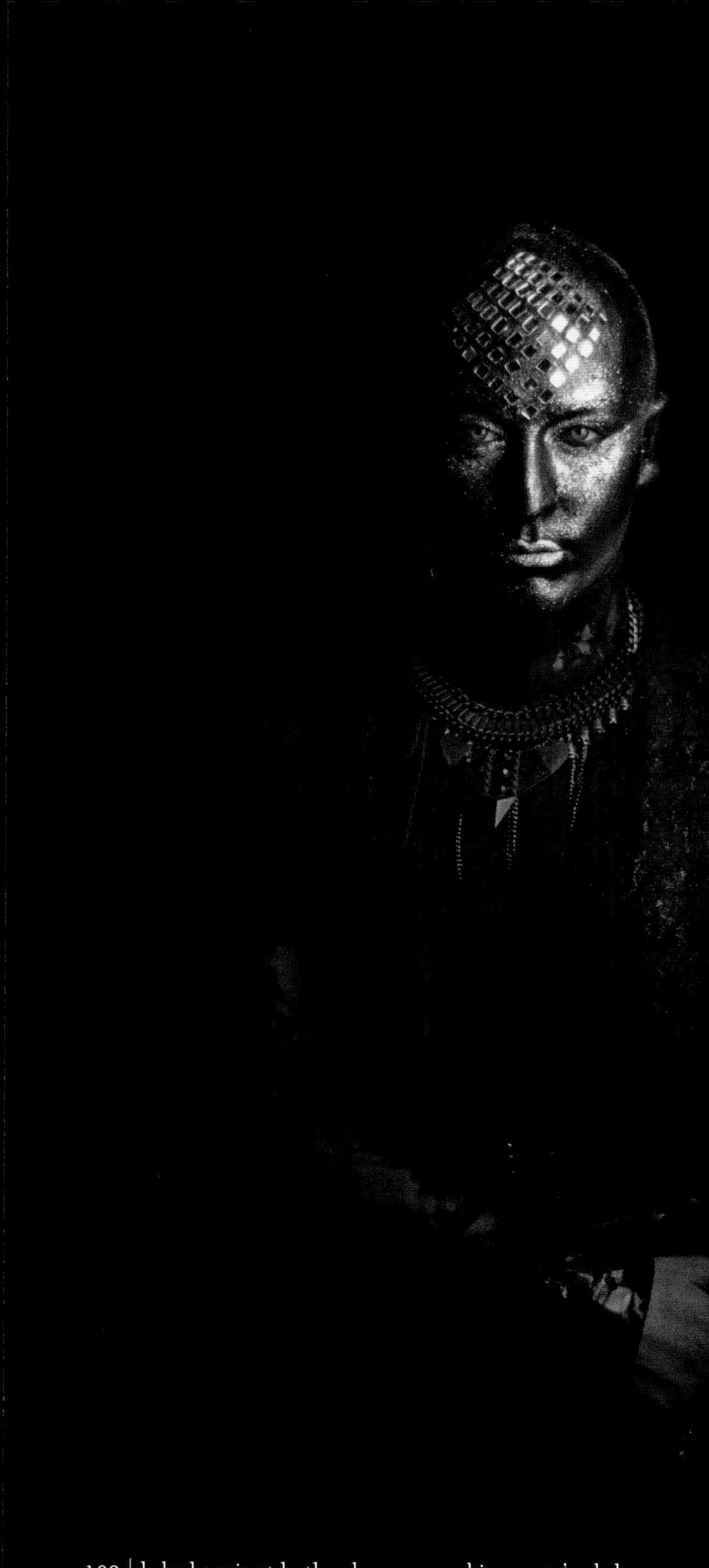

182 | luke harris at bethnal green working men's club

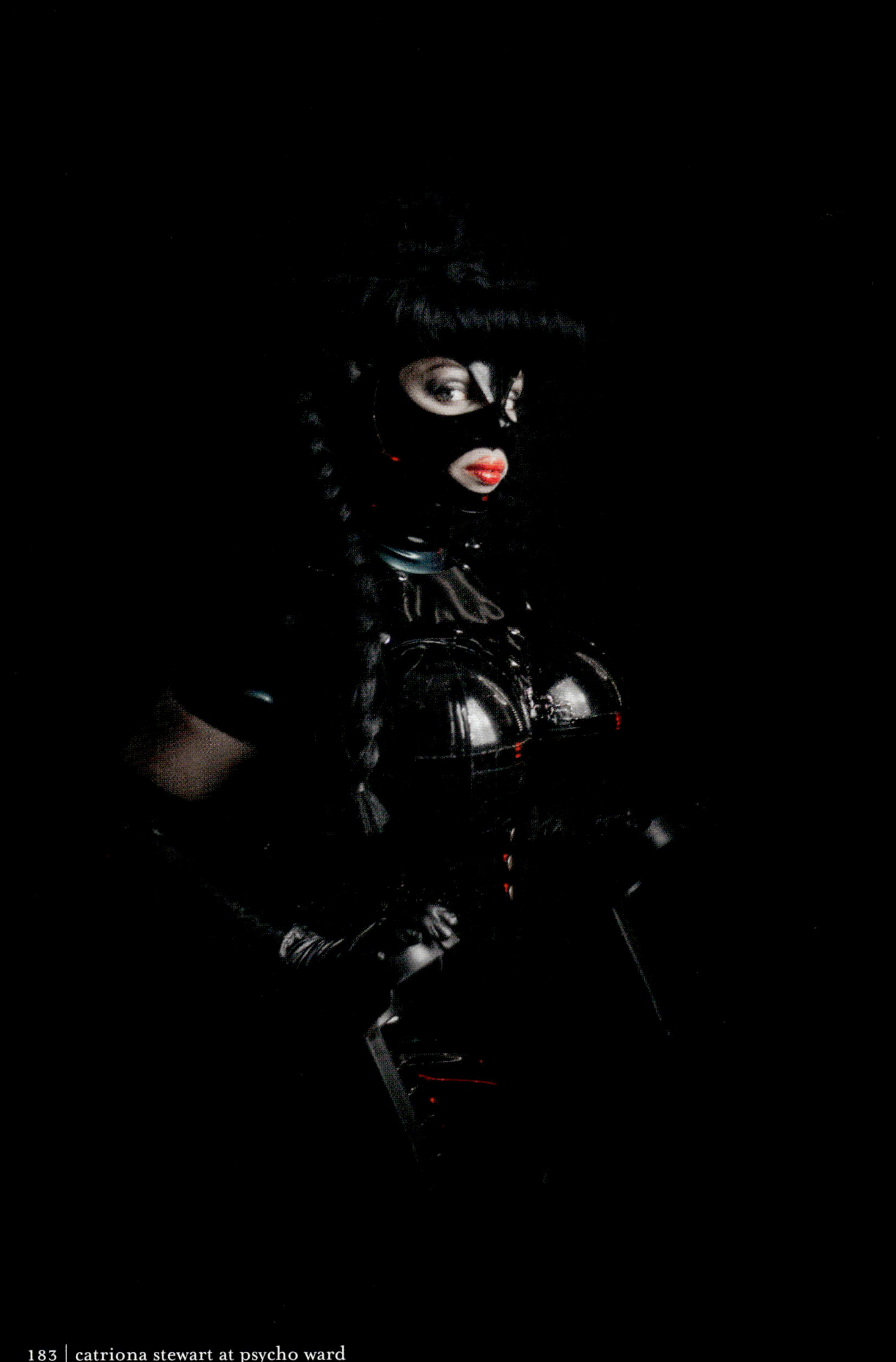

 | catriona stewart at psycho ward

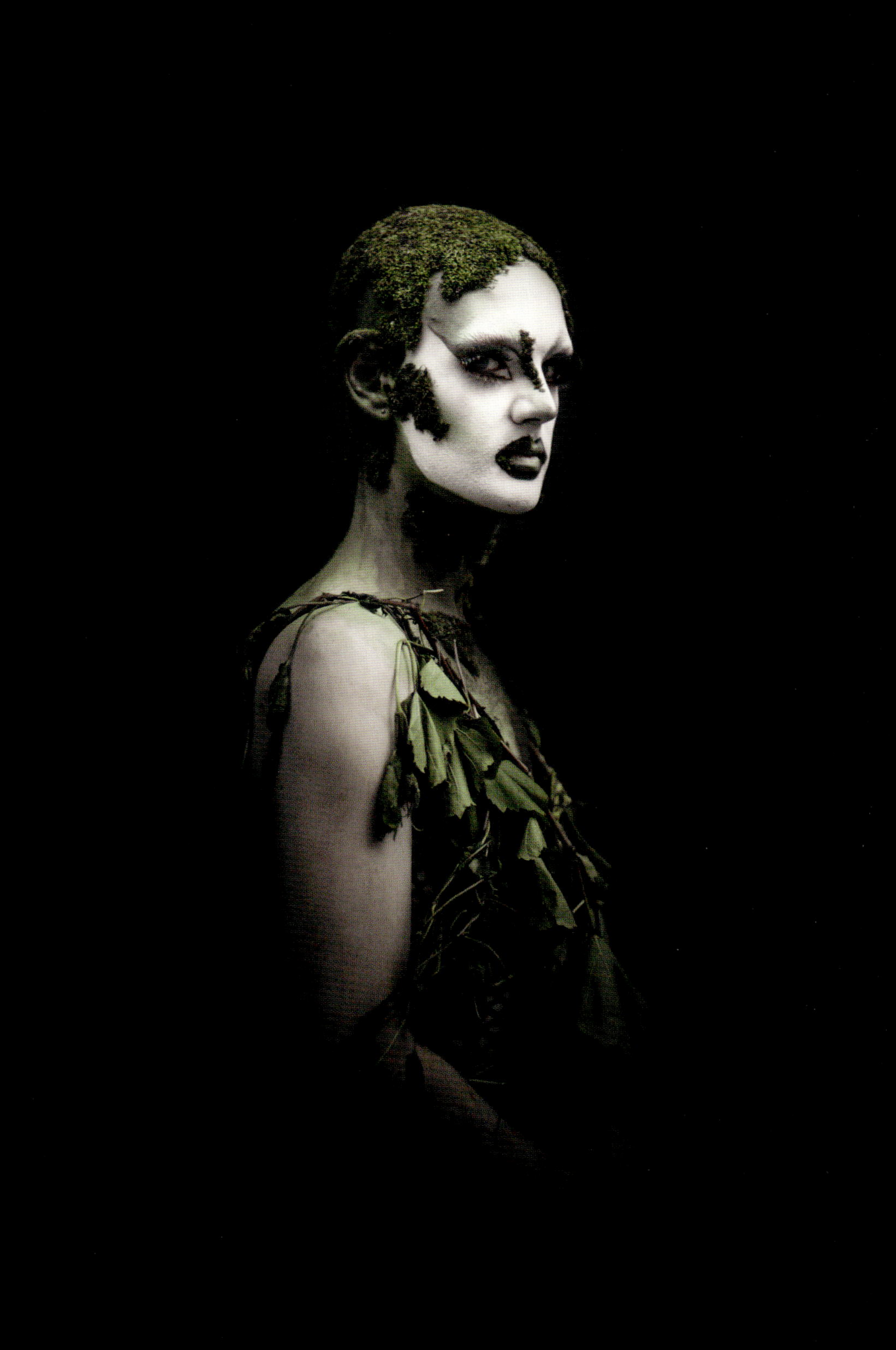

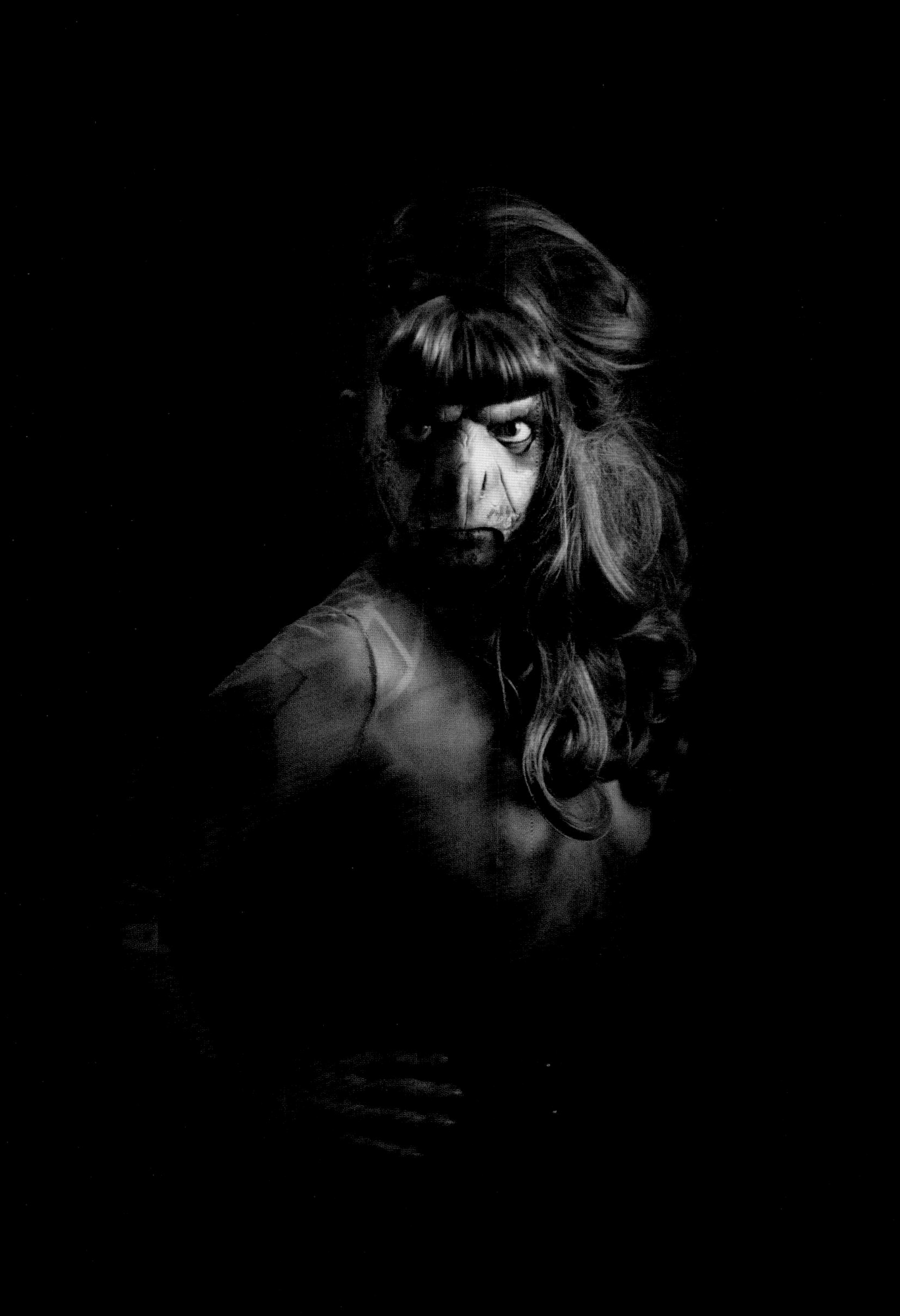

 | lolo brow at it's your funeral

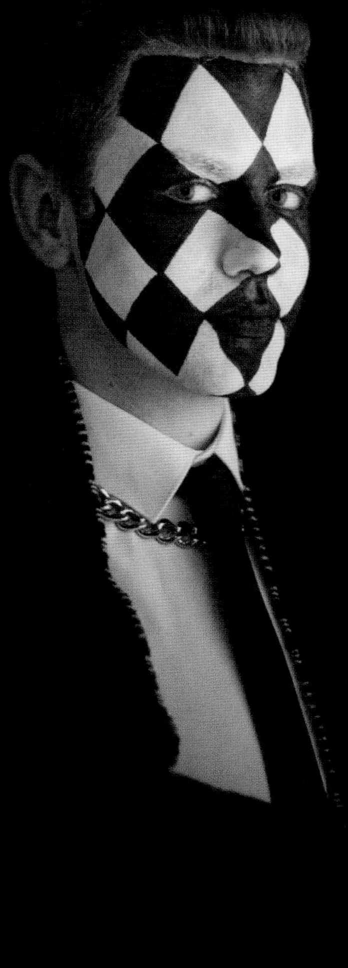

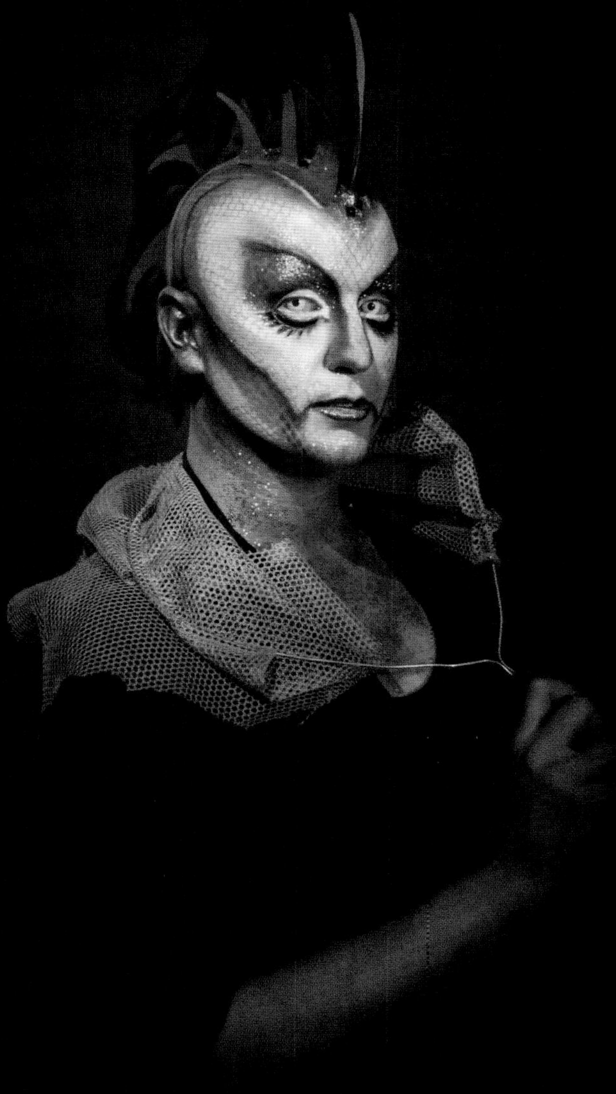

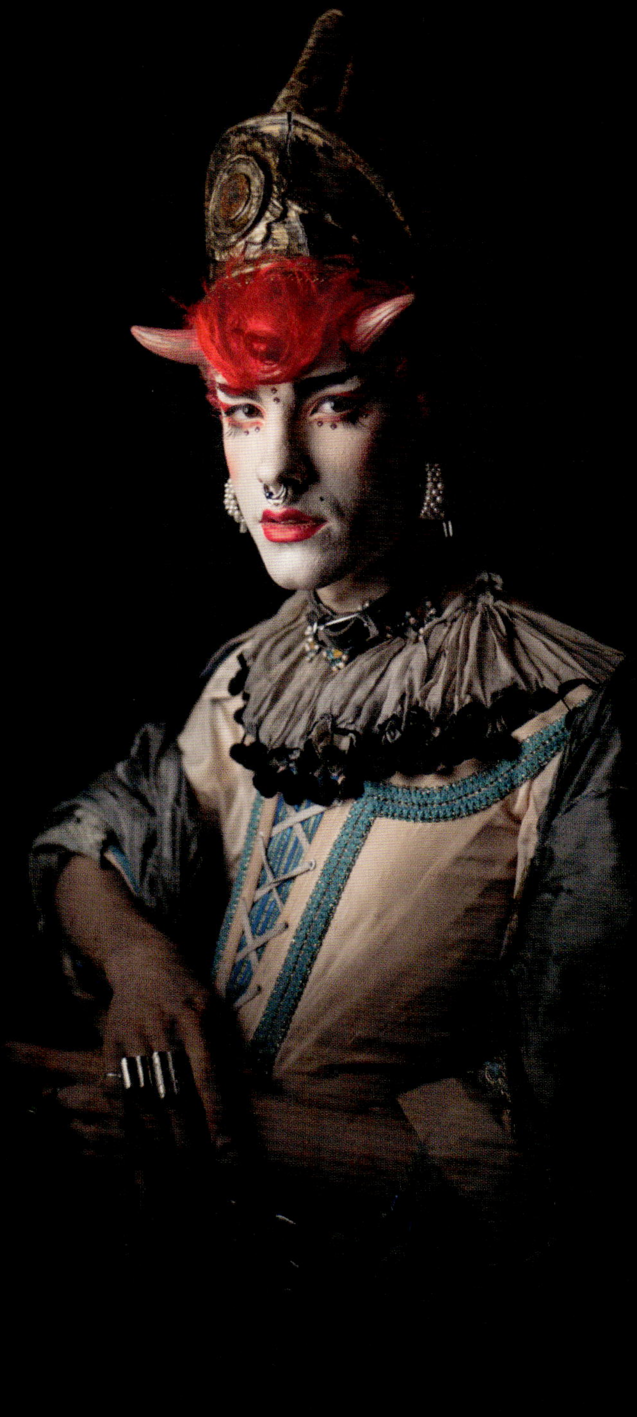

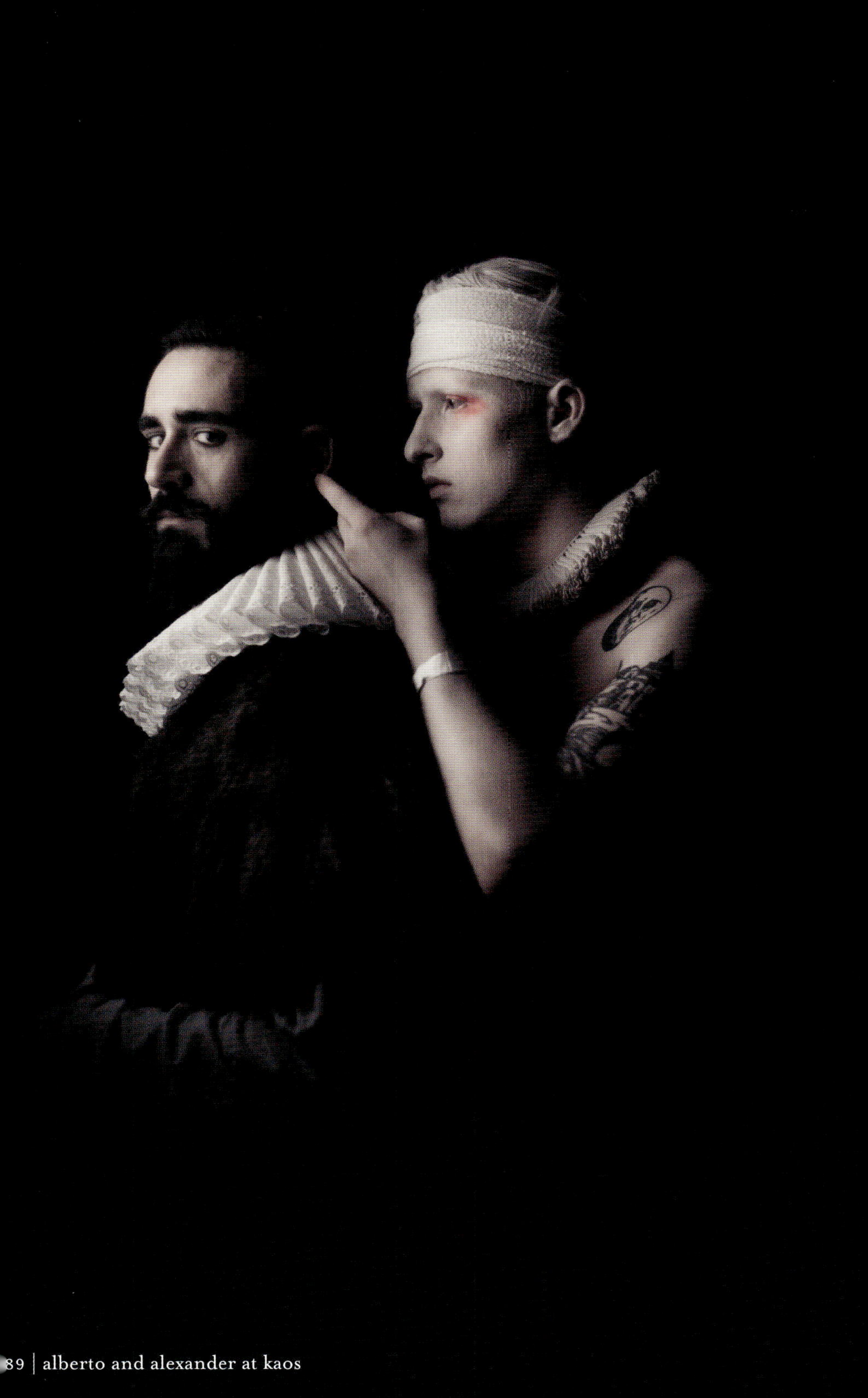

 | alberto and alexander at kaos

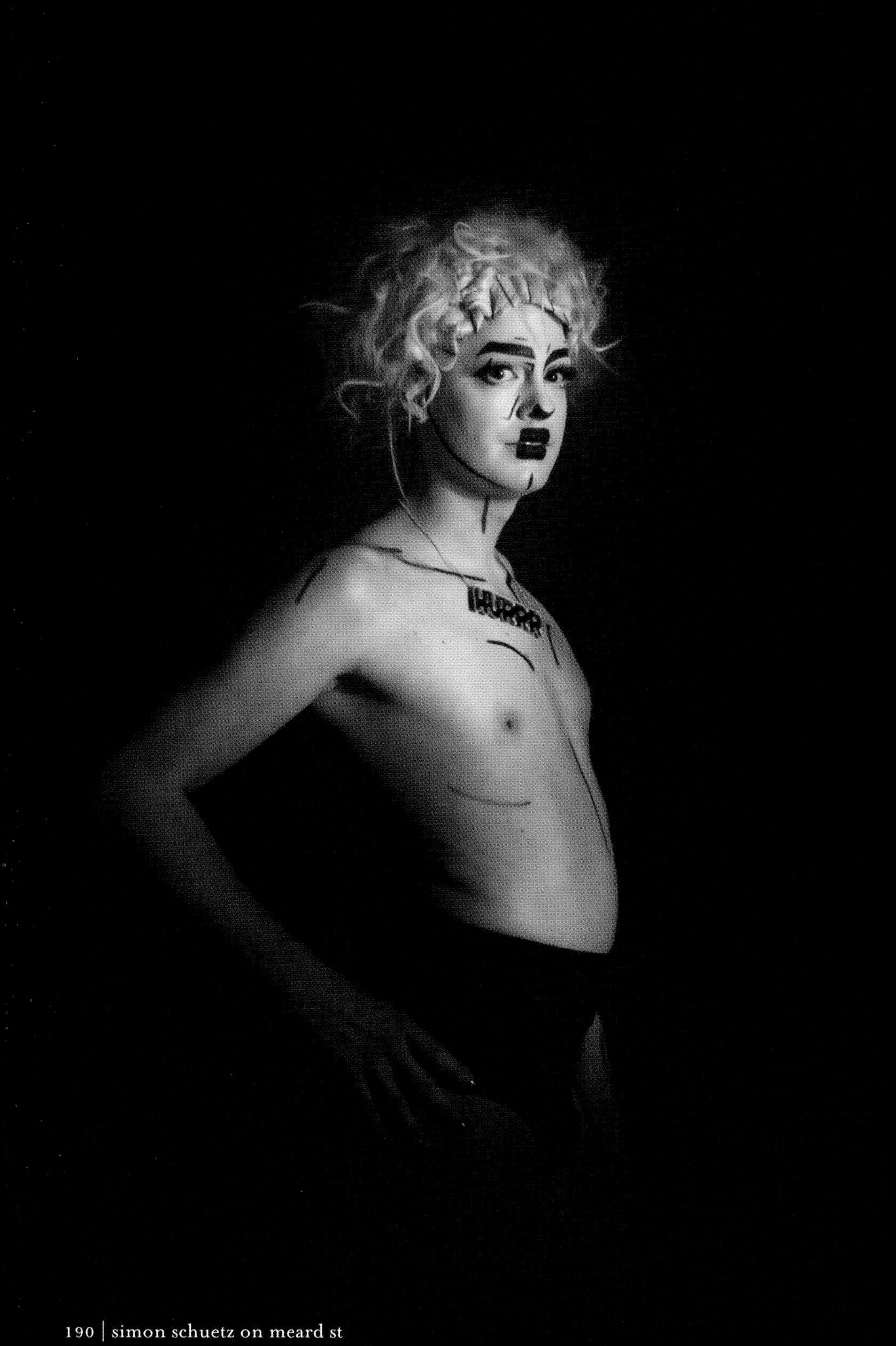

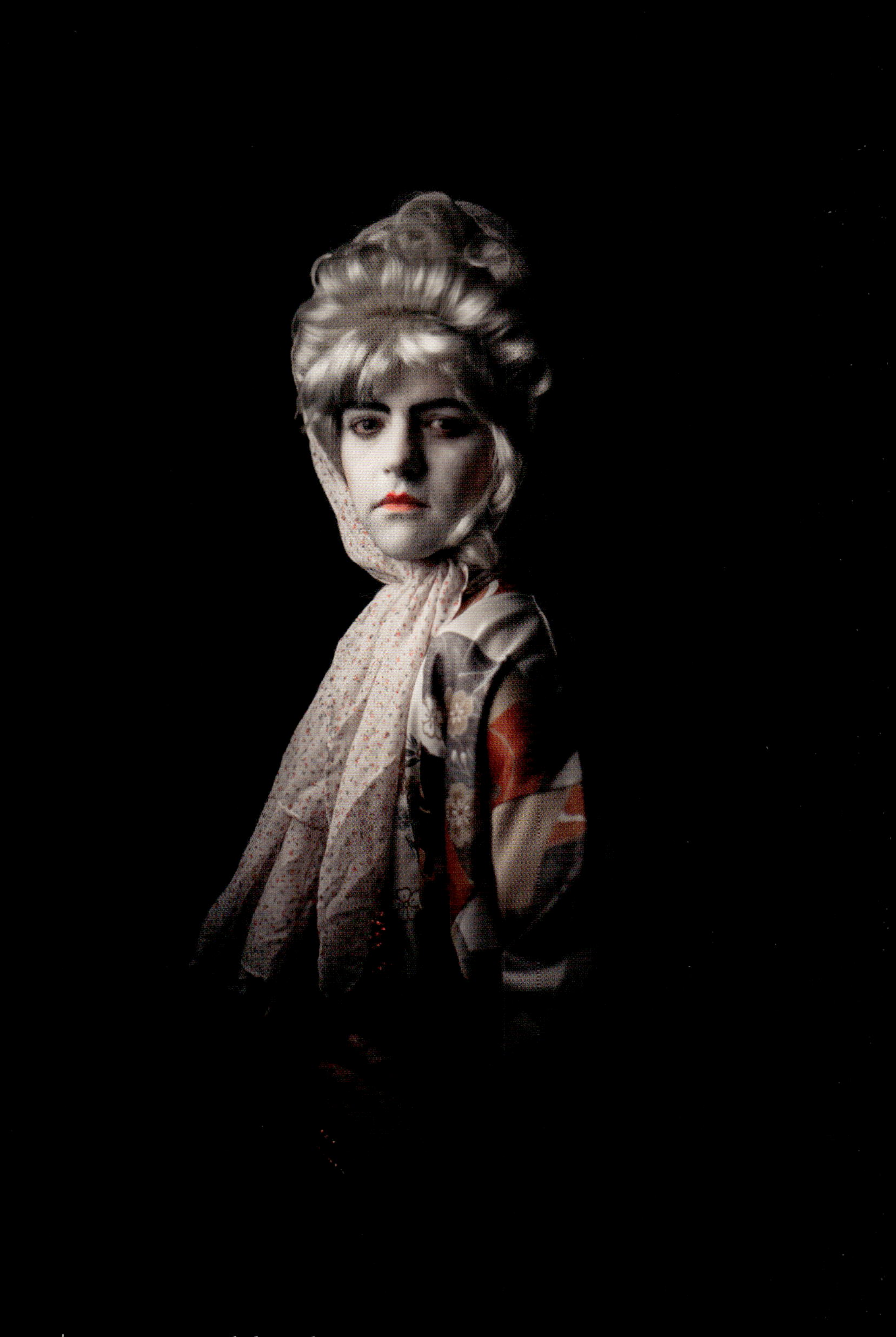

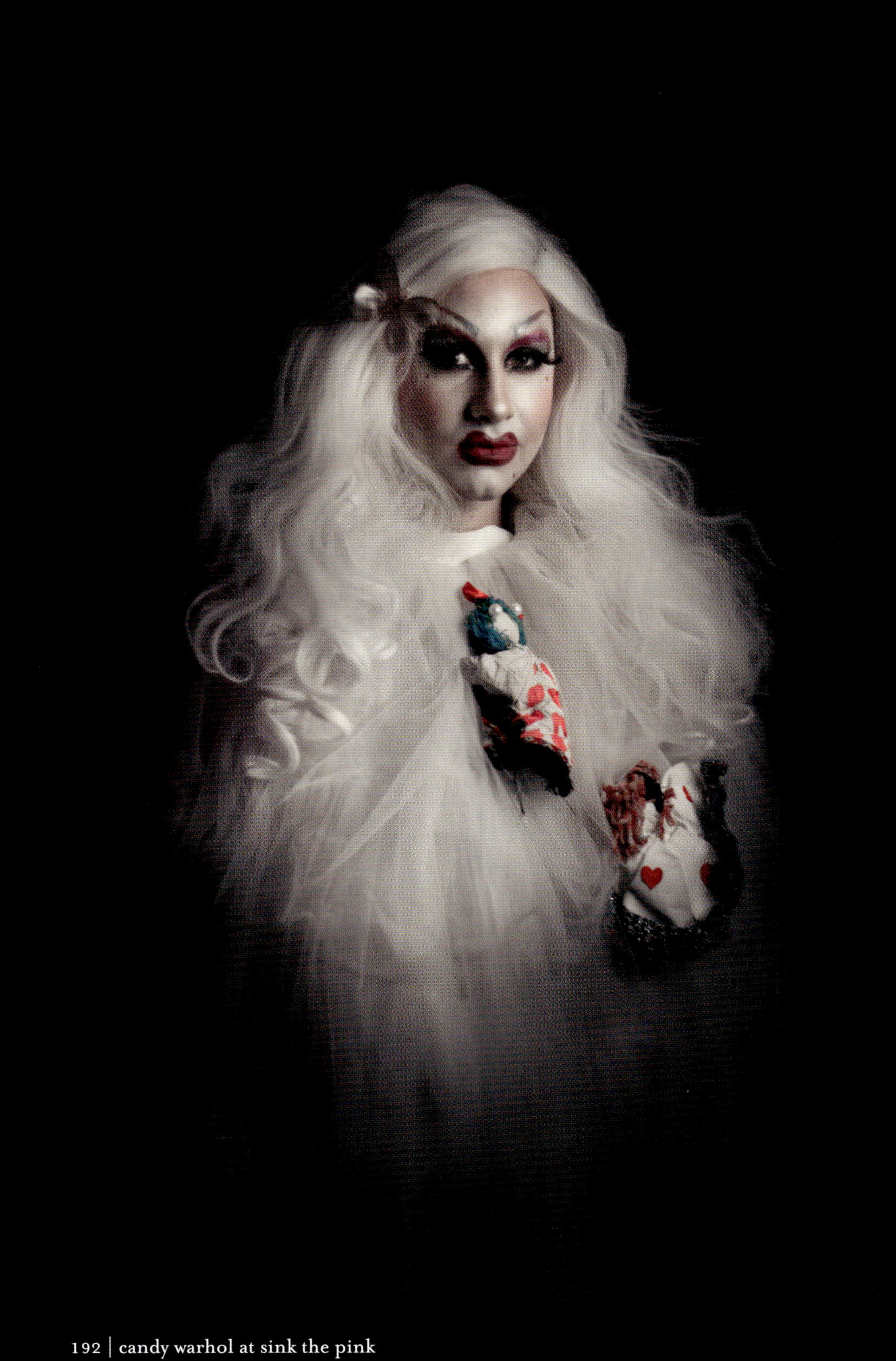

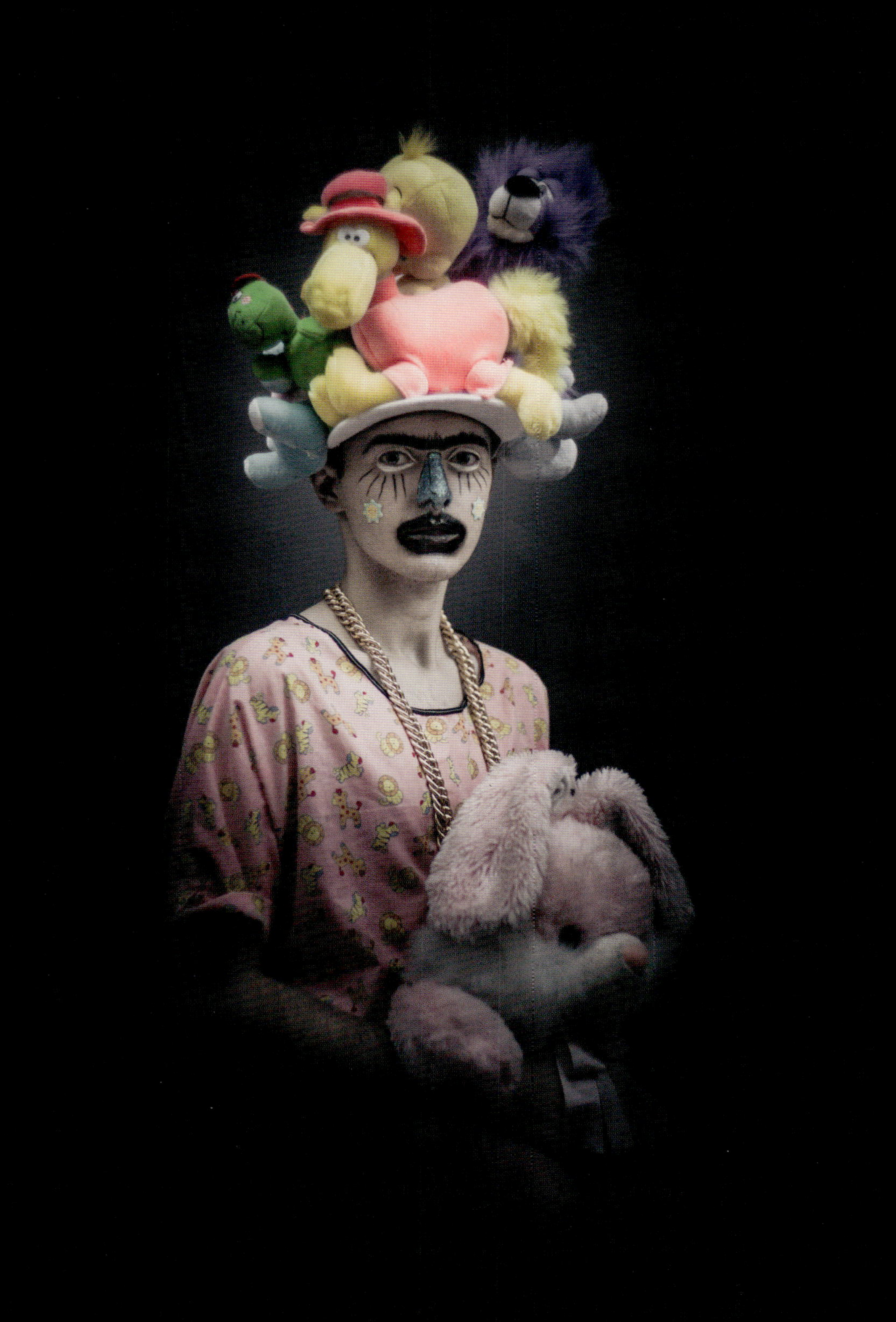

 | jason summerfield on brompton rd

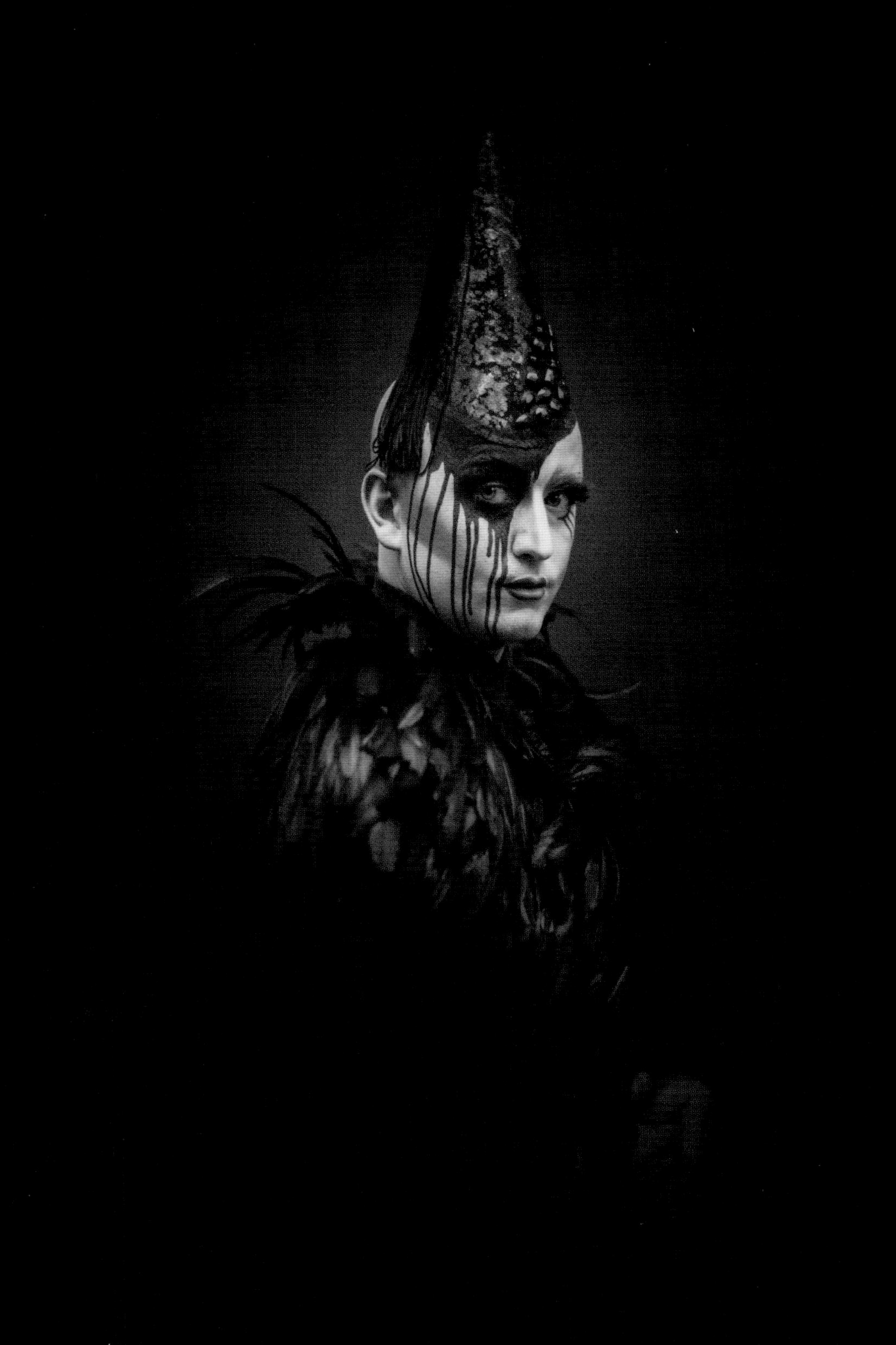

194 | luke harris on brompton rd

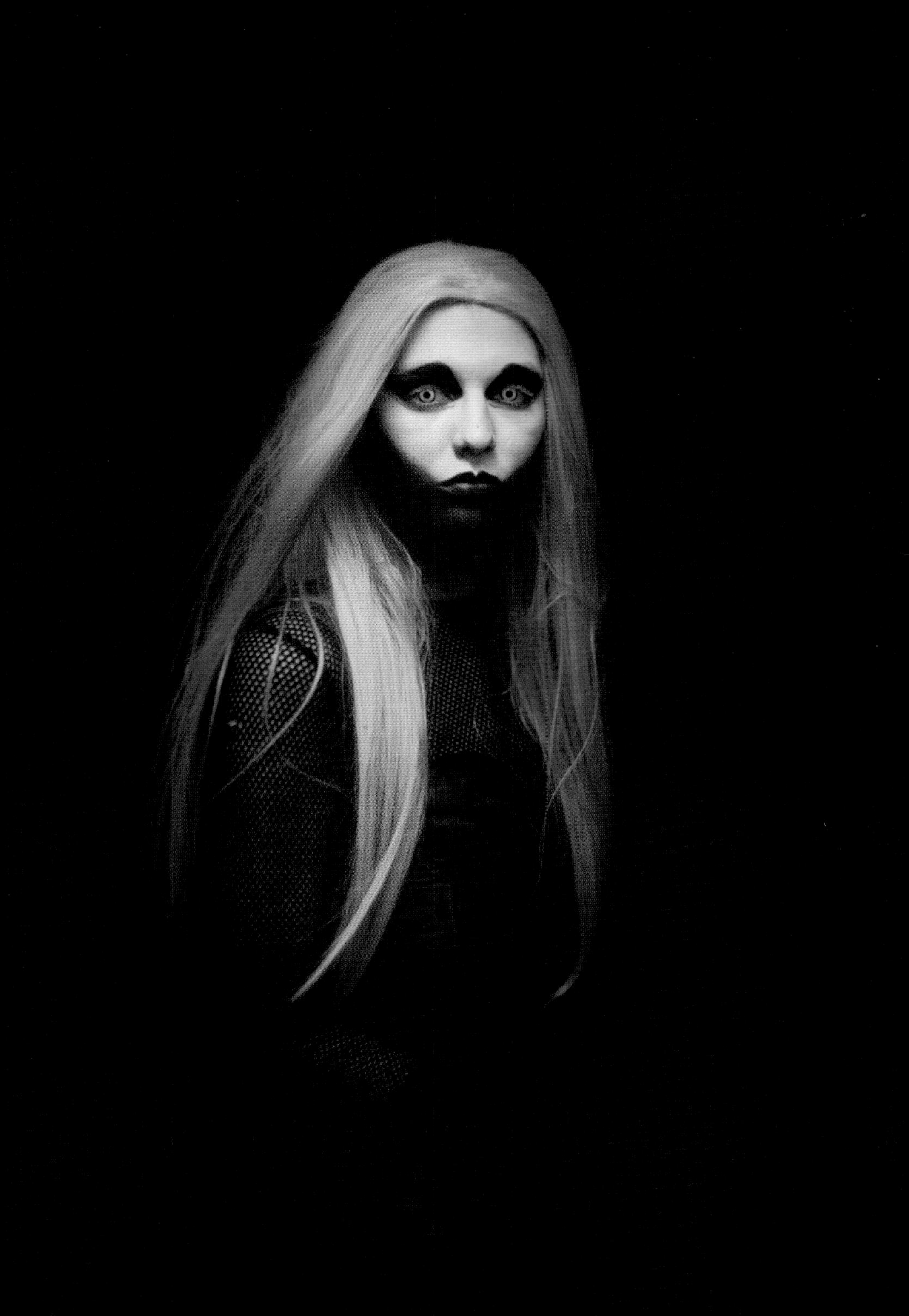

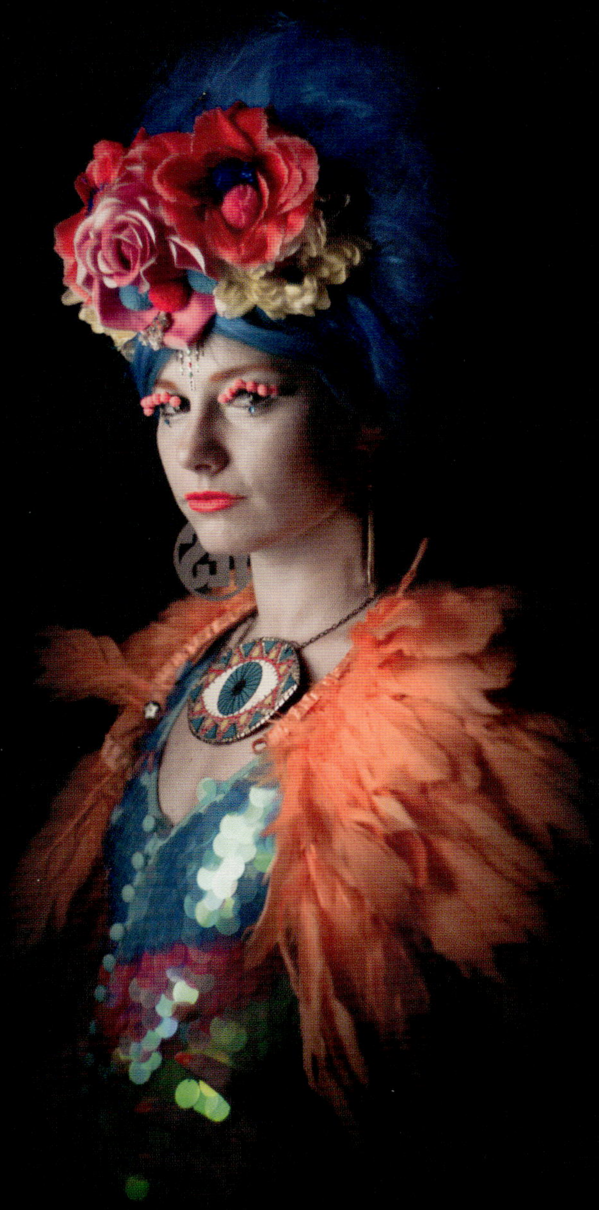

twinks burnett at sink the pink

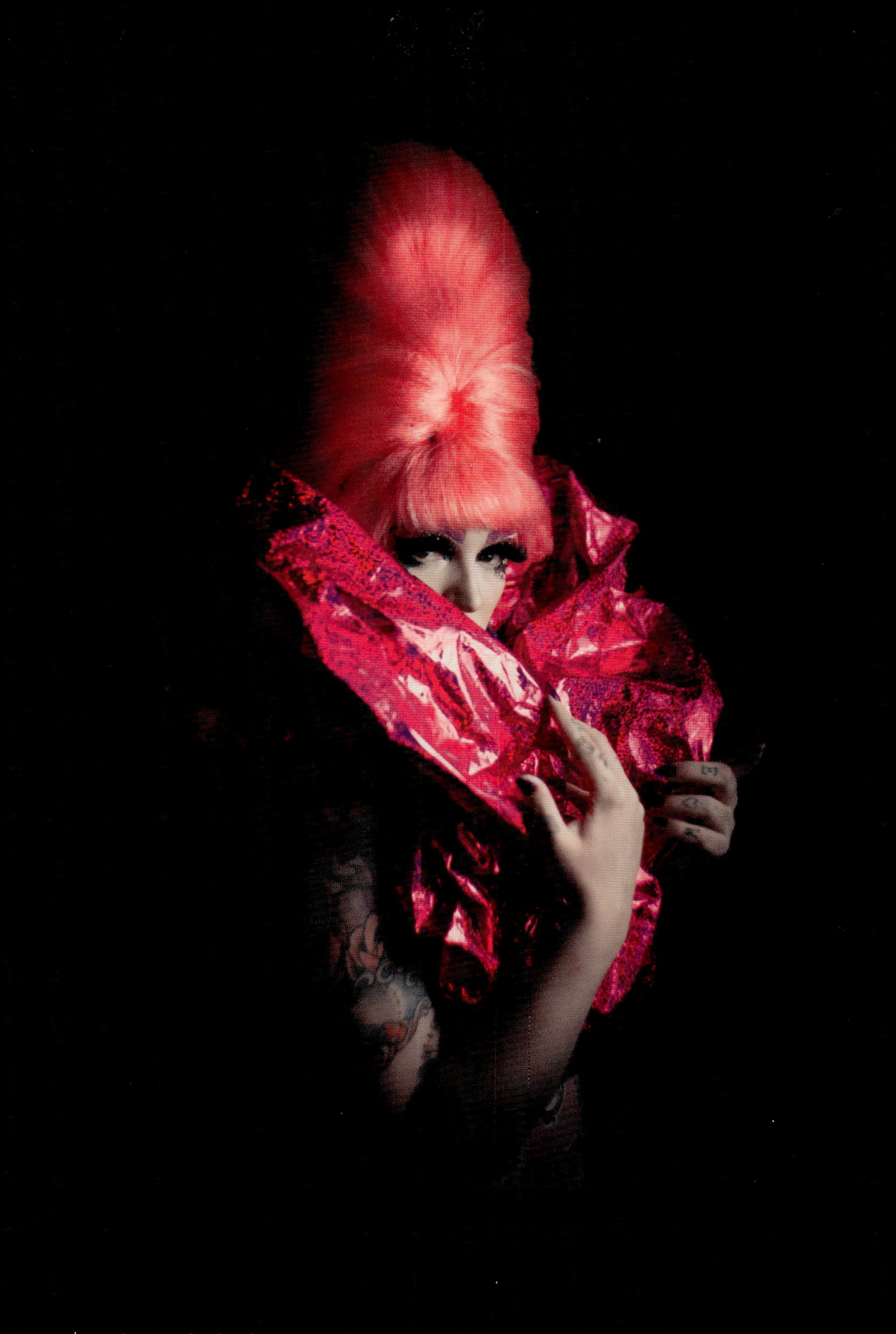

197 | tete bang at bethnal green working men's club

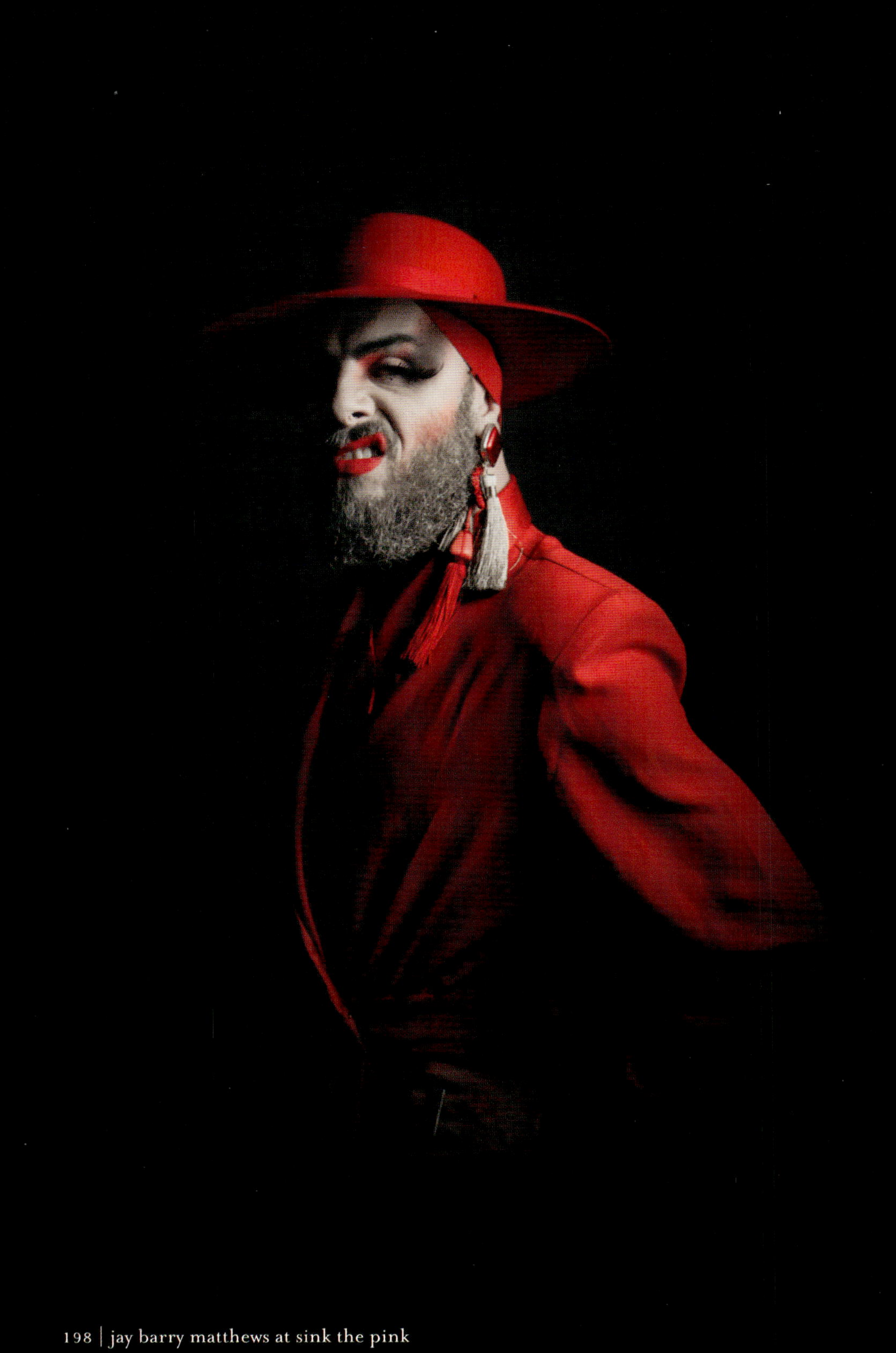

 | jay barry matthews at sink the pink

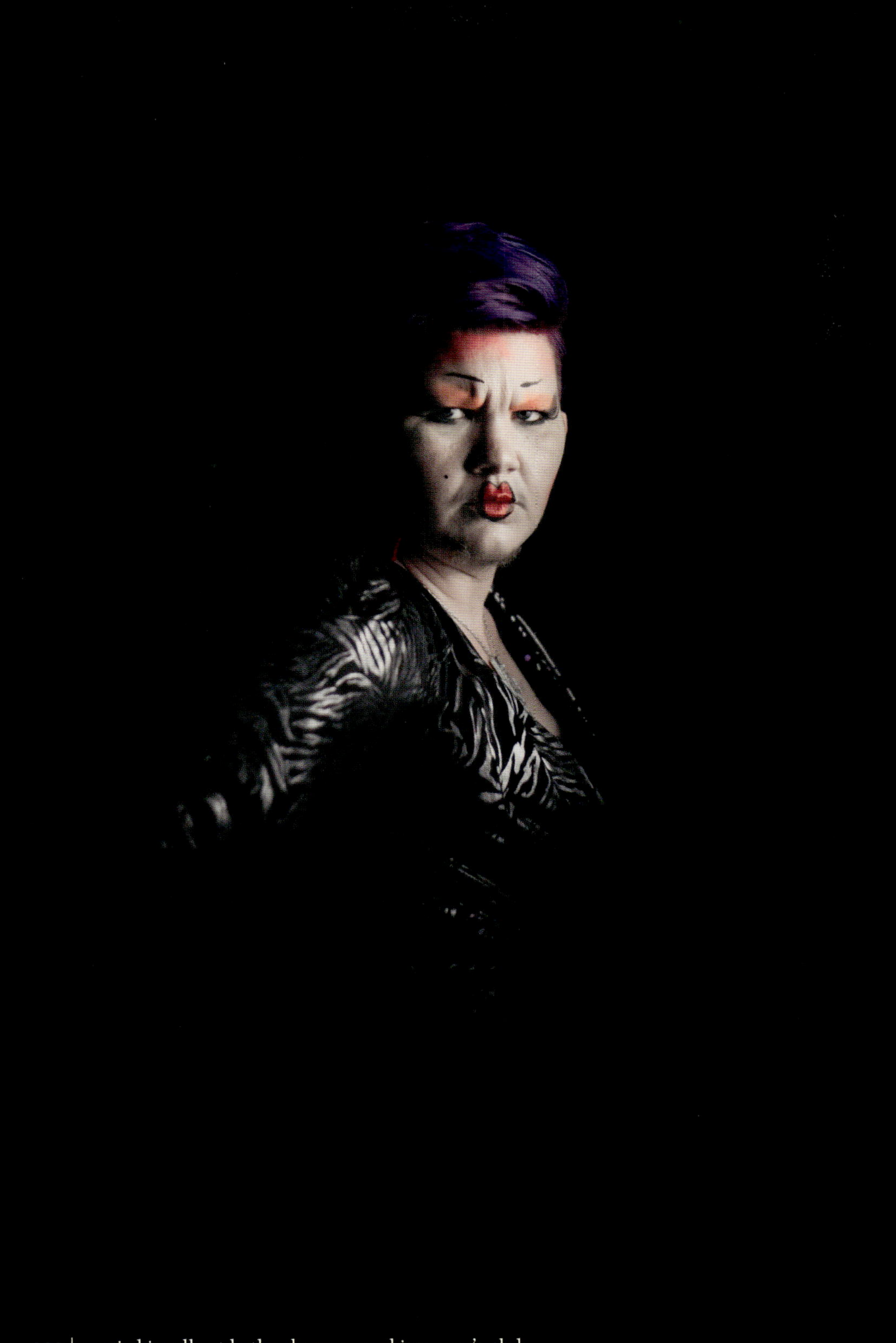

 maria kinsella at bethnal green working men's club

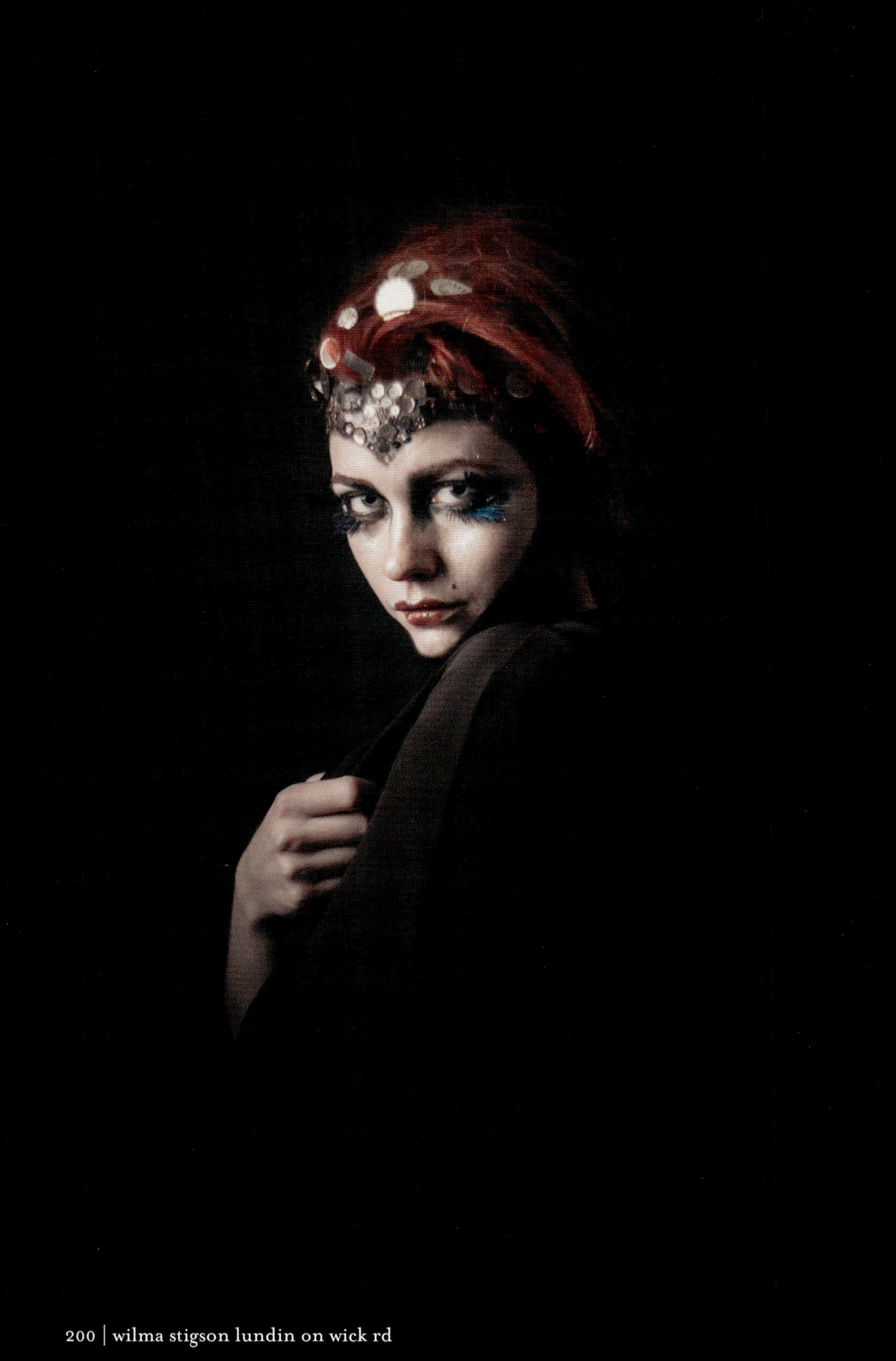

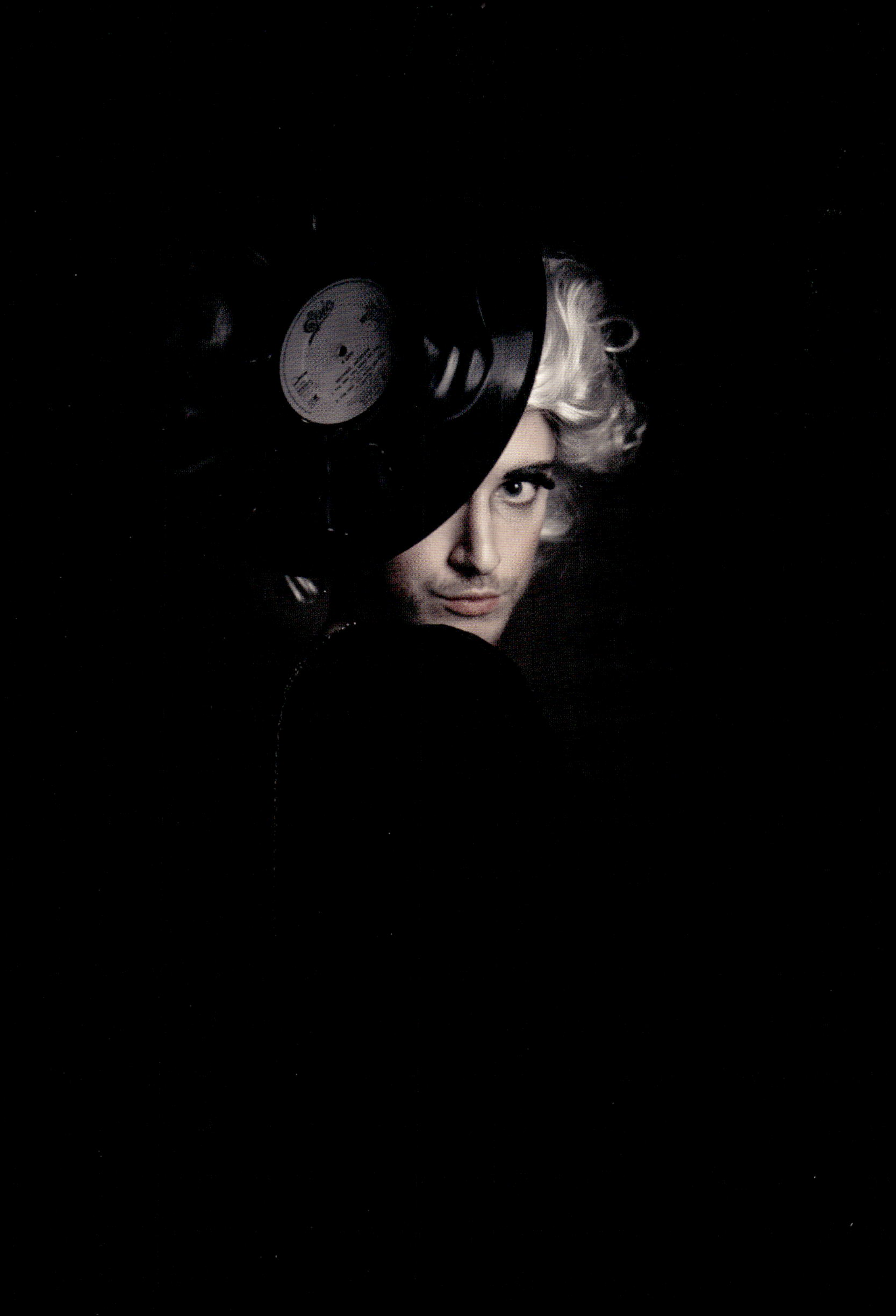

201 | barbara back at the sink the pink winter ball

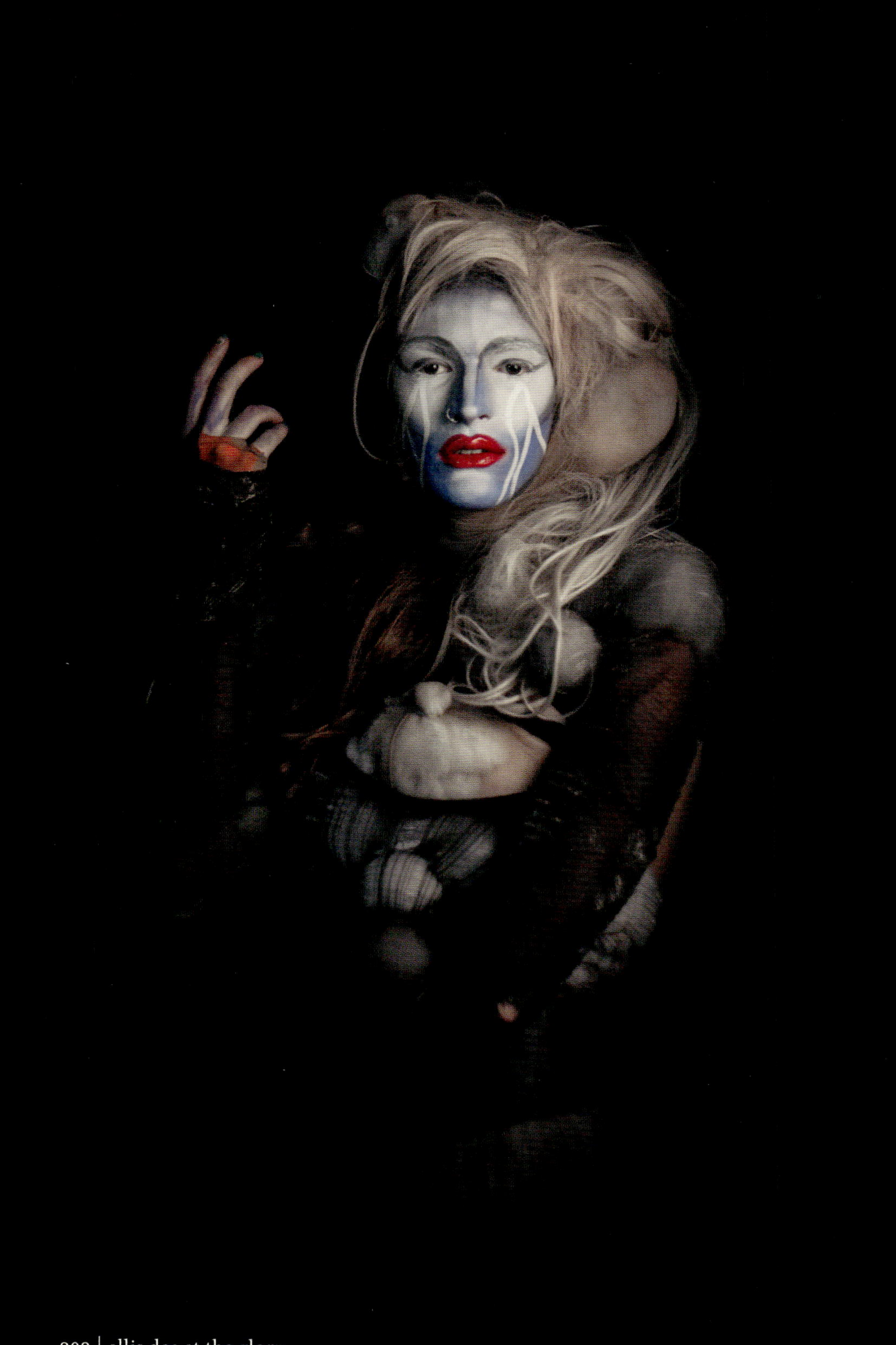

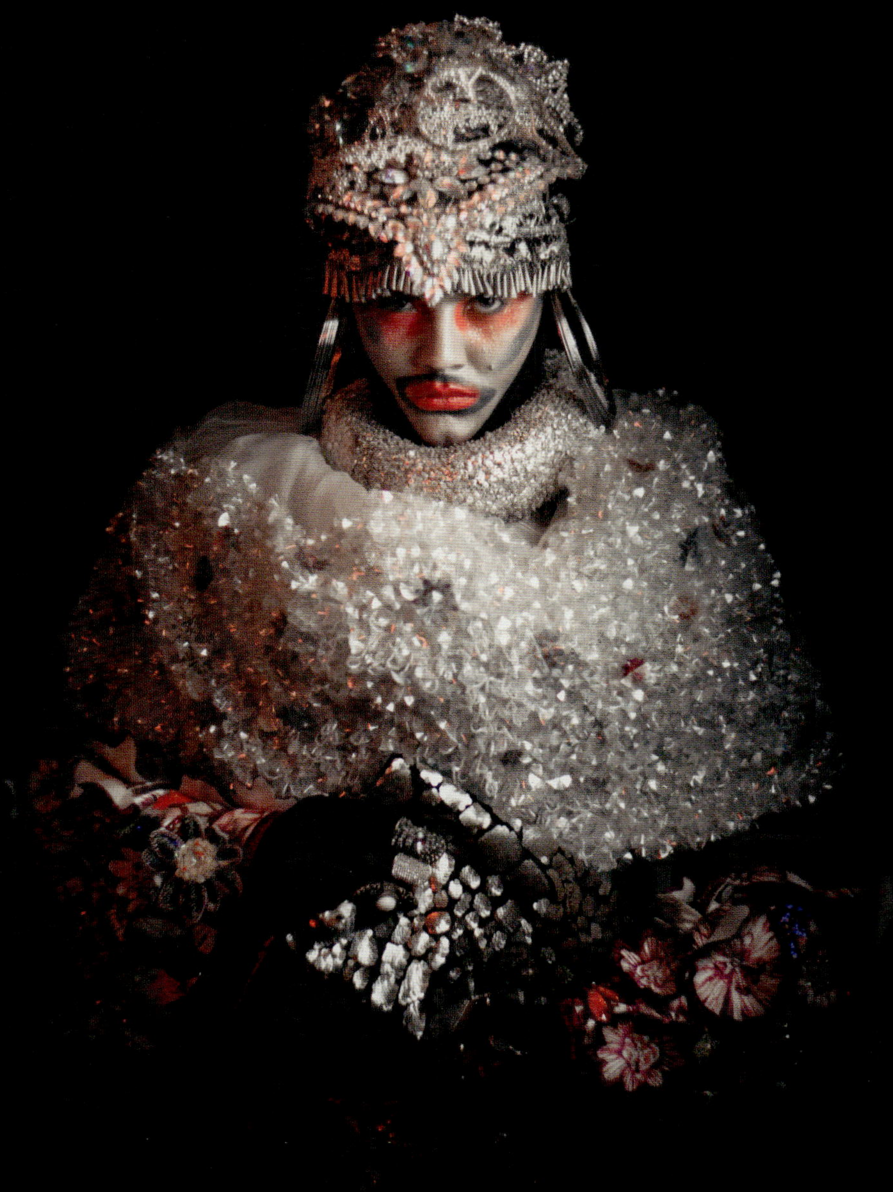

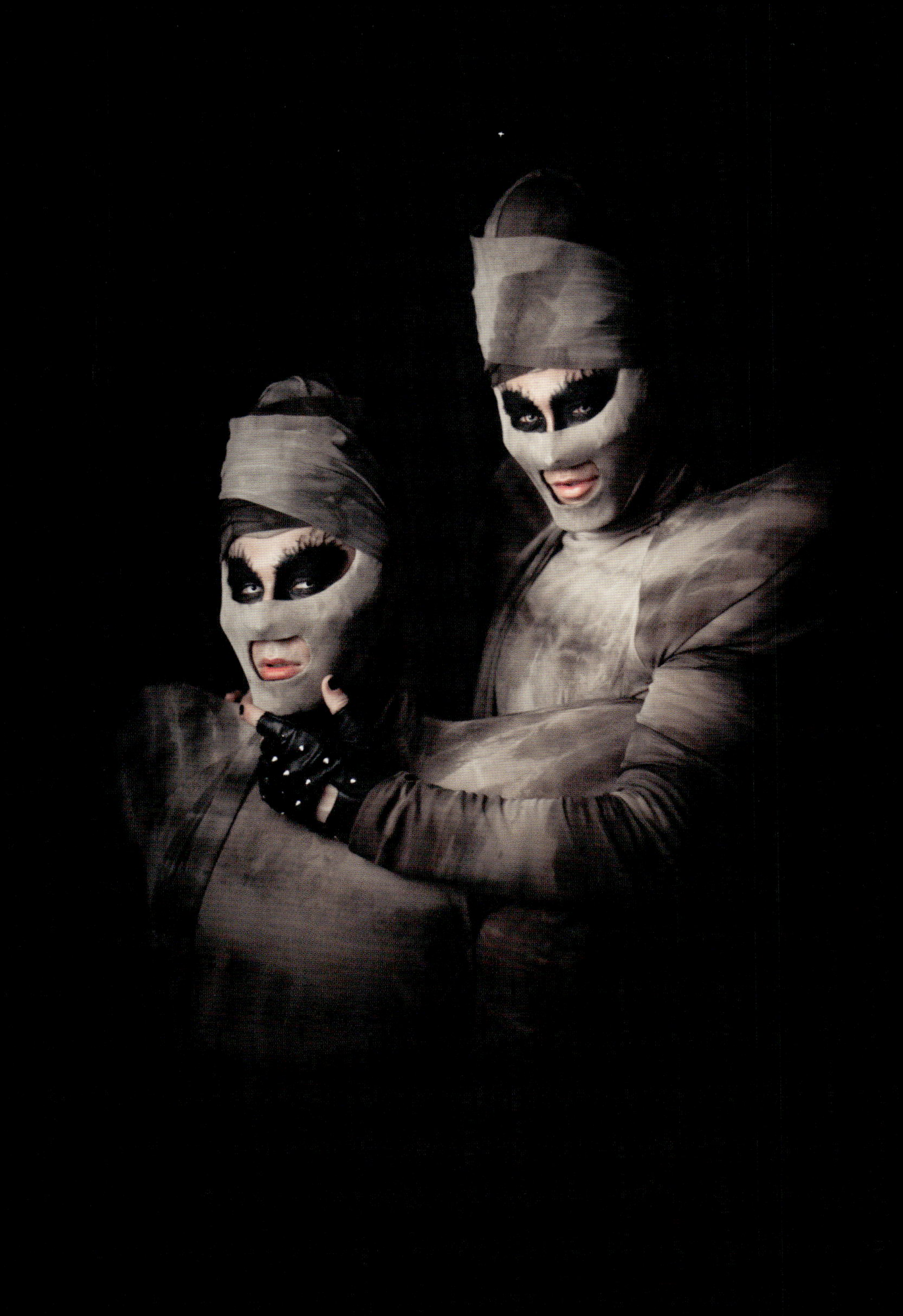

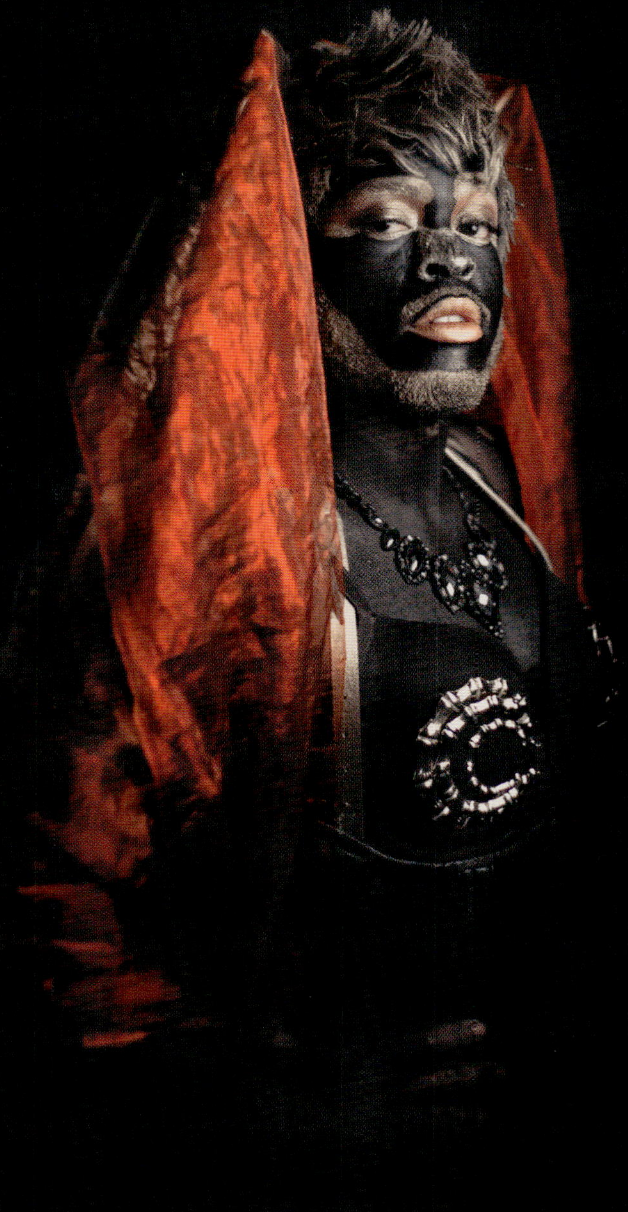

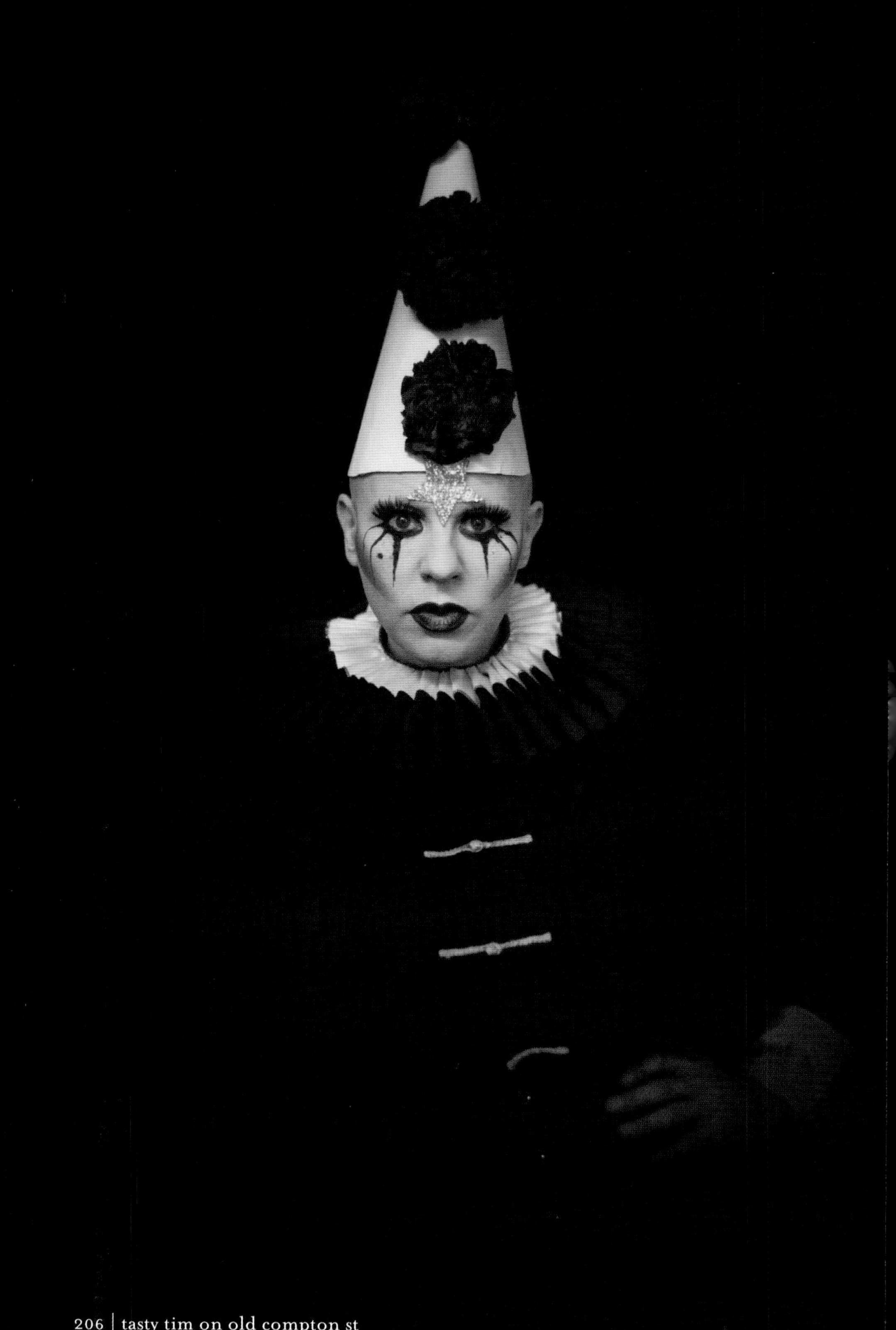

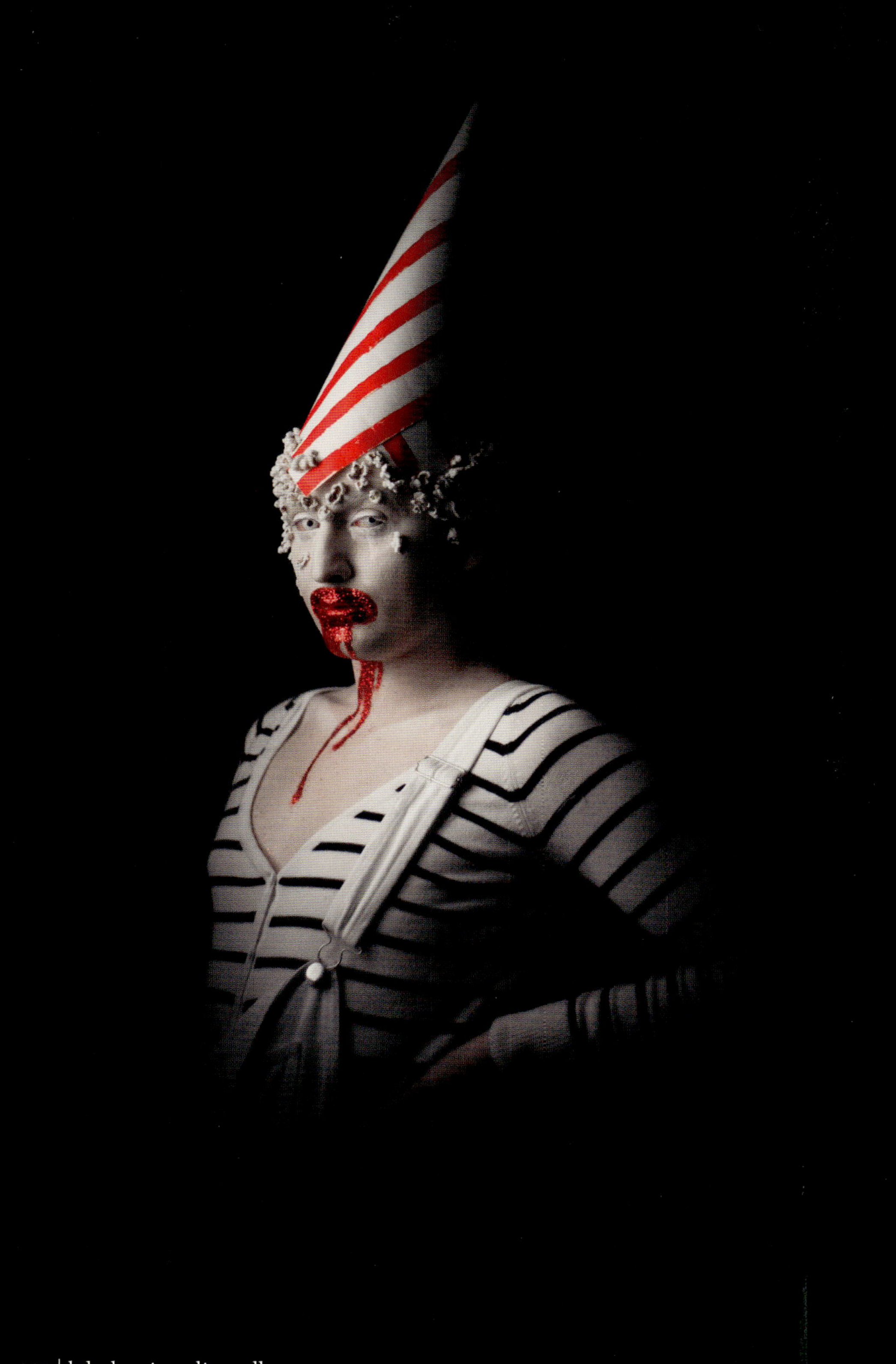

207 | luke harris at dingwalls

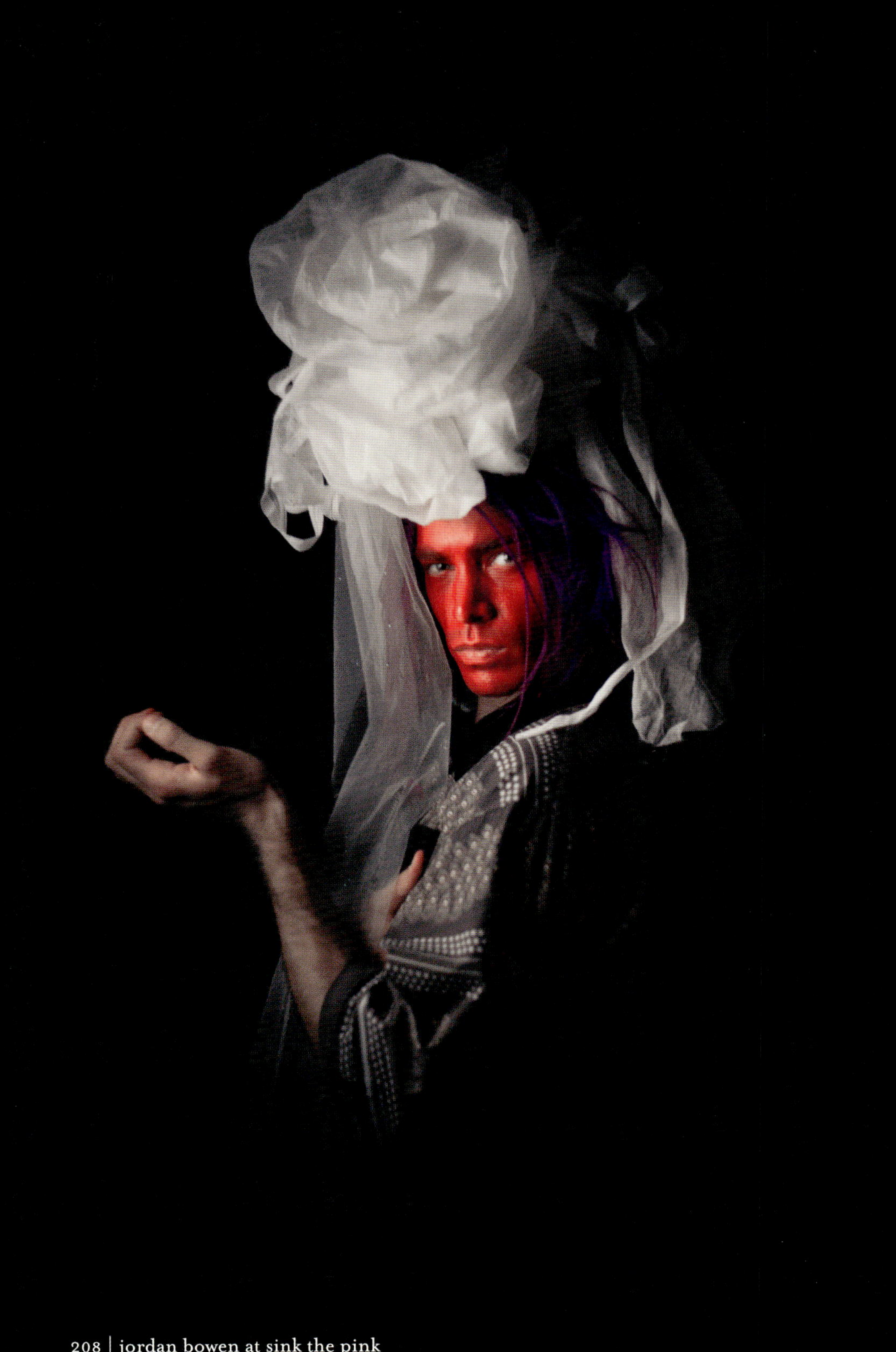

 jordan bowen at sink the pink

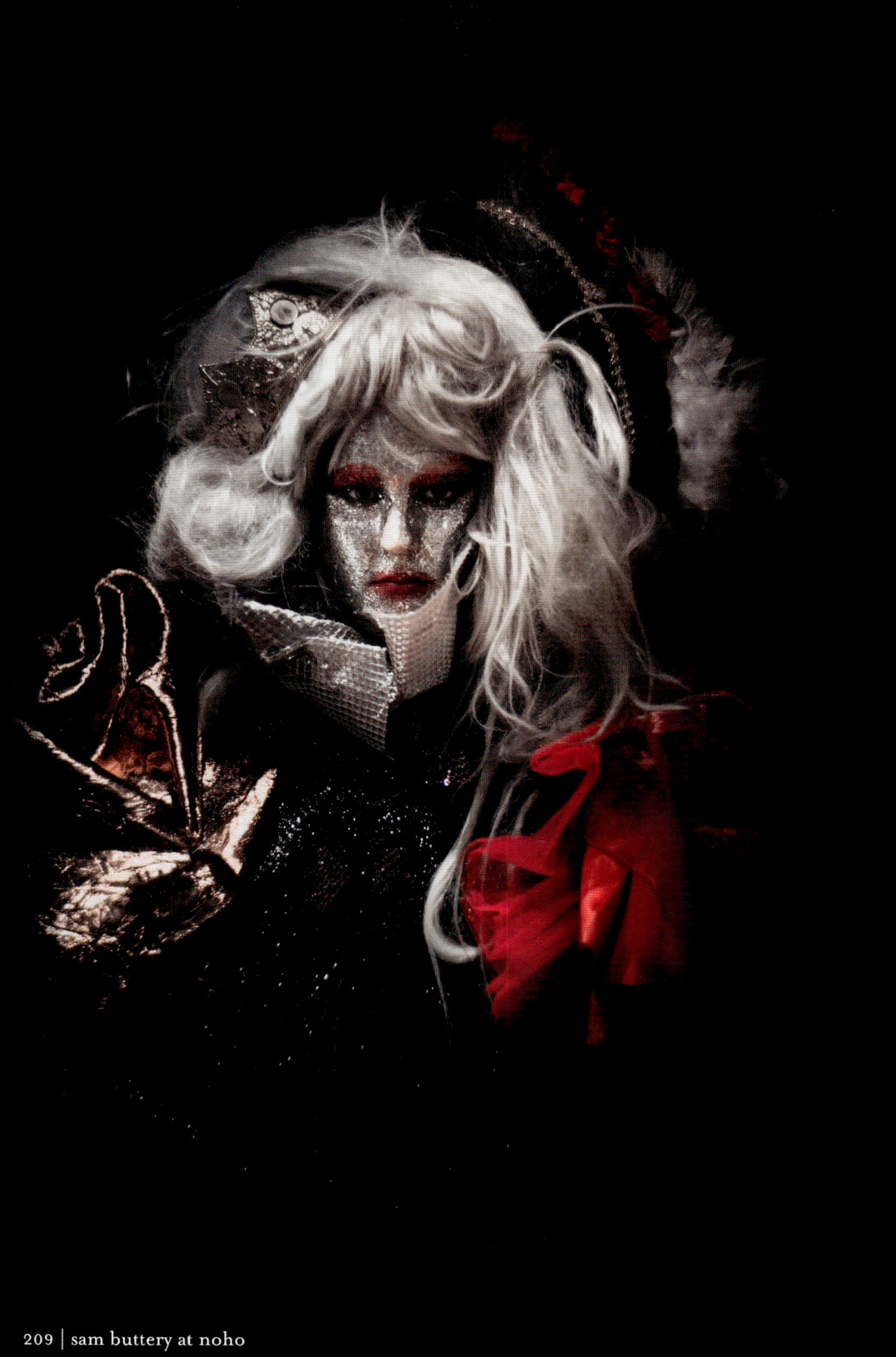

sam buttery at noho

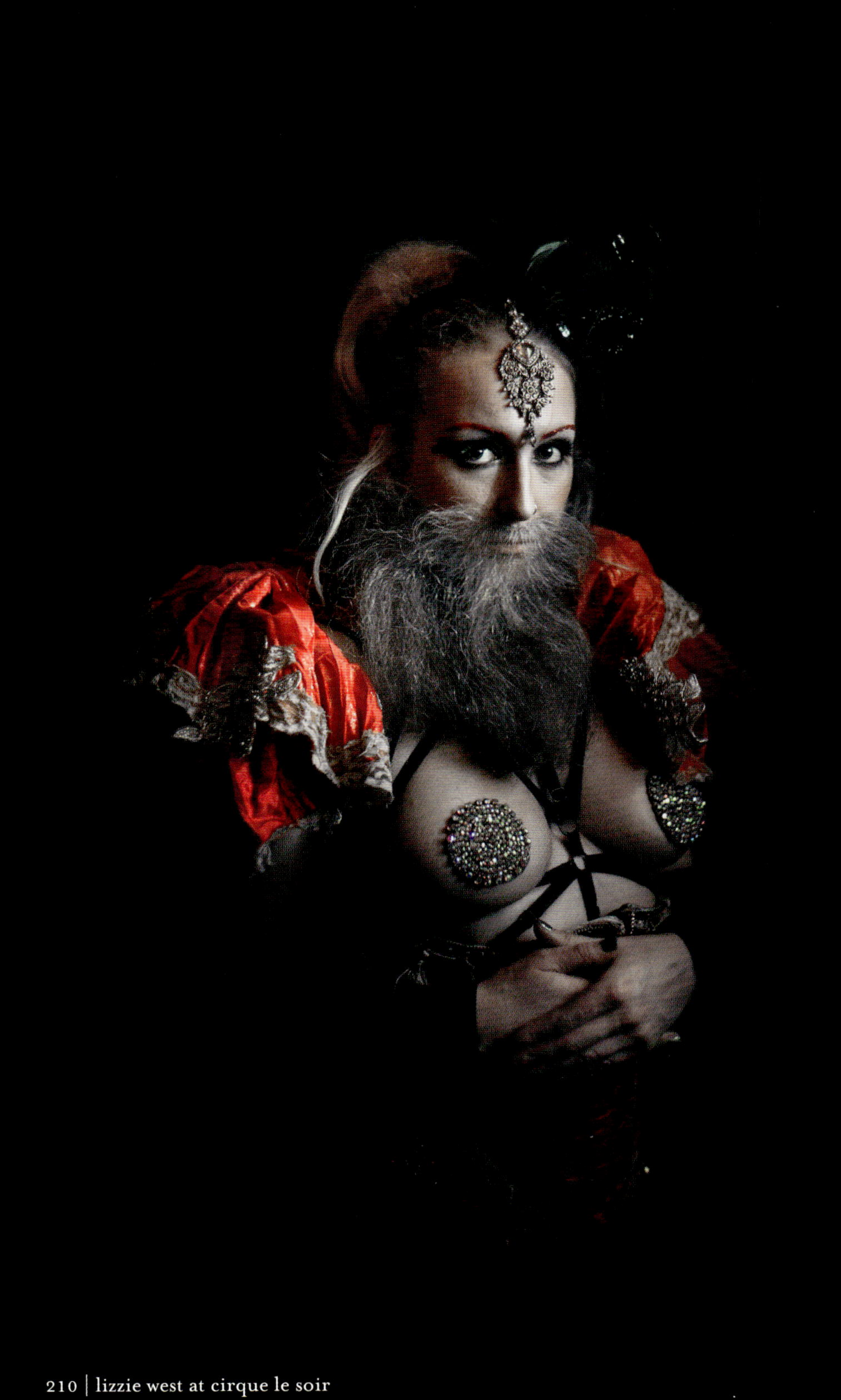

 | lizzie west at cirque le soir

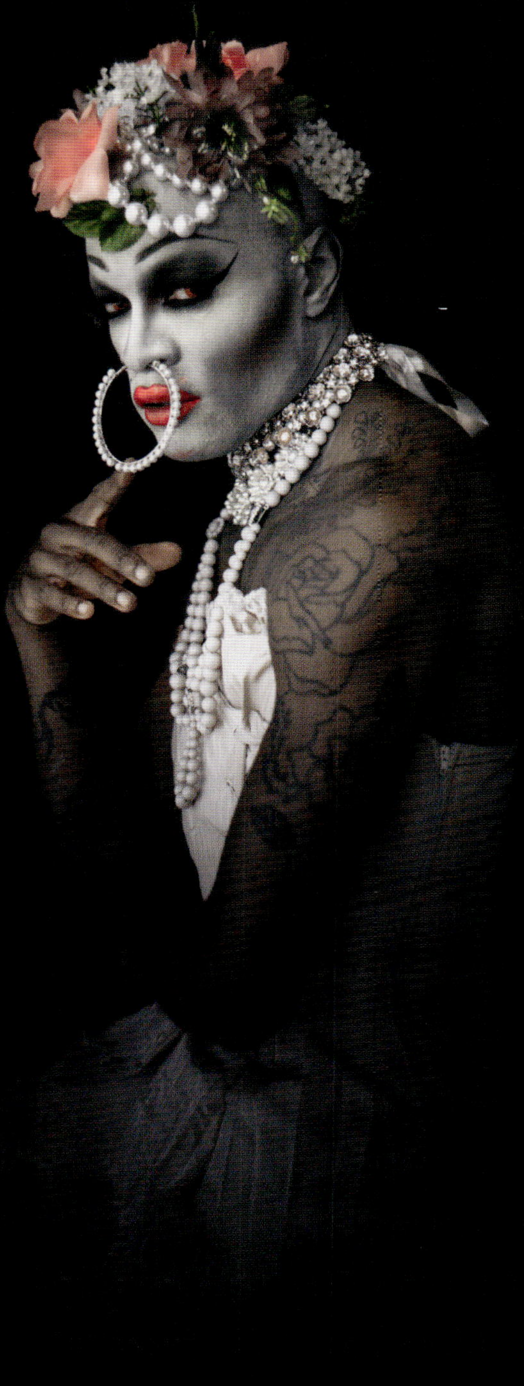

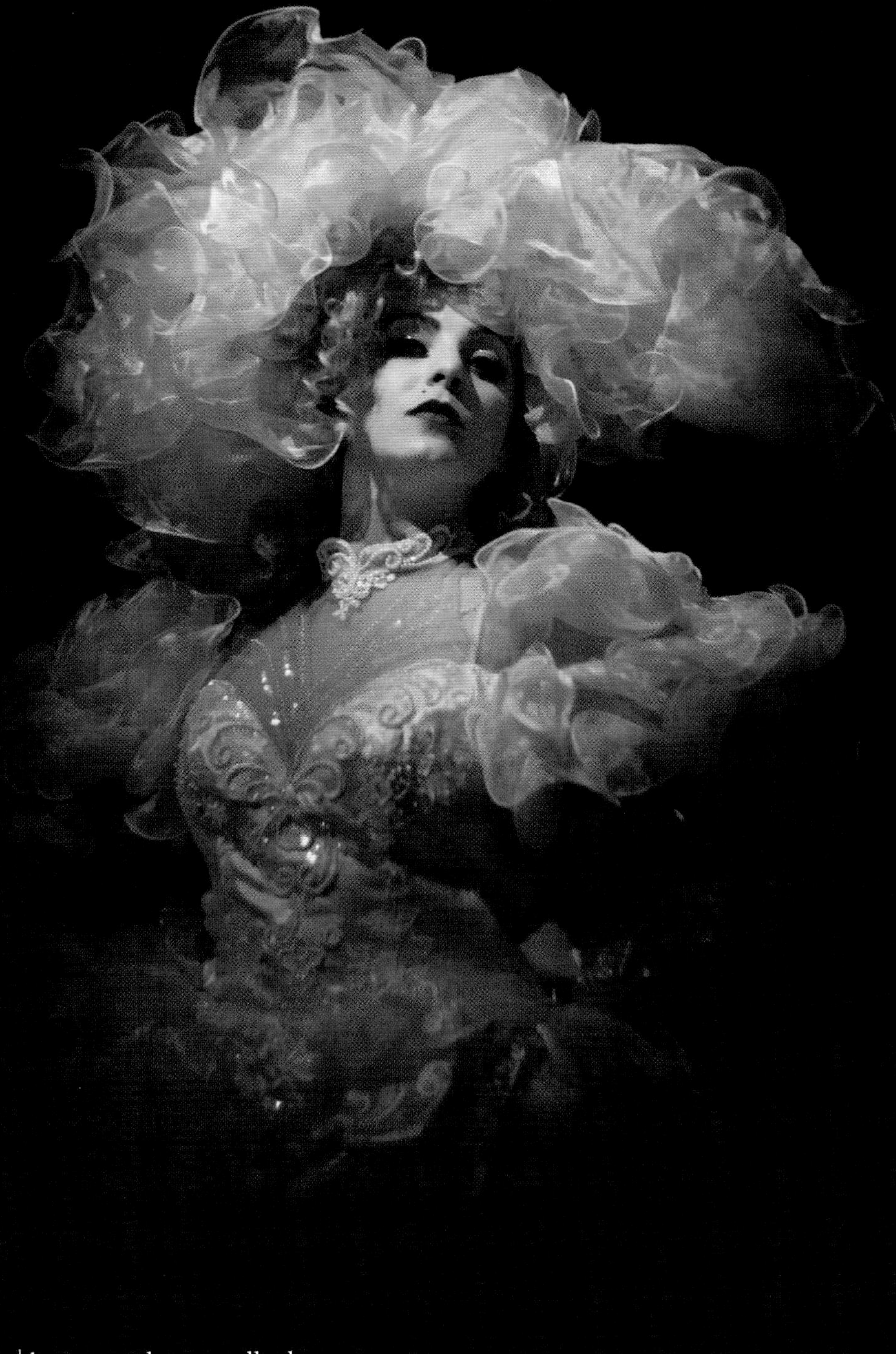

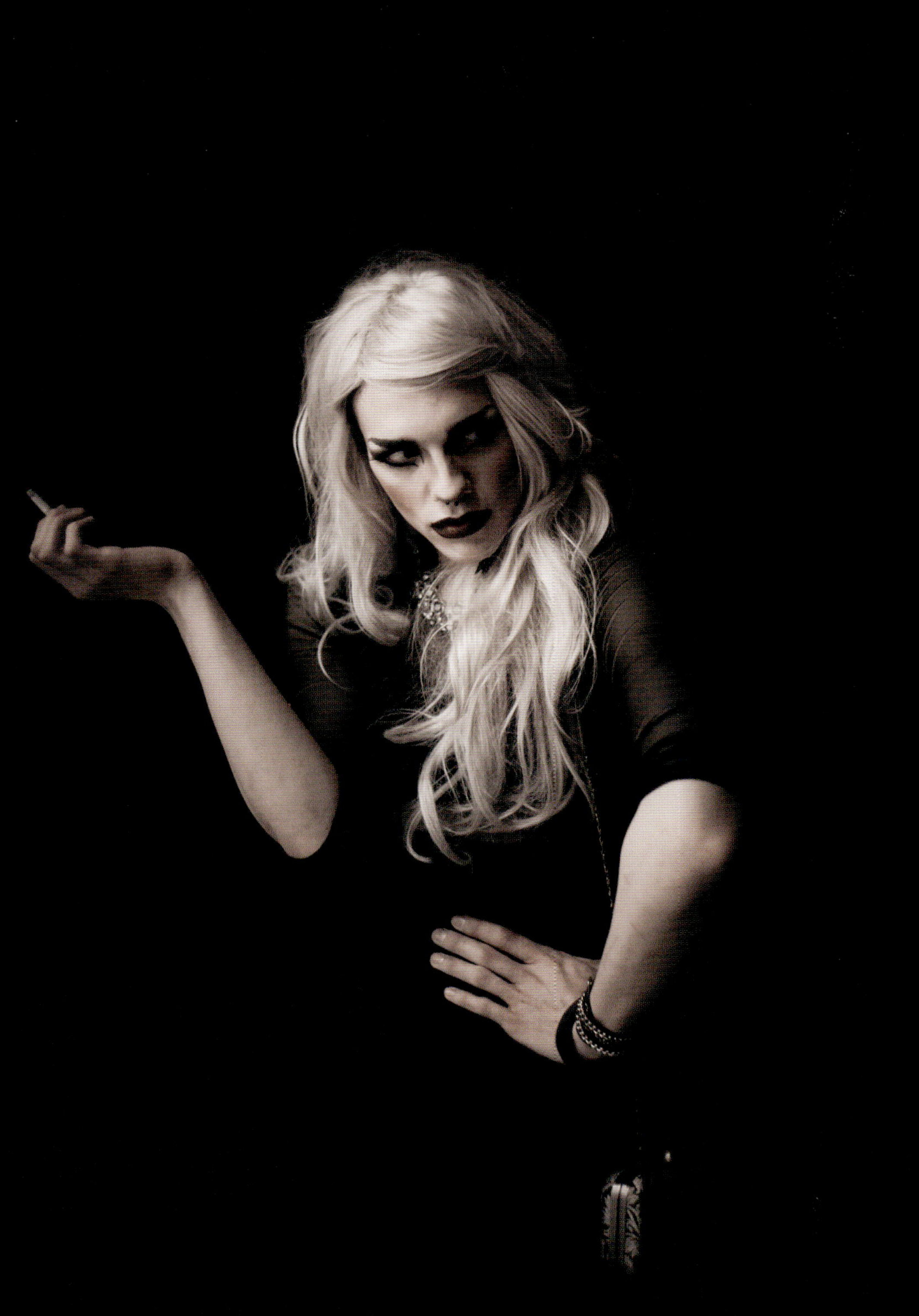

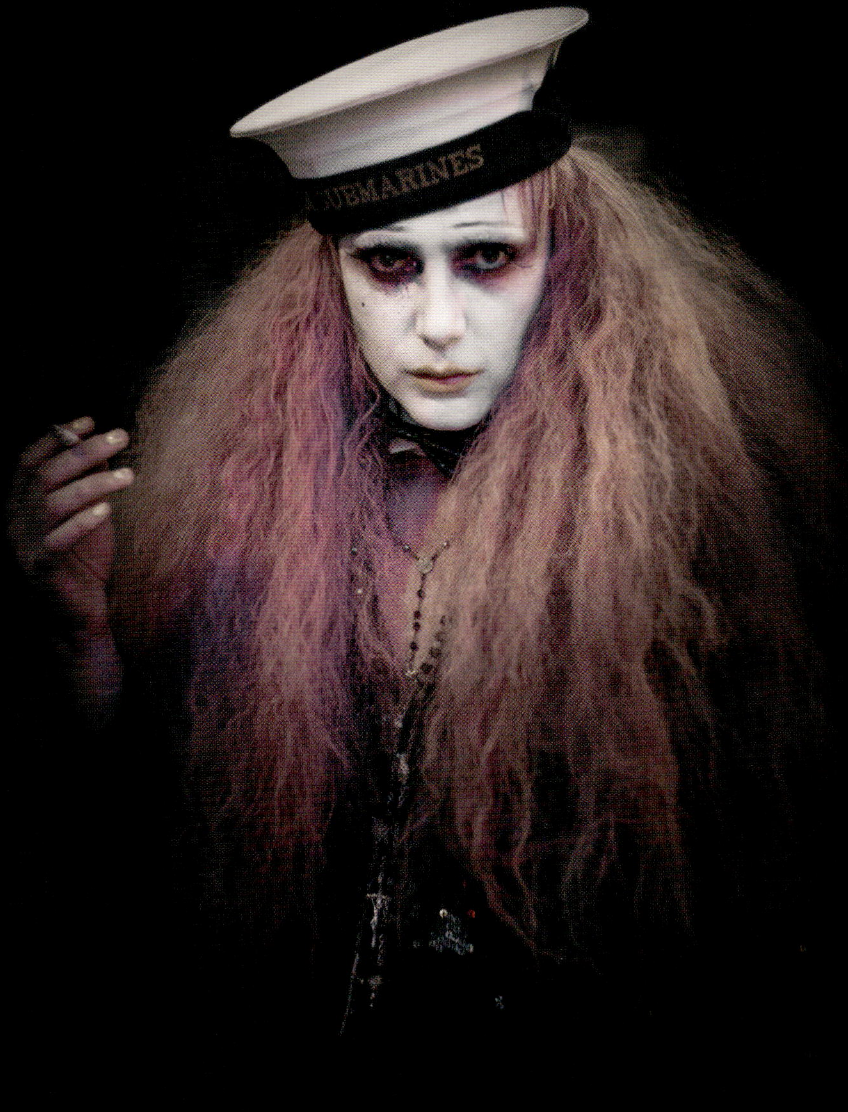
SUBMARINES

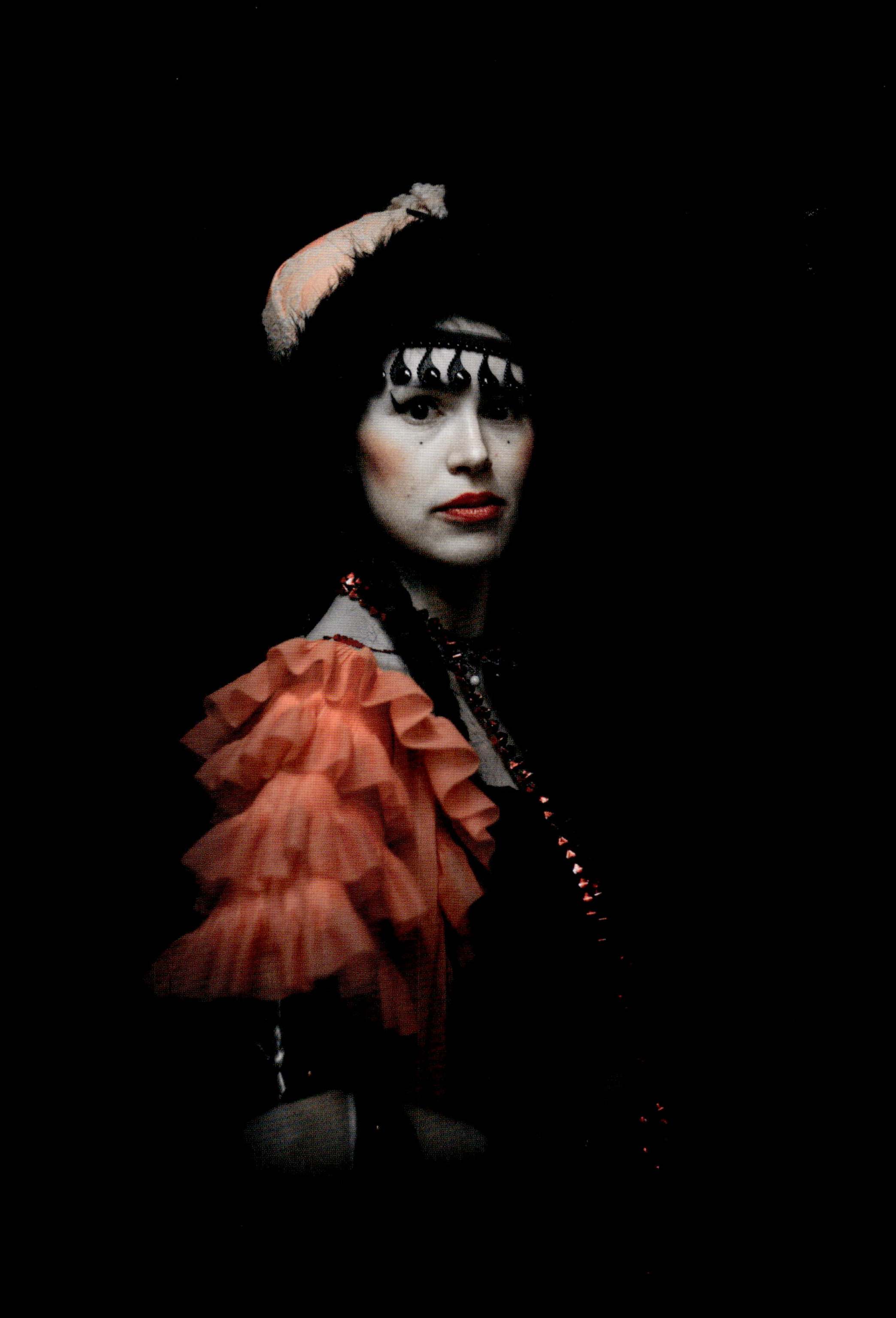

215 | loulou reloulou on kingsland rd

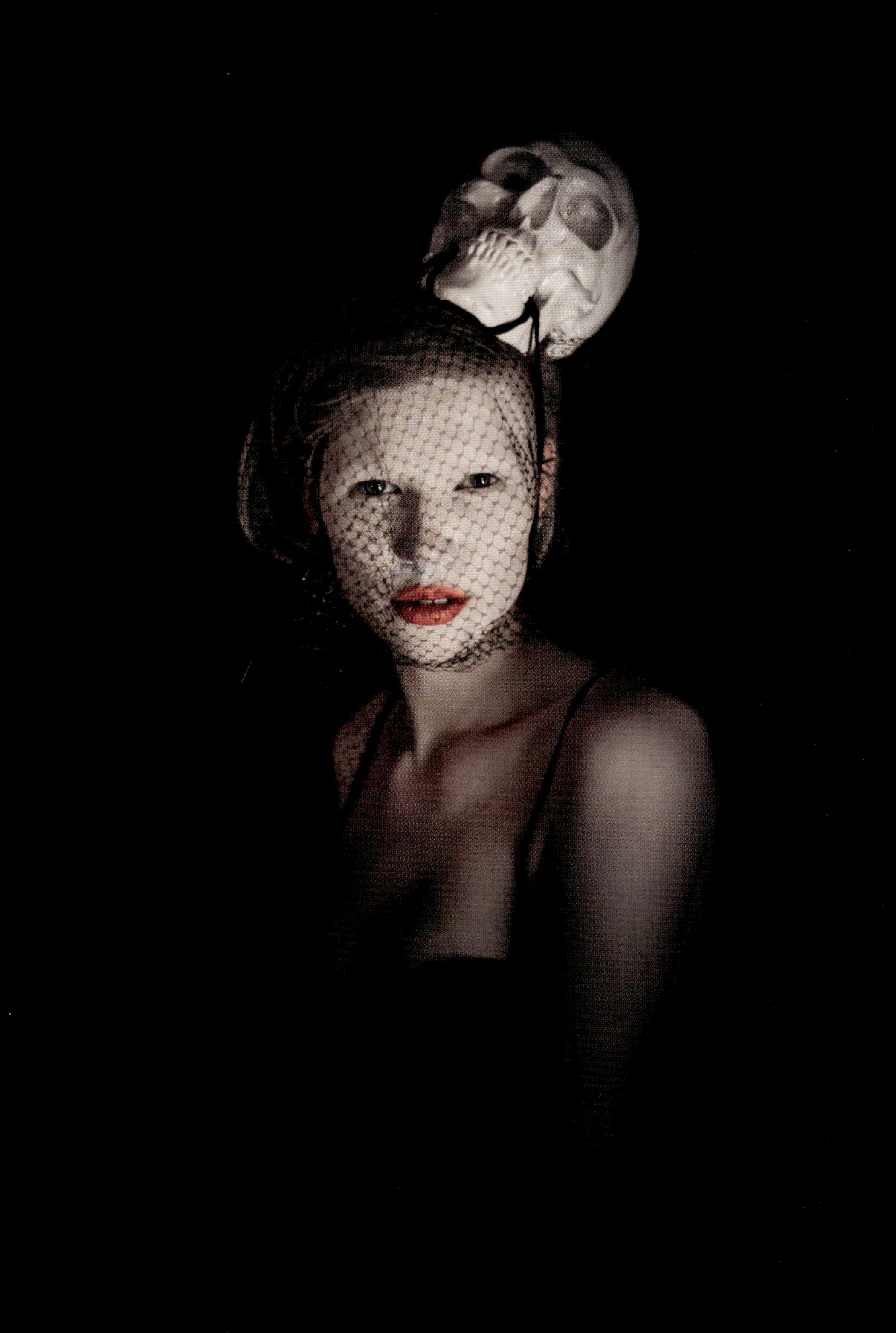

 | anni (with an 'i') at nun

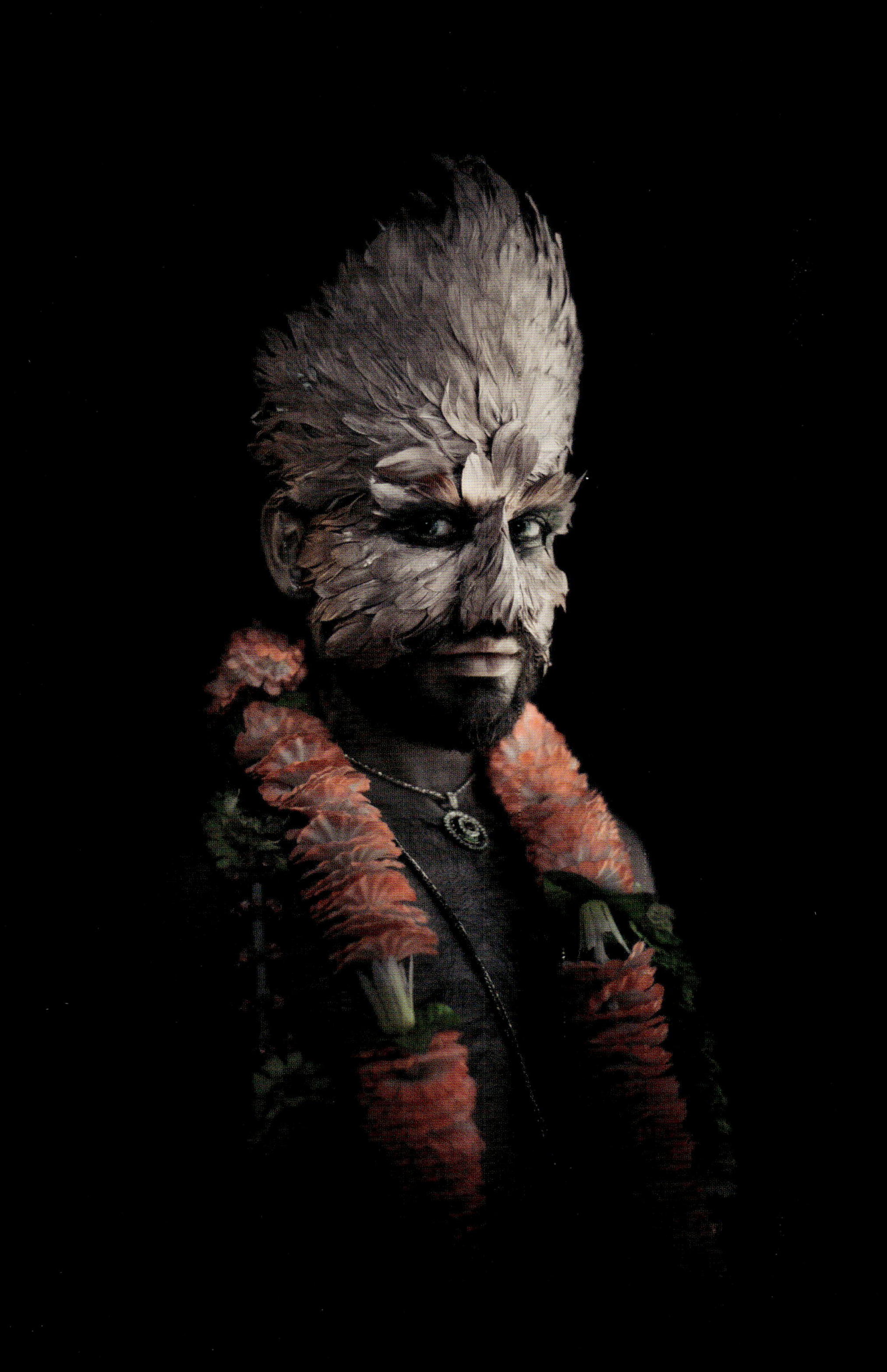

217 | nathan french on bethnal green rd

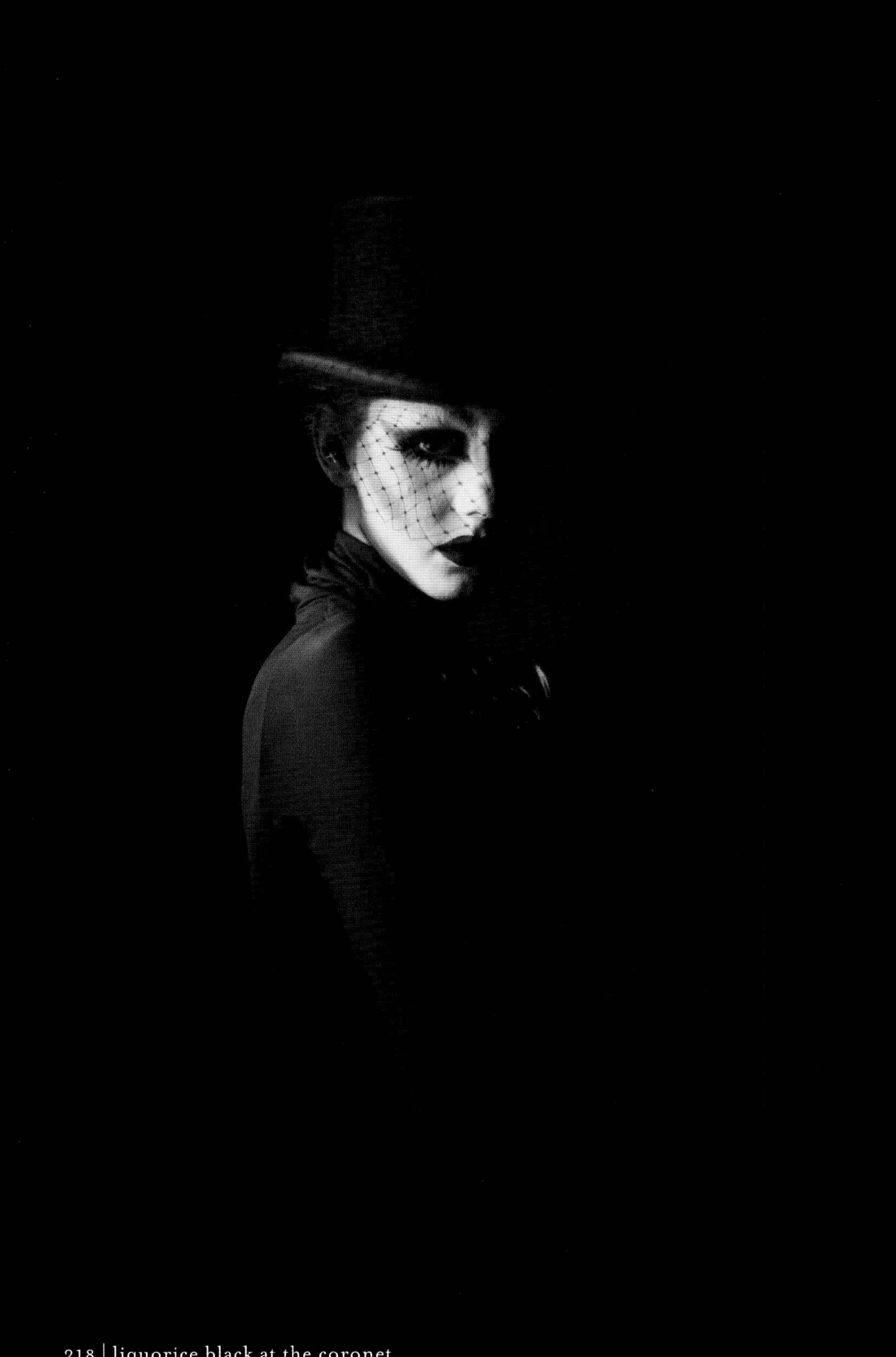

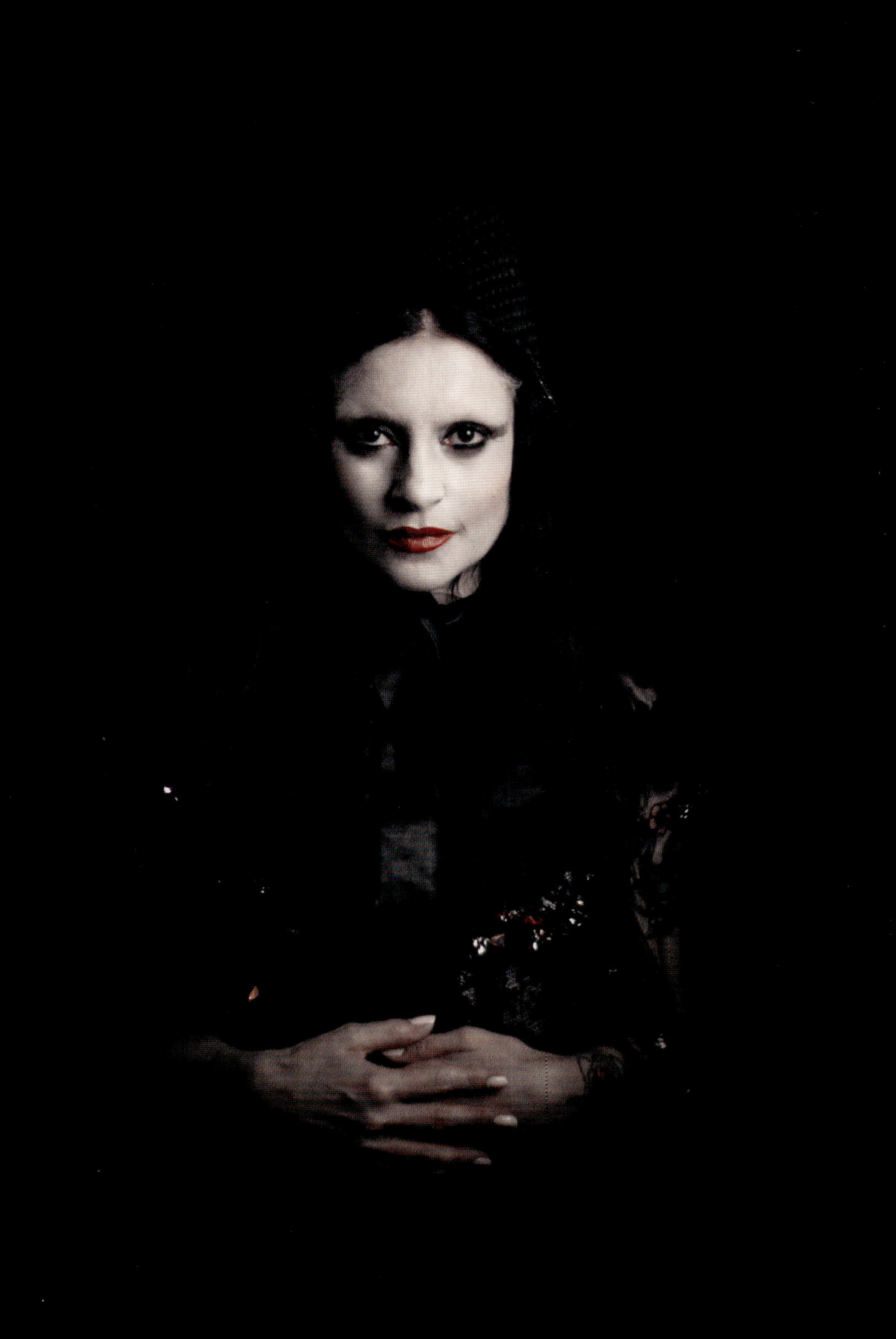

219 | princess julia at the amy grimehouse tudor realness ball

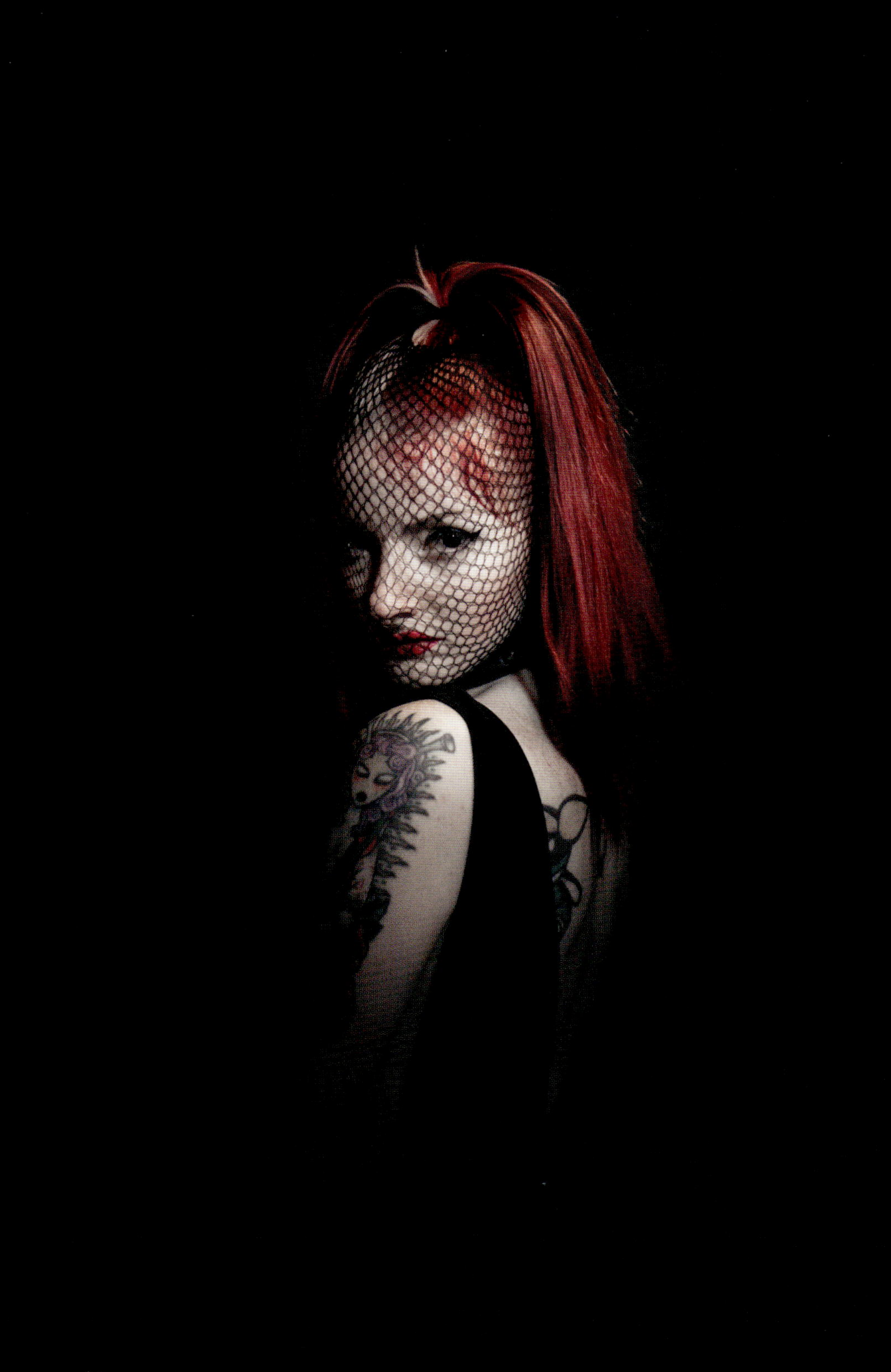

 happy valentine at cirque le soir

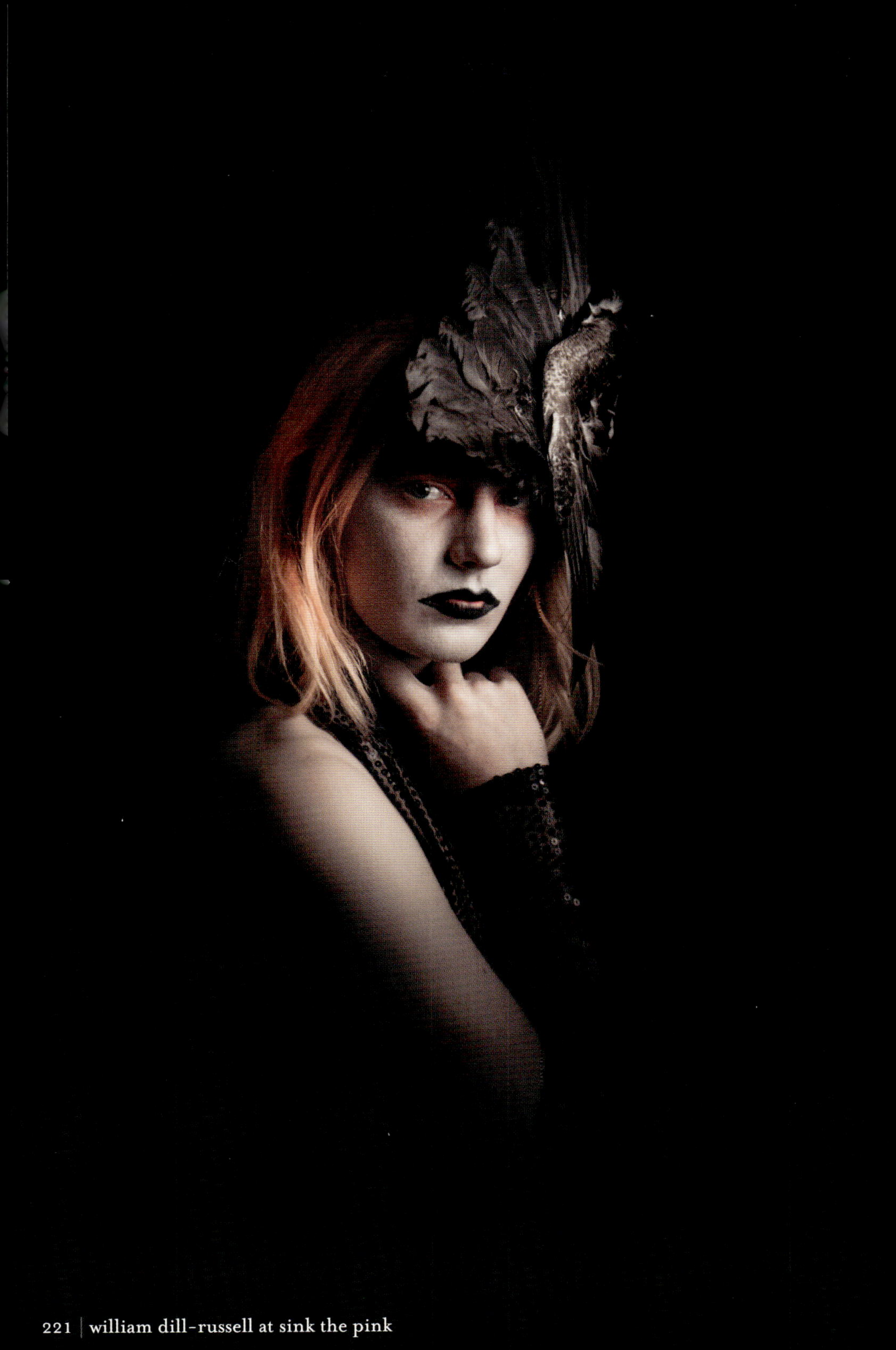

 | william dill-russell at sink the pink

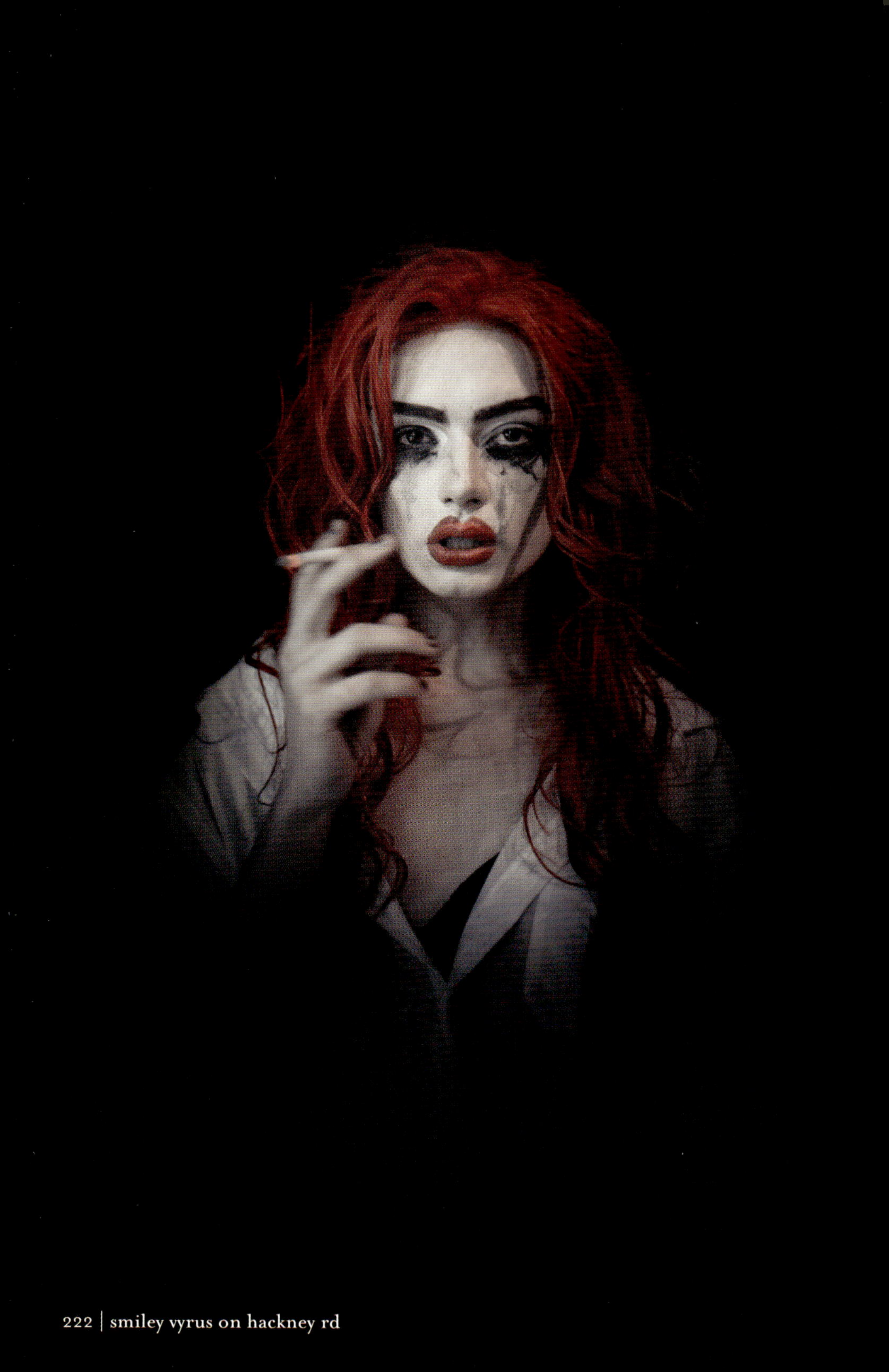

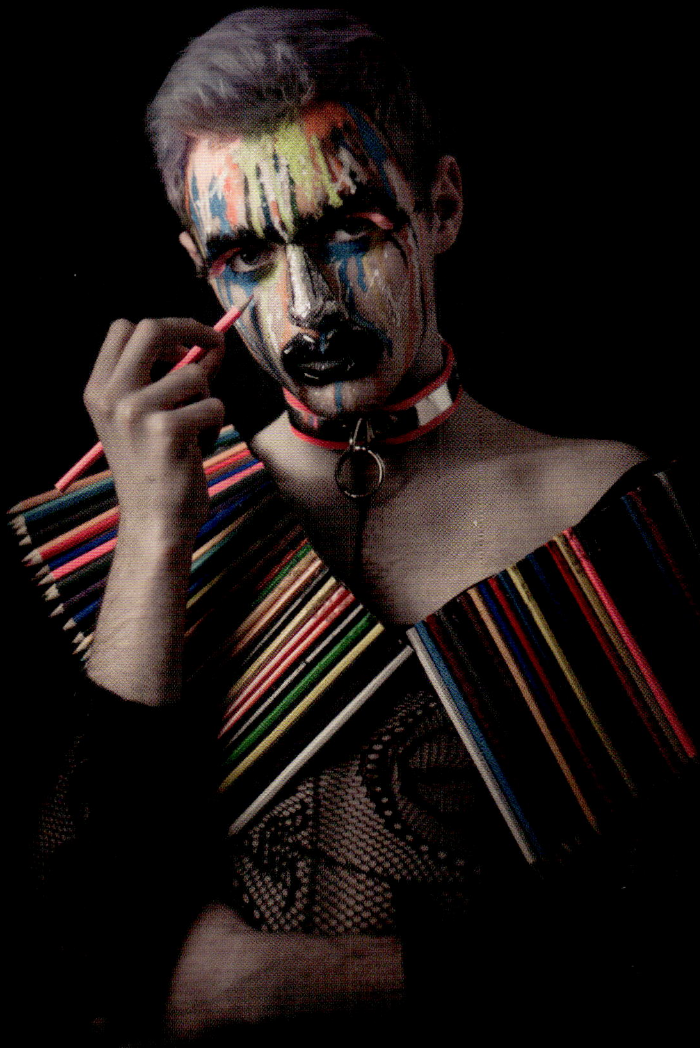

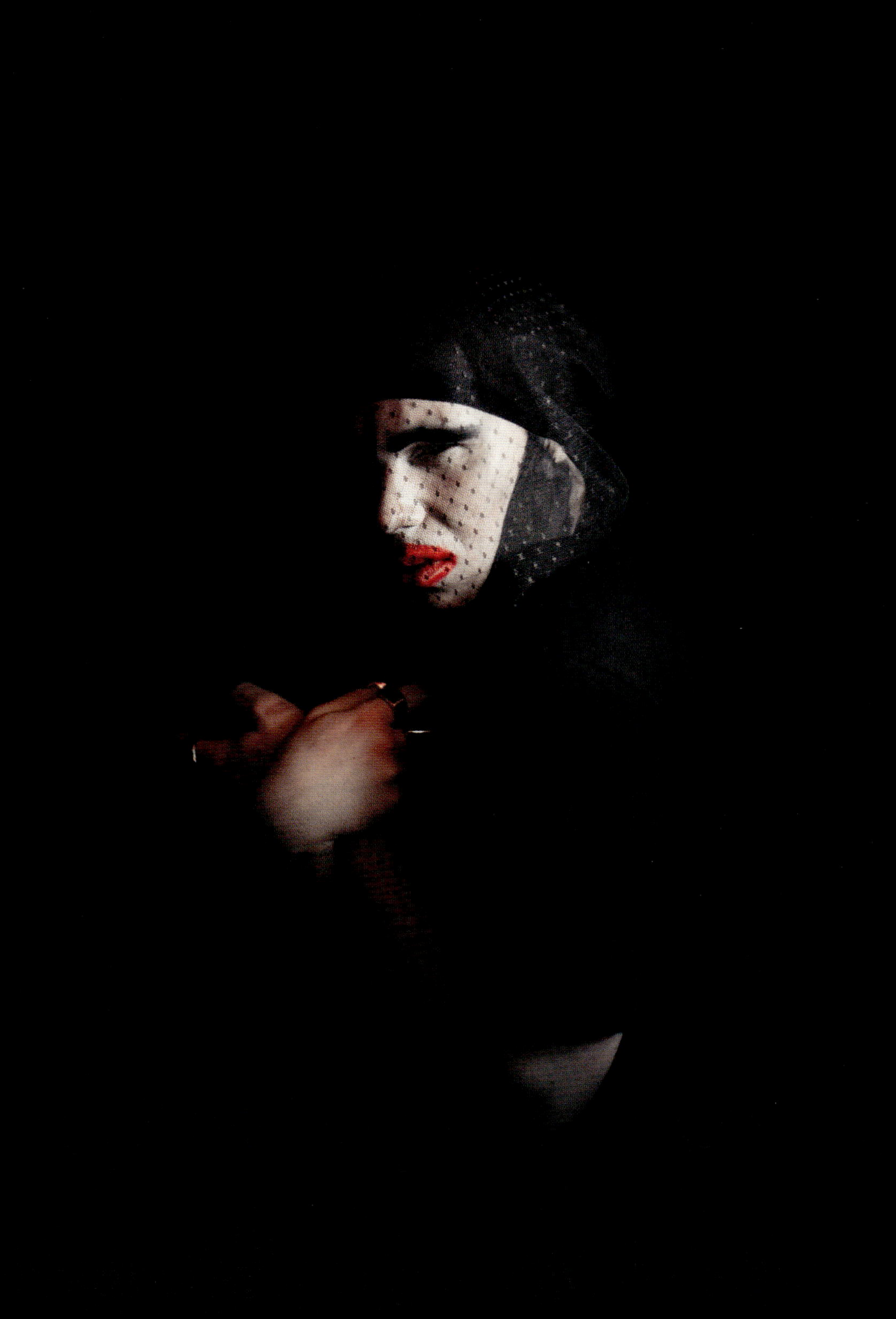

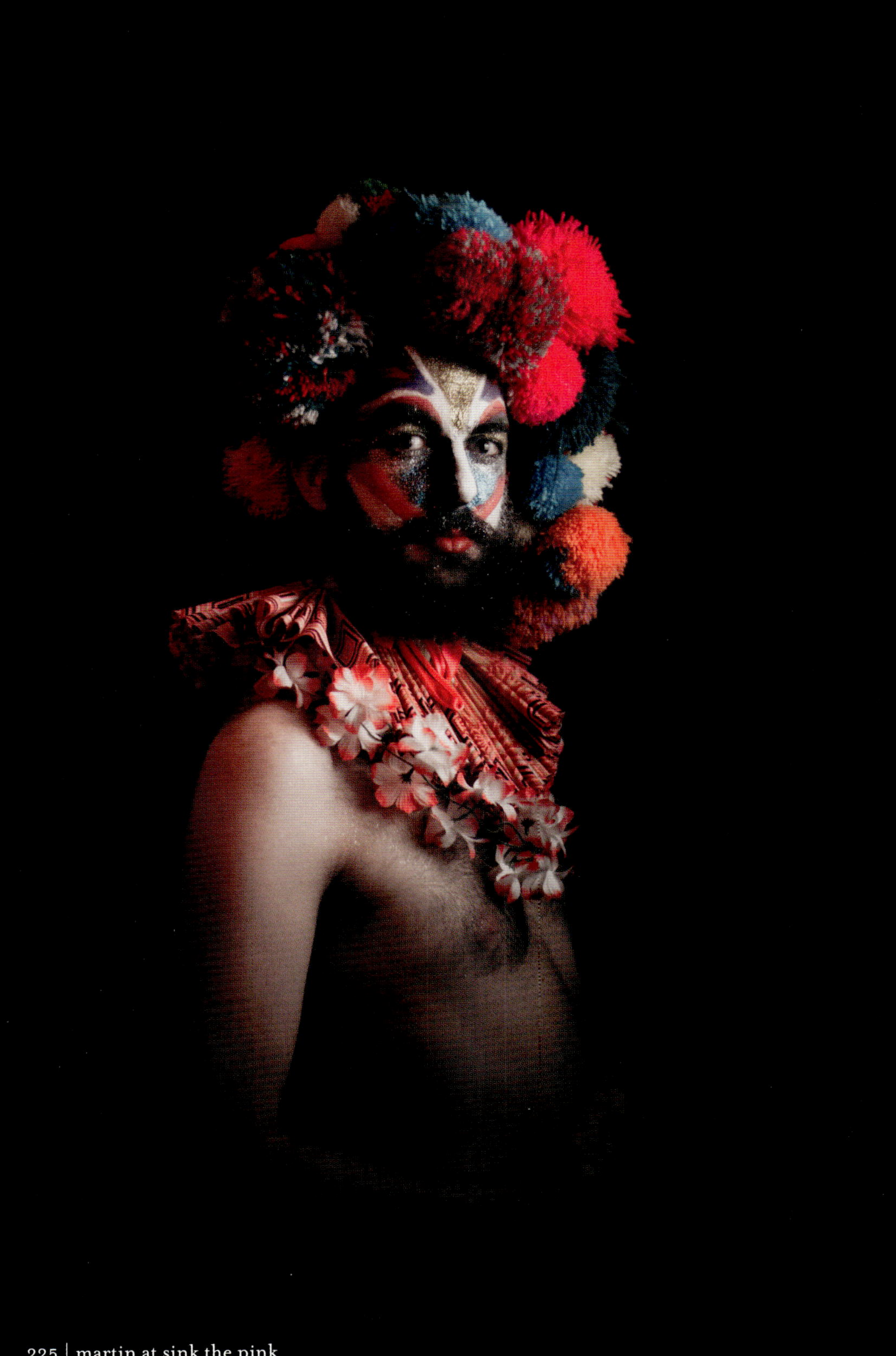

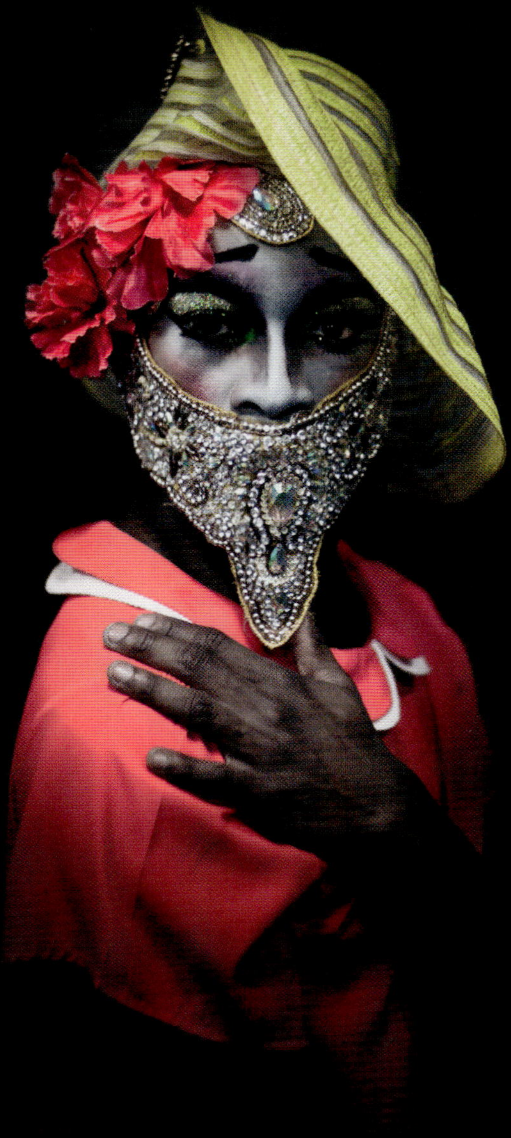

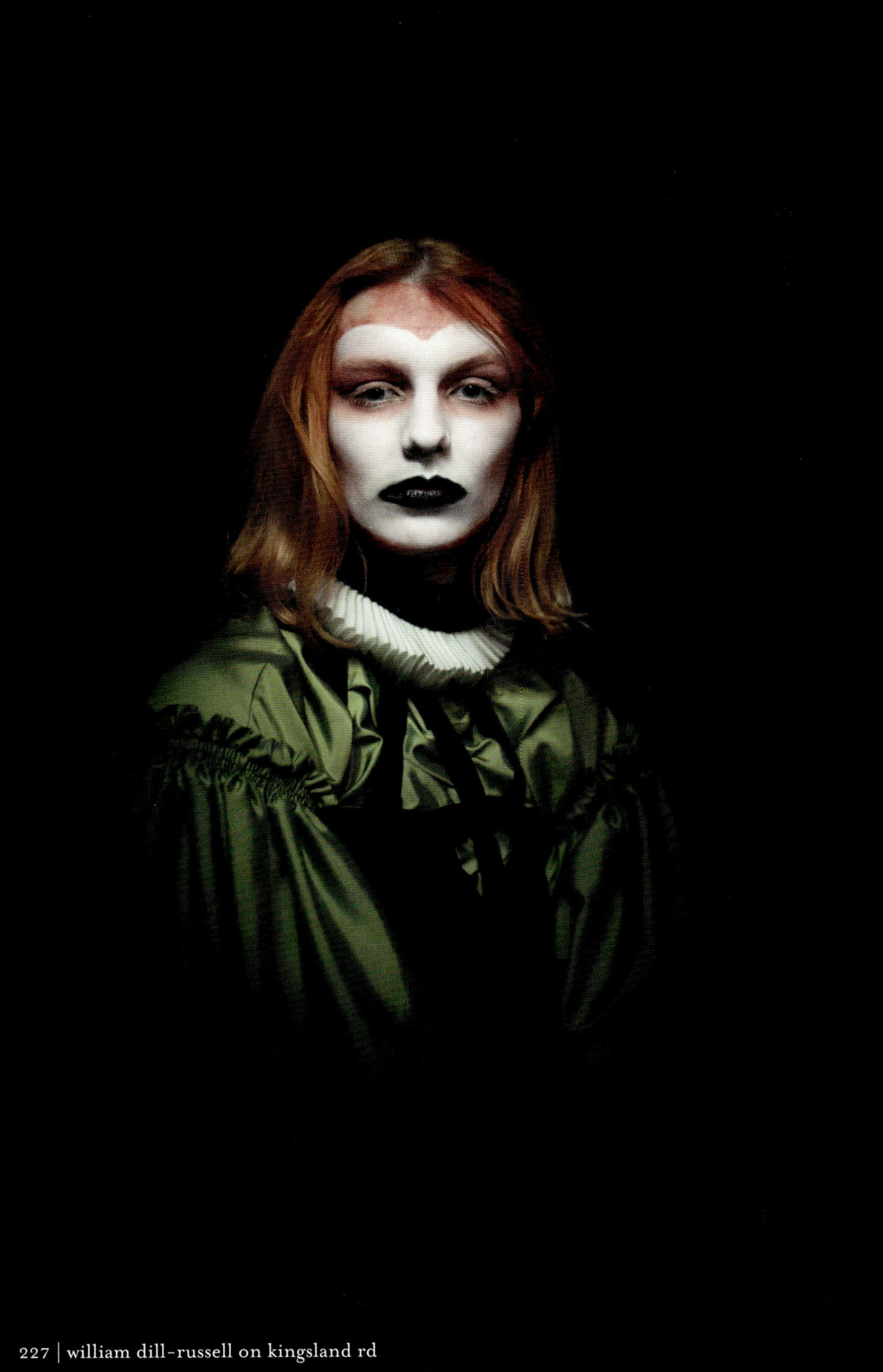

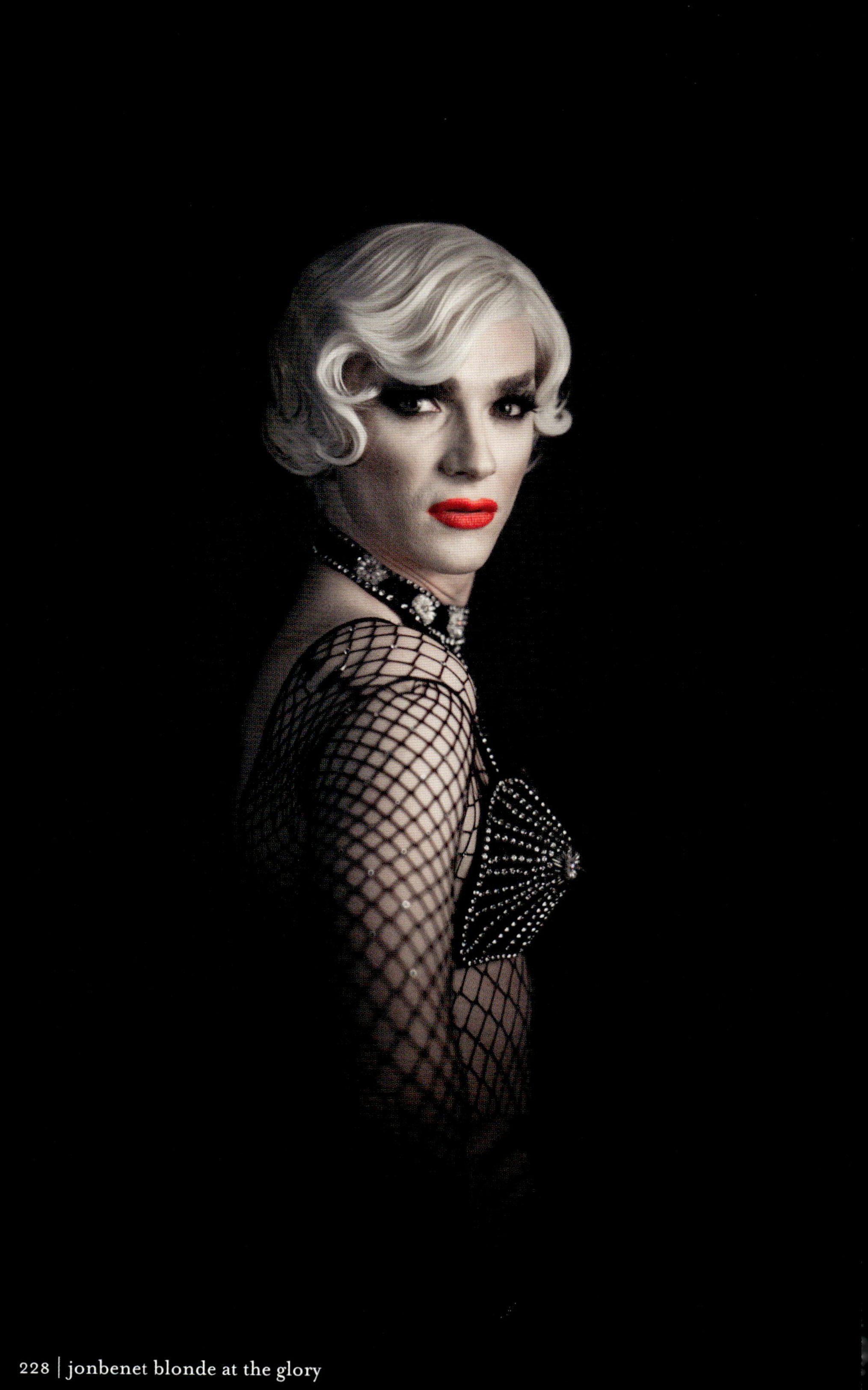

 jonbenet blonde at the glory

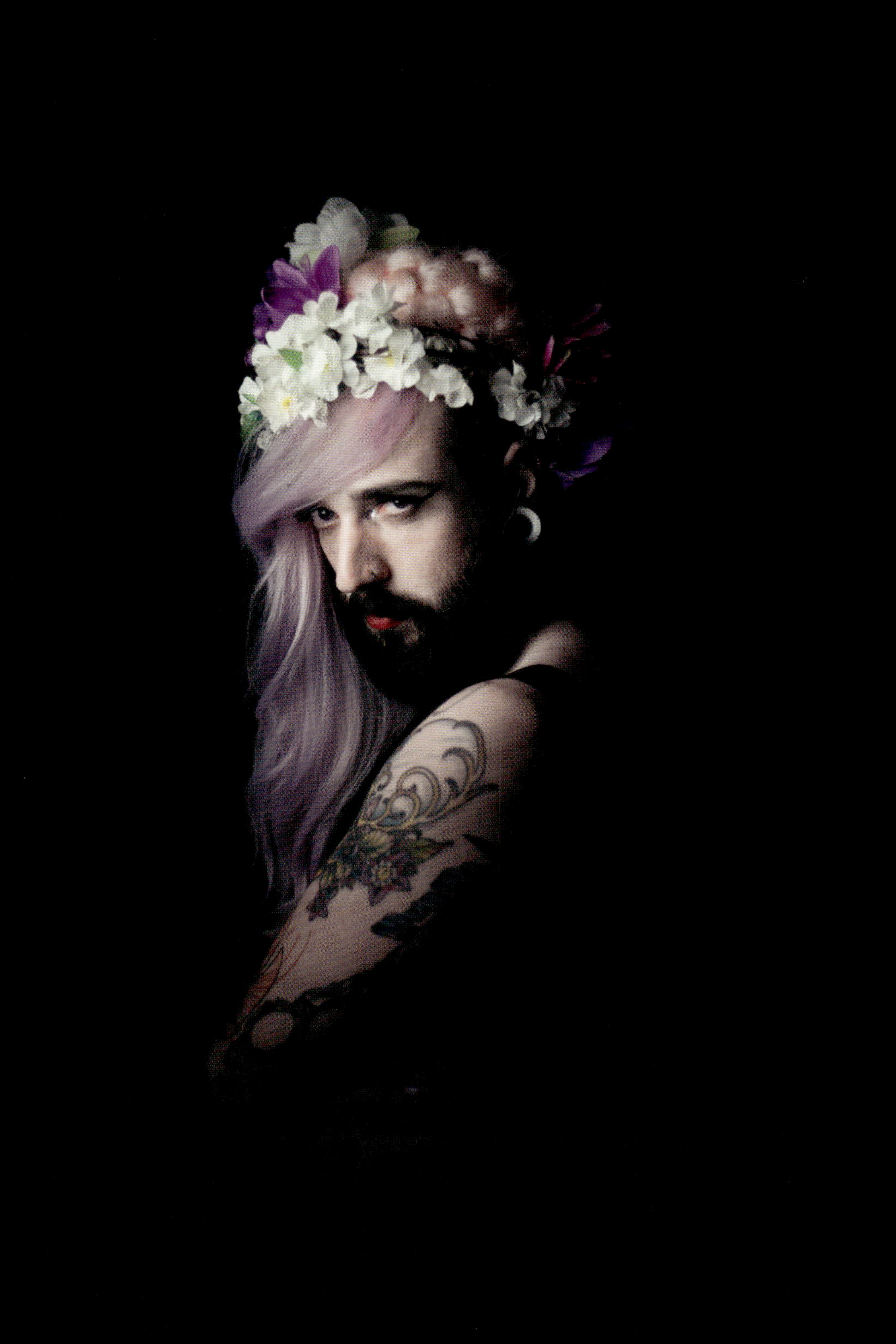

229 | andy beard at bethnal green working men's club

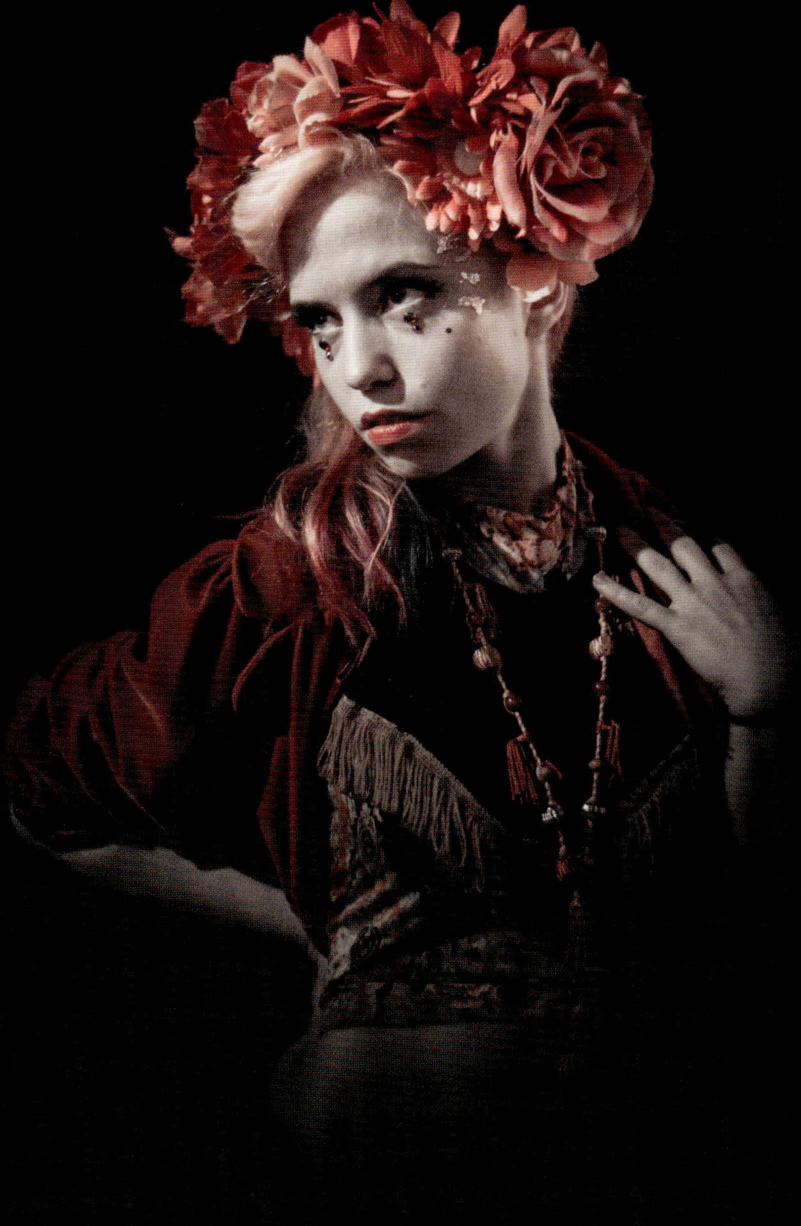

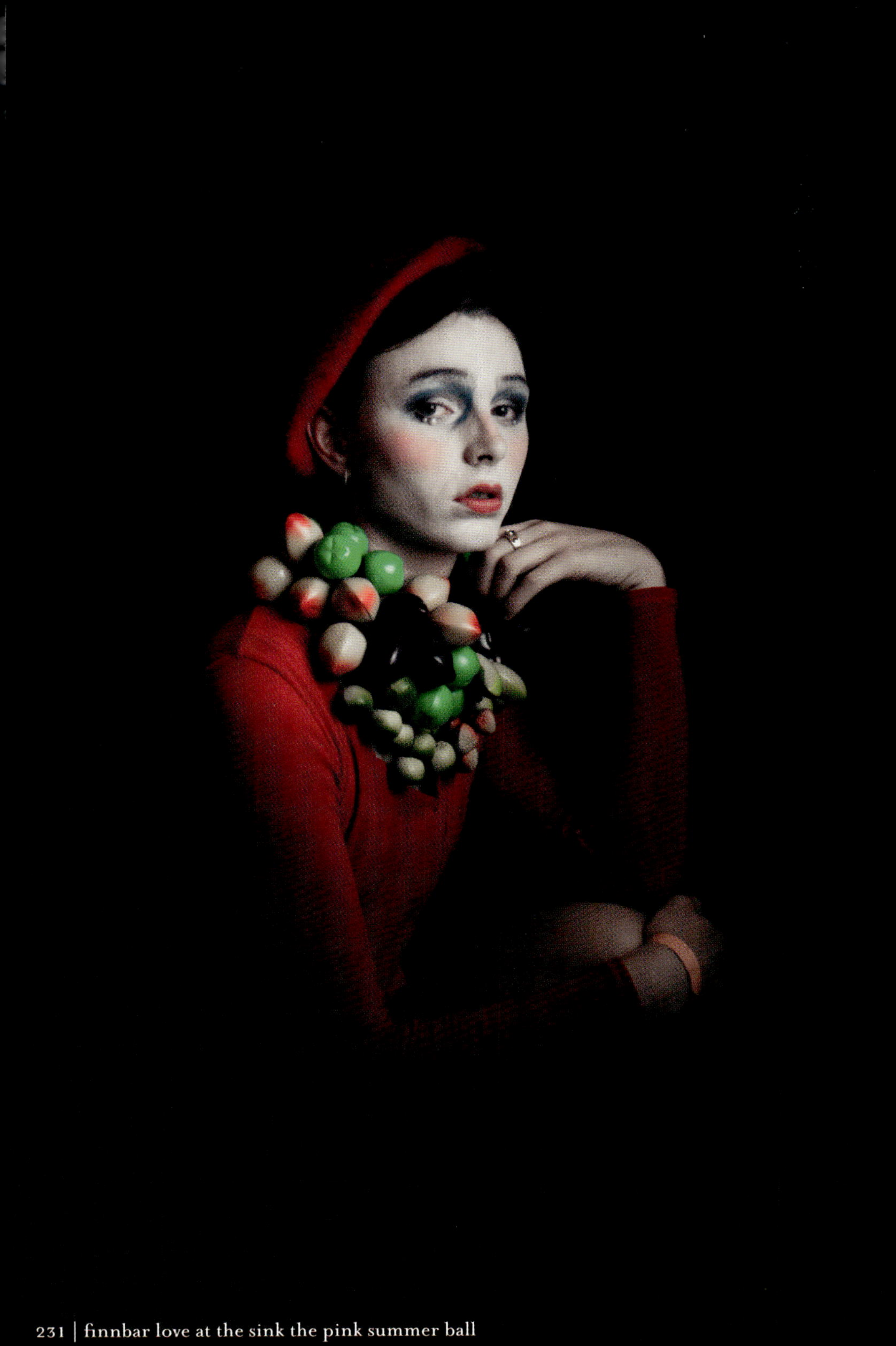

231 | finnbar love at the sink the pink summer ball

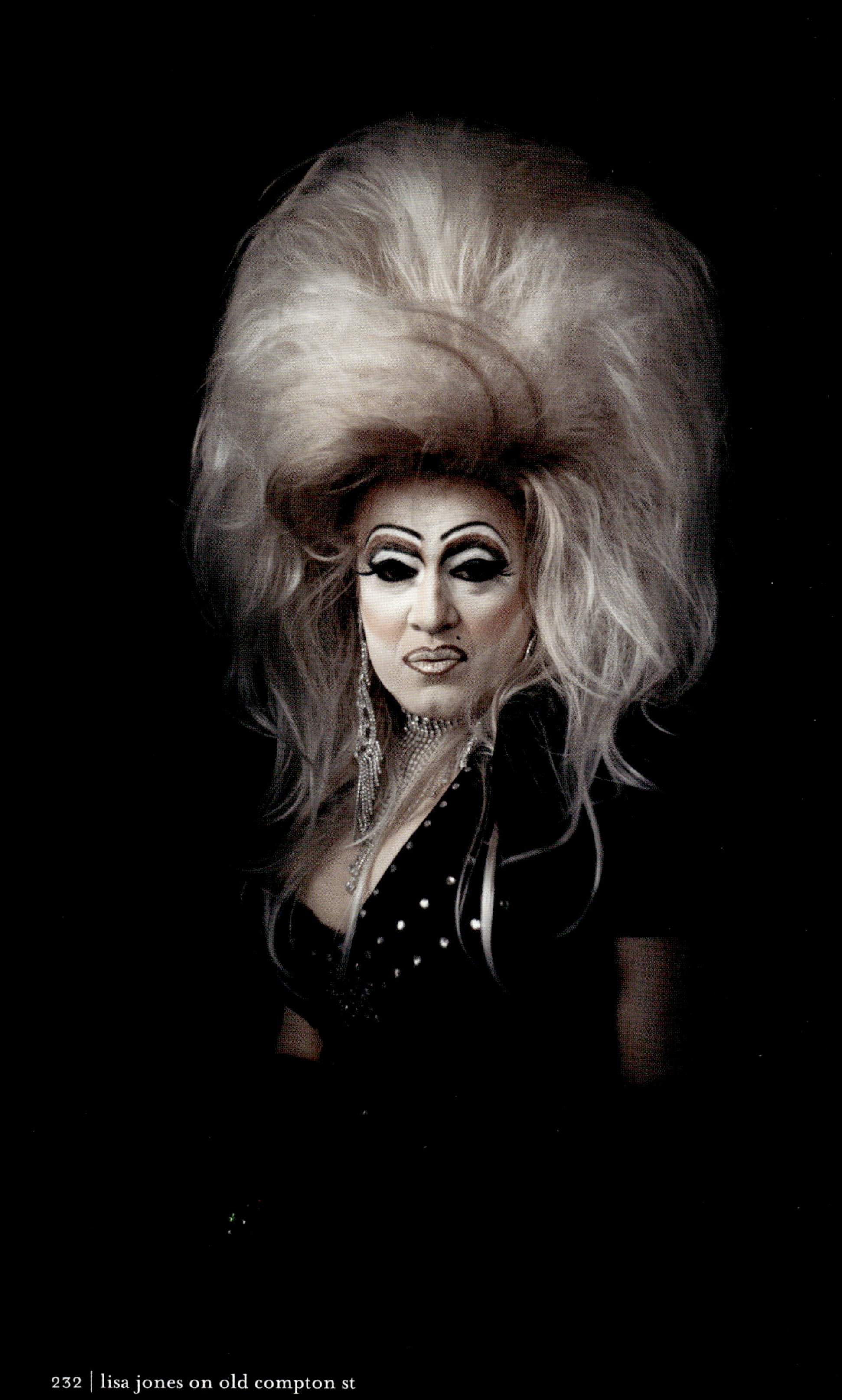

 lisa jones on old compton st

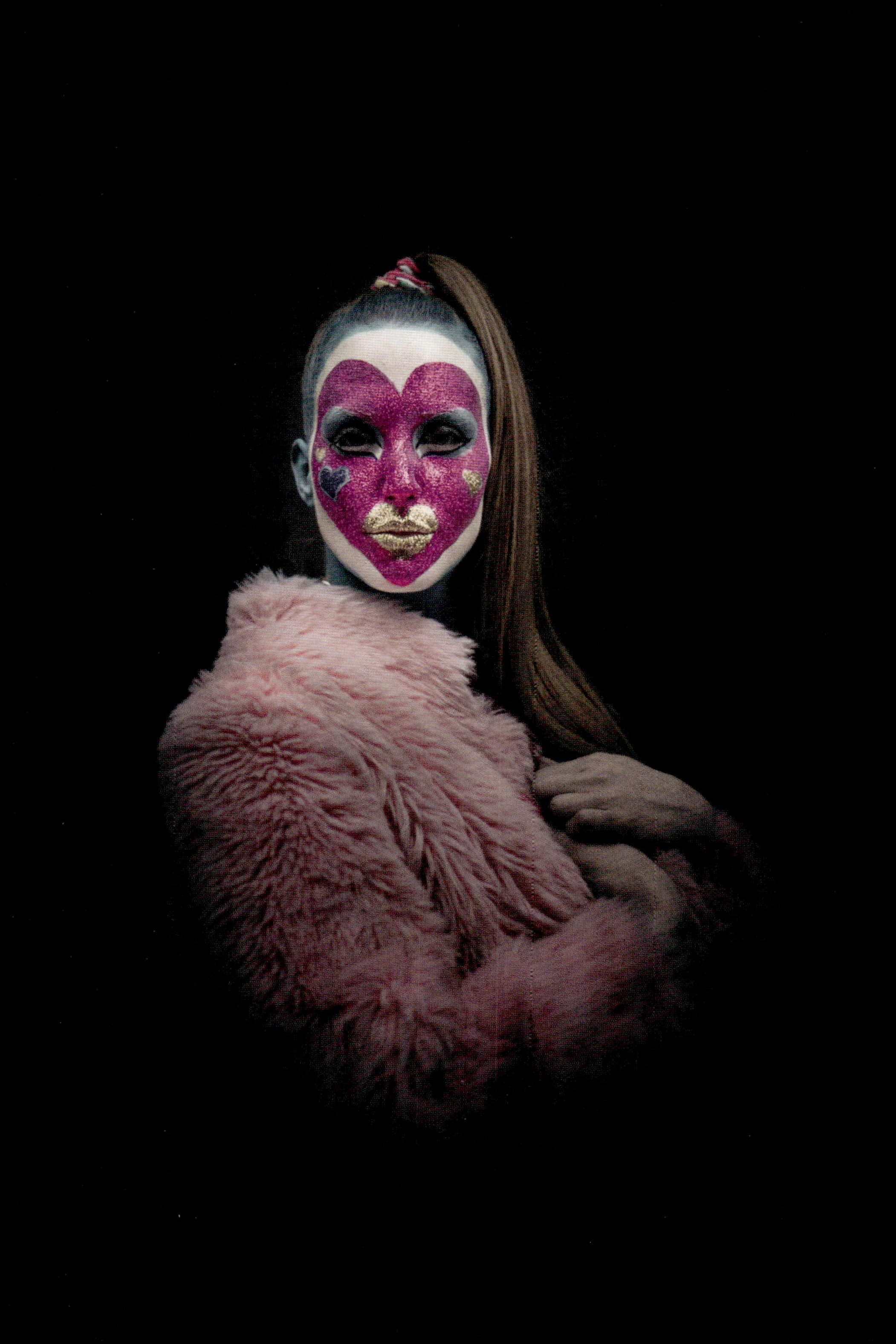

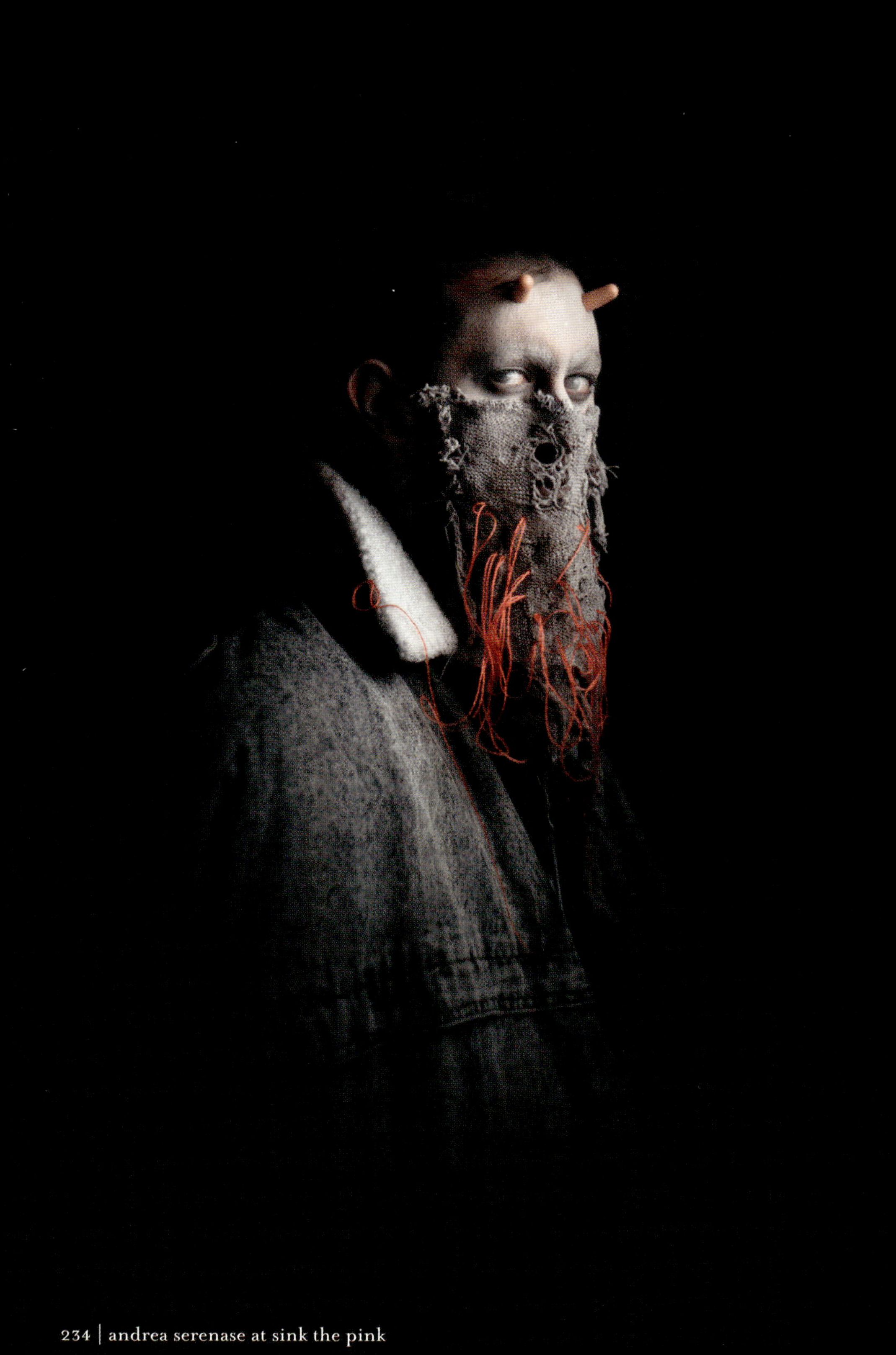

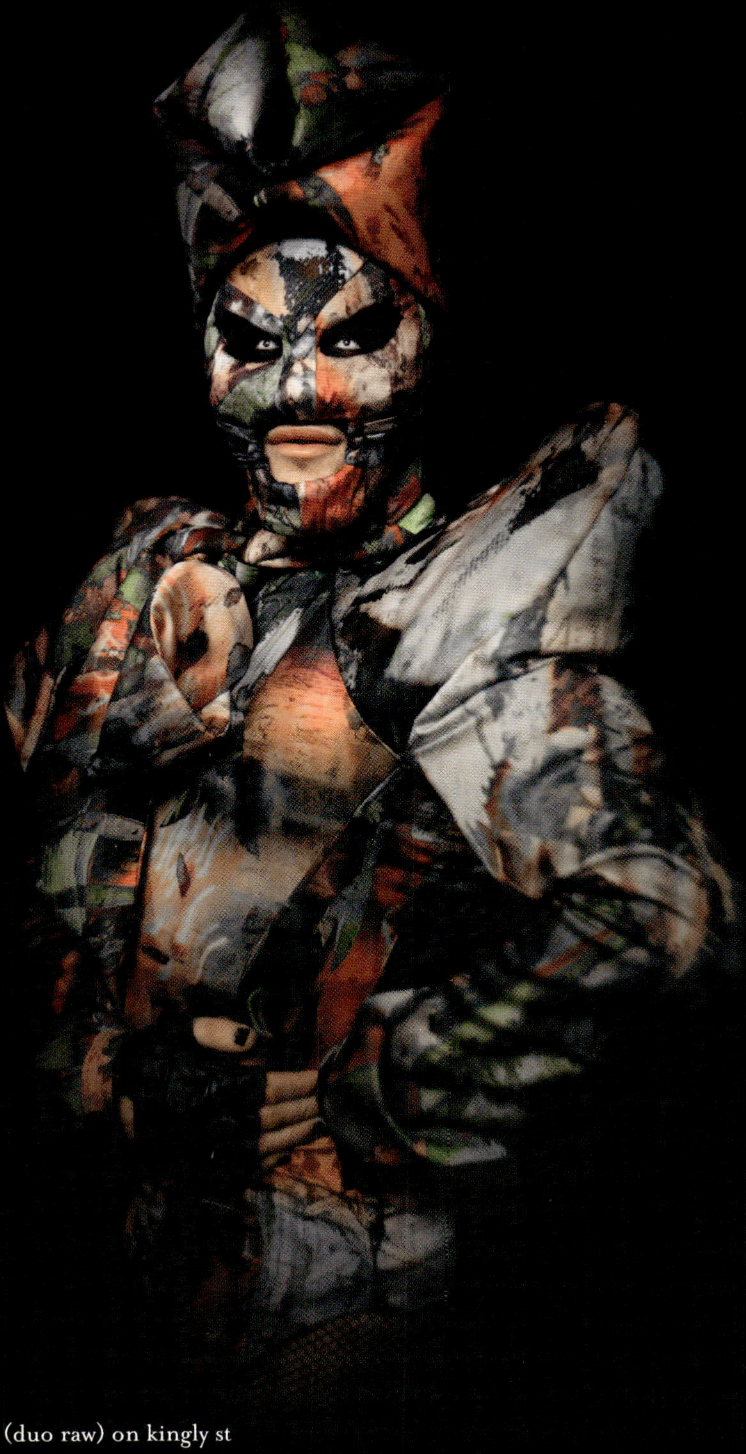

 | andreas (duo raw) on kingly st

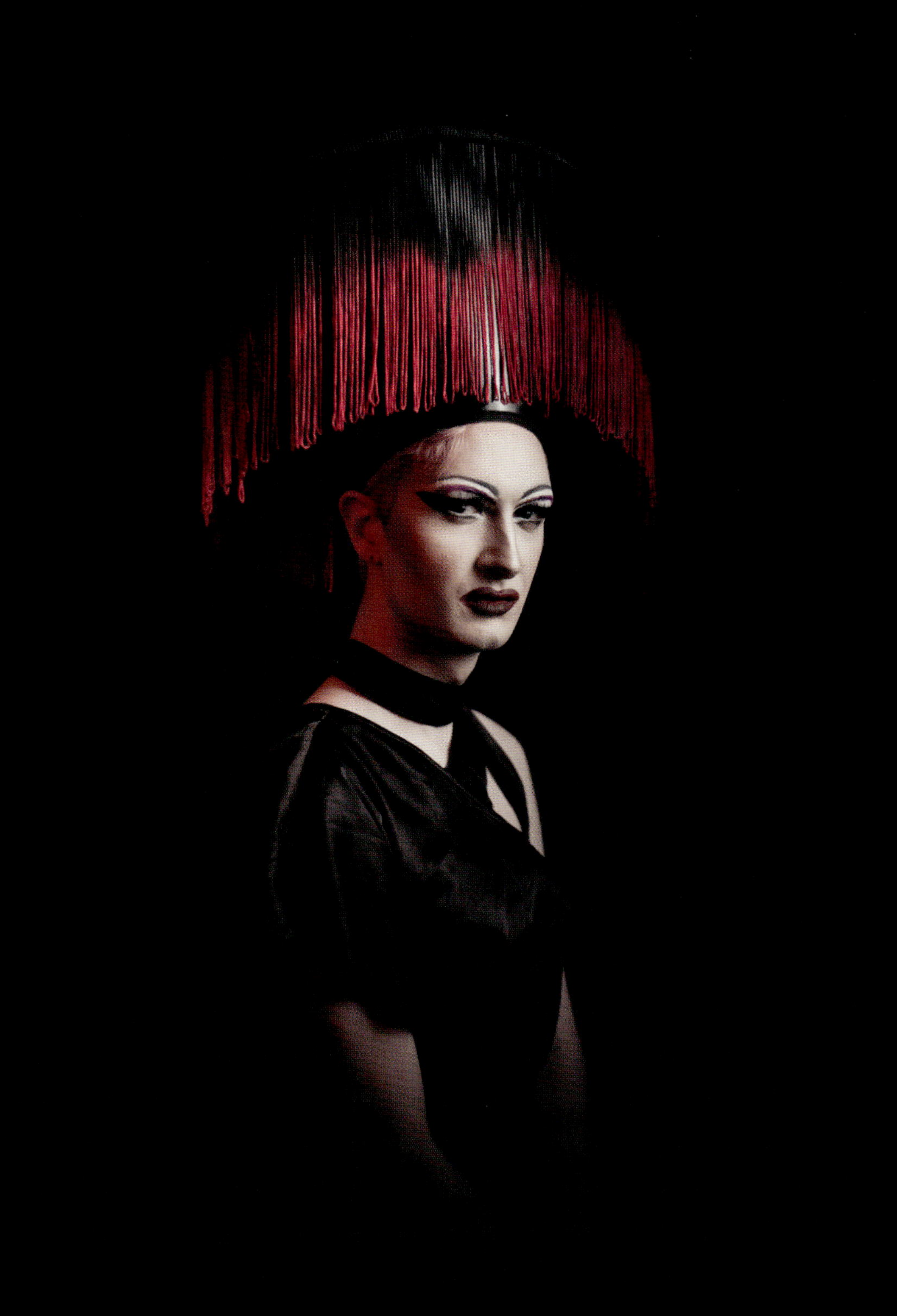

 | cola phalquero at the troxy

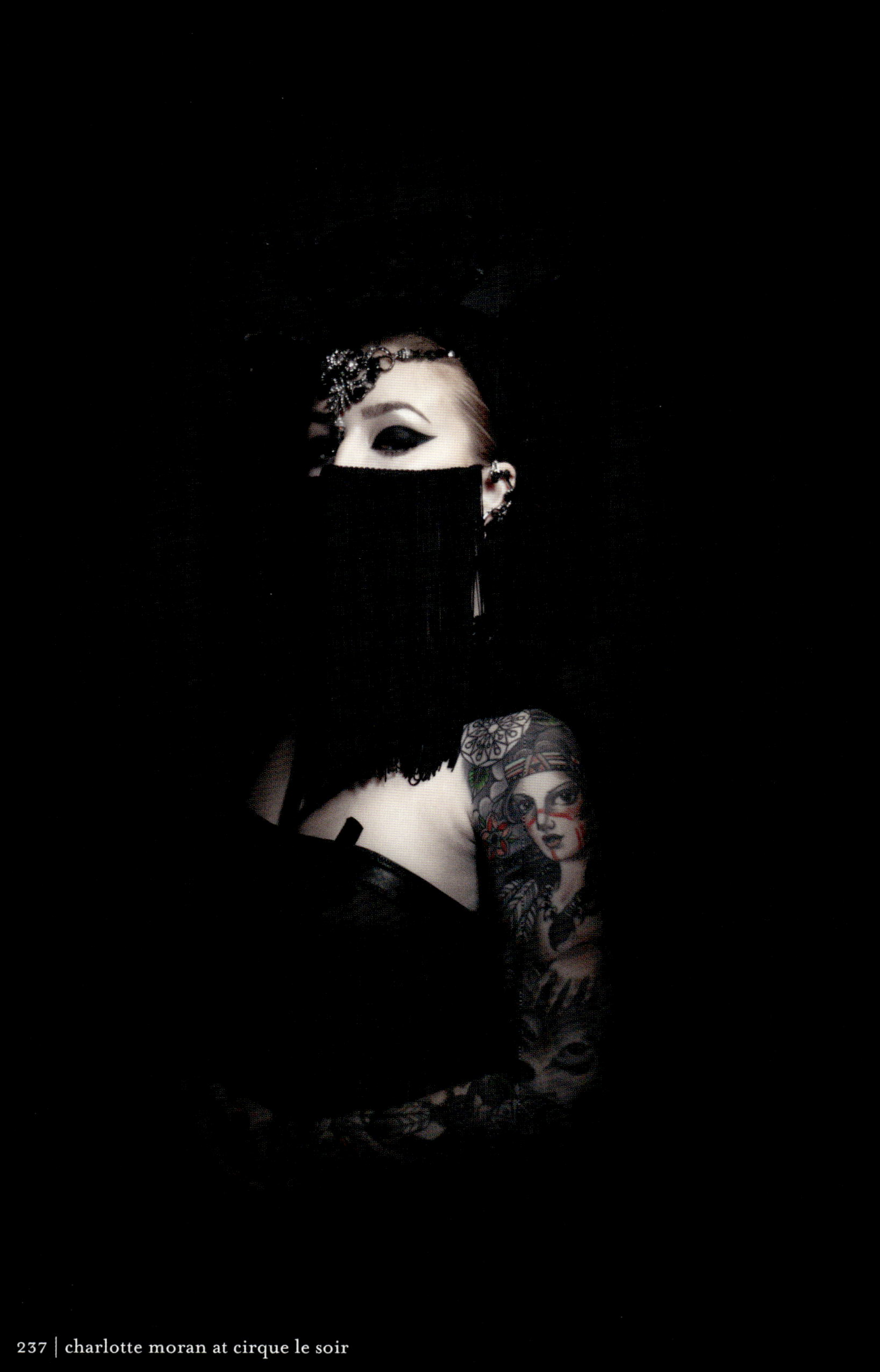

 | charlotte moran at cirque le soir

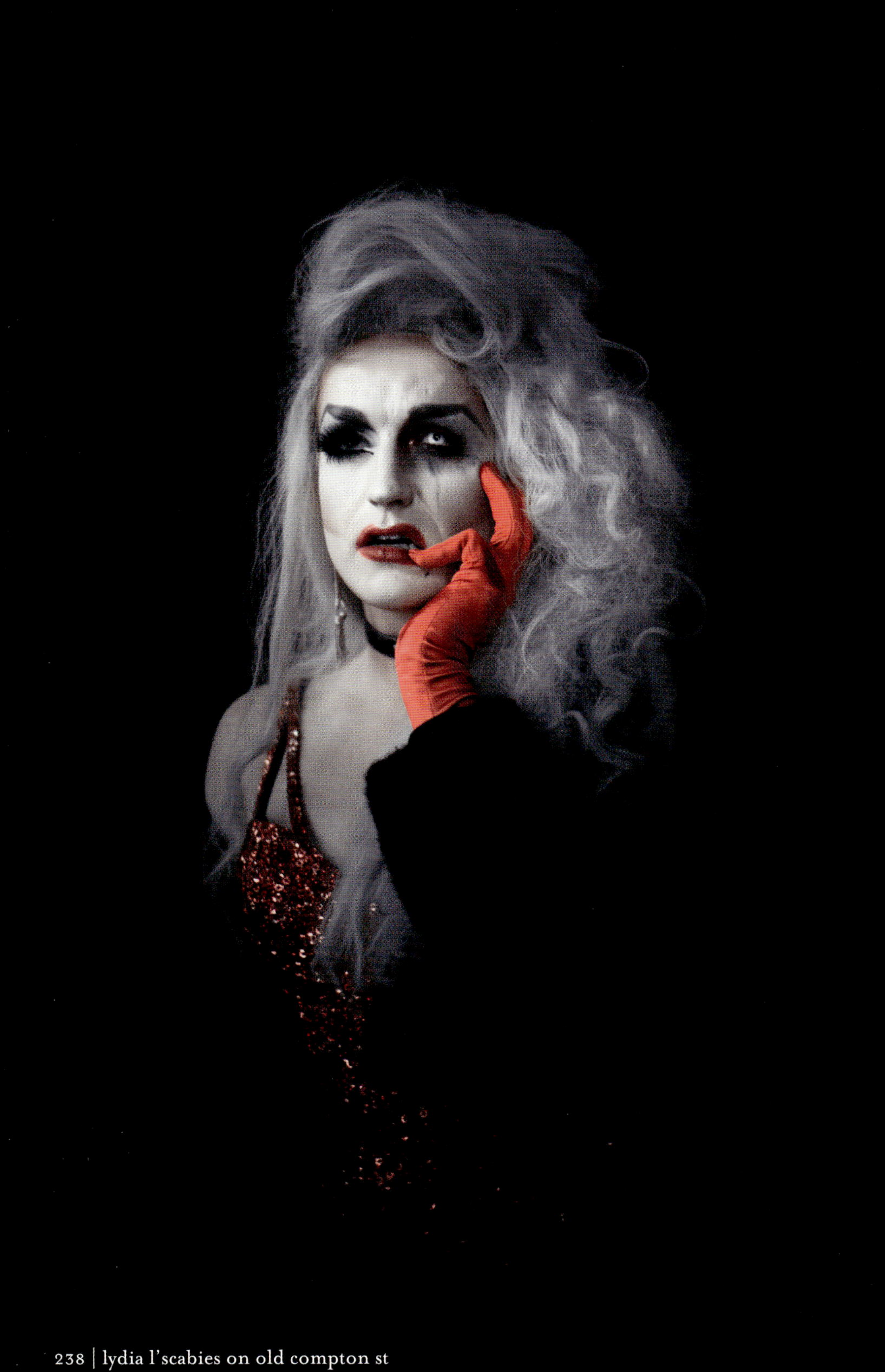

 lydia l'scabies on old compton st

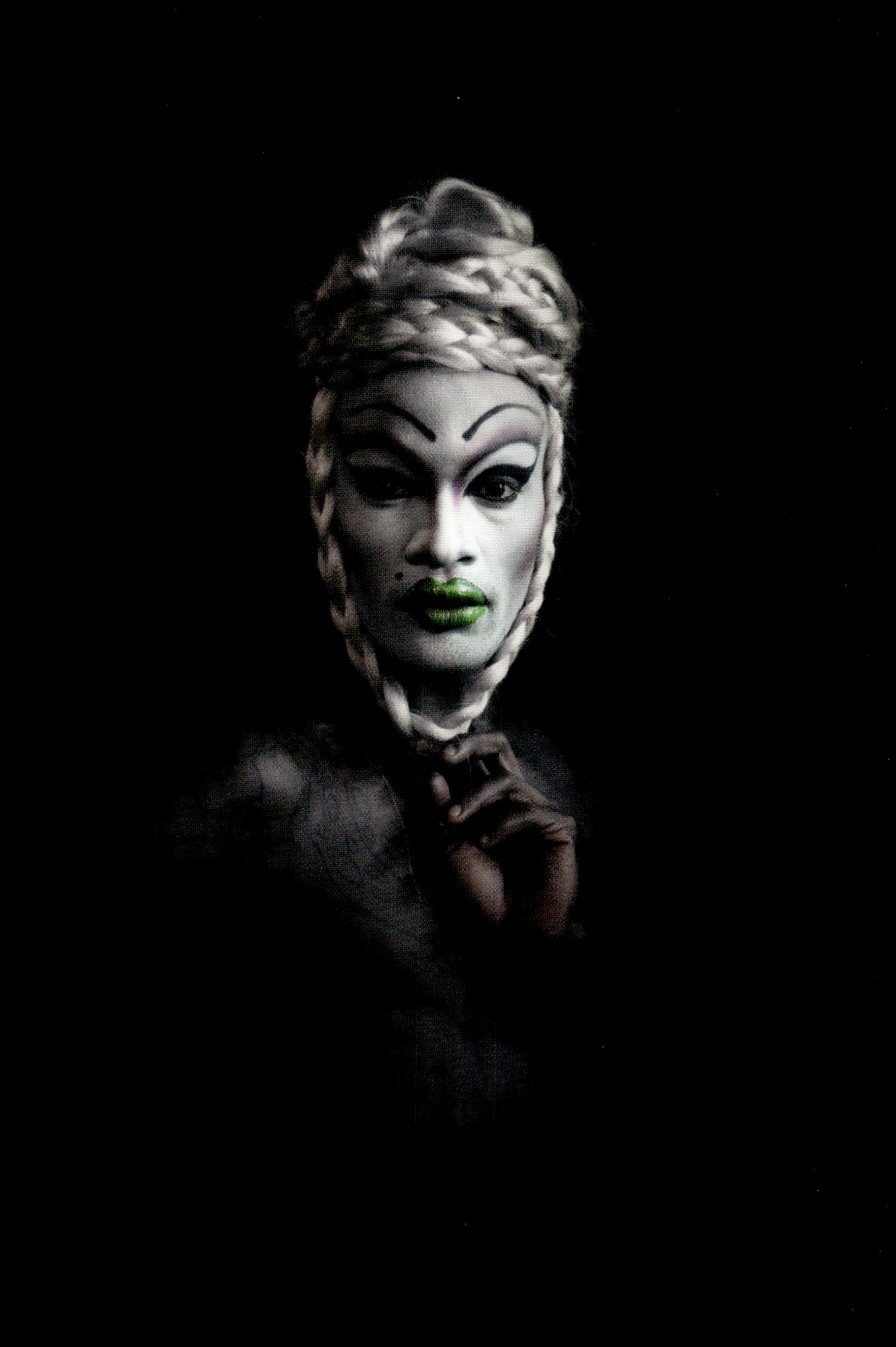

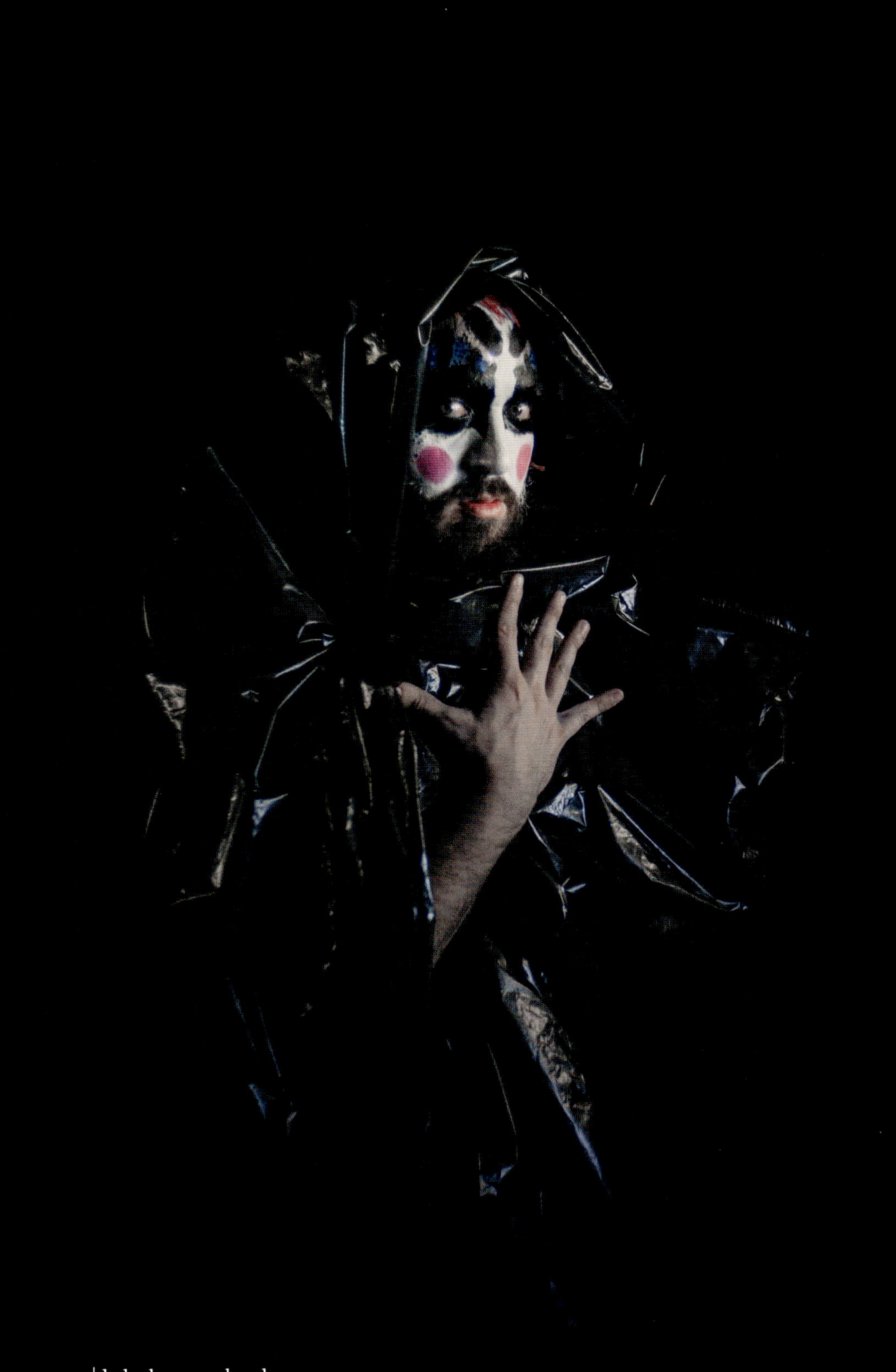

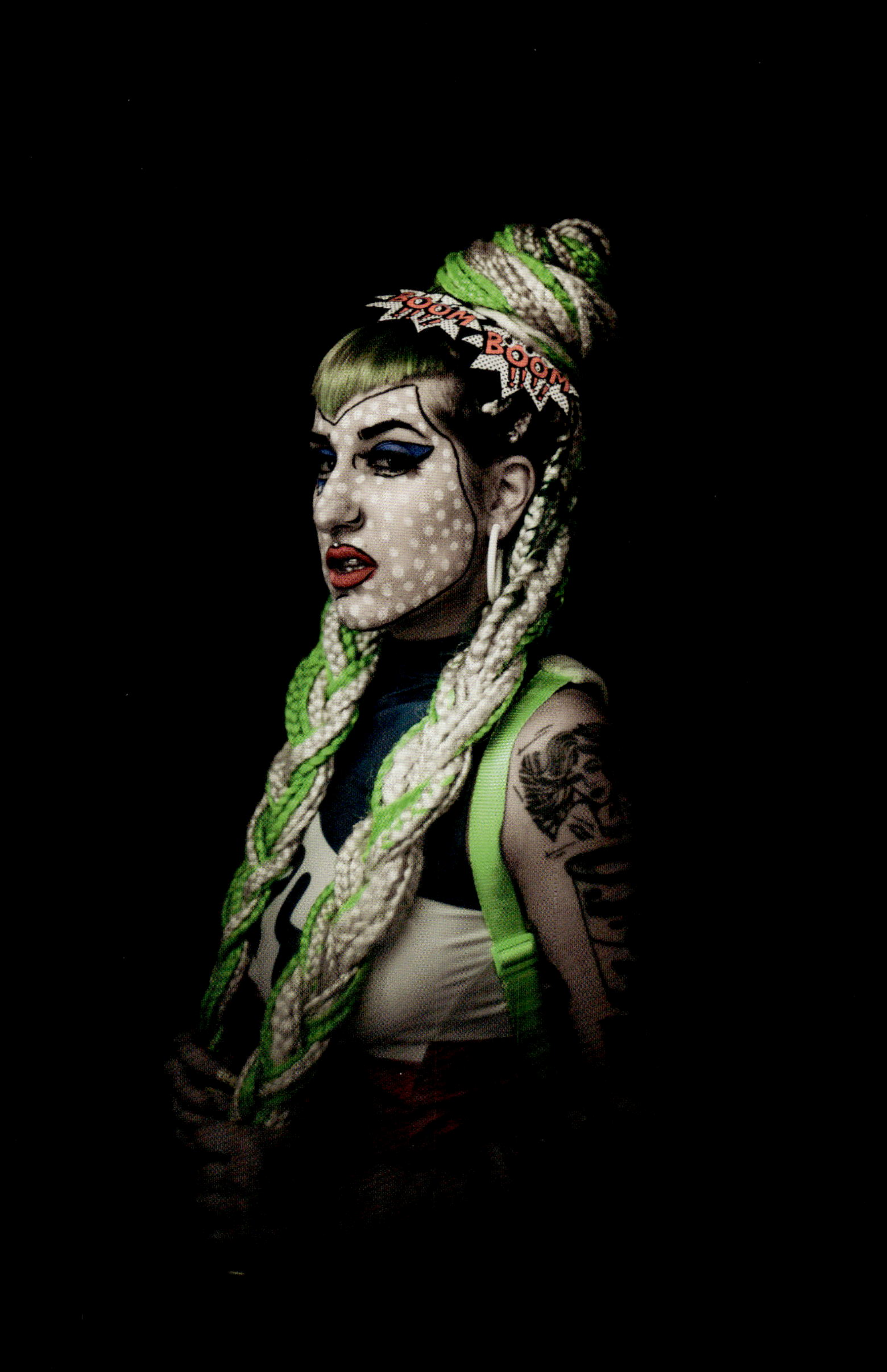

241 | kassandra powell on old compton st

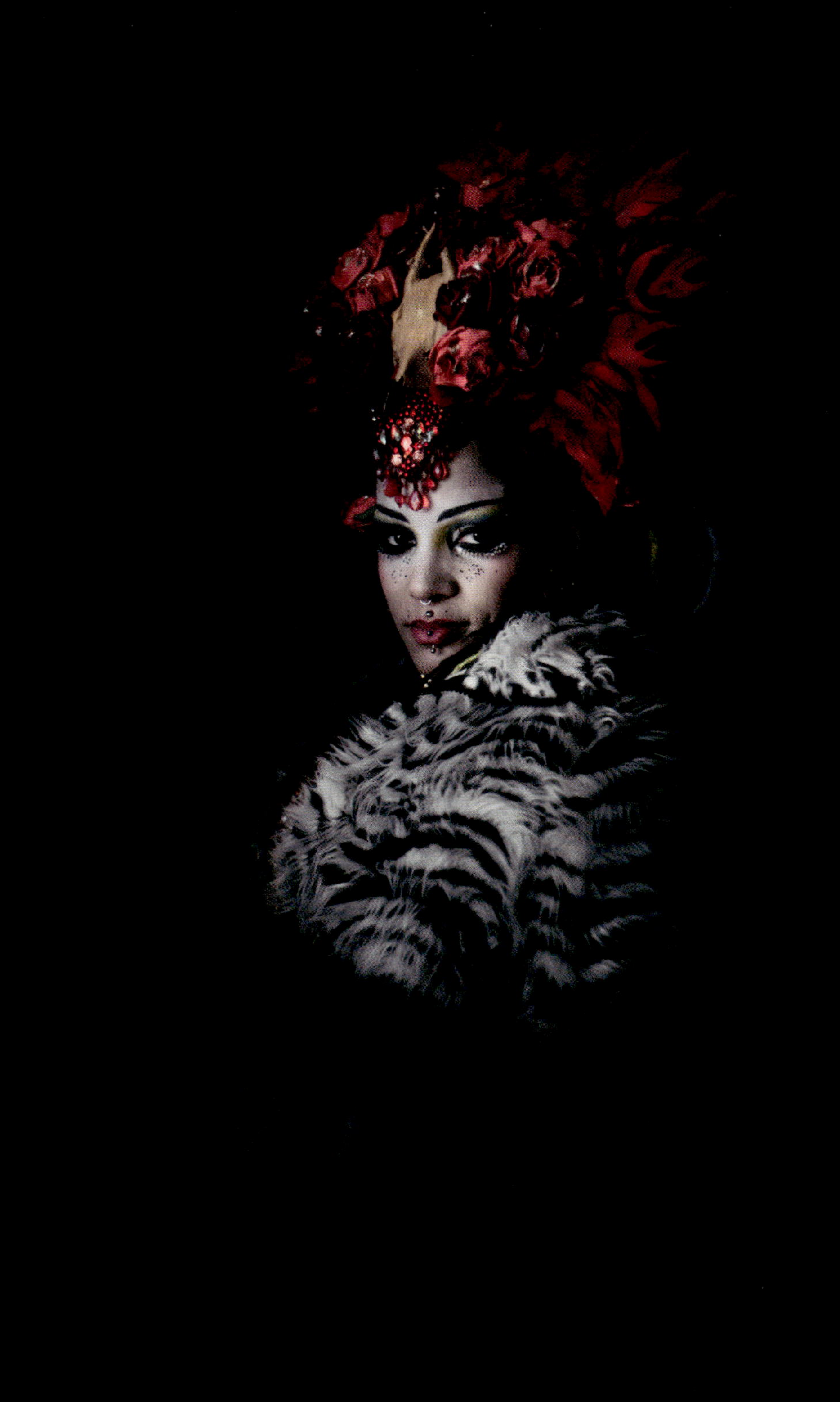

 jojo bones at egg london

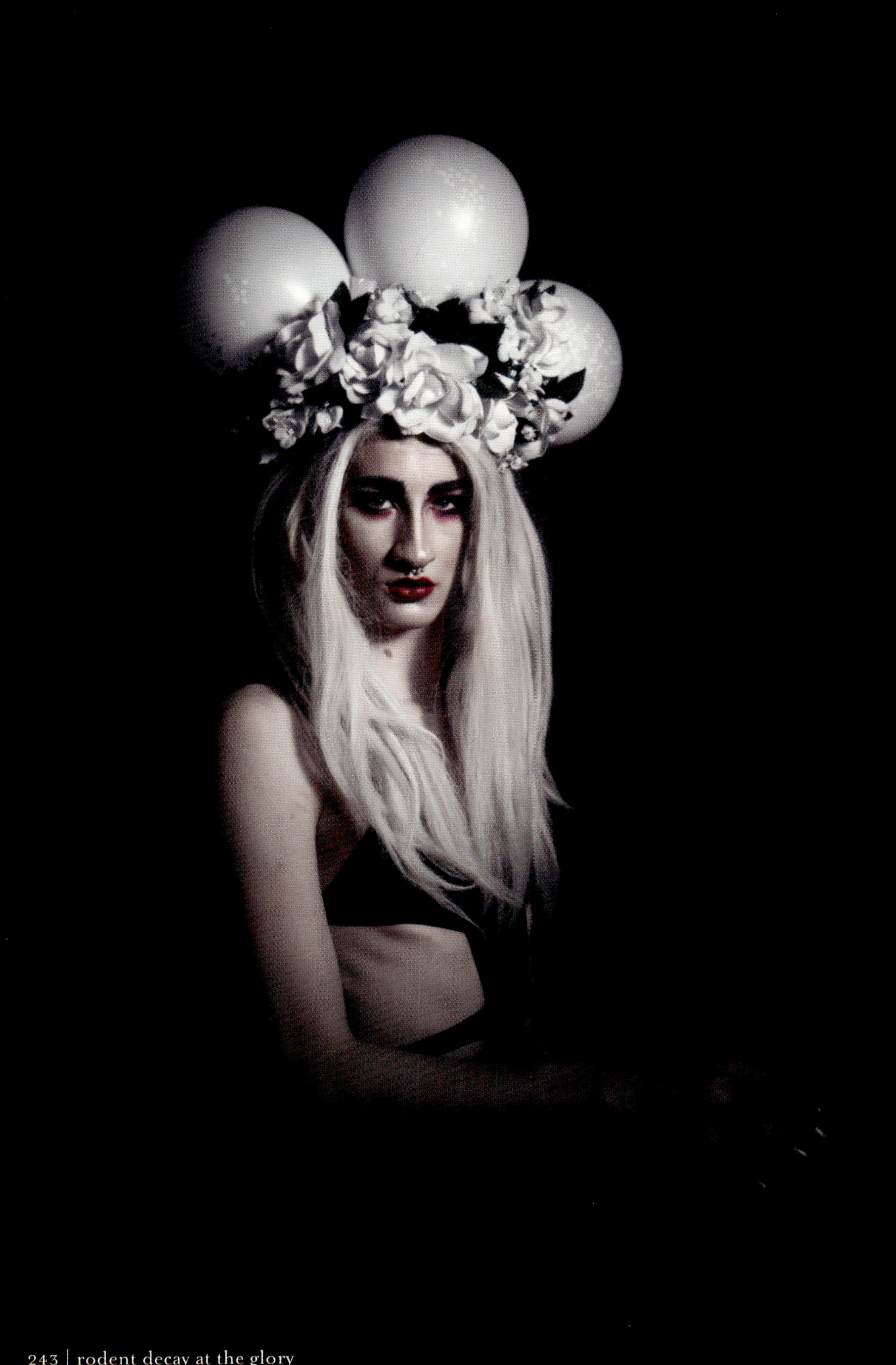

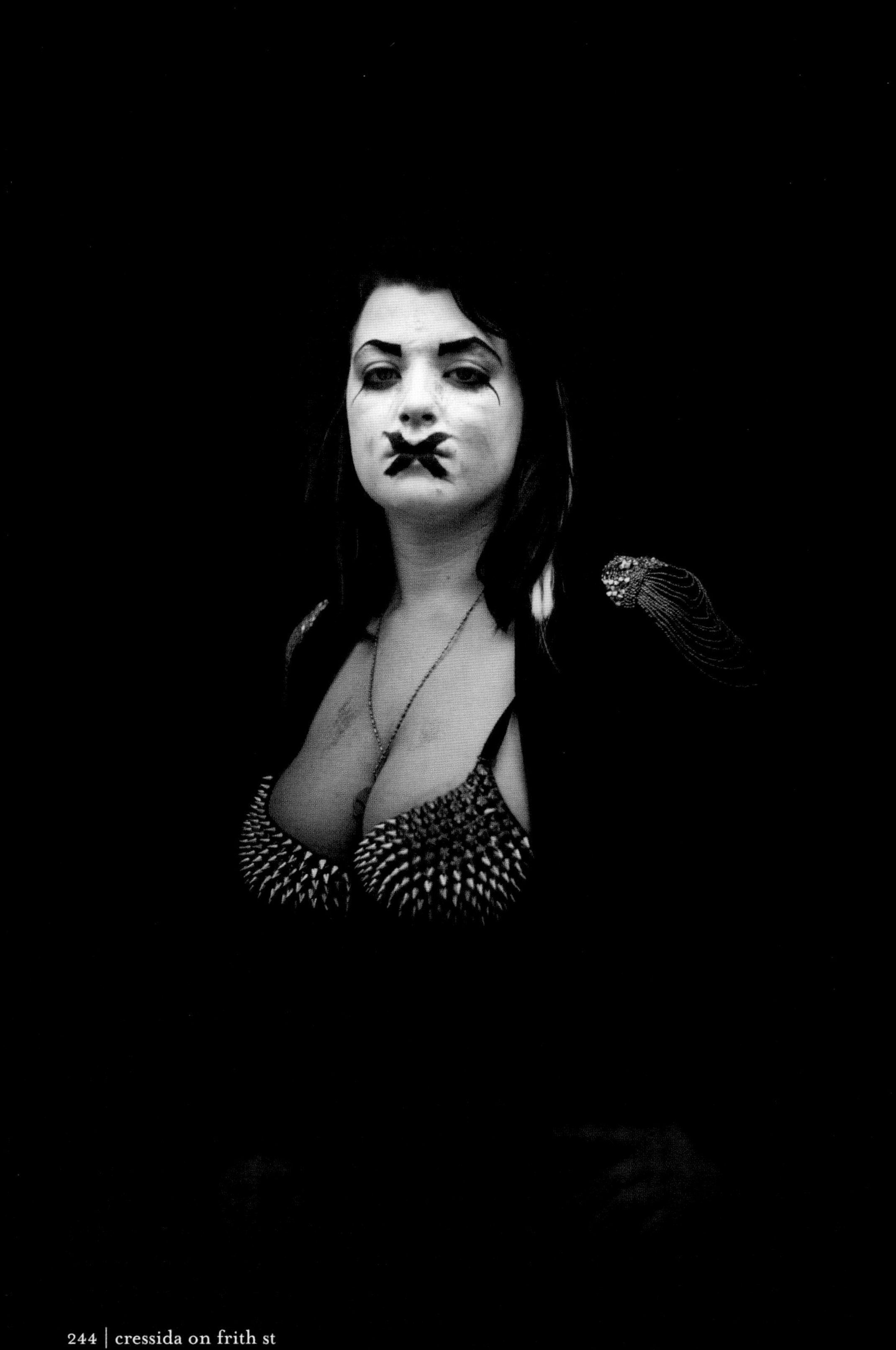

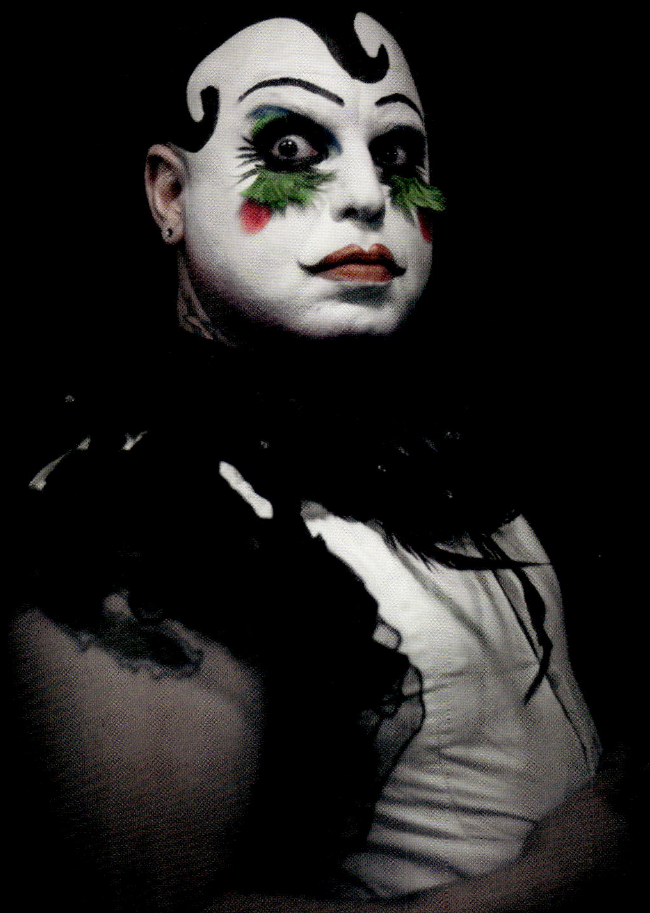

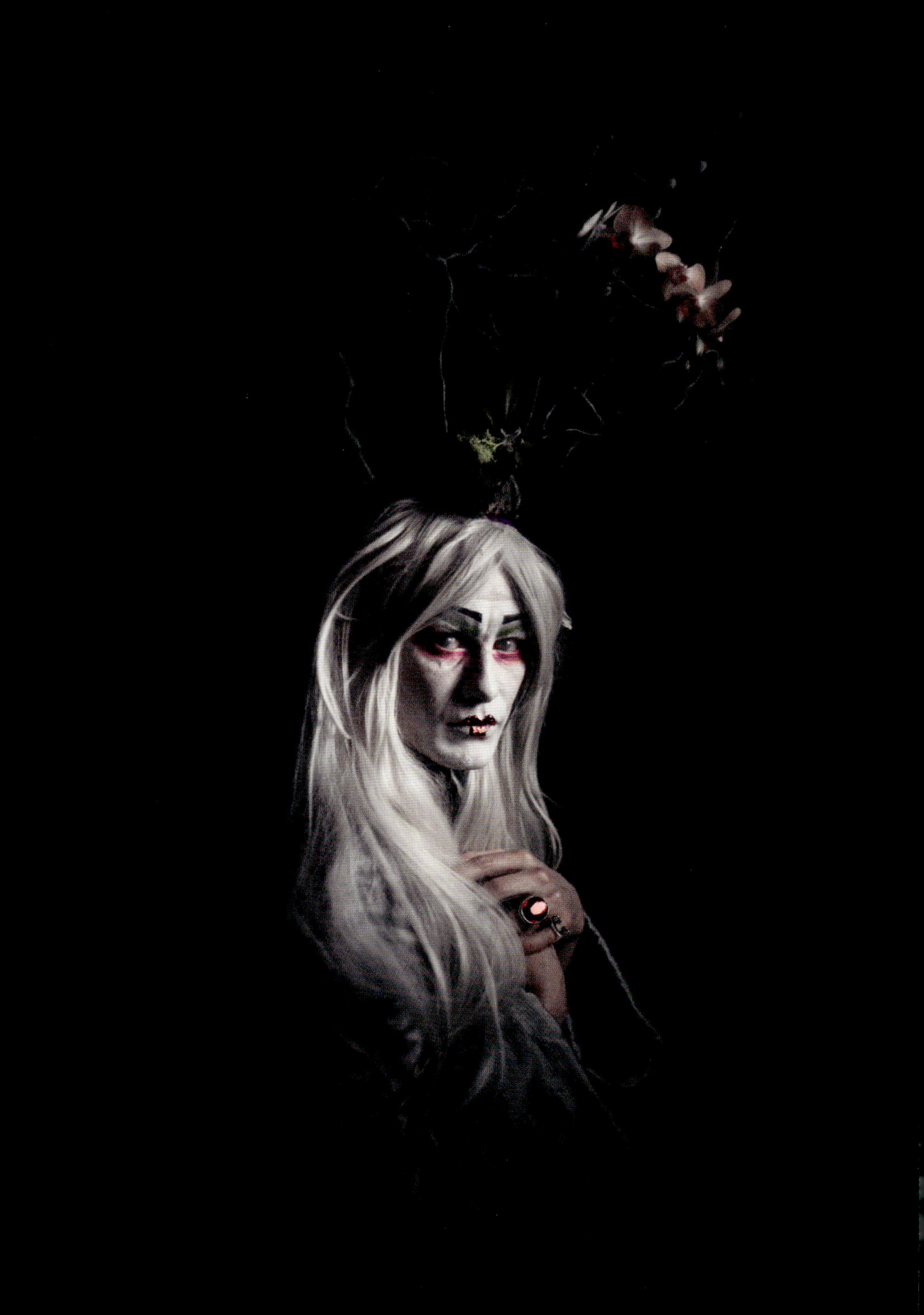

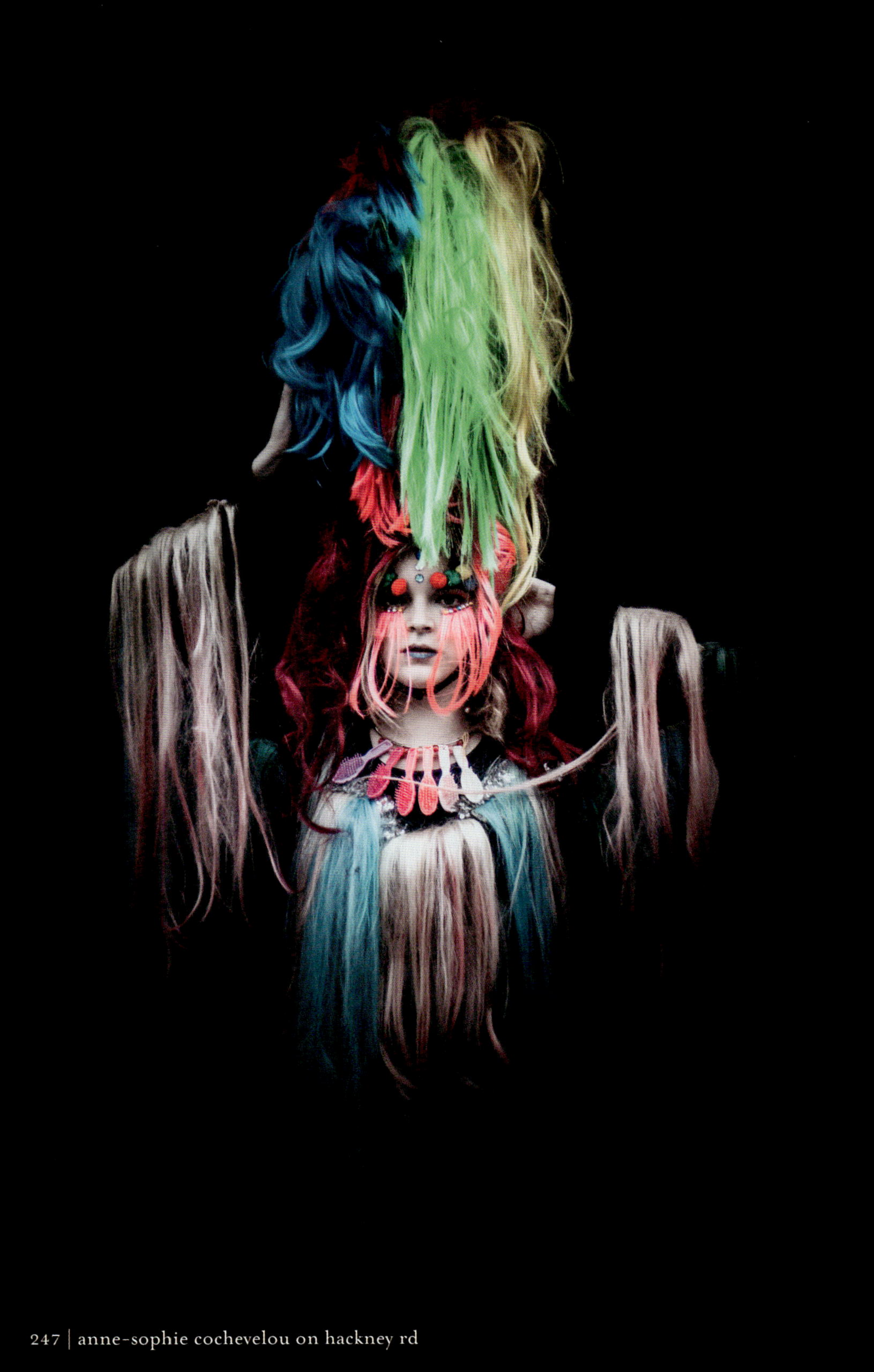

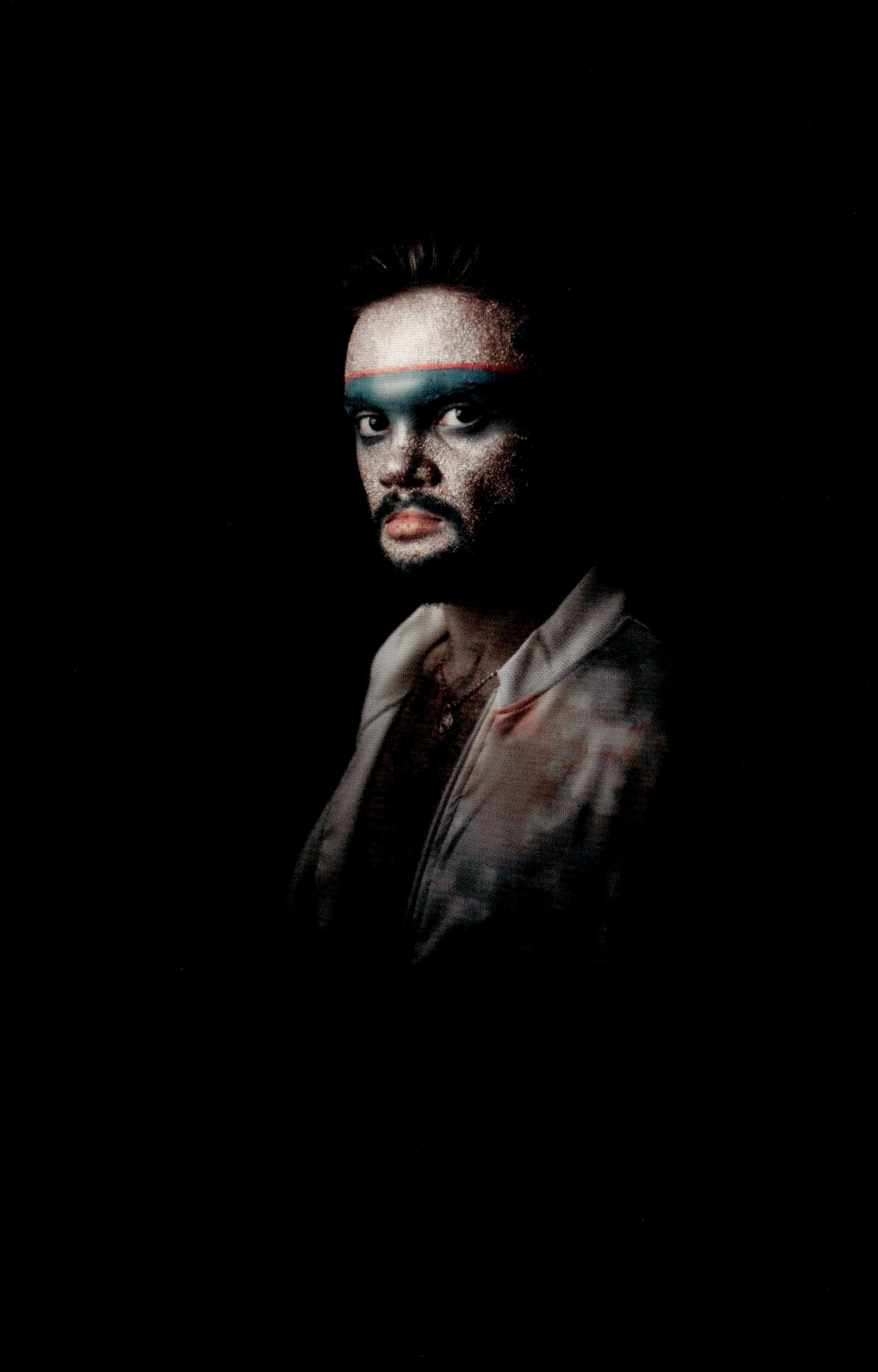

 | jacob alexander at wut? club

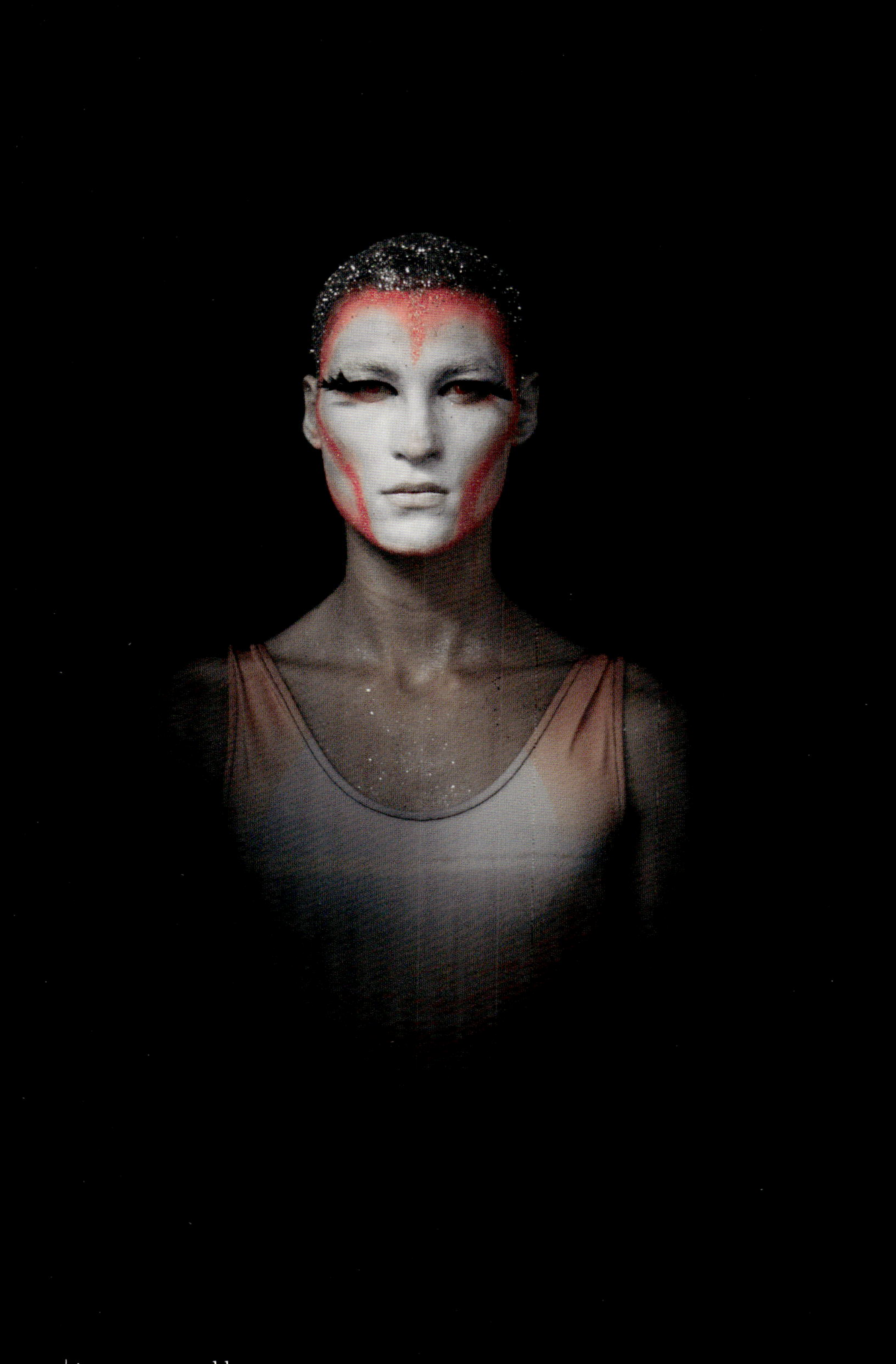

249 | james ross on old compton st

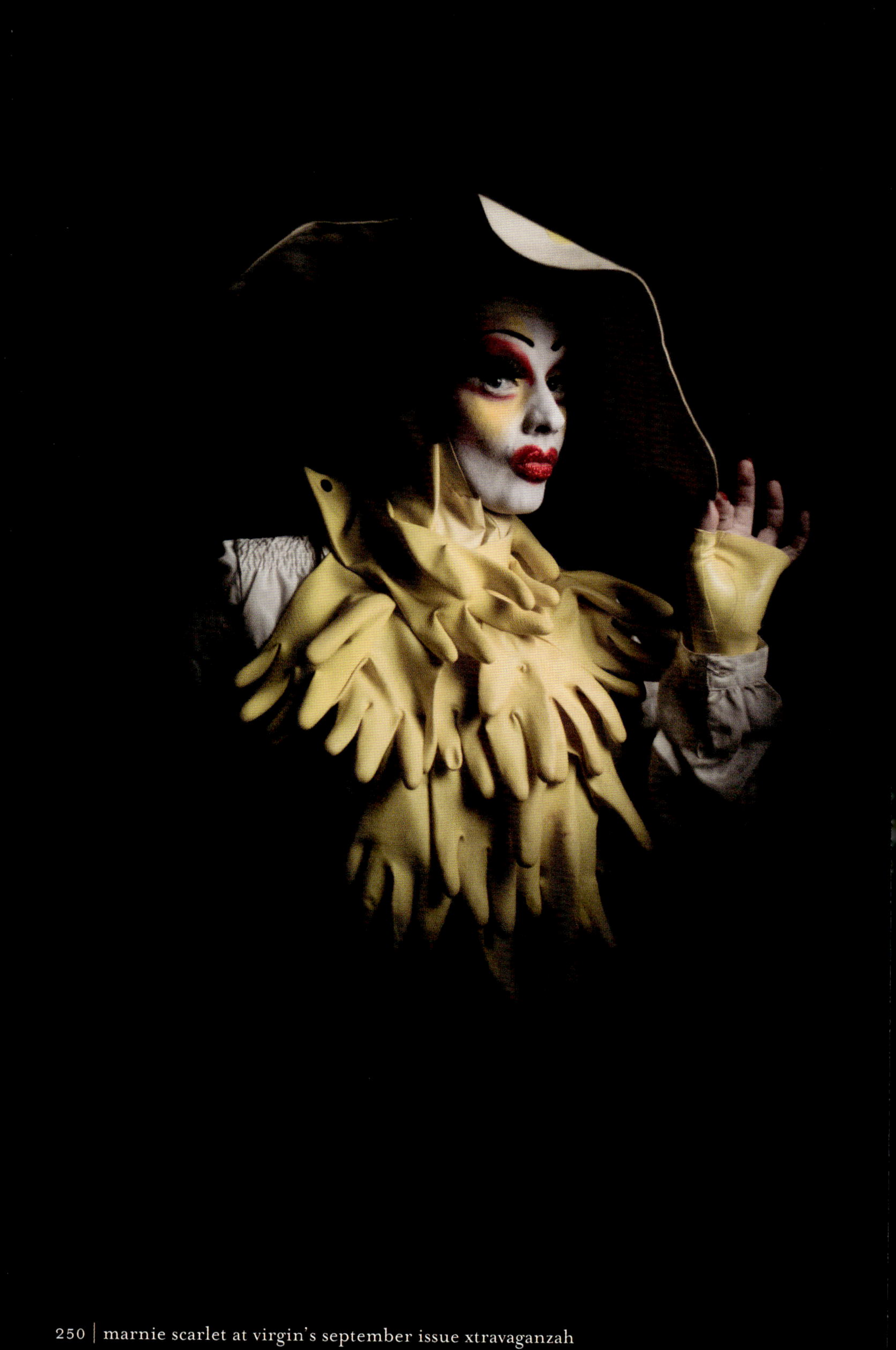

 | marnie scarlet at virgin's september issue xtravaganzah

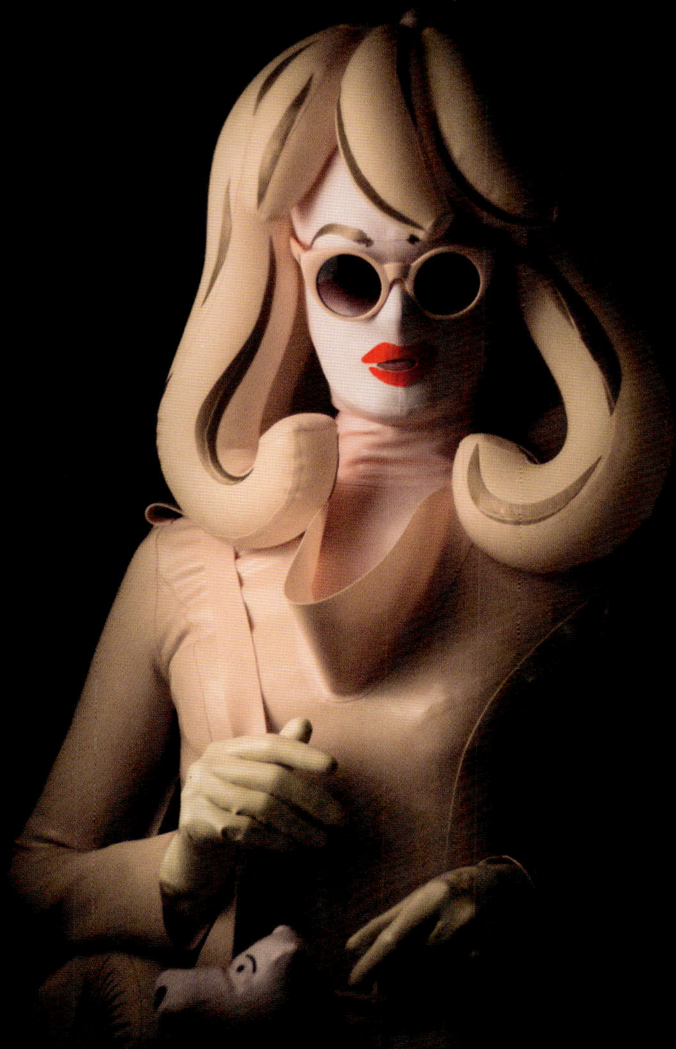

 pandemonia at the sorapol london fashion week show

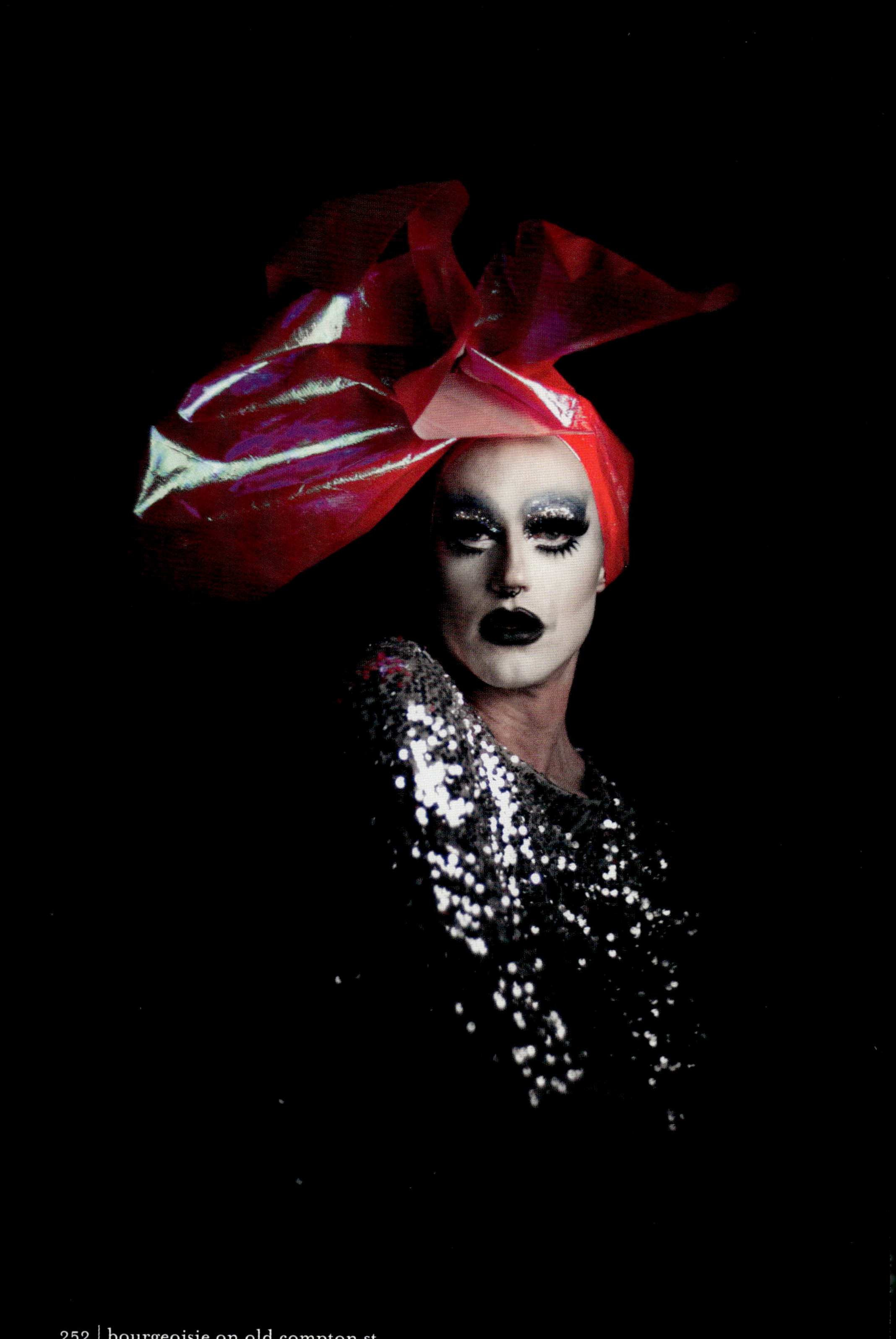

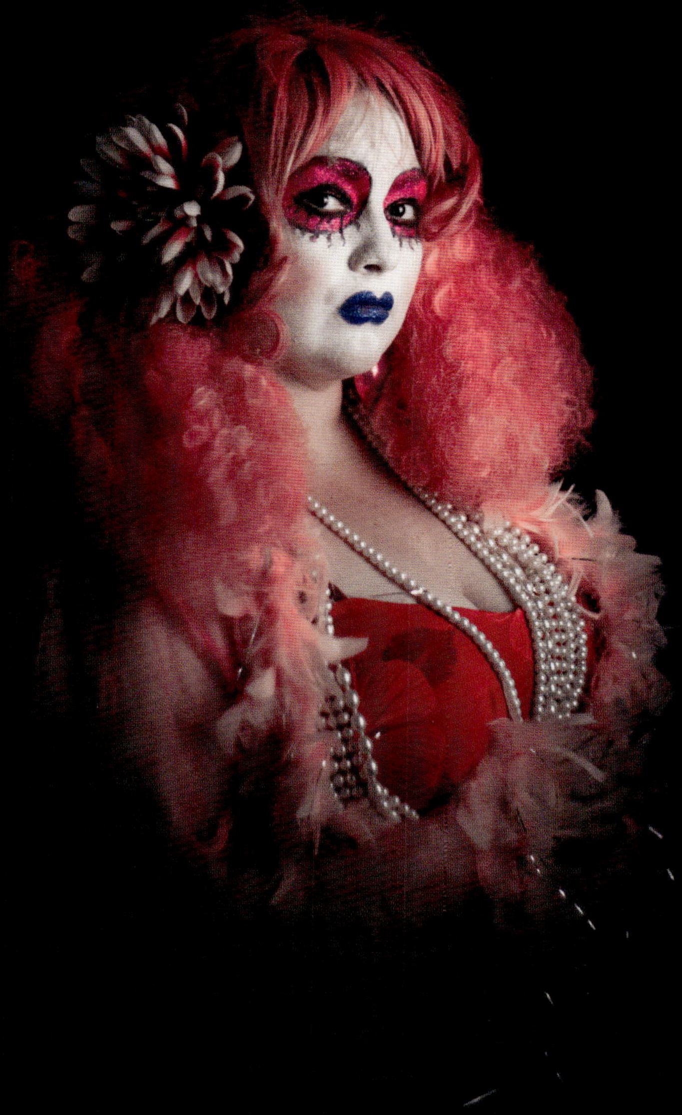

 | moan crawford at the amy grimehouse tudor realness ball

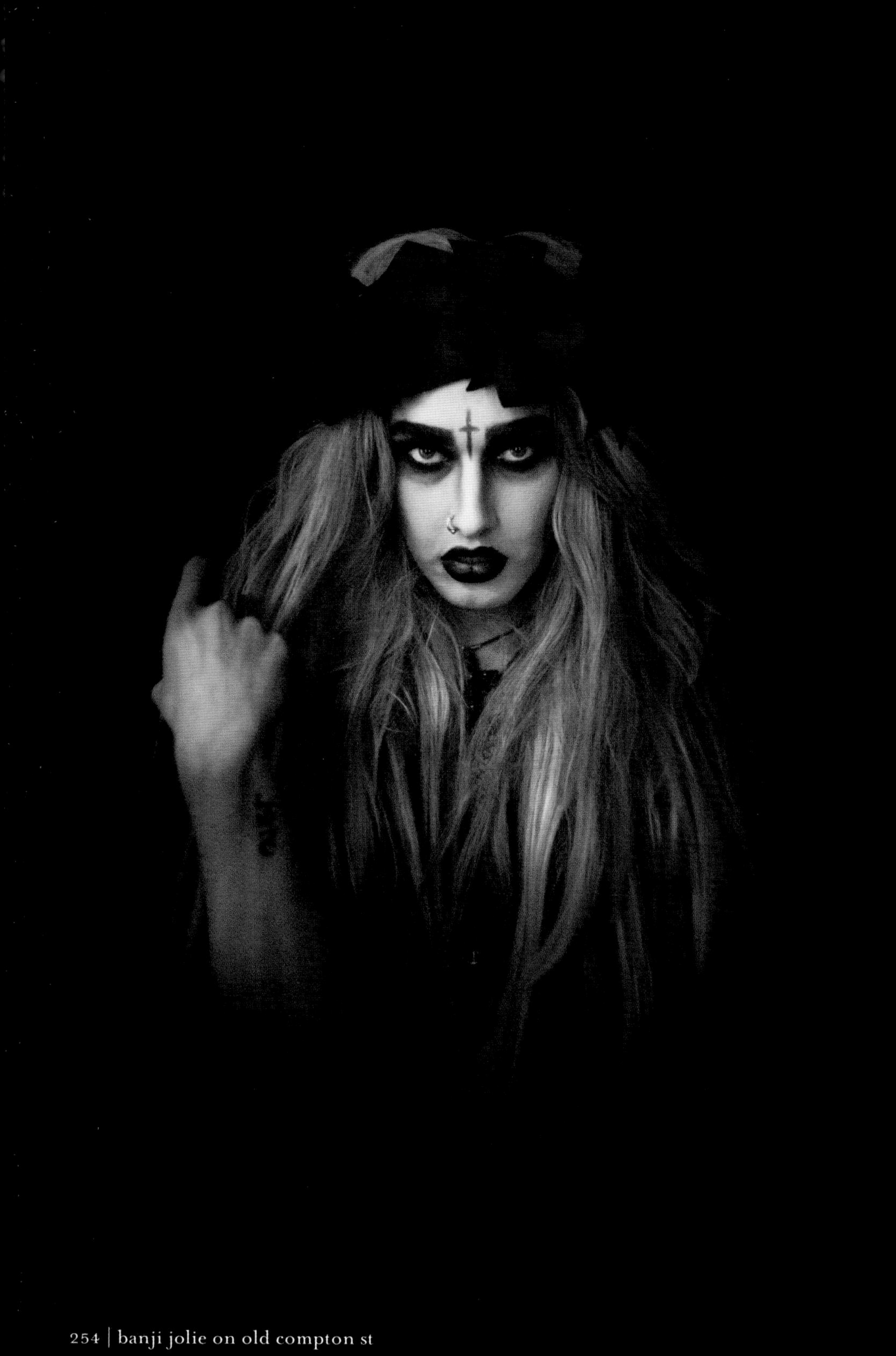

 banji jolie on old compton st

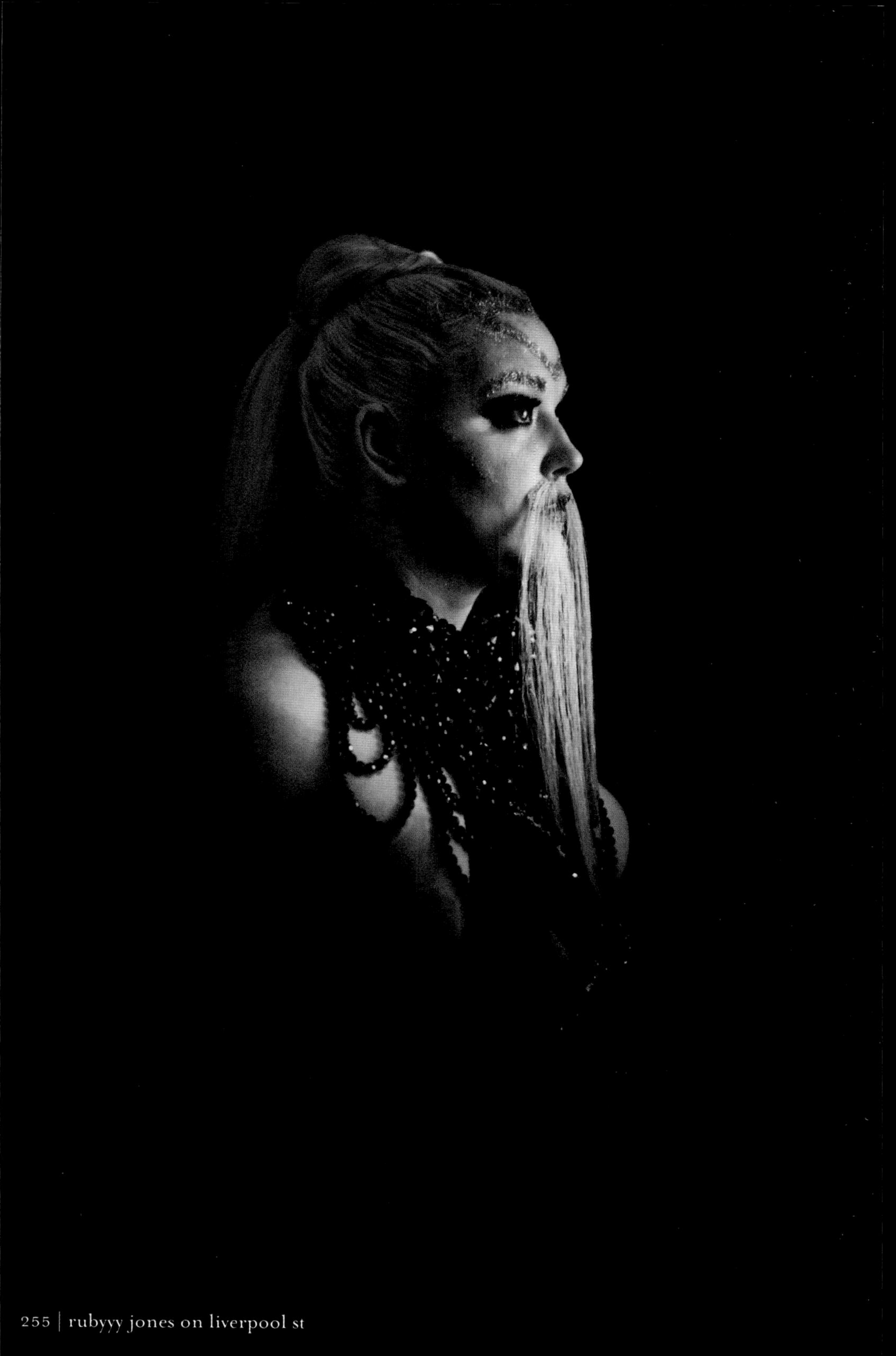

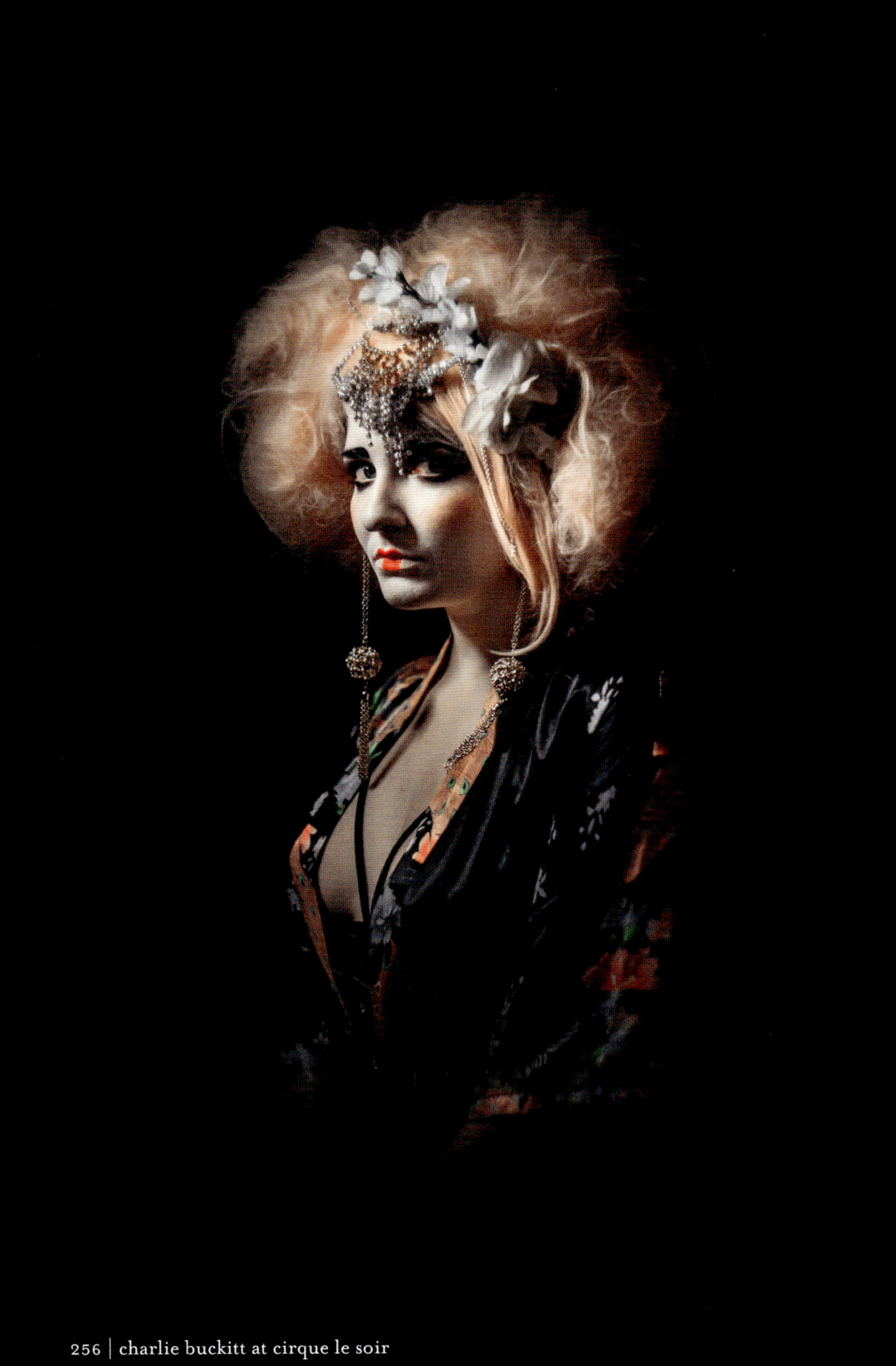

 charlie buckitt at cirque le soir

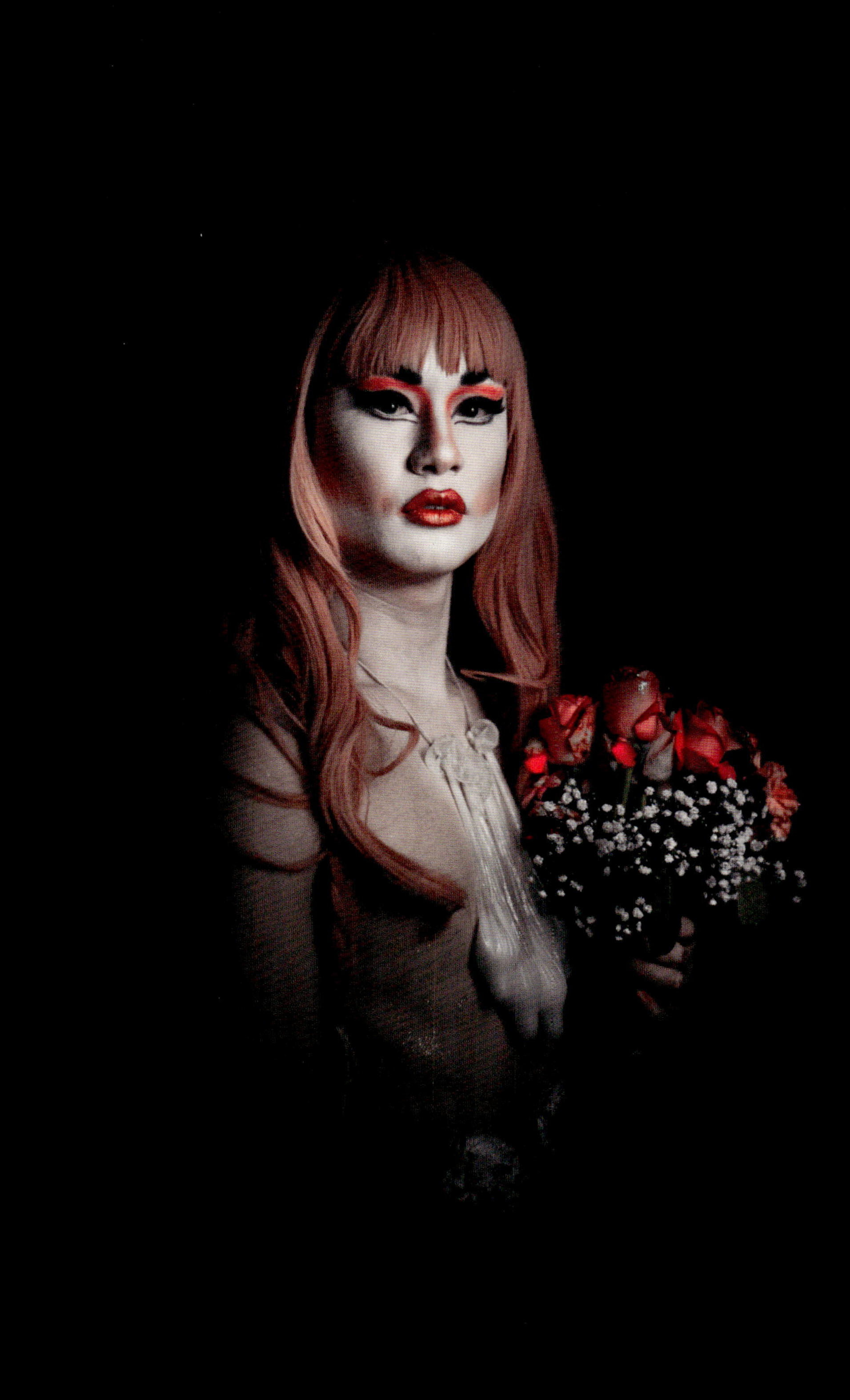

 | nekoko hime at the sink the pink winter ball

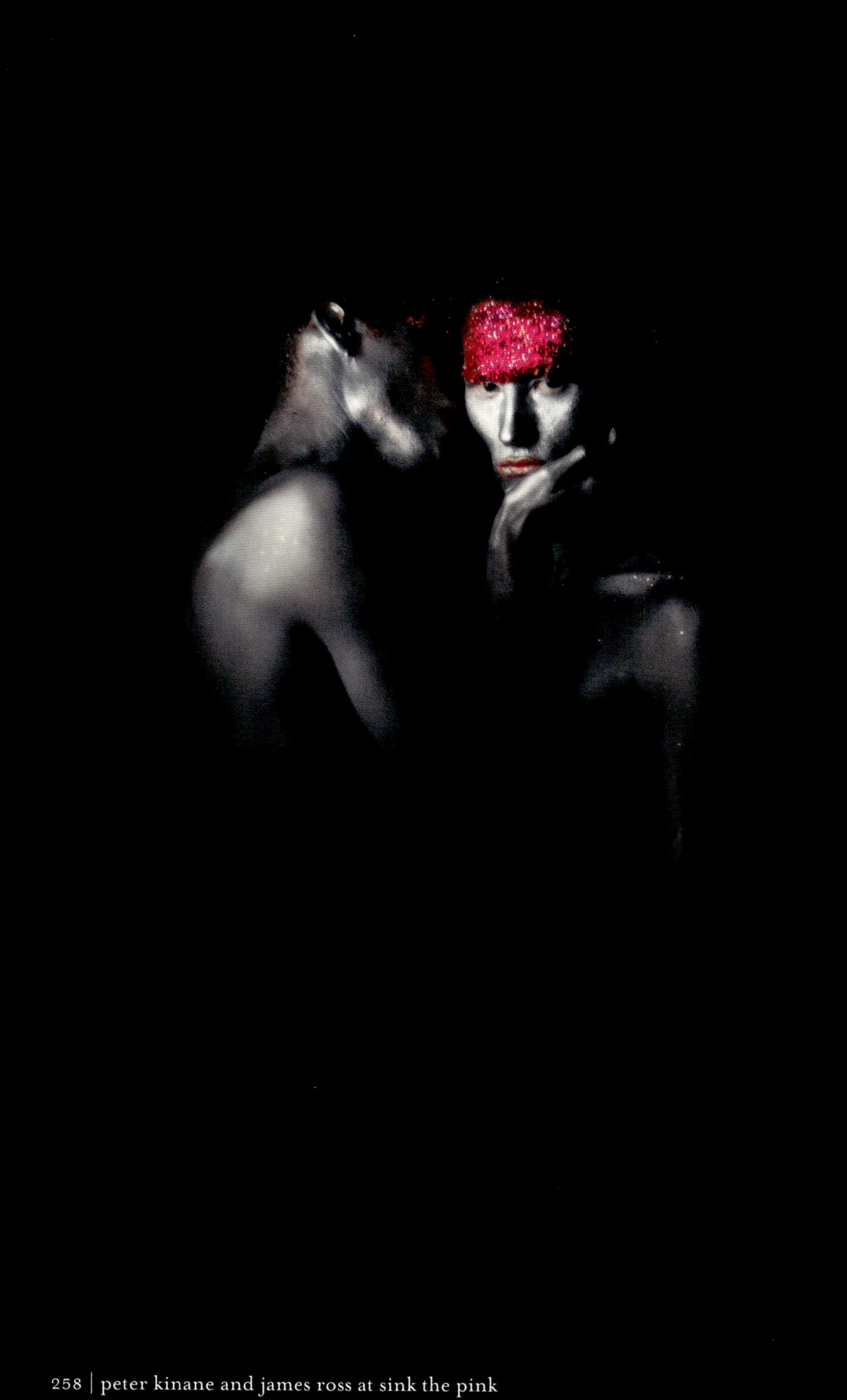

 | peter kinane and james ross at sink the pink

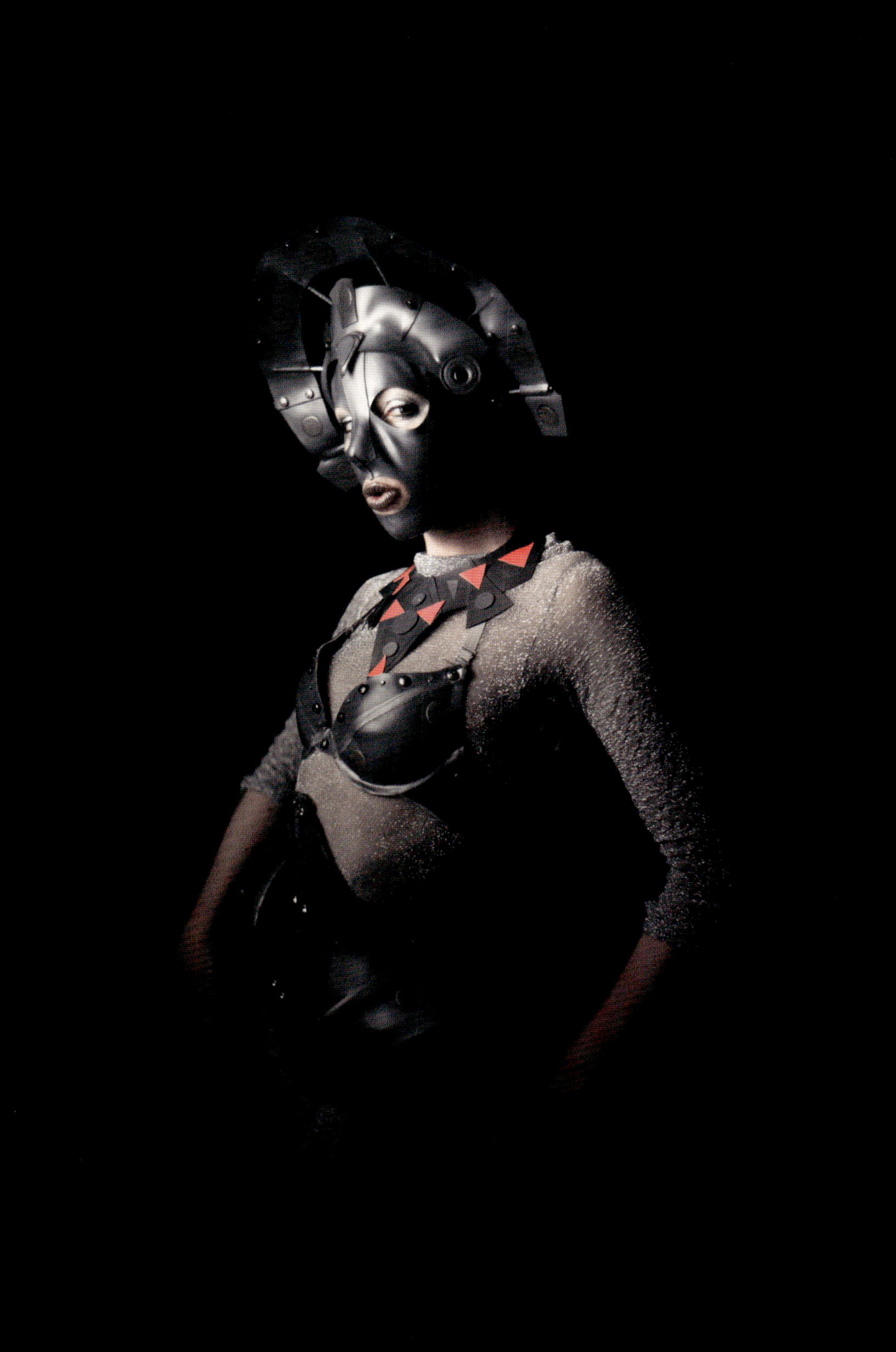

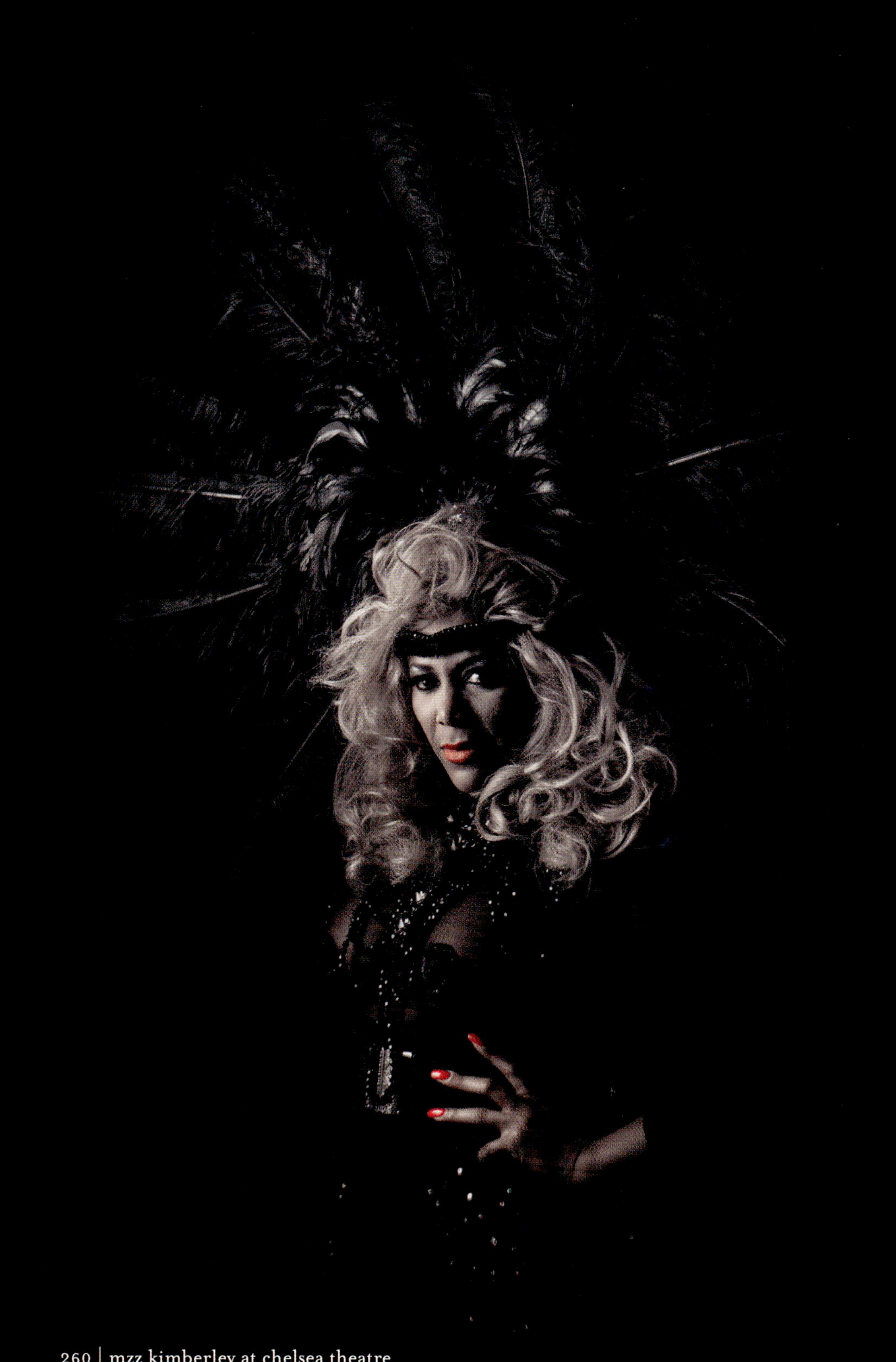

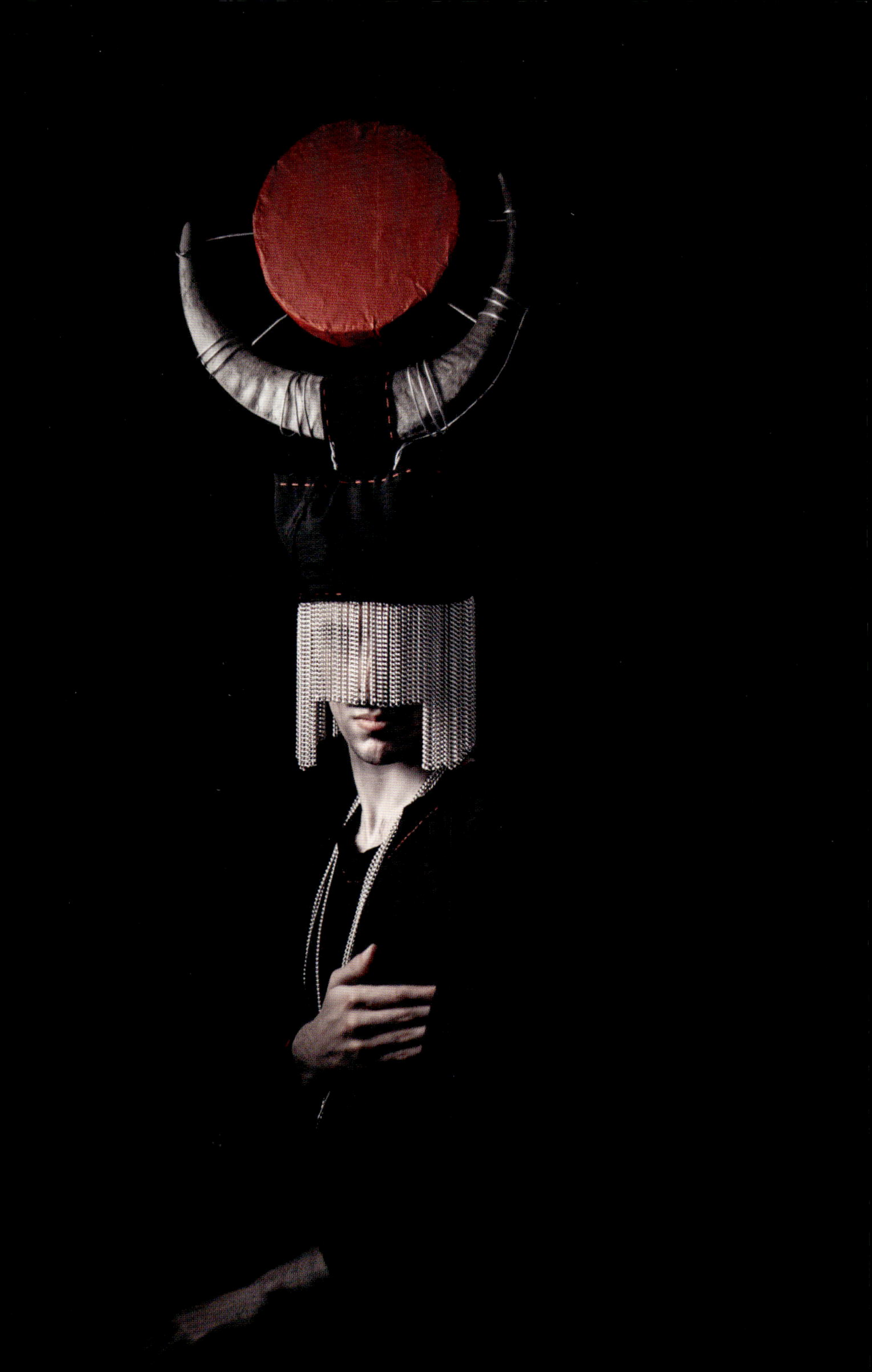

pedro merchán correas at kaos

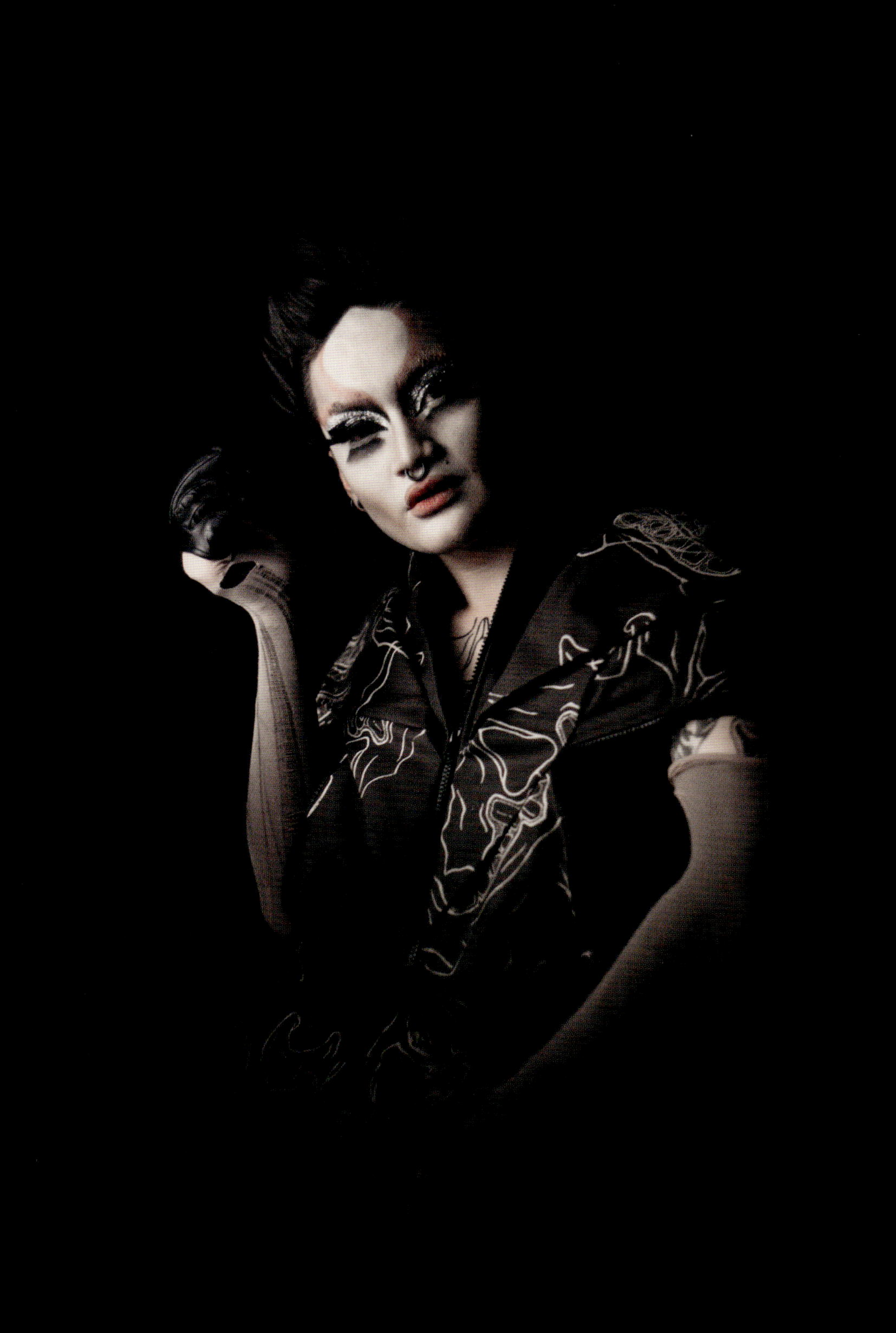

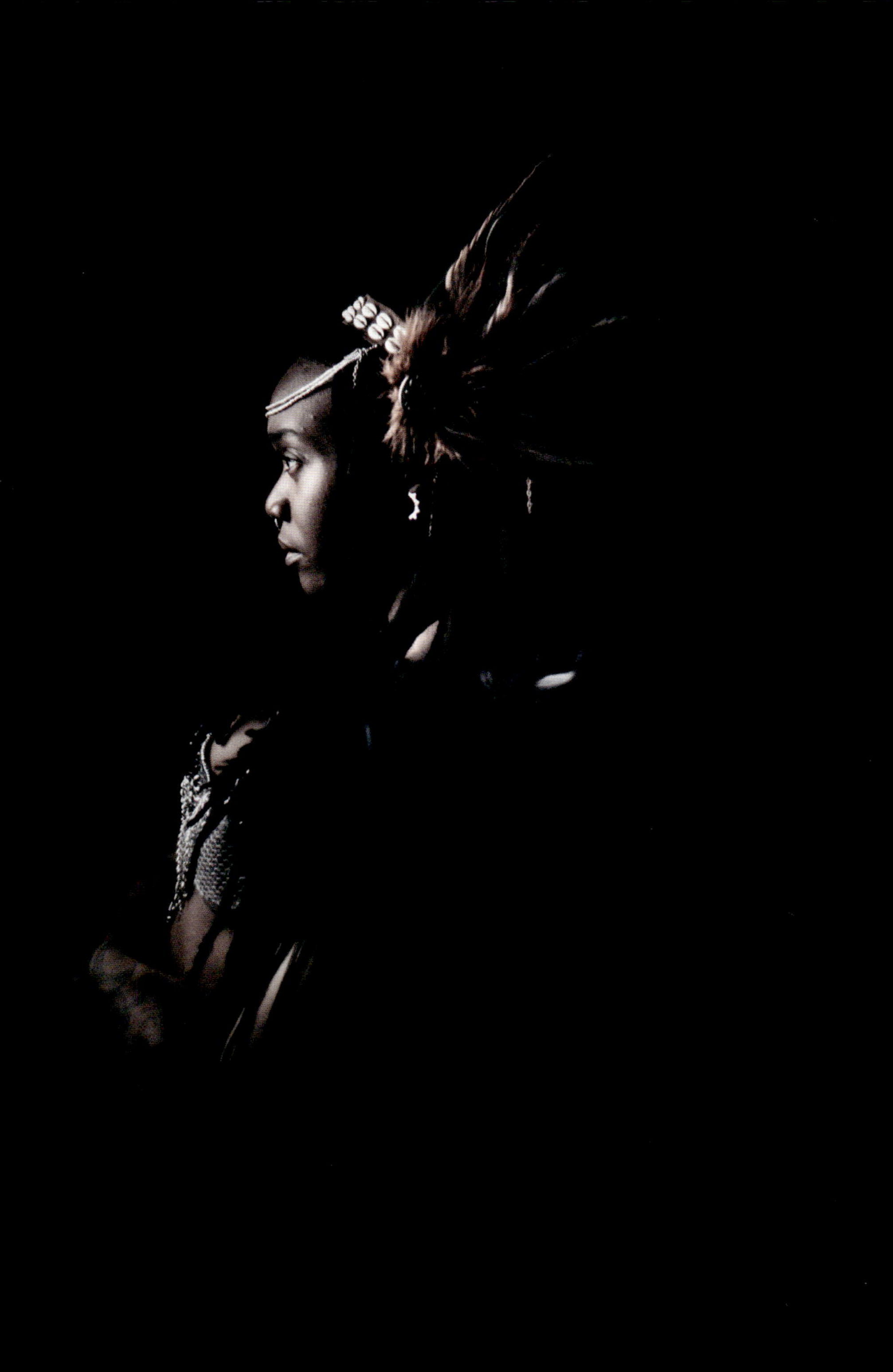

263 | lolo moni on hackney rd

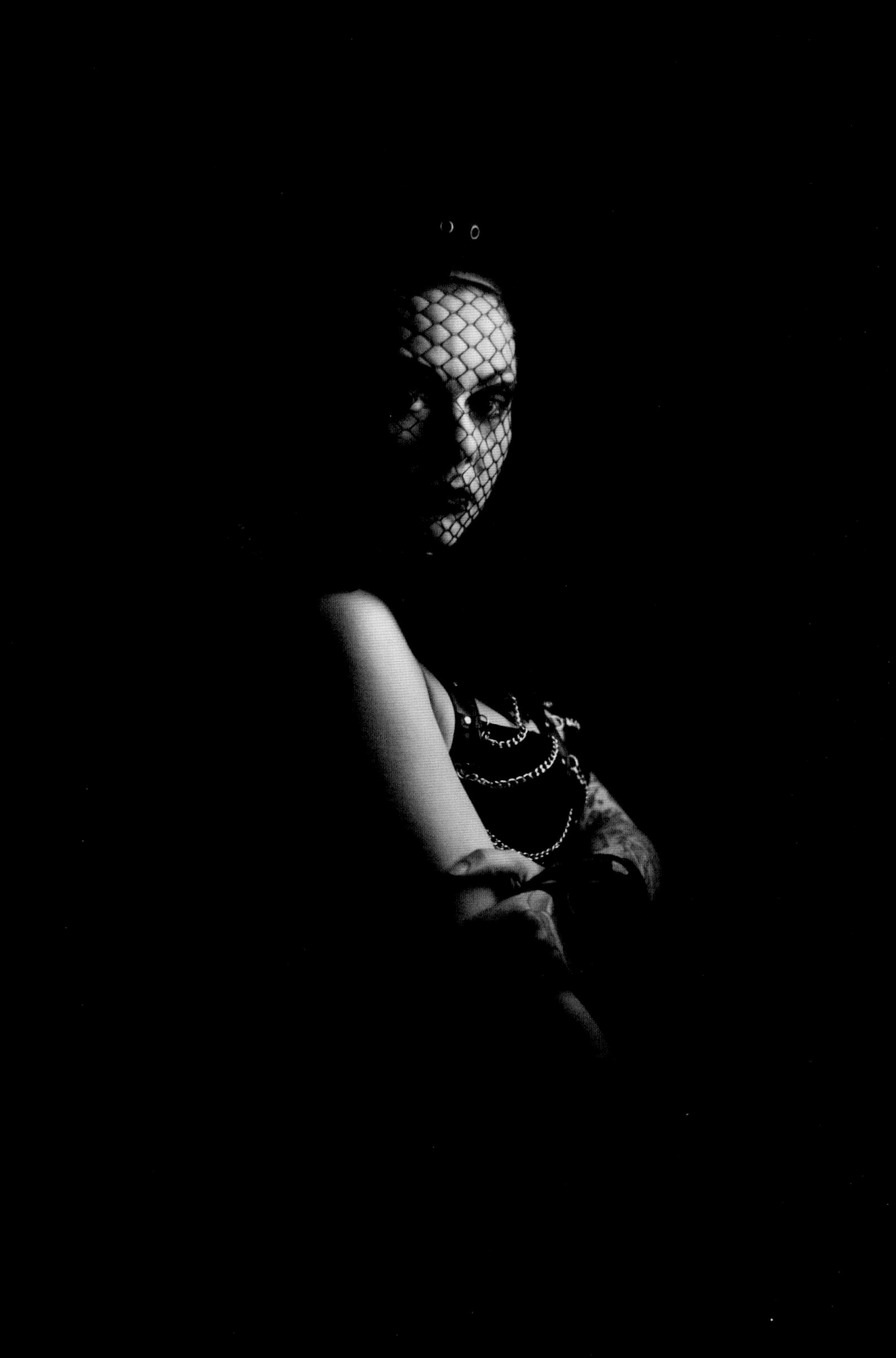

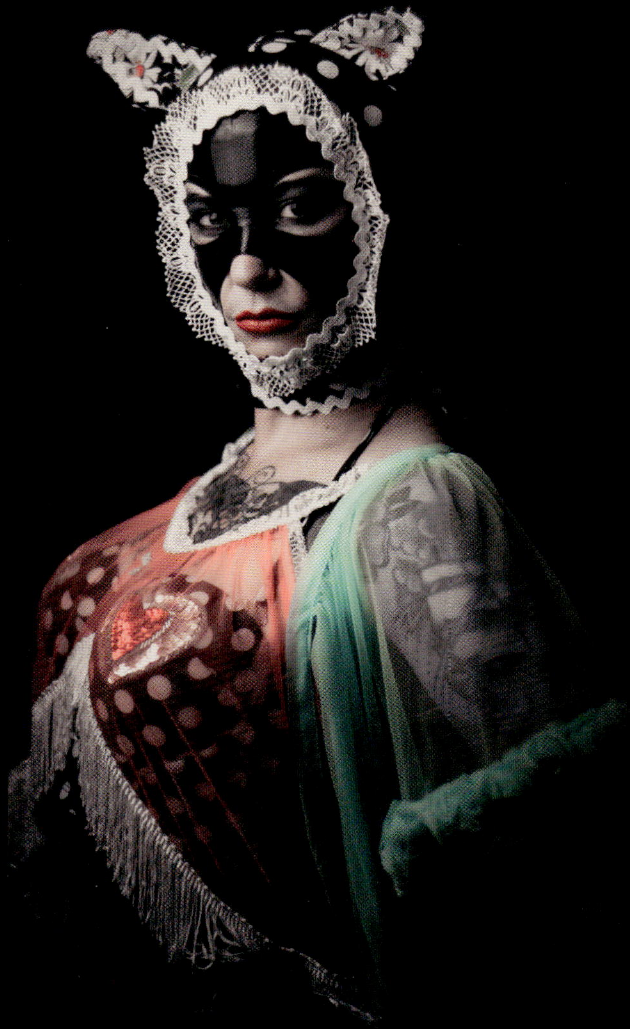

 kat toronto (miss meatface) at resistance gallery

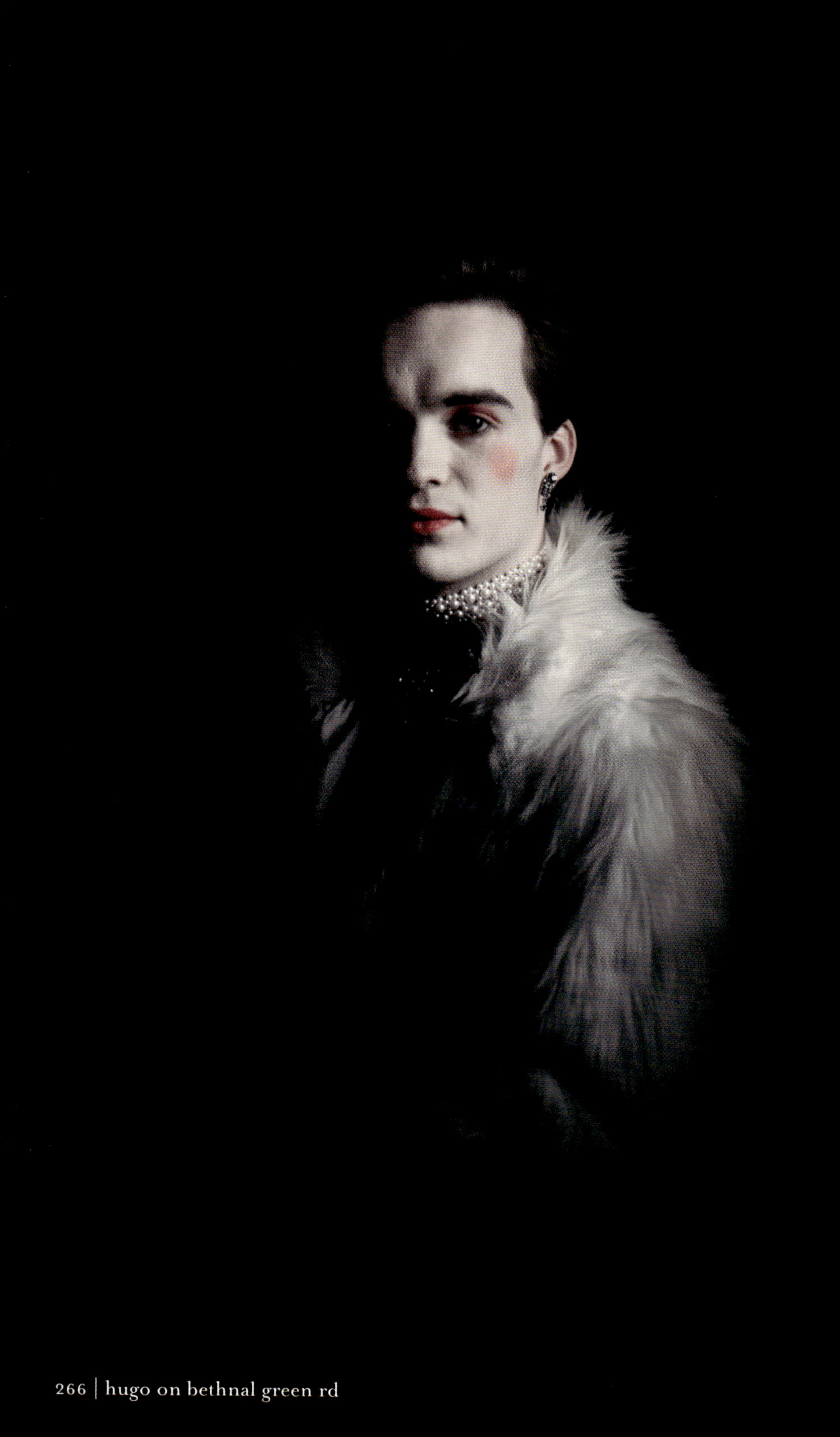

 hugo on bethnal green rd

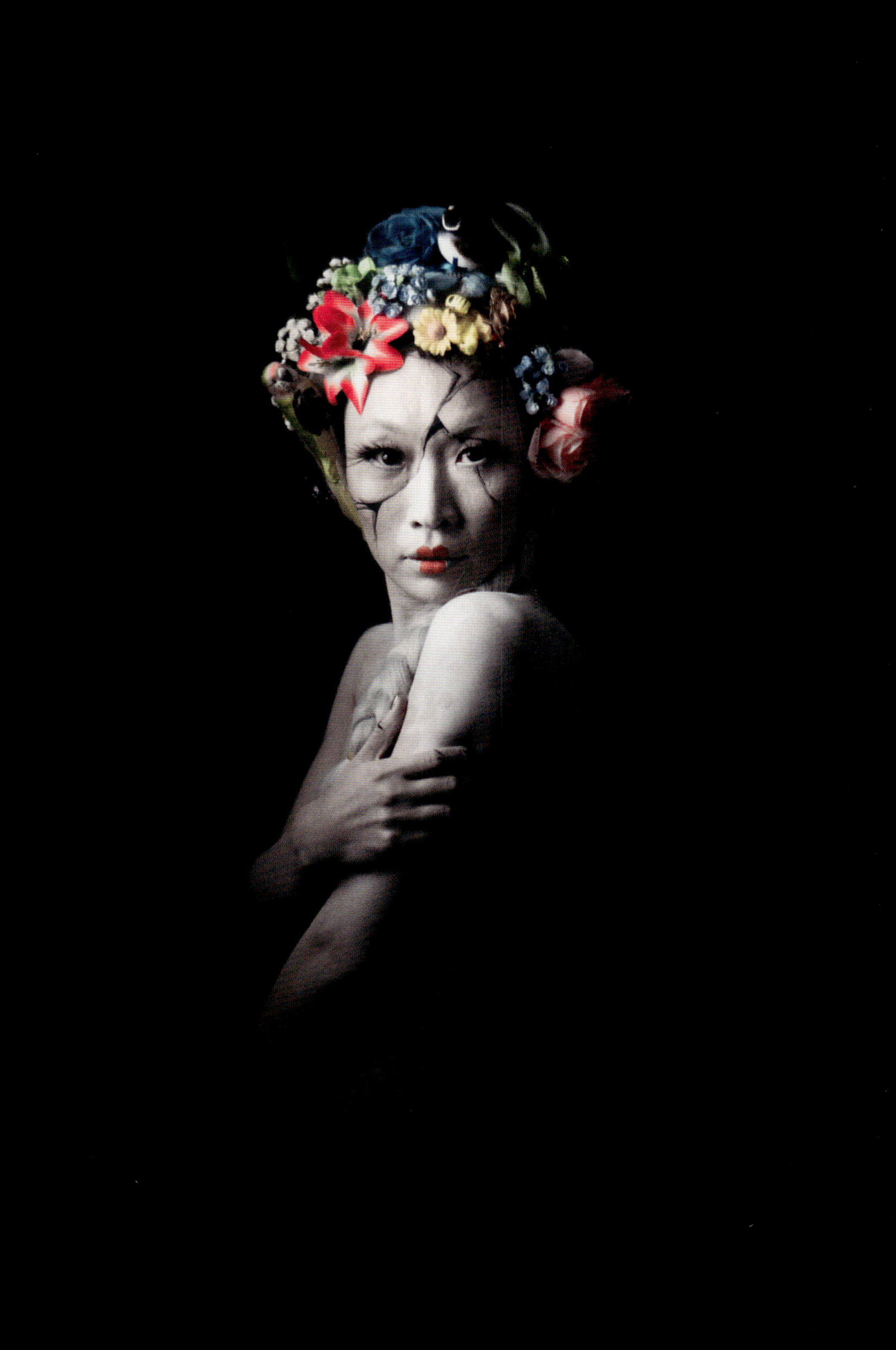

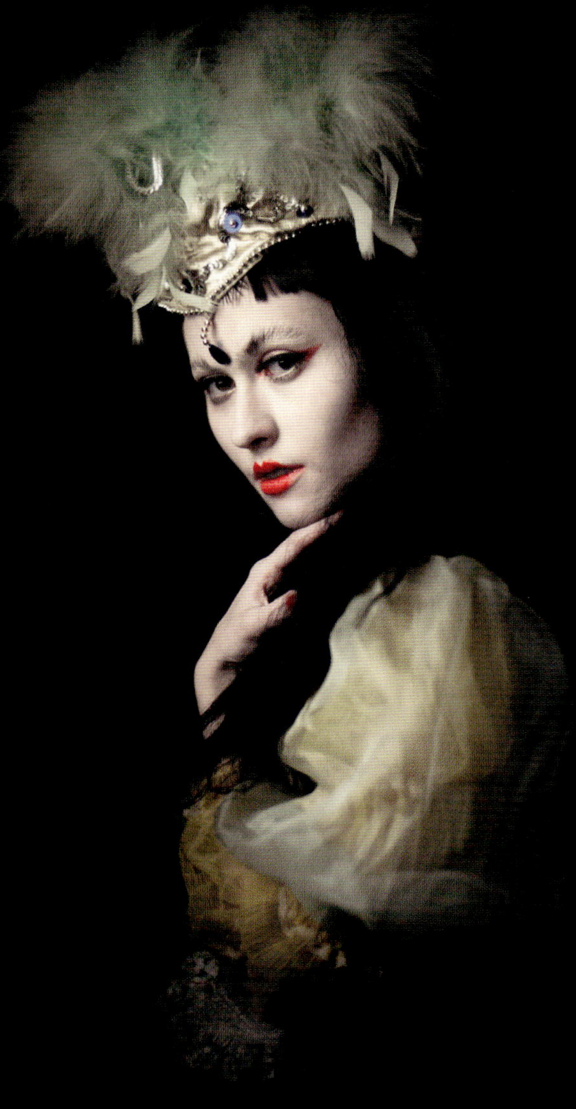

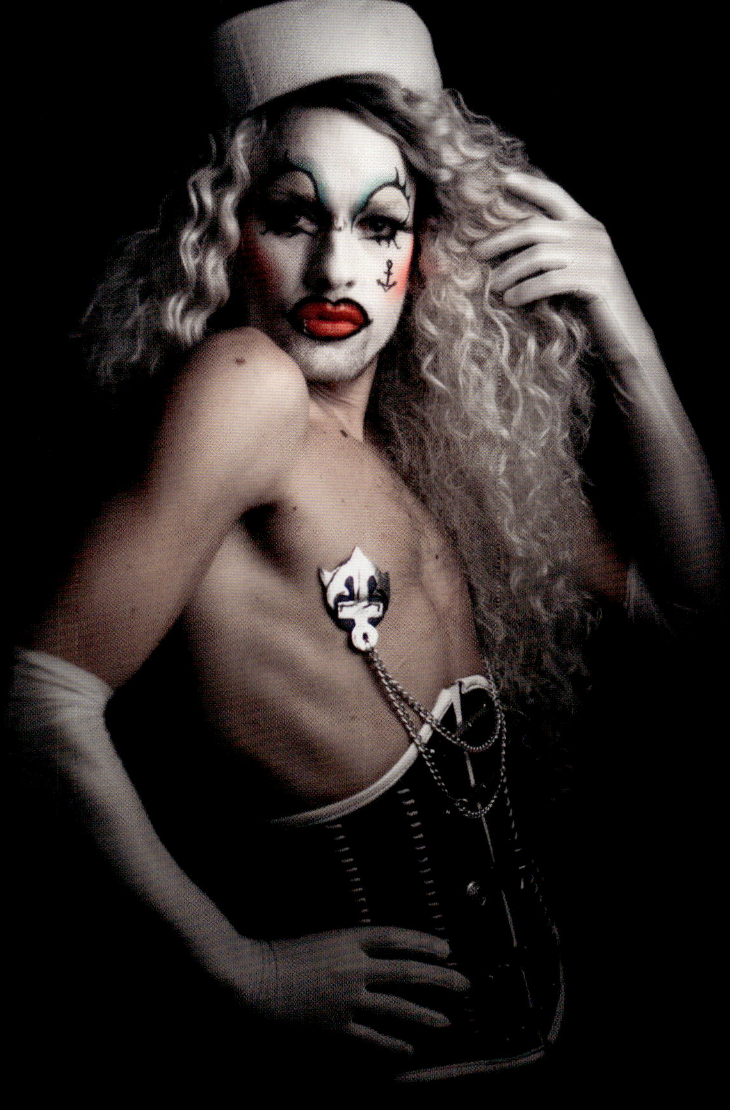

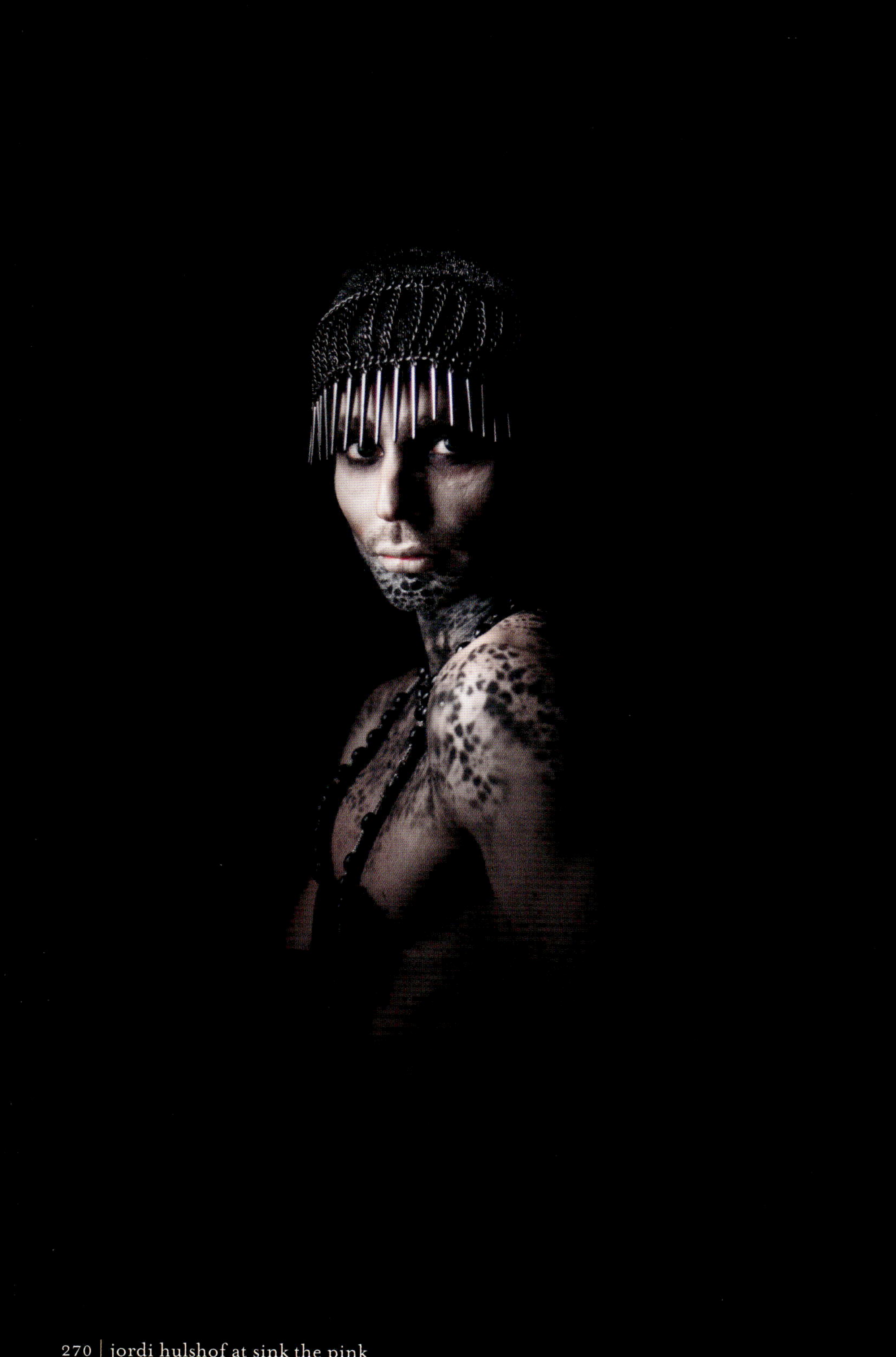

 | jordi hulshof at sink the pink

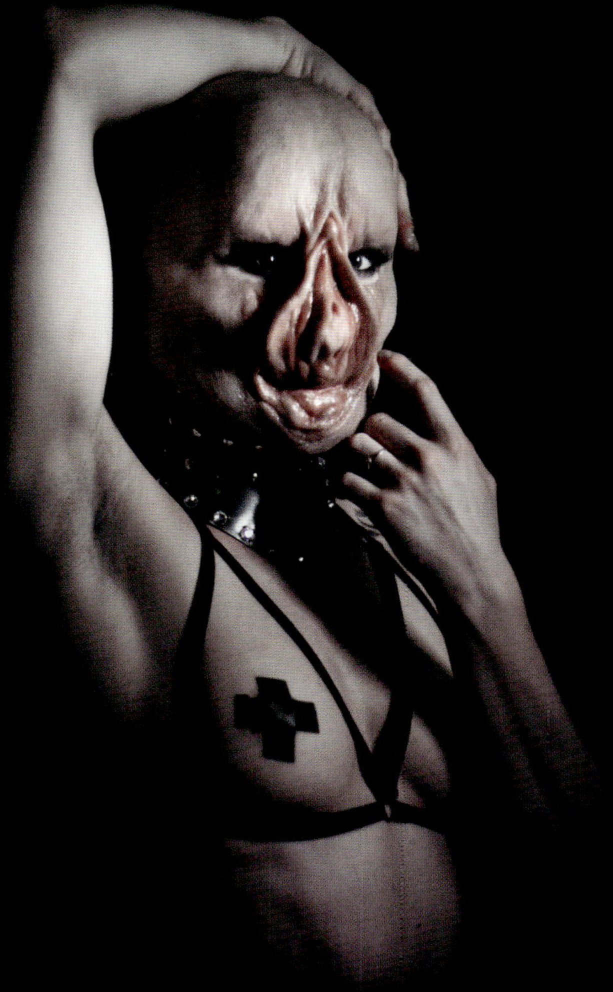

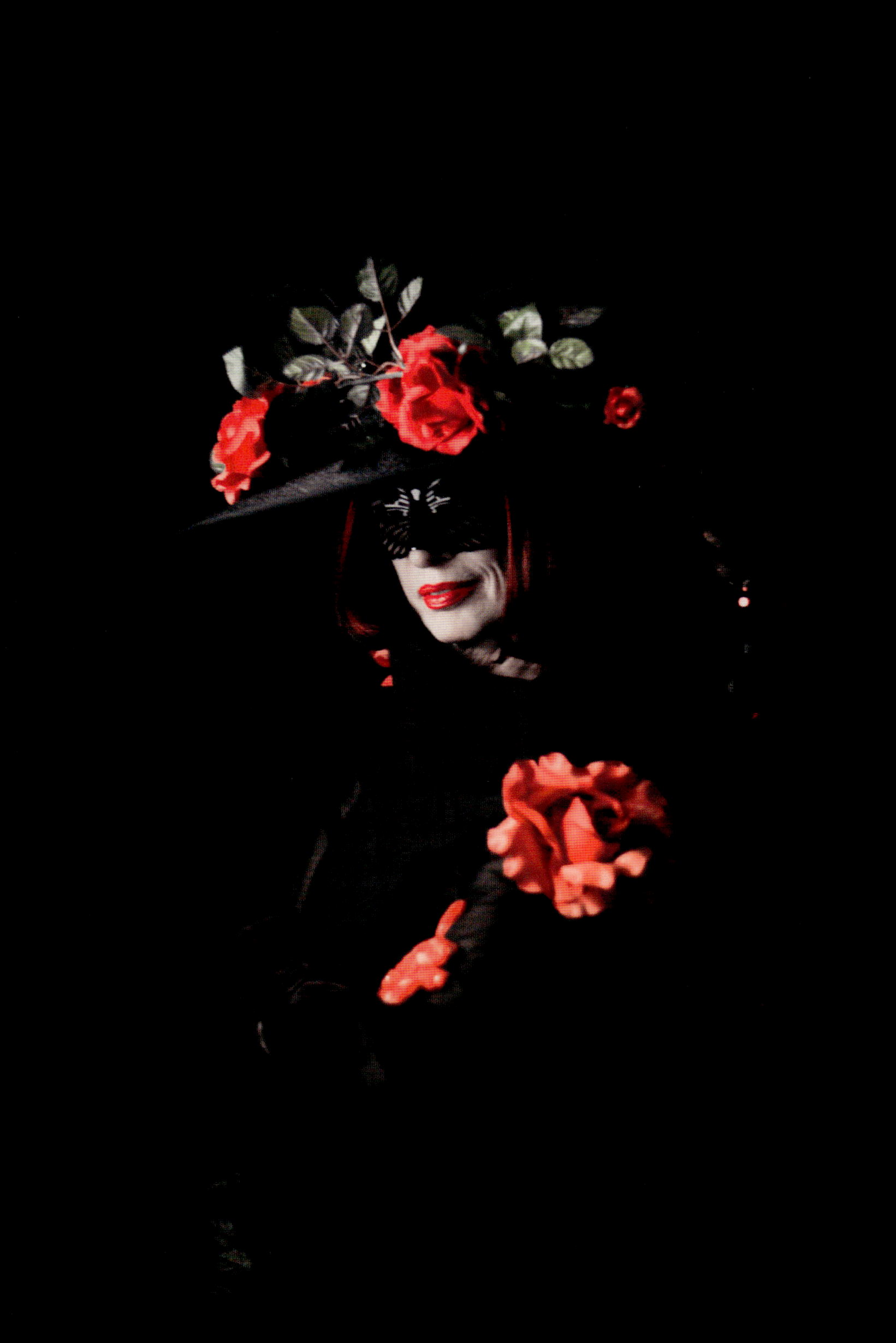

 | lady rosa at the sorapol london fashion week show

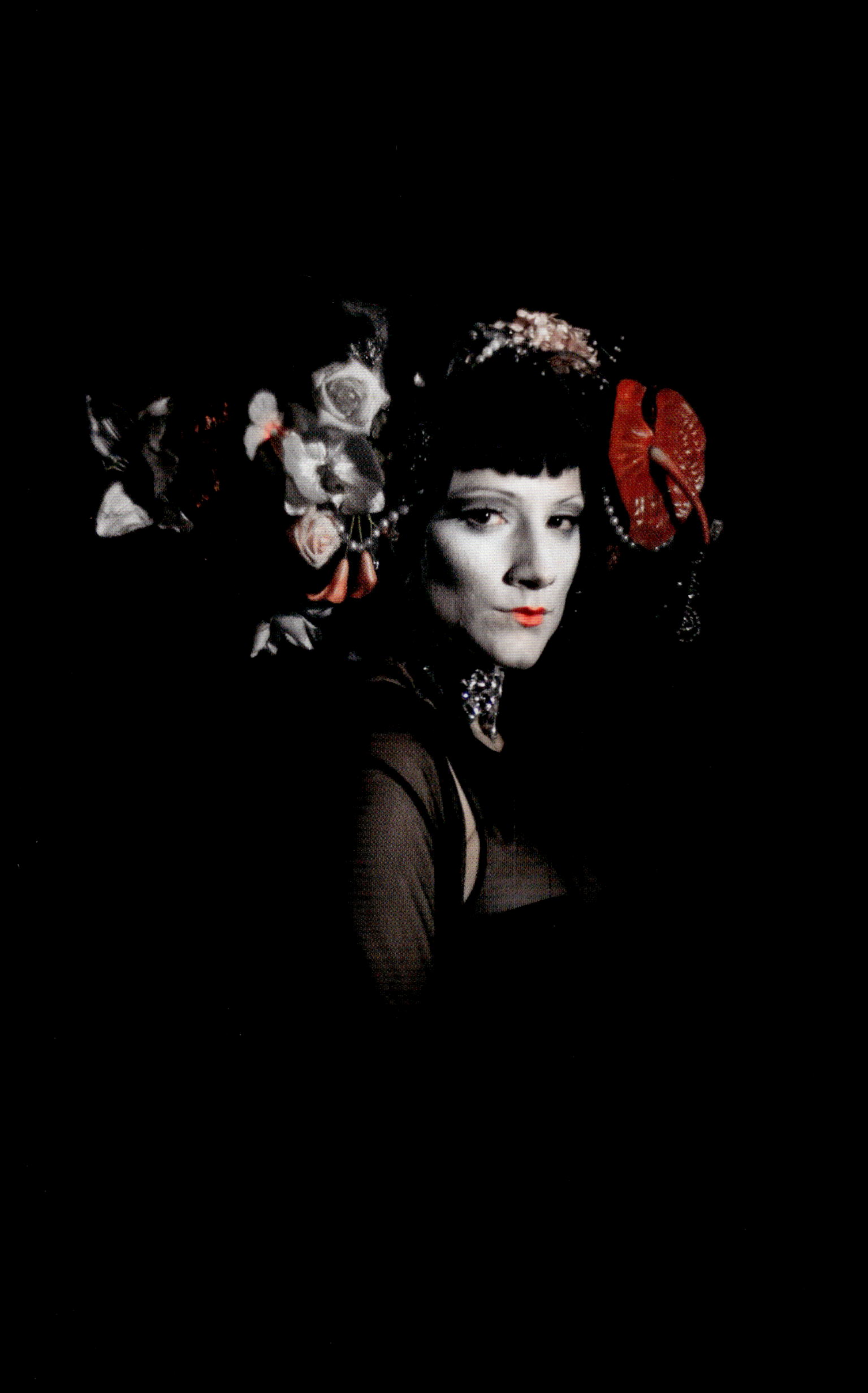

 | marta benaglia on bourchier st

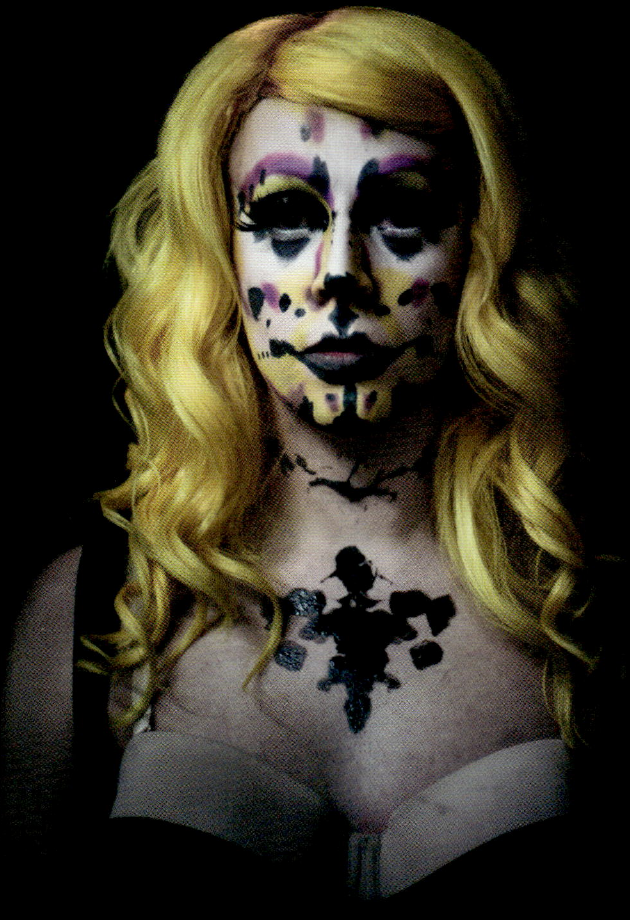

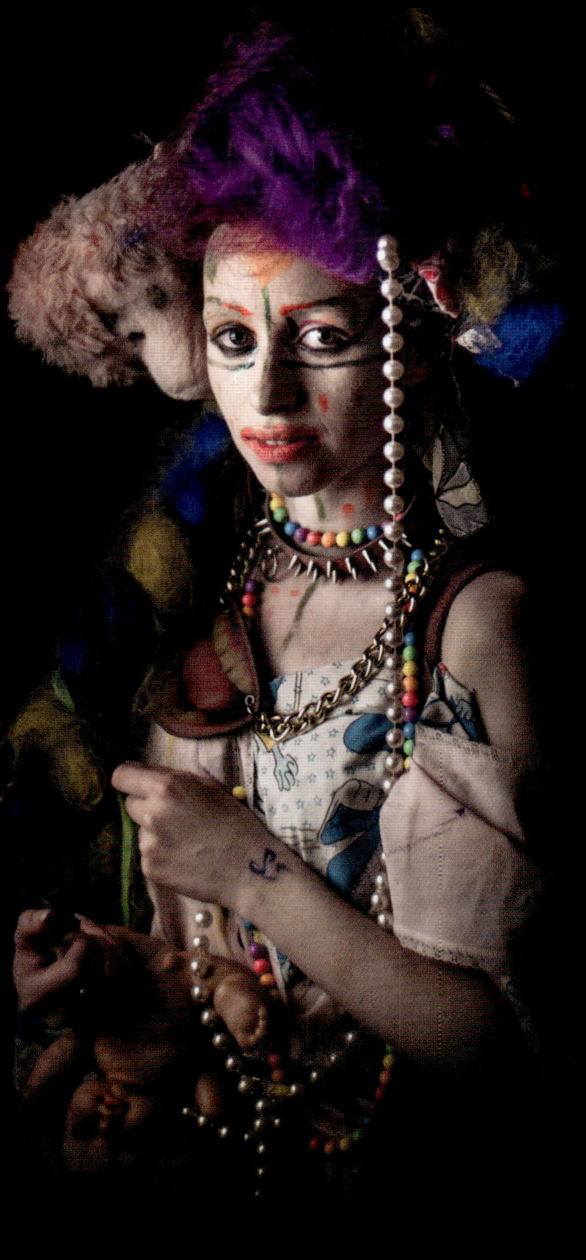

275 | naddy sane at wut? club

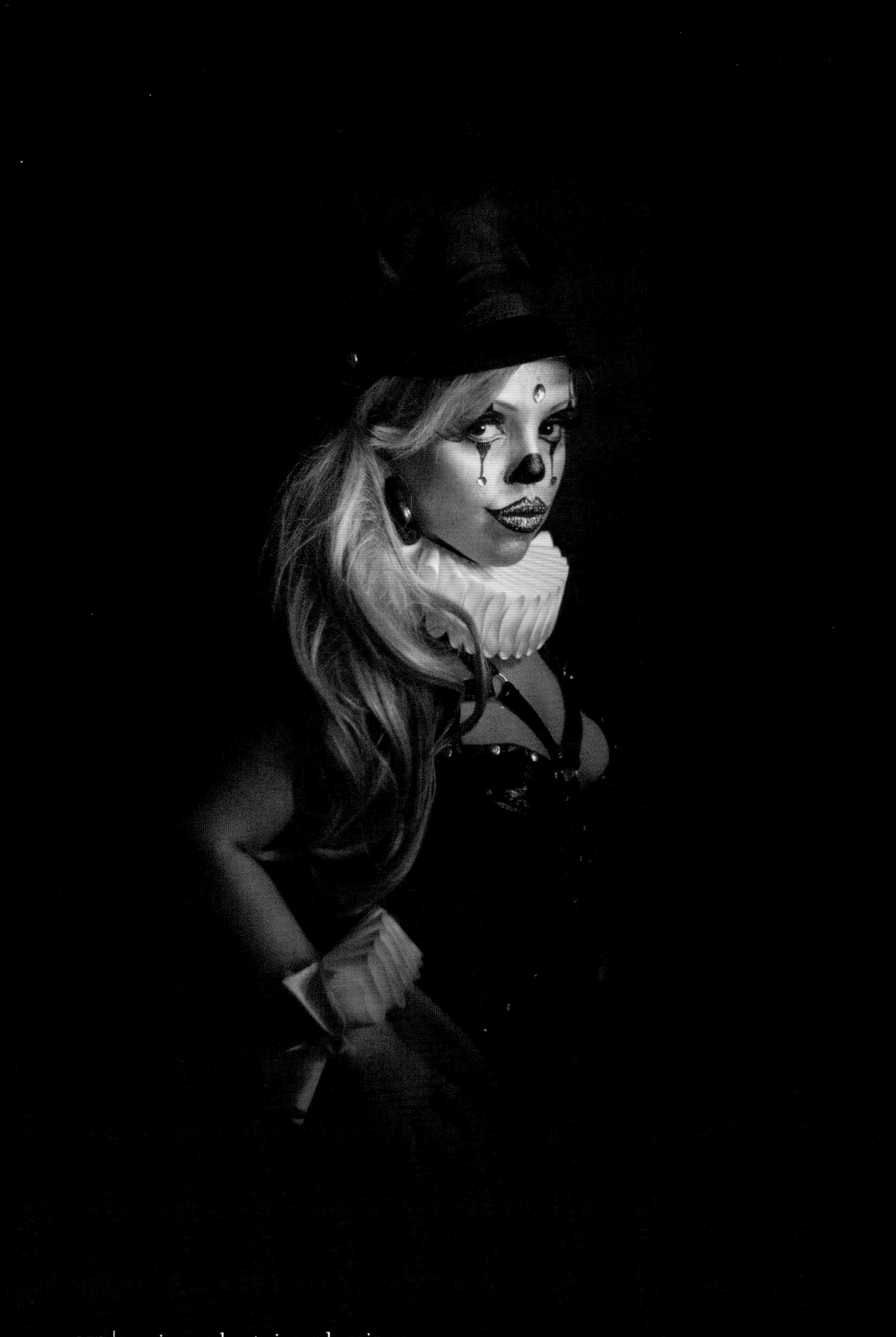

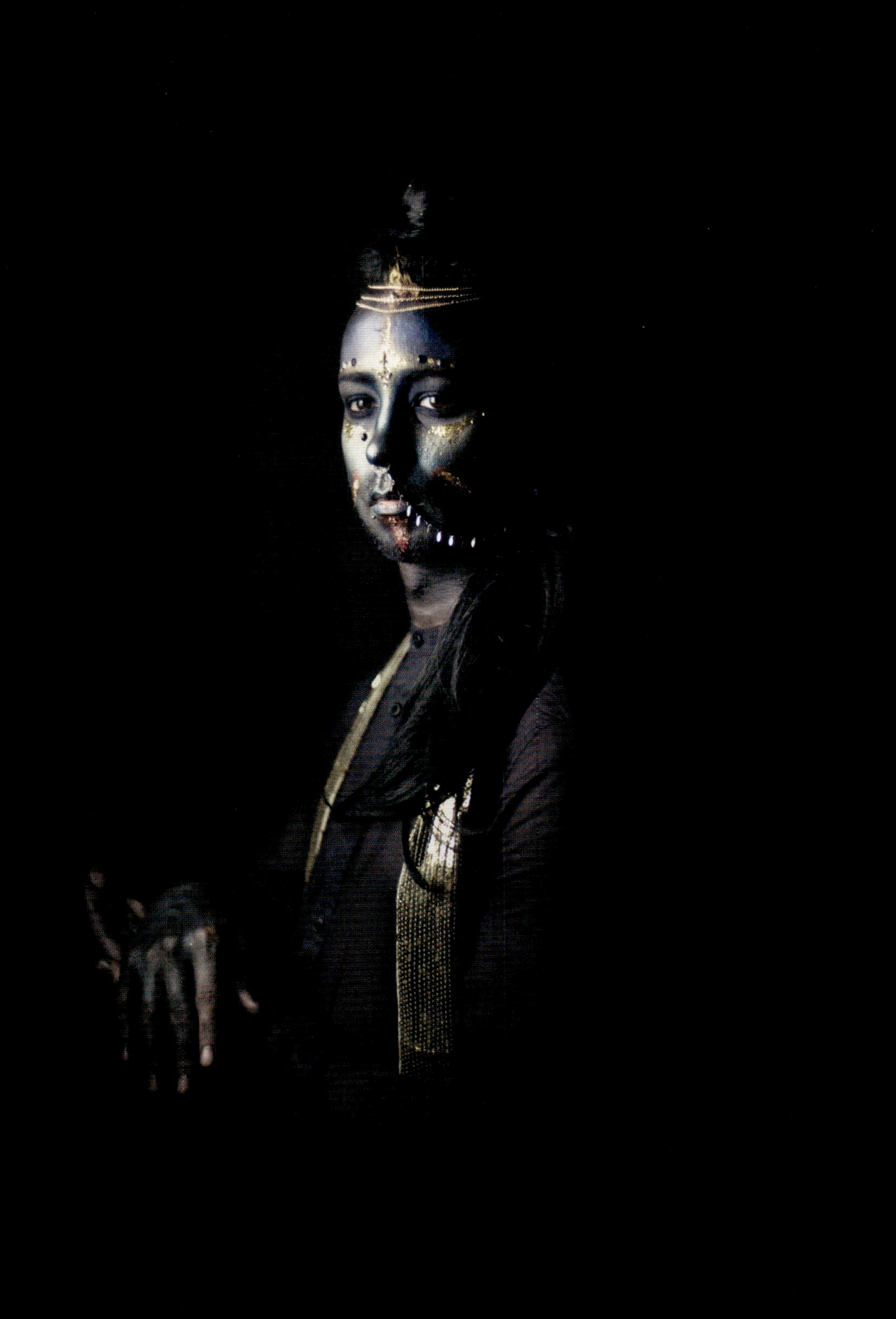

277 | leigh fontaine at sink the pink

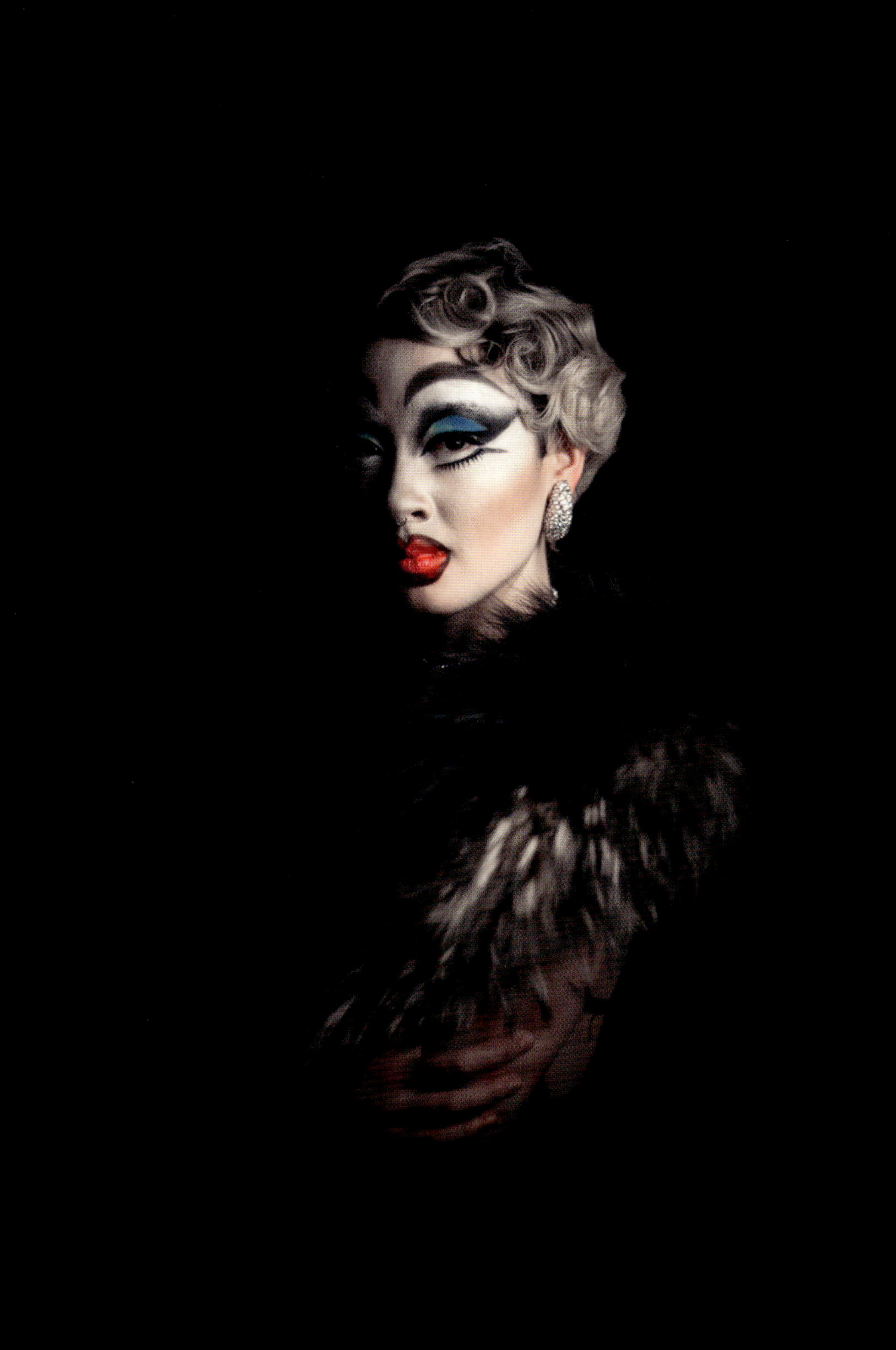

 victoria sin at bethnal green working men's club

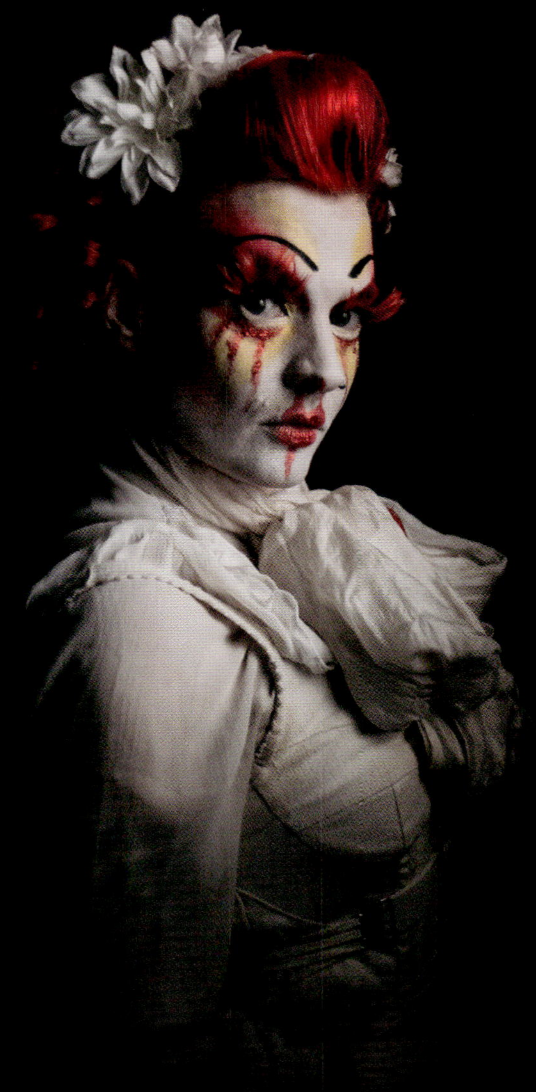

 | marnie scarlet at club pvc

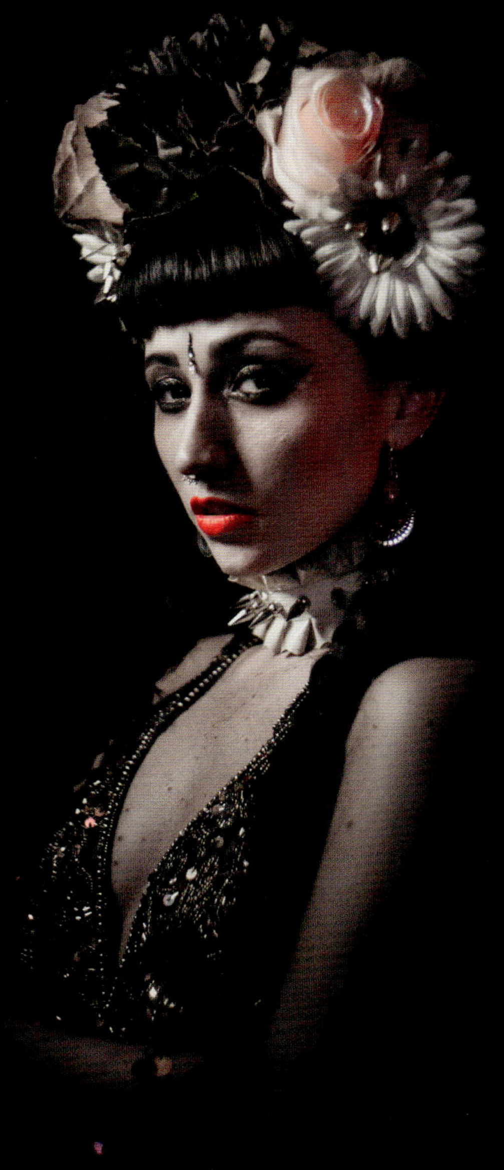

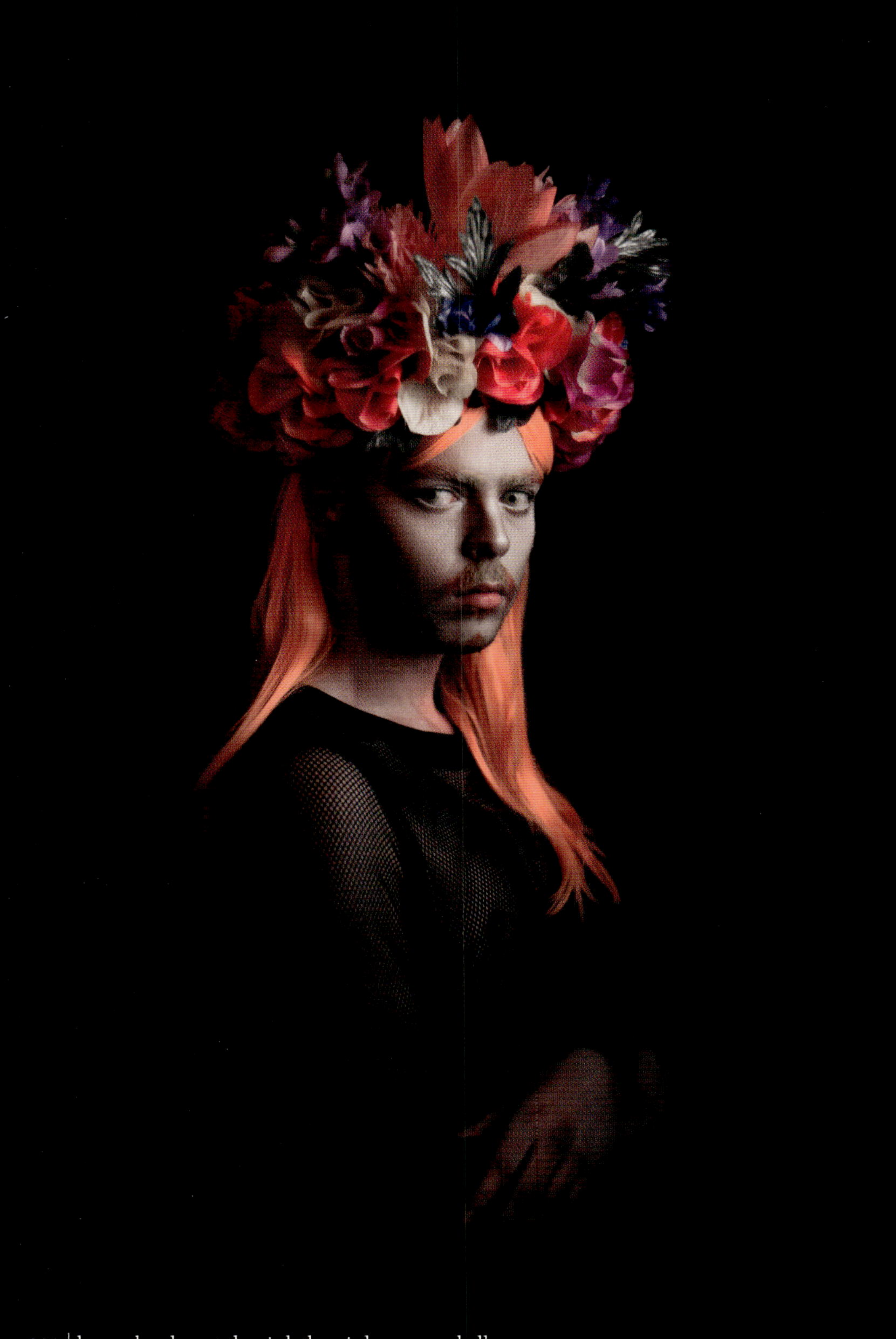

 | byron london at the sink the pink summer ball

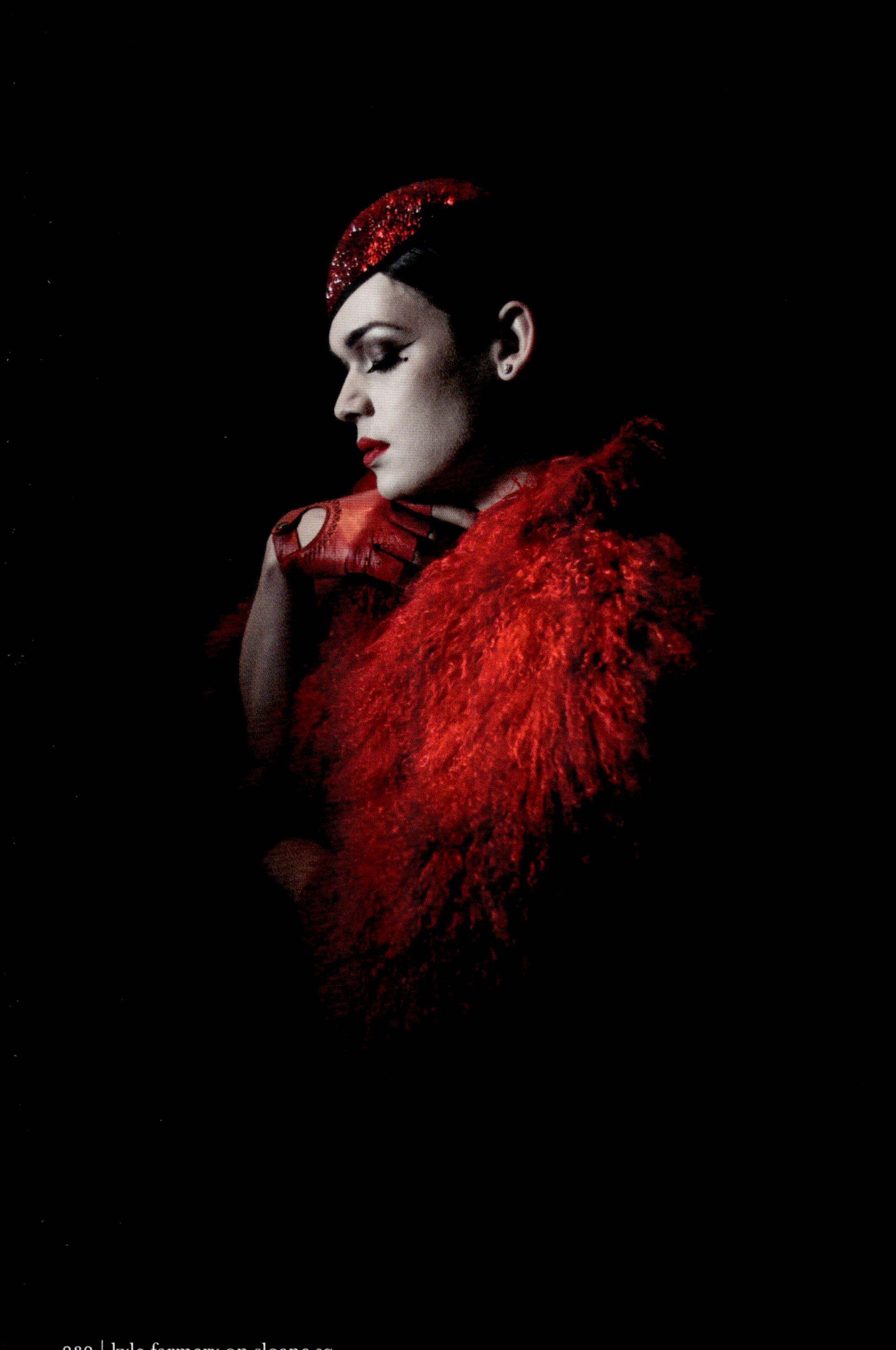

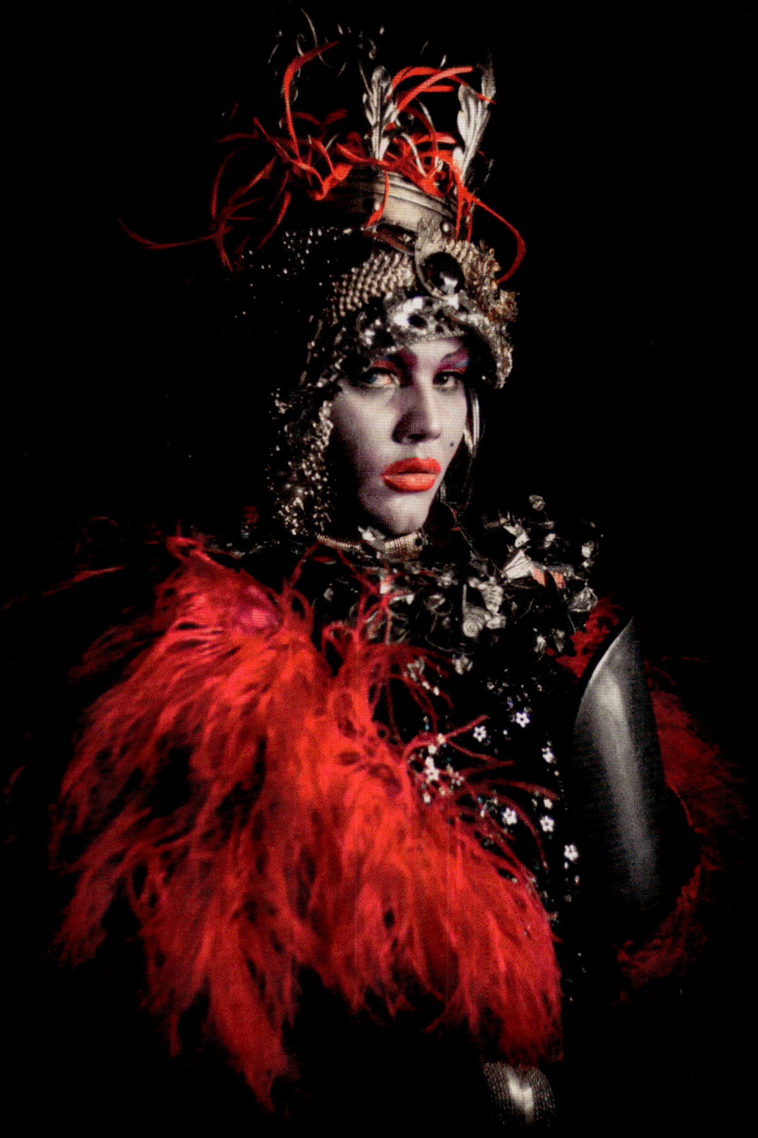

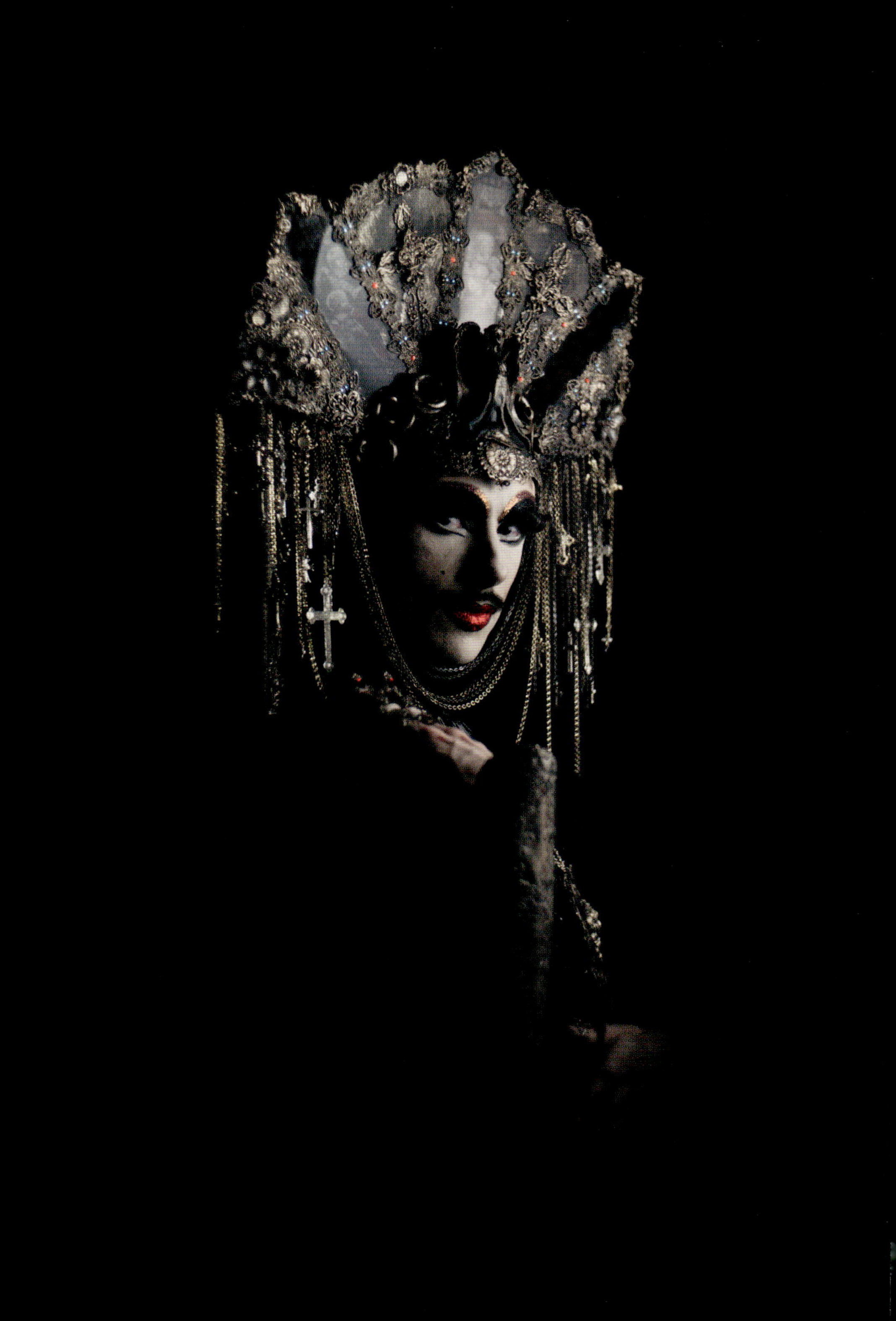

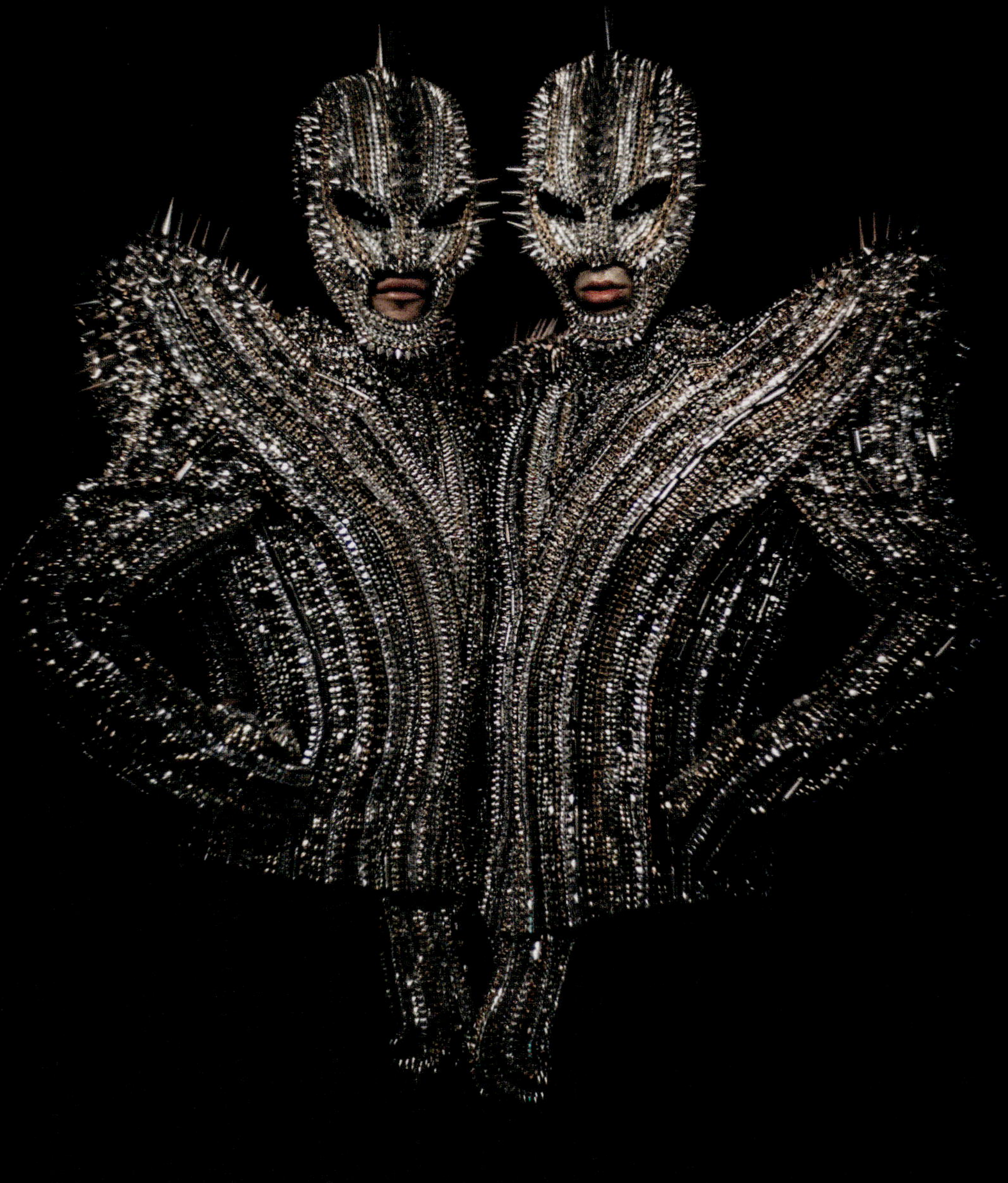

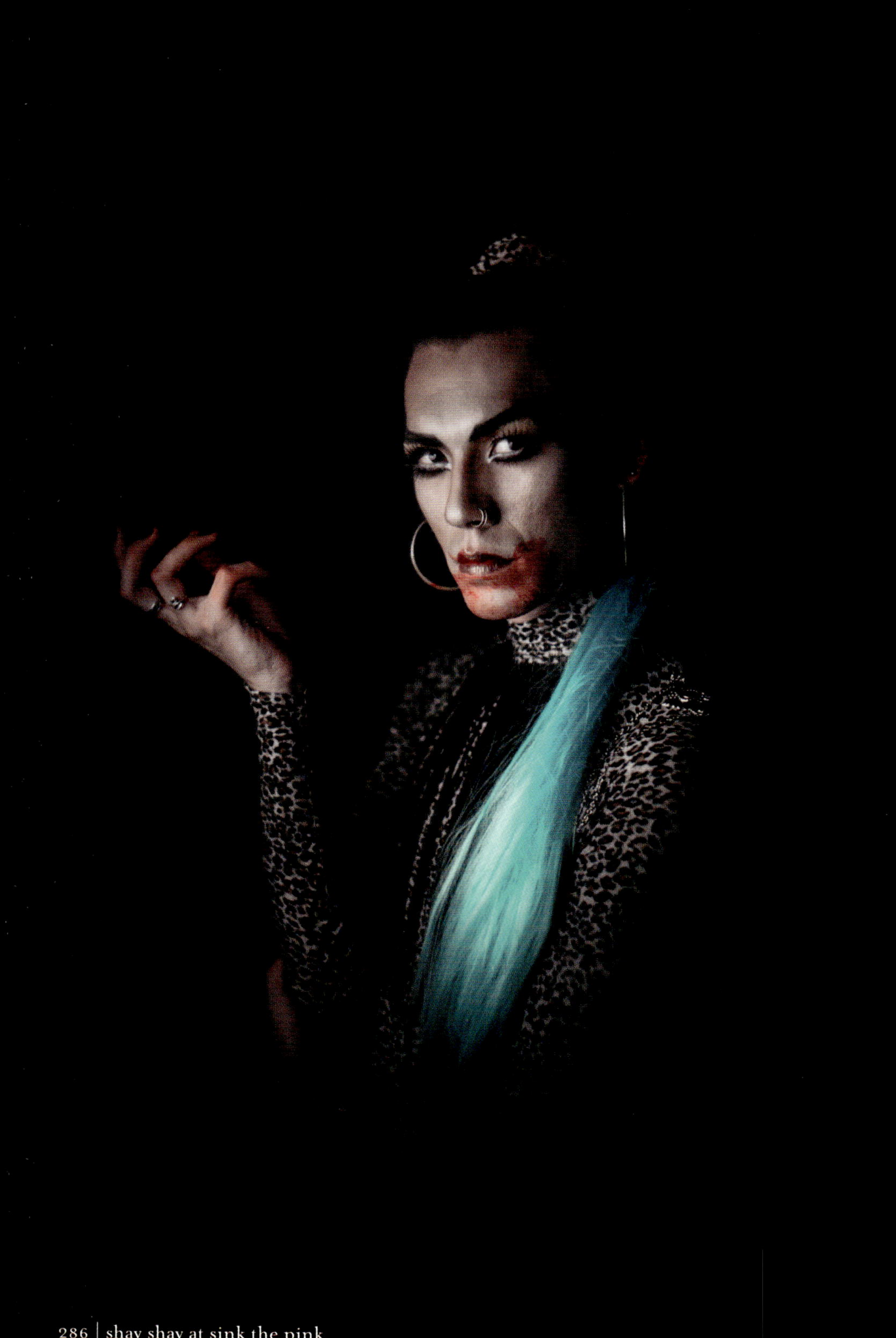

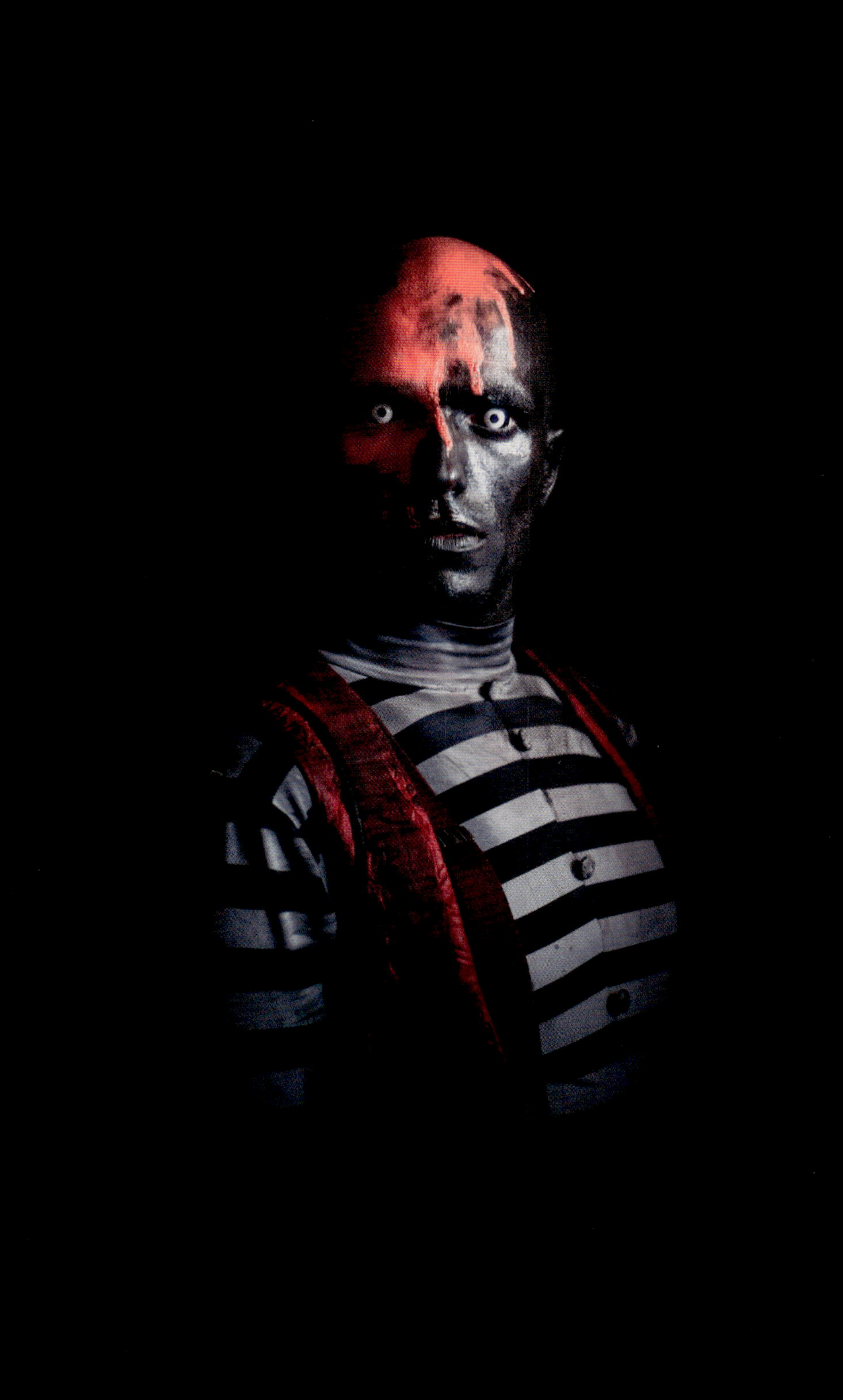

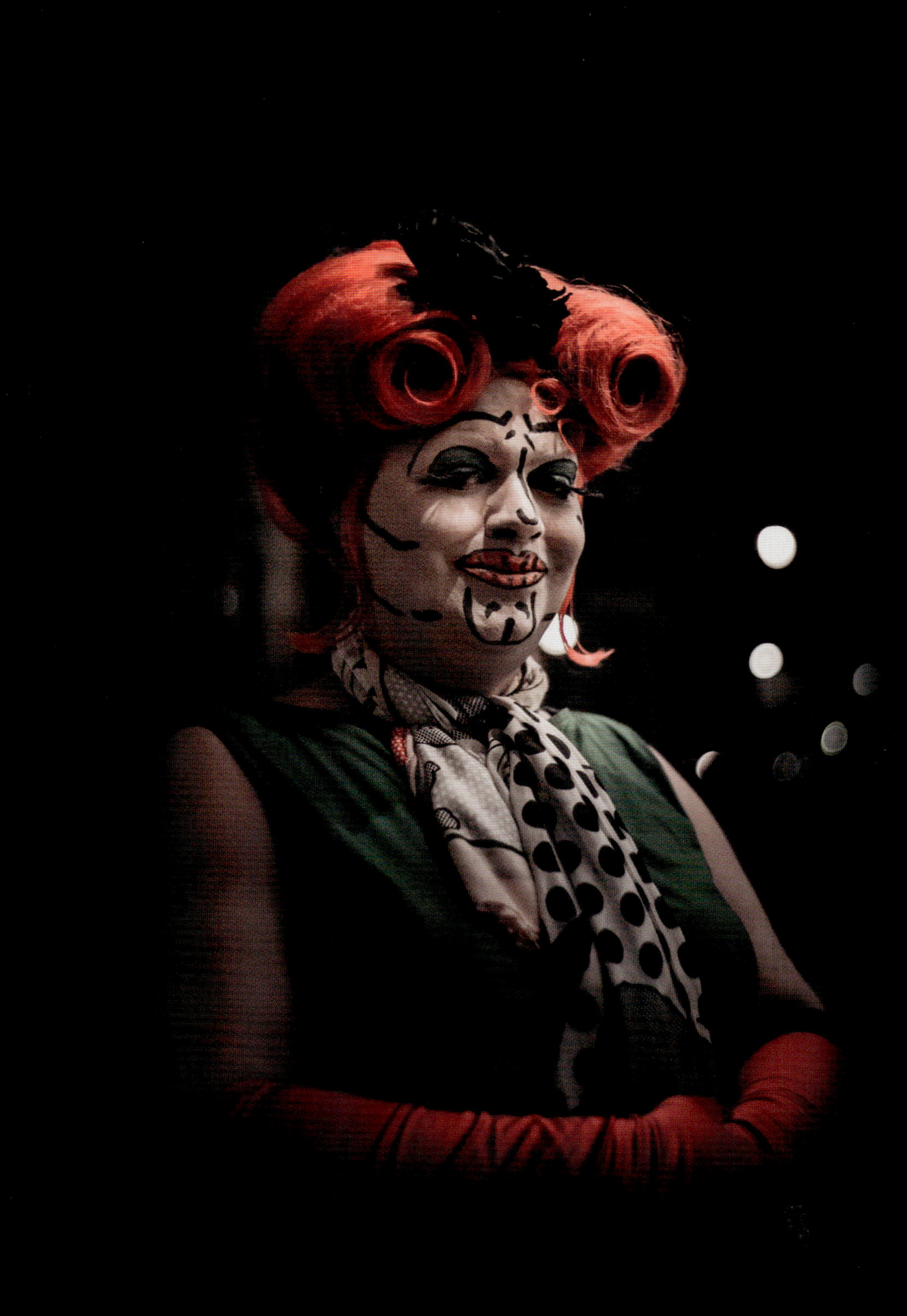

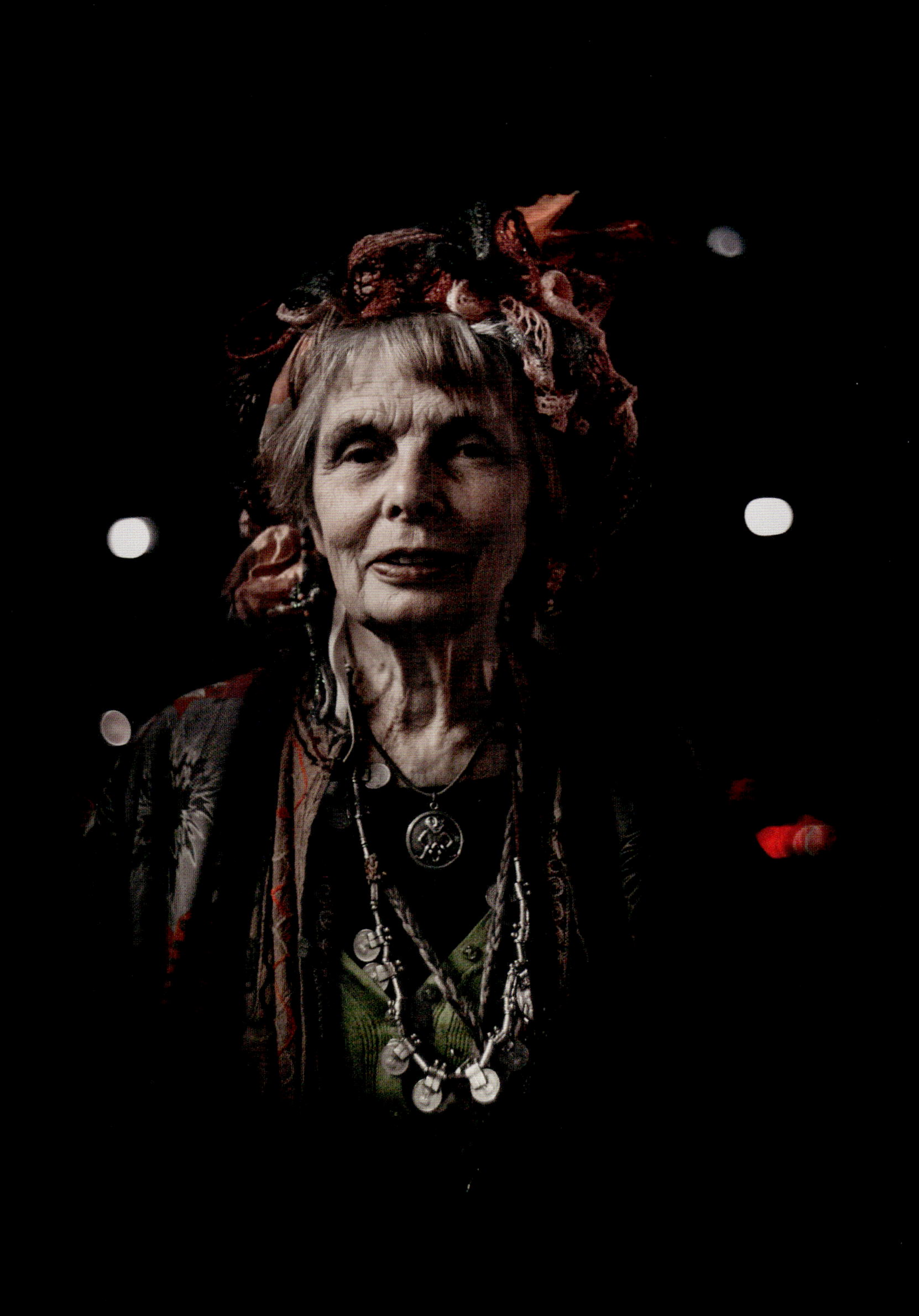

 raga woods on charing cross rd

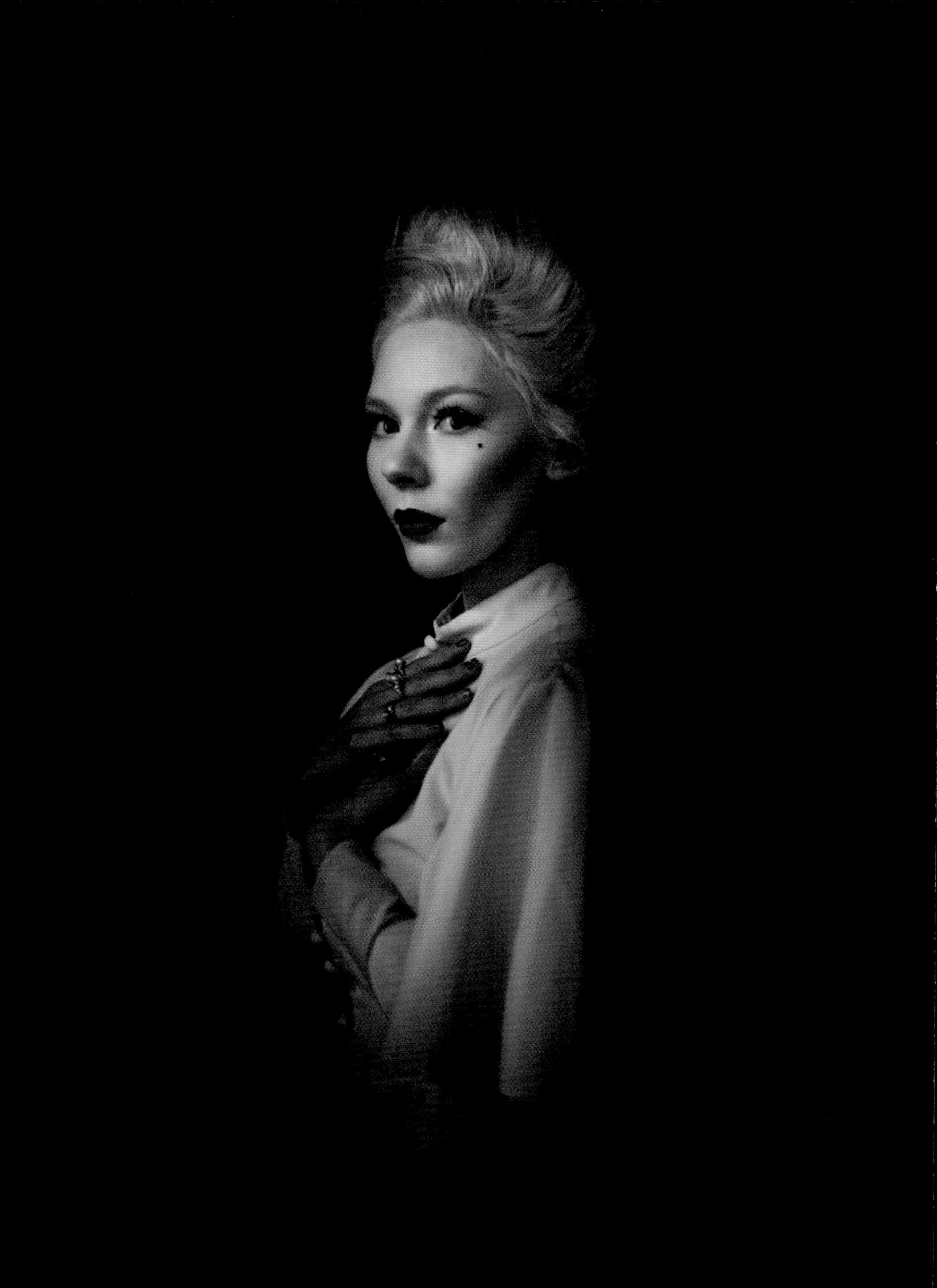

 ewa wilczynski on old compton st

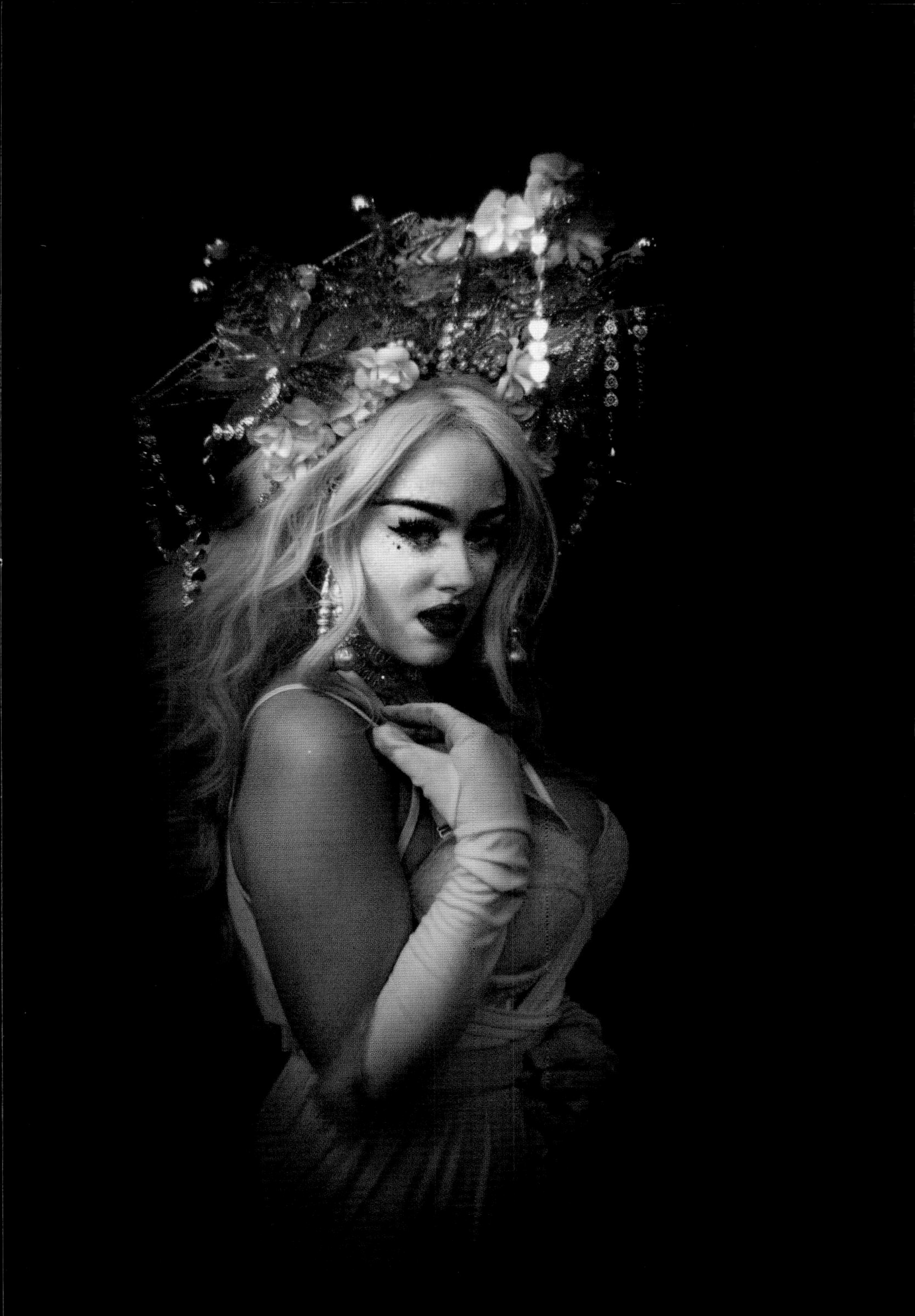

291 | bambi blue on old compton st

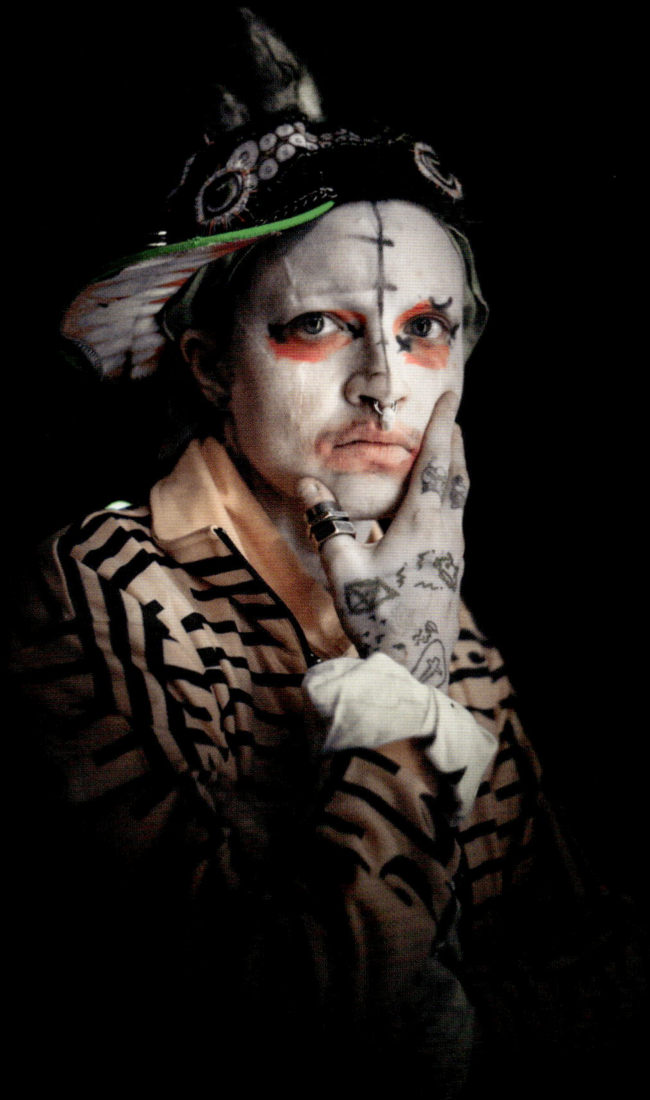

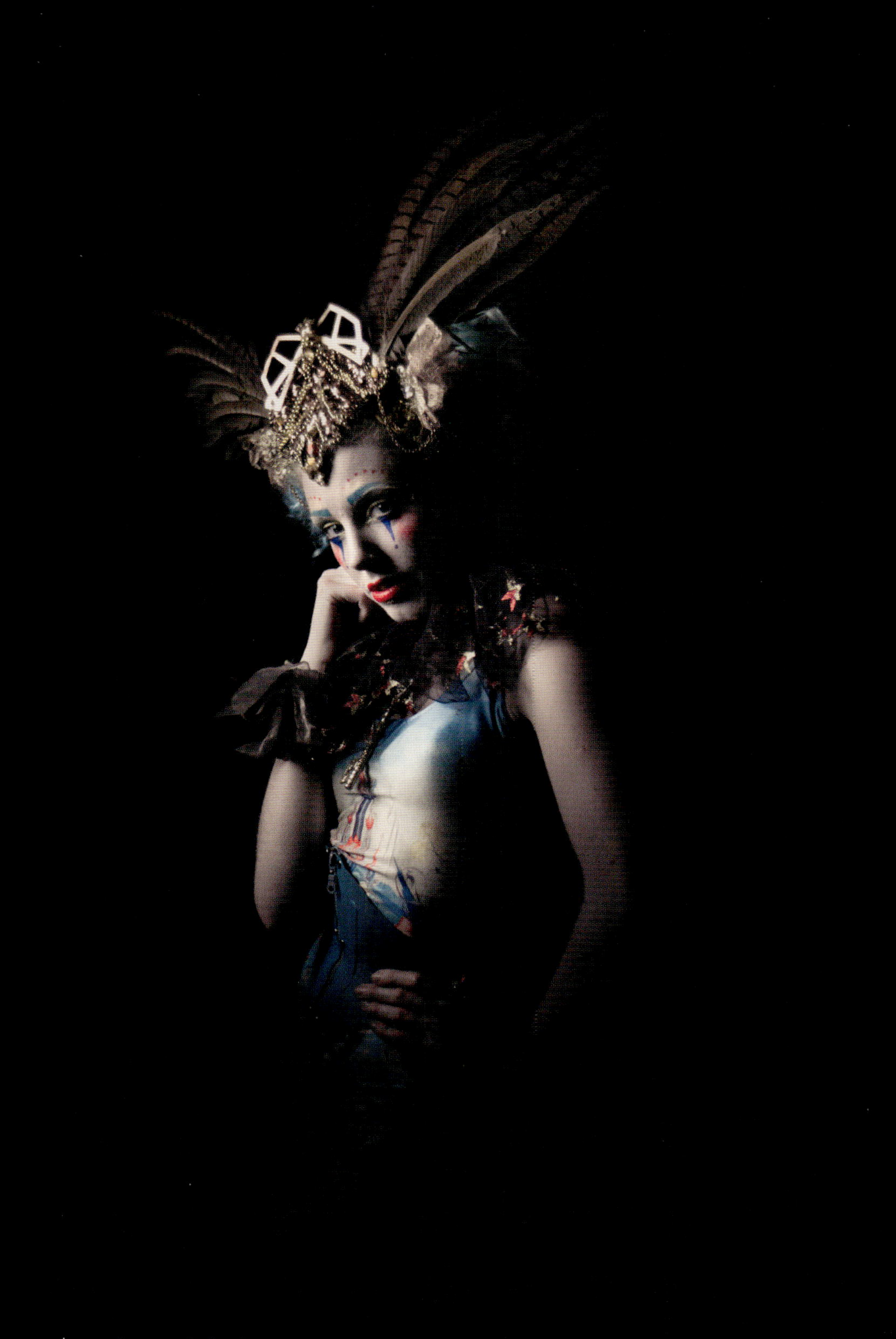

 | amy day at cult freak circus

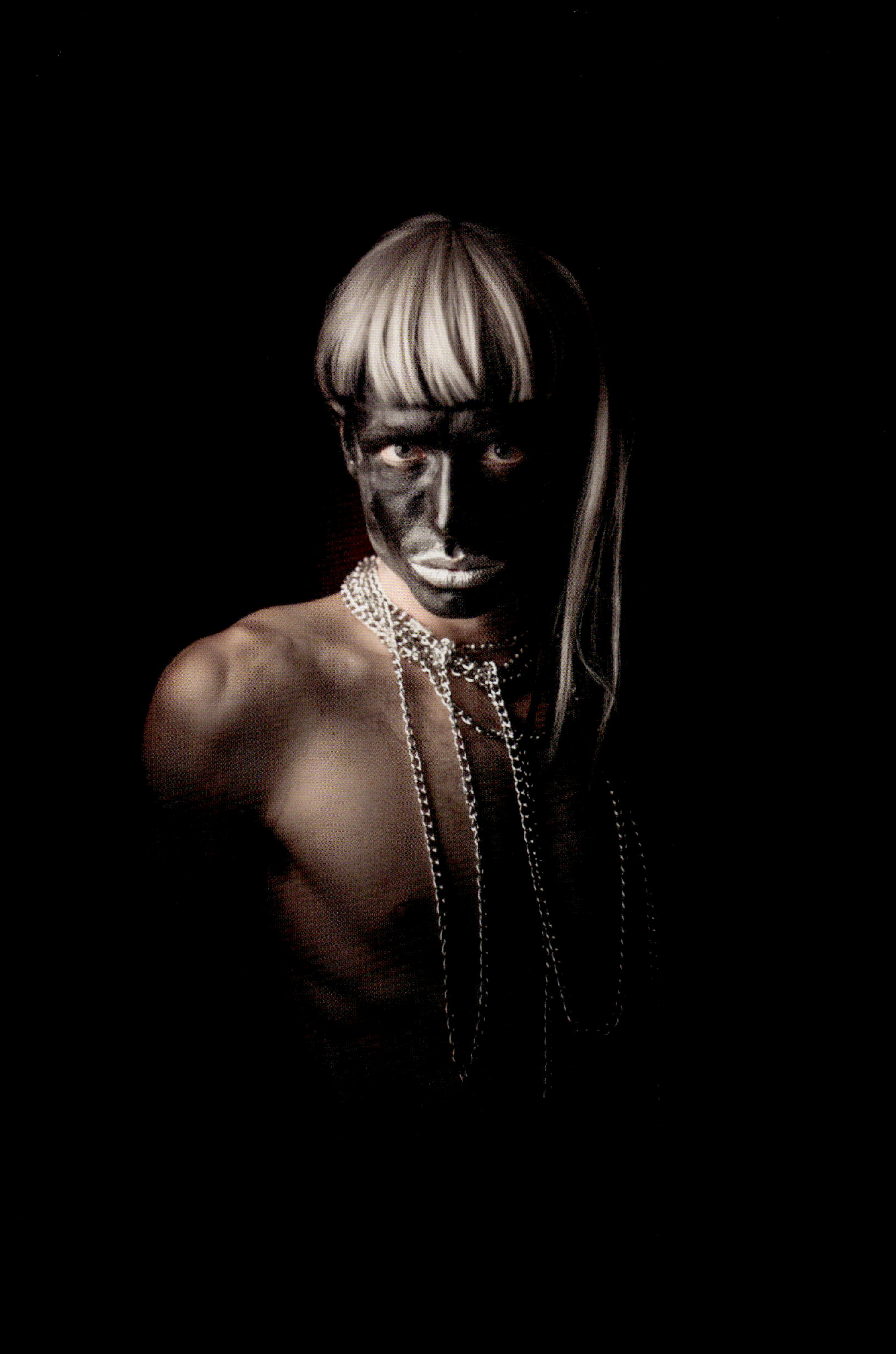

 ashley joiner at the charity monster ball

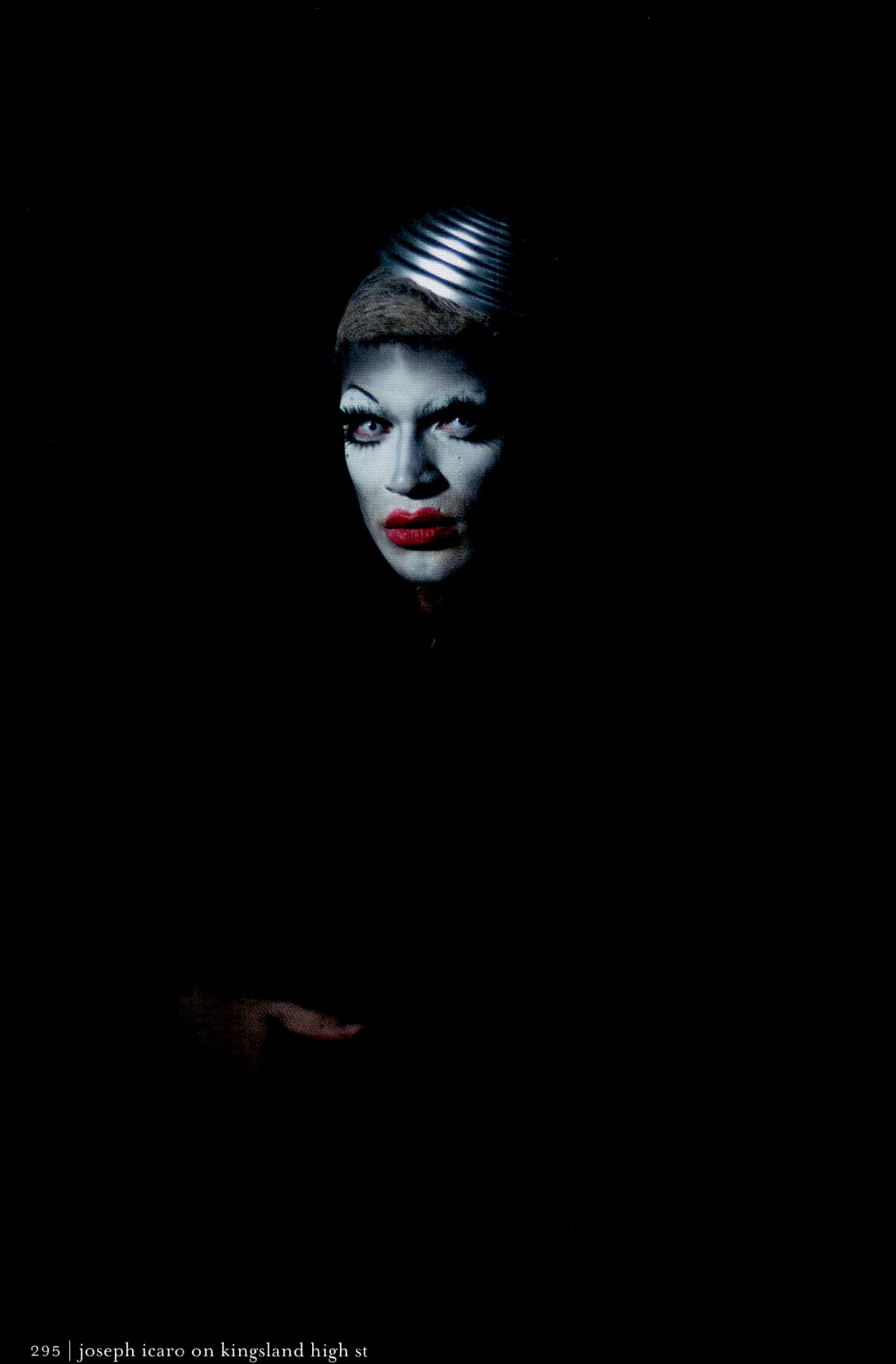

295 | joseph icaro on kingsland high st

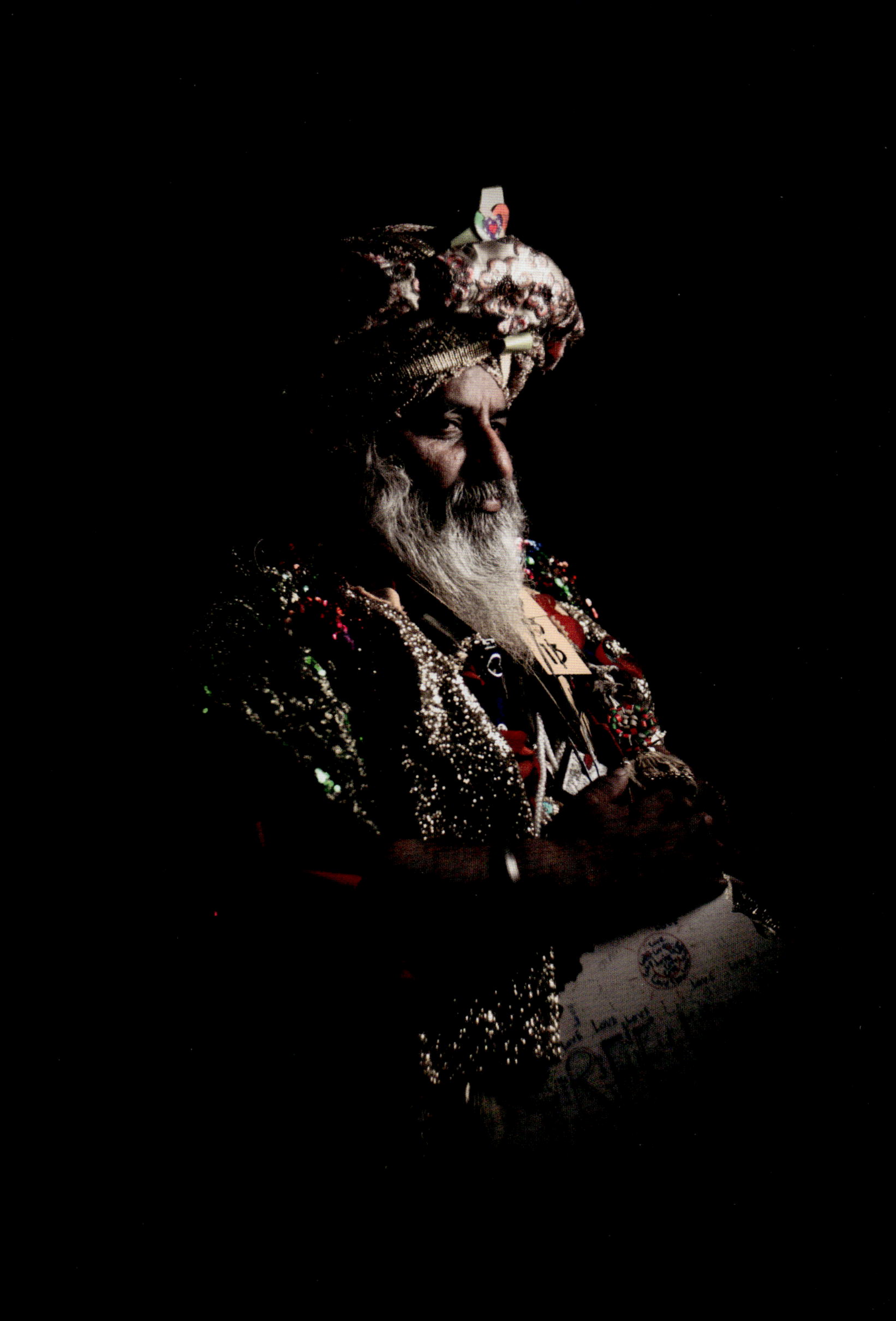

 | mukhtiar singh dhaliwal at lady rosa's trash emporium

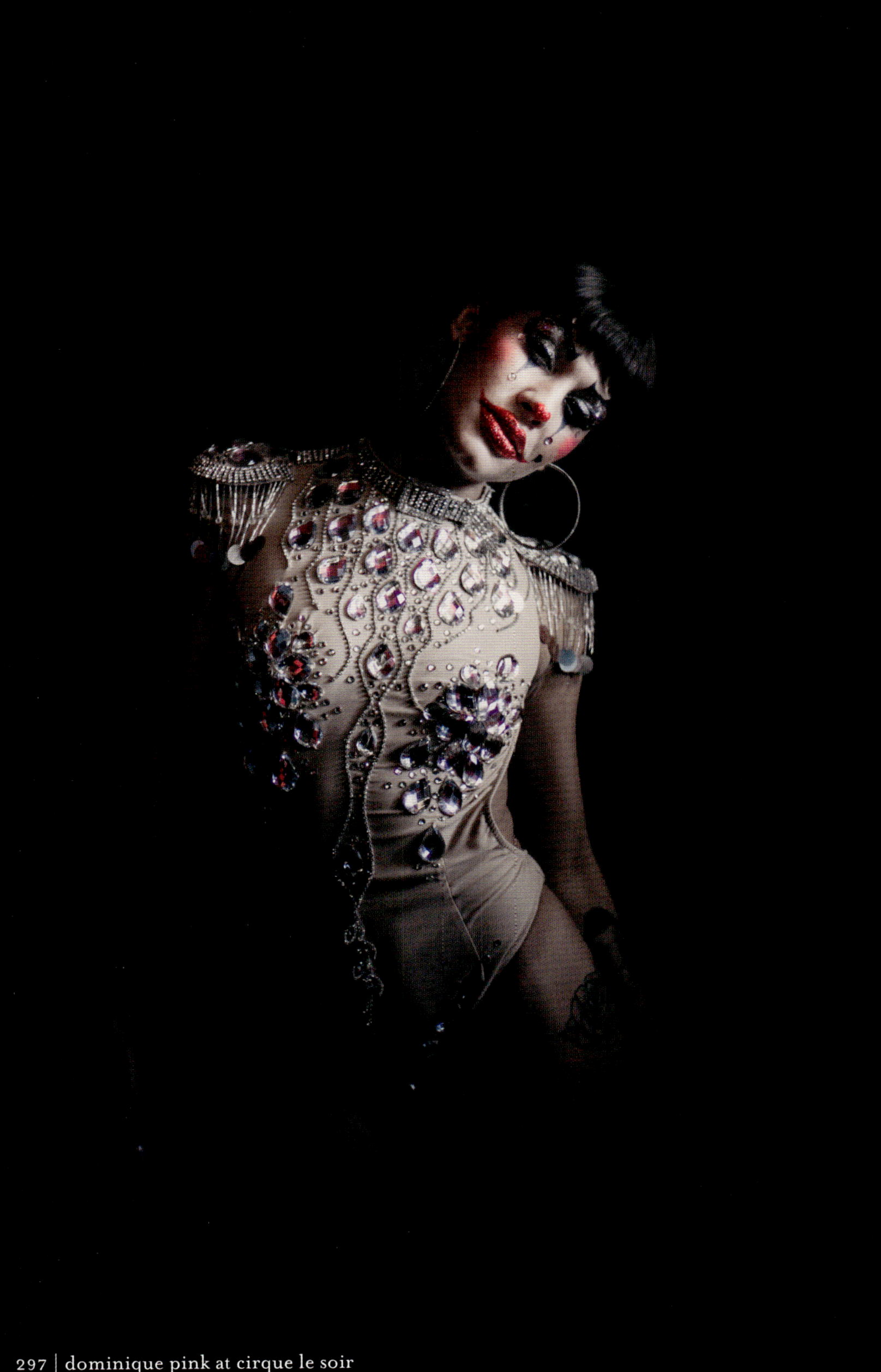

 | dominique pink at cirque le soir

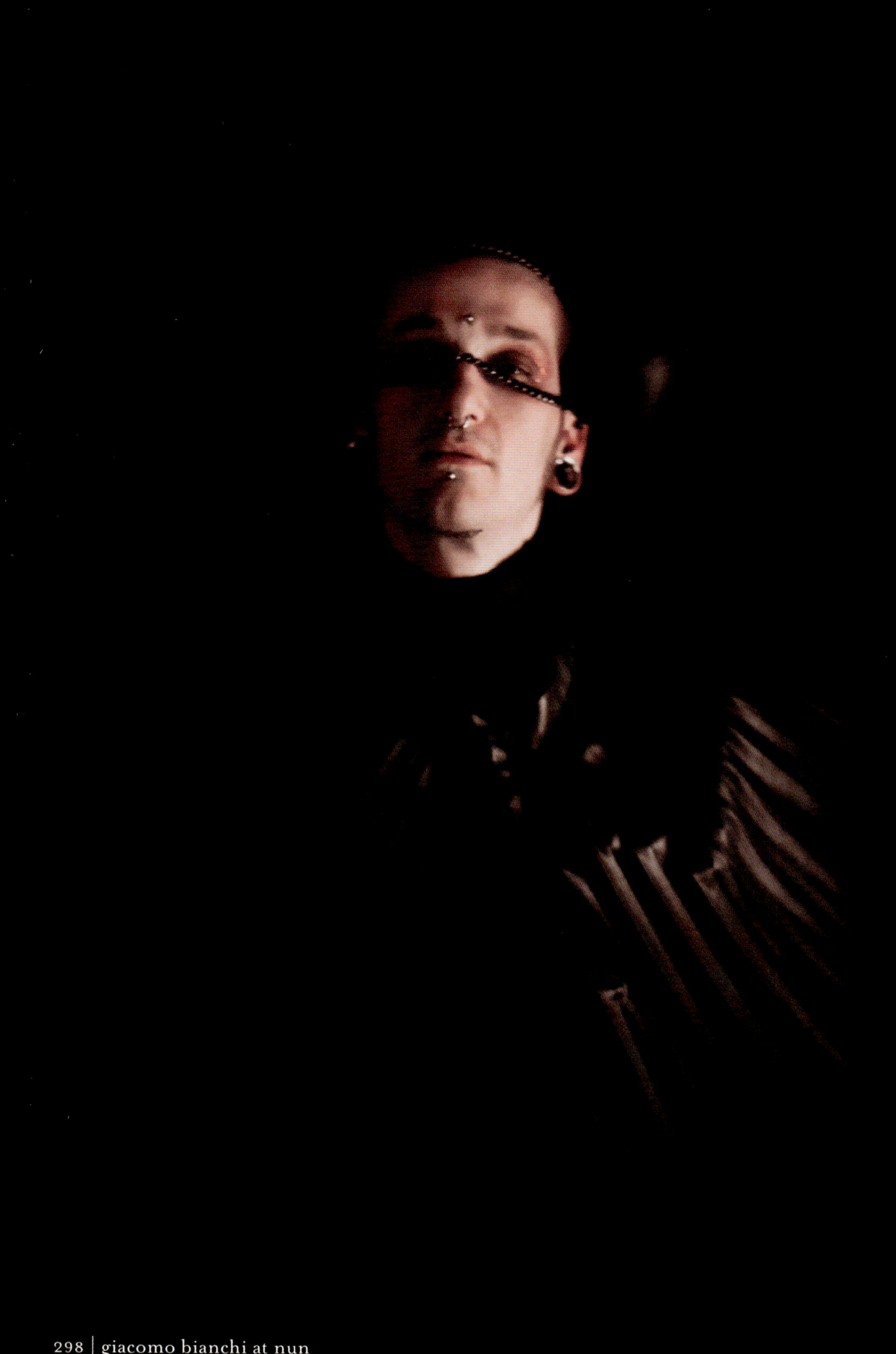

 | giacomo bianchi at nun

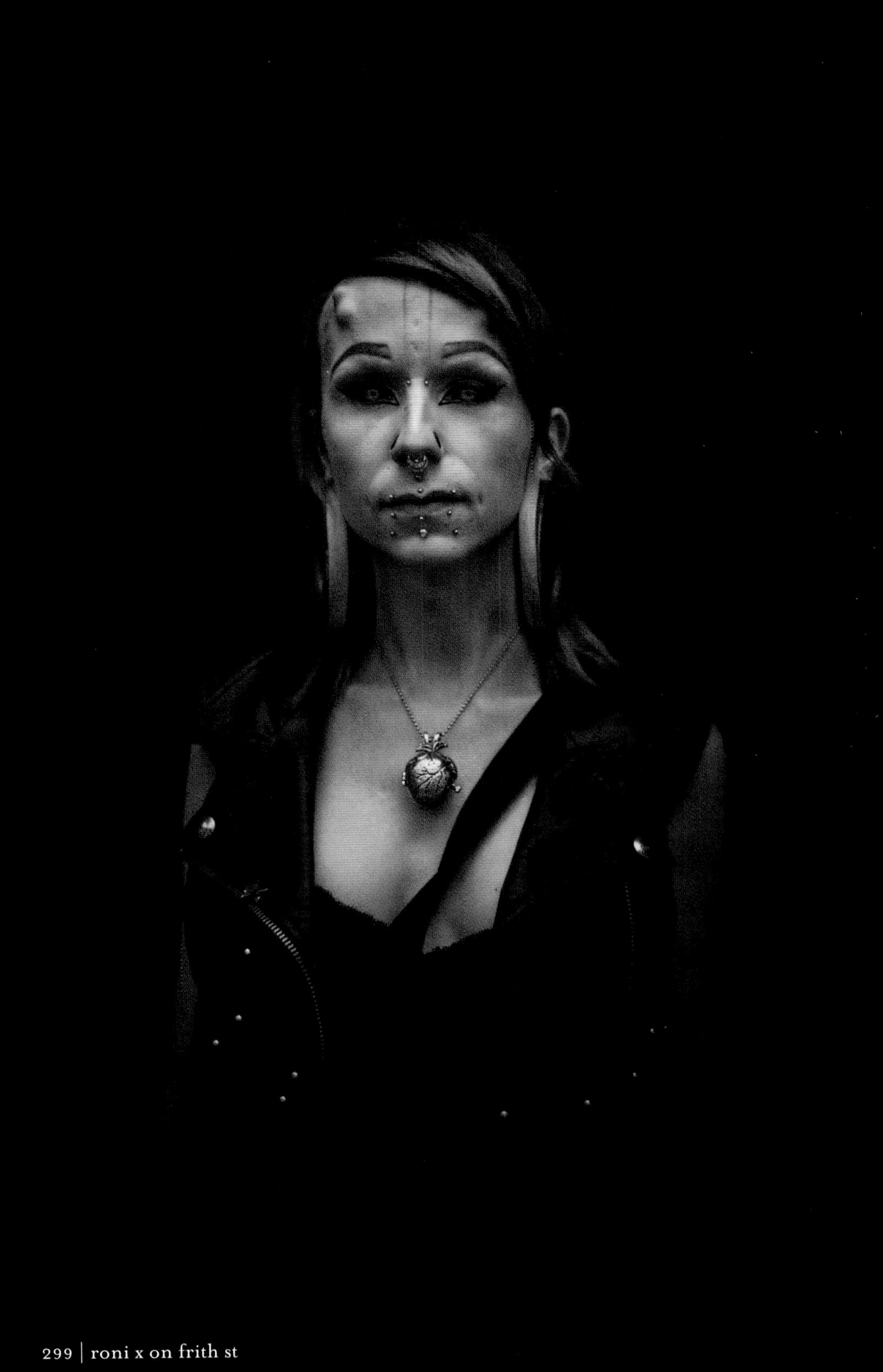

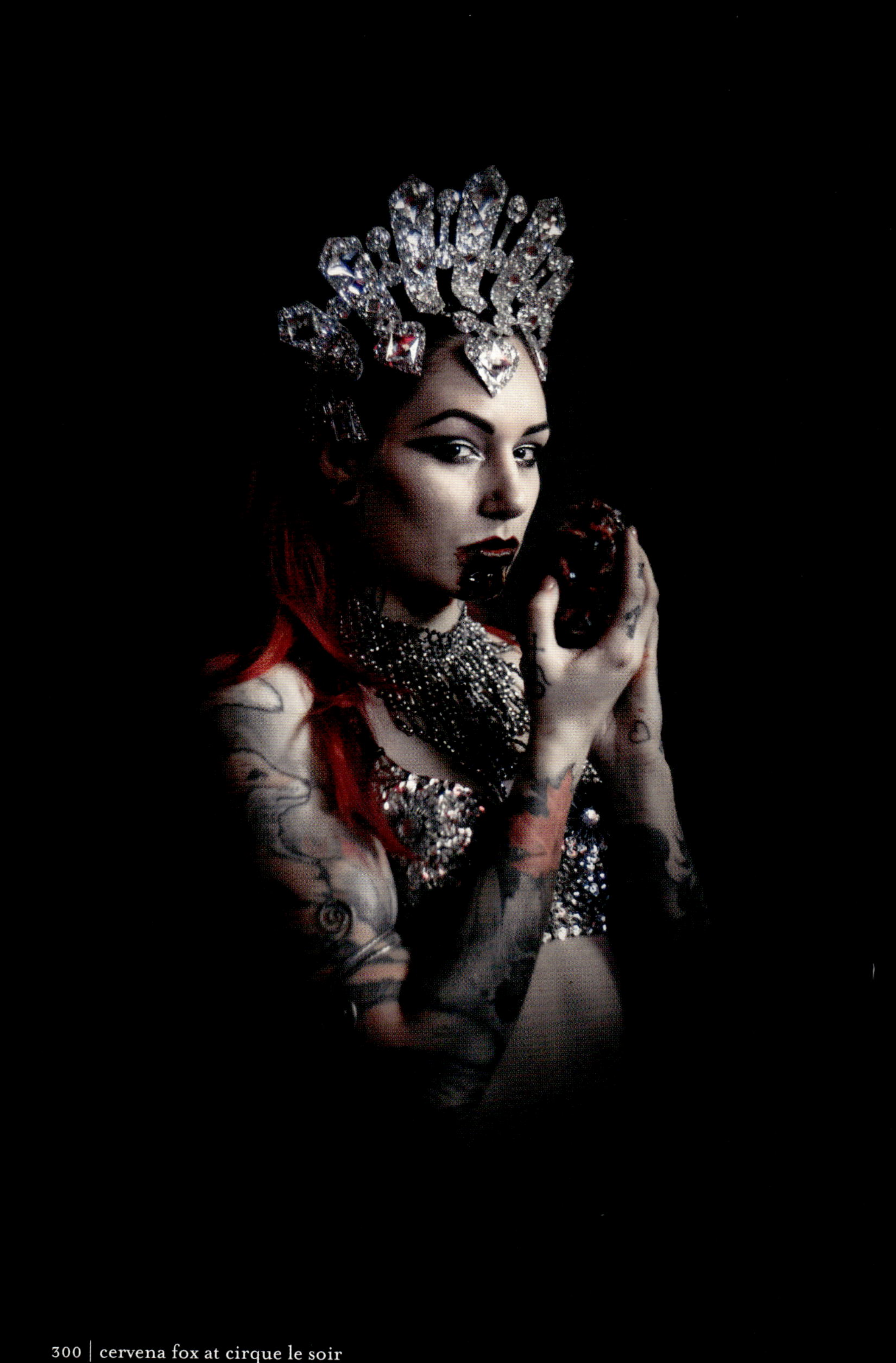

 | cervena fox at cirque le soir

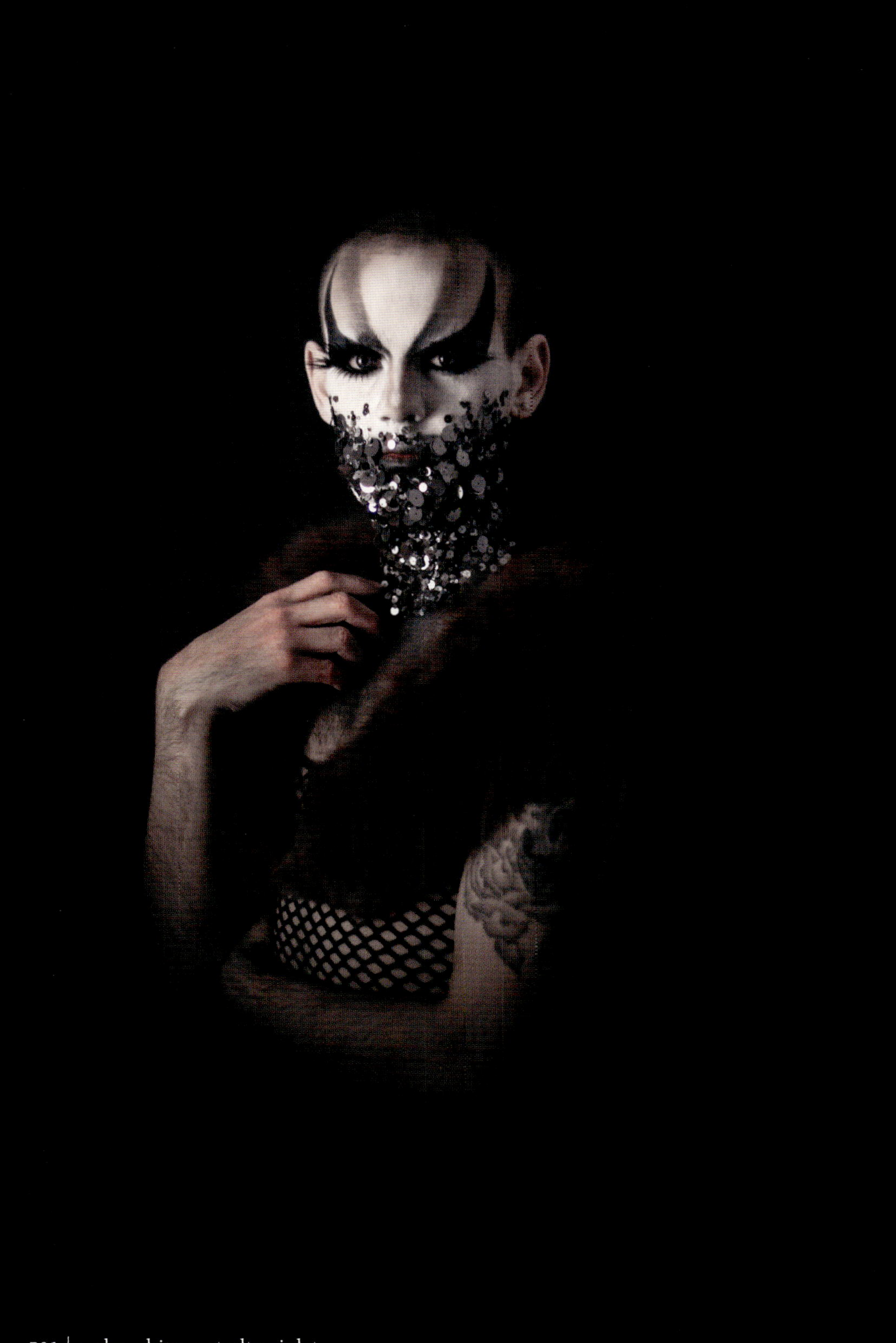

 | carlos whisper at ultraviolet

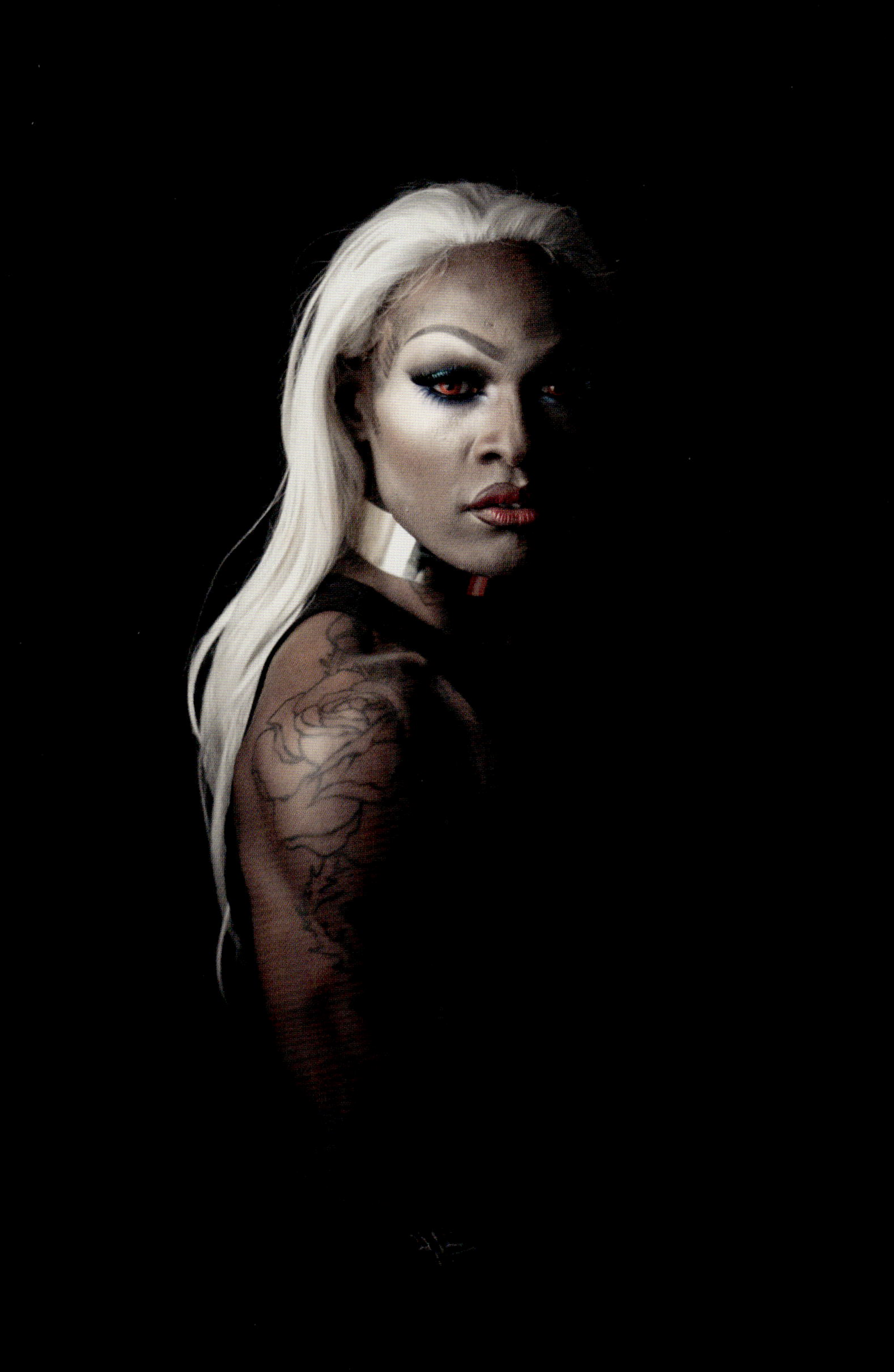

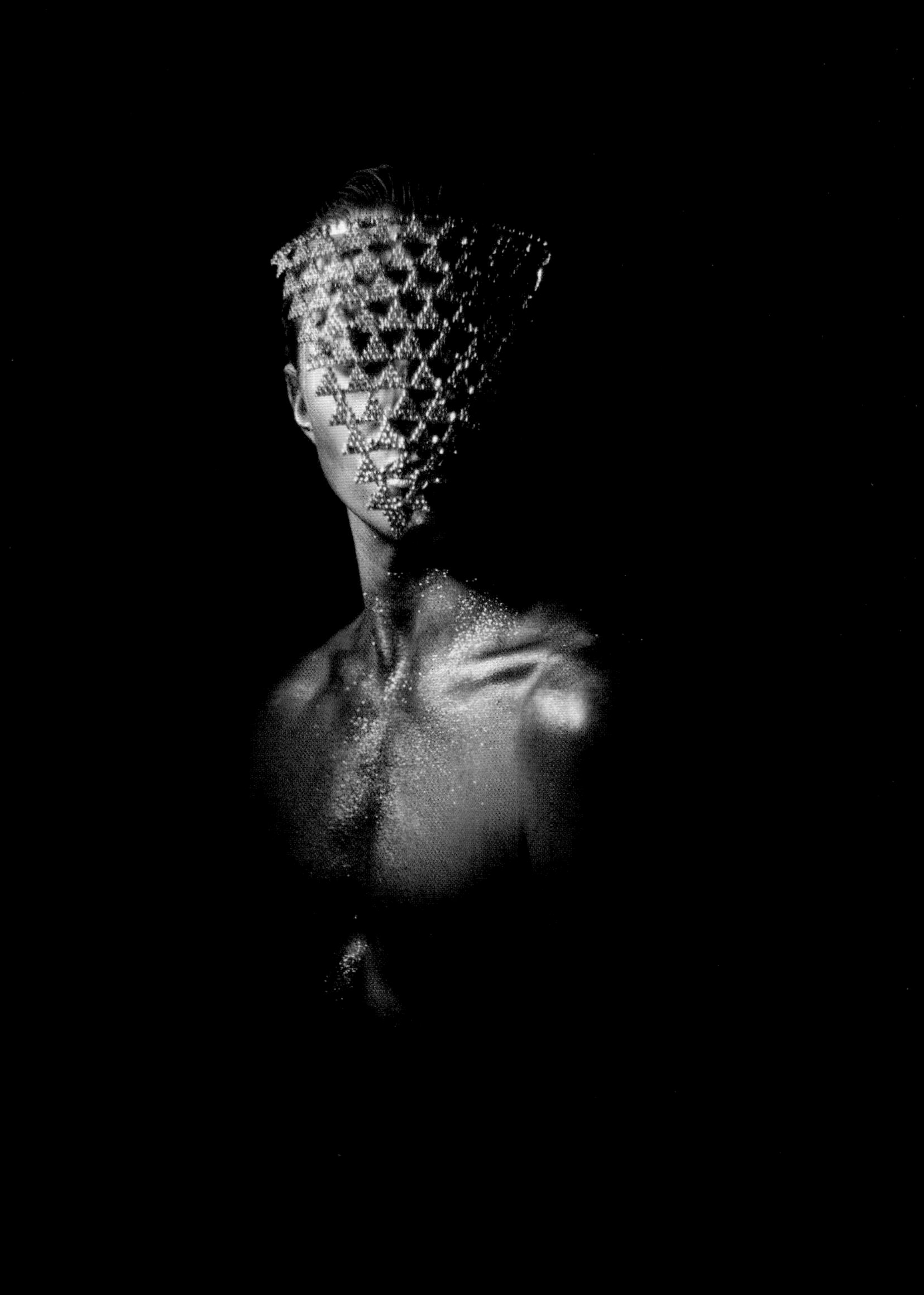

303 | benjamin milan at cirque le soir

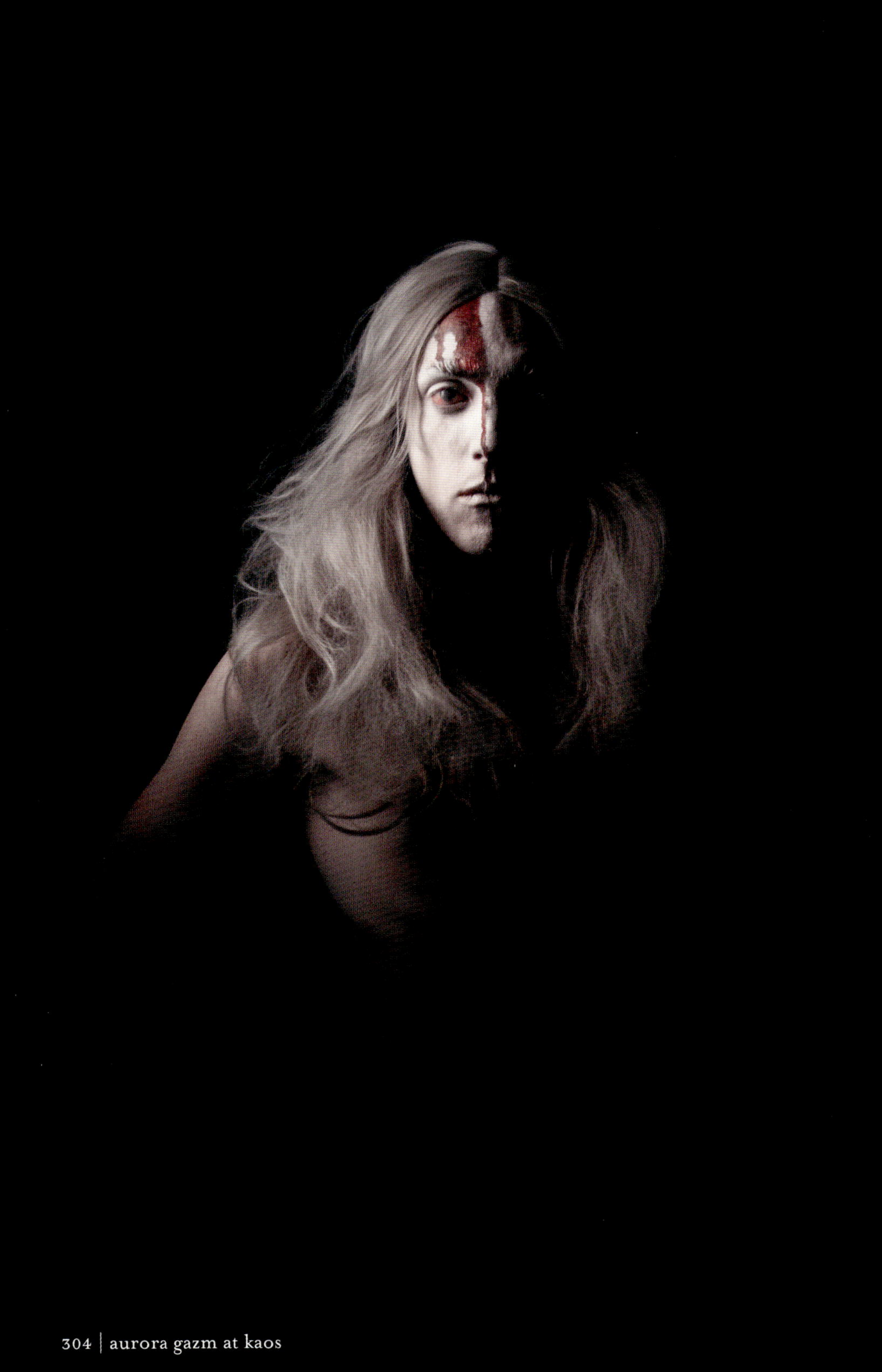

 aurora gazm at kaos

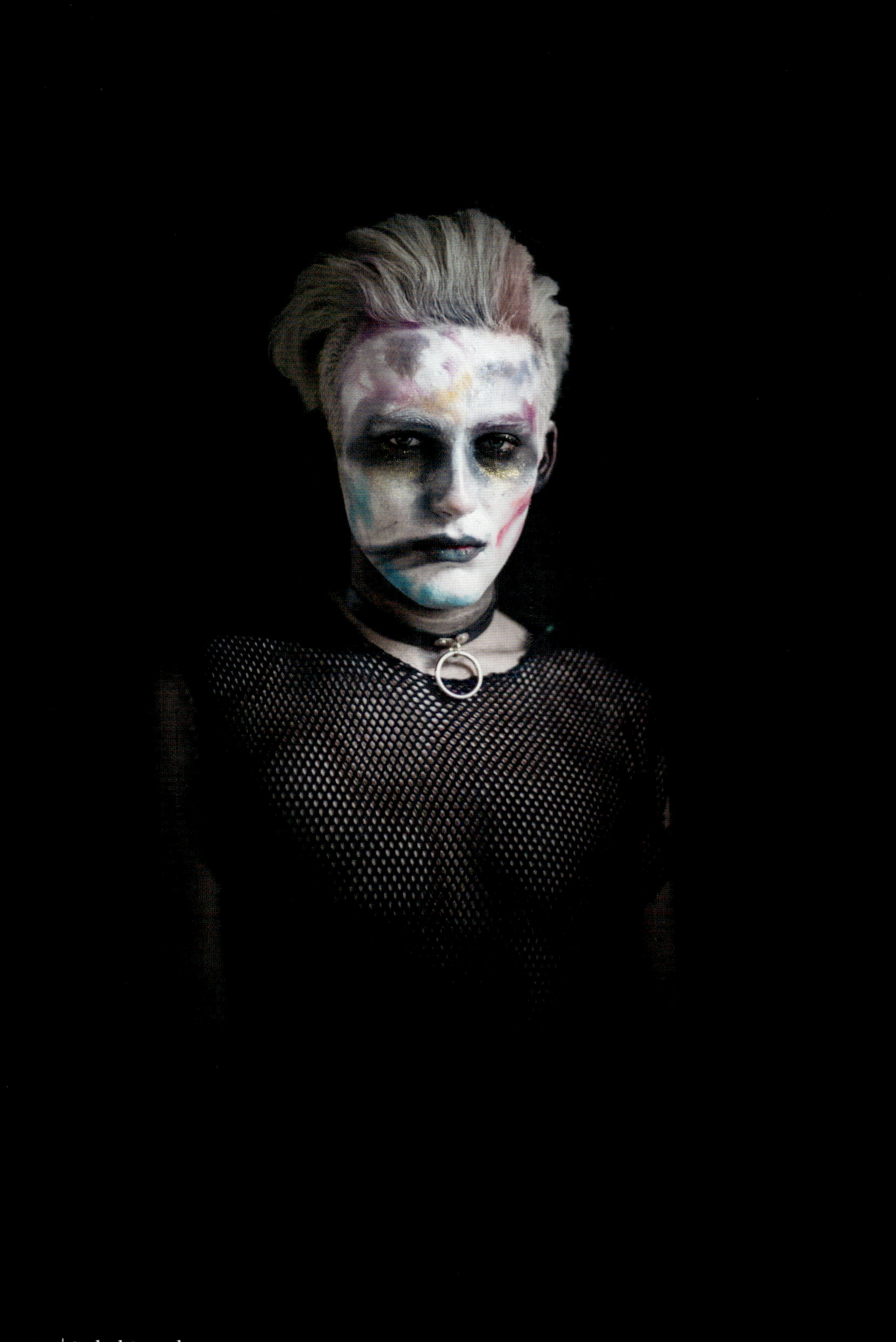

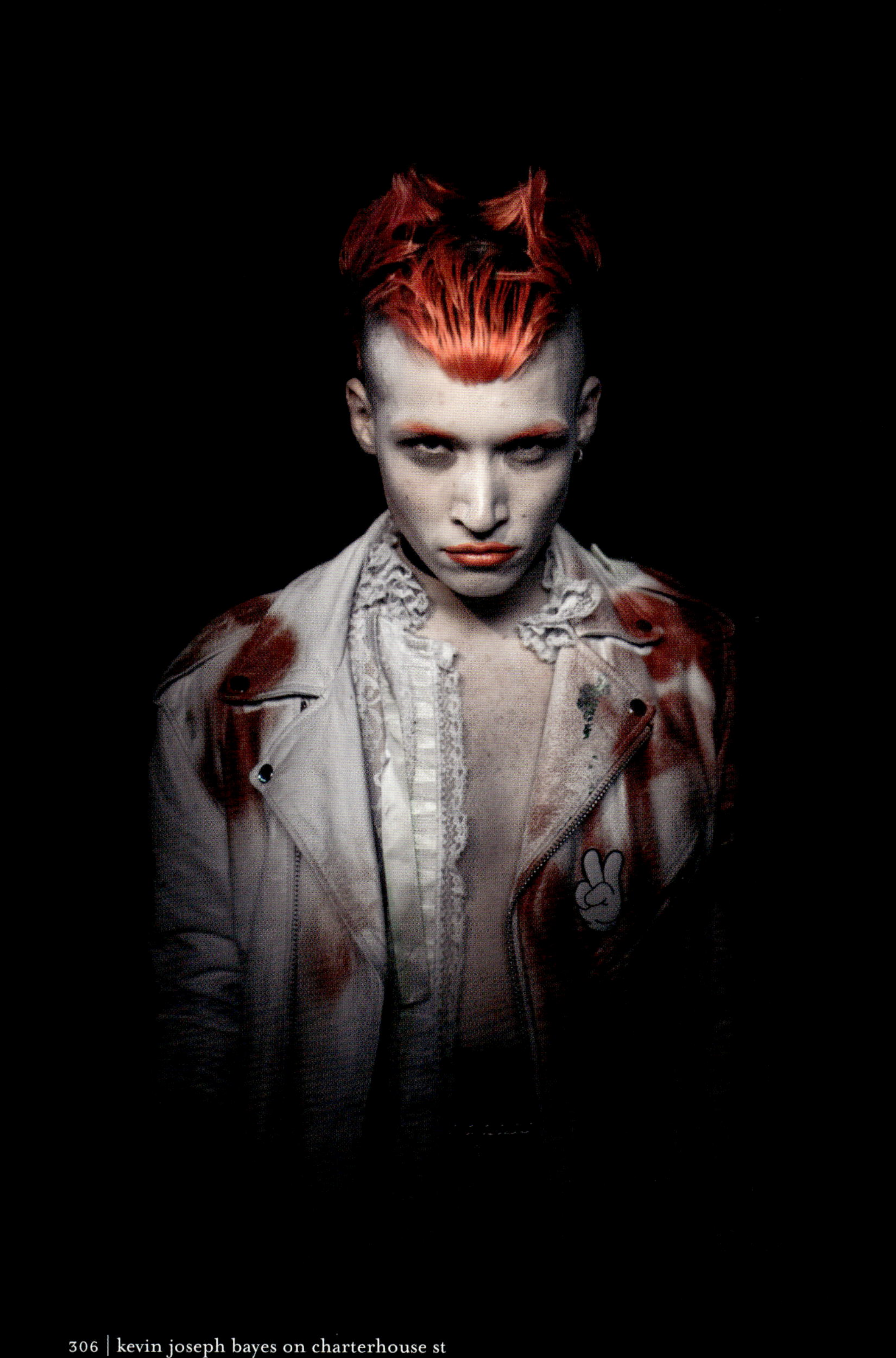

 kevin joseph bayes on charterhouse st

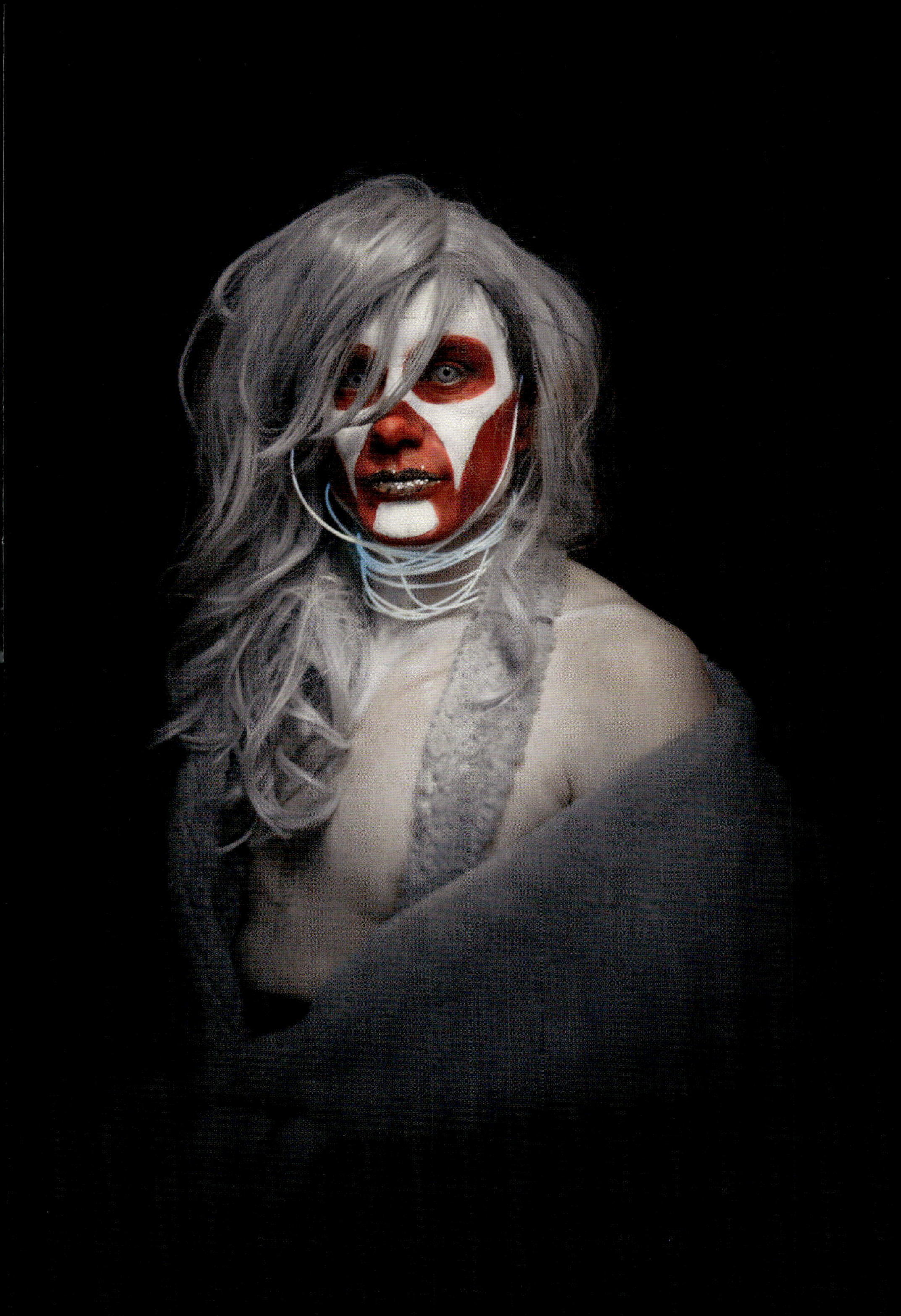

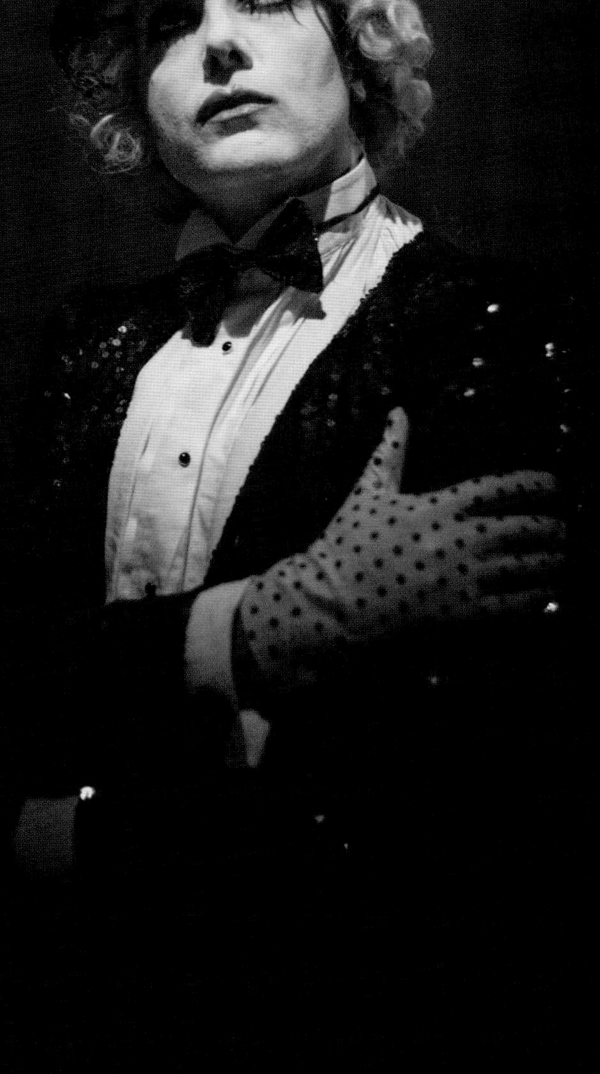

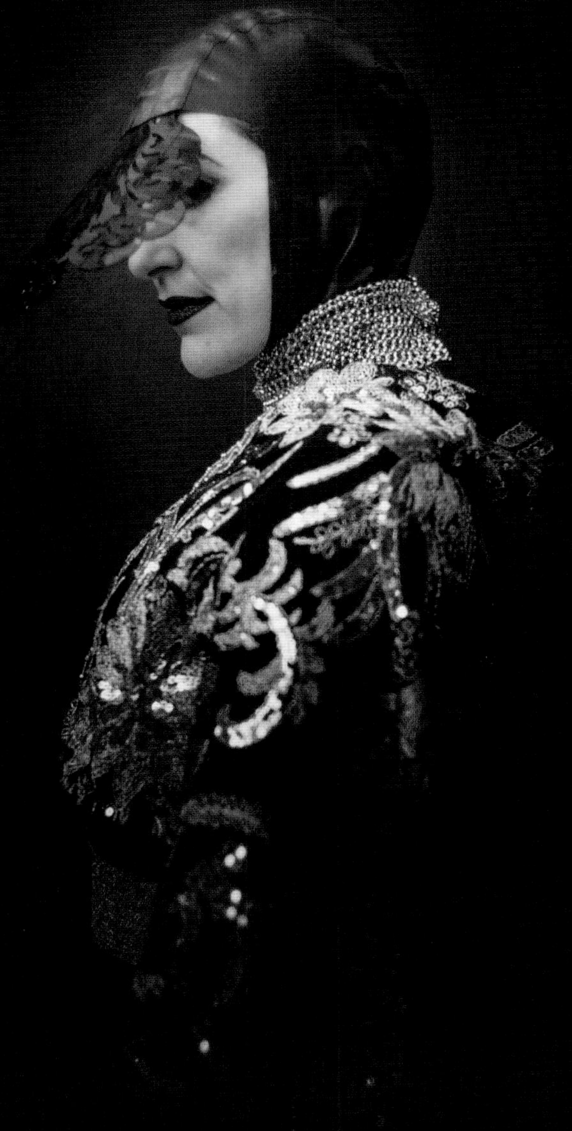

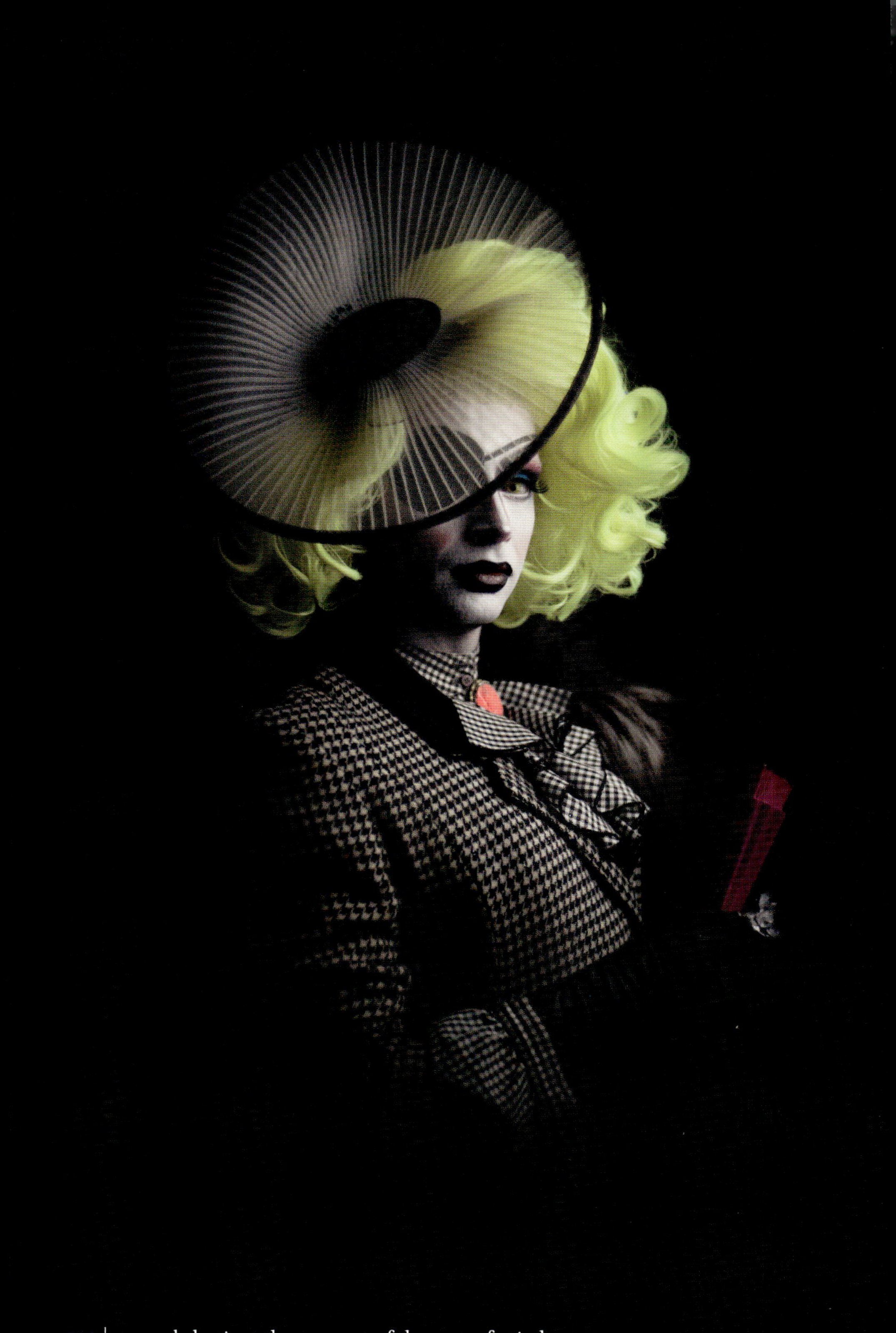

 anna phylactic at the queerest of the queer festival

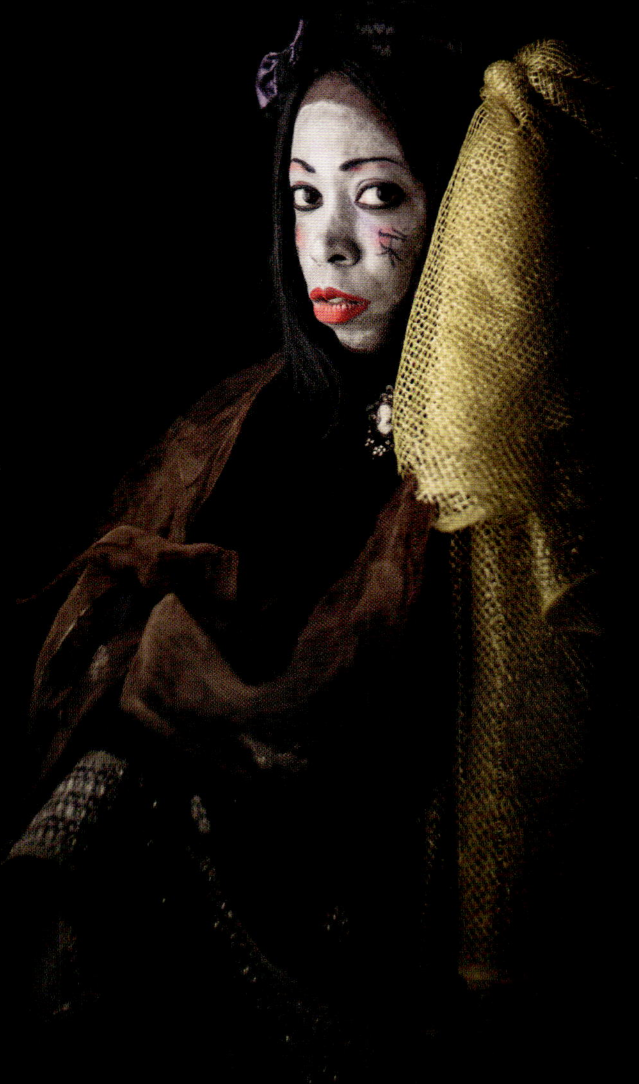

311 | jah geisha on dalston sq.

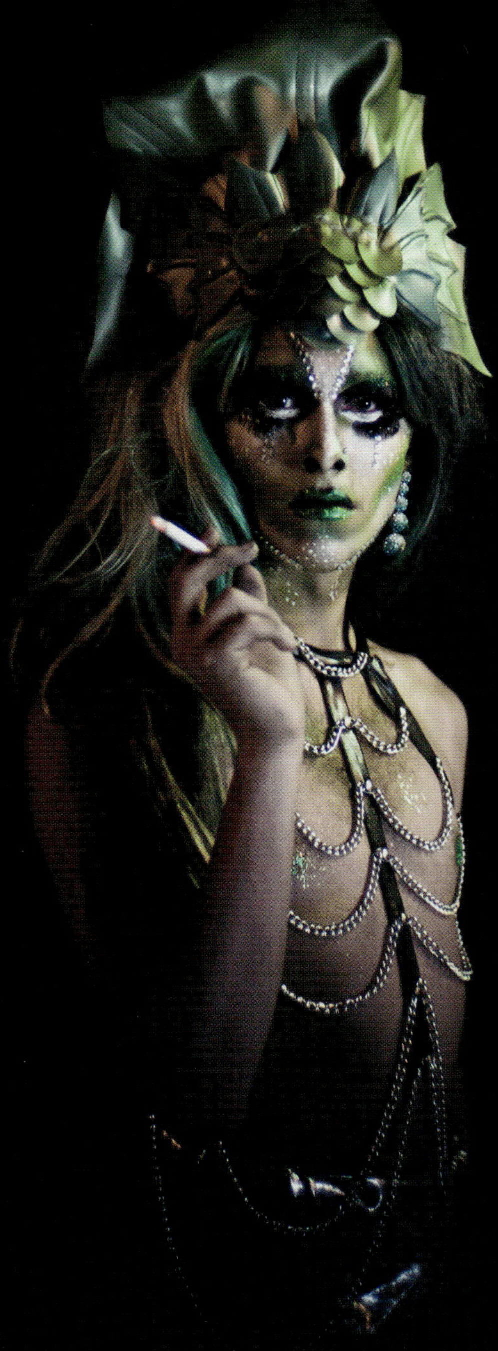

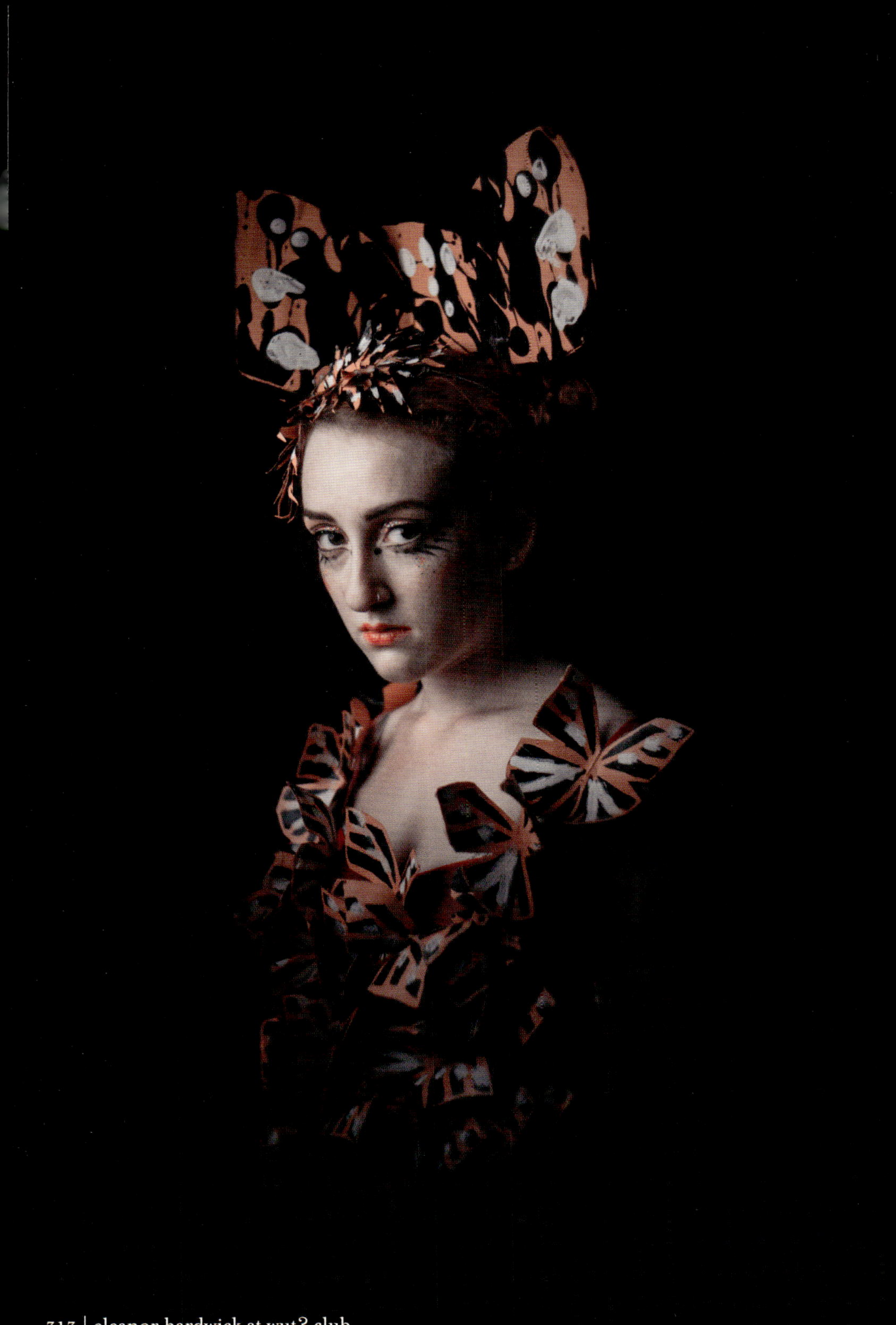

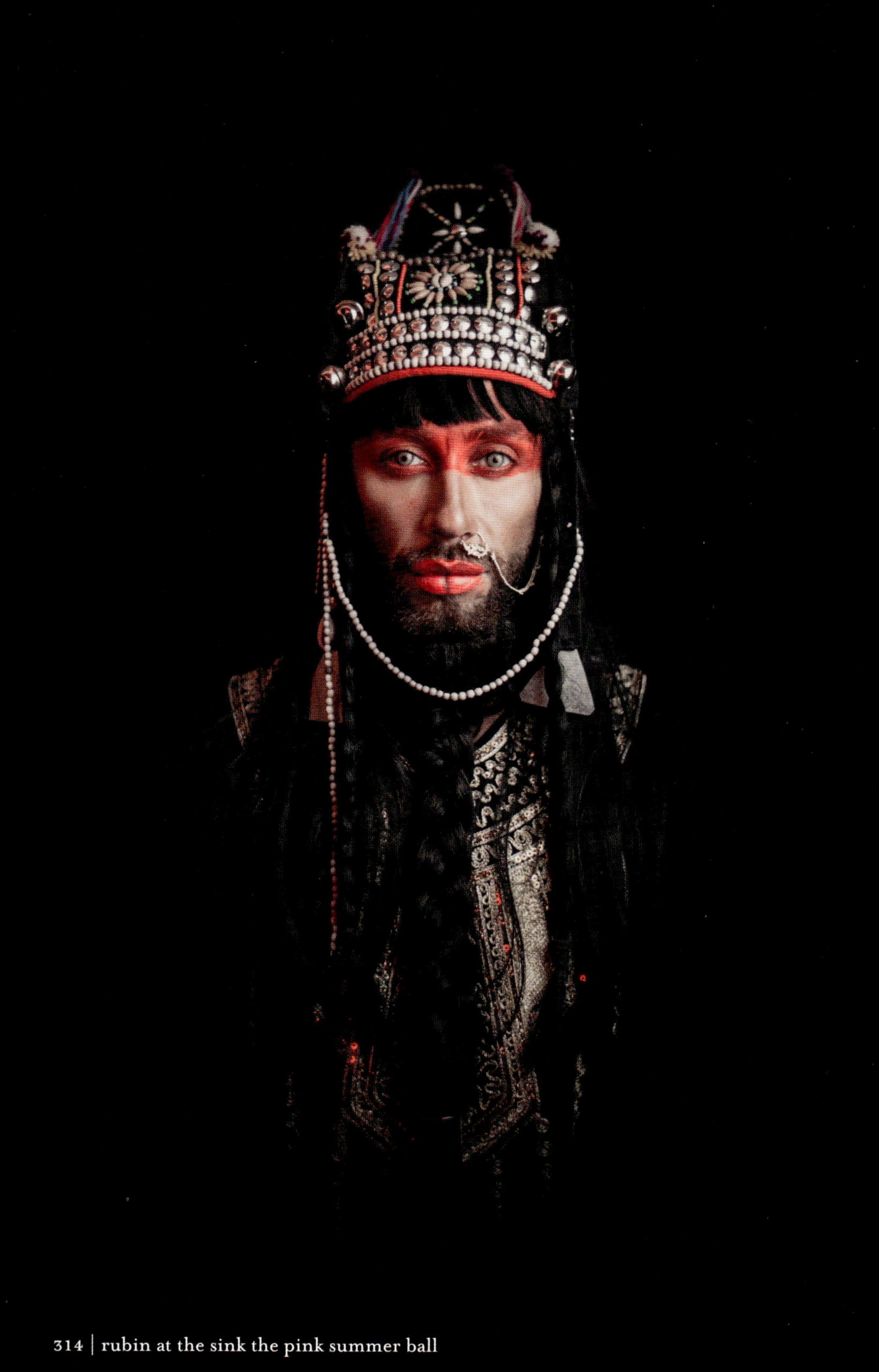

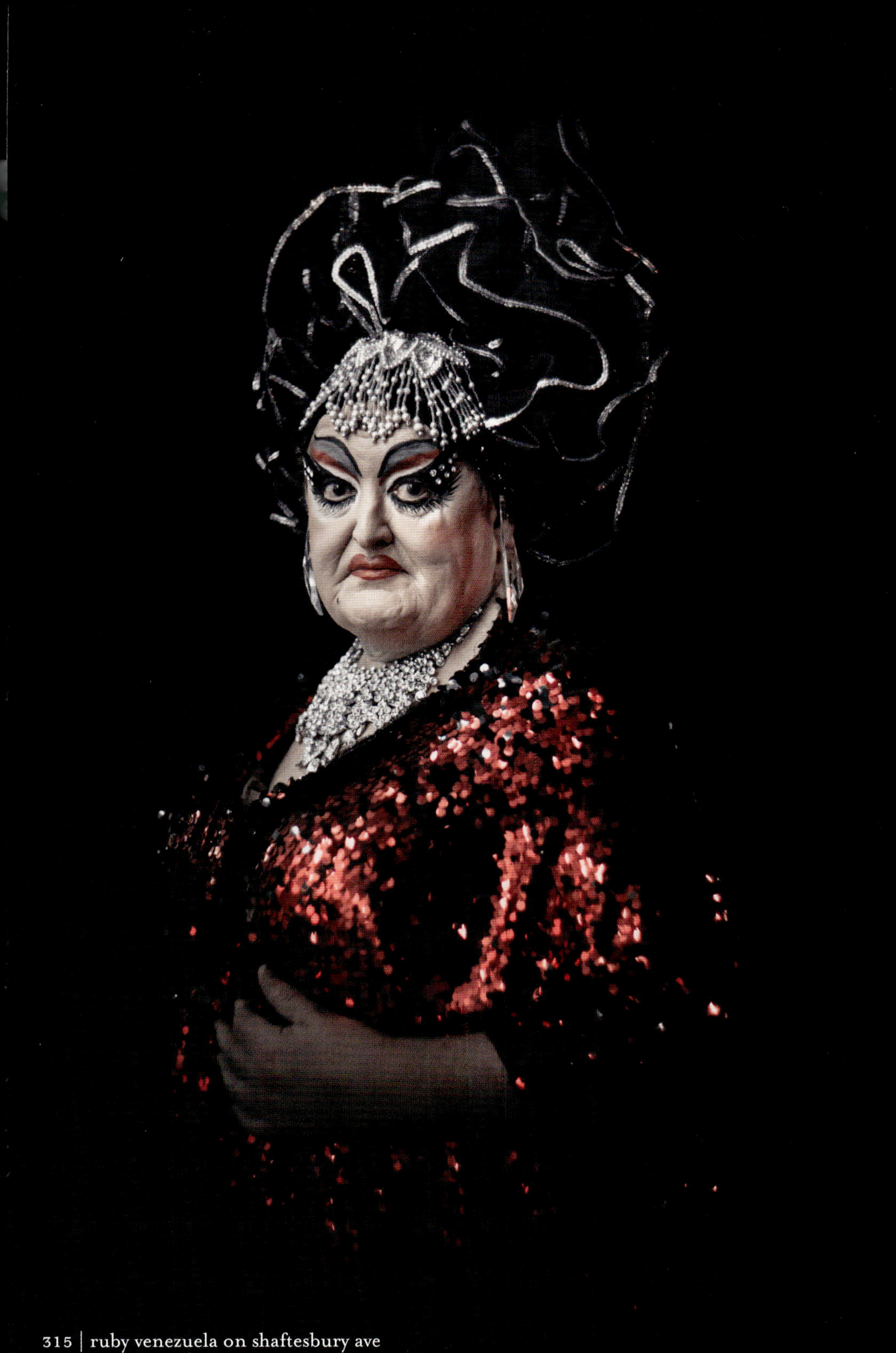

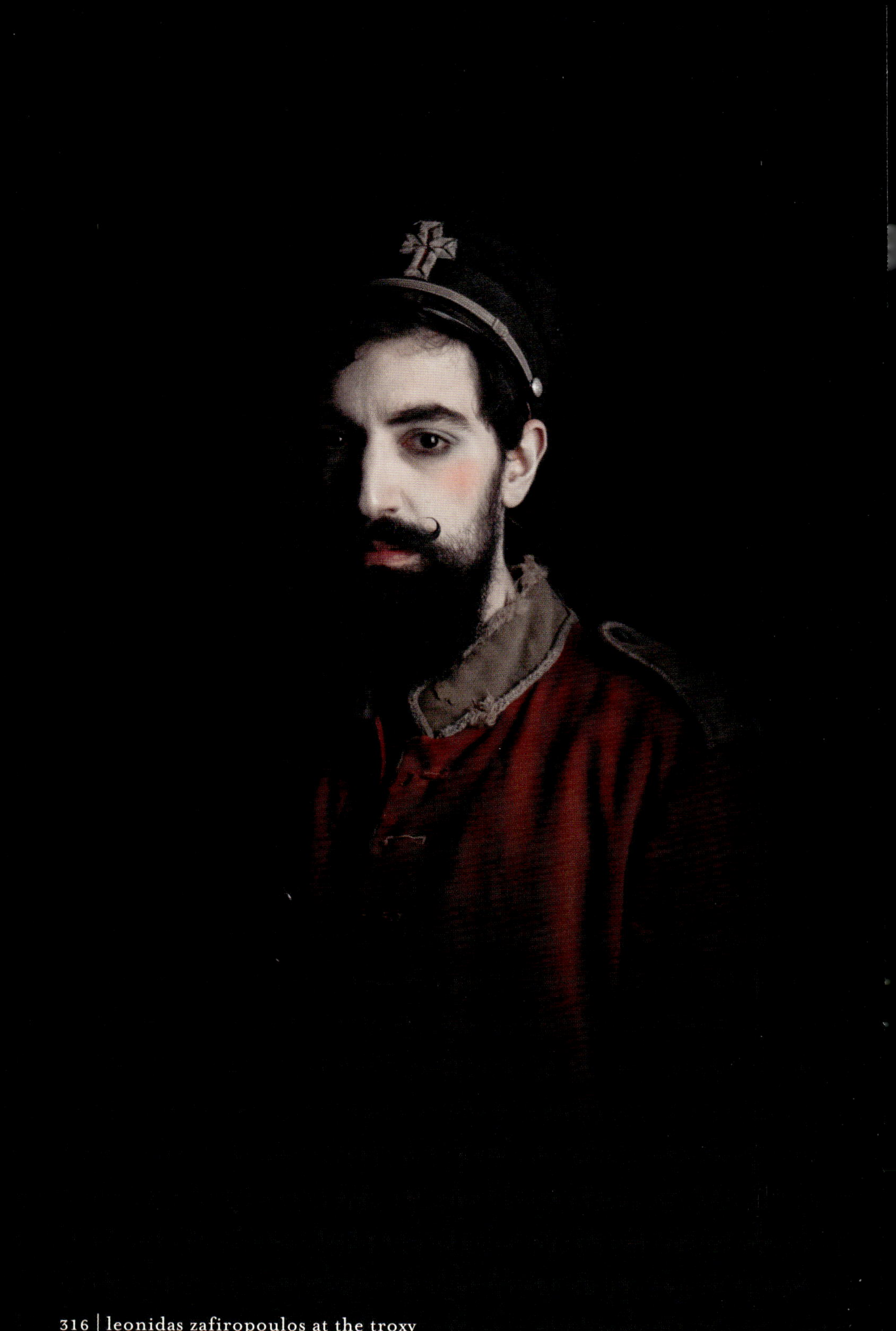

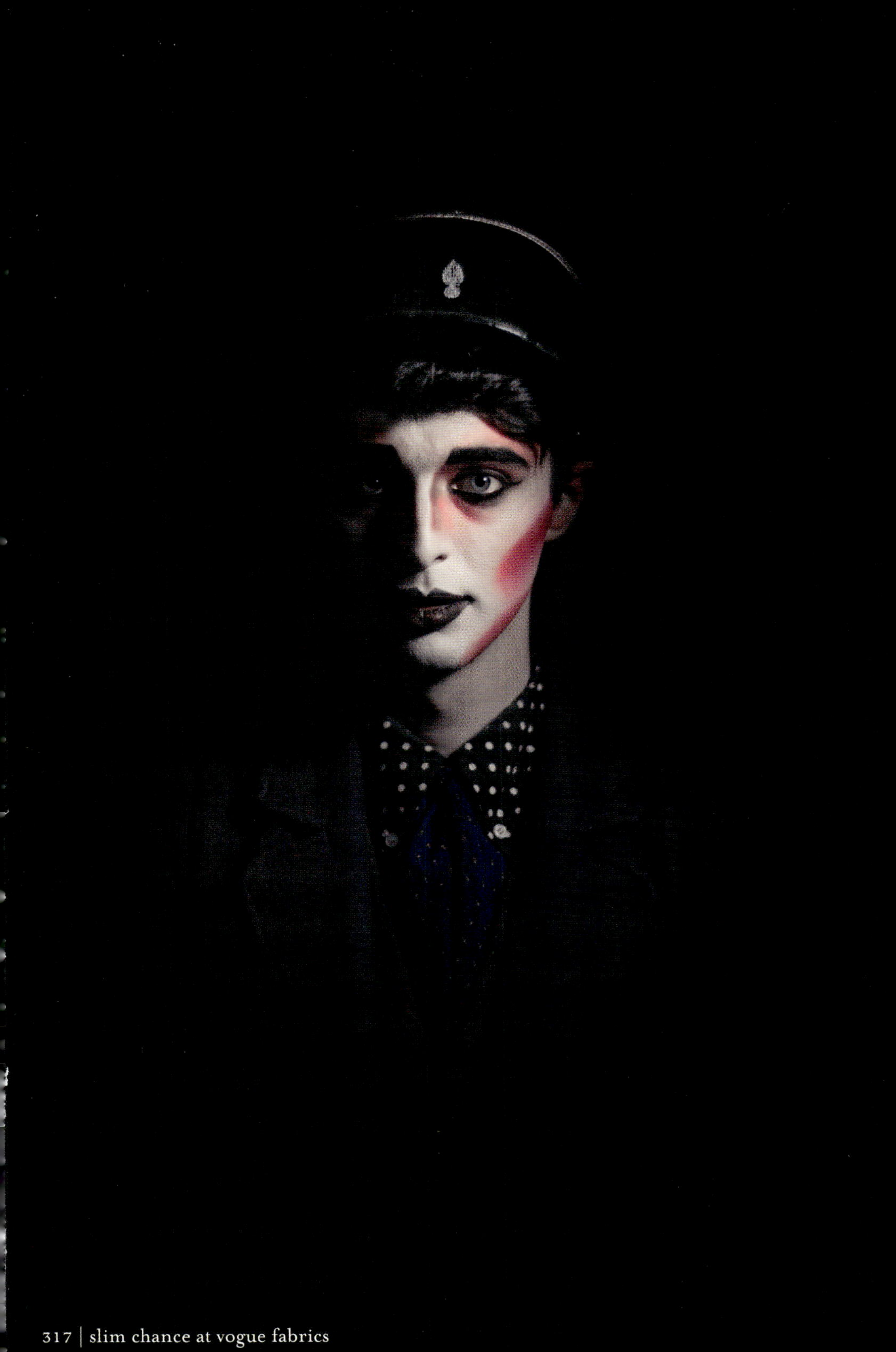

acknowledgements

I am absolutely indebted to everyone who let me take their photograph; who trusted me, a total stranger, when I approached them on the street or in a club, and who had the patience to humour me while I struggled to find the right light or background or was pernickety about their pose and/or expression.

There are too many people who have helped with the project to thank individually, but I'd like to extend my undying gratitude and love to the following: Maxi More for being so open and supportive, not to mention for coming up with the term 'Night Flowers' to describe a wonderful community; Chadd Curry, without whose warmth and openness this project may not have happened; Daniel Lismore for everything, but mostly for being extraordinary; Teru Kuwayama and the Instagram team for their support and encouragement; everyone who follows my Instagram feed, without whose interest and engagement I wouldn't have had the motivation to stay up late all those nights, out in the cold; Dave Thomas for his grace and approachability in helping out a total stranger; Boy George for his fabulous foreword and for being an absolute trailblazer and inspiration; Mia Apples, Alex Menace and the Amy Grimehouse crew; Jack Cullen and The Glory; Hugh Merrell, Nicola Bailey and Claire Chandler at Merrell Publishers; Lee Adams and everyone at KAOS; Gaffy Gaffiero; Rubyyy Jones; James Tailor; Charleene Rena, Camilla Bish, Boom Boom and everyone at Cirque le Soir; AKA UK and everyone else at my day job who pretended I wasn't a zombie after having only 3–4 hours of sleep each night for more than a year; EmiRihanna Litsa for her enlightening take on things; Mersedes Margoit for help with the filming; Amy Redmond, Glyn Fussell and the Sink the Pink crew; Kalypso Kampani for all her patience; my friends, family and most of all my wonderful mother, Maureen Frost, for her endless support, inspiration and encouragement. Thank you!

about the author

Damien Frost is an artist and graphic designer who works across the fields of painting, illustration, photography, and website and print design. Frost studied visual arts at the University of Newcastle, Australia, and has exhibited his paintings, illustrations, photography and digital work in Australia and the United Kingdom. He established his own studio/gallery, presented a show on community radio for several years, and was a founding member of Octapod, a community new media and arts organization in Newcastle, Australia. Frost produces the websites objectnotfound.net, a collection of found photographs, notes and letters, and artcrimes.net, which documents cases of modern iconoclasm. In recent years Frost's practice has focused predominantly on photography, and he has been documenting the alternative queer, performance and nightlife communities in London.

Frost currently lives in London, where he works as a graphic designer, creating posters for opera, ballet and theatre. His work can be viewed at

damienfrost.com
and
@harmonyhalo on Instagram

First published 2016 by Merrell Publishers, London and New York

Merrell Publishers Limited
70 Cowcross Street
London ECIM 6EJ

merrellpublishers.com

British Library Cataloguing in Publication Data.
A catalogue record for this book is available from the British Library.

ISBN 978-1-8589-4648-1

Produced by Merrell Publishers Limited
Art direction by Nicola Bailey
Designed by Damien Frost
Edited by Claire Chandler

Printed and bound in China

Front cover:
Daniel Lismore at Noho
Back cover:
Maxi More on Greek St; see p. 124
Page 2:
Maya Petrovna (with reflected self-portrait)
Endpapers:
Design by Damien Frost

Extract on p. 5:
'After All' by David Bowie. Lyrics © EMI Music Publishing, Sony/ATV Music Publishing LLC, Kobalt Music Publishing Ltd, Universal Music Publishing Group, BMG Rights Management US, LLC, Tintoretto Music

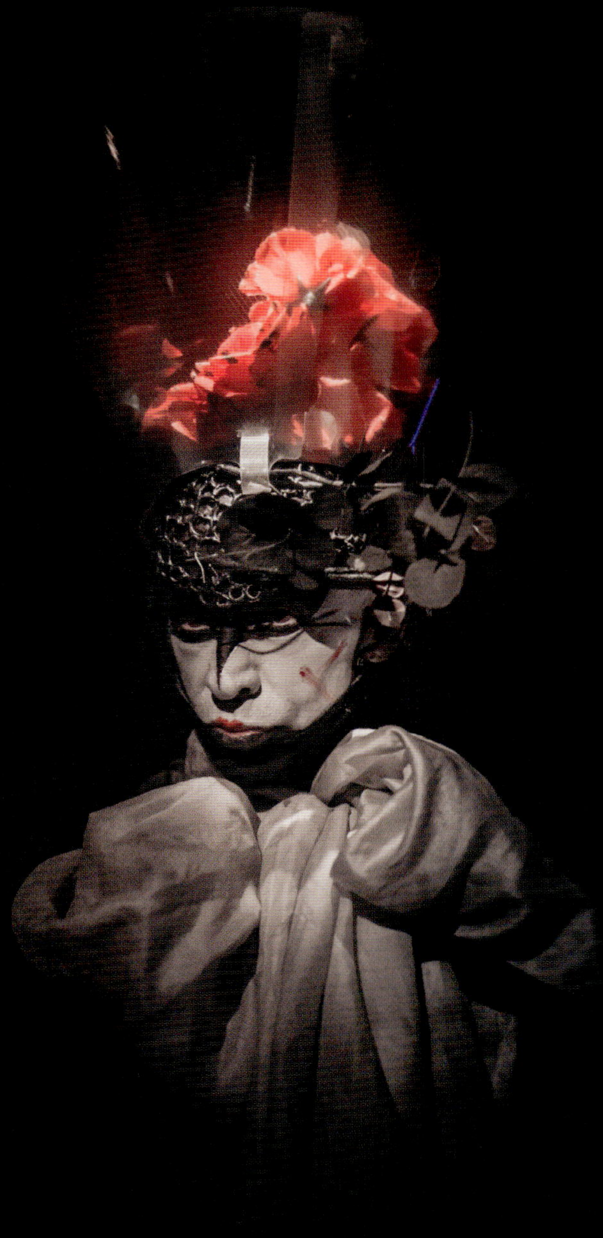

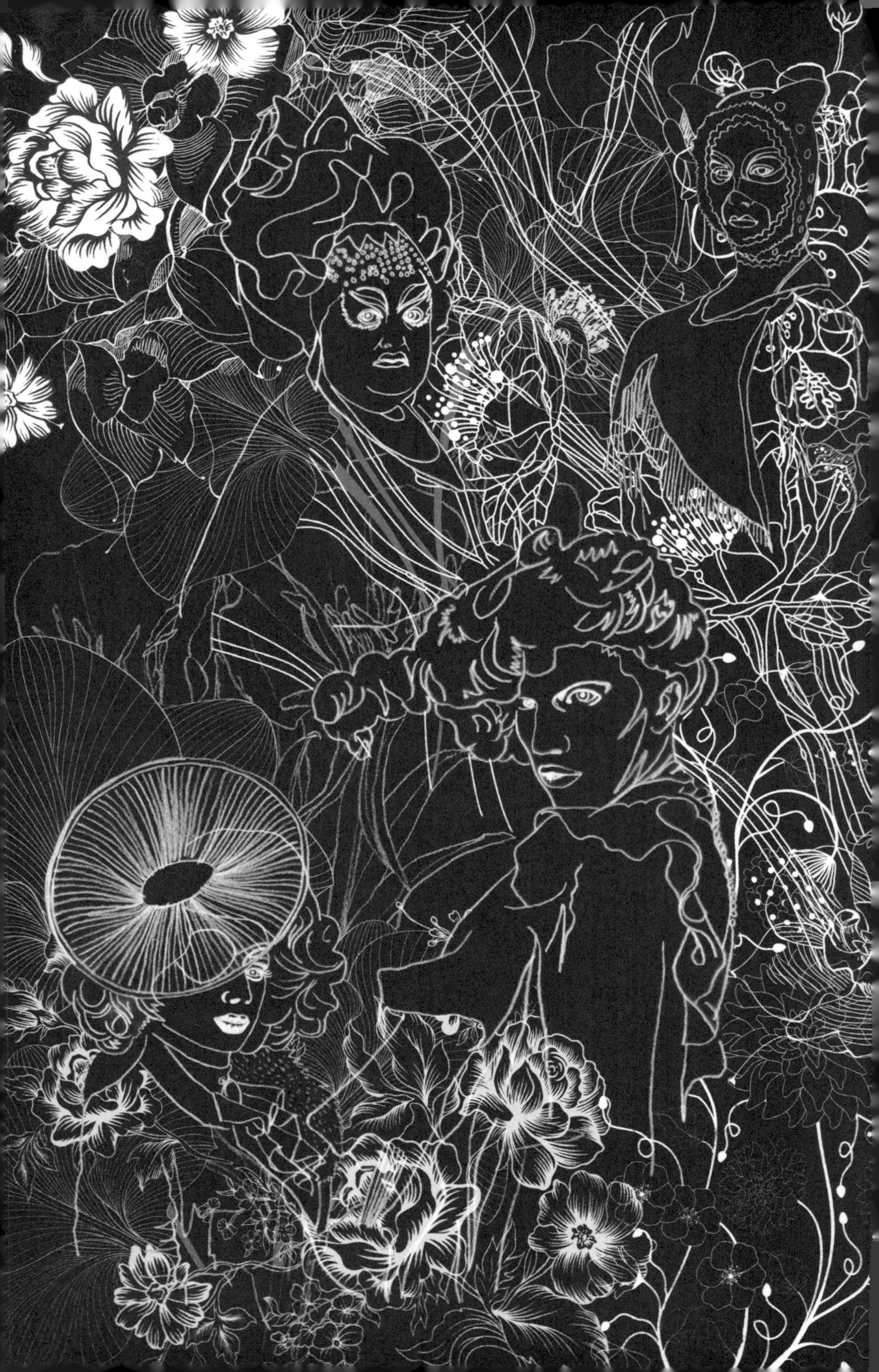